Frommer's®
Paris 2012

by Joseph Alexiou, Lily Heise, Sophie Nellis,
Kate van den Boogert & Meg Zimbeck
with Barbra Austin

WILEY

John Wiley & Sons, Inc.

Published by:
John Wiley & Sons, Inc.
111 River St.
Hoboken, NJ 07030-5774

ISBN 978-1-118-04597-8 (paper); ISBN 978-1-118-07686-6 (paper); 978-1-118-10279-4 (ebk); 978-1-118-10280-0 (ebk); 978-1-118-10281-7 (ebk)

Editor: Jennifer Polland
Production Editor: Jonathan Scott
Cartographer: Elizabeth Puhl
Photo Editor: Alden Gewirtz
Cover Photo Editor: Richard Fox
Design by Vertigo Design
Graphics, Layout, and Prepress by Wiley Indianapolis Composition Services
Front cover photo: Rainy Night at Place Edgar Quinet in Paris © Peet Simard/Terra/Corbis
Back cover photos: *Left:* Eiffel Tower ©Alterstock/Alamy Images. *Middle:* Pont des Arts and Seine River in Paris ©Art Kowalsky/Alamy Images. *Right:* Rodin's "The Thinker" ©Markel Redondo.

For information on our other products and services or to obtain technical support, please contact our Customer Care Department within the U.S. at 877/762-2974, outside the U.S. at 317/572-3993 or fax 317/572-4002.

Wiley also publishes its books in a variety of electronic formats. Some content that appears in print may not be available in electronic formats.

Manufactured in China

5   4   3   2   1

CONTENTS

LIST OF MAPS

ABOUT THE AUTHORS

Joseph Alexiou works as a freelance journalist, and he is the author of *Paris For Dummies.* His work has appeared in the *New York Press,* the *New York Observer,* and *Paper* magazine. He holds an MS from the Columbia University Graduate School of Journalism, and he lives in Brooklyn.

Lily Heise has been living in Paris for more than 10 years, having studied art in both Italy and France. She has extensive experience in the travel and culture sectors, from trip planning to leading tours and from exhibit curatorship to teaching film studies. She regularly reports on Paris culture news and events for local and international online and print publications. She lives in Montmartre and spends her free time exploring offbeat Paris and visiting the latest art exhibits.

Sophie Nellis came to Paris for a summer adventure in 2007. Four years later, she is still here. After completing an undergraduate degree in English Literature and History at Trinity College in Dublin, Ireland, her love affair with Paris led her to a Masters in Paris Studies at the University of Paris in London (ULIP). Here she specialized in 19th- and 20th-century Paris and wrote a dissertation on the history of Algerian immigration in Paris. She currently lives in Belleville and divides her time among writing, teaching, translating, and leading walking tours of Paris.

Kate van den Boogert is founding editor of the popular Paris blog gogoparis.com, an insider's guide to fashion, food, arts, gigs, and gossip in the French capital. Kate moved to Paris from Melbourne in 2000.

Meg Zimbeck is a food and travel writer and the Founding Editor of Paris by Mouth (www.parisbymouth.com), an online resource about eating and drinking in Paris with contributions from some of the most respected food and wine writers living in Paris. Originally from Kansas City (followed by Chicago and Boston), Meg has been based in Paris for years and has contributed to *Food & Wine,* the *Wall Street Journal, Budget Travel, BlackBook,* and *Hemispheres.*

Barbra Austin is a food writer, a pastry chef, and the Assistant Editor of Paris by Mouth. She conducted extensive research and wrote a dozen listings for the dining chapter.

ACKNOWLEDGMENTS

Thank you to my family and friends, especially the many Parisians who helped me along the way.

—Joseph Alexiou

I would like to thank Mike Nellis, Maureen Waugh, and Victoria for their unending support; Kate van den Boogert for her inspiration; and Michael Parker for all his encouragement during this particular project.

—Sophie Nellis

Special thanks to Paris by Mouth intern Catherine Down who provided fact-checking and other assistance for the dining chapter.

—Meg Zimbeck

Thank you to Jessica Langan-Peck and Chris Summers for their help editing portions of this book.

—Jennifer Polland

HOW TO CONTACT US

In researching this book, we discovered many wonderful places—hotels, restaurants, shops, and more. We're sure you'll find others. Please tell us about them, so we can share the information with your fellow travelers in upcoming editions. If you were disappointed with a recommendation, we'd love to know that, too. Please write to:

Frommer's Paris 2012
Wiley Publishing, Inc. • 111 River St. • Hoboken, NJ 07030-5774
frommersfeedback@wiley.com

ADVISORY & DISCLAIMER

Travel information can change quickly and unexpectedly, and we strongly advise you to confirm important details locally before traveling, including information on visas, health and safety, traffic and transport, accommodation, shopping, and eating out. We also encourage you to stay alert while traveling and to remain aware of your surroundings. Avoid civil disturbances, and keep a close eye on cameras, purses, wallets, and other valuables.

While we have endeavored to ensure that the information contained within this guide is accurate and up-to-date at the time of publication, we make no representations or warranties with respect to the accuracy or completeness of the contents of this work and specifically disclaim all warranties, including without limitation warranties of fitness for a particular purpose. We accept no responsibility or liability for any inaccuracy or errors or omissions, or for any inconvenience, loss, damage, costs, or expenses of any nature whatsoever incurred or suffered by anyone as a result of any advice or information contained in this guide.

The inclusion of a company, organization, or website in this guide as a service provider and/or potential source of further information does not mean that we endorse them or the information they provide. Be aware that information provided through some websites may be unreliable and can change without notice. Neither the publisher or author shall be liable for any damages arising herefrom.

FROMMER'S STAR RATINGS, ICONS & ABBREVIATIONS

Every hotel, restaurant, and attraction listing in this guide has been ranked for quality, value, service, amenities, and special features using a **star-rating system.** In country, state, and regional guides, we also rate towns and regions to help you narrow down your choices and budget your time accordingly. Hotels and restaurants are rated on a scale of zero (recommended) to three stars (exceptional). Attractions, shopping, nightlife, towns, and regions are rated according to the following scale: zero stars (recommended), one star (highly recommended), two stars (very highly recommended), and three stars (must-see).

In addition to the star-rating system, we also use **seven feature icons** that point you to the great deals, in-the-know advice, and unique experiences that separate travelers from tourists. Throughout the book, look for:

special finds—those places only insiders know about

fun facts—details that make travelers more informed and their trips more fun

kids—best bets for kids and advice for the whole family

special moments—those experiences that memories are made of

overrated—places or experiences not worth your time or money

insider tips—great ways to save time and money

great values—where to get the best deals

The following **abbreviations** are used for credit cards:

AE	American Express	**DISC**	Discover	**V**	Visa
DC	Diners Club	**MC**	MasterCard		

TRAVEL RESOURCES AT FROMMERS.COM

Frommer's travel resources don't end with this guide. Frommer's website, **www.frommers. com**, has travel information on more than 4,000 destinations. We update features regularly, giving you access to the most current trip-planning information and the best airfare, lodging, and car-rental bargains. You can also listen to podcasts, connect with other Frommers.com members through our active-reader forums, share your travel photos, read blogs from guidebook editors and fellow travelers, and much more.

THE BEST OF PARIS

By Kate van den Boogert & Meg Zimbeck

Paris is unique in that it is a major global city—home to more than 10 million people in the greater region—yet it manages to synthesize the rhythms of village life with those of a cosmopolitan world capital. Although the city is a center of European commerce, many shops are closed on Sundays, leaving time for lazy brunches or shopping excursions at a local market. Paris is the capital of fashion, art, and people-watching; a city where Chanel-clad ladies walk poodles along grand boulevards; a place where the waiters might be rude but the food is *délicieux*. Paris is all of that and more. Your love affair begins once you look beyond the Eiffel Tower, explore the back streets, and make Paris your own.

Things to Do Comfy shoes are essential for this city of a thousand walks, landscaped gardens, and cavernous galleries. Reserve your ticket for speedy access to the **Louvre,** which sidles up to the sculpture-dotted **Jardin des Tuileries.** Across the Seine on the **Left Bank,** take your pick from Impressionist hangout **Musée d'Orsay, Notre-Dame's** Gothic grandeur and **Musée Rodin**'s *Kiss* sculpture. Okay, you really *can't* leave without seeing Paris light up from the **Eiffel Tower,** open till midnight.

Restaurants & Dining Good food is a birthright and its appreciation a rite of passage in Paris, where a meal—sometimes even coffee—can last hours. For a memorable splurge, book one of the city's opulent three-star palace restaurants, like **Le Plaza Athenée** or **L'Astrance,** or book ahead for a table at one of the trendy *bistronomiques* that combine gastronomy with bistro pricing—**Frenchie, Le Chateaubriand, Rino,** and **Spring** are all hot right now.

Shopping Parisians luxuriate in shopping—bidding shopkeepers *bonjour* and pausing to *lèche-vitrines* ("lick the windows," or window shop). Saunter the boutiquey **Marais** for home-grown fashion, or voguish **rue Saint-Honoré,** home to concept store **Colette,** for more high-end labels. Where else can you find such palatial department stores as chic **Bon Marché,** Art Nouveau **Printemps,** or monumental **Galeries Lafayette**? Antiques, bric-a-brac, vintage Chanel—it's all at the charming **Porte de Vanves weekend flea market;** arrive early for bargains and stay for brunch.

Nightlife & Entertainment Ballet and opera at the glittering **Opéra Garnier,** Molière classics at the **Comédie Française,** and cancan at the (in)famous **Moulin Rouge**—Paris nightlife reaches from sublime to borderline sleazy. A young, trendy crowd parties around the **Bastille,** gay **Marais,** and the effortlessly hip bars in **Oberkampf,** where DJs play at industrial-chic **Nouveau Casino.** Dress to the nines to slip past picky doormen in clubs around

PREVIOUS PAGE: **A couple strolls along the picturesque quays of the Seine river.**

Champs-Élysées like celebrity-magnet **Le Baron,** and rock the Seine dancing to techno on moored party boat **Batofar.**

THE most unforgettable
TRAVEL EXPERIENCES

- **Whiling Away an Afternoon in a Parisian Cafe:** The cafes are where passionate meetings of writers, artists, philosophers, thinkers, and revolutionaries once took place—and perhaps still do. Parisians stop by their favorite cafes to meet lovers and friends, to make new ones, or to sit in solitude with a newspaper or book.

- **Taking Afternoon Tea à la Française:** Drinking tea in London has its charm, but the Parisian *salon de thé* is unique. Skip the cucumber-and-watercress sandwiches and delve into a luscious dessert such as the Mont Blanc, a creamy purée of sweetened chestnuts and meringue. The grandest Parisian tea salon is **Angélina,** 226 rue de Rivoli, 1er (✆ **01-42-60-82-00**).

- **Strolling Along the Seine:** Such painters as Sisley, Turner, and Monet have fallen under the Seine's spell. On its banks, lovers still walk hand in hand, anglers cast their lines, and *bouquinistes* (secondhand-book dealers) peddle their mix of postcards, 100-year-old pornography, and tattered histories of Indochina.

- **Spending a Day at the Races:** Paris boasts eight tracks for horse racing. The most famous and the classiest is **Hippodrome de Longchamp,** in the Bois de Boulogne, the site of the Prix de l'Arc de Triomphe and Grand Prix (p. 290). These and other top races are major social events, so you'll have to dress up.

Diners at Les Deux Magots cafe.

- **Calling on the Dead:** You don't have to be a ghoul to be thrilled by a visit to Europe's most famous cemetery, **Père-Lachaise** (p. 123). You can pay your respects to the resting places of Oscar Wilde, Yves Montand and Simone Signoret, Edith Piaf, Isadora Duncan, Frédéric Chopin, Marcel Proust, Jim Morrison, and others. Laid out in 1803 on a hill in Ménilmontant, the cemetery offers surprises with its bizarre monuments, unexpected views, and ornate sculpture.

- **Window-Shopping in the Faubourg St-Honoré:** In the 1700s, the wealthiest Parisians resided in the Faubourg St-Honoré; today, the quarter is home to stores catering to the rich, particularly on rue du Faubourg St-Honoré and avenue Montaigne. Even if you don't buy anything, it's great to window-shop big names such as Hermès, Dior, Chanel, Gaultier, Vuitton, Givenchy and Yves Saint Laurent. If you want to browse in the stores, be sure to dress the part. See chapter 7.

o **Exploring Ile de la Cité's Flower Market:** A fine finish to any day (Mon–Sat) spent meandering along the Seine is a stroll through the **Marché aux Fleurs,** place Louis-Lépine (p. 242). You can buy rare flowers, the gems of the French Riviera—bouquets that have inspired artists throughout the centuries. On Sundays, the area is transformed into the **Marché aux Oiseaux,** where you can admire rare birds from around the world.

o **Going Gourmet at Fauchon:** An exotic world of food, **Fauchon** (p. 258) offers more than 20,000 products from around the globe. Everything you never knew you were missing is in aisle after aisle of coffees, spices, pastries, fruits, vegetables, and much more. Take your pick: Scottish smoked salmon, preserved cocks' combs, Romanian rose-petal jelly, blue-red Indian pomegranates, golden Tunisian dates, dark morels from France's rich soil, century-old eggs from China, and a creole punch from Martinique, reputed to be the best anywhere.

o **Attending a Ballet or an Opera:** Take your pick between the rococo splendor of the majestic **Opéra Garnier** (p. 270) or the more modern **Opéra Bastille** (p. 270), France's largest opera house. Established in 1989, the Opéra Bastille presents opera and symphony performances in its four concert halls (its main hall seats 2,700). The Opéra Garnier is the home of the Paris Opera Ballet, one of the best companies in the world, and it hosts opera, classical concerts, and ballet performances inside its stunning gold and red velvet auditorium. Dress for the occasion, with pomp and circumstance.

o **Sipping Wine at Willi's:** Back in the early 1970s, the first-timer to Paris might have arrived with a copy of Hemingway's *A Moveable Feast* and, taking the author's endorsement to heart, headed for Harry's Bar at "Sank roo doe Noo." Harry's is still around but now draws an older, more conservative clientele. Today's chic younger expats head for **Willi's Wine Bar,** 13 rue des Petits-Champs, 1er (© **01-42-61-05-09;** p. 273). Here, the waitresses and long-haired young bartenders are mostly English. The place is like an informal

Enjoying *vin* at Willi's Wine Bar.

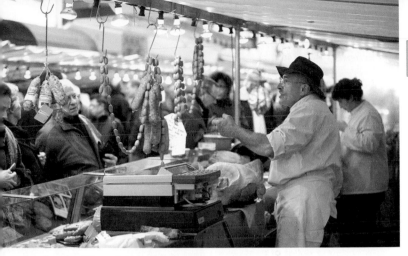

A meat vendor at the market on rue Montorgueil.

club for Brits, Australians, and Yanks, especially in the afternoon. Some 300 wines await your selection.

o **Checking Out the Marchés:** A daily Parisian ritual is ambling through one of the open-air markets to buy fresh food—perhaps a properly creamy Camembert or a ripe plum—to be eaten before sundown. Our favorite market is the Marché d'Aligre. During mornings at this grubby little cluster of food stalls, we've spotted some of France's finest chefs stocking up for the day.

THE most unforgettable
FOOD & DRINK EXPERIENCES

o **Eating illicit cheese:** Many varieties of French *fromage* (cheese) are actually illegal in the United States because they're made with raw, unpasteurized milk—this adds depth of flavor to the cheese. While in France, sample the oozy Brie de Meaux (or Brie de Melun, if it's available), the pungent washed rind cheese Epoisses, or a very young and tangy snow-white chèvre. Our favorite cheese shop is **Androuet** (37 rue de Verneuil; ✆ **01-42-61-97-55;** www.androuet.com) in the 7th arrondissement, though there are other locations around the city.

o **Pairing that cheese with a warm baguette:** Just across the street from the Androuet cheese shop in the 7e is the **Eric Kayser** bakery (p. 223). Run by an acclaimed Alsatian who has patented several

Fresh baguettes.

Picnicking in the Champ de Mars.

Sampling local wines.

bread-making techniques, this bakery sells at least four different types of baguette, all chewy and delicious.

o **Filling a box of chocolates:** It's impossible to walk into a chocolatarie and not be tempted to take home a box. Choose the size of the box, and then begin the fun task of pointing out whatever *pralinés* and *ganaches* you'd like to try. Our favorite *chocolatiers* are **Jacques Genin** (133 rue du Turenne, 3e; ✆ **01-45-77-29-01**) and **Patrick Roger** (108 boulevard Saint-Germain, 6e; ✆ **01-43-29-38-42**; www.patrickroger.com).

o **Going au naturel:** Natural wines, which are made from organic grapes and use few preservatives or stabilizing agents, are all the rage in Paris right now. The best place to learn about these (by drinking, of course) is **Vivant** (p. 203),

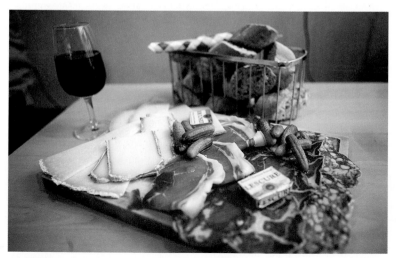

The makings of a Parisian meal: cheese, charcuterie, cornichons, bread, and wine.

a restaurant in the 10th arrondissement that's run by a leader in the *vins naturels* movement named Pierre Jancou.

o **Surrendering control:** Tasting menus that offer no choices are becoming increasingly popular in Paris's restaurants. If you're ready to put yourself in the hands of a talented chef, try **Le Chateaubriand** (p. 206), **La Bigarrade** (p. 197), or **Spring** (p. 183).

o **Having a picnic:** When the weather is nice, the banks of the Seine River and the Canal St-Martin and the city's many parks become lined with Parisians enjoying a picnic in the open air. Bring a baguette, some cheese, and a bottle of wine, and join the locals for some of the cheapest fun to be had in Paris.

THE best MUSEUMS

o **Palais de Tokyo:** The Palais de Tokyo is a contemporary "art mall" that displays radical emerging art—even its hours (noon–midnight) are radical. After its 2011 renovation and expansion, the museum has become even more monumental, with double the exhibition space. You're bound to see thought-provoking exhibitions that you'd be unlikely to see elsewhere. See p. 114.

o **Musée du Louvre:** The Louvre's exterior is a triumph of French architecture, and its interior shelters an embarrassment of art, one of the greatest treasure troves known to Western civilization. Of the Louvre's more than 300,000 paintings, only a small percentage can be displayed at one time. The museum maintains its staid dignity and timelessness even though thousands of visitors traipse daily through its corridors, looking for the *Mona Lisa* or the *Venus de Milo*. I. M. Pei's controversial Great Pyramid nearly offsets the grandeur of the Cour Carrée, but it has a real functional purpose. See p. 85.

o **Musée d'Orsay:** The spidery glass-and-iron canopies of a former railway station frame one of Europe's greatest museums of art. Devoted mainly to paintings of the 19th century, d'Orsay contains some of the most celebrated masterpieces of the French Impressionists, along with sculptures and decorative objects whose designs forever changed the way European artists

Musée du Louvre.

Centre Pompidou.

interpreted line, movement, and color. This is also where *Whistler's Mother* sits in her rocker. See p. 142.

o **Centre Pompidou:** "The most avant-garde building in the world," or so it is known, is a citadel of modern art, with exhibitions drawn from more than 40,000 works. Everything seemingly is here—from Calder's 1928 *Josephine Baker* (one of his earliest versions of the mobile) to a re-creation of Brancusi's Jazz Age studio. See p. 96.

o **Musée Jacquemart-André:** The 19th-century town house, with its gilt salons and elegant winding staircase, contains the best small collection of 18th-century decorative art in Paris. The building and its contents were a bequest to the Institut de France by the late Mme Nélie Jacquemart-André, herself an artist of note. See p. 112.

o **Musée National du Moyen Age/ Thermes de Cluny:** This museum houses some of the most beautiful medieval art still in existence. Dark, rough-walled, and evocative, the Cluny is devoted to the church art and castle crafts of the Middle Ages. It is more celebrated for its tapestries—among them the world-famed series of *The Lady and the Unicorn*. Here you can also visit the ruins of Roman baths, dating from around A.D. 200. See p. 130.

The Lady and the Unicorn tapestries.

o **Musée Marmottan Monet:** On the edge of the Bois de Boulogne, this museum is home to 130 paintings, watercolors, pastels, and drawings of Claude Monet, the "father of Impressionism." A gift of Monet's son Michel, the bequest is one of the greatest art acquisitions in France. Exhibited here is the painting *Impression: Sunrise,* which named the artistic movement. See p 113.

o **Musée Rodin:** Auguste Rodin, the man credited with freeing French sculpture from classicism, once lived at and had his studio in this charming 18th-century mansion across from Napoleon's tomb. Today, the house and its garden are filled with his works, including *The Thinker* crouched on his pedestal, the *Burghers of Calais,* and the writhing *Gates of Hell.* See p. 145.

THE best ACTIVITIES FOR FAMILIES

o **Best for Keeping the Kids Quiet: Les Catacombes,** a creepy underground ossuary, will have the kids transfixed. Wander through almost 2km (1¼ miles) of labyrinthine corridors lined with six million bones, transferred here from Parisian cemeteries over 200 years ago. In the past, it served as a quarry, where stone was extracted for building, and during World War II, the French Resistance used the tunnel system to outsmart the German soldiers. See p. 149.

o **Best for History:** Originally a royal garden dedicated to medicinal plants, the **Jardin des Plantes,** set within a park that includes the **Natural History Museum,** offers a mesmerizing overview of the history of both sea and land creatures and gives an insight into the impact of man on nature by spotlighting different extinct and endangered animals. There are also the recently reopened greenhouses, which present different natural and plant environments, from tropical rainforests to deserts; there's a space dedicated to geology and mineralogy; a Gallery of Paleontology which presents a fascinating collection of fossils and specimens, including dinosaurs, mammoths, and

Les Catacombes.

even the skeleton of Louis XV's pet rhinoceros! Plus there's a charming zoo, featuring over 900 animals, everything from wallabies to pink flamingos to orangutans. See p. 130.

Sleeping Beauty's Castle.

o **Best for Wearing the Kids Out:** Europe's most visited theme park, **Disneyland Paris,** offers total sensory overload for the whole family in its five lands: Main Street, U.S.A., Adventureland, Frontierland, Fantasyland, and Discoveryland. Fairy tales come alive in Sleeping Beauty's Castle, and adventurers will love Indiana Jones and the Temple of Peril. See p. 364.

o **Best for a Picnic: Parc des Buttes Chaumont,** a large 19th-century park built by Napoleon III, is full of exciting features that the kids will love, like cliffs, a suspension bridge leading to a romantic stone belvedere, a lake with ducks and swans, and a massive grotto with a thundering waterfall. There are pony rides, a merry-go-round, an adventure playground, and a puppet theater too. See p. 128.

o **Best Gross Out:** Rémy the rat from the animated 2007 film *Ratatouille* made his way up from the Paris sewers to take the reins of the restaurant made famous by his gastronomic hero, Auguste Gusteau. Take the kids on this smelly tour through **Les Egouts,** the city's sewers, and give them a new perspective on the city and its history. See p. 142.

o **Best Climb: Basilique du Sacré-Coeur,** an impressive neo-Byzantine basilica, crowns the Montmartre hill, the highest point in the city. Give your calf muscles a workout getting to the top: Take the Metro to Anvers and walk up the hill to the gardens surrounding the church; from there, the funicular can take you up to the church, where around 500 steps await to take you to the very top of the edifice, and its panoramic views of the city below. See p. 118.

o **Best Place to Run and Play: Parc de la Villette,** Paris's largest park, includes 10 astounding gardens that guarantee the whole family a memorable day. Here you'll find the Garden of Childhood Fears, with its mysterious musical forest; the Garden of Acrobatics, with games involving balance and movement; the Dragon Garden; the Garden of Mirrors; and more. The park includes vast open spaces ideal for picnics and games. See p. 128.

o **Best Photo Moment:** At the **Musée Grevin,** kids can pose for a snapshot with their favorite French hero, such as basketball star Tony Parker and singer Celine Dion. Take a tour of the history of France via 300 wax personalities, from Joan of Arc to King Louis XIV. There's also a discovery tour that takes you behind the scenes to learn how the wax dummies are made; here children can touch all the materials used, including the wax, glass eyes, and (real) hair! See p. 117.

- **Best for Thrill-Seekers:** For the summer months of July and August, the **Jardin des Tuileries** hosts a **funfair** (www.feteforaine-jardindestuileries.com), a special amusement park that boasts all the classic amusements such as a shooting gallery, trampolines, and a century-old wooden carousel. The enormous Ferris wheel provides superb views over Paris. See p. 82.

- **Best for a Hike:** **La Promenade Plantée,** a former railway line abandoned since 1969, has been transformed into a 4.5km (2.8-mile) pedestrian walkway that

Walking through La Promenade Plantée.

runs through the 12th arrondissement. It begins near Bastille at the Avenue Dausmenil and ends at the Bois de Vincennes. Have fun cutting through the city on this elevated green path, planted with all sorts of plants and trees. See p. 122.

THE best FREE & DIRT CHEAP PARIS

- **Meeting the Natives:** Meeting Parisians is one of the adventures of traveling to Paris—and it's free. Visitors often find Parisians brusque to the point of rudeness, but this hardened crust often protects a soft center. Compliment a surly bistro owner on her cuisine, and—9 times out of 10 —she'll melt before your eyes. Admire a Parisian's dog or praise a window display and you'll find a loquaciously knowledgeable companion. Try to meet a Parisian halfway with some kind of personalized contact. Only then do you learn their best qualities: their famed charm, their savoir-faire—and, yes, believe it or not, the delightful courtesy that marks their social life.

- **Attending a Free Concert:** Summer brings a Paris joy: free concerts in parks and churches all over the city. Pick up an entertainment weekly for details. Some of the best concerts are held at the **American Church in Paris,** 65 quai d'Orsay, 7e (© **01-40-62-05-00;** p. 271), which sponsors free concerts from September to June on Sunday at 5pm. You can also attend free concerts at **Eglise St-Merry,** 78 rue St-Martin, 4e (© **01-42-71-93-93;** p. 271). These performances are staged based on the availability of the performers, from September to July on Saturday at 9pm and again on Sunday at 4pm.

- **Hanging Out at Place des Vosges:** Deep in the Marais, place des Vosges is more an enchanted island than a city square. Laid out in 1605 by order of Henri IV, this lovely oasis is the oldest square in Paris. In the middle is a tiny park where you can sit and sun, listen to the splashing waters of the fountains, or watch the kids at play. On three sides is an encircling arcaded walk,

Strolling through the arcade at place des Vosges.

A contemporary art exhibit.

supported by arches and paved with ancient, worn flagstones. Sit sipping an espresso and people-watch as the day passes you by. See p. 103.

○ **Viewing Contemporary Art:** Space is too tight to document the dozens of art galleries that abound in Paris, but the true devotee will find that not all great art in Paris is displayed in a museum. There is a tendency, however, for owners to open galleries around major museums, hoping to lure the art lovers in. This is especially true around the Centre Pompidou, in the Marais. Our favorite galleries in the Marais include big guns **Emmanuel Perrotin,** 76 rue du Turenne, 3e (✆ **01-42-16-79-79;** www.galerieperrotin.com), and **Yvon Lambert,** 108 rue Vieille du Temple, 3e (✆ **01-42-71-09-330;** www.yvon-lambert.com). They display changing exhibits from both Parisian and international avant-garde artists. More traditional galleries are found in St-Germain-des-Prés, many along the Rue de Seine.

○ **Strolling the World's Grandest Promenade:** Pointing from place de la Concorde like a broad, straight arrow to the Arc de Triomphe at the far end, the **Champs-Élysées** (the main street of Paris) presents its grandest spectacle at night. Paris guidebook writers grow tired of repeating "the most in the world," but, of course, the Champs-Élysées is the world's most famous promenade. For the first third of the stroll from place de la Concorde, the avenue is lined by chestnut trees. Then it changes into a double row of palatial hotels and shops, office buildings, and endless sidewalk cafes.

○ **Cooling Off in the Jardin des Tuileries:** Parisians head to the Tuileries Gardens to cool off on a hot summer day. The park stretches on the Right Bank of the Seine from the place de la Concorde to the doorstep of the Louvre. This exquisitely formal garden was laid out as a royal pleasure ground in 1564, but was thrown open to the public by the French Revolution. Filled with statues (some by Rodin), fountains, and mathematically trimmed hedges, its nicest feature is a series of round ponds on which kids sail armadas of model boats. Stand on the elevated terrace by the Seine, enjoying panoramic views over Paris.

○ **Seeing Paris from a Bus:** Most tours of Paris are expensive, but for only 1.60€ you can ride one of the city's public buses traversing some of the most

Relaxing in the Jardin des Tuileries.

scenic streets. Our favorite is no. 29, which begins at historic Gare St-Lazare, subject of Monet's painting *La Gare St-Lazare* at Musée d'Orsay and featured in Zola's novel *La Bête Humainee*. Aboard no. 29, you pass the famous Opéra Garnier and proceed into the Marais district, passing by Paris's most beautiful square, place des Vosges. You end up at the Bastille district, home of the new opera. It's a close encounter with backstreet Paris and a cheap way to see the city without a tour guide's commentary.

THE best HISTORIC EXPERIENCES

- o **Invoking Ancient Rome at the Musée National du Moyen Age/Thermes de Cluny (Musée de Cluny):** This museum associates two historic edifices: the medieval Hôtel of the Abbots of Cluny and the ruins of the city's Gallo-Roman baths. These ancient thermal baths date from when the city—then known as Lutetia—was under Roman rule, between the 1st and 3rd centuries. *Thermae,* or municipal baths, were at the center of daily life in Roman society, providing a social forum for citizens. These ruins, along with the nearby outdoor amphitheater, are the only significant traces of the city's Roman period. See p. 130.

- o **Discovering the Oldest Church in Paris at St-Germain-des-Prés:** This is the oldest church in Paris, predating the Gothic Notre-Dame cathedral nearby by at least 600 years. The site was originally a Benedictine abbey founded in 542 by the Merovingian King Childebert to house a relic of the cross brought back from Spain. The Vikings pillaged the building in the 7th century, but the tower and nave were rebuilt 2 centuries later, and are now the only remaining vestiges of Romanesque architecture left in Paris. See p. 138.

The Conciergerie.

o **Remembering Marie Antoinette at the Conciergerie:** The seat of royal power for 400 years, from the 10th to the 14th centuries, this is the oldest royal palace in the capital. After Charles V abandoned the palace for a new residence in the current Marais, it was converted into a prison, and during the French Revolution, Marie Antoinette was held there before being guillotined. It's a great example of the architecture of the Middle Ages; don't miss the Gens d'Armes room, the Guard room, and the kitchens. On the northeastern corner you can still see the city's first public clock, installed in 1370. See p. 97.

o **Exploring the Musée du Louvre:** The history of the Louvre and the history of Paris are practically one. This emblematic building has dominated the center of the city since the 12th century, changing over the years from a medieval fortress (you can still see these foundations in the basement today) to the gargantuan palace it became under the Sun King, Louis XIV, in the 17th century. Today, the Louvre is one of the world's most important museums. See p. 85.

o **Commemorating Medieval Times at La Sainte-Chapelle:** This medieval monument on the Ile de la Cité was built to house Christ's crown of thorns, which King Louis

The stained-glass windows of Sainte-Chapelle.

IX (Saint Louis) bought from the emperor of Constantinople in the 13th century. Considered a veritable masterpiece of Gothic architecture, it features 600 sq. m (6,460 sq. ft.) of magnificent stained-glass windows. The architecture is so delicate that when you are inside the church, you feel as if you are in palace entirely constructed of colored glass. See p. 103.

o **Reliving the French Revolution at Place de la Bastille:** The Bastille prison once stood here, and its storming on July 14, 1789, signaled the start of the French Revolution. In 1794, the revolutionary authorities beheaded 75 enemies of the state with its guillotine. Today the Bastille Square remains a powerfully symbolic site for Parisians and many marches and demonstrations start or finish here. See p. 122.

o **Honoring Napoleon at the Arc de Triomphe:** Napoleon commissioned this triumphal arch in 1806 in homage to his military victories. It is decorated with reliefs and sculptures representing scenes from his epic battles, and is the centerpiece of the place Charles de Gaulle-Etoile. Twelve majestic avenues commence at the base of the monument, most of which bear the names of famous battles fought by Napoleon (for example, Friedland and Wagram). The view from the top is incredible. See p. 104.

o **Drinking with the literary greats at Café de Flore:** The Café de Flore has been at the center of the city's intellectual life since it opened its doors in 1887. The writer Charles Maurras wrote his book *Au signe de Flore* there. The cafe has been associated with poets Guillaume Apollinaire, Louis Aragon, and Jacques Prévert; philosopher Jean-Paul Sartre; and expat American writers Arthur Koestler, Ernest Hemingway, and Truman Capote. Today, you can still order a glass of *vin*, and toast to all the drinks, arguments, and ideas that have passed through this exceptional place. See p. 229.

THE best LOCAL EXPERIENCES

o **Picnicking on the Canal St-Martin:** On a nice day, pack a picnic lunch and head to the banks of the charming Canal St-Martin, where you'll find bohemian Parisians relaxing under the shady plane trees and dining with friends. See p. 117.

o **Feasting on Oysters and Chablis:** During oyster season (Sept–Apr), take the time for a briny lunch of *fines de claire* oysters washed down with a glass—or two—of Chablis, a white wine from Burgundy. Many bistros and brasseries serve oysters during this period—you'll know by the heaping mounds of oysters set up on tables in front of these establishments.

o **Easting Asian in Chinatown:** While most visitors don't associate Paris with Asian food, the city has an important Asian community originating primarily from China, Laos, Vietnam, and Cambodia. There are three different Chinatowns in the city; the two most important Chinatowns are located at Métro Belleville and in the 13th arrondissement near Metro Porte d'Ivry. Here you can eat well (and cheaply) while seeing a different side of the city. See p. 200.

o **Riding a Bike:** The city's small size and predominantly flat terrain make it ideal for cycling. The city government actively encourages bike riding: you'll see bike

Shopping at a local food market.

paths around the city, and there's even an efficient municipal bike rental system, the **Vélib'** (www.velib.paris.fr). It's an invigorating way to see the city.

o **Bathing in a Hammam:** Bathhouses are common in Paris; this custom was imported by Paris's important communities from Maghreb, where hammams are prevalent. The best known and perhaps most beautiful hammam is the one inside the **La Grande Mosquée de Paris.** Strip down (it's women or men only) and relax in the succession of increasingly hot steam rooms, before plunging into a cold pool. Finish off the experience with a cleansing mint tea. See p. 129.

o **Perusing the Local Food Markets:** Possibly everything there is to say about the charm of the city's local food markets has already been said—it's a delight for all the senses. Get inspired by the variety of fresh French produce, from its cheeses to charcuteries to fruits, vegetables, seafood, meats, and world-class bread. See p. 243.

o **Hitting the Sales:** Twice a year Paris shops sacrifice their current collections, with up to 75% reductions, to make way for new stock. Summer sales start in the last week of June, and winter sales

Bicycling along the Canal St-Martin.

start in early January. Parisians stock up on everything from clothes to home goods to electronics at these city-wide sales. See p. 266.

- **Taking an Aperitif:** The *apéro* (predinner drink) is a common ritual in Paris, where Parisian meet in their favorite local bars and bistros for a chat and a drink, usually around 7pm. The aperitif is meant to open the appetite, and classic examples include white wine, champagne, pastis, or vermouth. See p. 229.

THE best NEIGHBORHOODS FOR GETTING LOST

- **Montmartre:** Striding a hill atop Paris, Montmartre used to be a village of artists, glorified by masters such as Utrillo, and painted, sketched, sculpted, and photographed by 10,000 lesser talents. Today, it's overrun by tourists, building speculators, and nightclub entrepreneurs who moved in as the artists moved out. However, a few still linger and so does much of the villagelike charm. See p. 157.

- **Quartier Latin:** Over the Seine on the Left Bank, the Latin Quarter lies in the 5th arrondissement and consists of streets winding around the Paris University, of which the Sorbonne is only a part. The logical starting point is place Saint-Michel, right on the river. From here you can wander at leisure, getting lost as you discover the dog-legged cluster of alleys adjoining the river—rue de la Huchette, rue de la Harpe, rue St-Séverin. End up by strolling along boulevard St-Germain, lined with sophisticated cafes and shops. See p. 163.

A staircase in Montmartre.

- **Le Marais:** The vaguely defined maze of streets north of place de la Bastille, known as Le Marais, or "the Marsh," is an attraction in itself. During the 17th century, this was a region of aristocratic mansions, which lost their elegance when the fashionable set moved elsewhere. The houses lost status, but they remain standing and restored today, as the once-decaying Marais has been gentrified. Today, it's one of the most fashionable districts in Paris, home to funky shops, offbeat hotels, dozens of bistros, hot bars, and "gay Paree." See p. 168.

- **Ile St-Louis:** A footbridge behind Notre-Dame leads to this enchanting island on the Seine, full of tree-shaded quays, town houses with courtyards, and antiques shops. This smaller and more tranquil of the Seine islands has

A street in the Quartier Latin.

remained much as it was in the 17th century. Over the years, many illustrious French have called St-Louis home—none more famous than Voltaire. This is our favorite real estate for wandering in the whole city. See p. 91.

o **Ile de la Cité:** "The cradle of Paris," where the city was born, is actually an island shaped like a great ship in the middle of the Seine. The site of France's greatest cathedral, Notre-Dame, it invites exploration and wandering. Home to French kings until the 14th century, Cité still has a curiously medieval air, with massive gray walls rising up all around you, relieved by tiny patches of parkland. Sainte-Chapelle and the Conciergerie are both found on the island. See p. 91.

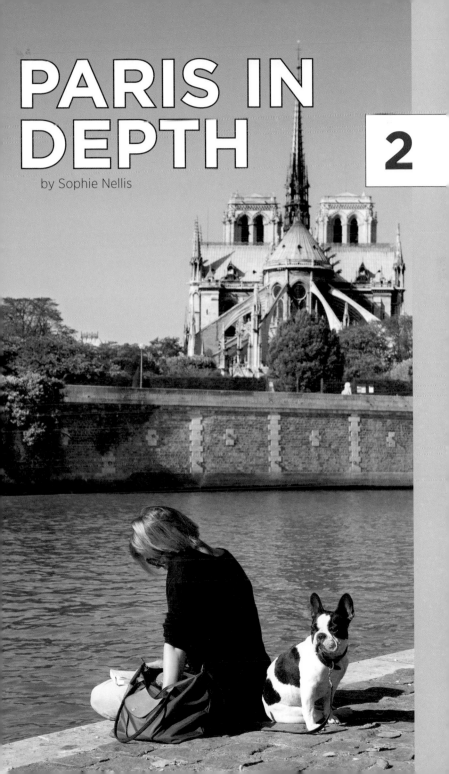

PARIS IN DEPTH

by Sophie Nellis

2

P aris is a city that is steeped in history, and its past is omnipresent throughout the city. Over the centuries, the city has been shaped by many great men, a few great women, and its rowdy and rebellious inhabitants: the Parisians. From Philippe Auguste, the first king to build a wall around the city, to François Mitterrand, the former French president responsible for I. M. Pei's glass pyramid in the Louvre, Paris's rulers have ensured their places in history by imprinting their tastes and their political visions on the city. But the Parisians have always been skeptical of authority. Whether they are building barricades, hurling cobblestones, or marching through the streets, Parisians have always made it clear that the city belongs to them. They remain very proud of Paris, and, thanks to the city's great art, fashion, and food, Parisians are some of the most cultured people on the planet.

However, over the past few decades, many Parisians have been complaining that the city has lost its soul, that it's turning into *Paris Ville-Musée* (Paris the Museum). Less edgy than Berlin and less hip than London, Paris seemed to be stagnating. But the city is fighting back, and is slowly reinventing itself as a 21st-century capital. From the young designers setting up shop in the 3rd arrondissement to the pioneering chefs who are experimenting with neo-bistrots, and from new sustainability initiatives—such as the Vélib' bike-rental program—to a growing immigrant population, the city is rapidly changing and Parisian traditions are being injected with a new sense of dynamism. The future of Paris is far from certain but one thing's for sure: Paris is a city on the move.

PARIS TODAY

Paris is a city of neighborhoods, each with its own distinct atmosphere. The center of the city remains a beautiful and elegant area that is also the center of business and culture. However, over the past few decades, many Parisians have been complaining that the city has lost its soul, and that it's turning into *Paris Ville-Musée* (Paris the Museum). Rising housing prices have made it virtually impossible for anyone other than the superwealthy to live in central Paris, and more neighborhoods are becoming gentrified. For a city that is infamous for its revolutions and rebellions, many Parisians complain that the city has become somewhat sanitized.

As very few people can afford to live in the city center, you'll find much more life in the outer arrondissements. In recent years, there's been a shift toward the northern and northeastern arrondissements, which were traditionally

PREVIOUS PAGE: **Relaxing on the Seine.**

home to the city's *quartiers populaires* (working-class districts). These neighborhoods tend to be edgy and dynamic, as prices are lower, rents are cheaper, and the nightlife is better. Here, you'll find a mix of students, artists, immigrants, middle-class families, and **bobos** (short for *bourgeois-bohèmes*, which means bourgeois bohemian). Who are the *bobos*? Usually liberal, the *bobos* are a creative and chic group, most of whom have a middle-class education and strong ambitions for success. Over the past decade, the *bobos* have been transforming the face of Paris, moving into the *quartiers populaires* and bringing with them chic boutiques, trendy bars, and organic restaurants. As more and more parts of Paris become gentrified, the *bobos* are now key players in the life and soul of the city.

Sadly, there are very few genuine *quartiers populaires* left in Paris. Since the 1960s, the city's working-class population and the majority of the region's immigrant population have been forced to live farther and farther outside of the city in the **banlieues** (suburbs). Northern suburbs such as St-Denis and Aubervilliers-La Courneuve are infamous for their sprawling housing estates (known as *cites*), poor transport connections, high unemployment, and high crime rate. Understandably, many young people living in these suburbs, particularly the children of immigrants, feel isolated and excluded from French society. These social tensions exploded in October 2005, when two teenage boys were electrocuted while hiding from police in an electricity substation in Clichy-sous-Bois. Their deaths sparked huge riots in the vast, run-down housing estates in the *banlieues*; the violence spread all over France, from Marseilles to Strasbourg, and lasted for several weeks. Since the 2005 riots, the *banlieues* have received a great deal of media attention but nobody is sure how to deal with what appears to be a profound sense of alienation. For young people living in these troubled suburbs today, little has changed. It remains very difficult to get a job in Paris if your address places you in one of the *cites*, and in some of the racially diverse estates in Clichy-sous-Bois, unemployment for those under 25 is as high as 40%.

However, some of the suburbs—such as Issy-les-Moulineaux, Levallois-Perret, and Montreuil—are quite nice, and many middle-class families have been leaving Paris for these more affordable locales. There are more than 10 million people living in the Parisian suburbs and only around 2.2 million in Paris. The *banlieues* are burgeoning, and many people believe that the solution to the museum-ification of Paris lies here. Consequently, one of the biggest challenges facing Paris today is how to better integrate the city into its surrounding suburbs. In April 2009, President **Nicolas Sarkozy** proposed an ambitious urban renewal project, **Le Grand Paris,** which aims to improve transportation and housing, while making Paris a greener, more sustainable 21st-century city. As part of this program, the city has accepted 10 proposals from various renowned architects—including Jean Nouvel, Roland Castro, and Richard Rogers—but has yet to decide on a specific plan of action. Ideas include a monorail-style metro running above the *périphérique* (the ring road that surrounds Paris, known as the *périph*) and green housing estates. This is an ambitious long-term project that will be implemented over the next decade, and the future of Greater Paris promises to be anything other than dull.

Sarkozy is not the only one with big ideas for the city's future. Paris's Socialist mayor **Bertrand Delanoë** is experimenting with new social housing projects. Challenging a 1977 by-law that limits the height of buildings within Paris to 37m (121 ft.), he is convinced that tower blocks offer the best solution to the housing crisis. Several sites, including Porte de la Chapelle in the 18e and the

Street musicians.

Masséna-Bruneseau district of the 13e, have been chosen as potential locations for 50m (164 ft.) and 200m (656 ft.) towers. In addition, Delanoë is a keen advocate of the so-called Triangle, a 200m-tall (657 ft.) glass office building to be built at the Porte de Versailles in the 15e; the designers are Herzog & de Meuron, the same firm who did London's Tate Modern. Another key building project is the redevelopment of Les Halles. Architects Patrick Berger and Jacques Anziutti plan to cover the shopping center with a giant canopy and transform the surrounding area into an urban garden. Work started on *le nouveau coeur de Paris* (the new heart of Paris) in January 2011.

Delanoë, who became mayor in 2001, was the first openly gay mayor of a European capital. He was reelected in 2008, and despite his failure to win Paris's bid for the 2012 Olympic Games, he is generally well liked and respected by Parisians. He's done a lot to improve the city, including implementing free Wi-Fi in many public places, and creating programs such as Paris Plage (a fake beach set up alongside the Seine in the summer) and La Nuit Blanche (an all-night arts festival in Oct). However, he's probably best known for his environmental initiatives. It was Delanoë who was responsible for both the highly popular **Vélib'** bike-rental program and the increase in the amount of bike lanes around the city. Encouraged by the success of the Vélib' program, he recently launched another green initiative, the **Autolib',** which will encourage Parisians to rent rather than own a car.

Green is not just a popular color with the mayor. Paris is currently undergoing a *bio* (organic) revolution, and being green, organic, and ethical is very much in fashion these days. You can find the health food store **Naturalia** in nearly every neighborhood, and all major supermarkets now offer their own ranges of both organic and environmentally friendly products. Restaurants that offer organic dishes are becoming increasingly popular, and organic wine is also in high demand. Twice a year Paris hosts the **Salon des vins des Vignerons Indépendants** (the Independent Winegrowers's Tradefair).

Paris remains a food lover's dream destination and Parisians are as passionate about food and eating out as ever. The big trend in Parisian dining at the moment is the **neo-bistrot.** Known for an innovative approach to cooking and a relaxed atmosphere, the neo-bistrot serves high-quality French food at reasonable prices (usually under 50€ per person). Rejecting the formalities of

Michelin-starred restaurants, the neo-bistrots try to be more casual. One French chef, Alain Senderens, even went so far as to reject his Michelin stars. Popular neo-bistrots include **Frenchie** in the 2e (p. 184), **Claude Colliot** in the 4e, **Le Comptoir du Relais** in the 6e (p. 216), and **Jadis** in the 15e (p. 224). Another interesting, and perhaps surprising, trend is the rising popularity of Anglo-Saxon food. **The Rose Bakery** in the 3e and 9e, **Bob's Juice Bar** in the 3e and 10e (p.190), and **Le Bal Café** in the 18e (p. 204), are all doing a pretty good job of introducing Parisians to the joys of British and American cuisine. See chapter 6 for more information on dining in Paris.

This Anglo-Saxon influence is not limited to food. Younger Parisians are a fairly international bunch, most of whom can speak English and are interested in traveling and working abroad. They are also interested in English music and culture. Despite the fact that at least 40% of the music played on the Paris radio stations has to be French—thanks to a 1994 law passed to protect French pop—more and more musicians are singing in English. Charlotte Gainsbourg, alternative rock band Phoenix, and electro-pop band Pony Pony Run Run are just a few examples of French musicians who sing in English.

Culturally, Paris still has a lot to offer. From opera houses to fashion houses and art galleries to theaters, culture remains an integral part of *la vie Parisienne*. Although the art scene is not as edgy or avant-garde as in London or New York, Paris remains an important city on the exhibition circuit, hosting several major exhibitions every year, as well as the **FIAC** (Foire International d'Art Contemporain) art fair in October. Many of Paris's museums and art galleries are world-famous and a must-see for visitors, but it's also worth going a little further afield to check out newer cultural spaces. The **104,** a cultural center located in the former Municipal Funeral Service warehouses in the 19e, has a number of artists in residence and organizes events, and the long-awaited **Cité de la Mode et du Design** (Fashion and Design Museum), which is part of the Docks en Seine

France's first couple: President Nicolas Sarkozy and Carla Bruni-Sarkozy.

Bicycling is a popular means of transportation in Paris.

THE new PARISIANS

Paris is often described as a melting pot, and the city is home to large numbers of immigrant communities. While some Parisians welcome immigrants and are keen to acknowledge the contributions that immigrants have made to French society, others have balked at the perceived drain on their resources and fear that immigrants are not prepared to integrate into French society.

Immigration first became a major political debate in the 1990s and since then it has become strongly associated with questions of national identity. Some would even go so far as to say that 21st-century France is suffering from an identity crisis. As a secular, republican state, France has always favored assimilation over multiculturalism. This is partly a result of the French concept of identity, which is based on the 1789 Declaration of the Rights of Man. If all citizens are equal, ethnicity and religion must remain outside of the political sphere, and all citizens are thus divested of their origins. Consequently, it is illegal to collect ethnic-based data in France and there are no statistics about the children of immigrants. In theory, if you are born in France, you're French.

In practice, however, it's very different and many second- and third-generation immigrants don't feel French. In November 2009, Sarkozy launched a debate about national identity. At the center of the debate was the question "What does it mean to be French?" The debate received a lot of media attention and public meetings were held across the country. However, many commentators felt that the debate ignored the colonial legacy, and that the real but unspoken question was "Can one be black, Arab, Asian and still be French?" The debate is particularly pertinent in Paris because the majority of Paris's immigrant populations live on the other side of the *périphérique* in the *banlieues.* This means that there is a physical, as well as psychological, divide between Parisians and the Paris region's immigrant population. What is sure is that if Le Grand Paris or other urban renewal projects are to succeed, they must include these new Parisians. The debate continues.

Key to this immigration debate is the position of Islam in France, which is home to the largest Muslim population in Europe—Muslims account for roughly 8% of the French population. In January 2010 the government began a campaign to ban the burqa (the veil that covers all of a woman's face). Sarkozy claimed that it was not welcome in France, a secular country that values gender equality. Once again, the campaign provoked an intense media debate and in May 2010 the burqa ban was approved. Any woman seen wearing a burqa in public risks being fined 150€, while husbands who force their wives to wear it face a fine of 15,000€ or even a prison sentence. Only about 2,000 women wear the burqa in France.

project in the 13e, is due to open in October 2011, just in time for Paris fashion week. Also worth a visit is the contemporary art gallery **Mac/Val** in the Parisian suburb of Vitry-sur-Seine.

Going to the cinema remains a popular pastime for Parisians, and there is at least one cinema in each of the 20 arrondissements. Compared to other capitals, you can still find a lot of independent, art house cinemas in Paris, and a diverse range of films are always on offer in the city. Filmmakers are as fascinated by Paris as ever—look out for Woody Allen's new film *Midnight in Paris* (2011), with a cameo appearance by France's first lady, Carla Bruni-Sarkozy. French film director Luc Besson is planning to open the **Cité Européene du Cinéma** in the old EDF (Electicité de France) buildings in the troubled suburb of St-Denis. The complex, which is due to be completed in 2012, will include nine production studios, ateliers, boutiques, and restaurants, and promises to give the national film industry a huge boost.

Paris has a strong literary history, and today writers continue to flock here and be inspired by the city. Some of the most famous contemporary Parisian writers are actually writers who came to Paris from former French colonies, including Tahar Ben Jelloun (from Morocco) and Assia Djebar (from Algeria). In 2010, Le Prix Goncourt, France's most prestigious literary award, was given to Michel Houellebecq for his novel *La carte et Le Territoire (The Map and the Territory)*; Houellebecq is one of France's most famous contemporary writers.

Paris's relationship with its suburbs, immigration, and national identity will undoubtedly be key issues in the 2012 French presidential election. Sarkozy is expected to run for a second term. Former French president Dominique de Villepin, Sarkozy's most vocal critic on the traditional right, has indicated that he will challenge his archrival in the upcoming presidential election. At press time, the Parti Socialiste (PS) had yet to vote on their presidential candidate (the primaries are in October 2011) but possible contenders are Ségolene Royale, who lost to Sarkozy in 2007; Martine Aubry, the leader of the Socialist Party; and Bertrand Delanoë. In January 2011, Marine Le Pen, the leader of the far-right, xenophobic Front National (FN) announced her intention to run for president. Her popularity in the polls has sparked a political panic reminiscent of 2002 when her father and predecessor Jean-Marie Le Pen reached the second round of the Presidential election against Chirac. Although Paris is a city in a state of flux, these social, political, and cultural changes are undoubtedly injecting Paris with a new sense of dynamism.

THE MAKING OF PARIS
The Origins of Paris

Early humans were roaming the plains of Paris and hunting deer, boar, and bears as early as 700,000 years ago. Several dugout canoes that were found in Bercy in the early 1990s and date from around 4500 B.C. revealed the importance of the river in the lives of these early societies. You can see some of these boats in the **Musée Carnavelet** (p. 100) in the Marais.

By 250 B.C., a tribe of Celts known as the **Parisii** had settled on the present-day Ile de la Cité. The Parisii were first and foremost river people and the Seine was a place of trade and exchange. The strategic location of the Parisii's fortified town, and the relative wealth of the community, soon attracted the attention of the Romans.

Roman Paris & Early Christianity (52 B.C.–A.D. 400)

By the time the Romans, led by Julius Caesar, conquered the Parisii in 54 B.C., much of southern Gaul had already fallen into Roman hands. The Roman occupation of Gaul was immortalized in the enormously popular *Asterix* comic books, written by René Goscinny and illustrated by Albert Uderzo. First published in

1959, the series follows a group of Gauls—led by Asterix and his friend Obelix—as they resist the Roman occupier.

Under the Romans, this thriving community became known as **Lutetia** (*Lutèce* in French). Most of the 8,000 inhabitants lived on the Left Bank, around today's Rue St-Jacques and Boulevard St-Michel. You can still see traces of Lutetia today: the site of the 15,000-seat amphitheater on Rue Monge, the **Arènes de Lutèce** (p. 129), has been preserved, and the remains of the Roman baths are in the **Thermes de Cluny** (p. 130).

Roman ruins at the Thermes de Cluny.

Christianity first came to Paris in the form of Saint Denis. In around A.D. 250 Denis was sent from Athens to Lutetia to convert the Gallo-Roman Parisians, who were notorious for their pagan ways. Denis founded the Parisian church and became the first Bishop of Paris. Beheaded near the Gallo-Roman temple of Mercury in Montmartre, legend has it that Denis picked up his head and carried it to the present-day suburb of St-Denis where he died. Denis's headless antics led to him becoming one of the Paris's patron saints.

Saint Geneviève, a pious virgin who is said to have defended Paris from Attila the Hun, is another important figure in Paris's history. From A.D. 275 onward, Lutetia was raided by wave after wave of barbarian invaders from across the Rhine river. Although the Romans managed to hold onto the town for two more centuries, Roman rule in Gaul began to disintegrate as a result of these Germanic invasions. In A.D. 451, Attila the Hun was threatening the city and its

DATELINE

250 B.C. Parisii tribe lives on the Ile de la Cité and trades along the Seine.	**1360s** Charles V moves into the Louvre, making it a royal palace.
52 B.C. Julius Caesar conquers the city during the Gallic Wars, renaming it Lutétia.	**1546** First stones of present-day Louvre laid under François I.
A.D.250 St-Denis beheaded in Montmartre.	**1559** Construction begins on Catherine de Médici's Palais des Tuileries; building facades in Paris move from half-timbered to more durable chiseled stonework.
486 Clovis, king of the Franks chooses Paris as his capital.	
987 Hugh Capet becomes first king of the Capetian dynasty.	**1572** The Wars of Religion reach their climax with the St. Bartholomew's Day massacre of Protestants.
1253 Robert de Sorbon establishes the Sorbonne, a theology college.	

inhabitants were preparing to flee. Thanks to the intervention of young Geneviève, who prayed for Paris and encouraged the people to stay and defend the city, Attila backed off and Paris was spared. She was less fortunate in 486, when, after a ten-year blockade, Geneviève had to surrender the city to Clovis, King of the Francs. There is a shrine dedicated to St-Geneviève in the church of **St-Etienne-du-Mont** (p. 134) in the 5e, and a statue of St Geneviève on the Pont de la Tournelle, which was created by Paul Landowski in 1928. Ever wary of invaders, you'll notice St-Geneviève is facing the east.

From Clovis to the Capetians (5th c.–10th c.)

Clovis, the first king of the Franks (a west Germanic tribe) ruled in the 5th century, choosing Paris as the capital of his kingdom. Clovis founded the **Merovingian dynasty,** which ruled from 486 to 752—all of its rulers were known for their violence and ferocity. Clovis's wife, Clotilde, persuaded him to convert to Christianity and a spate of church building began the Christianization of the city. In 511 Clovis's son, **Childebert,** commissioned the cathedral of St-Etienne, the forerunner of Notre Dame—its remains can be seen in the archaeological crypt under the Place du Parvis Notre Dame. Childebert was also responsible for bringing back the relics of Saint Vincent to Paris and placing them in a chapel on the Left Bank. He decided to build a basilica to house the relics, which eventually became known as **St-Germain-des-Prés;** over the following centuries it became the Left Bank's most powerful abbey.

The Merovingians were succeeded by the militaristic **Carolingian dynasty,** which ruled from 752 to 987. The most famous of the Carolingians was **Charlemagne,** who conquered half of Europe but chose Aix-la-Chapelle (in present-day Germany), rather than Paris, as his capital. Exposed and badly defended, Paris was vulnerable to invasion and was repeatedly sacked and pillaged by the Normans in the 9th century. Many of the churches that had been built in the 6th century were destroyed. In the absence of the Carolingian kings, Paris was ruled by the counts, and in 987 they elected a new king, **Hughes Capet.** This was the

1599 Henri IV endorses the Edict of Nantes, establishing religious toleration.

1615 Construction begins on the Palais du Luxembourg for Henri IV's widow, Marie de Médici.

1624 The Palais Royal is built in honor of Cardinal Richelieu.

1683 Louis XIV, the "Sun King," moves his court to the newly built Versailles.

1789 The French Revolution begins.

1793 Louis XVI and his Austrian-born queen, Marie Antoinette, are publicly guillotined.

1804 Napoleon Bonaparte crowns himself emperor of France and embellishes Paris further with neoclassical splendor.

1814 Aided by a coalition of France's enemies, especially England, the Bourbon monarchy under Louis XVIII is temporarily restored.

1848 A violent working-class revolution deposes Louis-Philippe, who's replaced by autocratic Napoleon III.

continues

Five Paris Historical Reads

Andrew Hussey, *Paris: The Secret History* (Bloomsbury, 2006)
Colin Jones, *Paris: The Biography of a City* (Viking, 2004)
Graham Robb, *Parisians: An Adventure History of Paris* (Norton & Co., 2010)
Rod Kedward, *La Vie en bleu, France and the French Since 1900* (Penguin, 2006)
Alistair Horne, *Seven Ages of Paris* (Knopf, 2002)

beginning of a new dynasty and a new era of great prosperity for Paris. Under the **Capetian dynasty,** which ruled France from 987 to 1328, Paris was once again the royal capital and the kings lived in a palace on the Ile de la Cité (on the site of the present-day Palais de Justice).

The Middle Ages (11th c.–15th c.)

During the Middle Ages, Paris flourished and became a center of politics, commerce, trade, religion, education, and culture. The "Queen of Cities" was divided into three parts: The Ile de la Cité remained the administrative heart of Paris and it was here that you could find the symbols of state power such as the royal palace and the cathedral; the Left Bank, thanks to the creation of the University of Paris, became associated with education and learning; and the Right Bank saw a boom in commercial activity and became associated with trade and commerce. These associations have continued throughout the history of Paris and, to a certain degree, remain true today.

The 12th and 13th centuries were a time of intense building activity, and it was in this period that **Gothic architecture** was born. Engineering developments had freed church architecture from the heavy, thick walls of Romanesque structures and allowed ceilings to soar, walls to thin, and windows to proliferate. Gothic interiors enticed churchgoers' gazes upward to high ceilings filled with light. Graceful buttresses and spires soared above town centers. The Gothic

---

DATELINE continued

1853 Napoleon III asks Baron Haussmann to modernize Paris.

1860s The Impressionist style of painting emerges.

1870 The Franco-Prussian War ends in the defeat of France.

1871 Insurrectionary government known as The Paris Commune takes over Paris from March to May.

1878–1937 Several international expositions add monuments to the Paris skyline, including the Tour Eiffel.

1914–18 World War I rips Europe apart.

1940 German troops invade Paris; the French government, under Marshal Pétain, evacuates to Vichy, while the French Resistance under Gen. Charles de Gaulle maintains symbolic headquarters in London.

1944 U.S. troops liberate Paris; Charles de Gaulle returns in triumph.

1954–62 War begins in Algeria and is eventually lost; refugees flood into Paris, and the nation becomes divided over its North African policies.

The Cathédrale de Notre-Dame is a prime example of Gothic architecture.

phase is believed to have begun with Abbot Sugar's rebuilding of the **Abbey of St-Denis** in the 1140s. However, it was the **Cathédrale de Notre-Dame** (p. 92) that made the style so influential. Work began on Notre Dame in 1163, and it took 2 centuries to be built; the Gothic style was preserved until the 17th century when, in the name of restoration, the church suffered a number of mutilations. Higher than any other building in the city, Notre Dame dramatically altered the skyline of medieval Paris and could be seen from miles around. The success of **Victor Hugo's epic novel *Notre Dame de Paris,*** published in 1831, led to a revival of interest in Gothic architecture and, more importantly, to the restoration of Notre Dame. This was carried out by renowned 19th-century architect Eugéne Viollet-le-Duc.

The monarch who did the most to consolidate Paris's reputation as a great city during the Middle Ages was **Philippe Auguste,** who ruled France from 1180 to 1223. He built the **Louvre** (p. 85), a 33m-high (108-ft.) tower that was used to defend the city from attack and survey the surrounding area (the word Louvre is thought to have come from the old French word *louver,* which meant stronghold). He was also responsible for the first covered market at **Les Halles** (p. 82), which strengthened the reputation of the Right Bank as a center of commerce and trade. His greatest achievement, however, was the military fortifications he constructed around the city from 1190 to 1213. Running from the Louvre to the lower Marais on the Right Bank and encompassing the site of the present-day Panthéon and the

1958 France's Fourth Republic collapses; General de Gaulle is called out of retirement to head the Fifth Republic.	**1994** Mitterrand and Queen Elizabeth II ride under the English Channel in the new Channel Tunnel.
1968 Paris's students start rioting in the Latin Quarter.	**1995** Jacques Chirac is elected president and Mitterrand dies the following year. Paris is crippled by a general strike and terrorists bomb the subway.
1981 François Mitterrand is elected France's first Socialist president since the 1940s; he's reelected in 1988.	
1989 Paris celebrates the bicentennial of the French Revolution.	**1999** On Christmas Day a violent storm assaults Paris and the Ile de France, damaging buildings and toppling thousands of trees.
1992 Euro Disney opens on the outskirts of Paris.	

continues

area around Odéon on the Left Bank, the **Philippe Auguste Wall** had the effect of consolidating and defining the space of the city. There are several places in Paris where you can see remains of this 12th-century wall, including Rue Clovis in the 5th arrondissement and Rue des Jardins St-Paul in the Marais.

By the time Philippe Auguste died in 1223, Paris was the undisputed cultural capital of Europe. This was largely due to its intellectual activity and the reputation of the University of Paris. In the 12th century, students from across Europe flocked to the city to study medicine, law, theology, and liberal arts. In 1253, Robert de Sorbon, a royal chaplain, established a new theology college that became known as the **Sorbonne.** It quickly became one of Paris's most prestigious colleges and a byword for the University of Paris. By 1300 there were 3,000 students living on the Left Bank, most of whom spoke Latin. This is how the Latin Quarter got its name.

The Hundred Years' War (1337–1453)

In 1328, Charles IV died without an heir, bringing an end to the Capetian dynasty—this marked the end of the medieval golden age and the beginning of a troubled period in the history of Paris. The late king's cousin, **Philippe de Valois** became king, marking the beginning of the Valois dynasty, but his claim was contested by Edward III of England—this instigated the **Hundred Years' War** between France and England. Although the Valois kings ultimately won the war, it nevertheless brought financial ruin to the city of Paris. To make matters worse, the **Black Death** (bubonic plague) arrived in Paris in 1348, killing several hundred Parisians a day. For the next century Paris was full of tension, violence, plots, and intrigue.

When Charles V came to the throne in 1364, he was determined to crush the unruly forces at work within the city, and decided to both strengthen and expand the Philippe Auguste Wall. On the Right Bank, the wall encompassed a new fortress, the **Bastille** (p. 122). Charles V was the first monarch to make the Louvre a royal residence. He moved there in the late 1360s and transformed it into a luxurious and official residence.

DATELINE continued

2002 France replaces its national currency, the franc, and switches to the euro, the new European currency.

2003 Attacks on French Jews mark the rise of anti-Semitism, the worst since World War II.

2005 Riots break out in the suburbs and spread across France.

2006 Massive demonstrations against a new labor law are held in Paris and other cities. Jacques Chirac revokes the law.

2007 Pro-American Nicolas Sarkozy becomes president of France, sparking riots.

2008 France bans smoking in public places.

2010 Economic woes and a battered euro plague France.

2012 French presidential election.

A divided CITY

The dichotomies of Paris/*banlieue* (suburbs), center/periphery, inside/outside are particularly pertinent to Paris because of the physical boundary that separates the 20 arrondissements of the city from the rest of the Paris region. There has been a marker distinguishing *intra muros* (inside the wall) from *extra muros* (outside the wall) since fortifications were built around Paris in A.D. 300. The **Philippe Auguste Wall,** built between 1190 and 1213, was predominantly a defensive measure but it also served to define and distinguish the city as a royal capital. Although the position and use of the fortifications changed throughout the centuries, the social geography of the city became increasingly determined by the existence of a barrier between Paris and the world outside. After the First World War, the **Thiers fortifications,** as the barrier was then known, were considered obsolete and were slowly dismantled over several decades. This was a golden opportunity to better integrate Paris into the surrounding *banlieues,* but what happened only served to reinforce the divide between the city and its suburbs. The space created by the removal of the ramparts was eventually used to build the *boulevard périphérique.* Although many modern cities are surrounded by a ring road, the history of Paris and its fortifications renders the *périph* a powerful symbol of the divide between the center and the suburbs of Paris—the inside and the outside. It could be read as a symbol of the social exclusion and alienation experienced by those living in the *banlieues,* far away from the luxury and glamour of Paris.

The Renaissance and the Wars of Religion (16th c.)

Military escapades in Italy in the early 16th century brought the Renaissance style to France. Italian **Renaissance architecture** was characterized by its use of symmetry, decorative facades, columns and pilasters, and domes. In France, the continuing prevalence of the Gothic style, combined with the need for steep roofs and tall chimneys, created a Renaissance style with a particular French emphasis; this later evolved into a style known as French Classicism. The Renaissance style was instigated by **François I,** whose greatest achievement in Paris was the **Louvre** (p. 85); a Renaissance-style palace was a very public affirmation of glory. In 1546, the medieval palace and fortress that were the existing Louvre were destroyed and the first stones of the present-day Louvre were laid by the architect Pierre Lescot in the Cour Carrée. For the next 3 centuries, François I's Renaissance palace served as the model for all subsequent extensions and additions to the Louvre.

The Reformation, the religious movement that established Protestantism and was begun by Martin Luther in Germany in 1517, had caused bitter conflict between Catholics and Protestants, known as Huguenots, in France. By the 1560s, this conflict had turned into civil war and the **Wars of Religion** lasted from 1562 to 1598. The bloodiest atrocity of the Wars of Religion, the **St. Bartholomew's Day Massacre,** took place in Paris on August 24, 1572. The scheming powerhouse at the heart of the French court, Catherine de Medici, had arranged for her daughter Marguerite de Valois to marry Henri de Navarre, a

The Louvre is a Renaissance-style palace.

Protestant aristocrat from the Bourbon family. While the official reason for the marriage was to join the two opposing religious forces in a union that would support the monarchy, Catherine had a number of hidden motives: there were a large number of Huguenots in Paris for the wedding, and on the morning of August 24, the tolling of the bell in St-Germain l'Auxerriois acted as a signal for the Catholics to start massacring Huguenots. Between 1,500 and 2,000 Huguenots were killed, but Henri de Navarre was spared, thanks to his wife. Marguerite de Valois's turbulent life and the massacre were the inspiration for **Alexandre Dumas's 1845 novel, *La Reine Margot*,** which in turn inspired the 1994 film adaptation of the same name.

Henri IV (1589–1610)

After a dark and turbulent century, Paris entered a dynamic period of growth in the late 16th century, under the guidance of Henri IV, and later, his son and successor Louis XIII. **Henri IV** became king in 1589, but it was 5 years before he entered Paris. Determined to win the Parisians over, the Huguenot king converted to Catholicism, announcing *"Paris vaut bien une messe"* ("Paris deserves a mass"). In 1599 he signed the Edict of Nantes, which ended the Wars of Religion and led to long-lasting religious toleration and diversity in France.

	Pierre Abélard

One of Paris's most famous medieval scholars was Pierre Abélard. After arriving in the city in 1108, Abélard quickly became one of most popular teachers and philosophers in Paris. He was employed by the canon of Notre Dame to tutor his niece, Héloïse, in theology and philosophy. Abélard and Héloïse fell in love and eloped to Brittany where they got married and had a son.

However, Abélard was not ready to swap academic life for domestic life and on his way back to Paris he sent Héloïse to a convent. Believing Abélard had abandoned his niece, Fulbert and a group of his cronies went to Abélard's house during the night and castrated him. Despite his scholarly brilliance, Abélard's reputation never quite recovered.

Five Paris Paintings

Eugène Delacroix, *La Liberté guidant le people* (1830)
Edouard Manet, *Olympia* (1863)
Claude Monet, *Le Pont de l'Europe–Gare St-Lazare* (1877)
Pablo Picasso, *Les Demoiselles d'Avignon* (1907)
Auguste Renoir, *Bal du moulin de la Galette* (1876)

Henri IV, known as *Le Vert Galant* (which roughly translates as "the old charmer") due to his fondness for the ladies, was very committed to Paris and was determined to restore the city to its earlier eminence. Like François I before him, he wanted the Louvre to be a testament to his power so he decided to link the Louvre with the Palais de Tuileries by building what is now known as the **Grande Galerie.** (In 1559 Catherine de Medici had ordered the construction of the Palais de Tuileries, which would have stood in between the current Jardin des Tuileries and the Arc de Triomphe du Carrousel.) This palace became the home of the reigning monarch while the Louvre was the symbol of state power.

Henri IV was also responsible for the building of the **place des Vosges** (then known as the Place Royale; p. 103), which transformed the Marais from a marshy wasteland to one of Paris's most fashionable areas. A number of the Marais's finest *hôtel particuliers* (private mansions) were built during this period.

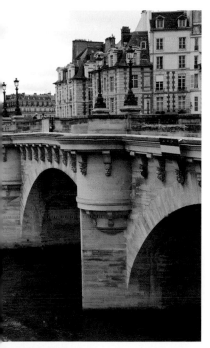

The Pont Neuf.

Arguably, Henri IV's most important contribution to Paris was the **Pont Neuf** (p. 95). It was the first stone bridge to cross the Seine, and the first bridge that did not have houses or shops on it. Its unprecedented length and width (232m x 22m/761 ft. x 72 ft.) made it the longest bridge in Paris. At the time, its name, which means New Bridge, was deserved. Today, as the other bridges across the Seine have all been replaced, it stands as the oldest bridge in Paris. Once completed, it became a hub of activity and in his *Tableau de Paris* in 1788, Louis-Sébastien Mercier declared the Pont Neuf to be "to the city what the heart is to the body: the center of movement and of circulation." Henri IV was assassinated by a Catholic fanatic called François Ravaillac while his carriage was stuck in traffic on the Rue de la Ferronerie (near Les Halles). However, the city continued to expand and the population continued to increase after his death.

The Sun King & Versailles (1638–1789)

Louis XIV, known as *le Roi Soleil* (the Sun King), became king in 1638 at the age of 4. He ruled until his death in 1715 at the age of 76, making him the longest ruling monarch in the history of Europe. His reign marked the peak of absolute monarchy in France, and he is famous for asserting "I am the State." Early in his reign, he was attracted to the idea that the glorification of the capital city would both add to prestige of his own dynasty and create a dominant royal presence. He built the two triumphal arches at Porte St-Denis and Porte St-Martin, and was responsible for the Baroque-style **Hôtel des Invalides** (p. 139), a complex of buildings designed to house injured and elderly soldiers from the king's army. The hospital of Salpêtrière in the 13e was built to shelter fallen women.

However, Louis XIV soon abandoned Paris for **Versailles.** He spent colossal sums of money enlarging the former hunting lodge of his father, Louis XIII. Built in the excessive Baroque style, Versailles is the embodiment of grandeur and indulgence. The French court officially moved there in 1683, and from then on Paris was eclipsed by the courtly goings on in Versailles. After the death of Louis XIV, the infant **Louis XV** lived in Paris for several years but soon scuttled back to Versailles. His successor, **Louis XVI** had no intention of living in Paris. Over the years various additions were made to the palace, including the Hall of Mirrors, the

Louis XIV (The Sun King).

Petit Trianon (which was built in the 1760s for Louis XV's mistress, Mme de Pompadour), and La Petite Ferme, where Louis XVI's wife, Marie Antoinette, played at being a milkmaid. **Sofia Coppola's 2006 film, *Marie Antoinette,*** despite its anachronisms and rock soundtrack, superbly captures the decadence and frivolity of Versailles and the last years of the *Ancien Régime.*

The Enlightenment (18th c.)

Despite the absence of the king, the 18th century was one of the most prestigious and dynamic periods in Paris's history. Paris became the unofficial capital of the **Enlightenment,** the age of rational humanism. Philosophers and intellectuals, such as **Rousseau** and **Voltaire,** gathered in coffeehouses and bars to criticize the monarchy and discuss alternative forms of government. The population soared from half a million in 1715 to more than 650,000 in 1789. Literacy rates were increasing and the number of books published increased threefold. This was also the heyday of the **Palais Royal** (p. 90); in the early 1780s, Philippe II, the duc d'Orléans, transformed his Parisian residence into a semipublic space that became the meeting place of intellectuals, prostitutes, and sexual adventurers.

The storming of the Bastille.

However, the increasing wealth of the city only served to highlight the vast gap between rich and poor. The ruling elite feared the *sans-culottes* (which means "without breeches"), members of the lower working classes who lived and worked in the warrenlike alleys around Rue du Faubourg St-Antoine (off the present-day Place de la Bastille). Rumors of the excess and decadence of Versailles led people to perceive the court as increasingly corrupt and immoral. From 1784 to 1787, Louis VXI aroused the hostility of the Parisian working classes by building the Farmers General Wall, a customs barrier. Anyone bringing products into the city from outside Paris had to pay a tax. When a riot started on July 14, 1789, the mob attacked the **Bastille** and various outposts of the Farmers General Wall, thus starting the French Revolution.

The French Revolution (1789–1799)

The storming of the Bastille, on July 14, 1789, was the beginning of the French Revolution. Although the events that took place in Paris during the revolution would change France forever, the face of the city itself changed very little.

 Five French Novels

Muriel Barbery, *The Elegance of the Hedgehog* (Europa Editions, 2008)
Michel Houellebecq, *Platform* (Knopf, 2003)
Victor Hugo, *The Hunchback of Notre-Dame* (1831)
Georges Perec, *Life: A User's Manual* (1978)
Emile Zola, *The Belly of Paris* (1873)

Instead, the city was "reclaimed" by the people. They were more interested in destroying the symbols of the *Ancien Régime* than building anything new. This was exemplified by the destruction of a number of churches and abbeys, the desecration of the royal tombs at the Saint-Denis basilica, and the symbolic decapitation of the statues of the kings on the facade of Notre-Dame (the revolutionaries mistook them for the kings of France but actually they represent the kings of Judah). Church bells were melted down to make cannonballs, churches were renamed or given a new function—Notre Dame became the Temple of Reason and the Eglise St-Germain was used to store gunpowder—and many streets across the city were given more revolutionary names. Place Louis XV became place de la Révolution—it was only given its current name, place de la Concorde, after the revolution.

In 1792 the revolution took a much more radical turn. The extremist **Jacobins,** led by Maximilien Robespierre, Georges Jacques Danton, and Jean-Paul Marat, instigated the period of the revolution known as **The Reign of Terror.** On January 21, 1793, Louis XVI was guillotined in the place de la Révolution. Marie Antoinette was kept prisoner in the Conciergerie, where the Revolutionary Tribunal presided over the revolution and decided who should be sent to the guillotine. Located next to Sainte-Chapelle on the Ile de la Cité, you can visit Marie Antoinette's cell in the **Conciergerie** (p. 97). She was executed in October 1793. By mid-1794, around 2,500 people had been beheaded in Paris.

Napoleon (1804–1814)

Taking advantage of the postrevolutionary chaos, **Napoleon Bonaparte** crowned himself emperor of the French in 1804. He famously declared that "Paris is short of monuments" and so "It must be given them." His desire to remake Paris into a city fit for an emperor led to an ambitious public building

The Arc de Triomphe.

program. From 1802 onward, canals—including Canal St-Martin—were built to ensure that the city had a clean water supply. In 1806, Napoleon decided to build the **Arc de Triomphe** (p. 104), which was intended to celebrate his victory at Austerlitz but was only completed two decades after his downfall, and a neo-classical "Temple to the Glory of the Great Army," which was never fully completed and later became **La Madeleine** (p. 111).

Although the emperor failed to reshape Paris in the way that he had hoped, his military prowess—and the fact that he preserved the changes brought about by the revolution—mean that even today the French still consider him to be a great national hero. His reign provides the backdrop for Victor Hugo's classic tale of social oppression and human courage, *Les Misérables.*

Food-wise, the 18th century was very important. It was during this period that the restaurant, as we know it today, first appeared. Thanks to the revolution, in the 1790s, chefs from aristocratic houses found themselves jobless and were forced to look for work. Many of them opened restaurants. Many restaurant conventions that we take for granted—such as flexible mealtimes, printed menus, and individualized meals—date from this period.

Napoleon III & Haussmann (1848–1870)

For several decades France gave the monarchy a second chance, but after the last French king, Louis-Philippe, abdicated in 1848, power fell into the hands of Louis Bonaparte, Napoleon's nephew. In December 1848, he was elected president, and by 1852, he had moved into the **Palais des Tuileries** (p. 82) and declared himself **Emperor Napoleon III.** In 1853, he appointed **Georges-Eugène Haussmann** as prefect of Paris, placing under his control a city that, monuments aside, had changed little since the Middle Ages. Inadequate housing meant there was huge overcrowding in the poorer parts of the city. There was no efficient sanitation system; the Seine was still being used as a sewer, and only one in five houses had access to running water. There were no straight roads through Paris and congestion increasingly disrupted the social and economic life of the city. Haussmann had a very prestigious position; he had no superior other than the emperor and the two men met every day. Napoleon III wanted to create a city that was modern, aesthetically beautiful, and a magnificent monument to his power. Ultimately though, Haussmann oversaw this transformation, and it was his name that has come to be associated with the Paris that emerged from it.

A Haussmann-style boulevard.

Haussmann improved circulation in the city by widening the streets and building the boulevards—a prime example of his work is the boulevard that was named after him, the Boulevard Haussmann in the 9e. He was responsible for the standardization of the Parisian facade: all the buildings in a block were linked by symmetrical wrought-iron balconies, creating a long, horizontal perspective—examples of this architecture can be seen on Boulevard St-Michel. He oversaw the renovation of the markets at **Les Halles** (p. 82) and the design of the eight iron- and glass-pavilions that were at the center of the project. He built 560km (348 miles) of sewers and vastly increased the amount of green space available to the public. Architecturally, Haussmann was inspired by French Classic architecture, but what distinguished Haussmann

The Flâneur

Idle strolling in London, Rome, or Madrid is simply idle strolling. Idle strolling in Paris is *flânerie*. The *flâneur* is an idle, aimless, and usually male stroller who wanders through the urban environment looking for distraction and pleasure. It was during the 19th century that the figure of the *flâneur* and the activity of *flânerie* became a key part of the Parisian experience. The archetypal Parisian *flâneur* was the poet Baudelaire, but modern writers are still inspired by this idea. Edmund White's book *The Flâneur* (Bloomsbury, 2001) uses the ideas of the *flâneur* and *flânerie* to delve into Paris's history and culture.

from those who had tried to reshape Paris in the past was the unprecedented scale of his transformation of the city.

However, not everybody was impressed by Haussmann, who described himself as a "demolition artist." He destroyed about 27,000 houses—including the house where he had grown up—and most of Medieval Paris was wiped off the map. The destruction of inner-city slums and the subsequent rise in property prices forced the working classes to move from the city center to the northeastern districts of the city. The poet Charles Baudelaire lamented the loss of *le vieux Paris* (old Paris) in his poem *Le Cygne* (The Swan), when he wrote "The old Paris is gone (the form a city takes more quickly shifts, alas than does the mortal heart)."

Haussmann, and his transformation of Paris, inspired many artists and writers. During the 19th century, Paris saw an extraordinary flourishing of art and literature, including the emergence of new forms of art. **Impressionism** was born during this time (you can see works by Impressionist artists such as Édouard Manet at the **Musée d'Orsay;** p. 142), as was **Literary Naturalism,** with writers like Émile Zola, one of the first pioneers of the French realist novel, paving the way. Both Zola and the Impressionists frequently took Haussmann's transformation of Paris as their subjects, and their work reveals much about Parisian modernity.

The Paris Commune (1871)

Perhaps what is most incredible about Napoleon III's and Haussmann's transformation of the city is how much was achieved in such a short period of time. The **Franco Prussian War** (1870–1871), in which Paris was occupied, led to the fall of Napoleon III. After 17 years as prefect, Haussmann was out on his ear. What followed remains one of the bloodiest periods of Paris's history. The new, moderate republican government signed a peace treaty with the Germans, which angered many Parisians. When the new president, Adolphe Thiers, ordered his soldiers to enter the city and take away its cannons, the working classes rose up in protest and the government was forced to flee to Versailles. The Parisians elected their own governing body, the **Commune,** and from March to May 1871, the working classes occupied the city. When the government troops were finally able to enter the city, they showed no mercy; 200,000 people were killed in a single week, which became known as *la semaine sanglante* (the bloody week). The fighting finished in **Père Lachaise** (p. 123), where 147 Communards were shot against the Mur des Fédérés.

Despite its short life, the Commune succeeded in leaving its mark on the city. Napoleon's column in place Vedôme was pulled down, the **Hôtel de Ville**

(p. 99) was set on fire, which destroyed all the state registers and archives, and the **Palais des Tuileries** (p. 82) was looted and burned to the ground. While the Hôtel de Ville was quickly rebuilt, the ruins of the Palais des Tuileries were swept away, making room for the gardens that we have today.

La Belle Époque (1880–1914)

Memories of the Commune were soon swept away as Paris entered the period known as *la belle époque* (the beautiful age). Lasting from roughly 1880 to World War I, it was only *after* the horrors of the war that journalists started referring to it as *la belle époque*. This was the era of the *Expositions Universelles* (the Great Exhibitions), during which Paris was visited by millions of people from across the globe. The highlight of the 1889 *Exposition Universelle* was the **Eiffel Tower** (p. 146). At a height of 320m (1,066 ft.), it was the tallest structure in the world when it was completed in 1899, and it remains the tallest structure in Paris. Many people hated the tower when it was first unveiled—it was supposed to be dismantled in 1909—but the tower remained, forever changing the Paris skyline. The stars of the 1900 *Exposition Universelle* were the **Grand Palais** (p. 110) and the **Petit Palais** (p. 115), which were built just off the Champs-Élysées. The huge iron- and glass-structure of the Grand Palais was typical of the architecture of the Industrial Age, and testified to the importance of these materials in 19th-century architecture.

In July 1900, the first **Métro** line was opened—Line 1—running from Vincennes to Porte Maillot. The station entrances were designed by Art Nouveau architect Hector Guimard. **Art Nouveau,** with its asymmetrical, curvaceous

An Art Nouveau–style Métro sign.

The Eiffel Tower undergoing construction.

designs based on organic forms, was a reaction against the Industrial Age. Only a few of Guimard's original Métro entrances survive, at Porte Dauphine and Abbesses.

Although Paris had been overtaken by London in terms of size, Paris remained Europe's cultural capital during *la belle époque*. This was the heyday of the **Impressionists Claude Monet, Auguste Renoir, Edgar Degas, Camille Pissarro,** and **Paul Cézanne.** They were given the name Impressionists by critics who felt that their paintings were an impression rather than a finished scene. Interested in the effects of light, the Impressionists often painted outside, capturing subjects in the countryside and Haussmann's Paris.

With its cheap rents, booze, and cabarets, **Montmartre** (p. 157) had become the home of the literary and artistic avant-garde. All the big artists of the day—including **Picasso** and **van Gogh**—lived, drank, and painted in Montmartre. From 1904 to 1912, Picasso lived at the Bateau-Lavoir, a former piano factory, and it was here that he painted *Les Demoiselles d'Avignon,* the painting that marked the beginning of cubism. This was the era of absinthe (also known as "the green fairy") and the **Moulin Rouge** (p. 278). **Toulouse-Lautrec's** paintings of cabarets, circus freaks, and prostitutes perfectly capture the wild, heady spirit of the time.

In December 1895, the Lumière brothers showed the first moving images of Paris to the customers of the Grand Café on Boulevard des Capucines. This was the birth of a new art form, and the beginning of the Parisian passion for **cinema.**

WWI & the Années Folles (1914–1938)

When the Germans broke through Belgium and entered France in September 1914, they very nearly made it to Paris. They were met by the French army at the **Battle of the Marne,** just 15km (9 miles) east of Paris. The Parisian taxi fleet came to the nation's rescue by taking 4,000 soldiers to the front. Paris was safe and by the end of that year, the fighting had turned into the trench warfare that came to characterize World War I. Although Paris itself suffered very little from 1914 to 1918, victory came at an high cost: Of the eight million French soldiers who fought in WWI, 1.3 million were killed, and another 1 million were crippled. In June 1919, the **Treaty of Versailles** was signed in the Hall of Mirrors in the **Palace of Versailles** (p. 347), officially bringing an end to the war.

In the interwar years, Paris became the avant-garde capital of

Sylvia Beach and Ernest Hemingway in front of Shakespeare & Co.

the world. All the great writers, artists, and thinkers of the day gathered in Paris during the **années folles** (mad years), and the city was a whirlwind of decadence and creativity. Montparnasse had become the cultural epicenter of Paris, and the artistic community gathered in bars around Montparnasse, including Rotunde, the Dôme, the Select, and the Coupole—all of which are still in business.

As Prohibition reached its peak in the U.S., American writers—including **Ernest Hemingway, F. Scott Fitzgerald, Henry Miller, Ezra Pound,** and **Gertrude Stein**—came to Paris in search of freedom, bohemia, and alcohol. It was here that Ernest Hemingway began his career as a writer, and his 1936 memoir, *A Moveable Feast,* is arguably the best Anglophone novel about 1920s Paris. When they weren't at the bars of Montparnasse, these writers gathered in the English-language bookshop **Shakespeare & Co.** (p. 247), run by a young American woman called **Sylvia Beach.** In July 1920, Sylvia met the Irish writer **James Joyce,** and in March 1921, she offered to publish his modernist masterpiece, *Ulysses*.

WWII & Occupation (1939–1944)

When World War II broke out, France believed that it would be protected by its concrete fortifications, known as the Maginot Line. However, in May 1940, the German army simply bypassed the fortifications and entered France by going through Belgium. Fear and panic led to a mass exodus from Paris toward the south of France, but by the autumn most Parisians had returned home. The chaos of this period is brilliantly portrayed in the first part of **Irène Némirovsky's novel *Suite Française;*** this book was never finished as Némirovsky died at the age of 39 in Auschwitz. A more romantic, but less historically accurate, portrayal of this time is the classic film *Casablanca.*

Paris was in German hands by June 1940. Although Parisians had to get used to rationing and the presence of both German soldiers and German street signs, Paris suffered little physical damage during the Occupation. As France was being liberated in 1944, Hitler famously gave the order for the retreating German army to blow up Paris, but the commander in charge, Von Cholitz, could not bring himself to destroy such a beautiful city.

The Occupation was a dark period in the history of both France and Paris, and it was many years before the French recognized the role they had played in the Holocaust. Anti-Semitism had been prevalent in France long before the Occupation, and the Germans found that many sections of society, as well as Marshall Pétain's Vichy Government, were more than happy to get involved in the deportation of the Jews. This culminated in July 1942, when the Parisian police rounded up 12,000 of the city's Jews. They were interned in the Vel' d'Hiv sports stadium before being deported to Auschwitz. Around 75,000 Jews were deported from France during the Occupation. Most of them passed through a temporary internment camp in Drancy, just outside Paris. The town of Drancy still exists and you can see it from the window of the RER B on your way out to Aéroport Roissy-Charles-de-Gaulle.

Les Trentes Glorieuses (1945–1975)

After the end of WWII, France embarked on a period of ambitious industrial modernization. The postwar economic boom that followed came to be known as *les trentes glorieuses* (the 30 glorious years). Wages were higher and increased spending on consumer goods radically changed the culture of everyday life, with more and more French households being equipped with television sets, washing machines, and cars. Women gained more independence, and younger people gained more freedom.

Many of the lifestyle changes brought about by *les trentes glorieuses* were explored in the films of the **French New Wave,** known as *la nouvelle vague,* which were a celebration of youth, Paris, and above all, cinema. New Wave film directors such as Jean-Luc Godard, François Truffaut, Claude Chabrol, and Agnès Varda used lighter, hand-held cameras to film in the streets rather than in studios; they challenged conventional editing practices and encouraged improvisation. It was through New Wave films, such as *À bout de souffle* (**Breathless**) and *Les Quatre Cents Coups* (**The 400 Blows**), that the world came to know the sights and sounds of Paris.

A scene from *À bout de souffle (Breathless)*.

The Algerian War (1954–1962)

Although daily life was improving at home, France's empire was falling apart abroad. After the French army was defeated in the 1954 **French Indochina War,** they entered the **Algerian War,** a long and bloody decolonization war in which Algeria fought France for its independence. The Algerian War lasted until 1962 and, like the Occupation, is one of the more shameful periods of French history. Although subsequent governments have never admitted it, torture was used as an interrogation technique by the French army during the Algerian War.

By 1954 there were 350,000 Algerians living in France, most of whom were in Paris. Although the postwar economic boom depended on an immigrant labor force, the Algerian War made life very difficult for the Algerian community in Paris. Tensions between the leaders of the community and the police escalated, culminating in a protest by 20,000 Algerians in Paris on October 17, 1961. Under the orders of Maurice Papon, the police opened fire on the crowds and savagely

---

 Five New Wave Films

François Truffaut, *Les Quatre Cents Coups* (1959)

Alain Resnais, *Hiroshima Mon Amour* (1959)

Jean-Luc Godard, *À bout de souffle* (1960)

Agnès Varda, *Cléo de 5 à 7* (1962)

François Truffaut, *Jules et Jim* (1962)

assaulted protesters. Over 11,000 Algerian men were arrested and the bodies of a number of Algerians were thrown into the Seine. It is thought that around 200 people died in the massacre, which is commemorated on a plaque on the Pont St-Michel.

Many immigrants who came to Paris during *les trentes glorieuses* found themselves living in *bidonvilles* (shantytowns) on the peripheries of the city. Slowly, those living in the *bidonvilles* were relocated to huge housing estates, known as *grandes ensembles,* in the *banlieues*. However, these poorly built housing estates soon became sites of spatial isolation and economic exclusion, and many people believe that the current problems in the *banlieues* date from this period.

May 1968

In May 1968, at Paris University at Nanterre, a university campus in the suburbs of Paris, students began to protest the campus's overcrowded and dilapidated buildings, occupying some of the buildings for days. When the ringleaders of the sit-in were brought before a disciplinary hearing held at the **Sorbonne** in Paris, a riot broke out on the Boulevard St-Michel and stones were thrown at police. As the protest gathered momentum, more and more students filled the streets, and TV crews arrived. Trade unions and secondary school students soon joined them. The streets were full of graffiti and slogans challenging society such as "Métro, boulot, dodo" ("subway, work, sleep") and "Sous les pavés, la plage" ("Under the paving stones, the beach"). Although the student riots are only the backdrop to **Bernardo Bertolucci's 2003 film *The Dreamers***, which tells the story of a young American student who gets caught up in a complicated conflict, the film captures the violence and the idealism of May '68.

By mid May, nine million people were on strike, and the protest threatened Charles de Gaulle's right-wing government. Police reacted to the protesters with violence, but somewhat surprisingly the revolts did not topple the government, as many feared; in June 1968, de Gaulle called an election, and his party won by an overwhelming majority. Although May '68 challenged capitalist society and revived the 19th-century tradition of Parisian militancy, ultimately it confirmed France's middle-class commitment to capitalist values. One of the leaders of the revolt, Daniel Cohn-Bendit, is now a member of the Green Party in the European Parliament.

Mitterand's Grand Projects (1981–1985)

De Gaulle was succeeded by two more right-wing presidents: Georges Pompidou and Valéry Giscard d'Estaing. So it was a huge event when the head of the Parti Socialiste (PS), **François Mitterrand,** won the presidential election in 1981; he remained president until 1995.

Like the great kings and emperors before him, Mitterand understood how important it was for a great leader to leave his mark on the city. With his heart set on prosperity, he launched a number of controversial initiatives known as the *Grands Projets* (big projects), including **I.M. Pei's glass pyramid in the Louvre** (p. 85), **La Grande Arche de La Défense** (p. 152), the **Opéra Bastille** (p. 270), and the **Bibliothèque Nationale de France (BNF)** in the 13e (p. 148). The use of glass in many of the *Grands Projets* was intended to express the idea of transparency. Like a lot of new buildings in Paris, many of the *Grands*

I.M. Pei's glass pyramid in the Louvre.

Projects were hated when they were first unveiled. One critic accused Mitterand of "treating the Louvre as if it were Disneyland." However, today these initiatives have been absorbed into the city's landscape, and Parisians have learned to appreciate the *Grands Projets*.

Contemporary Politics (1995–Present)

The 1990s were a difficult decade for Parisians. **Jacques Chirac** became president in 1995 but his presidency was almost immediately undermined by a series of strikes and protests that lasted for months on end. (These strikes were mainly in the public sector and were a response to Chirac's Prime Minister Alain Juppé's planned welfare cutbacks.) There was also a profound sense of fear in Paris, due to a wave of terrorist attacks in 1995. In July '95, the St-Michel Métro station was bombed, resulting in the death of 7 people and the injury of another 84 people. However, at the same time, Chirac wanted to improve Paris, so he commissioned the **Musée du quai Branly** (p. 144), which is dedicated to indigenous art from Africa, Asia, Oceania, and the Americas. The building was designed by renowned contemporary French architect Jean Nouvel and has a "living wall" on part of its exterior.

In early 2003, Chirac's decision to oppose the U.S.-led invasion of Iraq gained him popularity both abroad and at home. However, his failed attempt to reform the public sector in the spring and his mismanagement of the deadly heat wave in August—which killed 14,000 elderly people—aroused a great deal of criticism.

In October 2005, following the deaths of two teenagers in the suburb of Clichy-sous-Bois, riots broke out in the huge, run-down housing estates in the *banlieues*. Rioters—many of whom were the children of North African immigrants—torched cars, smashed buildings, and threw stones at the police. The violence spread all over France, from Marseilles to Strasbourg, and lasted for several weeks. Chirac was forced to declare a State of Emergency. **Nicolas Sarkozy,** then minister of the interior, intensified the anger of the rioters when he called them *"racaille"* (a very insulting expression, meaning "scum"). Sarkozy was elected president of France in 2007, and he has continued to take a hard line on immigration and national identity issues—these will undoubtedly be key topics of debate in the 2012 presidential election. Five years after these riots, many people feel that the tensions in the *banlieues* remain unresolved.

Politically, Sarkozy remains a divisive figure. His attempt to reform the pension system by raising the age of retirement from 60 to 62 caused a wave of strikes and protests across France in the autumn of 2010. Despite widespread opposition to the legislation, the French parliament approved the reforms in October 2010. His crackdown on France's Roma (Gypsy) population, which has led to the deportation of thousands of Roma, has been met with criticism on all sides of the social and political spectrum.

Outside of politics, Parisians tend to look at Sarkozy's personal life with ridicule. His marriage to Italian-French pop singer Carla Bruni-Sarkozy and his vacations with the rich and famous have earned him the title of the "bling bling president," and stories of his aides putting boxes behind podiums to make him seem taller during his speeches have been met with derision. Given how badly Sarkozy is currently doing in the polls, it remains to be seen whether the French will give him a second chance and reelect him in the upcoming 2012 French presidential election. One thing's for sure, he won't go without a fight.

WHEN TO GO

With an average of 27 million visitors per year, Paris is the most visited city in the world. Although the city is bustling year-round, the summer (July–Aug) is the worst time to visit, since most Parisians flee the city while most tourists crowd into the city then. Paris is probably most pleasant to visit in the spring (Apr–June) or fall (Sept–Nov), but it is also lovely during December, when the city is all lit up with Christmas lights. Annual fashion shows and trade fairs bring a lot of people to the city in September and October, so it may be difficult to find a hotel room during this period. Hotels in Paris rarely advertise off-season rates, but rooms are often a little less expensive during the cold, rainy period from November to February. Airfares are cheaper during these months, and more promotions are available; airfares rise in the spring and fall, peaking in the summer, when tickets cost the most.

Weather

Although you'll often hear French people complaining about the weather in Paris, Parisian weather is usually quite stable, and the surrounding region boasts one of the lowest annual rates of precipitation in the country (640mm/25in.). In

 Five Contemporary French Films

Mathieu Kassovitz, *La Haine* (1995)

Jean-Pierre Jeunet, *Amélie* (2001)

Michael Haneke, *Caché (Hidden;* 2005)

Julie Delpy, *2 Days in Paris* (2007)

Laurent Cantet, *Entre Les Murs (The Class;* 2008)

terms of weather, the best times to visit Paris are the spring (Apr–June) or the fall (Sept–Oct). Recently, Paris has seen extreme temperatures in both summer (when temperatures are around 90°F/30°C) and winter (when temperatures are around 30°F/below 0°C)—perhaps a result of global warming. The high temperatures in summer, combined with air pollution, make visiting Paris unbearable then—especially in the un-air-conditioned Métro.

For a reliable weather forecast, go to **Météo France** (www.meteofrance.com), **Weather.com,** or tune into local radio stations.

Paris's Average Daytime Temperatures & Rainfall

	JAN	FEB	MAR	APR	MAY	JUNE	JULY	AUG	SEPT	OCT	NOV	DEC
TEMP. °F	39	40	45	50	57	62	67	67	61	53	44	41
TEMP. °C	4	4	7	10	14	17	19	19	16	12	7	5
RAINFALL (IN.)	2.2	1.8	1.4	1.7	2.3	2.1	2.3	2.5	2.1	1.9	2.0	1.9
RAINFALL (MM)	56	46	36	42	57	54	59	64	55	50	51	50

Public Holidays

Holidays in France are known as *jours fériés.* Shops and banks are closed, as well as many (but not all) restaurants and museums. If a *jour férié* falls on a Thursday, for example, many French people *faire le pont* (literally "make the bridge") and take the Friday off work. For a list of major holidays, see "Fast Facts," p. 390.

Paris Calendar of Events

For an exhaustive list of events beyond those listed here, check http://events.frommers.com, where you'll find a searchable, up-to-the-minute roster of what's happening in cities all over the world.

JANUARY

January Sales. Over 1,000 shops, from boutiques to *grands magasins,* participate in the January sales, offering discounts as high as 70%. Sales are standardized in France, meaning shops can only open to bargain-hunters on authorized days, so if you want to grab the goods before anybody else, be there when the doors open (usually 10am). Sales begin around January 11 and last until mid-February.

International Circus Festival of Tomorrow. The annual International Circus Festival of Tomorrow at Paris's Pelouse de Reuilly (Métro: Liberté) offers the chance to catch the world's finest circuses under one roof. Young artists from such diverse schools as the Beijing Circus, the Moscow Circus, and France's own *Ecole Fratellini* compete at the festival in a bid to discover the stars of the future. To book, call ✆ **01-40-55-50-56;** www.cirquededemain.com. Four days at the end of January.

FEBRUARY

International Agricultural Show. Every February, the *terroir* (France's countryside) comes to Paris for the International Agricultural Show at the Porte de Versailles. It's a real institution (even the French president makes an official call) with exhibits featuring the top models of the animal world, meaty gastronomic delicacies from 22 French regions, leisure, hunting, and fishing displays. Order tickets in advance online at www.salon-agriculture.com or call ✆ **01-49-20-45-12.** Mid-February.

Six Nations Rugby. France faces its European rivals (England, Scotland, Wales, Ireland, and Italy) in the Six Nations rugby union internationals at the humongous *Stade de France*. The championship is the oldest rugby tournament in the world, having existed in one form or another for 120 years. Since the advent of the Six Nations, France has been the most successful country, so come along and see whether they can be beaten on home territory. Check www.stadedefrance.com or www.rbs 6nations.com for information. February and March.

MARCH

Paris Carnival. The annual *Carnaval de Paris* goes by many names, including the *Pantruche Carnaval,* the *Saint-Fargeau,* and the *Promenade du Boeuf Gras* (Fat Cow Parade). Led by the Fat Cow herself (yes, an actual cow), it revives an age-old tradition begun in 1274. Cheerful Parisians, trumpeters, and other musicians parade through the capital's streets to the Hôtel de Ville (Town Hall). Carnival buildup usually begins 1:30pm at Place Gambetta, and leaves at 3pm, arriving at the town hall at 7pm. For information, see www.carnavaldeparis. org. First Sunday of March.

Banlleues Blues. This annual music festival, in Paris's northern suburb of St-Denis, brings top-notch jazz and blues names to the traditionally culture-hungry suburbs. It's a fine way to discover lesser-known theaters as your feet swing to the sound of top-notch international musicians. Visit www.banlieuesbleues. org. Mid-March to mid-April.

Festival Chorus. Paris's Festival Chorus brings rock, pop, and French chanson to dozens of venues across the western Hauts-de-Seine suburb with some 120 artists taking part in more than 80 different concerts. The main stage is the Magic Mirror, an old-fashioned, circus-style big-top set on the esplanade between La Defense's modern towers.

Buy tickets in advance by calling ☏ **01-47-74-64-64;** www.chorus92.fr. Two weeks from mid- to late-March.

APRIL

Paris Marathon. The Paris Marathon offers runners the chance to take in some of the city's most famous landmarks (cheered on by thousands of spectators), including the Champs-Élysées, the Tuileries garden, and Place de la Bastille. If you'd like to get your kids involved, there is a 1.5km (1 mile) breakfast run for kids 5 to 10 years old, *La Course du P'tit Déj,* held the day before the marathon. Register for both online at www.parismarathon.com. One Sunday in April.

Salon des Réalités Nouvelles. The Parc Floral brings abstract art to the fore at its annual Salon des Réalités Nouvelles. More than 400 French and international avant-garde artists reveal the latest trends in the abstract world through their striking creations, which range from paintings and photos to weird and wonderful sculptures and installations. Once you've had your fill, the colorful flower beds of the Parc Floral beckon. For information, visit www.realitesnouvelles.org. Mid-April.

Foire du Trône. Europe's largest temporary carnival, the Foire du Trône at the Pelouse de Reuilly attracts around five million visitors every year. Though it has roots stretching from the 12th century, since the 1950s the event has grown to epic proportions—every year, visitors down enough beer to fill an Olympic swimming pool. With its flashing lights, pumping music, freak shows, and greasy aromas, the Foire du Trône is a world away from the cultural clichés of the French capital, and sometimes that is the best thing about it. Visit www. foiredutrone.com. Early April to the end of May.

MAY

Nuit des Musées. During the Nuit des Musées (Museum Night), the city's museums stay open until 1am, offering you a chance to see the Louvre, and hundreds more, for free. For information, visit http://nuitdesmusees.culture.fr. One Saturday mid-May.

St-Germain-des-Prés Jazz Festival. The *Rive Gauche,* Paris's traditional jazz quarter, swings as local and international musicians perform at this jazz festival. Playing everything from boogie-woogie to blues, free concerts are held in St-Germain square with ticketed concerts taking place in local libraries, cafes, concerts halls, and bars. Visit www.festivaljazzsaintgermainparis.com. Two weeks in May.

The French Open. For 2 weeks the world's best tennis players battle it out on Roland Garros's clay courts. The event is one of France's biggest sports competitions, so book in advance for a decent seat. The main matches are the most expensive, so if you want to save money, watch the unseeded players on the smaller courts—you could be watching the tennis stars of the future. Visit www.fft.fr/rolandgarros. Mid-May to early June.

Paris Wine Fair. Paris's Palais Brongniart (the city's beautiful neoclassical, former stock-exchange building) is the setting for the annual *Salon de la Revue du Vin de France* (French Wine Fair). Professionals and enthusiasts gather over 2 days to sample the country's best wines and some 200 winemakers attend— it's the perfect opportunity for you to learn how to tell your Bordeaux from your Bourgogne and build up your own dream cellar. Visit www.larvf.com. Mid-May.

JUNE

Jardin Shakespeare. Every year the Jardin Shakespeare in Paris's Bois de Boulogne hosts an open-air theater festival. Plays by the bard are performed in French and English, as well as works by other playwrights and the occasional concert or opera. The Jardin

Shakespeare is so-called because of its five miniature gardens, each named after a Shakespearean work—*Macbeth, Hamlet, The Tempest, As You Like It,* and *A Midsummer Night's Dream*—and you won't find a more charming spot for a summer night's entertainment. For information call ✆ **01-40-19-95-33;** www.jardinshakespeare.fr. June to September.

Paris Jazz Festival. This annual summer event presents a program of free jazz concerts in the beautiful surroundings of the Parc Floral. Gigs take place every Saturday and Sunday throughout June and July. The concerts begin at 3pm and are free to all those who have paid the standard park entry fee. Arrive early to ensure that you get one of the 1,500 seats available, or pack a picnic and bask by the park's miniature lake. Visit www.parisjazzfestival.fr. June to July.

Fête de la Musique. In Paris for the Fête de la Musique? Everywhere you go you'll hear music, from opera and jazz to techno and rock. The Fête unites big names at major venues with accordionists on street corners and choirs in church halls. All concerts are free and every year the Fête de la Musique website publishes a list of participating venues. For information, visit www.fetedelamusique.culture.fr. June 21.

Solidays. Solidarité SIDA is France's main charity promoting the cause of those with HIV. Its annual festival, Solidays, held at Paris's Hippodrome de Longchamp, has fast become one of the city's hippest cultural events attracting more than 100,000 visitors for a weekend of music and arts. Circus performers, fairground stalls, mime artists, and bungee jumpers create a festive atmosphere, but the real stars of the show are the musicians—big names from the international pop and rock scene. Visit www.solidays.org for information. Late June.

Gay Pride. The flamboyant Paris Gay Pride parade traditionally goes from

République to Beaubourg via the Marais, but final confirmation of the route is not usually given until the last minute. Paris has a large gay and lesbian population, with consequently one of the most liberal attitudes in France. Over the last few years the march has grown into a huge carnival, and the big day itself is the culmination of a series of events, including debates and masked balls. Visit www.accueil.gaypride.fr. Late June.

Paris Dance Festival. *Les Ftés de la Danse* provides a series of breathtaking ballet performances at the Belle Epoque Théâtre du Châtelet. A different world-renowned company is invited to perform every year. Expect everything from traditional ballet to contemporary modern dance. For information call ✆ **01-42-68-22-14** or visit www.lesetesdeladanse.com.

Bastille Day. France's national holiday commemorates the 1789 storming of the Bastille at the start of the French Revolution. Crowds line the Champs-Élysées for a military parade led by the president, during which jets fly in formation as top military brass bands march from the Arc de Triomphe to the Place de la Concorde. Later Parisians party until dawn as fireworks explode over the Trocadéro. July 14.

Paris Plage. Every summer, 3.2km (2 miles) of the Seine (near the Pont Neuf) are turned into Paris Plage, a beach complete with golden sand and tanning beds. There's free sports, such as volleyball, and entertainment, from comedy to hip-hop. A second stretch of beach, along the Canal de l'Ourcq, also draws crowds with yet more concerts, outdoor games, canoeing, and sand. For information, visit www.paris-plages.fr. July to August.

Open-air Cinema at La Villette. Each summer, film fans converge on Paris's Parc de la Villette for its 4-week Open-Air Cinema. Pack a picnic, and watch movies with the locals—some are dubbed or subtitled and some are "VO" (original language). Visit www.villette.com. Mid-July to mid-August.

Classique au Vert. World-class classical musicians gather to serenade around 1,500 tourists and Parisians in the leafy Parc Floral (Métro: Château de Vincennes) during this event. Pack a picnic and savor it on the lawn as the sound fills the air—or, if you want a spot under the bandstand get there around an hour before the concert. For information, visit www.classiqueauvert.fr. Weekends in August and September.

Arènes de Montmartre Festival. The Italian tradition of *commedia dell'arte* and traveling theater comes to Montmartre's Arènes (one of only two remaining Roman amphitheater ruins in Paris) for a 3-week festival. The Mystère Bouffe Theatre Company takes the lead with its colorful theatrical inventions. Plays are also performed in other spots around the Marais and the 10th and 20th arrondissements. For information, visit www.mysterebouffe.com.

Rock en Seine. This music festival, held in the Saint Cloud park just outside Paris (Métro: Boulogne Pont Saint-Cloud), offers a consistently excellent line-up of internationally renowned pop and rock stars, and its chilled-out atmosphere makes it a definite highlight of the city's musical calendar. Kids are welcome too, with a special "minirock" stage set aside for 6- to 10-year-olds. If you buy a festival pass, you can camp at the festival campsite (just bring your own tent). Visit www.rockenseine.com/en for information. Late August.

Techno Parade. The annual Techno Parade turns up the volume and quickens the pace on Paris's streets. Around 20 floats carrying 150 musicians, DJs, and performers turn out to dance their way along the 4.8km (3-mile) route. This huge event forms part of the *Rendez-vous* *électroniques* (Electronic Festival) and attracts 400,000 hardcore partygoers. Top DJs entertain the crowds with their mixing skills and decibel-defying sound systems. You can free your inner party animal afterwards too, in numerous bars and clubs across the capital. Visit www. technoparade.fr. Mid-September.

Journées du Patrimoine (Heritage Days). France's Heritage Days give visitors the chance to peek behind the doors of 14,000 buildings that are usually closed to the public. All over the country visitors can glimpse inside politicians' homes, private crypts and cellars, and the back-stage of theaters; many museums open their doors for free as well. Paris has so many wonderful buildings to discover that there are tremendous crowds, so expect to line up and be patient—the wait will be worth it. For a full program of what to see, check www. journeesdupatrimoine.culture.fr. Late September.

Paris-Versailles Walk. Walkers and runners have been taking part in the annual Paris-Versailles Walk, *Grande Classique,* for more than 30 years. It starts on the quay in front of the Eiffel Tower and ends 16km (10 miles) away at the Château de Versailles. Changing rooms and refreshments are available all along the route. Anyone over the age of 16 is invited to enter, but French regulations dictate that you need to send in a medical certificate to prove you're up to the challenge. You'll also need to enroll online beforehand at www.paris versailles.com. Late September.

Paris Autumn Festival. Encompassing opera, film, dance, and performing arts, Paris's Autumn Festival incorporates more high-powered contemporary arts events than some other cities see in a whole year. Dip into this festival at any point and you'll discover the best productions Paris has to offer. Languages range from Japanese and Russian to French, German, and English (subtitled where necessary in French), so choose your productions wisely. Visit www. festival-automne.com. September to December.

OCTOBER

Nuit Blanche. See Paris as you've never seen it before, when museums, monuments, cinemas, parks, and swimming pools stay open from dusk to dawn (for one night only) as thousands of revelers celebrate Nuit Blanche. The Métro stays open later, and night buses serve all the main arteries until dawn. Visit www. paris.fr. Early October.

Prix de l'Arc de Triomphe. Paris's Hippodrome de Longchamp stages the Prix de l'Arc de Triomphe, the jewel in the crown of French horse racing, attended by around 48,000 onlookers. Part of the prestigious World Series Racing Championship, the Arc is popular with Brits, who cross the channel to watch the action. In addition to the excitement of the race, expect a wonderful display of horses, hats, and enough champagne to sink a ship. For information, visit www. prixarcdetriomphe.com. Early October.

Montmartre Grape Harvest Fest. The 5-day Montmartre Grape Harvest Festival *(Fête des Vendanges de Montmartre)* celebrates the new Cuvée Montmartre vintage wine (produced on Montmartre's very slopes). Each year, thousands of revelers come to see short film screenings, listen to concerts, and drink *vin*. Stalls selling regional produce set up shop on the *Butte* (Montmartre's hill) and a colorful parade in honor of Bacchus fills the cobbled streets. Visit www. fetedesvendangesdemontmartre.com. Early October.

Salon du Chocolat. The Salon du Chocolat, at Paris's Porte de Versailles, is heaven for thousands of chocolate lovers who come to devour the international ambrosia and learn how it's made. You can also discover the latest in industry trends from a series of chocolate tastings, demonstrations, and symposiums

while watching *douceurs* and chocolatiers create their fineries. This is a popular
event so buy your ticket online before
you go at www.salon-du-chocolat.com.
Late October.

NOVEMBER
Orchestres en Fête. This annual classical
music festival is celebrated nationwide,
but as the capital city, Paris is the *real*
center for classical music. Expect classics and lesser-known contemporary
pieces played by 50-piece national
orchestras as well as more intimate con
certs by small Baroque ensembles in
venues across the city. For information
visit www.orchestresenfete.com. Mid- to
late November.

Les Nuits Capitales. This event celebrates Paris's nightlife scene, recognizing all music genres, like jazz,
electronica, hip-hop, rock, and pop. It's a
fine opportunity to dance the night away
in hip venues across the city and to discover new artists. *Tip:* All participating
venues offer reduced prices to those
registered on the Nuits Capitales'

website (www.nuitscapitales.com). Call
📞 **01-43-58-38-50.** Late November.

DECEMBER
High Heel Race. As far as wackiness
goes, Paris's High Heel Race is a winner.
Each year preselected teams of women
run as fast as they can in high heels
(without breaking their necks), at a different Parisian Monument. It's the final
leg of an international competition spon-
sored by the Sarenza shoe website. The
winner gets thousands of British pounds
to spend on Sarenza's shoes. Yes, it's
marketing, but it's all good fun, and
there is live music. For information, visit
www.highheelrace.co.uk. Early
December.

Ice-Skating. Get your skates on and get
down to Paris's ice rinks, which pop up
across Paris over the winter months.
You'll find a mix of tourists and locals
cutting up the ice, and best of all: it's
free (skate rentals cost around 5€).Visit
www.paris.fr for information. December
to early March.

SUSTAINABLE TOURISM

In an age when environmental, ethical, and social concerns are becoming more
important, Paris has embraced sustainability and has become a green city. It was
recently ranked one of the top 10 cities committed to ecological issues by the
European Green City Index.

The city of Paris has an excellent public transportation system, which is
cheap and user-friendly, and most Parisians get around the city by public transport. With 16 lines and 300 stations, the Paris **Métro** is an efficient system that
covers most of the city. Several Métro lines are currently being extended, as is the
Tramway network which is quiet, electric, and nonpolluting. There is also the
RER (*Réseau Express Régional*), the **Suburban Rail,** and a widespread network
of **buses.** Alternatively, since the city is relatively small, many people choose to
get around simply by walking.

Bertrand Delanoë, Paris's mayor since 2001, launched a series of initiatives aimed at making the city more environmentally friendly by reducing pollution and cutting down on traffic. In 2007, Delanoë introduced the **Vélib'** scheme
(www.velib.paris.fr), a public bicycle rental program; with thousands of bicycles
and bike rental stations spread throughout the city, it is a fast and inexpensive
way to get around the city, and you will see both Parisians and visitors taking
advantage of this program. Delanoë also expanded bike lanes throughout the city,
and today you'll see more cyclists and cycle lanes in Paris than ever before. Under

Delanoë's guidance, there are plans to introduce a similar car-sharing program called the **Autolib',** due to be launched in October 2011.

Paris is home to 400 green spaces, all of which are enhanced and maintained by the city council. The city is home to some beautiful parks, including the **Jardin du Luxembourg** in the 6e (p. 136) and the **Parc des Buttes Chaumont** in the 19e (p. 128), and these spaces offer a refuge from the urban environment. Over the last 15 years, the city government has spent a lot of money on transforming vacant land into parks (like Jardin Serge Gainsbourg at Porte des Lilas) and there are several parks currently undergoing renovation and expansion (like Parc Martin Luther King at Clichy Batignolles).

Many hotels in Paris have undertaken measures to preserve the environment, and those that have are awarded with a green label; in Paris, look for hotels with the title of *La Clef Verte* (Green Key; www.laclefverte.org) or the European Eco-Label. Both labels reward hotels that take a more environmental approach to water, energy and waste, and raise the awareness of their guests. In Paris, the **Best Western Premier Regent's Garden** (p. 309) boasts a European Eco-Label and the **Hôtel Radisson Blu Trocadéro Dokhan's** (p. 310) claims the title of *La Clef Verte,* among others. Although there are currently only a few hotels that boast such labels, sustainable tourism is becoming increasingly important in the hotel industry. Even if you don't stay at a green hotel, you can still do your bit: turn down the air-conditioning when you leave the room, request that your sheets aren't changed every day, and use your towels more than once. Laundry makes up around 40% of an average hotel's energy use.

Responsible tourism means leaving a city in the same condition as you found it. You can do this by not dropping litter and respecting the recently created color-coded garbage bin system: Yellow bins are for recyclable materials, including paper, plastic, and aluminum cans, while gray bins are for garbage. Support the local economy and culture of the city by shopping in smaller, neighborhood shops, and eating in local, family run restaurants rather than big chain stores and restaurants. Vegetarianism is still not particularly widespread in France, but organic food *(bio)* is becoming increasingly popular—look out for the *bio* tag in shops and restaurants. For more information about Paris's sustainability, go to http://en.parisinfo.com/sustainable-tourism.

TOURS

An organized tour can provide good background information on the city and help you get your bearings. There are a number of different tour options on offer in Paris, including boat tours, bus tours, and walking tours. Many visitors are looking for more and more creative ways of getting to know Paris. Whether you dream of learning to speak French or perfecting your French culinary skills, here are several ideas for exploring Paris in a different, more innovative, way.

Boat Tours

Whether you choose to explore the Seine or Paris's canals, a boat tour is a lovely way to see Paris. **Bateaux-Mouches** (© **01-42-25-96-10;** www.bateaux-mouches.fr; Métro: Alma-Marceau) cruises depart from Pont de l'Alma on the Right Bank of the Seine, and last for a little over 1 hour; cruises run regularly from 10:15am to 11pm from April to September, and from 11am to 9pm from October to March. Tickets cost 10€ and the commentary is in French and English.

On the other side of the river, in front of the Eiffel Tower, the **Bateaux Parisiens** (℃ **01-76-64-14-45;** www.bateauxparisiens.com; Métro: RER Champ de Mars Tour Eiffel), offers smaller boats that run every half hour from 10:30am to 10:30pm from April to September, and every hour from 10:30am to 10pm from October to March. The tour lasts for an hour, the commentary is available in 13 languages, and tickets cost 11€.

Vedettes du Pont Neuf (℃ **01-46-33-98-38;** www.vedettesdupontneuf. com; Métro: Pont Neuf) runs hour-long cruises from the Square du Vert Galant at the tip of the Ile de la Cité. Tickets cost 12€ and boats depart roughly every 30 minutes from 10:30am to 10:30pm from mid-March to October, and less regularly from November to mid-March.

The best canal cruise is **Canauxrama** (℃ **01-42-39-15-00;** www. canauxrama.com; Métro: Jaurés or Bastille), which tours the picturesque Canal St-Martin. Boats leave from Bassin de la Villette at 9:45am and 2.45pm, and from Bastille at 9:45am and 2:30pm; tickets cost 16€, and the cruise takes about 2½ hours The service runs daily from May to September.

Bus Tours

A bus tour is a good way to get orientated and see the major sites. **L'Open Tour** (℃ **01-42-66-56-56;** www.parislopentour.com) offers four bus route tours— Paris Grand Tour, Montmartre–Grands Boulevards, Montparnasse–St-Germain, and Bastille–Bercy—which run from around 9am to 8pm. A 1-day pass costs 29€, and a 2-day pass 32€. **Les Cars Rouge** (℃ **01-53-95-39-53;** www. carsrouges.com) offers a hop-on, hop-off trip that stops at nine sites, including the Eiffel Tower, the Louvre, Notre Dame, and the Champs-Élysées. Buses leave every ten minutes in summer and every 20 minutes in winter. The commentary is available in eight languages and a 2-day ticket is 24€.

Cooking Schools

Auguste Escoffier was one of the great pioneers of modern French cuisine, and one of the first chefs at Paris's Hôtel Ritz. **The Ritz-Escoffier Ecole de Gastronomic Française** (℃ **01-43-16-30-50;** www.ritzparis.com; Métro: Concorde, Opéra, Madeleine) offers demonstration classes of the master's techniques for amateurs, professionals, and even children. Classes are taught in French and English and last between 1 hour and 19 weeks, depending on the class. Prices start at 55€.

Le Cordon Bleu (℃ **01-53-68-22-50;** www.cordonbleu.edu; Métro: Vaugirard) is the most famous French cooking school—this is where Julia Child mastered the art of French cooking. The best-known courses last 10 weeks, after which you are awarded a certificate; prices start at 1,500€. If you'd prefer a less intense immersion, you can opt for a 2-hour demonstration class (prices start at 41€) or 4-day workshop (869€–930€). Classes are in English.

Less grand but equally enjoyable are the cooking classes offered by **La Cuisine Paris** (℃ **01-40-51-78-18;** www.lacuisineparis.com; Métro Hôtel de Ville), a friendly school, set up by a Franco-American team, that offers French cooking classes in both French and English. The calendar of classes is updated every month and prices range from 65€ for 2 hours to 150€ for 4 hours. Similarly, **Cook'n with Class** (℃ **01-42-55-70-59;** www.cooknwithclass.com, Métro: Château Rouge, Lamarck-Caulaincourt) offers a range of small-group classes, including walks to local markets. All classes are in English and prices range from 125€ for 3-hour classes to 185€ for 5-hour classes.

Cycling & Running Tours

2

Tours

PARIS IN DEPTH

Fat Tire Bike Tours (☎ 01-56-58-10-54; www.fattirebiketours.com/paris; Métro: RER Champ de Mars Tour Eiffel) offers a 4-hour day- and night-tour of Paris by bike; tickets cost 28€, including the bike rental. Tours leave from the south leg of the Eiffel Tower daily at 11am and 3pm from April to October and daily at 11am from November to March. This company also offers bike tours of Versailles and Monet's gardens in Giverny.

Paris à Vélo, C'est Sympa (☎ 01-48-87-60-01; www.parisvelosympa. com; Métro: Richard Lenoir) offers four 3-hour bike tours in French and English: Heart of Paris, Unusual Paris, Paris Contrasts, and for the early birds, Paris at Dawn. The tour schedule varies, so check the website for departure times. Tickets cost 34€, which includes bike rental and insurance.

Paris Running Tours (www.parisrunningtours.com; Métro: Alma-Marceau) offers jogging tours of the city. The standard tours—Paris West, Paris East, Paris North, and the popular Da Vinci Code tour—take participants on a 10km (6-mile) jog, and cost 50€. (Each additional runner costs 25€.)

Guided Tours

Paris is a dream come true for shopaholics. **Chic Shopping Paris** (☎ 06-77-65-08-01; www.chicshoppingparis.com) offers tours that are designed to give visitors a behind-the-scenes shopping experience. Focusing on new shops and discovering new trends, tours include a boutique tour, a Sunday shopping tour, and an arts and antiques tour of a flea market. All of the standard tours last for 4 to 4½ hours and cost 100€ per person, and custom tours are available.

Created by professional travel writer Heather Stimmler-Hall, **Secrets of Paris** (☎ 01-43-36-69-85; www.secretsofparis.com) offers private, customized tours of Paris. All tours are designed with the client, and each unique tour aims to reveal a previously unseen side of the city. Suggested themes include Multicultural Paris, Graffiti Art tours, and Paris After Dark. Prices range from 150€ to 600€, depending on the length of the tour.

Entrée to Black Paris (☎ 212/658-9351 in the U.S.; http://entree toblackparis.blogspot.com or www.discoverparis.net), which is affiliated with Discover Paris!, offers visitors the opportunity to discover the vibrant legacy Africans, African-Americans, and other peoples of African descent have left on France through a selection of self-guided, downloadable PDF itineraries. Subjects include Josephine Baker, star of the *La Revue Nègre* (The Black Revue), and the writer Richard Wright. Itineraries cost $25.

Hot Air Balloon Tours

A unique way to see the city from above is by a hot air balloon. Located in the Parc André Citroën in the 15e, **Ballon de Paris** (☎ 01-44-26-20-00; www.ballondeparis.com; Métro: Javel or Balard) has a hot air balloon that reaches an altitude of 150m (492 ft.) but remains tethered to the ground. Tickets cost 12€ Saturday and Sunday, 10€ Monday through Friday.

Language Classes

The **Alliance Française** (© **01-42-84-90-00;** www.alliancefr.org), a highly reputable nonprofit organization, offers French language classes at its Paris school. Evening courses (4 hr. per week) start at 53€, general French classes (9 hr. per week) start at 93€, and the intensive course starts at 213€; the price decreases per week the longer you stay. Reservations must be made at least 6 weeks in advance.

      Les Cours de Civilisation Française de la Sorbonne (© **01-44-10-77-00;** www.ccfs-sorbonne.fr) offers French-language classes for students of all levels. There are four semesters per year, and within each semester a range of different classes are offered. Prices vary depending on the course and the semester; a 2-week conversation class costs 260€, while the 12-week intensive summer session costs 2,750€.

Walking Tours

Paris was made for walking and the best way to discover the city is on foot. **Context** (© **01-72-81-36-35;** www.contexttravel.com) organizes small group and private walking tours led by scholars and experts. Tours range from general 2-hour orientation strolls to more focused themed walks, such as an in-depth tour of the Louvre or a gastronomic stroll. Prices range from 40€ to 85€ per person, depending on the walk. **Sight Seeker's Delight** (© **06-65-98-01-66;** www.sightseekersdelight.com) offers a range of walking tours, including one of the Seine, Montmartre, Jewish Paris, and Père-Lachaise. Prices vary between 20€ and 40€. **Paris Walks** (© **01-48-09-21-40;** www.paris-walks.com) organizes 2-hour walks of the city, based on either a theme or a neighborhood. Most of the walks cost 12€ and do not require a reservation, but some of the walks, such as the Chocolate Tour, are a little more expensive and need to be booked in advance.

3

SUGGESTED PARIS ITINERARIES

by Sophie Nellis

From the Louvre to the Eiffel Tower, Paris is home to some of the world's most famous museums and monuments. While all of these sights are well worth visiting, the city itself is much more than a mere collection of buildings. Visiting Paris is as much about soaking up the atmosphere as about sightseeing. With all the layers of history, it's easy to forget that Paris is a 21st-century capital, but some of the more recent additions to the city, such as the Vélib' biking scheme, have injected Paris with a new sense of dynamism.

Each of Paris's 20 arrondissements possesses a unique style and character. Our guide to the different neighborhoods of Paris will give you an insight into the city and help you decide where you want to stay and what you want to see. Once you arrive in Paris, try to explore as many neighborhoods as you can in order to appreciate the diversity of the city. Our suggested itineraries will help you organize your time and discover new sides to the city. If you only have a few days, you'll probably spend most of your time in the center of Paris, seeing the major sites. In a week, you'll be able to wander off the beaten track and explore some of Paris's neighborhoods in a bit more depth. And if you can stay for several weeks, you'll soon be an expert on *la vie parisienne*.

CITY LAYOUT

Compared to many capitals, Paris is surprisingly compact. The river Seine divides the city into the **Rive Droite** (**Right Bank**) to the north and the **Rive Gauche** (**Left Bank**) to the south. The larger Right Bank is where you find the city's business sector, stately monuments, and high-fashion industry. The smaller Left Bank has the publishing houses, universities, and a reputation as bohemian because students, philosophers, and creative types have been congregating here for centuries.

Paris is divided into 20 numbered municipal districts called **arrondissements.** The layout of these districts follows a distinct pattern. The first (abbreviated 1er for *premier*) arrondissement is the dead center of Paris, comprising an area around Notre-Dame and the Louvre. From there, the rest of the districts spiral outward, clockwise, in ascending order, like a snail shell. The lower the arrondissement number, the more central the location. If you want to be within walking distance of all the major sites and monuments, be sure to stay in one of the first eight arrondissements. There are only six arrondissements—the 5e, 6e, 7e, 13e, 14e, and 15e—on the Left Bank. The Right Bank is much larger, and it is composed of the remaining 14 arrondissements.

Most city maps are divided by arrondissement, and addresses include the arrondissement number (in Roman or Arabic numerals and followed by "éme" or "e", for example 10éme). Arrondissement numbers are key to locating an address in Paris, and this book lists addresses the way they appear in Paris, with the arrondissement number following the specific street address (for instance, 29 rue de Rivoli, 4e, is in the 4th arrondissement). Paris also has its own version of a zip code. The mailing address for a hotel is written as, for example, "Paris 75014." The last two digits, 14, indicate that the address is in the 14th arrondissement—in this case, Montparnasse. Arrondissements are indicated on the blue enamel street signs, above the street name.

Finding an address can be a complicated process in Paris, but once you know the arrondissement in which an address is located, finding that spot is much easier. Numbers on buildings running parallel to the Seine usually follow the course of the river east to west. On north-south streets, numbering begins at the river. To enter a building, you'll usually need a code for the outside door. Once inside, you'll need a letter indicating which staircase to take, the floor number, and the position of the apartment (right, left, last door, etc.). *Bis* and *ter* after a building number are the equivalent of "b" or "c" and indicate a separate address.

A good way to orient yourself is the Métro. As you're rarely more than a 10-minute walk away from a Métro station, it's easy to work out which part of Paris you're in by finding your nearest station.

There is a pull-out map showing Paris's neighborhoods at the back of this book. For a more detailed map of Paris, we recommend *Paris Pratique par arrondissement,* available at newsstands and bookshops for around 7€. This guide provides you with a Métro map and maps of each arrondissement, with all streets listed and keyed. Free maps of the Paris Métro, bus, and RER networks are available at all Métro stations.

NEIGHBORHOODS IN BRIEF
The Right Bank

LES HALLES, LOUVRE & PALAIS ROYAL (1ER & 2E)   Home to some of Paris's most important sites, the area around the **Louvre** and **Palais-Royal** is one of the most visited (but least residential) parts of the city. Whether you're strolling through the **Jardin des Tuileries** or admiring the classic beauty of the **Place Vendôme,** this is one of the most elegant neighborhoods in the city. It's also one of the most luxurious, with designer boutiques filling the arcades of the Palais-Royal and *haute couture* lining the sidewalks of the **rue St-Honoré. Rue de Rivoli,** the main street running through the 1st arrondissement, is one of the busiest streets in Paris, full of shops, cafes, and restaurants. For a little peace and quiet, head south for a walk along the banks of the Seine or take refuge in the gardens of the Palais-Royal.

North of the Palais-Royal is the **Bourse** (stock exchange). You'll find fewer tourists, but it still remains close to the center of the action. Like most financial districts, it's bustling and lively during the week but much quieter at weekends. To the east is **Sentier,** the traditional center of the wholesale clothing trade, and the picturesque, cobbled market street, **rue Montorgueil.** For a more classic shopping environment, explore the various passages (covered arcades) that the 2nd arrondissement is famous for.

Although the area around the **Forum des Halles** is currently being redeveloped by architect David Mangin, it remains one of central Paris's least attractive neighborhoods. The huge underground shopping center and

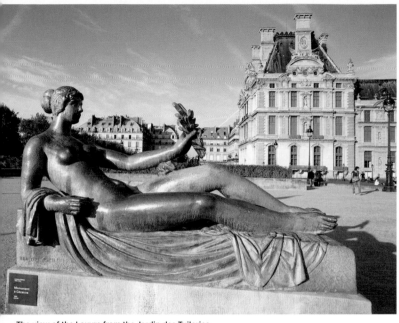

The view of the Louvre from the Jardin des Tuileries.

Métro/RER station means that Les Halles is always hectic and heaving with people. It's not the safest area and it's worth avoiding at night. The same is true of the seedy rue St-Denis, just east of Les Halles, as this is one of Paris's red light districts.

LE MARAIS, ILE ST-LOUIS & ILE DE LA CITÉ (3E & 4E) Located in the heart of the city, Paris's two islands could not be more different from each other. Although the **Ile de la Cité** does have some quieter spots, such as the Square du Vert-Galant, it is dominated by the majestic Gothic cathedral **Notre-Dame** and is visited by thousands of tourists every day. The **Ile St-Louis,** with its aristocratic town houses, is much calmer and more picturesque. Far removed from the hustle and bustle of Paris, the *quais* of the Ile St-Louis are perfect for a romantic stroll.

An old doorway on the Ile de la Cité.

59

RIGHT BANK
1 Les Halles, Louvre, & Palais Royal (1er & 2e)
2 Le Marais, Ile St-Louis & Ile de la Cité (3e & 4e)
3 Champs-Élysées & Western Paris (8e, 16e, & 17e)
4 Opéra & Canal St-Martin (9e & 10e)
5 Pigalle & Montmartre (18e)
6 République, Bastille & Eastern Paris (11e & 12e)
7 Belleville & Northeast Paris (19e & 20e)

LEFT BANK
8 Latin Quarter (5e)
9 St-Germain-des-Prés & Luxembourg (6e)
10 Eiffel Tower & Nearby (7e)
11 Montparnasse & Southern Paris (13e, 14e, 15e)

Paris Neighborhoods

↑ *To Roissy/Charles-de-Gaulle Airport*

ROUEN · ST-DENIS · AUBERVILLIERS

Porte de Clignancourt · Porte de la Chapelle · Porte d'Aubervilliers · Porte de la Villette

bd. Macdonald

Cité des Sciences et de l'Industrie

LA VILLETTE

Canal de l'Ourcq

18e

❺

Basilique du Sacré-Cœur

MONTMARTRE

bd. Ornano · bd. Barbès · bd. de Rochechouart

Porte de Pantin

LE PRÉ ST-GERVAIS

rue Riquet · place Marx · rue de Flandre · rue de la Villette

Bassin de la Villette

av. Jean Jaurès

19e

PARC DE BUTTES-CHAUMONT

Porte des Lilas

Gare du Nord · Gare de l'Est

rue La Fayette · bd. de Magenta

❹

10e

rue du Faubourg St-Martin · Canal St-Martin · bd. de la Villette

BELLEVILLE

❼

rue du Faubourg du Temple

MÉNILMONTANT

Porte de Bagnolet · A3

pl. de la République · av. de la République · bd. Voltaire

bd. de Belleville · bd. de Ménilmontant

20e

❶

Les Halles

rue de Sébastopol · rue de Turbigo

3e

❷

MARAIS

rue Rambuteau

Centre Pompidou

Hôtel de Ville

pl. des Vosges

ILE DE LA CITÉ

ILE ST-LOUIS

Notre-Dame

11e

CIMETIÈRE DU PÈRE-LACHAISE

bd. R. Lenoir · av. Philippe Auguste

Porte de Montreuil

BASTILLE

place de la Bastille

Opéra Bastille

rue de Faubourg St-Antoine

bd. Voltaire

NATION

pl. de la Nation

Cours de Vincennes

Porte de Vincennes

Porte de St-Mandé

LATIN QUARTER

Sorbonne

Panthéon

4e

av. Ledru-Rollin

bd. Diderot · av. Daumesnil

❻

JARDIN DES PLANTES

Gare d'Austerlitz

5e

❽

bd. St-Marcel

Gare de Lyon

12e

pl. Félix Eboué

bd. de Bercy

BERCY

Porte de Vincennes

Zoo de Vincennes *(closed until 2014)*

Porte Dorée

d. Arago · bd. Blanqui · av. des Gobelins · bd. de l'Hôpital · bd. Auriol

pl. d'Italie

Bibliothèque National de France

quai de Bercy

quai de la Gare

Seine

av. de Choisy · av. d'Italie · av. d'Ivry · bd. Masséna

13e

Porte de Charenton

BOIS DE VINCENNES

Porte de Bercy

d'Alésia

PARC DE MONTSOURIS

Cité universitaire

bd. Kellerman

Porte de Gentilly

↓ *To Orly*

GENTILLY

IVRY-SUR-SEINE

Porte d'Ivry · Porte d'Italie

CHARENTON

A4

0		1 mi
0	1 km	

The Marais is home to the city's Jewish community.

Having avoided Haussmann's 19th-century transformation of Paris, **Le Marais** has a more intimate atmosphere than other parts of Paris. The neighborhood became fashionable in the early 17th century when Henri IV commissioned the beautiful **Place des Vosges**, and it is full of aristocratic mansions (known as *hôtels particuliers*) that were built by the French aristocracy. After the French Revolution the area fell into disrepair, but in 1962, under Culture Minister André Malraux's law which permitted the preservation of historic quarters, Le Marais underwent a process of restoration and today it is one of Paris's trendiest neighborhoods.

Stretching across the 3rd and 4th arrondissements, the southern part of Le Marais is a lively area, full of elegant boutiques and small, contemporary art galleries. It's a great area for wining and dining, and very popular on Sundays as, unlike many other parts of Paris, most of the shops here are open. The area around **rue des Rosiers** has long been home to the city's Jewish community, while the **rues St-Croix-de-la-Bretonnerie, des Archives,** and **Vieille-du-Temple** are the center of Paris's gay and lesbian life. The northern part of the Le Marais, around the rue de Bretagne, is more up and coming but considerably quieter than the 4th.

CHAMPS-ÉLYSÉES & WESTERN PARIS (8E, 16E & 17E)   One of the most famous avenues in the world, the tree-lined **Avenue des Champs-Élysées** is the embodiment of Parisian grandeur. While strolling along the Champs-Élysées may be something of a disappointment thanks to the fast-food restaurants, overpriced cafés, and chain stores, leading off to the south are **Avenue George V** and **Avenue Montaigne,** home to *haute couture* boutiques and several of Paris's most luxurious hotels. Above the Champs-Élysées, around **Boulevard Haussmann,** you'll find a busy, commercial district and a lot less tourists.

Heading north you'll come to the picturesque **Parc Monceau** and the area known as **Batignolles.** This sophisticated neighborhood became fashionable during the 19th century, and is full of elegant Haussmannian-style buildings and wide avenues. Today, it's a wealthy, residential area. Nearby is **rue des Dames,** where there are a number of hip bars and restaurants.

There's a similar atmosphere in the 16th arrondissement, which is full of embassies, diplomats, and exclusive residences. Although there are several interesting museums, including the **Musée Guimet, Paris's Musée d'Art Moderne,** and the hip **Palais du Tokyo,** this bourgeois district can feel quite far from the action.

OPÉRA & CANAL ST-MARTIN (9E & 10E)   Sandwiched between the 2nd and 18th arrondissements, the 9th is a good base for exploring Paris's Right

Bank. The area around the **Opéra Garnier** is one of the busiest, most commercial areas of Paris. It's a great place for shopping, and it's where you'll find the famous 19th-century department stores **Galeries Lafayette** and **Printemps.** Heading east from Opéra you come to the area known as **Grands Boulevards,** which stretches from Boulevard Montmartre to Boulevard de Bonne Nouvelle. This was the epicenter of cafe and theater life during the 18th and 19th centuries, and although there is still lively nightlife here, the grandeur of Grands Boulevards has faded and the area can seem rather shabby and inauthentic.

The 10th arrondissement is one of Paris's most multiethnic neighborhoods, and the streets around **rue du Faubourg Saint-Denis** are home to large numbers of Indians, Pakistanis, Bangladeshis, West Indians, Africans, and Turks. It's a vibrant, thriving area and the **Passage Brady** is one of the best places in Paris to eat Indian and Pakistani food. However, the streets around Strasbourg St-Denis, Gare du Nord, and Gare de l'Est are not the safest parts of the city and should be avoided late a night. The main attraction of the 10th is the increasingly popular Canal Saint Martin. With its picturesque footbridges and cobbled, tree-lined *quais,* this is the ideal place for a summer picnic or Sunday stroll. There's a very *bobo* (short for *bourgeois bohemian*) atmosphere around here, thanks to the stylish boutiques and trendy bars and cafés.

PIGALLE & MONTMARTRE (18E)   Located on a hill, Montmartre's winding, narrow streets are a far cry from the wide avenues and boulevards of central Paris. Despite its distance from the center, **Montmartre**—or *la butte* (the hill), as it is affectionately referred to by locals—is one of the city's most popular neighborhoods for visitors and residents alike. At the end of the 19th century, Montmartre was full of avant-garde writers and artists, including Picasso, van Gogh, and Toulouse-Lautrec, who were attracted by the cheap rents and cheap booze. Despite the busloads of tourists who climb the hill to visit **Sacré-Coeur,** this area has retained its bohemian atmosphere and if you avoid the tourist traps—such as place du Tertre—you'll find plenty of charm and romance. There's a great selection of bars and restaurants around **rue des Abbesses** and **rue Lepic,** and one of the advantages of being a little farther away from the center is that the prices are lower.

Street performers in Montmartre.

Around **Pigalle** there are a number of good bars and well-known music venues. However, between Place Pigalle and Place Blanche, you'll discover the seedier side of this neighborhood with flashing neon signs advertising sex shops and adult-only cinemas. To the east of the 18th, around rue de la Goutte d'Or and Barbès Rochechouart, there is a large North African community. There's a lively atmosphere here but it's quite hectic, particularly on Saturdays when there is a popular fruit and vegetable market. If you do get off the Métro here, be wary of pickpockets. Located on the northernmost edge of the 18th is the city's most famous flea market, the **Marché aux Puces de Clignancourt.**

RÉPUBLIQUE, BASTILLE & EASTERN PARIS (11E & 12E) Until a few decades ago, the 11th and 12th arrondissements were home to Paris's working-class population. Despite the fact that this neighborhood has become gentrified, both place de la Bastille and place de la République remain symbolic places for the French Left and are often the scenes of large public demonstrations.

Politics aside, **République** and **Bastille** are well connected in terms of public transport and are popular places to go out at night. Although many of the bars around place de la Bastille are overpriced and overrated, the area between Goncourt, Menilmontant, Parmentier, and Oberkampf is young and hip, and boasts some of the best nightlife in the city. As you head farther south, the 11th becomes increasingly quiet and residential.

Place de la Bastille is dominated by the modern **Opéra Bastille,** which was met with mixed reactions when it opened in 1989. To the east of the place is the **rue du Faubourg St-Antoine,** which has been the center of the furniture-makers district for centuries. It's now a pleasant shopping street, but if you go up some of the side streets you can still find some artisans at work. In the southern part of the 12th is **Bercy Village.** Up until the 1980s, wine was unloaded from boats and stored in warehouses here, but the warehouses were recently renovated and are now home to shops and bars.

BELLEVILLE & NORTHEAST PARIS (19E & 20E) Traditionally a working-class district **Belleville** is home to large numbers of immigrants. North African Muslims and Jews, many of Tunisian origin, live alongside Chinese and Vietnamese immigrants, and Belleville is Paris's second Chinatown. Sadly, Paris property prices mean that this area, like many others before it, is slowly being gentrified. There's a lively atmosphere in Belleville, and if you climb rue de Belleville the park at the top of the hill offers spectacular views of Paris.

The 19th is not the most attractive of Paris's arrondissements, but there are some places that are worth visiting. At the top of the Canal St-Martin is the **Bassin de la Villette,** where two MK2 cinemas (MK2 is one of Paris's biggest movie theater chains) face each other across the canal. There's a pleasant atmosphere here during the summer, when people gather outside the local bars, picnicking or playing *pétanque.* If you continue along the Canal de l'Ourcq you'll reach the **Parc de la Villette,** which hosts an outdoor cinema festival in the summer and a jazz festival in September. A little farther south is one of Paris's loveliest green spaces, the **Parc des Buttes Chaumont.** If you continue south, the 19th becomes the 20th, a sprawling, predominantly residential district, some parts of which are not easily accessible on the Métro. There are a couple of good bars and music venues dotted around the 20th, but its main attraction is definitely the **Père**

Lachaise Cemetery, where the likes of Jim Morrison, Edith Piaf, and Chopin are buried.

The Left Bank

LATIN QUARTER (5E) From a historical perspective, the Latin Quarter is not to be missed. From the Roman settlement of Lutetia to the heady days of May 1968, layers of Parisian history are visible in the 5th arrondissement. Home to the **Sorbonne**—the administrative center of the University of Paris—the Latin Quarter has been associated with education and learning since the Middle Ages. Parts of it, particularly around rue Mouffetard and Place de la Contrescarpe, are filled with students, and there are a lot of art house cinemas here that give the neighborhood an offbeat, indie vibe. As you head farther south, you can see the quieter, more residential side of the 5th.

Its popularity with the expat community in the 1920s—Ernest Hemingway, Henry Miller, and James Joyce, among others—gave the Latin Quarter a romantic, literary edge. To relive this era, head to the charming English-language bookshop, **Shakespeare & Co.** (see p. 247), on rue de la Bûcherie. Sadly, however, very little of this Latin Quarter remains and many visitors are disappointed by how tacky and commercial parts of the 5th have become. The area around Place St-Michel and rue de la Huchette, although very central, is one of most touristy parts of the city. If you're looking for an authentic Parisian experience, avoid eating or drinking in any of the bars and restaurants around here.

ST-GERMAIN-DES-PRÉS & LUXEMBOURG (6E) Now one of the city's most exclusive neighborhoods, St-Germain oozes *Rive Gauche* glamour. For most of the 20th century, the area around the Eglise-St-Germain-des-Prés was

One of the many famous cafes in St-Germain-des-Prés.

the intellectual heartland of Paris, and everywhere you turn, you'll encounter historic and literary associations. Here you'll find three of Paris's most famous cafes, all within a few meters of one another. Known as **The Golden Triangle,** the **Brasserie Lipp, Les Deux Magots,** and **Café de Flore** were frequented by the likes of Hemingway and Picasso in the 1920s, and Jean-Paul Sartre and Simone de Beauvoir in the 1950s. Nowadays, you'll find more *haute couture* (Christian Dior, Louis Vuitton, and more) than highbrow culture.

There's a lively atmosphere in the narrow streets around St-Germain and **Odéon,** and this neighborhood boasts some great bars and restaurants. It gets much quieter towards the charming **Jardin du Luxembourg,** a 24-hectare (59-acre) park, the design of which is based in the Boboli Gardens in Florence. Full of 19th-century park furniture and allegorical statues, this is one of Paris's loveliest parks.

EIFFEL TOWER & NEARBY (7E)   Despite the fact that many people hated it when it was showcased at the 1889 Great Exhibition, the **Eiffel Tower** has become Paris's most famous symbol. The panoramic views from the top, and the sheer magnificence of the structure itself, attract thousands of visitors everyday. But where there are tourists there are pickpockets and you should be very vigilant when strolling around beneath the tower. Similarly, the Champ de Mars attracts some dodgy characters and it's not the safest place to hang out after dark.

The 7th arrondissement is a calm, elegant neighborhood. In the center you'll find the **Hôtel des Invalides,** where Napoleon's body was interred, the **Assemblée Nationale** (National Assembly), and a number of key government ministries. Although there are a lot of civil servants running around—or being chauffeured around—during the week, there's very little life at the weekends. There's a bit more of a buzz on either side of Invalides. The area around **rue St-Dominique** and **rue de Grenelle** is quite lively, and **rue Cler** is a popular, well-heeled market-street full of gourmet food shops and classy cafés. On the other side of the 7th, you'll find the elegant shopping street, **rue du Bac,** and on the rue des Sèvres, the beautiful, 19th-century department store, **Le Bon Marché.**

MONTPARNASSE & SOUTHERN PARIS (13E, 14E & 15E)   Montparnasse is a busy, commercial neighborhood dominated by the rather ugly **Montparnasse Tower,** which was built in the 1970s. It's still reasonably close to central Paris and is very well connected in terms of public transport. Along Boulevard Montparnasse you'll find several famous, Art Deco brasseries—La Coupole, Le Select, and Le Dôme—which were patronized by the all the movers and shakers of the interwar period, including Hemingway, Picasso, Lenin, and Trotsky.

As you head south, the 14th becomes increasingly residential and there's very little to see or do down here. The same is true for the 15th arrondissement, with the exception of the lively shopping district around **Métro La Motte Picquet Grenelle** and **rue du Commerce.** However, as you head east you'll see quite a different side of Paris in the 13th arrondissement. Equally as residential as the 14th and 15th, it's one of the few districts in the city where there are modern, high-rise tower blocks. Home to Paris's principal **Chinatown,** the area around Place d'Italie, Tolbiac, and Olympiades is a great place to come for authentic Chinese and Vietnamese food.

ITINERARIES

ICONIC PARIS

If you have limited time in Paris and want to sample the best the city has to offer, then this is the itinerary for you, taking you on a whistle-stop tour past 17 of the city's main attractions. If you don't linger too long in any one place, you could just about get through them all in a day—although why not take your time and spread things over 2 (or even 3) days? ***Start:*** *Métro to Cité on the Ile de la Cité. Exit the station, turn right and cross place Louis Lépine. You'll come to boulevard du Palais, where you'll see Sainte-Chapelle.*

1 ### SAINTE-CHAPELLE

This sublime Gothic chapel built in 1242 is renowned for its breathtaking stained-glass windows. There are often long lines so it's good to get here as early as you can. See p. 103.

Turn right as you exit Sainte-Chapelle. When you reach Pont St-Michel, turn left along Quai du Marché Neuf. Continue until you reach:

2 ### CATHÉDRALE DE NOTRE-DAME

One of the supreme masterpieces of Gothic art, the majestic Notre-Dame, built between 1163 and 1250, is the main reason to visit the Ile de la Cité. See p. 92.

Walk away from the cathedral on rue du Cloître Notre Dame, which runs along the left-hand side of Notre-Dame. Cross the Pont St-Louis to:

The spectacular stained-glass windows of Sainte-Chapelle.

3 ILE ST-LOUIS

Full of 17th-century aristocratic town houses, this small island is one of the calmest and most picturesque places in Paris. Stroll along rue Saint Louis en l'Ile, making sure to stop in at Maison Berthillon (nos. 29–31), Paris's most famous sorbet and ice-cream parlor. See p. 91.

Cross onto the Right Bank via either Pont Marie or Pont Louis-Philippe. Turn right and walk along the quays.

A quiet street in Ile St-Louis.

4 THE QUAYS OF THE SEINE

Walking along the quays, you'll encounter the most splendid panoramic views that Paris has to offer. The city has 37 bridges, many of them landmarks in their own right. Admire the Pont Neuf, the oldest and most evocative of Paris's fourteen bridges.

At the Pont des Arts, turn right into the Cour Carrée, where you'll see the:

5 MUSÉE DU LOUVRE

"I never knew what a palace was until I had a glimpse of the Louvre," wrote Nathaniel Hawthorne. The world's greatest art museum—and a former

Winged Victory.

Iconic Paris

17e

10e

3e

MARAIS

4e

ÎLE ST-LOUIS

ÎLE DE LA CITÉ

5e

LATIN QUARTER

2e

La Bourse

Forum des Halles

Hôtel de Ville

Hôtel-Dieu

Sorbonne

1er

Palais Royal

Opéra Garnier

La Madeleine

Gare St-Lazare

9e

8e

Arc de Triomphe

Grand Palais

Petit Palais

16e

Musée du Quai Branly

Tour Eiffel

15e

Musée du Louvre

Musée d'Orsay

Musée Rodin

Hôtel des Invalides

7e

6e

St-Germain-des-Prés

St-Sulpice

Palais du Luxembourg

0   1/4 mi
0   0.25 km

1 Sainte-Chapelle
2 Cathédrale de Notre-Dame
3 Île St-Louis
4 The Quays of the Seine
5 Musée du Louvre
6 Jardin des Tuileries
7 Place Vendôme
8 Opéra Garnier
9 Café de la Paix
10 Place de la Concorde
11 Arc de Triomphe
12 Eiffel Tower
13 Musée d'Orsay
14 Église-St-Germain-des-Prés
15 The Golden Triangle
16 Centre Pompidou
17 Sacré-Cœur

69

Place de la Concorde.

royal residence—the Louvre is the 1st arrondissement's main attraction. The museum's most famous works are the *Mona Lisa, Venus de Milo,* and *Winged Victory.* See p. 85.

Walk through the Cour Carrée and across the Cour Napoleon, admiring I. M. Pei's glass pyramid. Cross the Place du Carrousel to the:

6 JARDIN DES TUILERIES

It's worth strolling through this elegant French garden just to admire the sculptures and ornamental ponds. At the far end you'll find two galleries: the Jeu de Paume and the Orangerie.

Leave the gardens through one of the exits on the right, which will bring you to rue de Rivoli. Take rue de Castiglione north to:

7 PLACE VENDÔME

Home of the Ritz hotel and top-of-the-range jewelers, including Cartier and Bvlgari, this square is the embodiment of Parisian luxury. At the center is a column celebrating Napoleon's Battle of Austerlitz in 1806.

Cross the square and walk north on rue de la Paix, until you reach:

8 OPÉRA GARNIER

Be dazzled by the grand and ornate facade of the Opéra Garnier (p. 118), a testament to the excesses of the Second Empire.

9 Café de la Paix 🍵

On the left of the Opéra Garnier you'll see the glitzy **Café de la Paix** (corner of Place de l'Opéra and Boulevard des Capucines; ✆ **01-40-07-36-36;** www. cafedelapaix.fr), also designed by Charles Garnier in the 19th century. Why not stop for lunch or a luxurious coffee in this beautiful Paris institution? The menu is different (and cheaper) if you sit on either the indoor or outdoor terrace rather than inside the restaurant.

Arc de Triomphe.

Take Métro line 8 to Concorde, to:

10 PLACE DE LA CONCORDE

At the center of place de la Concorde is the 3,300-year-old Obelisk of Luxor. From here, you will have a spectacular view up the Champs-Élysées toward the Arc du Triomphe.

Walk northwest on the Champs-Élysées on the left-hand side, admiring the Petit Palais and the Grand Palais. At place Clemenceau take Métro line 1 to Charles de Gaulle-Étoile. Exit to see the:

11 ARC DE TRIOMPHE

Begun by Napoleon in 1806, this triumphal arch is modeled on ancient Roman arches, and is dedicated to the French army. Beneath it is the tomb of the Unknown Soldier. See p. 104.

From Charles de Gaulle-Étoile take Métro line 6 to Bir-Hakeim. Exit to see the:

12 EIFFEL TOWER

Towering above Paris's skyline, Gustave Eiffel's cast-iron tower built for the 1889 Great Exhibition is one of the city's greatest symbols. See p. 146.

Take the yellow RER C line from Champ de Mars Tour Eiffel to Musée D'Orsay. All lines of RER C will stop there but make sure your train is going in the right direction.

13 MUSÉE D'ORSAY

A former railway station, the Musée d'Orsay houses an internationally renowned collection of 19th-century art, including key works by the masters of French Impressionism. See p. 142.

The interior of the Musée d'Orsay.

Leaving the museum, turn left down rue de Bellechasse and then right onto boulevard Saint-Germain. Stroll along this elegant boulevard until you reach:

14 ÉGLISE-ST-GERMAIN-DES-PRÉS

This church is all that remains of the former Abbey of St-Germain. The clock tower dates from 1000 A.D., making it the oldest church in Paris. See p. 138.

15 The Golden Triangle ☕

Stop for an aperitif or a bite to eat at one of three elegant cafes known as The Golden Triangle: **Brasserie Lipp, Les Deux Magots,** and **Café de la Flore** (all of which are located on the Boulevard St-Germain, just a stone's throw away from the church). Admire the beautiful Art Deco interiors and if you're lucky enough to get a table on the terrace, indulge in a bit of people-watching.

Les Deux Magots cafe.

The Centre Pompidou.

From St-Germain-des-Prés take Métro line 4 to Les Halles. Take the rue Rambuteau exit and turn left as you come out of the station. Walk along rue Rambuteau, crossing Boulevard de Sebastopol, and on your right you'll see:

16 CENTRE POMPIDOU

Described by some early critics as a "wart" on the face of Paris, the Centre Pompidou (built in 1977) still arouses mixed reactions. Architecture aside, it contains the impressive Musée National d'Art Moderne and often puts on prestigious temporary exhibitions. See p. 96.

Walk back to Métro Les Halles and take line 4 to Barbès Rochechouart. Change onto line 2 for one stop, getting off at Anvers. Turn right up rue de Steinkerque and you'll find yourself at the foot of Sacré-Coeur. If you're feeling strong, brave the steps; if not you can use a Métro ticket to take the Funiculaire to:

17 SACRÉ-COEUR

Standing in front of this kitsch 19th-century basilica gives you a magnificent view over Paris, day or night (p. 118). After visiting Sacré-Coeur, explore the winding, narrow streets of Montmartre. As you head back down the hill, finish your tour with a drink in one of the bars along rue des Abbesses.

HEMINGWAY & 1920S PARIS

"If you're lucky enough to have lived in Paris as a young man, then wherever you go for the rest of your life, it stays with you, for Paris is a moveable feast." So opens *A Moveable Feast*, Ernest Hemingway's memoir of the years he spent in Paris in the 1920s. He was not the only soon-to-be-great Anglophone writer drawn to Paris during this time, and this tour will introduce you to some of the key players and places of this moveable feast. **Start:** *Place de la Contrescarpe.*

Shakespeare & Co. bookshop.

1 PLACE DE LA CONTRESCARPE

A Moveable Feast opens with a description of the grubby Café des Amateurs, which was located in this picturesque square. The cafe is no longer there, but there are plenty of student dives nearby on the rue Mouffetard.

Head northeast out of the square along rue Cardinal Lemoine.

2 RUE CARDINAL LEMOINE

Hemingway and his wife Hadley had the first Parisian apartment at no. 74. A little farther up, at no. 71, is where Irish writer **James Joyce** finished his modernist masterpiece *Ulysses* in the early 1920s.

Turn left onto rue Monge, which becomes rue Lagrange. At the river, go left. On your left you'll come to:

3 SHAKESPEARE & CO.

Opened in 1919 by a young American called **Sylvia Beach,** this wonderful English-language bookshop soon became a meeting place for the all the Anglophone writers who were in Paris in the 1920s, including Joyce, Hemingway, and **Ezra Pound.** In 1922, Sylvia decided to publish Joyce's *Ulysses*.

Continue along the Seine to St-Michel and take Métro line 4 to St-Germain-des-Prés.

Brasserie Lipp.

Hemingway & 1920s Paris

6e

ÎLE DE LA CITÉ

Cathédrale Notre-Dame

LATIN QUARTER

5e

MONTPARNASSE
14e

1 Place de la Contrescarpe
2 Rue Cardinal Lemoine
3 Shakespeare & Co.
4 Brasserie Lipp
5 Jardin du Luxembourg
6 La Closerie des Lilas

4 BRASSERIE LIPP

The 1920s saw the literary and artistic center of Paris shift from Montmartre in the north of Paris to the cafes and brasseries of St-Germain and Montparnasse in the south. **Brasserie Lipp** (151 Blvd. St-Germain; *01-45-48-53-91*), was one of Hemingway's favorite watering holes, and he occasionally came here to write.

Turn right out of Brasserie Lipp and right again onto rue Bonaparte. Cross rue de Vaugirard and continue along rue Guynemer. Opposite no. 4 is an entrance to the:

5 JARDIN DU LUXEMBOURG

Hemingway used to walk through the gardens on his way to visit renowned patron of the arts **Gertrude Stein** (who lived at 27 rue de Fleurus). When he was particularly strapped for cash, he used to hunt pigeons here with his son.

Exit the gardens on Boulevard St-Michel and take RER B to Port Royal.

6 LA CLOSERIE DES LILAS

Another of Hemingway's favorite cafes, **La Closerie des Lilas** (171 Blvd. Montparnasse; *C* 01-40-51-34-50) is where he and

Gertrude Stein.

the novelist **F. Scott Fitzgerald** planned a crazy trip to Lyon to recover Fitzgerald's car. Today it's quite an upmarket restaurant.

PARISIAN ARCHITECTURE THROUGH THE AGES

Thanks to Baron Haussmann's modernization of the city in the 19th century, in architectural terms Paris is more homogenous than most capitals. The uniformity of Haussmannian architecture is undoubtedly key to Paris's charm and beauty, but you don't have to look far to find traces of other styles and periods. **Start:** *Ile de la Cité.*

1 CATHÉDRALE DE NOTRE-DAME

Built between 1163 and 1250, but added to over the centuries, Notre-Dame is the archetypal Gothic cathedral. The key features of **Gothic** architecture were flying buttresses, rose windows, and if you venture inside, vaulted ceilings. See p. 92.

Head north along rue de la Cité. Cross the Seine and continue along rue St-Martin. Turn left onto rue de Rivoli. When you see the Louvre, turn left onto rue de l'Amiral de Coligny and go into the Cour Carrée.

The Gothic Cathédrale de Notre-Dame.

Parisian Architecture Through the Ages

Cimetière de Montmartre

av. de Clichy

r. Caulaincourt

Basilique du Sacré Coeur

MONTMARTRE

18e

bd. Barbès

17e

r. Pierre Fontaine

bd. de Clichy

r. Blanche

r. Notre-Dame de Lorette

bd. de Rochechouart

5

av. d'Amsterdam

r. de Clichy

Gare du Nord

r. La Fayette

bd. de Magenta

r. du Faubourg St-Martin

19e

Canal Saint-Martin

bd. de la Villette

Gare St-Lazare

8e

9e

r. Fayette

r. La

r. du Fbg. Montmartre

Gare de l'Est

r. d'Hauteville

bd. de Strasbourg

bd. de Magenta

10e

HÔPITAL ST-LOUIS

4

Opéra Garnier

r. du Faubourg du Temple

3

place Vendôme

av. de l'Opéra

r. de Richelieu

Jardin du Palais Royal

2e

Montmartre

bd. de Sébastopol

bd. de Turbigo

place de la République

av. de La République

11e

r. Saint-Honoré

r. de Rivoli

1er

Palais Royal

r. du Louvre

de

r.

3e

bd. Voltaire

bd. Richard Lenoir

Jardin des Tuileries

Musée du Louvre

2

r. de Rivoli

Forum des Halles

Centre Pompidou

Musée d'Orsay

Seine

bd.

MARAIS

r. de Rivoli

place de la Bastille

7e

bd. St-Germain

St-Germain-des-Prés

ÎLE DE LA CITÉ

1

4e

bd. Henri IV

Opéra Bastille

ÎLE ST-LOUIS

r. de Lyon

St-Sulpice

bd.

St Germain

6e

r. de Rennes

r. de Vaugirard

Sorbonne

12e

bd. Diderot

bd. Raspail

Jardin du Luxembourg

bd. St-Michel

LATIN QUARTER

CAMPUS DE JUSSIEU

Panthéon

Gare de Lyon

r. Monge

Jardin des Plantes

Seine

5e

Gare d'Austerlitz

bd. du Montparnasse

MONTPARNASSE

Cimetière du Montparnasse

14e

bd. de Port Royal

Arago

bd.

av. des Gobelins

bd. Saint-Marcel

r. de l'Hôpital

GROUPE HOSPITALIER PITIÉ-SALPÊTRIÈRE

6

bd. Vincent Auriol

13e

place d'Italie

1	Cathédrale de Notre-Dame
2	Musée du Louvre
3	Église de la Madeleine
4	Boulevard Haussmann
5	Métro Abbesses
6	Bibliothèque Nationale de France (BNF)

0   1/2 mi
0   0.5 km

MUSÉE DU LOUVRE

The left-hand side of the façade opposite you is oldest part of the Louvre. Built in the 1530s, it's a good example of **Renaissance** architecture. Admire the decorative bas-reliefs, the pilasters (shallow columns projecting from the wall), and the symmetry of the facade. See p. 85.

Take Métro line 1 from Louvre-Rivoli to Concorde. Change onto either line 8 or 12 to Madeleine.

3 **ÉGLISE DE LA MADELEINE**

Inspired by ancient Rome, Napoleon I ordered the construction of this **neoclassicist** temple. He intended it to be a "Temple to the Glory of the Great Army," but as it was incomplete when he fell from grace, it became a church and was consecrated in 1842.

Walk around the church and turn down rue Tronchet. At the end of the street you'll come to:

4 **BOULEVARD HAUSSMANN**

Named after the Baron who transformed Paris in the 19th century, this wide tree-lined boulevard demonstrates the key characteristics of **Haussmannian** architecture; look for wrought-iron balconies and the alignment of the windows and balconies to create a sense of perspective.

Boulevard Haussmann.

After you pass Printemps and Galeries Lafayettes on your left, turn left on rue de la Chaussée d'Antin to Trinité d'Estienne d'Orves. Take Métro line 12 to Abbesses.

5 MÉTRO ABBESSES

This is one of the only two original Métro entrances that are left in Paris (the other is at Porte Dauphine). Designed by Hector Guimard in 1900, the Paris Métro entrances were a classic example of the **Art Nouveau** style.

Take Métro line 12 to Madeleine and change onto line 14. Get off at Bibliothèque François Mitterand.

6 BIBLIOTHÈQUE NATIONALE DE FRANCE (BNF)

The towers of the Bibliothèque Nationale de France resemble open books.

Designed by **contemporary** architect Dominique Perrault, this huge library opened in 1996. The reading rooms are underground, while the books are housed in four glass towers—the shape of each tower is supposed to symbolize an open book.

4

EXPLORING PARIS

by Kate van den Boogert

The city of Paris has a long history: There has been civilization here for more than 2 millennia, ever since Julius Caesar's troops invaded the city in 52 B.C., snatching power from the Gaulish tribe, the *Parisii*. Two thousand years of art, architecture, war, religion, and politics—not to mention power, passion, and intrigue—has left its mark on the city. Paris counts hundreds of museums and monuments. There are irresistible stars such as the Louvre, *bien sûr*, but there are also many surprising, secret spots. It's a city that can transport you back centuries, where you can lose yourself in the labyrinth of royal power and opulence or get captivated by the violence of the French Revolution. Or the city can bring you up to date, with the most avant-garde art, design, and architecture that the world has to offer today. But the special thing about Paris is that just walking the streets feels like visiting the world's most magical museum.

The year 2012 will see the Musée d'Orsay and the Palais de Tokyo emerge from major revamps. The much-missed Musée Picasso, Musée de l'Homme, and Musée Galliera are to reopen to the public after years of renovations, while new institutions such as the Gaîté Lyrique settle into Paris's dense cultural landscape. Paris's transport and shopping hub Les Halles is in the middle of a massive overhaul, expected to finish in 2016.

Area by area, the following pages will highlight the best that Paris can offer, from iconic sights known the world over to quirky museums and hidden gardens, from 1,000-year-old castles to galleries celebrating the most challenging contemporary art, and from the must-sees to the only-if-you've-seen-everything-else-sees. Here, then, is the best of Paris's attractions.

PARIS'S TOP 14 SIGHTS & ATTRACTIONS

PREVIOUS PAGE: **A fountain in place de la Concorde.**

- Hôtel des Invalides/Napoleon's Tomb (p. 139)
- Jardin du Luxembourg (p. 136)
- Musée d'Orsay (p. 142)
- Musée du Louvre (p. 85)
- Musée du Quai Branly (p. 144)
- Palais de Tokyo (p. 114)
- Parc de la Villette (p. 128)
- Sainte-Chapelle (p. 103)
- Tour Eiffel (p. 146)

THE RIGHT BANK
Les Halles, Louvre & Palais Royal (1er & 2e)

Crowned by the Louvre, this central area that flanks the Seine packs in a high density of important museums, centered on the magnificent former royal palace and its expansive Jardin des Tuileries. Though the Louvre is on top of most visitors' to-do lists, don't forget that there are also some wonderful smaller museums close by, and great shopping too.

Jardin des Tuileries ★★ ☺ GARDEN   The spectacular statue-studded Jardin des Tuileries, bordering place de la Concorde, is as much a part of Paris as the Seine. Le Nôtre, Louis XIV's gardener and planner of the Versailles grounds, designed the gardens. Some of the gardens' most distinctive statues are the 18 enormous bronzes by Maillol, installed within the Jardin du Carrousel, a subdivision of the Jardin des Tuileries, between 1964 and 1965, under the direction of Culture Minister André Malraux.

About 400 years before that, Catherine de Médici ordered a palace built here, the **Palais des Tuileries;** other occupants have included Louis XVI (after he left Versailles) and Napoleon. Twice attacked by Parisians, it was burned to the ground in 1871 and never rebuilt. The gardens, however, remain. In orderly French manner, the trees are arranged according to designs, and even the paths

---

The New Les Halles

For eight centuries, **Les Halles** was the city's primary wholesale fruit, meat, and vegetable market. In the 19th century, Zola famously called it "the belly of Paris." The smock-clad vendors, beef carcasses, and baskets of vegetables all belong to the past, for the original market was torn down in the early '70s and relocated to a massive steel-and-glass edifice at Rungis, a suburb near Orly. Today, Les Halles includes the city's chief transportation hub and a major shopping complex, the **Forum des**

Halles (1–7 rue Pierre-Lescot, 1er). This large mall, much of it underground, contains shops, restaurants, and movie theaters. In 2010, the city embarked on a massive 810-million euro renovation program that will overhaul the underground shopping and transportation zones as well as the garden above. Renovations are slated to be completed in 2016, but the complex should remain open and operational during the renovations. For more information, visit www.parisleshalles.fr.

Attractions near Les Halles, the Louvre, Palais Royal & Opéra (1e, 2e, & 9e)

Cour Napoléon &
I. M. Pei Pyramid **9**
Fragonard Musée
du Parfum **6**
Jardin des Tuileries **6**
Jeu de Paume **4**
Musée de l'Orangerie **5**
Musée des Arts
Décoratifs **7**

Musée du Louvre **10**
Musée Grévin **3**
Opéra Garnier **2**
Palais Royal **8**
St-Eustache **12**
St-Germain l'Auxerrois **11**

Pedestrians only
Ⓜ Metro station
RER RER station
⊠ Post office

1/4 mi
0.25 km
To Canal St-Martin →

MARAIS

83

A video exhibit at Jeu de Paume.

are arrow-straight. Bubbling fountains break the sense of order and formality.

Each summer, over the months of July and August, the parks hosts a traditional **funfair** (www.feteforaine-jardindestuileries.com) alongside the rue de Rivoli—be sure to take a Ferris Wheel ride for excellent views.

Near place de la Concorde, 1er. ✆ **01-40-20-90-43.** Free admission. Daily Apr–May 7am–9pm; June–Aug 7am–11pm; Sept 7am–9pm; Oct–Mar 7:30am–7:30pm. Métro: Tuileries or Concorde.

Jeu de Paume ★★ MUSEUM After knowing many roles, this museum, in the northeast corner of the Tuileries gardens, has become a national center for photography and video, exploring "the world of images, their uses, and the issues they raise" from the 19th to the 21st centuries. It is one of the finest museums of its type in the world, and presents ever-changing exhibitions, many of them daringly avant-garde.

Originally, in this part of the gardens, Napoleon III built a ball court on which *jeu de paume,* an antecedent of tennis, was played—hence the museum's name. The most infamous period in the gallery's history came during the Nazi occupation, when it served as an "evaluation center" for works of modern art. Paintings from all over France were shipped to the Jeu de Paume; art condemned by the Nazis as "degenerate" was burned.

1 place de la Concorde, 8e. ✆ **01-47-03-12-50.** www.jeudepaume.org. Admission 8.50€ adults, 5.50€ students and children. Tues noon–9pm; Wed–Fri noon–7pm; Sat–Sun 10am–7pm. Métro: Concorde.

Musée de l'Orangerie ★★ MUSEUM In the Tuileries stands another gem among museums. It has an outstanding collection of art and one celebrated work on display: Claude Monet's exquisite *Nymphéas* (1915–27). The two galleries were purpose built by the French state to house eight massive murals by Monet, in which water lilies float amorphously on the canvas. The paintings are displayed as the artist intended them to be—lit by sunlight in large oval galleries that evoke the shape of the garden ponds at his former Giverny estate.

Creating his effects with hundreds and hundreds of minute strokes of his brush (one irate 19th-c. critic called them "tongue lickings"), Monet achieved unity and harmony, as he did in his Rouen Cathedral series and his haystacks. Artists with lesser talent might have stirred up "soup." But Monet, of course, was a genius. See his lilies and evoke for yourself the mood and melancholy as he experienced them so many years ago. Monet continued to paint his water landscapes right up until his death in 1926, although he was greatly hampered by failing eyesight.

The renovated building also houses the art collections of two men, John Walter and Paul Guillaume, who are not connected to each other, except that they were both married at different times to the same woman. Their collection includes more than 24 Renoirs, including *Young Girl at a Piano*. Cézanne is represented by 14 works, notably *The Red Rock,* and Matisse by 11 paintings. The highlight of Rousseau's nine works displayed here is *The Wedding,* and the dozen paintings by Picasso reach the pinnacle of their brilliance in *The Female Bathers.* Other outstanding paintings are by Utrillo (10 works in all), Soutine (22), and Derain (28).

It is possible to buy a joint ticket to both the Musée d'Orsay (p. 142) and the Musée de l'Orangerie, which is valid for 4 days and costs 13€.

Jardin des Tuileries, 1er. ✆ **01-44-77-80-07.** www.musee-orangerie.fr. Admission 7.50€ adults, 5€ students 25 and younger. Free 1st Sun of every month. Wed–Mon 9am–6pm. Métro: Concorde.

Musée des Arts Décoratifs ★★ MUSEUM   In the northwest wing of the Louvre's Pavillon de Marsan, this imposing museum is home to a treasury of furnishings, fabrics, wallpaper, objets d'art, and items displaying living styles from the Middle Ages to the present. Notable are the 1920s Art Deco boudoir, bath, and bedroom done for couturier Jeanne Lanvin by the designer Rateau, plus a collection of the works donated by Jean Dubuffet. Decorative art from the Middle Ages to the Renaissance is on the second floor; collections from the 17th, 18th, and 19th centuries occupy the third and fourth floors. The fifth floor has specialized centers, such as wallpaper and drawings, and exhibits detailing fashion, textiles, toys, crafts, and glass trends. The space also includes a lovely ground-floor shop, **107 Rivoli** (p. 246), selling all sorts of craft pieces, and a restaurant, Le Saut du Loup, which boasts an outdoor eating area in the Tuileries Gardens.

Palais du Louvre, 107 rue de Rivoli, 1er. ✆ **01-44-55-57-50.** www.lesartsdecoratifs.fr. Admission 9€ adults, 7.50€ ages 18–25, free for children 17 and younger. Tues–Wed, Fri 11am–6pm; Thurs 11am–6pm; Sat–Sun 10am–6pm. Métro: Palais-Royal or Tuileries.

Musée du Louvre ★★★ MUSEUM   The Louvre is the world's largest palace and museum, and it houses one of the greatest art collections ever. To enter, pass through I. M. Pei's controversial 21m (69-ft.) **glass pyramid ★**—a startling though effective contrast of the ultramodern against the palace's classical lines.

Musée du Louvre.

Viewing the *Mona Lisa.*

Commissioned by the late president François Mitterrand and completed in 1989, it allows sunlight to shine on an underground reception area with a complex of shops and restaurants.

People on one of those "Paris-in-a-day" tours try to break track records to get a glimpse of the Louvre's two most famous ladies: the beguiling ***Mona Lisa*** and the armless ***Venus de Milo*** ★★★. The herd then dashes on a 5-minute stampede in pursuit of ***Winged Victory*** ★★★, the headless statue discovered at Samothrace and dating from about 200 B.C. In defiance of the assembly line theory of art, we head instead for David's **Coronation of Napoleon,** showing Napoleon poised with the crown aloft as Joséphine kneels before him, just across from his ***Portrait of Madame Récamier*** ★, depicting Napoleon's opponent at age 23; she reclines on her sofa agelessly in the style of classical antiquity.

Then a big question looms: Which of the rest of the 30,000 works on display would you like to see?

Between the Seine and rue de Rivoli, the Palais du Louvre suffers from an embarrassment of riches, stretching for almost 1km (½ mile). In the days of Charles V, it was a fortress, but François I, a patron of Leonardo da Vinci, had it torn down and rebuilt as a royal residence. Less than a month after Marie Antoinette's head and body parted company, the Revolutionary Committee decided the king's collection of paintings and sculpture should be opened to the public. At the lowest point in its history, in the 18th century, the Louvre was home for anybody who wanted to set up housekeeping. Laundry hung in the windows, corners were pigpens, and families built fires to cook their meals in winter. Napoleon ended all that, chasing out the squatters and restoring the palace. In fact, he chose the Louvre as the site of his wedding to Marie-Louise.

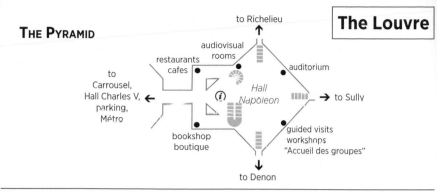

THE PYRAMID

to Richelieu

The Louvre

audiovisual rooms

restaurants cafes

to Carrousel, Hall Charles V, parking, Métro

auditorium

Hall Napóleon

→ to Sully

bookshop boutique

guided visits workshops "Accueil des groupes"

to Denon

THE WINGS

rue de Rivoli

Marly Horses (ground floor)

Richelieu

cour Napoléon

The Pyramid →

Sully *cour Carrée*

Denon

Venus de Milo (ground floor)

Mona Lisa (first floor)

Winged Victory (first floor)

So where did all these paintings come from? The kings of France, notably François I and Louis XIV, acquired many of them, and others were willed to or purchased by the state. Many contributed by Napoleon were taken from reluctant donors: The church was one especially heavy and unwilling giver. Much of Napoleon's plunder had to be returned, though France hasn't yet seen its way clear to giving back all the booty.

The collections are divided into seven departments: Egyptian Antiquities; Oriental Antiquities; Greek, Etruscan, and Roman Antiquities; Sculpture; Painting; Decorative Arts; and Graphic Arts. If you don't have to do Paris in a day, you might want to visit several times, concentrating on different collections or schools of painting. Those with little time should take a guided tour.

Acquired by François I to hang above his bathtub, Leonardo's **La Gioconda (Mona Lisa)** ★★★ has been the source of legend for centuries. Note the guard and bulletproof glass: The world's most famous painting was stolen in 1911 then found in Florence in 1913. At first, both the poet Guillaume Apollinaire and Picasso were suspected, but it was discovered in the possession of a former Louvre employee, who'd apparently carried it out under his overcoat. Two centuries after its arrival at the Louvre, the *Mona Lisa* in 2003 was assigned a new gallery of her own. Less well known (but to us even more enchanting) are Leonardo's **Virgin and Child with St. Anne** ★ and the **Virgin of the Rocks.**

Winged Victory.

After paying your respects to the "smiling one," allow time to see some French works stretching from the Richelieu wing through the entire **Sully wing** and even overflowing into the **Denon wing.** It's all here: Watteau's *Gilles* with the mysterious boy in a clown suit staring at you; Fragonard's and Boucher's

Venus de Milo.

rococo renderings of the aristocracy; and the greatest masterpieces of David, including his stellar 1785 *The Oath of the Horatii* and the vast and vivid *Coronation of Napoleon.* Only Florence's Uffizi rivals the Denon wing for its Italian Renaissance collection—everything from Raphael's *Portrait of Baltha-zar Castiglione* to Titian's *Man with a Glove.* Veronese's gigantic *Wedding Feast at Cana* ★, a romp of Venetian high society in the 1500s, occupies an entire wall (that's Paolo himself playing the cello).

Of the Greek and Roman antiquities, the most notable collections, aside from the *Venus de Milo* and *Winged Victory,* are fragments of a **Parthenon frieze** (in the Denon wing). In Renaissance sculpture, you'll see Michelangelo's *Esclaves (Slaves),* originally intended for the

Leaping Over the Louvre Line

If you don't want to wait in line for tickets to the Louvre, you can order tickets in advance by calling ℂ **08-92-68-46-94** or visiting **http://louvre.fnac spectacles.com**; tickets can be mailed to you, or you can pick them up at any Paris branch of the Fnac electronics chain. You can also order advance tickets and take a virtual tour at **www.louvre.fr**. Note that the Louvre is open until 10pm on Wednesday and Fridays—usually a quiet time to visit.

tomb of Julius II but sold into other bondage. The Denon wing houses masterpieces such as Ingres's *The Turkish Bath,* the **Botticelli frescoes** from the Villa Lemmi, Raphael's *La Belle Jardinière,* and Titian's *Open Air Concert.* The Sully wing is also filled with old masters, such as Boucher's *Diana Resting After Her Bath* and Fragonard's *Bathers.*

The **Richelieu wing ★★★** houses northern European and French paintings, along with decorative arts, sculpture, Oriental antiquities (including a rich collection of both Islamic and Far Eastern Art), and the Napoleon III salons. One of its galleries displays 21 works that Rubens painted in a space of only 2 years for Marie de Médici's Palais de Luxembourg. The masterpieces here include Dürer's *Self-Portrait,* van Dyck's *Portrait of Charles I of England,* and Holbein the Younger's *Portrait of Erasmus of Rotterdam.*

When you tire of strolling the galleries, you may like a pick-me-up at the Richelieu Wing's **Café Richelieu** (ℂ 01-47-03-99-68) or, under the arcades and overlooking Pei's pyramid, at **Café Marly,** 93 rue de Rivoli, 1er (ℂ **01-49-26-06-60**). Boasting Napoleon III opulence, the Marly is a perfect oasis. Try a cafe crème, a club sandwich, a pastry, or something from the bistro menu.

Veronese's *Wedding Feast at Cana.*

Contemporary Art & the Louvre

With all those centuries-old master-pieces grabbing the spotlight, the museum's contemporary works can get overlooked—but they're worth seeking out. In 2010, the museum unveiled a painted ceiling in the Salle des Bronzes by American artist Cy Twombly, the third contemporary artist who was commissioned to install a permanent work at the Louvre. (He was preceded by contemporary artists Anselm Kiefer and François Morellet.) Twombly's painting appears on the ceiling of one of the Louvre's largest galleries, and it covers more than 350 sq. m (3,770 sq. ft.). The ceiling depicts an immense blue sky that is dotted with spheres and white insets inscribed with the names of famous Greek sculptors.

34–36 quai du Louvre, 1er. Main entrance in the glass pyramid, Cour Napoléon. ☎ **01-40-20-53-17,** 01-40-20-50-50 for operator, or 08-92-68-46-94 for advance credit card sales. www.louvre.fr. Admission 10€, children 17 and younger free, free to all 1st Sun of every month. Sat–Mon and Thurs 9am–6pm; Wed and Fri 9am–10pm. 1½-hr. English-language tours (Mon and Wed–Sun) 9€, 6€ children 12 and younger with museum ticket. Métro: Palais-Royal–Musée du Louvre.

Palais Royal ★★ HISTORIC BUILDING   The Palais Royal was originally known as the Palais Cardinal, for it was the residence of Cardinal Richelieu, Louis XIII's prime minister. Richelieu had it built, and after his death it was inherited by the king, who died soon after. Louis XIV spent part of his childhood here with his mother, Anne of Austria, but later resided at the Louvre and Versailles. The palace was later owned by the duc de Chartres et Orléans (see Parc Monceau on p. 115), who encouraged the opening of cafes, gambling dens, and other public entertainment. Today the building is occupied by the French Culture Ministry.

The lovely **Jardin du Palais Royal** is at the center of the arcaded former palace, and features a fountain and gardens. Don't miss the main courtyard, close to the rue St Honoré, with the controversial 1986 Buren sculpture—280 prison-striped columns, oddly placed. The arcades of the Palais Royal have become a high fashion destination over the last few years, with high-end boutiques such as Marc Jacobs and Stella McCartney.

Rue St-Honoré, 1er. No phone. Free admission. Gardens daily 7:30am–dusk. Métro: Palais Royal–Musée du Louvre.

St-Eustache ★★ CHURCH   This Gothic and Renaissance church completed in 1637 is rivaled only by Notre-Dame. Mme de Pompadour and Richelieu were baptized here, and Molière's funeral was held here in 1673. The church has been known for organ recitals ever since Liszt played in 1866. Inside rests the **black-marble tomb** of Jean-Baptiste Colbert, the minister of state under Louis XIV; atop

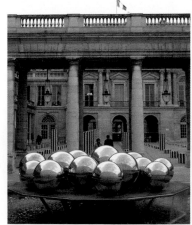

The courtyard of the Palais Royal.

the tomb is his marble effigy flanked by statues of *Abundance* by Coysevox and *Fidelity* by Tuby. Notable paintings are Rembrandt's **The Pilgrimage to Emmaus,** two versions of **Disciples d'Emmaüs** by Rubens, and a triptych by modern American painter Keith Haring—his last work before he died in 1990 of AIDS. The church has a side entrance on rue Rambuteau.

2 impasse St-Eustache, 1er. ✆ **01-42-36-31-05.** www.st-eustache.org. Free admission. Daily 9am–7pm; Sun 9am–7pm; Sun organ recitals 5:30pm. Métro: Les Halles

St-Germain l'Auxerrois ★★
CHURCH   Once it was the church for the Palais du Louvre, drawing an assortment of royalty, courtesans, men of art and law, and local artisans. Sharing place du Louvre with Perrault's colonnade, the church contains only the

The black-marble tomb of Jean-Baptiste Colbert, in St-Eustache.

foundation stones of its original 11th-century belfry. The chapel that had stood here was greatly enlarged in the 14th century by the addition of side aisles and became a beautiful church, with 77 sq. m (829 sq. ft.) of stained glass, including some rose windows from the Renaissance. The intricately carved **church-wardens' pews** are outstanding, based on 17th-century Le Brun designs. Behind them is a **15th-century triptych** and **Flemish retable,** so poorly lit you can hardly appreciate it. The organ was ordered by Louis XVI for Sainte-Chapelle. Many famous men were entombed here, including the sculptor Coysevox and the architect Le Vau. Around the chancel is an intricate **18th-century grille.**

The saddest moment in the church's history was on August 24, 1572, the evening of the St. Bartholomew Massacre. The tower bells rang, signaling the supporters of Catherine de Médici, Marguerite de Guise, Charles IX, and the future Henri III to launch a slaughter of thousands of Huguenots, who'd been invited to celebrate the marriage of Henri de Navarre to Marguerite de Valois.

2 place du Louvre, 1er. ✆ **01-42-60-13-96.** Free admission. Daily 8am–7pm. Métro: Louvre-Rivoli.

Le Marais, Ile St-Louis & Ile de la Cité (3e & 4e)

This historic neighborhood, home to royalty and aristocracy in the 17th and 18th centuries, preserves exceptional architecture—some of it dating back to the Renaissance. Its narrow, winding streets are from another age. While it features some blockbuster attractions, including the **Hôtel de Ville** and the **Centre Pompidou,** the Marais is notable for its density of charming smaller museums, where you hopefully won't be fighting through crowds. The two islands in the Seine—Ile St-Louis and Ile de la Cité—set the stage for some impressive medieval monuments, the **Cathédrale de Notre-Dame,** the **Conciergerie,** and the glorious **Sainte-Chapelle.** *Note:* the Musée Picasso, which has been closed for renovations over the past few years, should reopen in 2012.

Cathédrale de Notre-Dame.

Rose window at the Cathédrale de Notre-Dame.

Cathédrale de Notre-Dame ★★ CHURCH   Notre-Dame is the heart of Paris and even of the country itself: Distances from the city to all parts of France are calculated from a spot at the far end of place du Parvis, in front of the cathedral, where a circular bronze plaque marks **Kilomètre Zéro.**

The cathedral's setting on the banks of the Seine has always been memorable. Founded in the 12th century by Maurice de Sully, bishop of Paris, Notre-Dame has grown over the years, changing as Paris has changed; often falling victim to whims of taste. Its flying buttresses (the external side supports, giving the massive interior a sense of weightlessness) were rebuilt in 1330. Though many disagree, we feel Notre-Dame is more interesting outside than in, and you'll want to walk all around it to fully appreciate this "vast symphony of stone." Better yet, cross over the Pont au Double to the Left Bank and view it from the quai.

The histories of Paris and Notre-Dame are inseparable. Many prayed here before going off to fight in the Crusades. The revolutionaries who destroyed the Galerie des Rois and converted the building into a secular temple didn't spare "Our Lady of Paris." Later, Napoleon crowned himself emperor here, yanking the

Kilomètre Zéro.

crown out of Pius VII's hands and placing it on his own head before crowning his Joséphine empress (see David's *Coronation of Napoléon* in the Louvre). But carelessness, vandalism, embellishments, and wars of religion had already demolished much of the previously existing structure.

The cathedral was once scheduled for demolition, but because of the popularity of Victor Hugo's *Hunchback of Notre-Dame* and the revival of interest in the Gothic period, a movement mushroomed to restore the cathedral

Attractions in the Marais, Ile St-Louis & Ile de la Cité (3e & 4e)

Notre-Dame de Paris

Statue of Louis XIV
Ambulatory
Statue of Louis XIII
Pietà
High Altar
← To Treasury
Choir
Virgin & Child (13th cent.)
Statue of St. Denis
Virgin & Child (14th cent.)
Portal of the Cloisters
North Transept
Crossing
South Transept
Portal of St. Stephen
North Rose Window
South Rose Window
North Aisle
Nave
South Aisle
Entrance to the Towers
West Rose Window
Portal of the Virgin
Portal of the Last Judgment
Portal of St. Anne

to its original glory. The task was completed under Viollet-le-Duc, an architectural genius. The houses of old Paris used to crowd in on Notre-Dame, but during his redesign of the city, Baron Haussmann ordered them torn down to show the cathedral to its best advantage from the parvis. This is the best vantage for seeing the three sculpted 13th-century portals (the Virgin, the Last Judgment, and St. Anne).

On the left, the **Portal of the Virgin** depicts the signs of the zodiac and the coronation of the Virgin, an association found in dozens of medieval churches. The restored central **Portal of the Last Judgment** depicts three levels: the first shows Vices and Virtues; the second, Christ and his Apostles; and above that, Christ in triumph after the Resurrection. The portal is a close illustration of the Gospel according to Matthew. Over it is the remarkable **west rose window ★★**, 9.5m (31 ft.) wide, forming a showcase for a statue of the Virgin and Child. On the far right is the **Portal of St. Anne,** depicting scenes such as the Virgin enthroned with Child; it's Notre-Dame's best-preserved and most perfect piece of sculpture. Equally interesting (though often missed) is the **Portal of the Cloisters** (around on the left), with its dour-faced 13th-century Virgin, a survivor among the figures that originally adorned the facade. (Alas, the Child she's holding has been decapitated.) Finally, on the Seine side of Notre-Dame, the **Portal of St. Stephen** traces that saint's martyrdom.

If possible, see Notre-Dame at sunset. Inside of the three giant medallions warming the austere cathedral, the **north rose window ★★** in the transept, from the mid 13th century, is best. The main body of the church is typically Gothic, with slender, graceful columns. In the **choir,** a stone-carved screen from the early 14th century depicts such biblical scenes as the Last Supper. Near the altar stands the 14th-century *Virgin and Child ★*, highly venerated among Paris's faithful. In the **treasury** are displayed vestments and gold objects, including crowns. Exhibited is a cross presented to Haile Selassie, former emperor of Ethiopia, and a reliquary given by Napoleon. Notre-Dame is especially proud of its relics of the True Cross and the Crown of Thorns.

To visit the **gargoyles ★★** immortalized by Hugo, you have to scale steps leading to the twin **towers,** rising to a height of 68m (223 ft.). When there, you

Pont Neuf

Don't miss the ironically named **Pont Neuf (New Bridge)** at the tip of the Ile de la Cité island, opposite from Notre-Dame. The span isn't new—it's Paris's oldest bridge, begun in 1578 and finished in 1604. In its day, it had two unique features: It was paved, and it wasn't flanked with houses and shops. Actually, with 12 arches, it's not one bridge but two (they don't quite line up)—one from the Right Bank to the island and the other from the Left Bank to the island. At the **Musée Carnavalet** (p. 100), a painting called *The Spectacle of Buffoons* shows what the bridge was like between 1665 and 1669. Duels were fought on it, the nobility's great coaches crossed it, peddlers sold their wares, and entertainers such as Tabarin went there to seek a few coins from the gawkers. As public facilities were lacking, the bridge also served as a *de facto* outhouse.

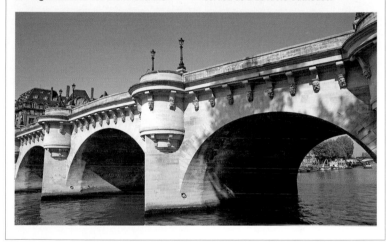

can inspect devils (some giving you the raspberry), hobgoblins, and birds of prey. Look carefully, and you may see hunchback Quasimodo with Esmeralda.

Approached through a garden behind Notre-Dame is the **Mémorial des Martyrs Français de la Déportation de 1945 (Deportation Memorial)**, out on the tip of Ile de la Cité. Here, birds chirp and the Seine flows gently by, but the memories are far from pleasant. The memorial commemorates the French citizens who were deported to concentration camps during World War II. Carved into stone are these blood-red words (in French): "Forgive, but don't forget." The memorial is open Monday to Friday 8:30am to 9:45pm, and Saturday to Sunday 9am to 9:45pm. Admission is free.

6 place du Parvis Notre-Dame, 4e. ☎ **01-53-10-07-02.** www.notredamedeparis.fr. Admission free to cathedral. Towers 8€ adults, 5€ seniors and ages 13–25, free for children 12 and younger. Treasury 3€ adults, 2.20€ seniors, 1.60€ ages 13–25, free for children 12 and younger. Cathedral year-round daily 8am–6:45pm (Sat–Sun 7:15pm). Towers and crypt daily 10am–6pm (until 11pm Sat–Sun June–Aug). Museum Wed and Sat–Sun 2–5pm. Treasury Mon–Fri 9:30am–6pm; Sat 9:30am–6:30pm; Sun 1:30–6:30pm. Métro: Cité or St-Michel. RER: St-Michel.

Centre Pompidou ★★★ MUSEUM
When it first opened in the 1970s, the Centre Pompidou was hailed as "the most avant-garde building in the world," and today it still continues to pack in the art-loving crowds—about six million people visit it each year.

Conceived by former French president Georges Pompidou and designed by architects Renzo Piano and Richard Rogers, this building originally opened in 1977, and it underwent a major renovation in 2000, which expanded and improved the space. The building's exterior is very

FROM TOP: Centre Pompidou; Brightly painted pipes on the facade of the Centre Pompidou.

bold: brightly painted pipes and ducts crisscross its transparent facade (green for water, red for heat, blue for air, and yellow for electricity), and an outdoor escalator flanks the building, freeing up interior space for exhibitions.

Inside, the big attraction is the impressive **Musée National d'Art Moderne (National Museum of Modern Art)** ★★, which is home to some 40,000 works from the 20th and 21st centuries—though only about 850 works can be displayed at one time. If you want to view some real charmers, seek out Calder's 1926 ***Josephine Baker,*** one of his earlier versions of the mobile, an art form he invented. You'll also find two examples of Duchamps's series of Dada-style sculptures he invented in 1936: ***Boîte en Valise*** (1941) and ***Boîte en Valise*** (1968). And every time we visit, we have to see Dalí's ***Hallucination partielle: Six images de Lénine sur un piano*** (1931), with Lenin dancing on a piano.

Other attractions inside the Centre Pompidou include: the **Bibliothéque Publique d'Information (Public Information Library),** a vast public library with a huge collection of French and foreign books, periodicals, films, music records, slides, and more; the **Institut de Recherche et de Coordination Acoustique-Musique (Institute for Research and Coordination of Acoustics/Music),** which brings together musicians and composers; the **Atelier Brancusi ★,** a minimuseum that recreates the Jazz Age studio of Romanian sculptor Brancusi; a movie theater; performance halls which often host concerts and events; shops; and restaurants. The Centre Pompidou holds regularly changing public exhibitions and events, so check their website for information.

Outside, there is a large open **forecourt,** which is a free "entertainment center" often featuring mimes, fire-eaters, circus performers, and sometimes musicians. Don't miss the nearby **Stravinsky fountain,** containing mobile sculptures by Tinguely and Niki de Saint Phalle.

Place Georges-Pompidou, 4e. ✆ **01-44-78-12-33.** www.centrepompidou.fr Admission 12€ adults, 9€ students, free for children 17 and younger. Wed–Mon 11am–10pm. Métro: Rambuteau, Hôtel de Ville, or Châtelet–Les Halles.

The Stravinsky fountain.

Conciergerie ★★ HISTORIC BUILDING   London has its Bloody Tower, and Paris has its Conciergerie. Even though the Conciergerie had a long regal history before the French Revolution, it was forever stained by the Reign of Terror and lives as an infamous symbol of the time when carts pulled up constantly to haul off fresh supplies of victims of Dr. Guillotin's wonderful little invention.

Much of the Conciergerie was built in the 14th century as an extension of the Capetian royal Palais de la Cité. You approach through its landmark twin towers, the **Tour d'Argent** (where the crown jewels were stored at one time) and **Tour de César,** but the **Salle des Gardes (Guard Room)** is the actual entrance. Even more interesting is the dark and foreboding Gothic **Salle des Gens d'Armes (Room of People at Arms),** utterly changed from the days when the king used it as a banquet hall. However, architecture plays a secondary role to the list of prisoners who spent their last days here. Few in its history endured tortures as severe as those imposed on Ravaillac, who assassinated Henri IV in 1610. In the Tour de César, he received pincers in the flesh and had hot lead and boiling oil poured on him like bath water before being executed. During the revolution, the Conciergerie became a symbol of terror to the nobility and enemies of the State. A short walk away, the Revolutionary Tribunal dispensed a skewed, hurried justice—if it's any consolation, the jurists didn't believe in torturing their victims, only in decapitating them.

The Conciergerie.

After being seized by a crowd of peasants who stormed Versailles, Louis XVI and Marie Antoinette were brought here to await their trials. In failing health and shocked beyond grief, *l'Autrichienne* ("the Austrian," as she was called with malice) had only a small screen (sometimes not even that) to protect her modesty from the gaze of guards stationed in her cell. By accounts of the day, she was shy and stupid, though the evidence is that on her death, she displayed the nobility of a true queen. (What's more, the famous "Let them eat cake," which she supposedly uttered when told the peasants had no bread, is probably apocryphal—besides, at the time, cake flour was less expensive than bread flour, so even if she said this, it wasn't meant coldheartedly.) It was shortly before noon on the morning of October 16, 1793, when the executioners arrived, grabbing her and cutting her hair, as was the custom for victims marked for the guillotine.

Later, the Conciergerie housed other prisoners, including Mme Elisabeth; Mme du Barry, mistress of Louis XV; Mme Roland ("O Liberty! Liberty! What crimes are committed in thy name!"); and Charlotte Corday, who killed Marat while he was taking a sulfur bath. In time, the revolution consumed its own leaders, such as Danton and Robespierre. Finally, one of Paris's most hated men, public prosecutor Fouquier-Tinville, faced the guillotine to which he'd sent so many others. Among the few interned here who lived to tell the tale was American Thomas Paine, who reminisced about his chats in English with Danton.

1 quai de l'Horloge, 4e. ℭ **01-53-40-60-80.** www.monum.fr. Admission 7€ adults, 4.50€ ages 18–25, free for children 17 and younger. Mar–Oct daily 9:30–6pm; Nov–Feb daily 9am–5pm. Métro: Cité, Châtelet, or St-Michel. RER: St-Michel.

Gaîté Lyrique ★ ☺ CULTURAL INSTITUTION This modern cultural institution, which is devoted to exploring mixed-media and digital art forms, opened in March 2011 to much fanfare. This museum hosts rotating exhibits that range from music and multimedia performances to design, fashion, and architecture to new media—there's even an interactive room dedicated to video

Hôtel de Ville.

games. This forward-thinking institution is located within a beautifully restored and updated 19th-century Parisian theater in the heart of the city.

3 bis rue Papin, 3e. 📞 **01-53-01-51-51**. www.gaite-lyrique.net. Tues–Sun 2–8pm. Métro: Réaumur Sébastopol.

Hôtel de Ville ★ HISTORIC BUILDING   On a large square with fountains and early-1900s lampposts, the 19th-century Hôtel de Ville isn't a hotel, but Paris's grandiose City Hall. The medieval structure it replaced had witnessed countless municipally ordered executions. Henri IV's assassin, Ravaillac, was quartered alive on the square in 1610, his body tied to four horses that bolted in opposite directions. On May 24, 1871, the Communards doused the City Hall with gas, creating a blaze that lasted for 8 days. The Third Republic ordered the structure rebuilt, with many changes, even creating a Hall of Mirrors evocative of that at Versailles. For security reasons, the major splendor of this building is closed to the public. There are changing art, architecture, design, and photography exhibitions (usually free admission), which can be accessed through the back entrance on rue Lobau. In winter, you'll find a skating rink on the piazza in front of the building.

29 rue de Rivoli, 4e. No phone for information. Free admission. Métro: Hôtel-de-Ville.

Maison de Victor Hugo ★ MUSEUM   Today, theatergoers who've seen *Les Misérables,* and even those who haven't read anything by Paris's 19th-century novelist, come to place des Vosges to see where Hugo lived and wrote. Some thought him a genius, but Cocteau called him a madman, and an American composer discovered that in his old age, he was carving furniture with his teeth! From 1832 to 1848, the novelist/poet lived on the second floor of the Hôtel Rohan Guéménée. The museum owns some of Hugo's furniture, as well as pieces that once belonged to Juliette Drouet, the mistress with whom he lived in exile on Guernsey, one of the Channel Islands.

Maison de Victor Hugo.

A salon in the Musée Carnavalet-Histoire de Paris.

Worth the visit are Hugo's drawings, more than 450, illustrating scenes from his own works. Mementos of the great writer abound, including samples of his handwriting, his inkwell, and first editions of his works. A painting of Hugo's 1885 funeral procession at the Arc de Triomphe is on display, as are many portraits and souvenirs of his family. Of the furnishings, a chinoiserie salon stands out. The collection even contains Daumier caricatures and a bust of Hugo by David d'Angers, which, compared with Rodin's, looks saccharine.

6 place des Vosges, 4e. ✆ **01-42-72-10-16.** www.musee-hugo.paris.fr. Free admission. Tues–Sun 10am–6pm. Métro: St-Paul, Bastille, or Chemin-Vert.

Maison Européene de la Photographie ★★ 🏛 MUSEUM   This major center for contemporary photography opened in the mid-1990s, and it features regularly changing photography exhibitions. The museum also has a permanent collection of about 15,000 works features works by well-known photographers such as Robert Frank and Raymond Depardon. You access the museum via a new wing built on the rue de Fourcy, but the majority of the museum is located within an 18th-century mansion, the Hôtel Hénault de Cantobre.

5-7 rue de Fourcy, 4e. ✆ **01-44-78-75-00.** www.mep-fr.org. Wed–Sun 11am–8pm. 7€ adults, 4€ students and seniors, free for children 7 and under. Free entry Wed 5–8pm. Métro: St-Paul.

Musée Carnavalet-Histoire de Paris ★★ ☺ MUSEUM   If you enjoy history, but history tomes bore you, spend some time here for insight into Paris's past, which comes alive in such details as the chessmen Louis XVI used to distract himself while waiting to go to the guillotine. The comprehensive and lifelike exhibits are great for kids. The building, a Renaissance palace, was built in 1544 and later acquired by Mme de Carnavalet. François Mansart transformed it between 1655 and 1661.

The palace is best known for one of history's most famous letter writers, Mme de Sévigné, who moved here in 1677. Fanatically devoted to her daughter (she moved in with her because she couldn't bear to be apart), she poured out nearly every detail of her life in her letters, virtually ignoring her son. A native of the Marais district, she died at her daughter's château in 1696. In 1866, the city of Paris acquired the mansion and turned it into a museum. Several salons cover the Revolution, with a bust of Marat, a portrait of Danton, and a model of the Bastille (one painting shows its demolition). Another salon tells the story of the captivity of the royal family at the Conciergerie, including the bed in which Mme Elisabeth (the sister of Louis XVI) slept and the Dauphin's exercise book.

Exhibits continue at the **Hôtel le Peletier de St-Fargeau,** across the courtyard. On display is furniture from the Louis XIV period to the early 20th century, including a replica of Marcel Proust's cork-lined bedroom with his actual furniture, including his brass bed. This section also exhibits artifacts from the museum's archaeological collection, including some Neolithic pirogues, shallow oak boats used for fishing and transport from about 4400 to 2200 B.C.

23 rue de Sévigné, 3e. ✆ **01-44-59-58-58.** www.carnavalet.paris.fr. Free admission. Special exhibits from 5€ adults, 4.20€ students and children. Tues–Sun 10am–6pm. Métro: St-Paul or Chemin Vert.

Musée Cognacq-Jay ★ MUSEUM   The founders of the defunct La Samaritaine department store, Ernest Cognacq and his wife, Louise Jay, were fabled for their exquisite taste. To see what they accumulated from around the world, head for this museum in the 16th-century Hôtel Denon, with its Louis XV and Louis XVI paneled rooms. Some of the 18th century's most valuable decorative works are exhibited, ranging from ceramics and porcelain to delicate cabinets and paintings by Canaletto, Fragonard, Greuze, Chardin, Boucher, Watteau, and Tiepolo.

In the Hôtel Donon, 8 rue Elzévir, 3e. ✆ **01-40-27-07-21.** www.cognacq-jay.paris.fr. Free admission to permanent collection; variable charges for temporary shows. Tues–Sun 10am–6pm. Métro: St Paul.

Musée d'Art et Histoire du Judaisme ★★ MUSEUM   Security is tight, but it's worth the effort. In the Hôtel de St-Aignan, dating from the 1600s, this museum of Jewish history has been handsomely and impressively installed. The development of Jewish culture is traced not only in Paris, but also in France itself, as well as in Europe. Many of the exhibitions are devoted to religious subjects, including menorahs, Torah ornaments, and ark curtains, in both the Ashkenazi and Sephardic traditions. For us, the most interesting documents relate to the notorious Dreyfus case. Also on parade is a collection of illuminated manuscripts, Renaissance Torah arks, and paintings from the 18th and 19th centuries, along with Jewish gravestones from the Middle Ages. The best display is of the artwork by leading Jewish painters and artists ranging from Soutine to Zadkine, from Chagall to Modigliani.

An exhibit at the Musée d'Art et Histoire du Judaisme.

Hôtel de St-Aignan, 71 rue du Temple, 3e. ✆ **01-53-01-86-53.** www.mahj.org. Admission 6.80€ adults, 4.50€ ages 18–26, free for children 17 and younger. Mon–Fri 11am–6pm; Sun 10am–6pm. Métro: Rambuteau.

Musée de la Chasse et de la Nature ★★ 🎁☺ MUSEUM   This surprising little "hunting and nature" museum explores the relationship between humans and nature via the art of hunting, which remains quite popular in France. Established by French industrialist and avid hunter Francois Sommer and his wife, Jacqueline, in 1964, the museum features a collection of art in different mediums that celebrates the natural world. There is also a large collection of stuffed animals—you'll see everything from pigeons to polar bears. The museum is housed in a beautiful 18th-century mansion, and it was last renovated in 2007.

2 rue des Archives, Hôtel de Mongelas, 3e. ✆ **01-53-01-92-40.** www.chassenature.org. Admission 6€ adults, 4.50€ students, children 17 and under free. Tues–Sun 11am–6pm. Métro: Rambuteau.

Musée de l'Histoire de France (Musée des Archives Nationales) ★ MUSEUM   The official home of the archives that reflect the convoluted history of France, this small but noteworthy palace was first built in 1371 as the **Hôtel de Clisson** and later acquired by the ducs de Guise, who figured prominently in France's bloody wars of religion. In 1705, most of it was demolished by the prince and princesse de Soubise, through their architect, the much-underrated Delamair, and rebuilt with a baroque facade. The princesse de Soubise was once the mistress of Louis XIV, and apparently, the Sun King was very generous, giving her the funds to remodel and redesign the palace into one of the most beautiful buildings in the Marais. *Tip:* Before entering through the building's main entrance, the gracefully colonnaded Cour d'Honneur (Court of Honor), walk around the corner to 58 rue des Archives, where you'll see the few remaining vestiges—a turreted medieval gateway—of the original Hôtel de Clisson.

In the early 1800s, the site was designated by Napoleon as the repository for his archives, and it has served that function ever since. The archives contain documents that predate Charlemagne. But depending on the policies of the curator, only some of them are on display at any given moment, and usually as part of an ongoing series of temporary exhibitions that sometimes spill out into the **Hôtel de Rohan,** just around the corner on the rue Vieille du Temple.

The turreted medieval gateway at the Musée de l'Histoire de France (Musée des Archives Nationales)

Within these exhibitions, you're likely to see the facsimiles of the penmanship of Marie Antoinette in a farewell letter she composed just before her execution; Louis XVI's last will and testament; and documents from Danton, Robespierre, Napoleon I, and Joan of Arc. The archives have the only known sketch of the Maid of Orléans that was completed during her lifetime. Even the jailers' keys from the long-since-demolished Bastille are here. Despite the undeniable appeal of the documents it shelters, one of the most intriguing aspects of this museum involves the layout and decor of rooms that have changed very little since the 18th century. One of the finest is the **Salon de la Princesse** (aka the Salon Ovale), an oval room with sweeping expanses of gilt and crystal and a series of artfully executed ceiling frescoes by Van Loo, Boucher, and Natoire.

In the Hôtel de Soubise, 60 rue des Francs-Bourgeois, 3e. *©* **01-40-27-60-96.** Admission 3€ adults, 2.30€ ages 18–25, free for children 17 and younger. Mon and Wed–Fri 10am–12:30pm and 2–5:30pm; Sat–Sun 2–5:30pm. Métro: Hôtel-de-Ville or Rambuteau.

Musée des Arts et Métiers ☺ MUSEUM

Paris's Arts and Industry museum was founded in 1794 within the church Saint-Martin-des-Champs. It features exhibits on the history of technological development. Highlights of its collection include an original version of Foucault's pendulum from 1851, which still swings eternally and that earned the museum a mention in Umbert Eco's novel *Foucault's Pendulum*. The museum includes an additional building adjacent to the abbey.

60 rue Réaumur, 3e. *©* **01-53-01-82-00.** www.arts-et-metiers.net. Admission 6.50€ adults, 4.50€ students, children under 18 free. Tues–Sun 10am–6pm (until 9:30pm Thurs). Métro: Arts et Métiers or Réaumur Sébastopol.

Place des Vosges ★★ ☺ SQUARE

The exquisite Place des Vosges was built by Henri IV and inaugurated in 1612 to celebrate the wedding of Louis XIII to Anne of Austria. It is Paris's oldest planned square and is in the heart of the Marais, actually marking the division between the 3rd and 4th arrondissements. Lined with large buildings of red brick and blue-tiled roofs, the square was previously named "Place Royale" under the reign of Henri IV, then "Place des Fédérés," "Place de la Fabrication-des-Armes," and "Place de l'Indivisibilité" during the French Revolution. It was only in 1800 that it was given the name it has today, in honor of the French department the Vosges. Adorned with Linden trees, water fountains, and an equestrian statue of Louis XIII, it makes a charming spot for a picnic *en famille*. There's free Wi-Fi here too.

4e. Métro: St-Paul.

Sainte-Chapelle ★★★ CHURCH

Countless writers have called this tiny chapel a jewel box, yet that hardly suffices. Go when the sun is shining, and you'll need no one else's words to describe the remarkable effects of natural light on Sainte-Chapelle. You approach the church through the Cour de la Sainte-Chapelle of the Palais de Justice.

Begun in 1246, the bi-level chapel was built to house relics of the True Cross, including the Crown of Thorns acquired by St. Louis (the Crusader King, Louis IX) from the emperor of Constantinople. (In those days, cathedrals throughout Europe were busy acquiring relics for their treasuries, regardless of their authenticity. It was a seller's, perhaps a sucker's, market.) Louis IX is said to have paid heavily for

Stained-glass windows in Sainte-Chapelle.

his relics, raising the money through unscrupulous means. He died of the plague on a crusade and was canonized in 1297.

You enter through the *chapelle basse* (lower chapel), used by the palace servants; it's supported by flying buttresses and ornamented with fleur-de-lis designs. The king and his courtiers used the *chapelle haute* (upper chapel), one of the greatest achievements of Gothic art; you reach it by ascending a narrow spiral staircase. On a bright day, the 15 stained-glass windows seem to glow with Chartres blue and wine-colored reds. The walls consist almost entirely of the glass, 612 sq. m (6,588 sq. ft.) of it, which had to be removed for safekeeping during the revolution and again during both world wars. In the windows' Old and New Testament designs are embodied the hopes and dreams (and the pretensions) of the kings who ordered their construction. The 1,134 scenes depict the Christian story from the Garden of Eden through the Apocalypse; you read them from bottom to top and from left to right. The great rose window depicts the Apocalypse.

Sainte-Chapelle stages **concerts** from March to November, daily at 7 and 8:30pm; tickets cost 19€ to 25€. Call ✆ **01-44-07-12-38** from 11am to 6pm daily for details.

Palais de Justice, 4 bd. du Palais, 4e. ✆ **01-53-40-60-80.** www.monum.fr. 8€ adults, 5€ ages 18–25, free 17 and younger. Mar–Oct daily 9:30am–6pm; Nov–Feb daily 9am–5pm. Métro: Cité, St-Michel, or Châtelet–Les Halles. RER: St-Michel.

Champs-Élysées & Western Paris (8e, 16e & 17e)

Money and power dominate this neighborhood and its emblematic avenue, the Champs-Élysées. There is also a wealth of exceptional museums here from the **Musée d'art Moderne,** a testament to Paris's Modernist glory days, to the **Palais de Tokyo,** a pioneering contemporary art space. In this area, you'll also find the **Maison Baccarat,** the **Musée Nissim de Camondo,** and the **Musée Jacquemart-André.**

American Cathedral of the Holy Trinity CHURCH   This cathedral is one of Europe's finest examples of Gothic Revival architecture and a center for the presentation of music and art. It was consecrated in 1886, and George Edmund Street, best known for the London Law Courts, created it. Aside from the architecture, you'll find remarkable pre-Raphaelite stained-glass windows illustrating the *Te Deum,* an early-15th-century triptych by an anonymous painter (probably a monk) known as the Roussillon Master; a needlepoint collection including kneelers depicting the 50 state flowers; and the 50 state flags in the nave. A **Memorial Cloister** commemorates Americans who died in Europe in World War I and all the victims of World War II. Documentation in several languages explains the highlights. The cathedral is also a center of worship, with a schedule of Sunday and weekday services in English. Les Arts George V, a cultural organization, presents reasonably priced choral concerts, lectures, and art shows.

23 av. George V, 8e. ✆ **01-53-23-84-00.** www.americancathedral.org. Free admission. Mon–Fri 9am–5pm. Métro: Alma-Marceau or George V.

Arc de Triomphe ★★ MONUMENT   At the western end of the Champs-Élysées, the Arc de Triomphe suggests an ancient Roman arch, only it's larger. Actually, it's the biggest triumphal arch in the world, about 49m (161 ft.) high and 44m (144 ft.) wide. To reach it, *don't try to cross the square,* Paris's busiest traffic hub. With a dozen streets radiating from the "Star," the roundabout has been called by one writer "vehicular roulette with more balls than numbers;" death is certain! Take the underground passage, and live a little longer.

Commissioned by Napoleon in 1806 to commemorate the victories of his Grand Armée, the arch wasn't ready for the entrance of his empress, Marie-Louise, in 1810 (he divorced Joséphine because she couldn't provide him an heir). It wasn't completed until 1836, under the reign of Louis-Philippe. Four years later, Napoleon's remains, brought from St. Helena, passed under the arch on their journey to his tomb at the Hôtel des Invalides. Since then, it has become the focal point for state funerals. It's also the site of the tomb of the Unknown Soldier, in whose honor an eternal flame burns.

The greatest state funeral was Victor Hugo's in 1885; his coffin was placed under the arch, and much of Paris came to pay tribute. Another notable funeral was in 1929 for Ferdinand Foch, commander of the Allied forces in World War I. The arch has been the centerpiece of some of France's proudest moments and some of its most humiliating defeats, notably in 1871 and 1940. The memory of German troops marching under the arch is still painful to the French. Who can forget the 1940 newsreel of the Frenchman standing on the Champs-Élysées weeping as the Nazi storm troopers goose-stepped through Paris? The arch's happiest moment occurred in 1944, when the liberation-of-Paris parade passed beneath it. That same

FROM TOP: **Arc de Triomphe; the view from the Arc de Triomphe.**

Attractions near the Champs-Élysées & Western Paris (8e, 16e & 17e)

American Cathedral of the Holy Trinity **12**	Musée d'Art Moderne de la Ville de Paris **11**
Arc de Triomphe **10**	Musée Jacquemart-André **15**
Bois de Boulogne **2**	Musée Marmottan Monet **3**
Cimetière de Passy **5**	Musée National des Arts Asiatiques Guimet **8**
Grand Palais **19**	
Jardin d'Acclimatation **1**	Musée Nissim de Camondo **14**
La Cité de l'Architecture et du Patrimoine **6**	Palais de Tokyo **7**
La Madeleine **17**	Parc Monceau **13**
Maison Baccarat **9**	Petit Palais **18**
Maison de Balzac **4**	Pinacothèque de Paris **16**

year, Eisenhower paid a visit to the tomb of the Unknown Soldier, a new tradition among leaders of state and important figures. After Charles de Gaulle's death, the French government (despite protests from anti-Gaullists) voted to change the name of this site from place de l'Etoile to place Charles de Gaulle. Today it's often known as place Charles de Gaulle–Etoile.

Of the sculptures on the monument, the best known is Rude's *Marseillaise,* or *The Departure of the Volunteers.* J. P. Cortot's *Triumph of Napoléon in 1810* and Etex's *Resistance of 1814* and *Peace of 1815* also adorn the facade. The monument is engraved with the names of hundreds of generals (those underlined died in battle) who commanded French troops in Napoleonic victories.

You can take an elevator or climb the stairway to the top, where there's an exhibition hall with lithographs and photos depicting the arch throughout its history, as well as an observation deck with an exceptional view.

Place Charles de Gaulle-Etoile, 8e. ✆ **01-55-37-73-77.** www.monum.fr. Admission 9€ adults, 5.50€ for those 18–24. Apr–Sept daily 10am–11pm; Oct–Mar daily 10am–10:30pm. Métro: Charles-de-Gaulle–Etoile. Bus: 22, 30, 31, 52, 73, or 92.

Bois de Boulogne ★★ ☺ PARK   One of the most spectacular parks in Europe is the **Bois de Boulogne,** often called the "main lung" of Paris. Horse-drawn carriages traverse it, but you can also drive through. You can discover its hidden pathways, however, only by walking. You could spend days in the Bois de Boulogne and still not see everything.

Porte Dauphine is the main entrance, though you can take the Métro to Porte Maillot as well. West of Paris, the park was once a forest kept for royal hunts. It was in vogue in the late 19th century: Along avenue Foch, carriages with elegantly attired and coiffured Parisian damsels would rumble along with their foppish escorts. Nowadays, it's more likely to attract run-of-the-mill picnickers. (Be careful at night, when hookers and muggers proliferate.)

When Napoleon III gave the grounds to the city in 1852, they were developed by Baron Haussmann. Separating Lac Inférieur from Lac Supérieur is the

The Bois de Boulogne.

Parc de Bagatelle.

Carrefour des Cascades ★ (you can stroll under its waterfall). The Lower Lake contains two islands connected by a footbridge. From the east bank, you can take a boat to these idyllically situated grounds, perhaps stopping off at the cafe/restaurant on one of them.

Restaurants in the *bois* are numerous, elegant, and expensive. The **Pré Catelan** ★ contains a deluxe restaurant of the same name (℃ **01-44-14-41-00**; www.precatelanparis.com), occupying a gem of a Napoleon III–style château, and also a Shakespearean theater in a garden planted with trees mentioned in the bard's plays. Nearby is **La Grande Cascade** (℃ **01-45-27-33-51**), once a hunting lodge for Napoleon III.

Jardin d'Acclimatation(℃**01-40-67-90-82**; www.jardindacclimatation. fr), at the northern edge of the park, is for children, with a zoo, an amusement park, and a narrow-gauge railway (see listing below for more information).

Two racetracks, the **Hippodrome de Longchamp** ★★★ and the **Hippodrome d'Auteuil,** are in the park. The Grand Prix is run in June at Longchamp (the site of a medieval abbey). Fashionable Parisians always turn out for this, the women in their finest haute couture. To the north of Longchamp is the **Grand Cascade,** an artificial waterfall.

In the western section of the *bois*, the 24-hectare (59-acre) **Parc de Bagatelle** ★ (℃ **01-43-28-47-63**) owes its existence to a bet between the comte d'Artois (later Charles X) and Marie Antoinette, his sister-in-law. The comte wagered he could erect a small palace in less than 3 months, so he hired nearly 1,000 craftsmen (cabinetmakers, painters, Scottish landscape architect Thomas Blaikie, and others) and irritated the locals by requisitioning all shipments of stone and plaster arriving through Paris's west gates. He won his bet. If you're here in late April, it's worth visiting the Bagatelle just for the tulips. In late May, one of the finest rose collections in Europe is in full bloom.

16e. Métro: Porte d'Auteuil, Les Sablons, Porte Maillot, or Porte Dauphine.

Cimetière de Passy CEMETERY   This cemetery runs along Paris's old northern walls, south and southwest of Trocadéro. It's a small graveyard sheltered by chestnut trees, but it contains many gravesites of the famous—a concierge at the gate can guide you. Painters **Edouard Manet** and **Romaine Brooks** and composer **Claude Debussy** are tenants. Many great literary figures since 1850 were interred here, including **Tristan Bernard, Jean Giraudoux,** and **François de Croisset.** Also present are composer **Gabriel Fauré;** aviator **Henry Farman;** actor **Fernandel;** and high priestess of the city's most famous literary salon, **Natalie Barney,** along with **Renée Vivien,** one of her many lovers.

2 rue du Comandant-Schloesing, 16e. ☏ **01-53-70-40-80.** Free admission. Mar–Nov Mon–Fri 8am–6pm, Sat 8:30am–6pm, Sun 9am–6pm; Nov–Feb Mon–Fri 8am–5:30pm, Sat 8:30am–5:30pm, Sun 9am–5:30pm. Métro: Trocadéro.

Grand Palais ★★ HISTORIC BUILDING Built for the 1900 Universal Exhibition, this giant exhibition hall spans a total area of 72,000 sq. m (775,000 sq. ft.), with the biggest glass roof in Europe—an elegant lighting solution, since the building was constructed prior to electricity. After years of renovations, the Grand Palais reopened in 2007, and today it hosts a changing array of sporting and cultural events, including FIAC (Paris's annual contemporary art fair), the Hermès horse jumping competition, and fashion shows; check their website for events. The Grand Palais faces the Petit Palais (p. 115).

1 Avenue Géneral Eisenhower, 8e. ☏ **01-44-13-17-17.** www.grandpalais.fr. Opening hours and admission prices vary according to the exhibitions and events. Métro: Champs-Élysées Clémenceau.

Jardin d'Acclimatation ★ ☺ AMUSEMENT PARK/GARDEN This 20-hectare (49-acre) children's park in the northern part of the Bois de Boulogne is the kind of place that amuses tykes and adults but not teenagers. The visit starts with a ride on a narrow-gauge train from Porte Maillot to the Jardin entrance, through a stretch of wooded park. The train operates at 10-minute intervals daily from 10:30am until the park closes; round-trip fare costs 2.70€. En route you'll find a **house of mirrors,** an **archery range,** a **miniature-golf course, zoo animals,** a **puppet theater** (performances Wed, Sat–Sun, and holidays), a **playground,** a **hurdle-racing course, junior-scale rides, shooting galleries,** and **waffle stalls.**

You can trot the kids off on a **pony** (Sat–Sun only) or join them in a **boat** on a mill-stirred lagoon. **La Prévention Routière** is a miniature roadway operated by the Paris police: Youngsters drive through in small cars equipped to start and stop, and are required by two genuine gendarmes to obey street signs and light changes. Inside the gate is an easy-to-follow map.

In the Bois de Boulogne, 16e. ☏ **01-40-67-90-82.** www.jardindacclimatation.fr. Admission 2.90€, free for children 3 and younger. Apr–Sept daily 10am–7pm; Oct–Mar daily 10am–6pm. Métro: Sablons.

Children's rides in the Jardin d'Acclimatation.

La Cité de l'Architecture et du Patrimoine ★ ☺ MUSEUM After a decade-long makeover, the City of Architecture and Heritage was opened by President Nicolas Sarkozy in 2007. With its trio of galleries and vast space, the museum is the largest architectural museum in the world. It lies in the east wing of the Palais de Chaillot on a hill overlooking a curve of the Seine, with panoramic views of Paris in all directions. The Eiffel Tower looms just across the river.

Exhibits are devoted to 12 centuries of French architecture, the most stunning of which is the reproduction of the **stained-glass window ★★** in the Gothic cathedral at Chartres. Other exhibits include a walk-in replica of Le

Rude's *Le Baptême du Christ* at La Madeleine.

Corbusier's mid-20th-century Cité Radieuse in Marseille.

In all there are 350 plaster cast reproductions of some of the greatest achievements in French architecture, going back to the Middle Ages. One gallery reproduces France's remarkable paintings and frescoes from the 12th to 16th centuries. A third gallery is devoted to modern architecture right up to a turn-of-the-millennium cultural center in New Caledonia in the South Pacific. Children can build their own architectural masterpieces with Legos and other materials.

1 place du Trocadéro, 16e. ✆ **01-58-51-52-00.** www.citechaillot.fr. Admission 8€ adults, 5€ students, free ages 18 and younger. Wed and Fri-Mon 11am-7pm; Thurs 11am-9pm. Métro: Trocadéro.

La Madeleine ★★ CHURCH   La Madeleine is one of Paris's minor landmarks, dominating rue Royale, which culminates in place de la Concorde. Though construction began in 1806, it wasn't consecrated until 1842. Resembling a Roman temple, the building was intended as a monument to the glory of the Grande Armée (Napoleon's idea, of course). Later, several alternative uses were considered: the National Assembly, the Bourse, and the National Library. Climb the 28 steps to the facade, and look back: You'll be able to see rue Royale, place de la Concorde and its obelisk, and (across the Seine) the dome of the Hôtel des Invalides. Don't miss Rude's *Le Baptême du Christ,* to the left as you enter.

Place de la Madeleine, 8e. ✆ **01-42-65-52-17.** www.eglise-lamadeleine.com. Free admission. Mon-Sat 9:30am-7pm; Sun services at 9:30, 11am, and 7pm. Métro: Madeleine.

Maison Baccarat ★★ MUSEUM   The fine French crystal maker Baccarat opened this magnificent Philippe Starck–designed flagship store and museum in 2003, in the former mansion of avant-garde art patron Marie-Laure de Noailles, who worked with artists like Salvador Dalí and Piet Mondrian. Starck integrated the building's avant-garde history with the more traditional style of Baccarat to design this whimsical building.

Baccarat first opened a glass factory, authorized by Louis XV, in 1764; in 1816, it began to manufacture crystal. The company quickly gained a reputation for its fine crystal works, and by the end of the 19th century, it was being commissioned to create pieces for various monarchies. One of those pieces—an elaborate 775kg (1,705-lb.) chandelier created for Czar Nicolas II—lights up an antechamber to this museum. Another sensational crystal chandelier adorns the entrance to the building—but this one is submerged in an aquarium. The design of the building is playful and contemporary, yet it still feels opulent and classic.

Maison Baccarat comprises a boutique on the ground floor selling the brand's tableware and jewelry, and an upstairs museum and restaurant, Cristal Room.

11 place des États-Unis, 16e. ✆ **01-40-22-11-00.** www.baccarat.com. Museum admission 5€ adults, 3.50€ seniors, free for ages 17 and under. Museum open Mon, Wed–Sat 10am–6.30pm. Métro: Iéna or Boissière.

An ornate chandelier at Maison Baccarat.

Maison de Balzac MUSEUM   In the residential district of Passy, near the Bois de Boulogne, sits this modest house with a courtyard and garden. Honoré de Balzac fled to this house in 1840, after his possessions and furnishings were seized, and lived there for 7 years (to see him, you had to know a password). If a creditor knocked on the rue Raynouard door, Balzac was able to escape through the rue Berton exit. The museum's most notable memento is Balzac's "screech-owl" (his nickname for his tea kettle), which he kept hot throughout the night as he wrote *La Comédie Humaine.* Also enshrined are Balzac's writing desk and chair, and a library of special interest to scholars. The little house is filled with caricatures of Balzac. A biographer once wrote: "With his bulky baboon silhouette, his blue suit with gold buttons, his famous cane like a golden crowbar, and his abundant, disheveled hair, Balzac was a sight for caricature."

47 rue Raynouard, 16e. ✆ **01-55-74-41-80.** www.balzac.paris.fr. Admission free for permanent collection. Special exhibition admission 4€ adults, 3€ seniors and students, 2€ ages 14–26, free for children 13 and younger. Tues–Sun 10am–6pm. Métro: Passy or La Muette.

Musée d'Art Moderne de la Ville de Paris ★★ MUSEUM   Paris's Modern Art Museum borders the Seine and is in fact housed in the Eastern Wing of the monumental Palais de Tokyo (p. 114), a building designed for the 1937 World Fair. The museum opened in 1961, and it is home to works of modern art, including Henri Matisse's "The Dance," Pierre Bonnard's "Nude in the Bath" and "The Garden," and Fernand Léger's "Discs." There are also works by Chagall, Rothko, Braque, Dufy, Picasso, Utrillo, and Modigliani. Seek out Pierre Tal Coat's *Portrait of Gertrude Stein,* and keep Picasso's version of this difficult subject in mind. The museum also presents excellent ever-changing exhibits on individual artists from all over the world or on contemporary international trends.

11 av. du Président-Wilson, 16e. ✆ **01-53-67-40-00.** www.mam.paris.fr. Free admission to general collections, temporary exhibition admission 5€–7€. Tues–Sun 10am–6pm. Métro: Iéna or Alma-Marceau.

Musée Jacquemart-André ★★ MUSEUM   This is the finest museum of its type in Paris, the treasure-trove of a couple devoted to 18th-century French paintings and furnishings, 17th-century Dutch and Flemish paintings, and Italian Renaissance works. Edouard André, the last scion of a family that made a fortune in banking and industry in the 19th century, spent most of his life as an army officer stationed abroad; he eventually returned to marry a well-known portraitist of government figures and the aristocracy, Nélie Jacquemart, and they went on to compile a collection of rare decorative art and paintings in this 1850s town house.

In 1912, Mme Jacquemart willed the house and its contents to the Institut de France, which paid for an extensive renovation and enlargement. The salons

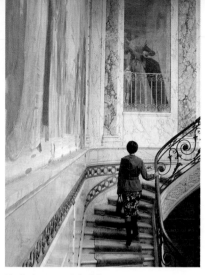

Musée Jacquemart-André.

drip with gilt and are the ultimate in *fin-de-siècle* style. Works by Bellini, Carpaccio, Uccelo, Van Dyck, Rembrandt (*The Pilgrim of Emmaus*), Tiepolo, Rubens, Watteau, Boucher, Fragonard, and Mantegna are complemented by Houdon busts, Savonnerie carpets, Gobelin tapestries, Della Robbia terra cottas, and an awesome collection of antiques.

Take a break with a cup of tea in Mme Jacquemart's high-ceilinged dining room, where you'll find the outstanding 18th-century Tiepolo frescoes of spectators on balconies viewing Henri III's 1574 arrival in Venice. Salads, tarts, *tourtes* (pastries filled with meat or fruit), and Viennese pastries are served during museum hours to a steady stream of tourist and school groups.

158 bd. Haussmann, 8e. ℭ **01-45-62-11-59.** www.musee-jacquemart-andre.com. Admission 10€ adults, 8.50€ children 7–17, free for children 6 and younger. Daily 10am–6pm. Métro: Miromesnil or St-Philippe-du-Roule.

Musée Marmottan Monet ★★ MUSEUM   In the past, an art historian or two would sometimes venture here to the edge of the Bois de Boulogne to see what Paul Marmottan had donated to the Académie des Beaux-Arts. Hardly anyone else did until 1966, when Claude Monet's son Michel died in a car crash, leaving a then $10-million bequest of his father's art to the little museum. The Académie suddenly found itself with 130-plus paintings, watercolors, pastels, and drawings. Monet lovers could now trace the evolution of the great man's work in a single museum. The collection includes more than 30 paintings of Monet's house at Giverny and many of water lilies, his everlasting fancy, plus **Willow** (1918), **House of Parliament** (1905), and a **Renoir portrait** of a 32-year-old Monet. The museum had always owned Monet's **Impression: Sunrise** (1872), from which the Impressionist movement got its name. Paul Marmottan's original collection includes fig-leafed nudes, First Empire antiques, assorted objets d'art, Renaissance tapestries, bucolic paintings, and crystal chandeliers. You can also see countless miniatures donated by Daniel Waldenstein. The works of other Impressionists are also included, among them Degas, Manet, Pissarro, Renoir, Auguste Rodin, and Alfred Sisley.

An exhibit at the Musée Marmottan Monet.

2 rue Louis-Boilly, 16e. ✆ **01-44-96-50-33.** www.marmottan.com. Admission 9€ adults, 5€ ages 8–24, free for children 7 and younger. Wed–Sun 11am–6pm; Tues 11am–9pm. Métro: La Muette. RER: Bouilainvilliers, line C.

Musée National des Arts Asiatiques-Guimet ★★ MUSEUM This is one of the most beautiful Asian museums in the world, and it houses one of the world's finest collections of Asian art. Some 3,000 pieces of the museum's 45,000 works are on display. The Guimet, opened in Lyon but transferred to Paris in 1889, received the Musée Indochinois du Trocadéro's collections in 1931 and the Louvre's Asian collections after World War II. The most interesting exhibits are Buddhas, serpentine monster heads, funereal figurines, and antiquities from the temple of Angkor Wat. Some galleries are devoted to Tibetan art, including fascinating scenes of the Grand Lamas entwined with serpents and demons.

An exhibit at the Musée National des Arts Asiatiques-Guimet.

6 place d'Iéna, 16e. ✆ **01-56-52-53-00.** www.guimet.fr. Admission 7.50€ adults, 5.50€ students, free for ages 17 and younger. Wed–Mon 10am–6pm. Métro: Iéna.

Musée Nissim de Camondo ★ 🎒 MUSEUM Visit this museum for fascinating insight into the decorative arts of the 18th century. Originally the home of Moïse de Camondo, a wealthy Parisian banker during the Belle Époque, this museum displays Camondo's excellent collection of 18th-century French furniture and decorative arts. (On his death, Camondo donated the home and its contents to the state in memory of his only son Nissim, who died in the First World War.) This museum offers an interesting glimpse into what a late 19th–century aristocratic home would have looked like; you'll see the home's enormous kitchen, hung with copper utensils, as well as spectacular furniture, clocks, chandeliers, vases and tableware. The museum is home to a silver dinner service commissioned by Catherine II of Russia from the silversmith Roettiers in 1770.

63 rue de Monceau, 8e. ✆ **01-53-89-06-40.** www.lesartsdecoratifs.fr. Admission 7€ adults, 5€ ages 18–25, free for children 17 and younger. Wed–Sun 10am–5:30pm. Closed Jan 1, May 1, Bastille Day (July 14), and Dec 25. Métro: Villiers.

Palais de Tokyo ★★★ ☺MUSEUM This art center, which opened in 2002, is one of the most original and avant-garde in Europe. Dedicated to "emerging" art and artists, the Palais de Tokyo emphasizes edgy, contemporary art and ideas. Its monumental raw concrete architecture immediately sets it apart from a classic museum, and its opening hours (noon to midnight) are radical too. The installations and vast open spaces invariably appeal to kids. The exhibits change frequently, so check to see what's showing—perhaps a video or sculpture exhibition, fashion events, or performance art. The space also includes a bookshop, a cafeteria, and a first-rate restaurant and bar. The museum is currently undergoing a renovation and expansion, which will double the museum's exhibition space.

13 av. du Président-Wilson, 16e. ☎ **01-47-23-54-01.** www.palaisdetokyo.com. Admission 6€ adults, 4.50€ students, free for ages 18 and younger. Tues–Sun noon–midnight. Métro: Iéna.

Parc Monceau ★ PARK   Much of Parc Monceau is ringed with 18th- and 19th-century mansions, some evoking Proust's *Remembrance of Things Past*. Carmontelle designed it in 1778 as a private hideaway for the duc d'Orléans (who came to be known as Philippe-Egalité), at the time the richest man in France. The duke was noted for his debauchery and pursuit of pleasure, so no ordinary park would do. It was opened to the public in the days of Napoleon III's Second Empire.

Monceau was laid out with an Egyptian-style obelisk, a medieval dungeon, a thatched farmhouse, a Chinese pagoda, a Roman temple, an enchanted grotto, various chinoiseries, and a waterfall. These fairy-tale touches have largely disappeared except for a pyramid and an oval naumachia fringed by a colonnade. Now the park is filled with solid statuary and monuments, including one honoring Chopin. In spring, the red tulips and magnolias are breathtaking.

35 boulevard de Courcelles, 8e. www.paris.fr. Free admission. 8am–sundown. Métro: Monceau or Villiers.

Petit Palais HISTORIC BUILDING   Like its neighbor the Grand Palais, the Petit Palais was built for the 1900 Universal Exhibition, and it became a fine arts museum in 1902. Designed by architect Charles Girault, the Petit Palais indeed feels like a "little palace." Its eclectic collections include paintings, sculpture, and objets d'art from ancient times through WWI. You'll see paintings by such French masters as Ingres, Delacroix, Manet, Monet, Courbet, and Sisley. The space also hosts temporary exhibits dedicated to everything from contemporary photography to fashion.

A room in the Musée Nissim de Camondo.

An exhibit at the Palais de Tokyo.

Parc Monceau.

Avenue Winston Churchill, 8e. ℭ **01-53-43-40-00.** www.petitpalais.paris.fr. Free admission to the permanent collections; charges vary for temporary exhibitions. Tues–Sun 10am–6pm. Métro: Champs-Élysées Clémenceau.

Pinacothèque de Paris MUSEUM   This privately funded gallery manages to rival some of the city's major institutions with its blockbuster shows—think Picasso, Pollock, or Munch—that get people lining up down the street. (The quietest days to visit are Mon and Wed, or at lunch time the rest of the week.) The impressive space covers 2,000 sq. m. (21,528 sq. ft.) over three levels, and is located between the two Fauchon delicatessens on the place de la Madeleine.

28 place de la Madeleine, 8e. ℭ **01-42-68-02-01.** www.pinacotheque.com. Daily 10:30am–6pm (until 8pm Wed). Admission 10€ adults, 8€ students. Métro: Madeleine.

Opéra & Canal St-Martin (9e & 10e)

The impressive **Opéra Garner** dominates its dynamic neighborhood, which delivers perhaps more opportunities for outstanding retail experiences than for cultural ones. But perhaps the greatest attraction in this area is the picturesque **Canal St-Martin** itself.

Fragonard Musée du Parfum MUSEUM   This perfume museum is in a 19th-century theater on one of Paris's busiest thoroughfares. As you enter the lobby through a courtyard, the scented air will remind you of why you're there—to appreciate perfume enough to buy a bottle in the ground-floor shop. But first, a short visit upstairs introduces you to the rudiments of perfume history. The copper containers with spouts and tubes were used in the distillation of

An exhibit in the Fragonard Musée du Parfum.

The Canal St-Martin

The Canal St-Martin is a picturesque waterway that connects the river Seine, near Bastille, to the Canal de l'Ourcq, near the Villette in the 19th arrondissement. When Parisians talk about *le canal*, they are usually referring to the popular stretch of the Quais Jemmapes and Valmy, which begins just above République and runs up by the Gare de l'Est. The canal was inaugurated in 1825 with the aim of bringing fresh drinking water to the heart of the city. During the 19th and early 20th centuries, this water highway attracted much commerce and

industry to the surrounding areas. Painter Alfred Sisley was inspired by this canal—you can admire his painting "Vue du canal Saint-Martin à Paris" (1870) at the Musée d'Orsay (p. 142). After almost being destroyed in the 1970s to make way for more roads, the canal was classified as a historic monument in 1993, and today, visitors can explore the canal at their leisure. If you'd like to take a scenic boat tour of the canal, contact **Paris Canal** (℃ **01-42-40-96-97;** www.paris canal.com) or **Canauxrama** (℃ **01-42-39-15-00;** www.canauxrama.com).

perfume oils, and the exquisite collection of perfume bottles from the 17th to the 20th century is impressive.

9 rue Scribe, 9e. ℃ **01-4742-04-56.** www.fragonard.com. Free admission. Mon–Sat 9am–6pm; Sun 9am–5pm. Métro: Opéra.

Musée Grévin ★ ☺ MUSEUM   The Grévin is Paris's number-one waxworks. This wax museum presents French history in a series of tableaux. Depicted are the 1429 consecration of Charles VII in the Cathédrale de Reims (armored Joan of Arc, carrying her standard, stands behind the king); Marguerite de Valois, first wife of Henri IV, meeting on a secret stairway with La Molle, who was soon to be decapitated; Catherine de Médici with Florentine alchemist David Ruggieri; Louis XV and Mozart at the home of the Marquise de Pompadour; and Napoleon

An exhibit in the Musée Grévin.   Opéra Garnier.

on a rock at St. Helena, reviewing his victories and defeats. Visitors will also find displays of contemporary sports and political figures, as well as 50 of the world's best-loved film stars.

Two shows are staged frequently throughout the day. The first, called the **"Palais des Mirages,"** starts off as a sort of Temple of Brahma and, through magically distorting mirrors, changes first into an enchanted forest and then into a fête at the Alhambra in Granada. A magician is the star of the second show, **"Le Cabinet Fantastique";** he entertains children of all ages.

10 bd. Montmartre, 9e. ✆ **01-47-70-85-05.** www.grevin.com. Admission 21€ adults, 18€ students, 13€ children 6–14, 10€ children 5 and younger. Mon–Fri 10am–6:30pm; Sat–Sun 10am–7pm. Ticket office closes at 5:30pm. Métro: Grands Boulevards.

Opéra Garnier ★★ OPERA HOUSE This neobaroque masterpiece was built in 1875, under Napoleon III, by architect Charles Garnier, and was known as the Palais Garnier. The stunning grand foyer, restored in 2004, is lined with mirrors and adorned with crystal chandeliers; it resembles the famous Galerie des Glaces at Versailles. It has a magnificent painted ceiling by Paul Baudry portraying themes from the history of music. The gilded auditorium has 1,900 seats and is lit by an immense crystal chandelier that hangs below a once-controversial ceiling painted by Marc Chagall in the 1960s. Today, the venue is home to the fine Paris Opera Ballet.

8 rue Scribe, 9e. ✆ **01-40-01-17-89.** www.operadeparis.fr. Admission 9€ adults, 5€ students, children under 10 enter for free. Daily 10am–5pm. Métro: Opéra.

Pigalle & Montmartre (18e)

Perched on the city's highest point, the **Sacré-Coeur** basilica may be the area's only significant monument, but Montmartre's cobblestone streets and unique, villagelike architecture are an attraction in themselves. The harmless red-light district of neighboring Pigalle can't be reduced to a single attraction either, but it is an exciting area to explore.

Basilique du Sacré-Coeur ★★ ☺ CHURCH Sacré-Coeur is one of Paris's most characteristic landmarks and has been the subject of much controversy.

Pigalle & Montmartre Attractions (18e)

Lamarck–Caulaincourt Ⓜ
r. Caulaincourt
r. Lamarck
r. Custine
Cimetière St-Vincent
r. S. Dereure
r. Paul Féval
Saint-
Parc de la Turlure
r. Lamarck
Mont Cenis
r. de la Bonne
r. Berquerel
av. Junot
sq. S. Buisson
r. de l'Abreuvoir
Vincent
r. de la Barre
des Saules
Musée de Montmartre
r. Cortot
r. du Chevalier de la Barre
r. Lamarck
Paul Albert
Cimetière de Montmartre
r. Joseph de Maistre
r. Tourlaque
r. Caulaincourt
Lepic
av. Junot
Girardon
Moulin de la Galette
r. St-Rustique
MONTMARTRE
Lepic
Norvins
r. St-Rustique
pl. J.B. Clément
place du Tertre
Basilique du Sacré-Coeur
r. de la Bonne
St-Pierre-de-Montmartre
Ⓔ
r. Poulbot
sq. Nadar
r. du Card. Dubois

② Ⓔ
r. J. de Maistre
Tholozé
d'Orchampt
r. Ravignan
r. Durantin
place E. Goudeau
place E. Goudeau
r. Berthe
Gabrielle
r. André Barsacq
FUNICULAR
r. Foyatier
sq. Willette
pl. St-Pierre
r. Ch. Nodier
Paul Albert
r. Burq
r. des Abbesses
r. des Trois Frères
Drevet
r. Tardieu
pl. S. Valadon
r. de Steinkerque
r. d'Orsel

Moulin Rouge
r. Puget
r. Coustou
r. Germain Pilon
r. Veron
Lepic
r. Planquette
sq. J. Rictus
place des Abbesses
Ⓜ Abbesses
r. de La Vieuville
r. Yvonne le Tac
r. des Abbesses
r. d'Orsel
place Ch. Dullin
r. Dancourt
r. des Martyrs
r. d'Orsel
r. Bochart de Saron
r. Briquet
Seveste

place Blanche Ⓜ Blanche
bd.
place A. Max Square Berlioz
r. de Blanche
r. Fontaine
r. Douai
Clichy
①
r. Houdon
Pigalle
place Pigalle
bd. de Rochechouart
Ⓜ Anvers
square d'Anvers
av. Trudaine

Basilique du Sacré-Coeur **4**
Cimetière de Montmartre **2**
Cimetière St-Vincent **3**
Musée de l'Erotisme **1**

|||| Steps
••••••• Funicular
Ⓜ Métro station

0 ———— 200 yds
0 ———— 200 m

One Parisian called it "a lunatic's confectionery dream." An offended Zola declared it "the basilica of the ridiculous." Sacré-Coeur has had warm supporters as well, including poet Max Jacob and artist Maurice Utrillo. Utrillo never tired of drawing and painting it, and he and Jacob came here regularly to pray. Atop the butte (hill) in Montmartre, its multiple gleaming white domes and campanile (bell tower) loom over Paris like a 12th-century Byzantine church. But it's not that old. After France's 1870 defeat by the Prussians, the basilica was planned as a votive offering to cure France's misfortunes. Rich and poor alike contributed money to build it. Construction began in 1876, and though the church wasn't consecrated until 1919, perpetual prayers of adoration have been made here day and night since 1885. The interior is brilliantly decorated with mosaics: Look for the striking Christ on the ceiling and the mural of his Passion at the back of the altar. The stained-glass windows were shattered during the struggle for Paris in 1944 but have been well replaced. The crypt contains what some of the devout believe is Christ's sacred heart—hence, the name of the church. Kids will delight in taking a turn on the merry-go-round, then taking the funicular up the hill to the church.

Insider's tip: Although the view from the Arc de Triomphe is the greatest panorama of Paris, we also want to endorse the view from the gallery around the inner dome of Sacré-Coeur. On a clear day, your eyes take in a sweep of Paris extending for 48km (30 miles) into the Île de France. You can also walk around

FROM TOP: Basilique du Sacré-Coeur; the dome of Basilique du Sacré-Coeur.

the inner dome, an attraction even better than the interior of Sacré-Coeur itself.

Place St-Pierre, 18e. ✆ **01-53-41-89-00.** www.sacre-coeur-montmartre.com. Free admission to basilica, joint ticket to dome and crypt 5€. Basilica daily 6am–11pm; dome and crypt daily 9am–6pm. Métro: Abbesses; take elevator to surface and follow signs to funicular.

Cimetière de Montmartre ★ CEMETERY This cemetery, established in 1795, lies west of Montmartre and north of boulevard de Clichy. Russian dancer **Vaslav Nijinsky,** novelist **Alexandre Dumas *fils*,** Impressionist **Edgar Degas,** and composers **Hector Berlioz** and **Jacques Offenbach** are interred here, along with **Stendhal** and lesser literary lights such as **Edmond** and **Jules de Goncourt** and **Heinrich Heine.** A more recent tombstone honors **François Truffaut,** film director of the *nouvelle vague* (new wave). We like to pay our respects at the tomb of **Alphonsine Plessis,** heroine of *La Dame aux Camélias,* and **Mme Récamier,** who taught the world how to lounge. **Émile Zola** was buried here, but his corpse was exhumed and promoted to the Panthéon in 1908. In 1871, the cemetery was used for mass burials of victims of the Siege and the Commune.

20 av. Rachel (west of the Butte Montmartre and north of bd. de Clichy), 18e. ✆ **01-53-42-36-30.** Mon–Fri 8am–6pm; Sat 8:30am–6pm; Sun 9am–6pm. Métro: La Fourche.

Cimetière St-Vincent CEMETERY   Because of the artists and writers who have their resting places in the modest burial ground of St-Vincent, with a view of Sacré-Coeur on the hill, it's sometimes called "the most intellectual cemetery in Paris"—but that epithet seems more apt for other graveyards. Artists **Maurice Utrillo** and **Théopile-Alexandre Steinlen** were buried here, as were musician **Arthur Honegger** and writer **Marcel Aymé.** More recently, burials have included the remains of French actor **Gabriello,** film director **Marcel Carné,** and painter **Eugène Boudin.**

6 rue Lucien-Gaulard, 18e. 📞 **01-46-06-29-78.** Mar 6–Nov 5 Mon–Fri 8am–6pm, Sat 8:30am–6pm, Sun 9am–6pm; Nov 6–Mar 5 Mon–Fri 8am–5:15pm, Sat 8:30am–5:15pm, Sun 9am–5:15pm. Métro: Lamarck-Caulaincourt.

Musée de l'Erotisme MUSEUM   A tribute to the primal appeal of human sexuality, this art gallery/museum is in a 19th-century town house that had been a raunchy cabaret. It presents a tasteful but risqué collection of art and artifacts, with six floors boasting an array of exhibits such as erotic sculptures and drawings. The oldest object is a palm-size Roman *tintinabulum* (bell), a phallus-shaped animal with the likeness of a nude woman riding astride it. Modern objects include resin, wood, and plaster sculptures by French artist Alain Rose and works by American, Dutch, German, and French artists. Also look for everyday items with erotic themes from South America (terra-cotta pipes shaped like phalluses) and the United States (a 1920s belt buckle that resembles a praying nun when it's fastened and a nude woman when it's open).

An exhibit from the Musée de l'Erotisme.

72 bd. de Clichy, 18e. 📞 **01-42-58-28-73.** www.musee-erotisme.com. Admission 9€ adults, children 17 and younger not permitted. Daily 10am–2am. Métro: Blanche.

République, Bastille & Eastern Paris (11e & 12e)

The two public squares, place de la République and place de la Bastille, provide a historical and geographical heart to these two largely residential neighborhoods.

Musée Edith Piaf 📷 MUSEUM   This privately run museum is filled with Piaf memorabilia such as photos, costumes, and personal possessions. The daughter of an acrobat, Giovanna Gassion grew up in this neighborhood and assumed the name of Piaf ("little sparrow"); her songs, such as "La Vie en Rose" and "Non, Je Ne Regrette Rien," eventually were heard around the world. You must phone in advance for the security code you need to buzz your way in.

5 rue Crespin-du-Gast, 11e. 📞 **01-43-55-52-72.** Free admission but donations appreciated. Mon–Wed 1–6pm; Thurs 10am–noon, but only by reservation. Métro: Ménilmontant.

La Maison Rouge ★ MUSEUM
Created by art collector Antoine
de Galbert, the "Red House" offers a
quality program of rotating exhibitions
focusing on contemporary
art. Solo shows alternate with thematic
shows, and many of the exhibitions,
conceived by independent
curators, are sourced from major
international private collections.
The charming space also includes a
cafe that is managed by the hip Rose
Bakery.

10 bd. de la Bastille, 12e. ☎ **01-40-01-08-81.** www.lamaisonrouge.org. Admission 7€ adults, 5€ ages 3 to 18 and senior citizens. Wed–Sun 11am–7pm (until 9pm Thurs). Métro: Quai de la Rapée.

La Promenade Plantée ★ ☺
WALK   Look up, above the Viaduc
des Arts running along the Avenue
Daumesnil, and you'll glimpse this
18th-century railway line. Unused
since 1969, this old railway line has
been converted into a 4.5km (2.8-mile)
pedestrian path that runs from
Bastille to the Bois de Vincennes.
This pleasant path is overrun with various fruit and nut trees, including lime and hazel, climbing plants, rosebushes, and other flowering plants.

Leaves from the beginning of Avenue Daumesnil, 12e.

Attractions near République, Bastille & Eastern Paris (11e & 12e)

Place de la Bastille

This square is symbolic of the French Revolution, which began here with the storming of the Bastille prison on July 14, 1789. (This date continues to mark Bastille Day, a French national holiday.) Almost nothing remains of the prison, except for a few foundations—you can see one from the platform of line 5 at Bastille Métro station. The statue in the middle of the square, the July Column, was inaugurated in 1840 in commemoration of the Trois Glorieuses, or 3 days of insurrections in 1830 that brought down

the French monarchy for a second time. The square's rich political symbolism makes it a preferred location for various public meetings and demonstrations, hosting everything from the Gay Pride Parade to Socialist Party events. Former president François Mitterrand even celebrated his 1981 election victory here. Note that the city's second national opera house, l'Opéra Bastille, is located on the southeastern rim of the square; it's regularly criticized for its architecture and reportedly average acoustics.

An exhibit from the Musée Edith Piaf.

Jogging on La Promenade Plantée.

Place de la République

The colossal bronze monument in the middle of the place de la République was inaugurated on July 14, 1883, in celebration of the French Republic. The figure of Marianne, a symbol of the French state, sits on a carved stone column that is decorated with allegories of *liberté, égalité,* and *fraternité.*

Marianne holds an olive branch as a symbol of peace in her right hand, and in her left, a tablet inscribed with the Rights of Man *(les Droits de l'Homme).* Because of its powerful symbolism, the monument is the preferred departure point for many left-wing demonstrations.

Belleville & Northeast Paris (19e & 20e)

Located on the edge of Paris, **La Villette** not only encompasses Paris's biggest park, Parc de la Villette, it is an exceptional 21st-century cultural compound including museums, concert halls, circus tents, and exhibition spaces that host a great year-round program. The lure of this former industrial zone is its outdoor attractions: In addition to La Villette, the renowned **Père-Lachaise cemetery** and the wonderful **Buttes Chaumont park** are also located in this area. Note that the area around the Belleville Métro station is also home to one of the city's bustling Chinatowns.

Cimetière du Père-Lachaise ★★★ ☺ CEMETERY   When it comes to name-dropping, this cemetery knows no peer; it has been called the "grandest address in Paris." Everybody from Sarah Bernhardt to Oscar Wilde to Richard Wright is resting here, along with Honoré de Balzac, Jacques-Louis David, Eugène Delacroix, Maria Callas, Max Ernst, and Georges Bizet. Colette was taken here in 1954; her black granite slab always sports flowers, and legend has it that cats replenish the roses. In time, the "little sparrow," Edith Piaf, followed.

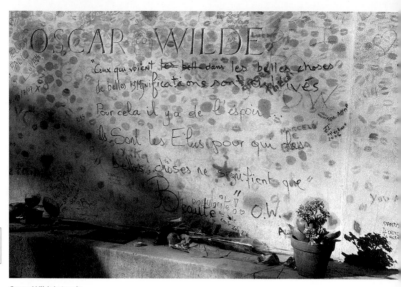

Oscar Wilde's tomb.

The lover of George Sand, poet Alfred de Musset, was buried under a weeping willow. Napoleon's marshals, Ney and Masséna, lie here, as do Frédéric Chopin and Molière. Marcel Proust's black tombstone rarely lacks a tiny bunch of violets (he wanted to be buried beside his friend/lover, composer Maurice Ravel, but their families wouldn't allow it).

Some tombs are sentimental favorites: Love-torn graffiti radiates 1km (½ mile) from the grave of Doors singer **Jim Morrison,** and could appeal to jaded teens. The great dancer **Isadora Duncan** came to rest in the Columbarium,

Cimetière du Père-Lachaise.

where bodies have been cremated and "filed" away. If you search hard enough, you can find the tombs of that star-crossed pair **Abélard** and **Héloïse,** the ill-fated lovers of the 12th century—at Père-Lachaise, they've found peace at last. Other famous lovers also rest here: A stone is marked **"Alice B. Toklas"** on one side and **"Gertrude Stein"** on the other; and eventually, France's First Couple of film were reunited when **Yves Montand** joined his wife, **Simone Signoret.**

Covering more than 44 hectares (109 acres), Père-Lachaise was acquired by the city in 1804. Nineteenth-century sculpture abounds, as each family tried to outdo the others in ostentation. Monuments also honor Frenchmen who died in the Resistance or in Nazi concentration camps. Some French Socialists still pay tribute at the **Mur des Fédérés,** the anonymous gravesite of the Communards who were executed in the cemetery on May 28, 1871. When these last-ditch fighters of the Commune, the world's first anarchist republic, made their final desperate stand against the troops of the French government, they were overwhelmed, lined up against the wall, and shot in groups. A few survived and lived hidden in the cemetery for years, venturing into Paris at night to forage for food.

A free map of Père-Lachaise is available at the newsstand across from the main entrance (additional map on p. 126).

16 rue de Repos, 20e. ☎ **01-55-25-82-10.** www.pere-lachaise.com. Mon–Fri 8am–6pm; Sat–Sun 8:30am–6pm (closes at 5pm Nov to early Mar). Métro: Père-Lachaise or Philippe Auguste.

Attractions in Belleville & Northeast Paris (19e & 20e)

Cimetière du Père-Lachaise **5**
Cité des Sciences et de l'Industrie **1**
Musée de la Musique **3**
Parc de la Villette **2**
Parc des Buttes Chaumont **4**

Cimetière du Père-Lachaise

Abélard & Héloïse **37**
Guillaume Apollinaire **5**
Pierre-Auguste Beaumarchais **30**
Hans Bellmer **24**
Sarah Bernhardt **9**
Georges Bizet **17**
Maria Callas **3**
Frédéric Chopin **36**
Colette **23**
Auguste Comte **34**
Jean Baptiste Camille Corot **11**
Honoré Daumier **10**
Jacques-Louis David **19**

Honoré de Balzac **16**
Eugène Delacroix **15**
Gustave Doré **14**
Isadora Duncan **6**
Paul Eluard **26**
Max Ernst **2**
Théodore Géricault **20**
Jean-Auguste-Dominique Ingres **13**
Jean La Fontaine **33**
René Lalique **12**
Lefebvre Masséna **29**
Amedeo Modigliani **28**
Molière **32**
Jim Morrison **35**

Alfred de Musset **21**
Edith Piaf **27**
Camille Pissarro **38**
Marcel Proust **4**
Gioacchio Antonio Rossini **22**
Rothschild family plot **39**
Henri de Saint-Simon **31**
Georges Seurat **18**
Simone Signoret & Yves Montand **8**
Gertrude Stein & Alice B. Toklas **25**
Oscar Wilde **1**
Richard Wright **7**

Cité des Sciences et de l'Industrie.

Cité des Sciences et de l'Industrie ★★ ☺ MUSEUM   A city of science and industry has risen here from unlikely ashes. When a slaughterhouse was built on the site in the 1960s, it was touted as the most modern of its kind. It was abandoned in 1974, and the location on the city's northern edge presented the government with a problem. What could be built in such an unlikely place? In 1986, the converted premises opened as the world's most expensive ($642-million) science complex, designed to "modernize mentalities" in the service of modernizing society. It is located within the Parc de La Villette compound (see below).

The place is so vast, with so many exhibits, that a single visit gives only an idea of the scope of the Cité. Busts of Plato, Hippocrates, and a double-faced Janus gaze silently at a tube-filled riot of high-tech girders, glass, and lights. The sheer dimensions pose a challenge to the curators of its constantly changing exhibits. Some exhibits are couched in Gallic humor—imagine using the comic-strip adventures of a jungle explorer to explain seismographic activity. **Explora,** a permanent exhibit, occupies the three upper levels of the building and examines four themes: the universe, life, matter, and communication. The Cité also has a **multimedia library,** a **planetarium,** and an **"inventorium"** for kids. The silver-skinned geodesic dome called **La Géode**—a 34m-high (112-ft.) sphere with a 370-seat theater—is the city's IMAX theater, regularly screening 3-D films on a giant 400 sq. m (4,305 sq. ft.) screen.

In the Parc de La Villette, 30 av. Corentine-Cariou, La Villette, 19e. ☏ **01-40-05-70-00.** www. cite-sciences.fr. Varied ticket options 11€–21€ adults, 8€–16€ ages 7–24, free 6 and younger. Tues–Sat 10am–6pm; Sun 10am–7pm. Métro: Porte de La Villette.

Musée de la Musique MUSEUM   In the stone-and-glass Cité de la Musique, this museum serves as a tribute and testament to music. You can view 4,500 instruments from the 16th century to the present, as well as paintings, engravings, and sculptures that relate to musical history. It's all here: cornets disguised as snakes, mandolins, lutes, zithers, music boxes, even an early electric guitar. Models of the world's great concert halls and interactive display areas give you a chance to hear and better understand musical art and technology. The museum is located within the Parc de la Villette (see below).

FROM LEFT: **An exhibit from the Musée de la Musique; Parc de la Villette.**

In the Cité de la Musique, 221 av. Jean-Jaurès, 19e. ℗ **01-44-84-44-84.** www.cite-musique.fr. Admission 8€ adults, 6.40€ students 18–25 and children 17 and younger. Tues–Sat noon–6pm; Sun 10am–7pm. Métro: Porte de Pantin.

Parc de la Villette ★★★ PARK   This modern 21st-century park, designed by architect Bernard Tschumi, cleverly combines nature and architecture. Twice the size of the Jardin des Tuileries, it is Paris's largest park. The Canal de l'Ourcq runs through the park, feeding into various waterfalls, fountains, and ponds. Two walkways crisscross the park: the first runs from the Porte de Pantin to the Porte de la Villette, and the second is elevated and runs along the southern bank of the canal. The park is famous for its 26 red "follies," a contemporary version of the 18th-century gazebo, which are both ornamental and functional. In the center of the park are large grassy areas known as the circle and the triangle, where people can relax; during the summer, the triangle hosts a popular outdoor cinema program.

211 avenue Jean Jaurès, 19e. ℗ **01-40-03-75-75.** www.villette.com. Daily 6am–1am. Métro: Porte de Pantin or Porte de la Villette.

Parc des Buttes Chaumont ★★ ☺ PARK   Napoleon III transformed a quarry into this magical park, full of almost ridiculous (if they weren't so charming) artificial features, such as lakes, waterfalls, and grottos—there's even an imitation of Etretat's coastline. Inaugurated during the 1867 World Fair, the Buttes Chaumont has century-old

Parc des Buttes Chaumont.

trees and is home to ducks, swans, geese, and fish. Parisians come here throughout the year to jog, walk their dogs, read books, picnic, or simply to hide out from the city. The park is home to two restaurants: **Rosa Bonheur** serves tapas-style snacks to a younger crowd, while **Le Pavillon du Lac** is a more serious dining affair with table service but equally lovely views. There are pony rides for the kids on weekends and Wednesdays, plus a puppet theater, a carousel, and two playgrounds.

Rue Manin, 19e. Open 7am–11pm May 1–Sept 30; 7am–9pm Sept 30–Apr 30. Métro: Botzaris or Buttes Chaumont.

THE LEFT BANK
Latin Quarter (5e)

This leafy neighborhood is defined by the medieval university at its heart: the Sorbonne. In fact, it gets its name from the Latin the students spoke in their classes there up until 1793. The Roman occupation, from 52 B.C. until A.D. 486, remains visible too; the rue Saint-Jacques and Boulevard Saint-Michel mark the former Roman cardo, and you can explore Roman ruins at the Cluny Museum.

Arènes de Lutèce ROMAN RUINS   Discovered and partially destroyed in 1869, this amphitheater is Paris's most important Roman ruin after the baths in the Musée de Cluny (p. 130). Today, the site is home to a small arena, not as grand as the original, and gardens. You may feel as if you've discovered a private spot in the heart of the city, but don't be fooled. Your solitude is sure to be interrupted, if not by groups of students playing soccer, then by parents pushing strollers down the paths. This is an ideal spot for a picnic; bring a bottle of wine and baguettes to enjoy in this vestige of the ancient city of Lutetia.

At rues Monge and Navarre, 5c. (✆ **01-40-71-76-60.** www.paris.fr. Free admission. Mon–Fri 8am–9pm, Sat–Sun 9am–9pm. Métro: Jussieu.

La Grande Mosquée de Paris ★ MOSQUE   This beautiful pink marble mosque was built in 1922 to honor the North African countries that had given aid to France during World War I. Today, North Africans living in Paris gather on Friday, the Muslim holy day, and during Ramadan to pray to Allah. Short tours are

given of the building, its central courtyard, and its Moorish garden; guides present a brief history of the Islamic faith. However, you may want to just wander around on your own and then join the students from nearby universities for couscous and sweet mint tea at the Muslim **Restaurant de la Mosquée de Paris** (✆ **01-43-31-18-14**), adjoining the grounds, open daily from noon to 3pm and 7 to 10:30pm.

2 bis place du Puits-de-l'Ermite, 5e. ✆ **01-45-35-97-33.** www.mosquee-de-paris.net. Admission 3€, free for children 7 and younger. Sat–Thurs 9am–noon and 2–6pm. Métro: Place Monge.

Sweet mint tea and baklava at the Restaurant de la Mosquée de Paris.

Musée de l'Institut du Monde Arabe ★ MUSEUM

Many factors have contributed to France's preoccupation with the Arab world, but three of the most important include trade links that developed during the Crusades, a large Arab population living today in France, and the memories of France's lost colonies in North Africa. For insights into the way France has handled its relations with the Arab world, consider making a trek to this bastion of Arab intellect and aesthetics. Designed in 1987 by architect Jean Nouvel and funded by 22 different, mostly Arab countries, it includes

The façade of the Musée de l'Institut du Monde Arabe.

expositions on calligraphy, decorative arts, architecture, and photography produced by the Arab/Islamic world, as well as insights into its religion, philosophy, and politics. There's a bookshop on site, a replica of a Medina selling high-quality gifts, art objects, and archival resources. Views from the windows of the on-site Moroccan restaurant encompass Notre-Dame, Ile de la Cité, and Sacré-Coeur. Guided tours start at 3pm Tuesday to Friday or at 4:30pm on Saturday and Sunday.

1 rue des Fossés St-Bernard, 5e. ℂ **01-40-51-38-38.** www.imarabe.org. Admission to permanent exhibitions 6€, 4€ students, free for children 11 and under. Tues–Sun 10am–6pm. Métro: Jussieu, Cardinal Lemoine, Sully-Morland.

Musée National d'Histoire Naturelle (Museum of Natural History) ★ ☺

MUSEUM This museum in the Jardin des Plantes, founded in 1635 as a research center by Guy de la Brosse, physician to Louis XIII, has a range of science and nature exhibits. At the entrance of the **Grande Gallery of Evolution,** two 26m (85-ft.) skeletons of whales greet you. Kids will love the display containing the skeletons of dinosaurs and mastodons, dedicated to endangered and vanished species. Galleries specialize in paleontology, anatomy, mineralogy, and botany. Within the museum's grounds are **tropical hothouses** containing thousands of species of unusual plant life and a **menagerie** with small animals in simulated natural habitats.

36 rue Geoffrey, 5e. ℂ **01-40-79-54-79.** www.mnhn.fr. Admission 9€ adults; 7€ students, seniors 60 and older, and children 4–13. Wed–Mon 10am–6pm. Métro: Jussieu or Gare d'Austerlitz.

Musée National du Moyen Age/Thermes de Cluny (Musée de Cluny) ★★ MUSEUM

Along with the Hôtel de Sens in the Marais, the Hôtel de Cluny is all that remains of domestic medieval architecture in Paris. Enter through the cobblestoned **Cour d'Honneur (Court of Honor),** where you can admire the flamboyant Gothic building with its vines, turreted walls, gargoyles, and dormers with seashell motifs. First, the Cluny was the mansion of a rich 15th-century abbot, built on top of/next to the ruins of a Roman bath. By 1515, it was the residence of Mary Tudor, widow of Louis XII and daughter of Henry VII and Elizabeth of York. Seized during the Revolution, the Cluny was rented in

Attractions in the Latin Quarter & Southern Paris (5e & 13e)

Hôtel-Dieu

St-Michel

place St-Michel

St-Michel–Notre-Dame

Cathédrale Notre-Dame

St-Michel

St-André des Arts

r. Suger

r. St-André des Arts

r. Serpente

bd. St-Germain

r. du Petit Pont

square R. Viviani

sq. Jean XXIII

ÎLE DE LA CITÉ

ÎLE ST-LOUIS

St-Paul

r. de Rivoli

r. de Fourcy

r. Charlemagne

r. St-Antoine

r. St-Paul

r. du Petit Musc

Pont Marie

voie Georges Pompidou

quai des Célestins

bd. Henri IV

4e

Sully-Morland

quai Henri IV

bd. Morland

quai de La Tournelle

pont de Sully

square Barye

Seine

Cluny–La Sorbonne

6e

r. Racine

Monsieur le Prince

Maubert–Mutualité

place Maubert

Quai de Montebello

r. Dante

r. Lagrange

r. du Sommerard

r. des Bernardins

r. de Poissy

r. de Pontoise

bd. St-Germain

r. des Fossés St-Bernard

Musée de la Sculpture en Plein Air

quai St-Bernard

Seine

sq. F. A. Mariette

Sorbonne

pl. de la Sorbonne

place Edmond Rostand

Luxembourg

r. Soufflot

place du Panthéon

Panthéon

LATIN QUARTER

sq. des Écoles

place Paul Langevin

Jardin Carré

Cardinal Lemoine

CAMPUS DE JUSSIEU
(Université Pierre-et-Marie-Curie, Université Paris Diderot, Institut de Physique du Globe de Paris)

Jussieu place Jussieu

Cuvier

Ménagerie

5e

r. de l'Estrapade

r. Clotilde

r. Descartes

r. Thouin

r. Rollin

r. Monge

place de la Contrescarpe

r. Lacépède

r. Linné

JARDIN DES PLANTES

Gare d'Austerlitz

place Monge

Place Monge

Grande Mosquée de Paris

Jardin des Plantes

Buffon

r. Geoffroy St-Hilaire

r. Censier

r. Daubenton

Censier-Daubenton

St-Marcel

GROUPE HOSPITALIER PITIÉ-SALPÊTRIÈRE

place A. Laveran

Église du Val-de-Grâce

VAL-DE-GRÂCE

HÔPITAL COCHIN

r. Claude Bernard

r. Berthollet

r. Broca

bd. de Port Royal

bd. Arago

r. du Fer à Moulin

bd. Saint-Marcel

Les Gobelins

av. des Gobelins

r. de l'Hôpital

r. Polivecau

r. Jeanne d'Arc

Campo Formio

r. de Campo Formio

R. Pinnel

Place d'Italie

place d'Italie

bd. Vincent Auriol

National

13e

9

Legend

- Arènes de Lutèce **5**
- Bibliothèque Nationale de France, Site Tolbiac/François Mitterrand **9**
- La Grande Mosquée de Paris **6**
- Manufacture Nationale des Gobelins **8**
- Musée de l'Institut du Monde Arabe **2**
- Musée National d'Histoire Naturelle (Museum of Natural History) **7**
- Musée National du Moyen Age/Thermes de Cluny (Musée de Cluny) **1**
- Panthéon **4**
- Roman Baths **1**
- St-Etienne-du-Mont **3**

The Lady and the Unicorn tapestries.

1833 to Alexandre du Sommerard, who adorned it with medieval artworks. After his death in 1842, the government bought the building and the collection.

This collection of medieval arts and crafts is superb. Most people come to see ***The Lady and the Unicorn*** tapestries ★★★, the most acclaimed tapestries of their kind. All the romance of the age of chivalry—a beautiful princess and her handmaiden, beasts of prey, and house pets—lives on in these remarkable yet mysterious tapestries discovered only a century ago in Limousin's Château de Boussac. Five seem to deal with the senses (one, for example, depicts a unicorn looking into a mirror held by a dour-faced maiden). The sixth shows a woman under an elaborate tent with jewels, her pet dog resting on an embroidered cushion beside her, with the lovable unicorn and his friendly companion, a lion, holding back the flaps. The background forms a rich carpet of spring flowers, fruit-laden trees, birds, rabbits, donkeys, dogs, goats, lambs, and monkeys.

The other exhibits range widely: Flemish retables; a 14th-century Sienese John the Baptist and other sculptures; statues from Sainte-Chapelle (1243–48); 12th- and 13th-century crosses, chalices, manuscripts, carvings, vestments, leatherwork, jewelry, and coins; a 13th-century Adam; and recently discovered heads and fragments of statues from Notre-Dame de Paris. In the fan-vaulted medieval chapel hang tapestries depicting scenes from the life of St. Stephen.

Downstairs are the ruins of the **Roman baths,** from around A.D. 200. The best-preserved section is seen in room X, the frigidarium (where one bathed in cold water). Once it measured 21×11m (69×36 ft.), rising to a height of 15m (49 ft.), with stone walls nearly 1.5m (5 ft.) thick. The ribbed vaulting here rests on consoles evoking ships' prows. Credit for this unusual motif goes to the builders of the baths, Paris's boatmen. During Tiberius's reign, a column to Jupiter was found beneath Notre-Dame's chancel and is now on view in the court; called the "Column of the Boatmen," it's believed to be the oldest sculpture created in Paris.

6 place Paul Painlevé, 5e. ℂ **01-53-73-78-00.** www.musee-moyenage.fr. Admission 8.50€ adults, 6.50€ youths 18–25. Wed–Mon 9:15am–5:45pm. Métro: Miromesnil or St-Philippe-du-Roule.

Panthéon ★★ CHURCH   Some of the most famous men in French history (Victor Hugo, for one) are buried here on the crest of the mount of St. Geneviève. In 1744, Louis XV vowed that if he recovered from a mysterious illness, he'd build a church to replace the Abbaye de St. Geneviève. He recovered but took his time fulfilling his promise. It wasn't until 1764 that Mme de Pompadour's brother hired Soufflot to design a church in the form of a Greek cross with a dome reminiscent of St. Paul's in London. When Soufflot died, his pupil Rondelet carried out the work, completing the structure 9 years after his master's death.

After the revolution, the church was converted to a "Temple of Fame" and became a pantheon for the great men of France. Mirabeau was buried here, though his remains were later removed. Likewise, Marat was only a temporary tenant. Voltaire's body was exhumed and placed here—and allowed to remain. In the 19th century, the building changed roles so many times—a church, a pantheon, a church again—that it was hard to keep its function straight. After Hugo was buried here, it became a pantheon once again. Other notable men entombed within are Rousseau, Soufflot, Zola, and Braille. Only one woman has so far been deemed worthy of placement here: Marie Curie, who joined her husband, Pierre. Most recently, in 1996, the ashes of André Malraux were transferred to the Panthéon because, according to former French president Jacques Chirac, he "lived [his] dreams and made them live in us." As Charles de Gaulle's culture minister, Malraux decreed the arts should be part of the lives of all French people, not just Paris's elite.

Before entering the crypt, note the striking frescoes: On the right wall are scenes from Geneviève's life, and on the left is the saint with a white-draped head looking out over medieval Paris, the city whose patron she became, as well as Geneviève relieving victims of famine with supplies.

Place du Panthéon, 5e. ✆ **01-44-32-18-00.** www.monum.fr. Admission 8€ adults, 5€ ages 18–25, free for children 17 and younger. Apr–Sept daily 10am–6:30pm; Oct–Mar daily 10am–6pm (last entrance 45 min. before closing). Métro: Cardinal Lemoine or Maubert-Mutualité.

The Panthéon.

St-Etienne-du-Mont ★★ CHURCH Once there was an abbey here, founded by Clovis and later dedicated to St. Geneviève, the patroness of Paris. Such was the fame of this popular saint that the abbey proved too small to accommodate the pilgrimage crowds. Now part of the Lycée Henri IV, the Tour de Clovis (Tower of Clovis) is all that remains of the ancient abbey—you can see the tower from rue Clovis. Today, the task of keeping St. Geneviève's cult alive has fallen on this church, practically adjoining the Panthéon. The interior is Gothic, an unusual style for a 16th-century church. Building began in 1492 and was plagued by delays until the church was finally finished in 1626.

The interior of St-Etienne-du-Mont.

Besides the patroness of Paris, such men as Pascal and Racine were entombed here. Because of the destruction of church records during the French Revolution, church officials aren't sure of the exact locations in which they're buried. St. Geneviève's tomb was destroyed during the revolution, but the stone on which her coffin rested was discovered later, and her relics were gathered for a place of honor at St-Etienne. The church possesses a remarkable early-16th-century **rood screen:** Crossing the nave, it's unique in Paris—called spurious by some and a masterpiece by others. Another treasure is a wood **pulpit,** held up by Samson, clutching a bone in one hand, with a slain lion at his feet. The fourth chapel on the right when you enter contains impressive 16th-century stained glass.

1 place St-Geneviève, 5e. ℭ **01-43-54-11-79.** Free admission. With the exception of some of France's school holidays, when hours may vary slightly, the church is open year-round as follows: Mon noon–7:30pm; Tues–Fri 8:45am–7:30pm; Sat 8:45am–7:45pm; Sun 8:45am–12:15pm and 2:30–7:45pm. Métro: Cardinal Lemoine or Luxembourg.

St-Germain-des-Prés & Luxembourg (6e)

This neighborhood in the 6th arrondissement was the postwar home of existentialism, associated with great writers and philosophers Jean-Paul Sartre, Simone de Beauvoir, Albert Camus, and an intellectual bohemian crowd that gathered at **Café de Flore** or **Les Deux Magots** (p. 231). St-Germain-des-Prés still retains an intellectually stimulating bohemian street life, full of many interesting bookshops, art galleries, *caveau* (basement) clubs, bistros, and coffeehouses. But the stars of the area are two churches, **St-Germain-des-Prés** and **St-Sulpice,** and the **Musée National Eugène Delacroix.**

Institut de France HISTORIC BUILDING Designed by Louis Le Vau, this dramatic baroque building with an enormous cupola is the seat of all five academies that dominate France's intellectual life—Française, Sciences, Inscriptions et Belles Lettres, Beaux Arts, and Sciences Morales et Politiques. The members of the Académie Française (limited to 40), guardians of the French language referred

Attractions in St-Germain-des-Prés, Luxembourg & Montparnasse (6e, 14e & 15e)

to as "the immortals," gather here. Many are unfamiliar figures (though Jacques Cousteau and Marshall Pétain were members), and the academy is remarkable for the great writers and philosophers who have *not* been invited to join—Balzac, Baudelaire, Diderot, Flaubert, Descartes, Proust, Molière, Pascal, Rousseau, Zola, to name only a few. The cenotaph was designed by Coysevox for Mazarin.

23 quai de Conti, 6e. ✆ **01-44-41-44-47.** www.institut-de-france.fr. Free admission (guests can walk into courtyard only). Daily 9am–6pm. Métro: Louvre-Rivoli.

Jardin du Luxembourg ★★ ☺ GARDEN   Hemingway once told a friend that the Jardin du Luxembourg "kept us from starvation." He related that in his poverty-stricken days in Paris, he wheeled a baby carriage (the vehicle was considered luxurious) through the garden because it was known "for the classiness of its pigeons." When the gendarme went across the street for a glass of wine, the writer would eye his victim, preferably a plump one; lure him with corn; "snatch him, wring his neck"; and hide him under the blanket. "We got a little tired of pigeons that year," he confessed, "but they filled many a void."

The Luxembourg has always been associated with artists, though children, students, and tourists predominate nowadays. Watteau came this way, as did Verlaine. In 1905, Gertrude Stein would cross them to catch the Batignolles/Clichy/Odéon omnibus, pulled by three gray mares, to meet Picasso in his studio at Montmartre, where he painted her portrait.

Marie de Médici, the wife of Henri IV, ordered the **Palais du Luxembourg** built on this site in 1612, shortly after she was widowed. A Florentine by birth, the regent wanted to create another Pitti Palace, where she could live with her "witch" friend, Leonora Galigal. Architect Salomon de Brossee wasn't entirely successful, though the overall effect is Italianate. Alas, the queen didn't get to enjoy the palace, as her son, Louis XIII, forced her into exile when he discovered she was plotting to overthrow him. She died in poverty in Cologne. For her palace, she'd commissioned 21 paintings from Rubens, which glorified her life, but they're now in the Louvre. It is extremely difficult to visit the palace, because it is the chamber of French senators. A few visits are organized throughout the year

Jardin du Luxembourg.

but there is no schedule. But you can call ☎ **01-44-54-19-49** and take a chance. Even so, when tours are offered only 30 tickets are available. The cost is 8€ per person.

You don't really come to the Luxembourg to visit the palace; the gardens are the attraction. For the most part, they're in the classic French tradition: well groomed and formally laid out, the trees planted in patterns. Urns and statuary on pedestals—one honoring Paris's patroness, St. Geneviève, with pigtails reaching to her thighs—encircle a central water basin. Kids can sail a toy boat, ride a pony, or attend an occasional Grand Guignol puppet show. And you can join a game of *boules* (lawn bowling) with a group of men who wear black berets and have Gauloises dangling from their mouths.

Place Edmond Rostand, Place André Honnorat, rue Guynemer, rue de Vaugirard, 6e. 8am–dusk. Métro: Odéon; RER: Luxembourg.

Musée National Eugène Delacroix ★ MUSEUM   This museum is for Delacroix groupies. If you want to see where he lived, worked, and died, this is worth at least an hour. Delacroix (1798–1863) is something of an enigma to art historians. Even his parentage is a mystery. Many believe Talleyrand was his father. One biographer saw him "as an isolated and atypical individualist—one who respected traditional values, yet emerged as the embodiment of Romantic revolt." Baudelaire called him "a volcanic crater artistically concealed beneath bouquets of flowers." The museum is on one of the Left Bank's most charming squares, with a romantic garden. A large arch on a courtyard leads to Delacroix's studio—no poor artist's studio, but the creation of a solidly established man. Sketches, lithographs, watercolors, and oils are hung throughout. If you want to see more of Delacroix's work, head to the Chapelle des Anges in St-Sulpice (p. 138).

6 place de Furstenberg, 6e. ☎ **01-44-41-86-50.** www.musee-delacroix.fr. Admission 5€ adults, free for children 17 and younger. Wed–Mon 9:30am–5pm. Métro: St-Germain-des-Prés or Mabillon.

Musée Zadkine MUSEUM   This museum near the Jardin du Luxembourg was once the home of sculptor Ossip Zadkine (1890–1967), and his collection has been turned over to the city for public viewing. Included are some 300 pieces of sculpture, displayed in the museum and the garden. Some drawings and tapestries are also exhibited. At these headquarters, where he worked from 1928 until his death, you can see how he moved from "left wing" cubist extremism to a renewed appreciation of the classic era. You can visit his garden for free even if you don't want to go into the museum—in fact, it's one of the finest places to relax in Paris on a sunny day, sitting on a bench taking in the two-faced *Woman with the Bird.*

100 bis rue d'Assas, 6e. ☎ **01-55-42-77-20.** www.zadkine.paris.fr. Free admission to permanent collections. Tues–Sun 10am–6pm. Métro: Notre-Dame des Champs or Vavin.

 Gregorians Unplugged

St-Germain-des-Prés stages wonderful concerts on the Left Bank; it boasts fantastic acoustics and a marvelous medieval atmosphere. The church was built to accommodate an age without microphones, and the sound effects will thrill you. For more information, call ☎ **01-55-42-81-33** or visit www.eglise-sgp.org. Arrive about 45 minutes before the performance if you'd like a front-row seat. Tickets are 15€ to 50€.

St-Germain-des-Prés church.

Delacroix's famous frescoes in St-Sulpice.

St-Germain-des-Prés ★★ CHURCH   It's one of Paris's oldest churches, from the 6th century, when a Benedictine abbey was founded here by Childebert, son of Clovis. Alas, the marble columns in the triforium are all that remain from that period. The Normans nearly destroyed the abbey at least four times. The present building has a Romanesque nave and a Gothic choir with fine capitals. At one time, the abbey was a pantheon for Merovingian kings. Restoration of the site of their tombs, **Chapelle de St-Symphorien,** took place in 1981, when unknown Romanesque paintings were discovered on the triumphal arch. Among the others interred here are Descartes (his heart, at least) and Jean-Casimir, the king of Poland who abdicated his throne. The Romanesque tower, topped by a 19th-century spire, is the most enduring landmark in St-Germain-des-Prés. Its church bells, however, are hardly noticed by the patrons of Les Deux Magots across the way.

3 place St-Germain-des-Prés, 6e. ✆ **01-55-42-81-33.** www.eglise-sgp.org. Free admission. Mon-Sat 8am–7:45pm; Sun 9am–8pm. Métro: St-Germain-des-Prés.

St-Sulpice ★★ CHURCH   Pause first outside St-Sulpice. The 1844 fountain by Visconti displays the sculpted likenesses of four bishops of the Louis XIV era: Fenelon, Massillon, Bossuet, and Flechier. Work on the church, at one time Paris's largest, began in 1646. Though laborers built the body by 1745, work on the bell towers continued until 1780, when one was finished and the other left incomplete. One of the priceless treasures inside is Servandoni's rococo **Chapelle de la Madone (Chapel of the Madonna),** with a Pigalle statue of the Virgin. The church has one of the world's largest organs, comprising 6,700 pipes; it has been played by musicians such as Marcel Dupré and Charles-Marie Widor.

The real reason to come here is to see the Delacroix frescoes in the **Chapelle des Anges (Chapel of the Angels),** the first on your right as you enter. Look for his muscular Jacob wrestling (or dancing?) with an effete angel. On the ceiling, St. Michael is having some troubles with the Devil, and yet another mural depicts Heliodorus being driven from the temple. Painted in Delacroix's final years, the frescoes were a high point in his baffling career. If these impress you, pay the painter tribute by visiting the Musée Delacroix (see above).

Rue St-Sulpice, 6e. ℰ **01-42-34-59-98.** Free admission. Daily 8:30am–8pm. Métro: St-Sulpice.

Eiffel Tower & Nearby (7e)

The **Eiffel Tower** has become a symbol for Paris itself. For years it remained the tallest man-made structure on earth, until skyscrapers such as the Empire State Building surpassed it. After admiring and climbing the elegant structure, stroll west along the river to two other important attractions: the **Musée du Quai Branly** and the **Musée d'Orsay.**

Hôtel des Invalides/Napoleon's Tomb ★★ HISTORIC BUILDING In 1670, the Sun King decided to build this "hotel" to house soldiers with disabilities. It wasn't an entirely benevolent gesture, considering that the men had been injured, crippled, or blinded while fighting his battles. When the building was finally completed (Louis XIV had long been dead), a gilded dome by Jules Hardouin-Mansart crowned it, and its corridors stretched for miles. The best way to approach the Invalides is by crossing over the Right Bank via the early-1900s Pont Alexander-III and entering the cobblestone forecourt, where a display of massive cannons makes a formidable welcome.

Before rushing on to Napoleon's Tomb, you may want to visit the world's greatest military museum, the **Musée de l'Armée.** In 1794, a French inspector started collecting weapons, uniforms, and equipment, and with the accumulation of war material over time, the museum has become a documentary of man's self destruction. Viking swords, Burgundian battle axes, 14th-century blunderbusses, Balkan *khandjars,* American Browning machine guns, war pitchforks,

Hôtel des Invalides.

salamander-engraved Renaissance serpentines, a 1528 Griffon, musketoons, grenadiers—if it can kill, it's enshrined here. As a sardonic touch, there's even the wooden leg of General Daumesnil, the governor of Vincennes, who lost his leg in the battle of Wagram. Oblivious to the irony of committing a crime against a place that documents man's evil nature, the Nazis looted the museum in 1940.

Among the outstanding acquisitions are suits of armor worn by the kings and dignitaries of France, including Louis XIV. The best are in the new Arsenal. The most famous one, the "armor suit of the lion," was made for François I. Henri II ordered his suit engraved with the monogram of his mistress, Diane de Poitiers, and (perhaps reluctantly) that of his wife, Catherine de Médici. Particularly fine are the showcases of swords and the World War I mementos, including those of American and Canadian soldiers—seek out the Armistice Bugle, which sounded the cease-fire on November 7, 1918, before the general cease-fire on November 11. The west wing's Salle Orientale has arms of the Eastern world, including Asia and the Mideast Muslim countries, from the 16th century to the 19th century. Turkish armor (look for Bajazet's helmet) and weaponry, and Chinese and Japanese armor and swords are on display.

Then there's that little Corsican who became France's greatest soldier. Here you can see the death mask Antommarchi made of him, as well as an oil by Delaroche painted at the time of Napoleon's first banishment (Apr 1814) and depicting him as he probably looked, paunch and all. The First Empire exhibit displays Napoleon's field bed with his tent; in the room devoted to the Restoration, the 100 Days, and Waterloo, you can see his bedroom as it was at the time of his death on St. Helena. The Turenne Salon contains other souvenirs, such as the hat Napoleon wore at Eylau; the sword from his Austerlitz victory; and his "Flag of Farewell," which he kissed before departing for Elba.

You can gain access to the **Musée des Plans-Reliefs** through the west wing. This collection shows French towns and monuments done in scale models (the model of Strasbourg fills an entire room), as well as models of military fortifications since the days of the great Vauban.

A walk across the Cour d'Honneur (Court of Honor) delivers you to the **Eglise du Dôme,** designed by Hardouin-Mansart for Louis XIV. The architect began work on the church in 1677, though he died before its completion. The dome is the second-tallest monument in Paris (the Tour Eiffel is the tallest, of course). The hearse used at the emperor's funeral on May 9, 1821, is in the Napoleon Chapel.

To accommodate **Napoleon's Tomb ★★★**, the architect Visconti had to redesign the church's high altar in 1842. First buried on St. Helena, Napoleon's remains were exhumed and brought to Paris in 1840 on the orders of Louis-Philippe, who demanded that the English return the emperor to French soil. The remains were locked inside six coffins in this tomb made of red

Napoleon's Tomb.

Eiffel Tower & Nearby Attractions (7e)

Hôtel des Invalides/
Napoleon's Tomb **6**
Les Egouts (Sewers of Paris) **3**
Musée d'Orsay **5**
Musée du quai Branly **2**

Musée Rodin **7**
Palais Bourbon/
Assemblée Nationale **4**
Tour Eiffel **1**

Finnish porphyry, with a green granite base. Surrounding it are a dozen Amazon-like figures representing Napoleon's victories. Almost lampooning the smallness of the man, everything is done on a gargantuan scale. In his coronation robes, the statue of Napoleon stands 2.5m (8¼ ft.) high. The grave of the "King of Rome," his son by his second wife, Marie-Louise, lies at his feet. Surrounding Napoleon's Tomb are those of his brother, Joseph Bonaparte; the great Vauban, who built many of France's fortifications; World War I Allied commander Foch; and the *Vicomte* de Turenne, the republic's first grenadier (actually, only his heart is entombed here).

Place des Invalides, 7e. ℭ **01-44-42-37-72.** www.invalides.org. Admission to Musée de l'Armée, Napoleon's Tomb, and Musée des Plans-Reliefs 9€ adults, 7€ students, free for children 17 and younger. Oct 1–Mar 31 Mon–Sat 10am–5pm, Sun 10am–5:30pm; Apr 1–Sept 30 Mon, Wed–Sat 10am–6pm, Sun 10am–6:30pm, Tues 10am–9pm; June–Aug daily 10am–7pm. Closed Jan 1, May 1, Nov 1, and Dec 25. Métro: Latour-Maubourg, Varenne, Invalides, or St-Francois-Xavier.

Les Egouts ★ ☺ HISTORIC SEWER   Some sociologists assert that the sophistication of a society can be judged by the way it disposes of waste. If so, Paris receives good marks for its mostly invisible sewer network. Victor Hugo is credited with making them famous in *Les Misérables:* Jean Valjean takes flight through them, "all dripping with slime, his soul filled with a strange light." Hugo also wrote, "Paris has beneath it another Paris, a Paris of sewers, which has its own streets, squares, lanes, arteries, and circulation."

In the early Middle Ages, drinking water was taken directly from the Seine, and wastewater poured onto fields or thrown onto the unpaved streets transformed the urban landscape into a sea of smelly mud. Around 1200, the streets were paved with cobblestones, and open sewers ran down the center of each. These open sewers helped spread the Black Death, which devastated the city. In 1370, a vaulted sewer was built on rue Montmartre, draining effluents into a Seine tributary. During Louis XIV's reign, improvements were made, but the state of waste disposal in Paris remained deplorable.

During Napoleon's reign, 31km (19 miles) of sewer were constructed beneath Paris. By 1850, as the Industrial Revolution made the manufacture of iron pipe and steam-digging equipment more practical, Baron Haussmann developed a system that used separate channels for drinking water and sewage. By 1878, it was 580km (360 miles) long. Beginning in 1894, the network was enlarged, and laws required that discharge of all waste and storm-water runoff be funneled into the sewers. Between 1914 and 1977, an additional 966km (600 miles) were added. Today, the network of sewers is 2,093km (1,300 miles) long.

The city's sewers are constructed around four principal tunnels, one 5.5m (18 ft.) wide and 4.5m (15 ft.) high. It's like an underground city, with the street names clearly labeled. Sewer tours begin at Pont de l'Alma on the Left Bank, where a stairway leads into the city's bowels. Visiting times might change during bad weather, as a storm can make the sewers dangerous. The tour consists of a film, a small museum visit, and then a short trip through the maze. *Warning:* The smell is pretty bad, especially in summer, but kids should love the gross-out factor.

Pont de l'Alma, 7e. ℭ **01-53-68-27-81.** Admission 4.20€ adults; 3.40€ seniors, students, and children 5–16; free for children 4 and younger. May–Sept Sat–Wed 11am–5pm; Oct–Apr Sat–Wed 11am–4pm. Métro: Alma-Marceau. RER: Pont de l'Alma.

Musée d'Orsay ★★★ MUSEUM   Architects created one of the world's great museums from an old rail station, the neoclassical Gare d'Orsay, across the Seine from the Louvre and the Tuileries. Don't skip the Louvre, of course, but come

Manet's *Olympia*, at the Musée d'Orsay.

here even if you have to miss all the other art museums in town. The Orsay boasts an astounding collection devoted to the watershed years 1848 to 1914, with a treasure-trove by the big names plus all the lesser-known groups (the symbolists, pointillists, nabis, realists, and late romantics). The 80 galleries also include Belle Époque furniture, photographs, objets d'art, and architectural models.

A monument to the Industrial Revolution, the Orsay is covered by an arching glass roof allowing in floods of light. It displays works ranging from the creations of academic and historic painters such as Ingres to romanticists such as Delacroix, to neorealists including Courbet and Daumier.

The museum's Impressionist and post-Impressionist galleries, as well as the four floors of the "Pavillon Amont," recently underwent a major renovation, which enlarged exhibition spaces and improved displays. The Impressionists still draw the crowds to this museum. Led by Manet, Renoir, and Monet, the Impressionists shunned ecclesiastical and mythological set pieces for a light-bathed Seine, faint figures strolling in the Tuileries, pale-faced women in hazy bars, and even vulgar rail stations such as the Gare St-Lazare. And the Impressionists were the first to paint that most characteristic feature of Parisian life: the sidewalk cafe, especially in the artists' quarter of Montmartre.

The most famous painting from this era is Manet's 1863 **Déjeuner sur l'herbe (Picnic on the Grass),** whose forest setting with a nude woman and two fully clothed men sent shock waves through respectable society when it was first exhibited. Two years later, Manet's **Olympia** created another scandal by depicting a woman lounging on her bed and wearing nothing but a flower in her hair and high-heeled shoes; she's attended by an African maid in the background. Zola called Manet "a man among eunuchs."

One of Renoir's most joyous paintings is here: the **Moulin de la Galette** (1876). Degas is represented by his paintings of racehorses and dancers; his 1876 cafe scene, **Absinthe,** remains one of his most reproduced works. Paris-born Monet was fascinated by the effect of changing light on Rouen Cathédrale and brought its stone bubbles to life in a series of five paintings; our favorite is *Rouen Cathédrale: Full Sunlight.* Another celebrated work is by an American, Whistler's *Arrangement in Grey and Black: Portrait of the Painter's Mother,* better known as *Whistler's Mother.* It's said that this painting heralded modern art, though many critics denounced it at the time because of its funereal overtones. Whistler was content to claim he'd made "Mummy just as nice as possible."

You'll also see works by Matisse, the cubists, and the expressionists in a setting once used by Orson Welles to film a nightmarish scene in *The Trial,* based on Kafka's unfinished novel. You'll find Millet's sunny wheat fields, Barbizon landscapes, Corot's mists, and Tahitian Gauguins.

1 rue de Bellechasse or 62 rue de Lille, 7e. ✆ **01-40-49-48-14.** www.musee-orsay.fr. Admission 8€ adults, 5.50€ ages 18–24, free ages 17 and younger. Joint ticket to this museum and the Musée de l'Orangerie (p. 84) 13€. Tues–Wed and Fri–Sun 9:30am–6pm; Thurs 9:30am–9:45pm. Closed Jan 1 and Dec 25. Métro: Solférino. RER: Musée d'Orsay.

Musée du quai Branly ★★★ ☺
MUSEUM   The architect Jean Nouvel said he wanted to create something "unique, poetic, and disturbing." And so he did with the opening of this $265-million museum, which took a decade to launch. There was even scandal: The terra-cotta figures from Nigeria turned out to be smuggled. At long last, under one roof nearly 300,000 tribal artifacts from Africa, Asia, Oceania, and the Americas have been assembled. Galleries stand on sculpted pillars that evoke totem poles. Set in a lush, rambling garden on the Left Bank in the shadow of the Eiffel Tower, this is the greatest museum to open in Paris since Pompidou.

FROM TOP: **The facade of the Musée d' Orsay; an exhibit from the Musée du quai Branly.**

Housed in four spectacular buildings with a garden walled off from the quai Branly are the art, sculpture, and cultural materials of a vast range of non-Western civilizations, separated into different sections that represent the traditional cultures of Africa, East and Southeast Asia, Oceania, Australia, the Americas, and New Zealand. The pieces here come from the now-defunct Musée des Arts Africains et Oceaniens, from the Louvre, and from the Musée de l'Homme. Temporary exhibits are shown off in boxes all along the 183m-long (600-ft.) exhibition hall.

Incredible masterpieces are on display made by some very advanced traditional civilizations; some of the most impressive exhibits present tribal masks of different cultures, some of which are so lifelike and emotional in their creation that you can feel the fear and elation involved in their use, which is well documented by descriptions in English. The exhibitions are very engaging for children. Allow 2 hours for a full visit, also take a stroll in the carefully manicured garden, or have a café au lait in the small cafeteria across from the main building. There are numerous entrances to the museum grounds from the area near the Eiffel Tower; the main entrance is on quai Branly.

27-37 quai Branly and 206-208 rue de Université, 7e. (C) **01-56-61-70-00.** www.quaibranly.fr. Admission 8.50€ adults, 6€ seniors and students 18-26, free for children 17 and younger. Tues-Wed and Sun 11am-7pm; Thurs-Sat 11am-9pm. Métro: Alma-Marceau. RER: Pont d'Alma.

Musée Rodin ★★ ☺ MUSEUM   Today Rodin is acclaimed as the father of modern sculpture, but in a different era, his work was labeled obscene. The world's artistic taste changed, and in due course, in 1911, the French government purchased Rodin's studio in this gray-stone, 18th-century mansion in the Faubourg St-Germain. The government restored the rose gardens to their 18th-century splendor, making them a perfect setting for Rodin's most memorable works.

In the courtyard are three world-famous creations. Rodin's first major public commission, **The Burghers of Calais,** commemorated the heroism of six citizens of Calais who in 1347 offered themselves as a ransom to Edward III in return for ending his siege of their port. Perhaps the single best-known work, **The Thinker,** in Rodin's own words, "thinks with every muscle of his arms, back, and legs, with his clenched fist and gripping toes." Not completed when Rodin died, **The Gate of Hell,** as he put it, is "where I lived for a whole year in Dante's *Inferno.*"

The Thinker, at the Musée Rodin.

Inside, the sculptures, plaster casts, reproductions, originals, and sketches reveal the freshness and vitality of a remarkable artist. You can almost see his works emerging from marble into life. Everybody is attracted to **Le Baiser (The Kiss),** of which one critic wrote, "The passion is timeless." Upstairs are two versions of the celebrated and condemned **Nude of Balzac,** his bulky torso rising from a tree trunk (Albert E. Elsen commented on the "glorious bulging" stomach). Included are many versions of his **Monument to Balzac** (a large one stands in the garden), Rodin's last major work. Other significant sculptures are the soaring **Prodigal Son; The Crouching Woman** (the "embodiment of despair"); and **The Age of Bronze,** an 1876 study of a nude man modeled after a Belgian soldier. (Rodin was falsely accused of making a cast from a living model.) Generally overlooked is a room devoted to Rodin's mistress, Camille Claudel, a towering artist in her own right. She was his pupil, model, and lover, and created such works as **_Maturity, Clotho,_** and the recently donated **_The Waltz_** and **_The Gossips._** The little alley behind the Musée Rodin winds its way down to a pond with fountains, flower beds, and even sand pits for children. It's one of the most idyllic hidden spots in Paris.

In the Hôtel Biron, 79 rue de Varenne, 7e. ✆ **01-44-18-61-10.** www.musee-rodin.fr. Admission 6€ adults, 5€ ages 18–25, free for children 17 and younger. Apr–Sept Tues–Sun 9:30am–5:45pm; Oct–Mar Tues–Sun 10am–5:45pm. Métro: Varenne, Invalides, or St-Francois-Xavier.

Palais Bourbon/Assemblée Nationale ★ HISTORIC BUILDING

The French parliament's lower house, the Chamber of Deputies, meets at this 1722 mansion built by the duchesse de Bourbon, a daughter of Louis XIV. You can make reservations for one of two types of visits as early as 6 months in advance. Hour-long tours on art, architecture, and basic French government processes are given Monday, Friday, and Saturday. They're in French (in English with advance booking). You may also observe sessions of the National Assembly, held Tuesday afternoon and all day Wednesday and Thursday beginning at 9:30am. Remember, this is a working government building, and all visitors are subject to rigorous security checks.

33 quai d'Orsay, 7e. ✆ **01-40-63-64-08.** www.assemblee-nationale.fr. Free admission. Hours vary, so call ahead. Métro: Assemblée Nationale.

Tour Eiffel ★★★ ☺ MONUMENT

This is without doubt one of the most recognizable structures in the world. Weighing 7,000 tons, but exerting about the same pressure on the ground as an average-size person sitting in a chair, the wrought-iron tower wasn't meant to be permanent. Alexandre Gustave Eiffel, the French engineer whose fame rested mainly on his iron

Tour Eiffel.

bridges, built it for the 1889 Universal Exhibition. (Eiffel also designed the framework for the Statue of Liberty.) Praised by some and denounced by others (some called it a "giraffe," the "world's greatest lamppost," or the "iron monster"), the tower created as much controversy in the 1880s as I. M. Pei's glass pyramid at the Louvre did in the 1980s. What saved it from demolition was the advent of radio—as the tallest structure in Europe, it made a perfect spot to place a radio antenna.

The tower, including its antenna, is 317m (1,040 ft.) high. On a clear day you can see it from 65km (40 miles) away. An open-framework construction, the tower unlocked the almost unlimited possibilities of steel construction, paving the way for skyscrapers. Skeptics said it couldn't be built, and Eiffel actually wanted to make it soar higher. For years it remained the tallest man-made structure on earth, until skyscrapers like the Empire State Building surpassed it.

We could fill an entire page with tower statistics. (Its plans spanned 5,400 sq. m/58,000 sq. ft. of paper, and it contains 2.5 million rivets.) But forget the numbers. Just stand beneath the tower, and look straight up. It's like a rocket of steel lacework shooting into the sky.

From December to February, it is possible to ice-skate inside the Eiffel Tower. Skating takes place on an observation deck 57m (188 ft.) above ground. The rectangular rink is a bit larger than an average tennis court, holding 80 skaters at once. Rink admission and skate rental are free, after you pay the initial entry fee below.

To get to **Le Jules Verne** (✆ **01-45-55-61-44**), the second-platform restaurant, take the private south foundation elevator. You can enjoy an aperitif in the piano bar and then take a seat at one of the dining room's tables, all of which provide an inspiring view. The menu changes seasonally, offering fish and meat dishes that range from filet of turbot with seaweed and buttered sea urchins to veal chops with truffled vegetables. Reservations are recommended.

Champ de Mars, 7e. (✆ **01-44-11-23-23.** www.tour-eiffel.fr. Admission to 2nd landing 8€, 3rd landing 13€. Stairs to 2nd floor 4.50€. Sept–May daily 9:30am–11:45pm; June–Aug daily 9am–12:45am. Sept–June stairs open only to 6:30pm. Métro: Trocadéro, Ecole Militaire, or Bir Hakeim. RER: Champ de Mars–Tour Eiffel.

TIME OUT AT the tower

To see the Eiffel Tower best, don't sprint—approach it gradually. We suggest taking the Métro to the Trocadéro stop and walking from the Palais de Chaillot to the Seine to get the full effect of the tower and its surroundings; then cross the Pont d'Iéna and head for the base, where you'll find elevators in two of the pillars—expect long lines. (When the tower is open, you can see the 1889 lift machinery in the east and west pillars.) You visit the tower in three stages: The first landing provides a view over the rooftops, as well as a cinema museum showing films, restaurants, and a bar. The second landing offers a panoramic look at the city. The third landing gives the most spectacular view; Eiffel's office has been re-created on this level, with wax figures depicting the engineer receiving Thomas Edison.

Montparnasse & Southern Paris (13e, 14e & 15e)

For the "Lost Generation," life centered around the cafes of Montparnasse, at the border of the 6th and 14th arrondissements. Hangouts such as the **Dôme, Coupole, Rotonde,** and **Sélect** became legendary, as artists—especially American expats—turned their backs on touristy Montmartre. Picasso, Amedeo Modigliani, Man Ray, and Hemingway frequented this neighborhood, as did Fitzgerald when he was poor (when he was rich, you'd find him at the Ritz). William Faulkner, Archibald MacLeish, Joan Miró, James Joyce, Ford Madox Ford, and even Leon Trotsky spent time here. Today Montparnasse plays second fiddle to St-Germain-des-Prés, though the Jean Nouvel–designed **Fondation Cartier** remains a real stand out. A different French architect, Dominique Perrault, is behind the massive new national library out in the 13th arrondissement, which signals the resurrection of this former industrial heartland.

Bibliothèque Nationale de France, Site Tolbiac/François Mitterrand
LIBRARY   The French National Library opened in 1996 with a futuristic design by Dominique Perrault (a quartet of 24-story towers evoking the look of open books); this is the last of the *grands projets* of the late François Mitterrand. It boasts the same grandiose scale as the Cité de la Musique and houses the nation's literary and historic archives; it's regarded as a repository of the French soul, replacing outmoded facilities on rue des Archives. The library incorporates space for 1,600 readers at a time, many of whom enjoy views over two levels of a garden-style courtyard that seems far removed from Paris's urban congestion.

This is one of Europe's most user-friendly academic facilities, emphasizing computerized documentation and microfiche—a role model that will set academic and literary priorities well into the future. The public has access to as many as 180,000 books, plus thousands of periodicals, with an additional 10 million historic (including medieval) documents available to qualified experts. Though the appeal of this place extends mainly to serious scholars, a handful of

The towers of the Bibliothèque Nationale de France, Site Tolbiac.

KIKI DE MONTPARNASSE

One of the most notable characters in Montparnasse was **Kiki de Montparnasse** (born Alice Prin; 1901–1953). She was raised by her grandmother in Burgundy until her mother called her to Paris to work. Here she adopted her new name and iconic look (a bowl cut, black rimmed eyes, and red lips), and became a model and muse for the Montparnasse

artists. She posed for artists including Amedeo Modigliani, Tsuguoharu Foujita, and Alexander Calder. She was Man Ray's lover and favorite model in the early '20s—his famous "Violin d'Ingres" is, in fact, a photograph of Kiki, and you can see it at the Musée d'Art Moderne. (On display at the same museum is Calder's 1930 mobile named "Kiki de Montparnasse ou Masque.") She sang at the Jockey Club, and in 1936, she opened her own cabaret on rue Vavin known as *Chez Kiki* to locals. In her black hose and garters, she captivated dozens of men, among them Frederick Kohner, who went so far as to title his memoirs *Kiki of Montparnasse*. Kiki later wrote her own memoirs, with an introduction by Hemingway. Papa called her "a Queen," noting that it was "very different from being a lady."

special exhibits might interest you, as well as concerts and lectures. Concert tickets rarely exceed 15€; a schedule is available at the library.

Quai François-Mauriac, 13e. ☎ **01-53-79-59-59.** www.bnf.fr. Admission 3.50€. Children 15 and under not admitted. Mon 2-8pm; Tues-Sat 10am-7pm; Sun 1-7pm. Closed Sept 8-21. Métro: Bibliothèque François-Mitterrand

Cimetière du Montparnasse ★ CEMETERY   In the shadow of the Tour Montparnasse, this debris-littered cemetery is a burial ground of yesterday's celebrities. A map to the left of the main gateway will direct you to the gravesite of its most famous couple, **Simone de Beauvoir** and **Jean-Paul Sartre.** Others resting here include **Samuel Beckett; Guy de Maupassant; Pierre Larousse** (famous for his dictionary); **Capt. Alfred Dreyfus;** auto tycoon **André Citroën;** sculptors **Ossip Zadkine** and **Constantin Brancusi;** actress **Jean Seberg;** composer **Camille Saint-Saëns;** photographer **Man Ray;** poet **Charles Baudelaire,** who wrote about "plunging into the abyss, Heaven or Hell"; and American intellectual and activist **Susan Sontag,** who was interred here in 2005.

3 bd. Edgar-Quinet, 14e. ☎ **01-44-10-86-50.** Mon–Fri 8am–6pm; Sat 8:30am–6pm; Sun 9am–6pm (closes at 5:30pm Nov–Mar). Métro: Edgar-Quinet.

Les Catacombes ★ HISTORIC INTEREST   Every year, about 50,000 visitors explore some 910m (2,986 ft.) of tunnel in these dank catacombs to look at six million ghoulishly arranged, skull-and-crossbones skeletons. First opened to the public in 1810, this "empire of the dead" is now illuminated with electric lights over its entire length. In the Middle Ages, the catacombs were quarries, but by the end of the 18th century, over-crowded cemeteries were becoming a menace to public health. City officials decided to use the catacombs as a burial ground, and the bones of several million persons were transferred here. In 1830, the prefect of Paris closed the catacombs, considering them obscene and indecent. During World War II, the catacombs were the headquarters of the French Resistance.

1 place du Colonel Henri Rol-Tanguy, 14e. ✆ **01-43-22-47-63.** www.catacombes-de-paris. fr. Admission 8€ adults, 6€ seniors, 4€ ages 14–25, free for children 13 and younger. Tues–Sun 10am–5pm. Métro: Denfert-Rochereau.

Skulls in Les Catacombes.

Fondation Cartier ★★ MUSEUM This is a special place. The fine jeweler Cartier commissioned Pritzker Architecture Prize–winning architect Jean Nouvel to design a headquarters for its art foundation, and the result in an airy glass and steel structure. Once you enter the building—passing under a vertical plant wall—you will encounter a range of themed exhibitions from both French and international artists. The foundation is known for presenting art from stars better known for their success in other fields, like Patti Smith or David Lynch. There is also a wild-looking garden surrounding the building, which is a pleasure to walk though.

261 bd Raspail, 14th. ✆ **01-42-18-56-50.** www.fondation.cartier.fr. Admission 8.50€ adults, 5.50€ students and seniors. Tues–Sun 11am–8pm (until 10pm Tues). Métro: Raspail

Manufacture Nationale des Gobelins ★ MUSEUM Did you know a single tapestry can take 4 years to complete, employing as many as three to five full-time weavers? The founder of this dynasty, Jean Gobelin, came from a family of dyers and clothmakers; in the 15th century, he discovered a scarlet dye that made him famous. By 1601, Henri IV imported 200 weavers from Flanders to make tapestries full time. Until this endeavor, the Gobelin family hadn't made any tapestries. Colbert, Louis XIV's minister, bought the works, and under royal patronage the craftsmen set about executing designs by Le Brun. After the revolution, the industry was reactivated by Napoleon. Today, Les Gobelins is a viable business entity, weaving tapestries for museums and historical restorations around the world. Throughout most of the week, the factories are closed to casual visitors, who are never allowed to wander at will. But if you'd like insight into this medieval craft, you can participate, 3 days a week (Tues, Wed, Thu), in one of two guided tours, each lasting 90 minutes and each conducted in French. The factory also includes the **Galerie des Gobelins,** which displays exhibits that are generally sourced from the extraordinary furniture and arts collections of the Mobilier National.

42 av. des Gobelins, 13e. ✆ **01-40-13-46-46.** www.mobiliernational.culture.gouv.fr. Tues–Sun 10am–6pm. Métro: Gobelins.

A weaver working in the Manufacture Nationale des Gobelins.

Musée Bourdelle ★ 🎒 MUSEUM   Here you can see works by Rodin's star pupil, Antoine Bourdelle (1861–1929), who became a celebrated artist in his own right. Along with changing exhibitions, the museum permanently displays the artist's drawings, paintings, and sculptures, and lets you wander through his studio, garden, and house. The original plaster casts of some of his greatest works are on display, but what's most notable here are the 21 studies of Beethoven. Though some of the exhibits are poorly captioned, you'll still feel the impact of his genius.

18 rue Antoine-Bourdelle, 15e. ✆ **01-49-54-73-73.** www.bourdelle.paris.fr. Admission 7€ adults, 3.50€ ages 14-26, free for children 13 and younger Tues–Sun 10am 6pm. Métro: Montparnasse-Bienvenüe.

Tour Montparnasse ☺ ARCHITECTURE   Completed in 1973 and rising 206m (676 ft.) above the skyline, the Tour Montparnasse was denounced by some as "bringing Manhattan to Paris." The city soon passed an ordinance outlawing any further structures of this size in the heart of Paris. Today, the modern tower houses an underground shopping mall, as well as much of the infrastructure for the Gare de Montparnasse rail station. You can ride an elevator up to the 56th floor (where you'll find a bar and restaurant) and then climb three flights to the roof terrace. The terrific view encompasses virtually every important Paris monument, including Sacré-Coeur, Notre-Dame, and La Défense.

33 avenue de Maine, 15e. ✆ **01-45-38-52-56.** www.tourmontparnasse56.com. Admission 11€ adults, 8€ students, 4.70€ children 7-15, Free for children 6 and younger. Apr–Sept daily 9:30am–11:30pm, Oct–Mar daily 9:30am–10:30pm. Métro: Montparnasse-Bienvenüe.

BEYOND CENTRAL PARIS

With regular Métro, train, and bus service, it is easy to access the major attractions outside of Paris, like Basilique St-Denis and La Grande Arche de la Défense. For more attractions outside of Paris, see chapter 10.

Basilique St-Denis.

La Grande Arche de La Défense.

Basilique St-Denis ★★ CHURCH   In the 12th century, Abbot Suger placed an inscription on the bronze doors here: "Marvel not at the gold and expense, but at the craftsmanship of the work." France's first Gothic building that can be precisely dated, St-Denis was constructed between 1137 and 1281 and was the "spiritual defender of the State" during the reign of Louis VI ("the Fat"). The facade has a rose window and a crenellated parapet on the top similar to the fortifications of a castle. The stained-glass windows—in stunning mauve, purple, blue, and rose—were restored in the 19th century.

The first bishop of Paris, St. Denis became the patron saint of the monarchy, and royal burials began here in the 6th century and continued until the Revolution. The sculpture designed for the **tombs**—some two stories high—spans French artistic development from the Middle Ages to the Renaissance. (There are guided tours in French of the Carolingian-era crypt.) François I was entombed at St-Denis, and his funeral statue is nude, though he demurely covers himself with his hand. Other kings and queens here include Louis XII and Anne de Bretagne, as well as Henri II and Catherine de Médici. Revolutionaries stormed through the basilica during the Terror, smashing many marble faces and dumping royal remains in a lime-filled ditch in the garden. (These remains were reburied under the main altar during the 19th c.) Free organ concerts are given on Sundays at 11:15am.

1 rue de la Légion d'honneur, St-Denis. ✆ **01-48-09-83-54.** http://saint-denis.monuments-nationaux.fr/en. Admission 7€ adults, 4.50€ seniors and students 18–25, free for children 17 and younger. Apr–Sept Mon–Sat 10am–6:15pm, Sun noon–6:15pm; Oct–Mar Mon–Sat 10am–5pm, Sun noon–5:15pm. Closed Jan 1, May 1, Dec 25. Métro: St-Denis.

La Grande Arche de La Défense MONUMENT   The sprawling satellite suburb of La Défense was built as a dedicated business district over 3 decades from the late '50s, just outside Paris, across the river from the 16th arrondissement. La

The Royal Heart of the Boy Who Would Be King

In a bizarre twist, following a Mass in 2004, the heart of the 10-year-old heir to the French throne, Louis XVII, was buried at **Saint-Denis Basilica,** near the graves of his parents, Marie Antoinette and Louis XVI. The heart was pickled, stolen, returned, and 2 centuries later, DNA tested. More than 2 centuries of rumor and legend surrounding the child's death were put to rest. Genetic testing has persuaded even the most cynical historians that the person who might have been the future Louis XVII never escaped prison. The boy died of tuberculosis in 1795, his body ravaged by tumors. The child's corpse was dumped into a common grave, but not before a doctor secretly carved out his heart and smuggled it out of prison in a handkerchief. The heart of the dead boy was compared with DNA of hair trimmed from Marie Antoinette during her childhood in Austria. It was a perfect match.

Grande Arche, a massive steel-and-masonry arch rising 35 stories, was designed as its architectural centerpiece and was inaugurated in 1989. It was built with the blessing of the late François Mitterrand and extends the magnificently engineered straight line linking the Louvre, the Arc de Triomphe du Carrousel (a monument between the Louvre and the Tuileries Gardens), the Champs-Élysées, the Arc de Triomphe, the Avenue de la Grande Armée, and the place du Porte Maillot. The arch is ringed with a circular avenue patterned after the one around the Arc de Triomphe. The monument is tall enough to shelter Notre-Dame beneath its heavily trussed canopy.

1 place du parvis de La Défense, Puteaux, 16e. **(?)** **01-49-07-27-27.** www.grandearche.com. Métro: Grande Arche de la Défense.

ESPECIALLY FOR KIDS

Paris is not always the easiest city to navigate with children, but kids will still love many of the museums, parks, and attractions the city has to offer. If you're staying on the Right Bank, take the children for a stroll through the **Jardin des Tuileries** (p. 82), where there are donkey rides, ice-cream stands, and a marionette show; at the circular pond, you can rent a toy boat. On the Left Bank, similar treats exist in the **Jardin du Luxembourg** (p. 136). After a visit to the Eiffel Tower, you can take the kids for a donkey ride in the **Champ de Mars.**

A Paris tradition, **puppet shows** are worth seeing for their colorful productions; they're a genuine French child's experience. At the Jardin du Luxembourg, or the Buttes Chaumont, puppets reenact plots set in Gothic castles and Oriental palaces; some critics say the best puppet shows are held in the Champ de Mars.

On Sunday afternoon, many French families head to the **Butte Montmartre** to bask in the fiesta atmosphere. You can join in: Take the Métro to Anvers, and walk to the *funiculaire* (the cable car that carries you up to Sacré-Coeur). When up top, follow the crowds to place du Tertre, where a Sergeant Pepper–style band will usually be blasting off-key and you can have the kids' pictures sketched by local artists. You can take in the views of Paris from the various vantage points and treat your children to ice cream. For a walking tour of Montmartre, see chapter 5.

Riding the carousel in the Jardin du Luxembourg.   A traditional puppet show.

Your kids may want to check out the Gallic versions of Mickey Mouse and his pals, so see chapter 10, "Side Trips from Paris," for **Disneyland Paris.**

Here is our list of top attractions that children will enjoy:

The Montmartre *funiculaire*.

Basilique du Sacré-Coeur (p. 118)

Bois de Boulogne (p. 108)

Cimetière du Père-Lachaise (p. 123)

Cité des Sciences et de l'Industrie (p. 127)

Gaîté Lyrique (p. 98)

Jardin d'Acclimatation (p. 110)

Jardin des Tuileries (p. 82)

Jardin du Luxembourg (p. 136)

La Cité de l'Architecture et du Patrimoine (p. 110)

La Promenade Plantée (p. 122)

Le Musée du quai Branly (p. 144)

Les Egouts (p. 142)

Musée Carnavalet-Histoire de Paris (p. 100)

Riding a pony at the Jardin d'Acclimatition.

The "Beach" of Paris

Relaxing under a palm tree on a chaise lounge sounds more Caribbean than Parisian, but a nearly 4.8km (3-mile) stretch of sandy shore opens along the Seine each summer. With the Eiffel Tower looming in the background, visitors and locals can enjoy the *plage* (beach; see picture), splash in fountains, swing in hammocks, play volleyball, or enjoy a picnic. Just don't go into the polluted water of the murky Seine.

STROLLING AROUND PARIS

by Sophie Nellis

5

LE CONSULAT

Although it's tempting to take the Métro around Paris, the best way to explore the city is on foot. Walking along the Seine, strolling around the Jardin du Luxembourg, or indulging in some idle *flânerie* (aimless wandering through an urban environment) along the Grands Boulevards will not only open your eyes to Paris's charm and beauty, but will enable you to discover the city's rich history. Paris is full of surprises and hidden treasures. In this chapter we suggest three walking tours around different Parisian neighborhoods: Montmartre, the Marais, and the Latin Quarter.

For more walking tours see *Frommer's 24 Great Walks in Paris*.

WALKING TOUR 1: MONTMARTRE

START:	**Place des Abbesses (Métro: Abbesses).**
FINISH:	**Place Blanche (Métro: Blanche).**
TIME:	**2 hours (not including stops). It's a 3km (2-mile) trek.**
BEST TIME:	**During the day.**
WORST TIME:	**After dark.**

Known as much for its villagelike atmosphere as for its monuments, Montmartre is one of the most picturesque areas in Paris. Its name has always been the subject of much disagreement. During the Gallo-Roman period, the hill (or *la butte* as the French like to call it) was known both as Mount Mercury and Mount Mars. However, it was Saint Denis, one of Paris's patron saints, who made the hill famous. Denis was the first bishop of Paris and he was beheaded by the Romans in Montmartre in A.D. 250. Legend has it that he miraculously picked up his head and carried it to the Paris suburb now known as Saint Denis. Thus, another possible origin of the name is the Mount of Martyrs.

At the end of the 19th century, Montmartre was full of painters, writers, and musicians—all of whom were attracted by Montmartre's authentic atmosphere and cheap rents. The neighborhood soon gained a reputation for bohemia and creativity. Toulouse-Lautrec painted Montmartre as a district of cabarets, circus freaks, and prostitutes. This seedy side of Montmartre is still very much visible—the area between Place Blanche and Place Pigalle is full of sex shops, sex shows, and prostitutes.

1 PLACE DES ABBESSES

In 1134 King Louis *Le Gros* (the Fat) founded an abbey at the top of the hill. Place des Abbesses is named after the various abbesses who ran the abbey

FACING PAGE: **Montmartre at night.**

Le Bateau-Lavoir.

that was located in this square. They all came from wealthy, aristocratic families. During the French Revolution, the 46th abbess, Louise de Montmorency-Laval, was guillotined and the abbey was pillaged. Her crime? The elderly abbess was found guilty of "blindly and deafly plotting against the revolution."

Admire the beautiful Métro entrance at Abbesses. Designed by Hector Guimard in 1900, the Paris Métro is one of the rare examples of the Art Nouveau style found in the city. At 36m (118 ft.) underground, this is the deepest Métro station in Paris.

With your back to the Métro, turn right and cross Place des Abbesses. Go along rue des Abbesses and turn up rue Ravignan, which leads to tree-studded place Emile-Goudeau. At no. 11bis–no. 13 is:

2 LE BATEAU-LAVOIR (BOAT WASHHOUSE)

This building, known as the cradle of cubism, was given the nickname *Le Bateau-Lavoir* by the poet Max Jacob, who noticed a line of washing when he came here for the first time. The building was originally used to manufacture pianos but in 1889, 10 artists' studios were installed. Picasso lived at the Bateau-Lavoir from 1904 to 1912, and it was here that he painted *Les Demoiselles d'Avignon*, the painting that marked the beginning of cubism. Other famous residents included Kees Van Dongen, Max Jacob, and Juan Gris. The city of Paris acquired the building in 1965 and it was classified as a historic monument, only to be destroyed by a fire in 1960. Reconstructed in 1978, it now houses 25 ateliers.

Continue up the hill along rue Ravignan. Turn left into Place Jean-Baptiste-Clément and go up the hill. Here rues Norvins, St-Rustique, and des Saules collide. Take rue Norvins and turn right down rue Poulbot. At no. 11 you come to:

3 ESPACE DALÍ MONTMARTRE

The phantasmagoric world of **Espace Dalí Montmartre** (℡ **01-42-64-40-10;** www.daliparis.com) features 300 original Dalí works, including his famous 1956 lithograph of Don Quixote. Open daily from 10am to 6pm.

Walking Tour 1: Montmartre

18e

9e

	200 yds
0	200 m

1 Place des Abbesses
2 Le Bateau-Lavoir
3 Espace Dalí Montmartre
4 Place du Calvaire
5 Place du Tertre
6 St-Pierre
7 Sacré-Coeur
8 Musée Montmartre
9 Montmartre Vineyard
10 Au Lapin Agile
11 Moulin de la Galette
12 Café des Deux Moulins ☕
13 Moulin Rouge

|||| Steps
⌁⌁⌁⌁ Funicular
Ⓜ Métro station

Rue Poulbot crosses the tiny:

4 PLACE DU CALVAIRE

Place du Calvaire (Calvary Sq.) is believed to be named after a large cross that once stood here. This square offers a panoramic view of the rooftops of Paris, and the greenery on the steps of the rue du Calvaire is typical of the more rural side of Montmartre. The artist/painter/lithographer Maurice Neumont lived at no. 1 (a plaque is fixed to the door).

An exhibit at Espace Dalí Montmartre.

Portrait artists on Place du Tertre.

Turning your back on the view, walk along rue du Calvaire to:

5 PLACE DU TERTRE

The site of Montmartre's first town hall (built in 1890), this old square is always overflowing with tourists. Look out for **La Mère Catherine** at no. 6, one of the oldest restaurants in the square. It was here that the word *bistrot* was invented. On March 30, 1814, a group of Russian soldiers were eating here and demanded a drink, "bystro" (which means "quick" in Russian). Thus, *bistrot* came to refer to a restaurant where you could get a quick bite to eat. Since the late 19th century, Place du Tertre has been associated with art and artists, and there are still a lot of street artists floating around. (You'll be asked countless times if you want your portrait sketched.) Despite its proximity to Sacré-Coeur, the square has lost a lot of its charm and can seem rather gaudy and inauthentic.

Turn right off the square on Place Jean Marais to:

6 ST-PIERRE

Consecrated by Pope Eugène III in 1147, this church, along with St-Germain-des-Près, is one of Paris's oldest buildings. St-Pierre had two uses: the eastern part was reserved for the Abbey of Montmartre, while the western part was a parish church. Thanks to this second, more community-orientated function, St-Pierre was spared destruction during the revolution. The current facade dates from 1775, and the three bronze doors that represent the three patron saints of the Church—Saint Pierre in the center, Our Lady on the right, and Saint Denis on the left—were added in 1980. The small cemetery next door is only open to the public on November 1.

From St-Pierre, turn left and then right into rue Azaïs. Continue until:

7 SACRÉ-COEUR

The Roman-Byzantine style basilica marks the Paris skyline with its colossal proportions. Despite pollution, the church remains white, thanks to the Souppes stone with which it was built. Resistant as granite, it exudes calcite when it comes into contact with rainwater. See p. 118 for more information.

Sacré-Coeur.

Facing the basilica, take the street running along the left-hand side of the church (rue du Cardinal-Guibert); then turn left onto rue du Chevalier-de-la-Barre and right onto rue du Mont-Cenis. Continue along this street to rue Cortot, then turn left. At no. 12 is the:

8 MUSÉE MONTMARTRE

Musée Montmartre (© **01-49-25-89-37;** www.museedemontmartre.fr) presents a collection of mementos from the neighborhood, and retraces the history of the area from the Abbey through the Paris Commune and into the 20th century. Great artists such as Duffy, van Gogh, Renoir, and Suzanne Valadon and her son, Utrillo, occupied this house at the end of the 19th century, and it was here that Renoir put the final touches to his famous *Moulin de la Galette*. Open Wednesday to Sunday 11am to 6pm.

From the museum turn right on rue Cortot. Make another right onto rue des Saules. On your right you'll see:

9 MONTMARTRE VINEYARD

The Benedictine Abbey that was founded in Montmartre in the 12th century encouraged the plantation of vines. Two centuries later they covered the hills of Montmartre, and wine remained one of this area's main sources of income until the 19th century. This vineyard was planted in 1933 to oppose construction that had been planned in the neighborhood. It produces gamay and pinot noir grape varieties, and a grape-harvesting festival called *la Fête des Vendanges,* is held in Montmartre every October.

A street performer in Montmartre.

At the intersection of rue des Saules with rue St-Vincent is one of the most visited and photographed corners of **la butte**. Here, on one corner, sits the famous:

10 AU LAPIN AGILE

This villagelike house opened as a cabaret in 1860. Owned by the Sals family, it was known as the Cabaret des Assassins. Madame Sals was an excellent cook, renowned for her *lapin gibelotte* (rabbit casserole). Around 1800, the satirical artist André Gill created a sign featuring a rabbit jumping out of a casserole dish, brandishing a bottle of wine (you can see the original in the Musée Montmartre). The cabaret was given the name Le Lapin à Gill, after the artist, which gradually became **Au Lapin Agile.** All of the Montmartre artists used to come here to sing and play the guitar, including Picasso, Utrillo, Braque, Modigliani, Apollinaire, and Jacob.

Turn left on rue St-Vincent. At Place Constantin-Pecqueur climb up the stairs. Go straight ahead along rue Girardon. At the junction with rue Lepic is the:

11 MOULIN DE LA GALETTE

This windmill is known as the **Moulin Radet**, and is now part of a restaurant. Around the corner on rue Lepic is the **Moulin Blute Fin.** Built in the 17th century, these windmills were used to produce flour until the late 19th century, when they became dance halls. People came to sing, dance, and eat *galettes* (a type of crepe), and as a result each of the windmills became known as a Moulin de la Galette. It was the Blute-Fin that was immortalized in oil in Renoir's *Le Moulin de la Galette* (the painting is now in the Musée d'Orsay). Toulouse-Lautrec, van Gogh, Picasso, and Utrillo were also regulars at the dance halls.

Turn right onto rue Lepic (the Blute-Fin is opposite no. 88) and continue to no. 54. From 1886 to 1888, van Gogh lived here with his beloved brother, Theo. It was during this period that he first discovered Impressionism. Follow the street as it winds down the hill toward the Boulevard.

12 Café des Deux Moulins ☕

Most of the restaurants around Place du Tertre are unabashed tourist traps. If you're looking for somewhere more authentic to eat and drink, head toward rue des Abbesses or rue Lepic, where there are a number of nice cafes and restaurants. Named after the two surviving windmills, the **Café des Deux Moulins,** 15 rue Lepic**,** 18e (✆ **01-42-54-90-50**), has charming 1950s decor, mirrored walls, and Art Deco details. It became a neighborhood icon when it featured in the 2001 film *Amélie,* starring Audrey Tautou. Serving traditional French food and open daily from 7am to 2am, this cafe is worth a visit.

Follow the street until it meets Boulevard de Clichy. To the right is:

13 MOULIN ROUGE

Established in 1889, Le Moulin Rouge was named after the local windmills and the huge wooden windmill built above the entrance. The cabaret soon gained a reputation for highly provocative dancing, most notably the cancan. The French actress and singer Mistinguett began her career here in *La Revue de Femme* in 1907. The Moulin Rouge was immortalized in the artwork of Toulouse-Lautrec and in Baz Luhrmann's 2001 film, *Moulin Rouge.* The windmill and the cancan are still here, but the rest has become an expensive, slick variety show with an emphasis on undraped women. See p. 278.

Moulin Rouge.

WALKING TOUR 2: **THE LATIN QUARTER**

START:	**Boulevard St-Michel (Métro: Cluny).**
FINISH:	**St-Étienne-du-Mont (nearest Métro: Cardinal Lemoine).**
TIME:	**1½ hours (not including stops). The distance is about 2km (1¼ miles).**
BEST TIME:	**Monday to Saturday from 11am to 11pm.**
WORST TIME:	**Sunday morning, when everybody else is asleep.**

One of the oldest areas of Paris, the 5th arrondissement was the heart of Roman Paris during the Roman occupation of France (from the 1st c. B.C. to the 5th c. A.D.). You can still see traces of this period as you walk around. It became known as the Latin Quarter during the Middle Ages, when most of its residents were either students or clergymen who spoke Latin. Long associated with education and learning, it is here that you'll find the most famous branch of the Université de Paris, the Sorbonne, and the prestigious Collège de France. However, the revolutionary days of May '68 are long gone, and although the 5th has retained a certain degree of youthful charm and romance, parts of it have become very touristy.

1 **BOULEVARD ST-MICHEL**

Nicknamed Boul' Mich by locals, this is the main street of the Latin Quarter. Opened in 1855, Boulevard St-Michel was one of the first boulevards to be built under Baron Haussmann, the man responsible for the modernization and redevelopment of Paris in the 19th century. Haussmann wanted the city to be organized around a huge central crossroads, called *la grande croisée,* at the center of which was Place du Châtelet. The rue de Rivoli was the east-west axis, Boulevard Sebastopol the northern axis, and Boulevard St-Michel achieved the southern leg. Just over a century later, the student uprisings of May '68 began here. The Latin Quarter was suddenly full of would-be revolutionaries, and residents witnessed violent clashes between protesters and police.

5

STROLLING AROUND PARIS

The Latin Quarter

At the junction of Boulevard St-Michel and Boulevard St-Germain, head north until you reach:

2 PLACE ST-MICHEL

At the center of the Place St-Michel is the huge fountain built by Gabriel Davioud in 1860, featuring a sculpture of Saint Michel slaying the dragon. This was the scene of frequent skirmishes between the Germans and the Resistance in the summer of 1944, and there is a plaque dedicated to those who fought here in front of the fountain. This is a popular meeting place, and the square is often full of amateur break-dancers and street performers.

Place St-Michel.

Cross Boulevard St-Michel and go down:

3 RUE DE LA HUCHETTE

This street is now one of the most touristy streets in Paris, and you should avoid the fast food and Greek-style restaurants down here. However,

Rue de la Huchette.

Walking Tour 2: The Latin Quarter

ÎLE DE LA CITÉ

1e

4e

6e

start here

5e

LATIN QUARTER

finish here

1 Boulevard St-Michel
2 Place St-Michel
3 Rue de la Huchette
4 Rue du Chat-qui-Pêche
5 St-Séverin
6 St-Julien-le-Pauvre
7 La Fourmi Ailée 🍴
8 Musée de Cluny
9 Sorbonne
10 Panthéon
11 St-Étienne-du-Mont

walking along this narrow street will give you an idea of what Paris looked like during the Middle Ages, when most Parisian streets were between 2 and 5m (6½–16 ft.) wide. Few streets like this one remain. At no. 23 is the tiny **Théâtre de la Huchette,** which is famous for having shown Eugene Ionesco's absurdist double bill of *The Lesson* and *The Bald Soprano* continuously since 1957. At no. 5 is the legendary jazz club **Caveau de la Huchette.** Established in 1946, this was the first club in Paris where jazz was played, and jazz legends such as Sidney Bechet and Lionel Hampton have played here.

Before you reach No. 5, branching off rue de la Huchette to your left is:

4 RUE DU CHAT-QUI-PÊCHE

This tiny alleyway is said to be the narrowest street in Paris, and also dates back to the Middle Ages. Before the *quai* was built, the Seine sometimes flooded the cellars of the houses, and legend has it that an enterprising cat took advantage of its good fortune and went fishing in the confines of the cellars—hence the street's name, which means "Street of the Cat Who Fishes."

Rue du Chat-qui-Pêche.

At the end of rue de la Huchette, turn right up rue du Petit Pont and continue to:

5 ST-SÉVERIN

Named after a 6th-century hermit, St-Séverin was built from 1210 to 1230 and reconstructed in 1448. Before entering, walk around the church to examine the gargoyles, birds of prey, and reptilian monsters projecting from its roof. These features explain why this church is an example of Flamboyant Gothic architecture. The bell tower is home to the oldest bell in Paris, which dates back to 1412, and next door is the city's only remaining charnel house, a place which houses the bones and bodies of the dead.

Where rue du Petit Pont becomes rue St-Jacques, cross over the street to rue Galande and look back over your shoulder at the spires of St-Séverin. Then turn back to the small church in front of you:

6 ST-JULIEN-LE-PAUVRE

A chapel has stood on this spot since the 6th century, but the current church dates back to the 12th century. It's now owned by the followers of the Melchite Greek rite, a branch of the Byzantine church. St-Julien-le-Pauvre is known for putting on great classical concerts—if you're interested, there are posters near the door. The garden in front of the church has the best view of Notre-Dame and is home to the oldest tree in Paris; it's an acacia tree that was brought to Paris from Guyana in 1680 (it's fenced off and supported).

Continue along rue Galande and turn left down rue du Fouarre to:

7 La Fourmi Ailée ♨

At no. 8 rue du Fouarre is **La Fourmi Ailée** (*(C* **01-43-29-40-99**), a charming restaurant and tea room. Because it has clouds painted on the ceiling and books lining the walls, you're bound to leave here feeling calm, refreshed, and inspired. Open for lunch and dinner, and serving tea all day, La Fourmi Ailée serves typical French cuisine with a surprising number of good vegetarian options. Open daily noon to midnight.

As you leave the cafe, backtrack along rue du Fouarre, which turns into rue Danté. At the junction, turn right onto Boulevard St Germain. Turn left on rue de Cluny until you come to Place Paul Painlevé.

8 MUSÉE DE CLUNY

Even if you're not particularly interested in medieval history and the origins of Paris, it's worth dropping into the Musée de Cluny to see the allegorical *The Lady and the Unicorn* tapestries and the remains of the Roman baths. See p. 130.

With the museum behind you, cross the square to rue des Écoles, where you'll see the main entrance to the Sorbonne. Don't forget to look back and admire the Musée de Cluny from afar.

9 SORBONNE

One of the most famous academic institutions in the world, the Sorbonne was founded in 1253 by Robert de Sorbon, St. Louis's confessor, as a theology college. By the next century it had become the most prestigious university in the West, attracting such professors as Thomas Aquinas and Roger Bacon, and such students as Dante, Calvin, and Longfellow. Following May 1968, when the Sorbonne was occupied by rebellious students, the University of Paris was split up into different faculties located in different parts of Paris. The current building dates from the early 1900s, and if you look at the side of the building on rue St-Jacques, you can see the names of the different academic subjects inscribed above the windows.

From rue des Écoles, turn right up rue St-Jacques. When you reach rue Soufflot, turn left. At the street's end is Place du Panthéon:

10 PANTHÉON

Sitting atop Mont St-Geneviève, this former church is now a nonreligious mausoleum, and the final resting place of such distinguished figures as Hugo, Zola, Rousseau, Voltaire, Curie. See p. 133.

Facing the Panthéon, walk around the left-hand side of the building until you come to Place Ste-Geneviève. In front of you is:

The Sorbonne.

St-Étienne-du-Mont.

11 ST-ÉTIENNE-DU-MONT

This church is home to a very elaborate shrine dedicated to Saint Geneviève, one of Paris's two patron saints. In 451, Attila the Hun was threatening to enter Paris. The city's elders advised people to flee, but a young woman named Geneviève encouraged them to remain and fight. Miraculously, Attila chose not to come to Paris and Geneviève was credited with saving the city. This church also contains Paris's only rood screen (a fancy wooden screen that divides the chancel and the nave). The church itself was built between 1492 and 1626, and is thus a curious mix of Gothic and Renaissance architecture.

To get to Métro Cardinal Lemoine, go past the church along rue Clovis and turn left onto rue du Cardinal Lemoine.

WALKING TOUR 3: THE MARAIS

START:	**Hôtel de Ville (Métro: Hôtel de Ville).**
FINISH:	**Métro Saint Paul.**
TIME:	**2½ hours (not including stops). The walk is about 4km (2½ miles).**
BEST TIME:	**Every day, during the day. Sunday is a very popular day to visit the Marais.**
WORST TIME:	**Toward dusk, when shops and museums are closed and it's too dark to admire the architectural details. Also, Saturday is the Jewish Sabbath so the area around rue des Rosiers can be quite quiet.**

By the late 16th century, the marshy area east of the Louvre was the only part of central Paris that remained undeveloped. It wasn't until the 17th century that the Marais (meaning marsh) became one of Paris's choicest neighborhoods. This was largely thanks to Henri IV, who commissioned the building of Place des Vosges in 1605. The success of the square made the Marais a fashionable area for the aristocracy and led to the construction of many *hôtels particuliers* (mansions) in the surrounding neighborhood. However, the popularity of the Marais began to wane towards the end of the 17th century when Louis XIV moved his court to Versailles, and after the Revolution, the once-elegant *hôtels* deteriorated into working-class tenements. In 1969, the Marais was the first district of Paris to be declared a historic district by Culture Minister André Malraux. This led to the restoration of its *hôtels,* which today are museums, archives, and libraries.

Today, the Marais (which covers the 3rd and 4th arrondissements) is trendy again, and loved by visitors and residents alike. It's a great area for window-shopping at trendy boutiques, up-and-coming galleries, and eclectic stores, and it's one of the few neighborhoods where shops are open on Sundays. It's long been a center for Paris's Jewish community and you'll find Jewish shops and businesses around rues des Rosiers, Pavée, and des Écouffes. More recently, it has become Paris's center of gay and lesbian life, particularly on rues St-Croix-de-la-Bretonnerie, des Archives, and Vieille-du-Temple.

1   **HÔTEL DE VILLE**

In 1532, François I commissioned an Italian architect to build a prestigious town hall in the Renaissance style. However, due to the Wars of Religion the building wasn't finished until 1628. During the Paris Commune the Hôtel de Ville was set on fire and it burned for 8 days, destroying all the art works,

Hôtel de Ville.

state registers, and archives inside. However, almost as soon as it was destroyed, the new government—the Third Republic—decided to construct a newer, grander building with a reproduction of the Renaissance façade. The building you can see today was inaugurated on July 13, 1882, but it looks much the same as it would have in 1628. The facade is decorated with 378 works by 230 sculptors, including Rodin. During the summer there are often screenings of big sporting events in front of the Hôtel de Ville, and in the winter the square is home to Paris's most popular ice rink.

With your back to Hôtel de Ville, walk left. Turn left at the quai and walk along the river and then turn left again onto rue Lobau. On your right you'll come to Place Saint Gervais:

2 EGLISE ST-GERVAIS-ST-PROTAIS

Named after the twins Gervais and Protais who were martyred in Milan under the rule of Emperor Nero, this is one of the oldest parishes on the Right Bank. The church was built in 1494 and typifies the late Gothic style. The facade, however, was added much later—in 1616—and is an example of early French classicism. On March 29, 1918, the church was hit by a German shell and 88 people were killed when the roof collapsed. This was the worst single incident involving a loss of civilian lives during the German bombardment of Paris in 1918.

To better admire the Gothic parts of the St-Gervais, turn right down rue de Brosse and then left onto rue de l'Hôtel de Ville. When you reach rue des Barres, turn left and you'll find yourself at the back of the church. Continue up the street until you reach rue François Miron. Turn right and walk along this street.

3 RUE FRANÇOIS MIRON

At **no. 11** and **no. 13** are two half-timbered houses that were built in the 14th century. You'll see a plaque on the front of each one; no. 11 was known as the *Maison à l'enseigne du Faucheur* (the house with the sign of the reaper) and no. 13 was the *Maison à l'enseigne du Mouton* (the house with the sign of the sheep). These names refer to hand-painted signs, which date from the 13th century, and were used to locate buildings before street signs and house numbers existed. Both buildings are perfect examples of gabled houses with their narrow facades, ground floors built from stone, and half-timbered upper stories, and they give us an insight into what Parisian houses would have looked like during the Middle Ages.

If you cross over to the other side of the street and continue until no. 68, you'll see the facade of the:

4 HÔTEL DE BEAUVAIS

In the 13th century the Cistercian Abbey of Chaalis (Oise) used this building as a town house when the monks traveled to Paris. In 1654, Pierre de Beauvais and his wife Catherine-Henriette Bellier moved here, having commissioned an architect to build them a sumptuous *hôtel*. The *hôtel* was inaugurated on August 26, 1660, when Louis XIV and his new wife, Marie-Thérèse, entered Paris. Anne of Austria (Louis's mother), Cardinal Mazarin, and the queen of England all stood on the balcony here to watch

Walking Tour 3: The Marais

Musée d'Art et d'Histoire du Judaïsme

Archives Nationales

Musée de l'Histoire de France

Musée Picasso — 13

Centre Pompidou

3e

place de Thorigny

start here — 1

place de l'Hôtel de Ville

Hôtel de Ville — 1

MARAIS — 12

4e

15 — r. des

14 — Rosiers

16

finish here — St-Paul

place des Vosges square Louis XIII — 9

11

3 — François Miron

2

4

St-Paul

8

10

ÎLE DE LA CITÉ

Cathédrale Notre-Dame

5

6

7

Seine

ÎLE ST-LOUIS

1 Hôtel de Ville	**6** Philippe Auguste Wall	**12** Musée Carnavalet
2 Eglise St-Gervais-St-Protais	**7** Village St-Paul	**13** Musée Picasso
3 Rue François Miron	**8** Hôtel de Sully	**14** Rue des Rosiers
4 Hôtel de Beauvais	**9** Place des Vosges	**15** Chez Hanna
5 Hôtel de Sens	**10** Maison de Victor Hugo	**16** Rue Pavée
	11 Rue des Francs-Bourgeois	

Pedestrians only
Ⓜ Métro station
⊠ Post office

0 — 200 yds
0 — 200 m

the procession as it came down rue François Miron. If the doors are open, go in and admire the courtyard.

From here you need to backtrack along the rue François Miron until you come to rue de Jouy. Turn left down this street and continue until you come to a junction. Cross over the street onto rue Charlemagne and turn right almost immediately onto rue du Figuier. At no. 1 is:

5 HÔTEL DE SENS

Now home to a public library, this building is one of only two civil buildings from the Middle Ages still standing in Paris (the other is the Hôtel de Cluny). Until 1622, Paris was a diocese that was dependent on the

171

Hôtel de Sens.

archdiocese of Sens in Burgundy, and when the archbishops of Sens came to Paris, they stayed in this *hôtel,* built between 1498 and 1507. One of the *hôtel's* most famous residents was Marguerite de Valois, whose life inspired Alexandre Dumas's 1845 novel *La Reine Margot.* Daughter of Henri II and Catherine de Medici, she married Henri de Navarre (who became Henri IV) in 1572. Their marriage was later annulled by the Pope, and Henri IV married Marie de Medici in 1600. After a long exile, Marguerite de Valois returned to Paris in 1605 and lived in the Hôtel de Sens for a year. Known for her great beauty, she scandalized society by having numerous affairs with younger men. The gates of the **Bibliothèque Forney (© 01-42-78-14-60)** are open Tuesday to Saturday 1 to 7pm.

At the junction of rue Figuier and rue du Fauconnier, cross rue du Fauconnier and go down rue de l'Ave Maria. Turn left onto rue des Jardins St-Paul. Behind the basketball courts is the:

6 PHILIPPE AUGUSTE WALL

An extraordinary piece of the Philippe Auguste Wall, which includes a small tower, has been conserved in the Marais. Before departing for the crusades in 1190, King Philippe Auguste wanted to assure that Paris was properly defended, so he ordered the construction of a wall around the city. Over the centuries the wall gradually expanded as Paris flourished. The old walls were torn down and new ones were constructed, the last of which were the Thiers Fortifications (built 1841–44); this wall ran around the edge of Paris's 20 arrondissements. In the 1960s, after the Thiers Fortifications had been torn down, the vacant land was used to build the ring road that runs around Paris, known as the *périph*. Thus, there has been a physical boundary separating Paris and its suburbs since the 12th century. The Philippe Auguste Wall was constructed with limestone dating from the Lutetian era (43–49 million years ago). At that time Paris had a tropical climate with palm trees, crocodiles, and exotic fish, and fossils of crustaceans and mollusks have been found in the stone.

Turn right into the courtyard at the green sign advertising the Village St-Paul:

7 VILLAGE ST-PAUL

Based around several adjoining courtyards, the Village St-Paul is a collection of small art galleries, quirky shops, and trendy cafes and restaurants. In the 1360s Charles V built himself a royal residence here, the Hôtel Saint-Pol. Charles believed that the *hôtel's* proximity to both the Bastille prison and the Philippe Auguste Wall would guarantee its security. This residence remained popular with the monarchy until the reign of François I, who couldn't bear its proximity to the nearby sewers. The *hôtel* was abandoned in 1543. Today, this is one of the most peaceful corners of the Marais and a great place to wander around if you're looking for an unusual gift.

After you've explored, leave through the archway opposite to the one by which you entered. You'll come out onto rue St-Paul. Turn left up this street, admiring the variety of shops on your way. Look out for the English-language bookshop The Red Wheelbarrow at no. 22. Turn right onto rue Saint-Antoine. If you cross the road, at no. 62 you'll see:

8 HÔTEL DE SULLY

Designed by Jean Androuet de Cerceau in 1624, the Hôtel de Sully is typical of the late French Renaissance style. The Duc de Sully, Henri IV's minister of finance, bought the building in 1634. After a strait-laced life as the "accountant of France," Sully broke loose in his declining years, adorning himself with garish jewelry and a young bride who had a fondness for very young men. The *hôtel* was bought by the state in 1944 and is now home to the *Centre des Monuments Nationaux*, which preserves historic monuments across France. Open daily from 9am to 7pm.

The Hôtel de Sully has two courtyards. At the far-right corner of the second courtyard there is an arch (opening hours are the same as Hôtel de Sully) that leads to:

9 PLACE DES VOSGES

The square was commissioned by Henri IV in 1605 but when he died in 1610 it was not yet finished. It was inaugurated in 1612 for the double wedding of Louis XIII to Anne of Austria and Elisabeth of France (the king's sister) to the future Philippe IV of Spain—that's why there's a statue of Louis XIII hidden among the trees in the center of the square's formal garden. Place des Vosges was the first public square in Paris. Henri IV told his courtiers that they could come and build their houses around the square, but that they had to respect certain rules, such as using brick (which was, and still is, quite unusual in Paris). But the aristocrats wanted to cut corners and you'll notice that some of the arcaded pavilions are not made from brick but painted plaster. The square was named Place Royale until the Revolution, when it became Place d'Indivisibilité. In 1799 it was renamed Place des Vosges after the *département* of Vosges that raised the most taxes for the revolutionary wars.

10 MAISON DE VICTOR HUGO

The square's most famous resident was undoubtedly Victor Hugo. Hugo lived at no. 6 from 1832 to 1848, when he went into voluntary exile on the Channel Islands after the rise of Napoleon III. It was here that he began his masterpiece *Les Misérables*. Hugo's former home is now a museum (✆ **01-42-72-10-16;** www.musee-hugo.paris.fr) and literary shrine.

If you leave the Place des Vosges by its northwest corner, you'll find yourself on:

11 RUE DES FRANCS-BOURGEOIS

One of the key arteries running through the Marais, the rue des Francs-Bourgeois marks the border between the 3rd and 4th arrondissements. Jack Kerouac suggested that the name meant "street of the outspoken middle-classes" but it actually refers to the *francs bourgeois*—poor members of the bourgeoisie who were exempt from paying taxes. You won't find many poor people here today though, as the rue des Francs-Bourgeois is one of the chicest streets in the Marais, full of elegant boutiques and designer brands. Some of the shops have retained their original façades; check out the pretty "boulangerie" at no. 23.

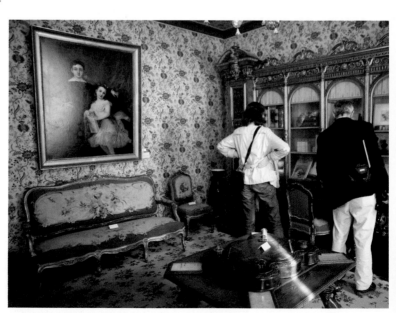

A room in the Maison de Victor Hugo

Musée Carnavalet.

At the junction with rue de Sévigné, turn right. On your left you'll see the:

12 MUSÉE CARNAVALET

This 16th-century mansion is the most important and well-known of all the Renaissance *hôtels* in the Marais. It is now a museum (℡ 01-44-59-58-58; www.paris.fr) dedicated to the history of Paris and the French Revolution (p. 100). The entrance is on rue de Sévigné.

Turn right up rue Payenne and then left onto rue du Parc Royal. You'll come to Place de Thorigny. If you turn right up rue Thorigny on your left you'll see:

13 MUSÉE PICASSO

The museum occupies the Hôtel Salé (*salé* means salty) and the name comes from the *hôtel's* first owner Pierre Aubert de Fontenay, who was responsible for collecting the salt tax. The museum is closed until spring 2012 for renovations so check on its status at the time of your visit (℡ 01-42-71-25-21; www.musee-picasso.fr).

Backtrack along rue Thorigny, and turn right onto rue de la Perle. Turn left on rue Vieille du Temple. Cross the rue des Francs-Bourgeois, passing a covered market called the Marché des Blancs Manteaux on your left. Turn left into:

14 RUE DES ROSIERS

This street, which was named after the rosebushes planted in neighboring gardens, is one of the most colorful and popular streets of the Marais. It has been the historic heart of Jewish Paris since the 12th century, and you'll find an intriguing blend of Ashkenazi and Sephardic traditions. Here you'll see

Rue des Rosiers.

everything from Eastern European bakeries to North African falafel restaurants. Sephardic Jews from North Africa have sought refuge here since the end of WWII and the collapse of the French colonial empire. To a certain degree, they replenished Paris's Jewish population, a significant proportion of whom were rounded up by the Nazis and the French police and deported to concentration camps during WWII. Like many streets in the Marais, the rue des Rosiers has become quite a trendy place to shop in recent years and you'll find a number of nice boutiques here.

15 Falafel Break ☕

The rue des Rosiers is famous for its delicious falafel. If it's summer, you can get falafel to go and continue your exploration of the Marais, pita bread in hand. But if you'd like to sit down, try **Chez Hanna** (54 rue des Rosiers; ℓ **01-42-74-74-99;** see picture). The menu is full of Jewish specialties, there's a friendly atmosphere, and the food is very reasonably priced. Open Tuesday to Sunday 11am to midnight.

At the end of rue des Rosiers, turn right onto rue Pavée.

16 RUE PAVÉE

This street dates from the Middle Ages. It got its current name in 1450 when it became one of the first streets to be paved over. At **no. 10** is the **Agoudas Hakehilos Synagogue,** built by Art Nouveau architect Hector Guimard (who was also responsible for designing the Paris Métro) in 1913. The building of this synagogue really tested Guimard's skills as an architect because he had to work with a piece of land measuring only 5m by 23m (16×75 ft.). To give the impression of a more ample facade, he built continuous pilasters (slightly projecting columns) and narrow windows.

Continue down the rue Pavée and you'll come to Métro St-Paul.

WHERE TO EAT

By Meg Zimbeck,
with Barbra Austin

P aris has always been a haven for high-rolling gastro-nomes who collect luxury restaurants like playing cards. That's still the case today. Whether you're looking for an opulent culinary experience or edgy, provocative cook-ing, Paris's range of quality restaurants—from three-star restaurants to casual bistros—remains unmatched by any other city in the world.

Although Paris has long been home to high end gourmet restaurants, a growing number of affordable, high-end bistros serving gourmet food have entered Paris's culinary scene—this is the bistronomy movement. For more than a decade now, chefs who have trained under three-star chefs have been leaving these "palace" restaurants to open more reasonably priced neo-bistrots, where you can get a three-course meal for about 30€ to 40€. Combining classic technique with an emphasis on fresh, seasonal ingredients, this new generation of chefs is revital-izing the culinary scene.

One important challenge remains, even at the informal bistro level: getting in. Paris restaurants tend to be small in size, and they rarely offer multiple seat-ings during a lunch or dinner service. The result is a smaller number of available seats, and these are often reserved in advance. Reservations are a very good idea at most of the restaurants we recommend, but you needn't worry about booking weeks in advance. The majority will have space if you call the same day or a few days in advance. Ask your hotel concierge to help if you can't manage the tele-phone, but don't shy away from this step if food is an important part of your Paris visit. The quality of what you can "stumble in" and find, versus what you can experience when you reserve, is radically different.

best RESTAURANT BETS

o **Best for Romance**: **Lasserre** (p. 194), with its over-the-top opulence and retractable ceiling, is an obvious setting for romance. A more affordable romantic option is **La Crèmerie** (p. 218), an old milk shop-turned-wine bar on the left bank, with beautiful tiles and an intimate atmosphere.

o **Best for Families**: For kids who are tired of tasting new things, **Breakfast in America** (p. 214) is a haven of recognizable favorites like hamburgers, milk-shakes, and all-day breakfast. Set inside the city's biggest park, **Rosa Bon-heur** (p. 210) allows parents to sample various tapas on a large, outdoor terrace while their kids play in the park.

o **Best Splurge**: **Passage 53** (p. 182), inside the city's oldest covered passage-way, is bursting with postcard charm—it also has delicious, yet modern, cui-sine, and it just received its second Michelin star. Among the three-star Michelin splurges, we're most taken with **L'Arpège** (p. 219).

o **Best Value**: Located just a few blocks from each other in the Marais, the **Breizh Café** (p. 190) and the **Café des Musées** (p. 188), are the places to

PRICE CATEGORIES

Very Expensive	Main dishes 50€ and up
Expensive	Main dishes 30€–50€
Moderate	Main dishes 15€–30€
Inexpensive	Main dishes Under 15€

go when you want to fill up on authentic French comfort food for under 20€ a head.

o **Best Service**: Of all the lavish three-star restaurants in Paris, **Guy Savoy** (p. 194) is widely thought to have the most warm and gracious service. On the other side of town, and the other end of the gastronomic spectrum, the restaurant **Fish** (p. 215) is always a warm and friendly place to go, and the largely expatriate waitstaff are a great help for those who don't speak French.

o **Best Classic Bistro**: In a city with so many excellent bistros, it's difficult to choose a favorite, but we'll narrow it down to **Le Régalade** (p. 215), **Le Bistrot Paul Bert** (p. 208), and **Chez l'Ami Jean** (p. 222). Book in advance for any of these three.

o **Best for Sunday Dinner**: Many restaurants in Paris are closed on Sundays, but **L'Atelier de Joël Robuchon** (p. 198) is open every day of the year, and **Goumard** (p. 182), also open on Sundays, is a fun place to indulge in some fresh oysters.

o **Best Steak Frites**: Run by a former butcher, **Le Severo** (p. 227) serves some of the city's best steak frites, along with *côtes de boeuf,* and other massive cuts of beef. **Le Relais de L'Entrecôte** (p. 218) is a fun dining option that serves multiple refills of steak and fries.

o **Best for Young, Inventive Chefs**: The top restaurants for innovative and modern French cuisine are **Le Chateaubriand** (p. 206), **Frenchie** (p. 184), and **Saturne** (p. 183). Book a few weeks in advance if you want a taste of what's new in Paris.

o **Best for Wine Enthusiasts**: If what's in your glass is just as important as what's on the plate, we recommend a visit to **Le Verre Volé** (p. 203), **Les Papilles** (p. 214), **Vivant** (p. 203), **Le Chapeau Melon** (p. 210), or **Le Baratin** (p. 210)—all of these places take wine seriously.

THE RIGHT BANK
Les Halles, Louvre & Palais Royal (1er & 2e)

Les Halles takes its name from the soaring food pavilions that once stood on this spot as part of the city's largest outdoor market. That market, which writer Émile Zola famously nicknamed "the belly of Paris," has since moved to the suburbs, but Les Halles still has plenty of gourmet offerings today. Three of the city's most heralded newcomers—Yam'Tcha, Spring, and La Régalade–St. Honoré—have opened here in recent years. Just to the north, the 2nd arrondissement has also become a hotbed of restaurant activity, with Saturne, Frenchie, and Passage 53 drawing foodies from all across the city.

Restaurants near Les Halles, the Louvre & Palais Royal (1er & 2e)

Au Pied de Cochon **17**
Aux Lyonnais **7**
Carré des Feuillants **2**
Chez Georges **15**
Coinstôt Vino **10**
Frenchie **13**
Goumard **1**
Juveniles **4**
La Régalade-
St. Honoré **19**
La Tour de Monthléry
(Chez Denise) **21**
Le Grand Véfour **5**
Le Vaudeville **11**
L'Hédoniste **14**

Macéo **6**
Olio Pane Vino **16**
Passage 53 **9**
Pinxo **3**
Racines **8**
Saturne **12**
Spring **20**
Yam'Tcha **18**

Pedestrians only
Ⓜ Metro station
RER RER station
⊠ Post office

VERY EXPENSIVE

Carré des Feuillants MODERN FRENCH   When chef Alain Dutournier turned this 17th-century convent between the place Vendôme and the Tuileries into a restaurant, it was an overnight success. The interior is artfully simple and has a vaguely Asian feel, with a series of small, monochromatic dining rooms that are mostly outfitted in tones of off-white and black overlooking a flowering courtyard and a glass-enclosed kitchen. You'll find a sophisticated reinterpretation of cuisine from France's southwest, using seasonal ingredients and lots of know-how. Some of the best dishes include roasted rack of milk-fed Pyrenees lamb cooked in a clay pot, or slices of John Dory with potatoes and tender cabbage lasagna. Milk-fed veal with flap mushrooms and purple artichokes is yet another specialty. For dessert try the mango and passion fruit ravioli.

14 rue de Castiglione (near place Vendôme and the Tuileries), 1er. ℂ **01-42-86-82-82.** www.carredesfeuillants.fr. Reservations required far in advance. Main courses 70€–88€; tasting menus 160€–200€. AE, DC, MC, V. Mon–Fri noon–2:30pm and 7:30–10pm. Closed Aug. Métro: Tuileries, Concorde, Opéra, or Madeleine.

Le Grand Véfour TRADITIONAL FRENCH   Tucked inside the Palais Royal and boasting one of the most beautiful restaurant interiors in Paris, Le Grand Véfour remains a history-infused citadel of classic French cuisine. This restaurant has been around since the reign of Louis XV. Napoleon, Danton, Hugo, Colette, and Cocteau dined here—as the brass plaques on the tables testify—and it's still a gastronomic experience. Guy Martin, chef for the past decade, continues to serve the restaurant's signature dishes like Prince Rainier III pigeon and truffled oxtail parmentier alongside new dishes that feature more contemporary flavors like yuzu and tonka bean. Other specialties are noisettes of lamb with star anise, Breton lobster with fennel, and cabbage sorbet in dark-chocolate sauce. The desserts are often grand, such as the *gourmandises au chocolat* (medley of chocolate), served with chocolate sorbet.

17 rue de Beaujolais, 1er. ℂ **01-42-96-56-27.** www.grand-vefour.com. Reservations required far in advance. Main courses 75€–125€; fixed-price lunch 88€; fixed-price dinner 268€. AE, DC, MC, V. Mon–Fri 12:30–1:45pm and 8–9:30pm. Closed Aug 2–30. Métro: Louvre–Palais-Royal or Pyramides.

EXPENSIVE

Goumard SEAFOOD   Opened in 1872, this landmark is one of Paris's leading seafood restaurants, with much of its seafood arriving daily from Brittany. Seafood platters—laden with mussels, crabs, shrimp, and many different oysters—are a specialty here. Fresh fish, such as Dover sole with buttery potatoes, and roasted lobster with celery root purée and chestnut cream, are other delicious options. With polished wooden panels and a collection of Lalique crystal fish in artificial aquariums, the decor creates the impression of being on a transatlantic ocean liner. The unusual restrooms, with commodes designed by Art Nouveau master cabinetmaker Majorelle, have been classified as a historic monument.

9 rue Duphot, 1er. ℂ **01-42-60-36-07.** www.goumard.com. Reservations required far in advance. Main courses 29€–82€; fixed-price menus 39€ and 59€. AE, DC, MC, V. Daily 11:30am–12:30am. Métro: Madeleine or Concorde.

Passage 53 ★★ MODERN FRENCH   After a stint at L'Astrance (p. 195), chef Shinichi Sato joined forces with famous butcher Hugo Desnoyer to open this petite restaurant inside the city's oldest covered passage. Start with a splash of Jacquesson Champagne before diving into a tasting menu that might begin with pink cubes of raw veal topped with a bracing and briny raw oyster. Up next, you might be served some pristine fish or a *civet* (a type of stew) of wild hare served with chocolate sauce. Flavors are bold and clear, and the technical skill on display is impressive. End the meal with a delicious tart with the thinnest-possible pastry crust.

53 passage des Panoramas, 2e. (**01-42-33-04-35.** www.passage53.com. Reservations recommended. Fixed-price lunch 45€; fixed-price dinner 85€. MC, V. Tues–Sat noon–10 pm. Métro: Grands Boulevards.

Saturne ★★ MODERN FRENCH   The young chef at the helm of this new restaurant is devoted to his ingredients, sourcing them carefully and cooking them with a sense of respectful restraint. Sven Chartier's cooking is bright and fresh, and at times his food looks more similar to Nordic cuisine than the French tradition in which he trained. The blonde wood decor and glass roof create an airy environment where diners can enjoy the sparse compositions, such as mackerel with charred leeks and squid with blinis and oyster mousse. The wine list assembled by sommelier Ewan Lemoigne leans toward natural, organic wines.

17 rue Notre-Dame-des-Victoires, 1er. (**01-42-60-31-90.** Reservations recommended. Fixed-price dinner 37€; fixed-price lunch 35€. MC, V. Mon–Fri noon–2pm and 8–10pm. Métro: Bourse.

Spring ★★ MODERN FRENCH   The most media-hyped restaurant in Paris was created by young American chef Daniel Rose. Spring initially opened in a remote Pigalle location, but after garnering rave reviews from French critics, Rose moved the restaurant to this new space near the Louvre. Today, Spring has a 16th-century wine cave, an underground wine bar with vaulted ceilings, an open kitchen, and a sleek modern dining room. The fixed-price tasting menu is improvisational—it changes nearly every day—but it might begin with a little beignet of fried sole, followed by roasted pigeon or sweetbreads with wild mushrooms. Desserts are deconstructed and usually come in threes—it might be a crustless lemon tart or berries floating in a tea made from the pit of a peach. The wine list is well chosen but it only offers a few moderately priced bottles.

6 rue Bailleul, 1er. (**01-45-96-05-72.** www.springparis.fr. Reservations required. Fixed-price dinner 64€; fixed-price lunch 23€. MC, V. Wed–Fri noon–3pm and 8–10:30pm; Tues and Sat 8–10:30pm. Métro: Louvre-Rivoli.

Yam'Tcha ★★★ MODERN FRENCH/CHINESE   A seat at this modern restaurant, on an ancient side street in Les Halles, is one of the city's most difficult to reserve. That has something to do with the small number of tables, but it is mostly due to the fact that Chef Adeline Grattard has received almost universal acclaim for her Franco-Chinese cooking. After spending time at the Michelin three-starred restaurant L'Astrance, Grattard set out on her own in 2009 and has been solidly booked ever since. The dishes on her prix-fixe menus reflect the seasons and change regularly; a recent menu included a flash-seared lobster with corn coulis, and a bouillon of beef with foie gras that one French critic called "the best dish of the year." Both wine and tea pairings (Yam'Tcha means "drink tea") are available. Reserve a month in advance for lunch and more than three months in advance for dinner.

4 rue Sauval, 1er. (**01-40-26-08-07.** Reservations required far in advance. Fixed-price lunch 50€; fixed-price dinner 85€. AE, MC, V. Métro: Louvre-Rivoli.

MODERATE

Au Pied de Cochon TRADITIONAL FRENCH   Their famous onion soup and namesake specialty (grilled pigs' feet with béarnaise sauce) still lure visitors, and where else in Paris can you get such a good meal at 3am? Other specialties include a platter named after the medieval patron saint of sausage makers, *la temptation de St-Antoine,* which includes grilled pig's tail, pig's snout, and half a pig's foot, all served with béarnaise and french fries and *andouillettes* (chitterling sausages) with béarnaise. Two flavorful but less unusual dishes: a *jarret* (shin) of pork, caramelized in honey and served on a bed of sauerkraut, and grilled pork ribs with sage sauce. On the street outside, you can buy fresh oysters.

6 rue Coquillière, 1er. ✆ **01-40-13-77-00.** www.pieddecochon.com. Main courses 18€–50€. AE, DC, MC, V. Daily 24 hr. Métro: Les Halles or Louvre.

Aux Lyonnais LYONNAIS/TRADITIONAL FRENCH   The Belle Époque interior at this *bouchon* (a Lyon-style bistro) is undeniably charming and provides plenty of postcard appeal for the tourists who populate this restaurant. The kitchen, which is overseen but not frequented by star chef Alain Ducasse, does justice to Lyonnais classics like *quenelles de brochet* (fish dumplings with crayfish sauce) and *tablier de sapeur* (fried breaded tripe). Service, however, can be hurried and robotic—don't be surprised to see a bill slapped down before you've finished your first bite of soufflé.

32 rue St-Marc, 2e. ✆ **01-42-96-65-04.** www.auxlyonnais.com. Reservations required. Main courses 20€–25€; 3-course fixed-price menu 34€. AE, DC, MC, V. Tues–Fri noon–1:30pm and Tues–Sat 7:30–10pm. Métro: Grands-Boulevards.

Chez Georges TRADITIONAL FRENCH   Food writer Alexander Lobrano calls Chez Georges "the gastronomic equivalent of the little black dress—unfailingly correct, politely coquettish, and impeccably Parisian." Until very recently, Chez Georges was managed by three generations of the same family, but the change in management hasn't dampened the restaurant's popularity, and at lunch it's still packed with businesspeople who come for their dose of *la cuisine bourgeoise* (comfort food). Waiters bring around bowls of appetizers, such as celery rémoulade, to get you started. You can follow with grilled turbot in a béarnaise sauce cassoulet, or *pot-au-feu* (beef simmered with vegetables). The sweetbreads with morels and cream are a delight.

1 rue du Mail, 2e. ✆ **01-42-60-07-11.** Reservations required. Main courses 23€–34€. AE, MC, V. Mon–Fri noon–2pm and 7:30–10pm. Métro: Bourse.

Coinstôt Vino WINE BAR   This cool wine bar occupies a corner spot in the historic Passage des Panoramas—Paris's oldest covered passage, if not its prettiest. Stop here for a glass or bottle of "natural" wine—unfiltered and unsulfured—from Guillaume Duprés's eclectic wine list. The menu is made up mainly of small plates; you'll find everything from oysters in season to cheese and charcuterie. There are usually also a few hot dishes. There are tables and counter seats in the main room, as well as some seating out in the passage.

26 passage des Panoramas, 2e. ✆ **01-44-82-08-54.** Reservations recommended. Main courses 15€–35€. MC, V. Mon noon–2pm; Tues–Fri noon–2pm and 6–11pm; Sat 6–11pm. Métro: Grands Boulevards.

Frenchie ★★ 🎁 MODERN FRENCH   Greg Marchand acquired the nickname Frenchie when he left his native France to work for Jamie Oliver in

England and later at New York's Gramercy Tavern. In 2009, Marchand returned to Paris and opened up this tiny bistro in an unfashionable part of the Sentier. Word spread quickly about the delicious and wonderfully priced cuisine, and Frenchie began to win various "Best Bistro" awards and features in magazines. As a result, this simple place requires booking (at least) several months in advance. Marchand's cooking remains astonishingly good. Starters like house-smoked fish with pickled vegetables are bright and clean, and main dishes—like duck with blood orange and dandelion—manage to be both comforting and provocative. Desserts, like a cheesecake composed of *Brillat-Savarin* (a delicious triple cream cheese), are never too sweet.

5 rue du Nil, 2e. 𝄢 **01-40-39-96-19.** www.frenchie-restaurant.com. Reservations required far in advance. Fixed-price dinner 38€. MC, V. Mon–Fri 7–10:30pm. Métro: Sentier.

La Régalade–St. Honoré ★★ TRADITIONAL FRENCH/BISTRO   It used to be that fans of the bistro La Régalade had to travel to the southern edge of the 14th arrondissement in order to enjoy the cooking of Bruno Doucet. Not anymore. In 2010, Doucet opened a second restaurant under the Régalade banner right on the rue Saint-Honoré. Now you can enjoy famously comforting dishes like sautéed morel mushrooms in cream with parsley and crispy croutons or farm-raised pork belly with a creamy interior and crispy skin. Just as at the restaurant down south, the same "help-yourself" crock of homemade pork terrine arrives with *cornichons* (gherkin pickles) and butter as you sit down to the table. Desserts, as you can imagine, are sometimes hard to face after all that pork fat, but they're included in the three-course prix fixe for a remarkable 33€.

123 rue Saint-Honoré, 1er. 𝄢 **01-42-21-92-40.** Reservations required. Fixed-price dinner 33€. MC, V. Mon–Wed noon–2:30pm and 7–10:30pm; Thurs–Fri noon–2:30pm and 7–11:30pm. Métro: Louvre-Rivoli.

La Tour de Montlhéry (Chez Denise) ★★ TRADITIONAL FRENCH/BISTRO   Diners looking for the classic Paris bistro experience come to this raucous old dining room near Les Halles. Chez Denise (as the locals call it) stays open late and serves sturdy platters of *côte de boeuf* (a giant rib steak), grilled marrow bones, and brochettes of grilled meat so long they look like swords. The long-aproned waiters are used to encountering English speakers, but Chez Denise hasn't yet lost its bawdy, authentic local vibe. This might not be, however, the place to bring your vegetarian friend.

5 rue des Prouvaires, 1er. 𝄢 **01-42-36-21-82.** Reservations recommended. Main courses 22€–25€; fixed-price dinner 50€. MC, V. Mon–Fri noon–3pm and 7:30pm–5am. Closed July 15–Aug 15. Métro: Les Halles.

Le Vaudeville BRASSERIE   Adjacent to La Bourse (stock exchange), this brasserie retains its marble walls and Art Deco carvings from 1918. In summer, diners can eat on a terrace adorned with geraniums. The place is boisterous and informal, often welcoming groups of six or eight diners at a time. The roster of platters includes a salad of crayfish and asparagus points, grilled Dover sole, smoked salmon, sauerkraut, and grilled meats—there's even stewed calf's head. Three dishes reign as enduring favorites: fresh grilled codfish with mashed potatoes and truffle juice, fresh *escalope* of warm foie gras with grapes or raspberries, and fresh pasta with morels. While the decor isn't quite as stunning as Bofinger (p. 188), Le Vaudeville is generally thought to have some of the best food among the surviving Paris brasseries.

29 rue Vivienne, 2e. ℂ **01-40-20-04-62.** www.vaudevilleparis.com. Reservations recommended in the evenings. Main courses 16€–30€; fixed-price menu 40€–50€. AE, DC, MC, V. Daily noon–3pm and 7pm–1am. Métro: Bourse.

L'Hédoniste ★ 🍴 MODERN FRENCH   This contemporary restaurant was opened in late 2010 by a French food writer and his wife. The pair renovated a charming spot in the Sentier and brought in Sébastien Dubrulle to run the kitchen. Dubrulle's cooking can be both inventive (marinated sea scallops with radish and turnip) and comforting (duck confit on a bed of whipped potatoes with toasted hazelnuts). The wine list reflects the current demand among Parisians for natural (organic, unadulterated) wine and contains many reasonably priced bottles.

14 rue Léopold Bellan, 2e. ℂ **01-40-26-87-33.** www.lhedoniste.com. Reservations recommended. Main courses 23€–24€. MC, V. Tues–Sat 12:30–2pm and 8–10pm. Métro: Sentier.

Macéo MODERN FRENCH   With a light and airy dining room overlooking the entrance to the Palais Royal, Macéo is a beautiful setting for lunch or dinner. Chef Thierry Bourbonnais produces food that's consistently delicious, like scallops with parsnip purée, leeks, and dates or seared venison with winter vegetables. This place also provides a vegetarian tasting menu—something that's almost unheard of in meat-obsessed Paris. Mark Williamson (who owns the nearby Willi's Wine Bar) has put together an outstanding wine list here. Make time after your meal for a stroll in the gardens of the Palais Royal (p. 90).

15 rue des Petits-Champs, 1er. ℂ **01-42-97-53-85.** www.maceorestaurant.com. Reservations recommended. Main courses 26€–30€; fixed-price dinners at 33€, 38€, and 48€. MC, V. Mon–Fri noon–2pm and 7:30–11pm; Sat 7:30–11pm. Métro: Pyramides.

Pinxo SOUTHWESTERN FRENCH/BISTRO   This is the informal bistro that's associated with Alain Dutournier's much more expensive Carré des Feuillants restaurant (p. 182). At Pinxo, diners are encouraged to use their hands (*pinxo* means "to pinch" in the chef's southwestern dialect) and to share with their tablemates. This is relatively easy because anything that appears on a plate is replicated three times, often with variations. The cuisine is robust and celebrates the prized Aquitaine breed of cow—you can have it grilled, sliced thin as carpaccio, or served with black truffles. Other delicious options include milk-fed lamb from the Pyrenees and a baby squid stuffed with pigs' feet, porcini mushrooms, and cocoa beans. The decor at Pinxo is minimal, with a wooden floor, white walls, and views that extend directly into an all-black open kitchen.

In the Plaza-Paris-Vendôme Hôtel, 9 rue d'Alger, 1er. ℂ **01-40-20-72-00.** www.pinxo.fr. Reservations recommended. Main courses 19€–28€; fixed-price lunch 21€. AE, MC, V. Daily 12:15–2:30pm and 7:15–11:30pm. Métro: Tuileries.

Racines TRADITIONAL FRENCH   Fans of unadulterated wines come here to sip special bottles within the city's oldest covered passage and to enjoy the cooking of Nicolas Gauduin. This young chef, who has passed through the kitchens of l'Arpège and Laurent, selects fresh ingredients and cooks them with restraint. Be sure to book ahead, even at lunchtime, because its proximity to a lot of media headquarters makes Racines a popular hangout for journalists. Well, that, and the wine.

8 passage des Panoramas, 2e. ℂ **01-40-13-06-41.** Reservations recommended. Main courses 20€–35€. MC, V. Mon–Fri noon–2:30pm and 7–10:30pm. Métro: Grands Boulevards.

Can You Dine Badly in Paris?

The answer is an emphatic yes. Our mailbox fills with complaints from readers who've encountered haughty service and paid outrageous prices for swill. Often, these complaints are about restaurants catering to tourists. Avoid them by following our suggestions or looking in nontouristy areas for new discoveries. If you ask Parisians for recommendations, specify that you're looking for restaurants where *they* would dine, not where they think you, as a tourist, would dine.

INEXPENSIVE

Juveniles SCOTTISH/INTERNATIONAL A short stroll from the Louvre and the Opéra, Juveniles is the domain of Tim Johnston, a friendly Scotsman who offers hearty food and one of the most international wine lists in the city. Diners come here for both haggis and traditional French charcuterie, along with cooked sausages and buttery mashed potatoes. The cheeses are pungent, and the food pairs well with the full-bodied Australian and Spanish red wines that are stacked in wooden crates all around. The staff is bilingual and friendly.

47 rue de Richelieu, 1er. ✆ **01-42-97-46-49.** Reservations recommended. Main dishes 8€–18€; tapas from 6€–13€. MC, V. Mon–Sat 7–11pm and Tues–Sat noon–3pm. Métro: Pyramide or Palais Royal.

Olio Pane Vino ITALIAN Francesco, the ruggedly handsome guy who runs this place, is the embodiment of Italian hospitality. He's pretty good in the kitchen, too, turning out new fresh pasta creations each day to satisfy devoted customers who come back regularly. Order a glass of Prosecco and an antipasti platter to start—it might include bresaola with Parmesan, grilled vegetables, or *vitello tonnato* (veal covered in a creamy tuna-flavored cream sauce)—and then choose from one of the several pasta dishes on offer every day. Good tiramisu and a fun crowd make this a hard place to dislike. The central location near Les Halles doesn't hurt either.

44 rue Coquillière, 1er. ✆ **01-42-33-21-15.** Reservations recommended. Main courses 13€–17€. MC, V. Mon–Wed and Sat noon–2:45pm; Thu–Fri noon–2:45pm and 7:45–10:30pm. Métro: Les Halles.

Le Marais, Ile St Louis & Ile de la Cité (3e & 4e)

The Marais is packed with contemporary art galleries and cutting-edge fashion boutiques, but our favorite restaurants in this neighborhood are utterly traditional, whether they're serving the city's best roast chicken (L'Ami Louis) or classic dishes from the Basque region (Au Bascou), Brittany (the Breizh Café), or Provence (Chez Janou). Any stroll through the historic Jewish quarter around the rue des Rosiers requires a stop at L'As du Fallafel for the beloved (and messy) falafel sandwich.

VERY EXPENSIVE

L'Ami Louis ♟ TRADITIONAL FRENCH L'Ami Louis was one of Paris's most famous brasseries in the 1930s, thanks to its excellent French food, like foie gras and roast chicken, served in copious portions and its charming "brown gravy" decor. In more recent years, thanks to regular visits from celebrities and politicians, L'Ami Louis has become a bastion of conspicuous consumption. However, prices are high—Louis boasts the most expensive roast chicken in Paris (78€)—and reservations are hard to come by without the help of a five-star concierge.

32 rue du Vertbois, 3e. ✆ **01-48-87-77-48.** Reservations required far in advance. Main courses 43€–78€. AE, DC, MC, V. Wed–Sun noon–1:30pm and 8–11:30pm. Métro: Temple.

EXPENSIVE

Benoit TRADITIONAL FRENCH   There's something weighty about this historical monument; every mayor of Paris has dined here since the restaurant was founded in 1912. Today Benoit is owned by the Alain Ducasse group, and therefore prices are a bit higher than you'd normally expect for bistro fare, but the food is still delicious. Traditional crowd-pleasers include turbot roasted in the Basque style, filet of sole, and *tête de veau* (head cheese) with a *ravigote* sauce.

20 rue St-Martin, 4e. ✆ **01-42-72-25-76.** Reservations required. Main courses 24€–43€; fixed-price lunch 38€. AE, DC, MC, V. Daily noon–2pm and 7:30–10pm. Métro: Hôtel-de-Ville.

MODERATE

Au Bascou BASQUE   The succulent cuisine of France's "deep southwest" is the specialty here, where art objects, paintings, and tones of ocher celebrate the beauty of the region, and hanging clusters of pimentos add spice to the air. Try *pipérade basquaise* (a spicy omelet loaded with peppers and onions), pimentos stuffed with purée of codfish, and *axoa* (a stew of veal shoulder, peppers, and onions). Also noteworthy are the *soupions* (baby squid) sautéed with chorizo.

38 rue Réaumur, 3e. ✆ **01-42-72-69-25.** Reservations recommended. Main courses 17€; fixed-price lunch menu 19€. AE, DC, MC, V. Mon–Fri noon–2pm and 7:30–10:30pm. Métro: Arts-et-Métiers.

Bofinger 🍴 ALSATIAN/BRASSERIE   Opened in the 1860s, Bofinger is the oldest Alsatian brasserie in town, but it's grown tired and stale over the years. Nevertheless, it's packed every night because of its stunning interior. If the food isn't what it used to be, the atmosphere for some will be worth trekking over here: it's a Belle Époque dining palace, resplendent with brass and stained glass. Affiliated with La Coupole, Julien, and Brasserie Flo, the restaurant has updated its menu but retained the most popular traditional dishes, such as *choucroute* (sauerkraut and sausages) and *sole meunière* (sole in lemon butter sauce). Other popular items include foie gras pressed with artichoke and celery and fresh oysters in season.

5-7 rue de la Bastille, 4e. ✆ **01-42-72-87-82.** www.bofingerparis.com. Reservations recommended. Main courses 15€–35€; fixed-price menu 25€–32€. AE, DC, MC, V. Mon–Fri noon–3pm and 6:30pm–1am; Sat–Sun noon–1am. Métro: Bastille.

Café des Musées 🍴 TRADITIONAL FRENCH/BISTRO   Close to both the Picasso museum and the Musée Carnavalet, Café des Musées boasts a good location, good food, and good prices—a rare combination in any part of Paris, but particularly in the Marais. The menu offers honest renderings of bistro classics, such as house-made terrines, steak frites, and a raspberry *dacquoise* (layer cake) for dessert. It also serves unpretentious wines in a bustling corner spot that expands to the sidewalk when the weather permits.

Restaurants in the Marais, Ile St-Louis & Ile de la Cité (3e & 4e)

49 rue de Turenne, 3e. ✆ **01-42-72-96-17**. Reservations recommended. Main courses 20€–35€; fixed-price dinner 20€; fixed-price lunch 13€. MC, V. Daily noon–3pm and 7–11pm. Métro: St. Paul.

Jaja MODERN FRENCH/BISTRO   Tucked into a charming courtyard in the southern Marais, this new bistro has quickly become a favorite among the foodies and style hounds of the neighborhood. It's a place to be seen, sure, but also a place to eat well for not much money, especially at lunch. Jaja's take on the hot dog (an artisanal sausage topped with pungent cheese) and the croque-monsieur (ham and cheese grilled sandwich) are playful and delicious. Stick to the basics here, and wash them down with wine from Jaja's very well-curated wine list.

3 rue Sainte-Croix-de-la-Bretonnerie, 4e. ✆ **01-42-74-71-52.** www.jaja-resto.com. Reservations recommended. Main courses 15€–24€; fixed-price lunch 16€. Mon–Sun noon–2:30pm and 8–11pm. Métro: Hotel de Ville.

L'Ambassade d'Auvergne AUVERGNAT/TRADITIONAL FRENCH   When you enter this rustic tavern through a bar that's heavy with oak beams, hanging hams, and ceramic plates, you feel immediately like you've been transported to the Auvergne. This homey restaurant showcases the culinary bounty of France's most isolated region, which produces some outstanding charcuterie and cheese. For mains, try the pork braised with cabbage, turnips, and white beans or grilled tripe sausages with mashed potatoes and Cantal cheese with garlic. Nonpork specialties include pan-fried duck liver with gingerbread, perch steamed in verbena tea, and roasted rack of lamb with wild mushrooms.

22 rue de Grenier St-Lazare, 3e. ✆ **01-42-72-31-22.** www.ambassade-auvergne.com. Reservations recommended. Main courses 17€–23€; fixed-price menus at 38€, 55€, and 65€. AE, MC, V. Daily noon–2pm and 7:30–10:30pm. Métro: Rambuteau.

Le Pamphlet 🗡 SOUTHWESTERN FRENCH/TRADITIONAL FRENCH   Alain Carrère has been called the most underrated chef in town, and his restaurant remains one of the only places you find nice linens, polite service, and classic cooking for less than 45€ a head. The menu changes regularly, but it might begin with rillettes of rabbit with crayfish, a thick cream of crabmeat soup garnished with baby peas, or a thin potato tart with marinated wild salmon and fine herbs. Mains might include fresh fish or properly cooked risotto.

38 rue Debelleyme, 3e. ✆ **01-42-72-39-24.** Reservations required, usually 48 hr. in advance for dinner. Fixed-price menu 35€–45€. MC, V. Tues–Fri noon–2:30pm and 7:30–11pm; Sun–Mon 7:30–11pm. Métro: Filles du Calvaire.

INEXPENSIVE

Bob's Juice Bar VEGETARIAN   Join the mix of *bobos*, fashion types, and Anglos at a communal table at this playful *bio* (organic) canteen for a refreshing, organic vegetarian lunch. Giant salads with greens and grains, a satisfyingly spicy veggie burger, curries, and soups are featured on the revolving menu. Pair it with a shot of wheatgrass or a freshly made smoothie. Go early on the weekends to avoid the brunch crunch.

74 rue des Gravilliers, 3e. ✆ **09-52-55-11-66.** www.bobsjuicebar.com. Reservations not required. Lunch 3.50€–8.50€. MC, V. Mon–Fri 8am–3pm; Sat–Sun 10am–4pm. Métro: Arts et Metiers.

Breizh Café ★ 🗡 CRÊPERIE/CAFÉ   This popular spot in the Marais serves crepes like you've never had them before. Run by a Breton-Japanese couple, this warm and modern wood-paneled space that is decorated with funky Japanese art has friendly service and quality food. Start with oysters or go straight to a savory buckwheat *galette,* which is crisp and nutty and filled with high-quality organic ingredients, such as farm fresh eggs, Bordier butter, and seasonal produce. Sip on one of the artisanal ciders, and save room for a sweet crepe, drizzled with chocolate or salted butter caramel. Reservations highly recommended.

109 rue Vieille du Temple, 3e. ✆ **01-42-72-13-77.** www.breizhcafe.com. Reservations recommended. Main courses 5.50€–11€. MC, V. Wed–Sat noon–11pm; Sun noon–10pm. Métro: Filles du Calvaire.

Chez Janou PROVENÇAL/BISTRO   On one of the 17th-century streets behind place des Vosges, a pair of cramped but cozy dining rooms filled with memorabilia from Provence make up this loud and somewhat raucous bistro. The service is brusque and sometimes hectic, but the sunny food, such as ratatouille and duck breast with rosemary, and boisterous clientele make for a fun and inexpensive night out.

2 rue Roger-Verlomme, 3e. ✆ **01-42-72-28-41.** www.chezjanou.com. Reservations recommended. Main courses 14€–18€; fixed-price lunch 15€. AE, MC, V. Daily noon–3pm and 7:30pm midnight. Métro: Chemin Vert.

L'As du Fallafel ★ FALAFEL/LIGHT FARE   You can distinguish the "king of falafel" from other pretenders on the street by the presence of a long line snaking away from the dark green shop front. Join the line (it moves fast) for a sandwich to go, or push through into one of two dining rooms and ask for a table. There are many options on the menu, including chicken shawarma and lamb kabobs, but you want the falafel sandwich. Stuffed with light and crispy balls of falafel (fried chickpeas) and topped with grilled eggplant and fresh salad, this really is one of the most delicious cheap bites in town. With a plate of fries to share and an Israeli beer, you can escape for less than 10€ per person. Note that L'As is closed Friday night and all day Saturday to honor the Jewish Sabbath.

34 rue des Rosiers, 4e. ✆ **01-48-87-63-60.** Reservations not accepted. Main courses 5€–16€. Sun–Thurs 11am–11:30pm; Fri 11am–5pm. Métro: St. Paul.

Tartes Kluger TRADITIONAL FRENCH/BAKERY   Occupying a loftlike space in the northern Marais, Tartes Kluger is a wonderful place to stop for lunch in between visits to the surrounding galleries and fashion boutiques. Two long communal tables are littered with glossy magazines and populated mostly by chic young women. They come to dine on Catherine Kluger's savory tarts (similar to a quiche), which are made from organic ingredients. Tarts include flavors such as feta, zucchini, and Parmesan or duck confit with turnips and potatoes, and are served with a fresh green salad. Finish up with a sweet tart, such as mango coconut, almond plum, or dark chocolate mousse.

6 rue de Forez, 3e. ✆ 01-53-01-53-53. www.tarteskluger.com. Reservations not required. Tarts 5€–7€; fixed-price lunch 12€; brunch 25€. MC, V. Mon–Thurs 11am–7pm; Fri–Sat 11am–8pm; Sun 11am–4pm. Métro: Temple.

Champs-Élysées & Western Paris (8e, 16e & 17e)

The posh avenues that radiate from the Champs-Élysées are home to some of the most expensive and elegant dining in the city. If you're looking to splurge on a lavish gastronomic experience, this is the right neighborhood. Dress sharp and

Bar des Théâtres **16**	La Bigarrade **21**	L'Astrance **12**	Les Tablettes **10**
Caïus **4**	La Cuisine **7**	Le Bouchon et	Michel Rostang **2**
Cristal Room **13**	La Maison Blanche **15**	l'Assiette **1**	Pierre Gagnaire **8**
Garnier **20**	L'Atelier Etoile de	Le Bristol **19**	Rech **3**
Guy Savoy **6**	Joël Robuchon **9**	Le Cinq **14**	Restaurant Plaza Athénée
Hiramatsu **11**	Lasserre **18**	Le Hide **5**	(Alain Ducasse) **17**

be ready to drop at least 100€ per head, unless you book a table at one of few moderate tables like Caïus, Le Hide, or Le Bouchon et l'Assiette.

VERY EXPENSIVE

Guy Savoy ★★ TRADITIONAL FRENCH   Guy Savoy is undoubtedly one of the top chefs in France, and his namesake restaurant caters to diners who want a three-star experience they can understand. You won't find molecular hijinks or a ton of unfamiliar ingredients here—just beautiful dishes composed of luxury ingredients and accented by what many feel is the best service in town. The signature starter is a bowl of truffled artichoke soup topped with shavings of aged Parmesan and served with a truffle buttered brioche for dipping. The menu changes seasonally but might include baby peas with poached quail's egg, or Breton lobster served inside a cloud of (dry ice) vapor. Don't be shy when the outstanding cheese cart comes around because the kind servers are happy to box up any desserts that you don't finish.

18 rue Troyon, 17e. ℭ **01-43-80-40-61.** Fax 01-46-22-43-09. www.guysavoy.com. Reservations for dinner required 1 month in advance; 2–3 days in advance for lunch. Main courses 75€–230€; fixed-price lunch 110€ and *menu dégustation* (tasting menu) 298€, 360€, and 480€. AE, DC, MC, V. Tues–Fri noon–2pm; Tues–Sat 7–10:30pm. Métro: Charles-de-Gaulle–Etoile or Ternes.

Hiramatsu TRADITIONAL FRENCH   Other than the fact that chef Hiroyuki Hiramatsu and most of his staff are Japanese, the only Asian touch at this restaurant is a hot, wet towel that arrives before the meal, in the Japanese style. Everything else is unabashedly French: the contemporary dining room, seating just 40, that's outfitted in mostly monochromatic tones of black and white; the rows of windows, each of which is set with shimmering panes of red-and-blue cut glass; and a polite staff wearing gray-and-white uniforms. Menu items change frequently, but are always artfully presented. Try pigeon breast with foie gras (flavored with strong coffee and cocoa), lobster with spinach wine sauce, or chops of veal with vegetables.

52 rue de Longchamps, 16e. ℭ **01-56-81-08-80.** www.hiramatsu.co.jp. Reservations required. Main courses 52€–112€; fixed-price lunch 48€ and fixed-price dinner 95€–130€. AE, DC, MC, V. Mon–Fri 12:30–1:30pm and 7:30–9:30pm. Métro: Trocadéro.

La Cuisine MODERN FRENCH   The latest addition to designer Philippe Starck's stable of dining rooms is La Cuisine, a new restaurant inside the Royal Monceau hotel (p. 308). The room is eye-catching and busy, full of modern art and artful design touches like a "to-do" list scribbled on a lamp shade. The cooking of chef Laurent André is delicious though not particularly inventive, but that seems to suit the well-heeled clientele that comes in from the nearby suburbs. Dishes are visually stunning—especially the "baroque" soft boiled egg with shrimp and porcini mushrooms. Desserts are all signed by Pierre Hermé, one of the most respected pastry chefs in the city.

37 avenue Hoche, 8e. ℭ **01-42-99-88-00.** www.leroyalmonceau.com. Reservations recommended. Fixed-price dinner 90€–150€. Daily noon–10:30pm. Métro: Etoile.

Lasserre TRADITIONAL FRENCH   This elegant restaurant was a bistro before World War II and has since become a legend. The main salon stretches two stories high, with a mezzanine on each side. Tall, silk-draped arched windows frame the tables set with fine porcelain, gold-edged crystal glasses, and silver candelabras. The ceiling is painted with white clouds and a cerulean sky, but in good weather, the staff slides back the roof to reveal the real sky. The faces of Audrey Hepburn and Marlene Dietrich have given way to young British royals and statuesque models from Brazil. Chef Christophe Moret, who previously worked under Ducasse at the Plaza Athenée, is a master of taste and texture, and he's brought renewed life to this swank citadel. Try the langoustines in a ginger-lime spiked seafood bouillon, truffled sea bass, young pigeon stuffed with truffles and served with turnips in lapsang-souchong tea, or the Brittany lobster with chestnut, salsify, and pumpkin. For dessert, try the roasted figs with olive oil and lime sorbet.

17 av. Franklin D. Roosevelt, 8e. ✆ **01-43-59-02-13.** Fax 01-45-63-72-23. www.restaurant-lasserre.com. Reservations required far in advance. Main courses 56€–95€; fixed-price lunch 75€; fixed-price dinner 185€. AE, MC, V. Thurs–Fri noon–2pm; Mon–Sat 7:30–10pm. Closed Aug. Métro: Franklin-D-Roosevelt.

L'Astrance ★★★ MODERN FRENCH   This small and charming spot is owned by two former employees (some say "disciples") of megachef Alain Passard, scion of L'Arpège; Christophe Rohat supervises the dining room, while Pascal Barbot is a true culinary force in the kitchen. The menu changes seasonally, but might include an unusual form of "ravioli," wherein thin slices of avocado encase a filling of seasoned crabmeat, all of it accompanied by salted almonds and a splash of almond oil. Other delights to the palate include turbot flavored with lemon and ginger, or sautéed pigeon with potatoes au gratin. The signature dish is a galette of thinly sliced raw mushrooms and verjuice-marinated foie gras with hazelnut oil and lemon comfit.

4 rue Beethoven, 16e. ✆ **01-40-50-84-40.** Reservations required months in advance. Main courses 24€–38€; fixed-price lunch 70€–120€; fixed-price dinner 120€–290€. AE, DC, MC, V. Tues–Fri 12:15–1:30pm and 8:15–9pm. Closed Aug. Métro: Passy.

Le Bristol ★★ MODERN FRENCH   Inside one of the most opulent three-star dining rooms in Paris in the Bristol Hotel (p. 305), the cuisine of Chef Eric Frechon continues to delight even the most experienced gastronomes. Frechon is particularly gifted with seafood, as evidenced by dishes such as sole stuffed with mushrooms and cooked in mussel jus, wild turbot served with a ravioli of pork lard and clams, and sea bass with oyster tartare. Another excellent dish is veal sweetbreads cooked in a tobacco leaf and served with a purée of anise-scented Jerusalem artichoke. Superb service and a strong wine list complete what is widely regarded as one of the best fine dining experiences in Paris.

112 rue Faubourg St. Honoré, 8e. ✆ **01-53-43-43-40.** www.lebristolparis.com. Reservations required. Main courses 68€–240€; fixed-price dinner 230€; fixed-price lunch 85€. AE, MC, V. Daily 12:30–2:30pm and 7–10:30pm. Métro: Miromesnil.

Le Cinq ★★ MODERN FRENCH   Since it was established in 1928 in honor of the king of England, there has always been a world-class dining venue associated with the Hotel George V. Today, the grand decor of this high-ceilinged room evokes the Grand Trianon at Versailles. Critics have been lavishing Chef Eric Briffard with praise, saying that he's a shoe-in to regain the restaurant's third Michelin star. Briffard trained under both Joël Robuchon and Alain Ducasse and cooks with precision and expertise. The menu changes frequently, but you may start with something like abalone and razor clams with algae butter and fried watercress, and move on to a main dish of venison with smoky bacon and a chocolaty peppercorn sauce.

In the Four Seasons Hotel George V, 31 av. George V, 8e. ℂ **01-49-52-71-54.** www.fourseasons. com. Reservations recommended 4 weeks in advance for dinner, 1 week in advance for lunch. Main courses 78€–135€; fixed-price lunch 78€–160€; fixed-price dinner 160€–230€. AE, DC, MC, V. Daily 12:30–2:30pm and 7–10:30pm. Métro: George V.

Michel Rostang TRADITIONAL FRENCH   Michel Rostang is one of Paris's most renowned old-school chefs, the fifth generation of a distinguished French "cooking family." His restaurant contains four dining rooms paneled in mahogany, cherrywood, or pearwood, some with frosted Lalique crystal panels. Changing every season, the menu offers modern improvements on *cuisine bourgeoise*. Truffles are the dish of choice in midwinter, and in spring you'll find racks of suckling lamb from the salt marshes of France's western coast; in autumn, look for pheasant, venison, and the infamous *lièvre* (wild hare)—Rostang is widely regarded as a master of wild game. Year-round staples include quail eggs with sea urchins, fricassee of sole, quenelles of whitefish with a lobster sauce, roasted scallops with chestnut gnocchi, or foie gras with roasted mandarins.

20 rue Rennequin, 17e. ℂ **01-47-63-40-77.** www.michelrostang.com. Fax 01-47-63-82-75. Reservations required 1 week in advance. Main courses 64€–88€; fixed-price lunch 76€; fixed-price dinner 169€. AE, DC, MC, V. Tues–Fri noon–2:30pm; Mon–Sat 7:30–10:30pm. Closed 3 weeks in Aug. Métro: Ternes.

Pierre Gagnaire ★★★ MODERN FRENCH   Veteran food writer Patricia Wells once said "there is no chef more creative than Pierre Gagnaire," and that sentiment has been echoed by countless other writers and fans. Of all the three-star chefs working in Paris today, Gagnaire is by far the most playful and experimental. He spent years collaborating with molecular gastronomy pioneer Hervé This to create boundary-pushing dishes with unusual textures and forms. The menu changes regularly, but recent meals have featured lobster hidden under brightly colored blankets of vegetable gel, and raw clams on a bed of sweet and sour pumpkin. One tip if you plan to order a la carte: each *plat* is actually made up of four to five dishes, so ordering both a starter and a main dish may yield more food than you could possibly eat. Perhaps it's not a bad thing that the desserts here are not as strong as you'll find at other three-star restaurants.

6 rue Balzac, 8e. ℂ **01-58-36-12-50.** Fax 01-58-36-12-51. www.pierre-gagnaire.com. Reservations required. Main courses 65€–165€; fixed-price lunch 105€; fixed-price dinner 265€. AF, DC, MC, V. Mon–Fri noon–1:30pm; Sun–Fri 7:30–10pm. Métro: George V.

Restaurant Plaza Athénée (Alain Ducasse) ★★ TRADITIONAL FRENCH   This three-star restaurant bears the name of internationally renowned chef Alain Ducasse and serves as the flagship of his restaurant empire. The globe-trotting chef is rarely here himself, but he has left his kitchen in the capable hands of Christophe Saintagne. A special emphasis is placed on "rare and precious ingredients"; the chef whips up flavorful and very expensive combinations of caviar, lobster, crayfish, and truffles (both black and white). Dishes may include sea scallops with salsify and black truffles, duck liver "pot au feu," or sole meunière with Belgian endives. The wine list is superb, with selections deriving from the best vintages of France, Germany, Switzerland, Spain, California, and Italy. The dining room, designed by Patrick Jouin and featuring a jaw-dropping "deconstructed" chandelier, is among the most beautiful in Paris.

In the Hôtel Plaza Athénée, 25 av. Montaigne, 8e. ℂ **01-53-67-65-00.** Fax 01-53-67-65-12. www.alain-ducasse.com. Reservations required 4–6 weeks in advance. Main courses 70€–175€;

Master Chef Alain Ducasse continues to expand his empire with the opening of **BE, 73 bd. de Courcelles, 8e (ℓ 01-46-22-20-20; Métro: Courcelles)**. Short for *Boulangerie Epicerie*, BE is part bakery and part upmarket deli. As a baker, Eric Kayser is famous in Paris, and he sells some 400 products from all over the globe, including 15 varieties of French bread baked fresh at least eight times a day. You can stop off here for the makings of a picnic, costing about 20€ to 30€ per person, depending on your selection. There are only 22 seats—if a table is free, grab it. You can eat an array of freshly made salads for 6€ to 9€, delicious homemade soups at 5€, and some of the best and most delectable sandwiches in Paris, from 4 € to 8€. Of course, if you want some walnut oil from the Dordogne or some lavender honey from Moustiers-Ste-Marie, they are standing on the shelves as well. Open Monday to Saturday 7am to 8pm.

fixed-price menu 260€–360€. AE, DC, MC, V. Thurs–Fri 12:45–2:15pm; Mon–Fri 7:45–10:15pm. Closed mid-July to Aug 25 and 10 days in late Dec. Métro: Alma-Marceau.

EXPENSIVE

Cristal Room MODERN FRENCH The Taittinger family of champagne fame has opened this Baccarat crystal–laden room in a former town house of the art patron Marie-Laure de Noailles. She was known as the benefactor of such artists as Man Ray and Salvador Dalí. For the new restaurant setting, Philippe Starck was called in to create the bling-bling decor, and the kitchen works under the (sometimes) direction of Guy Martin, who also oversees Le Grand Véfour (p. 182). It's definitely more about the scene than what's on the plate (the restaurant has two other locations in Moscow and Tokyo, if that tells you anything), but the kitchen still manages to put out pleasing dishes such as crusty veal sweetbreads and filet of turbot with roasted fresh walnuts.

11 place des Etats-Unis, 16e. ℓ **01-40-22-11-10.** www.baccarat.com/en/the-world-of-baccarat/bars-restaurants/cristal-room.htm. Reservations required. Main courses 37€–40€; fixed-price lunch 29€–55€; fixed-price dinner 99€–149€. AE, MC, V. Mon–Sat 12:15–2:15pm and 7:15–10:30pm. Métro: Boissière.

Garnier BRASSERIE/SEAFOOD If you're looking for a great brasserie, whether for the gleaming decor, the beautiful seafood, or the fact that it's open on Sunday, Garnier ranks among this city's most beloved. Towering silver platters of seafood are the thing here—load one up with oysters, mussels, crabs, clams, and anything else that strikes your fancy. Order a nice crisp bottle of Sancerre and settle in for a long feast. You can also stop by Garnier to pick up a crate of oysters to go if you prefer to slurp the bivalves in your hotel room. Just be sure to leave a tip for housekeeping.

111 rue St. Lazare, 8e. ℓ **01-43-87-50-40.** Reservations recommended. Main courses 27€–50€; fixed-price dinner 35€. MC, V. Mon–Sun noon–2:30pm and 7–11pm. Métro: Gare St. Lazare.

La Bigarrade MODERN FRENCH The cooking of Christophe Pelé has been described by some critics as "poetic" and "inspired," and by others as overrated. When he's on, and he often is, Pelé's experimental cooking rivals some of the best chefs in Paris. When he's not, however, 85€ seems like an awful lot to pay for a fixed-price menu that offers no choices and not a lot of food.

The setting, out near the northern edge of the 17th, is inarguably pretty, and the service is kind and attentive. Book well in advance if you'd like to take a chance on one of the most challenging young chefs working in Paris today.

106 rue Nollet, 17e. ✆ **01-42-26-01-02.** www.bigarrade.fr. Reservations required. Fixed-price dinner 85€; fixed-price lunch 45€. Mon 8:30–9pm; Tues–Fri 12:30–1:30pm and 8:30–9pm. Métro: Brochant.

La Maison Blanche PROVENÇAL/TRADITIONAL FRENCH   Jacques and his twin brother, Lauren Pourcel, were two of the most famous chefs in the southerly province of Languedoc before heading north to Paris. The setting of this place would be the envy of any restaurant in the world: positioned on the uppermost (seventh) floor of the Art Deco–style Theatre des Champs-Élysées, it has contemporary white and purple decor, sweeping views across the Seine, and two dining rooms. Clientele tends to be rich, non-French, and a bit pretentious, but in light of the brilliant food and the sublime setting, who cares? The menu changes with the inspiration of the chefs and the seasons, but stellar examples include such starters as crispy filet of red mullet with coriander-flavored baby vegetables or a small tart of duck foie gras with roasted rhubarb and peach. An especially good fish specialty is filet of John Dory in candied lemon vinaigrette with stuffed olives, or a rack of Aveyron lamb with cracked wheat and mushroom compote.

15 av. Montaigne, 8e. ✆ **01-47-23-55-99.** www.maison-blanche.fr. Reservations required. Main courses 38€–73€; fixed-price lunch 55€. AE, DC, MC, V. Mon–Fri noon–2pm; daily 8–11pm. Métro: Alma-Marceau.

L'Atelier Etoile de Joël Robuchon ★★ MODERN FRENCH   Chef Joël Robuchon recently expanded his empire with the addition of this second Atelier restaurant inside the Drugstore Publicis complex. Diners flock to this new location, just off the Champs-Élysées, for its high-flying gastronomy served by way of small sharable plates in a fun, unstuffy setting. Critics have raved about dishes of foie gras in port jelly with Parmesan cream, sea urchin with wasabi mousse, and black cod in a bouillon of daikon radish and yuzu zest. As at the original Left Bank location, reservations are accepted here only for lunch or for extremely early and late dinner seatings; for everyone else, it's first come, first served.

133 avenue des Champs-Élysées, inside the Publicis complex, 8e. ✆ **01-47-23-75-75.** www.joel-robuchon.net. Reservations accepted for lunch at 11:30am and 2pm, and dinner at 6:30pm. Small plates 14€–65€; 9-course tasting menu 150€. AE. Daily 11:30am–3:30pm and 6:30pm–midnight. Métro: Etoile.

Les Tablettes ★ MODERN FRENCH/PROVENÇAL   In a spot formerly occupied by La Table de Joël Robuchon, Chef Jean-Louis Nomicos recently opened Les Tablettes, a modern restaurant where the menu is presented on an iPad (*tablette,* in French). Nomicos's cooking has a modern edge, but is firmly based in the classic French tradition (he was most recently at Lasserre, p. 194). Loyalty to his Provençal roots is evident in dishes like sea scallops with bouillabaisse jus or filet of beef with black olives. The signature dish that has critics raving, however, is a "royale" of sea urchin and fennel. The 58€ lunch menu, which includes water, wine, and coffee, is a great introduction to fine dining in Paris.

16 ave Bugeaud, 16e. ✆ **01-56-28-16-16.** www.lestablettesjeanlouisnomicos.com. Reservations recommended. Main courses 65€–165€; fixed-price dinner 80€; fixed-price lunch 58€. AE, MC, V. Daily noon–2:30pm and 7:30–10:15pm. Métro: Victor Hugo.

Rech BRASSERIE/SEAFOOD   Chef Alain Ducasse has brought new life to this brasserie, founded in 1925, which today specializes in shellfish. The original Alsatian brasserie features have been retained, including the Art Deco furnishings—even the oyster shucker on the sidewalk. The previous owner, August Rech, believed in offering a limited but very select menu, and that tradition continues today. The specialty here is a gleaming platter of *fruits de mer*, but you can also order half a dozen different kinds of succulent fresh oysters. Poached skate wing appears with garlic and caper butter, and you can also order a grilled entrecôte with béarnaise sauce. For dessert, patrons order what might be the largest éclair served in Paris.

62 av. des Ternes, 17e. ✆ **01-45-72-29-47.** www.restaurant-rech.fr. Reservations required. Main courses 24€–45€; fixed-price lunch 34€. AE, DC, MC, V. Mon–Sat noon–3pm and 7–10pm. Closed July 25–Aug 15. Métro: Ternes.

MODERATE

Bar des Théâtres TRADITIONAL FRENCH   Its local patrons in the 8th arrondissement have long called this bar/restaurant "The Temple of the God Steak Tartare." For those daring souls who still eat this blood-rare red meat specialty, this long-established restaurant is said to make the best dish. Even though it's situated in the most lethally priced district of Paris, over the years it has kept its prices reasonable. Across the street is the Théâtre des Champs-Élysées, and many of its performers, especially actors and musicians, make the bar their "local" while appearing here. The chef also specializes in a delectable *magret de canard* (breast of duckling), and you can even order caviar and foie gras, but those items would put this into a very expensive category. Better settle for the sauerkraut.

6 av. Montaigne, 8e. ✆ **01-47-23-34-63.** Reservations recommended. Main courses 13€–22€. AE, DC, MC, V. Daily noon–1am. Closed Aug. Métro: Alma Marceau.

Caïus TRADITIONAL FRENCH   This chic place near the Arc de Triomphe, popular for business lunches and dinners, also draws well-heeled residents and visiting shoppers. The dining room is ringed with wood paneling, banquettes, and teakwood chairs and provides a showcase for Jean-Marc Notelet's comforting cuisine. Dishes like marinated and roasted sardines or sea bream with braised Belgian endives and root vegetables are evidence of Notelet's skill with seafood, but he's also good on dry land, serving a delicious confit of beef with fava beans and whipped celery rave with almond milk.

6 rue d'Armaillé, 17e. ✆ **01-42-27-19-20.** Reservations recommended. Main courses 19€–31€; fixed-price lunch 23€; fixed-price dinner 39€. AE, DC, MC, V. Mon–Sat noon–2:30pm; Mon–Sat 7:30–11pm. Métro: Argentine.

Le Bouchon et l'Assiette TRADITIONAL FRENCH   This relatively new bistro in the 17th is serving imaginatively tweaked French classics, such as *boudin noir* (blood sausage) with cauliflower and preserved lemon, foie gras with red cabbage and hazelnuts, sea scallops with caramelized turnips, and a wonderful steak with pepper sauce. Desserts are simple but delicious, with options including rice pudding, a nut-studded chocolate mousse, or a traditional *gâteau Basque*. It's a wonderful neighborhood joint that's relatively easy to book, and the prices, especially at lunchtime, are easy to digest.

127 rue Cardinet, 17e. ✆ **01-42-27-83-93.** Reservations recommended. Tues–Sat noon–2:30pm and 7:30–10:30pm. Main courses 18€; fixed-price dinner 33€; fixed-price lunch 22€. Métro: Malesherbes.

Chinatown Paris Style

Although it's not widely known, Paris does, in fact, have a Chinatown. **Quartier Chinois,** a 5-minute walk from Place d'Italie, centers on avenue d'Ivry in the 13th arrondissement. (To get there, take the Métro to Porte d'Ivry or Place d'Italie in the 13e.) About 250,000 Asian people live in the Quartier Chinois, and a slew of Asian food stores, restaurants, and markets cater to the growing population. **Tang Frères** (44 avenue d'Ivry, 13e; ☏ **01-44-06-61-86**) is the largest Asian-food market in Europe—here you'll find rows of teas and spices from China. Spend a morning exploring here and stick around for lunch at **Le Mer de Chine** (159 des Rentiers, 13e; ☏ **01-45-84-22-49**), serving the best Cantonese cuisine in Paris.

Le Hide ★ 🎁 TRADITIONAL FRENCH   This bistro near the Eiffel Tower was included in a recent top-10 list by *Le Figaro* (a local newspaper) of "overlooked tables" whose high quality merits more media attention than they have received. The still-hidden restaurant takes its name from chef Hide Kobayashi, who describes his food as French bistro cooking. The cuisine is certainly French, but a few of the recipes hint at his Japanese origins. Kobayashi perfected his craft in the kitchens of some of the world's greatest chefs, including Joël Robuchon. The menu changes regularly, and main courses, like fricassee of rabbit flavored with mustard or sweetbreads in cream with truffles, all carry the same price tag. In a neighborhood full of expensive and unmemorable restaurants, Le Hide is one of the best options for well-executed French bistro cuisine at an affordable price.

10 rue du General Lanrezac, 17e. ☏ **01-45-74-15-81.** www.lehide.fr. Reservations required. Main courses 16€; fixed-price menu 22€–29€. MC, V. Mon–Fri noon–3pm and Mon–Sat 7–10:30pm. Métro: Charles-de-Gaulle–Etoile.

Opéra & Canal St-Martin (9e & 10e)

This area is filled with good-value bistros and wine bars, and is populated by a younger, cooler set. Le Verré Vole, Vivant, and Coinstôt Vino serve meals centered on natural wine, and Philou and Le Pantruche are notable new, affordable bistros.

EXPENSIVE

Wally Le Saharien ALGERIAN   Head to this dining room—lined with desert photos and tribal artifacts crafted from ceramics, wood, and weavings—for an insight into the spicy, slow-cooked cuisine that fueled the colonial expansion of France into North Africa. The prix-fixe dinner menu begins with a trio of starters: spicy soup, stuffed and grilled sardines, and a savory pastilla of pigeon in puff pastry. Next comes any of several kinds of couscous or a *méchouia* (slow-cooked tart). Merguez, the cumin-laden spicy sausage of the North African world, factors importantly into any meal, as do homemade pastries.

36 rue Rodier, 9e. ☏ **01-42-85-51-90.** Reservations recommended. Main courses 35€–57€; fixed-price lunch 21€; fixed-price dinner 44€. MC, V. Tues–Sat noon–2pm and 7–10:30pm. Métro: Anvers.

MODERATE

Casa Olympe PROVENÇAL/GREEK   Serious foodies make their way to the 9th to feast on the wares of an original cook. Olympe Versini earned a Michelin

Restaurants near Opéra & Canal St-Martin (9e & 10e)

Casa Olympe 2	El Nopal 9	Philou 11	
Charlier 5	La Grille 7	Vivant 6	
Chez Grenouille 1	Le Pantruche 3	Wally Le	
Chez Michel 8	Le Verre Volé 10	Saharien 4	

star at the age of 29 and dazzled some of the most discerning palates of *tout* Paris in Montparnasse before opening this unassuming 32-seat dining room. Critics cite the earthiness of her cooking as evoked by her duck ravioli bathed in a jus reduction or her heavenly foie gras terrine brazenly studded with split vanilla beans. From head to hoof, she serves most parts of the pig—and does so with gusto. Her langoustine ravioli is modish but not excessively so, and her beef tenderloin with peppercorn sauce is one of the best versions of this time-honored dish.

48 rue St-Georges, 9e. ⓒ **01-42-85-26-01.** www.casaolympe.com. Reservations required. Fixed-price menu 33€ and 43€. MC, V. Mon–Fri noon–2pm and 8–11pm. MC, V. Métro: St-Georges.

Chez Grenouille TRADITIONAL FRENCH   Chef Alexis Blanchard has won prizes for his terrines and boudins, so you'll find all manner of charcuterie on the menu here, plus dishes such as suckling pig with foie gras, duck parmentier, sweetbreads, oxtail, and pigs' feet, plus a fish dish or two for lighter eaters. It's true that the ambience leaves something to be desired; the main dining room is woefully outdated, and the room downstairs is even worse. But what's on the plate might be enough of a draw, at least for carnivores. Finish with the sinfully boozy baba au rhum for two.

52 rue Blanche, 9e. ⓒ **01-42-81-34-07.** www.restaurant-chezgrenouille-paris.com. Reservations recommended. Main courses 20€–32€; fixed-price lunch Mon–Fri 25€. MC, V. Mon–Fri noon–3pm and 7–11pm; Sat 7–11pm. Métro: Trinité.

Chez Michel ★★ BRETON   Chef Thierry Breton prepares outstanding dishes from his native Brittany for diners that come from all over Paris and through the nearby Eurostar train hub at Gare du Nord. Breton recently ripped out a few tables and installed a massive oven in the dining room itself. He's now offering a four-course prix-fixe menu with homey options like braised lamb, a chicken pot pie that's studded with foie gras, and other slow-baked specialties. For dessert, try the copious rice pudding or the awe-inspiring Paris-Brest.

10 rue de Belzunce, 10e. ⓒ **01-44-53-06-20.** Reservations required. Fixed-price menu 32€. MC, V. Tues–Fri 11:45am–3pm and Mon–Fri 6:45pm–midnight. Métro: Gare du Nord.

La Grille SEAFOOD/TRADITIONAL FRENCH   This nine-table restaurant, with its historically classified 200-year-old wrought-iron grills, seems to be a holdover from another age. For at least a century after the French Revolution, fishermen from Dieppe used this place as a springboard for carousing and cabaret-watching after delivering their fish to Les Halles market. Since the late 1960s, the charming, outspoken M. and Mme Cullérre have run this restaurant. The holy grail at La Grille is an entire turbot prepared tableside with an emulsified white butter sauce. Other recommended dishes are seafood terrine, *boeuf bourguignon* (braised beef in red-wine sauce), and a brochette of scallops in white butter.

80 rue du Faubourg-Poissonnière, 10e. ⓒ **01-47-70-89-73.** Reservations required. Main courses 17€–66€. AE, MC, V. Mon–Sat noon–2:15pm and 7:30–9:30pm. Métro: Poissonnière.

Le Pantruche ★ 🎁 TRADITIONAL FRENCH/BISTRO   This new bistro near Pigalle received rave reviews when it opened in early 2011, impressing critics with the friendly atmosphere, affordable prices, and better-than-average bistro fare. Dishes include a rich celery root soup, tender glazed beef cheeks, oyster tartare, and a classic Grand Marnier soufflé. Although it's dressed like a humble neighborhood joint, Franck Baranger's cooking puts Le Pantruche in another league altogether.

3 rue Victor Massé, 9e. ℂ **01-48-78-55-60.** Reservations recommended. Fixed-price dinner 32€; fixed-price lunch 17€. Mon–Fri noon–2:30pm and 7:15–10:30pm. Métro: Pigalle.

Le Verre Volé ★★ WINE BAR/MODERN FRENCH   This wine bar, along the charming Canal Saint-Martin, has been open for more than 10 years, but it recently added a second dining room annex and brought in some real culinary talent in the form of Chef Delphine Zampetti. The sharable plates of charcuterie and cheese are still on the menu, but more inventive fare like octopus carpaccio, smoked swordfish, and pâté en croûte with pigeon and foie gras are also offered. Select a bottle of wine from the shelves that line the walls, and enjoy it (for a nominal corkage fee) in this informal and fun setting. It may be a casual place, but the popularity of the Verre Volé requires that you reserve in advance.

67 rue de Lancry, 10e. ℂ **01-48-03-17-34.** www.leverrevole.fr. Reservations recommended. Main courses 25€–30€; plate of the day 16€. MC, V. Daily 12:30–2pm and 7:30–10:30pm. Métro: Jacques Bonsergent.

Philou ★★ 🏠 TRADITIONAL FRENCH/BISTRO   Residents of the Canal Saint-Martin neighborhood rejoiced when Philippe Damas opened this charming bistro in 2010. This reasonably priced bistro serves superior bistro cooking, including sautéed porcini mushrooms, roasted grouse stuffed with foie gras, steak with root vegetables, and a delicious Mont Blanc (chestnut) dessert. The wine list wins major points for including many affordable but respected small producers. Service, which usually includes a visit from the amiable chef, is attentive and kind, and the updated bistro interior is very cool. All in all, one of our favorite openings in recent years.

12 avenue Richerand, 10e. ℂ **01-42-38-00-13.** Reservations recommended. Fixed-price dinner 25€; fixed-price lunch 15€. Tues–Sat noon–2:30pm and 8–10:30pm. Métro: Jacques Bonsergent.

Vivant ★ TRADITIONAL FRENCH/ITALIAN   Reflecting the mixed heritage of owner Pierre Jancou, this new restaurant in an up-and-coming part of the 10th arrondissement serves French and Italian homey fare. Jancou has a gift for uncovering and restoring beautiful, historic spaces (his previous projects include Racines in the 2nd, p. 186, and La Crèmerie in the 6th, p. 218), and Vivant—dressed up in colorful tiles that date from 1903—is no exception. As soon as you enter the door, you hear the swish-swish of a Berkel slicing machine—cured Italian ham is a requisite beginning to any meal here. Jancou is a major figure in the natural wine movement and the wine list offers some of the most interesting, hard-to-find bottles in the country. Complete your visit with an espresso pulled from the most beautiful 1950s coffee machine you've ever seen.

43 rue des Petites Ecuries, 10e. ℂ **01-42-46-43-55.** Reservations recommended. Main courses 15€–25€. MC, V. Mon–Fri noon–2:30pm and 8–10:30pm. Métro: Château d'Eau.

INEXPENSIVE

Chartier TRADITIONAL FRENCH/BRASSERIE   Opened in 1896, this unpretentious *fin-de-siècle* restaurant is now an official historic monument featuring a whimsical mural with trees, a flowering staircase, and an early depiction of an airplane (it was painted in 1929 by an artist who traded his work for food). The menu follows brasserie-style traditions, including items you might not dare to eat—beef tartare, chitterling sausages, tongue of beef with spicy sauce—as well as some classic temptations, like duck confit. The waiter will steer you through such dishes as *choucroute* (sauerkraut), *pavé* (a thick slice of rump steak), and at least five kinds of fish. High gastronomy this isn't, but you can't beat Chartier for a cheerful night on the cheap.

7 rue du Faubourg Montmartre, 9e. © **01-47-70-86-29.** www.restaurant-chartier.com. Main courses 9€–12€. AE, DC, MC, V. Daily 11:30am–10pm. Métro: Grands-Boulevards.

El Nopal MEXICAN There are only two stools at this tiny taqueria, but in good weather you can take your burritos, tacos, quesadillas, and freshly mashed guacamole to go, and find a spot along the nearby Canal Saint-Martin for your picnic. The tortillas are handmade, the salsa is hot, and the *aqua fresca* hits the spot on a sunny day. The grilled steak or chicken tacos are fantastic, but almost everything can be made vegetarian. Just ask: Claudia and Alejandro speak at least three languages.

3 rue Eugène Varlin, 10e. © **07-86-39-63-46.** Reservations not required. Main courses 6.50€. No credit cards. Mon–Thurs 11:30am–3pm and 6–10pm; Fri 11:30am–3pm and 6–11pm; Sat 5–11pm; Sun 11:30am–9pm. Métro: Chateau Landon.

Pigalle & Montmartre (18e)

Montmartre today is home to a good number of reputable restaurants—especially Le Bal Café and La Table d'Eugene. However, if you're looking for a good meal, avoid the place du Tertre, where hopeful portrait artists sit waiting for tourists with their easels.

MODERATE

Chéri Bibi ⚑ TRADITIONAL FRENCH Decorated with flea-market finds and featuring an affordable menu of classic French fare, Cheri Bibi has become the unofficial canteen for the young and artsy Montmartre crowd. The chalkboard menu includes rustic dishes like *boudin noir* (blood sausage), andouillette, head cheese, and steak frites. This might not be the place to bring a vegetarian friend. A crowd often gathers around the restaurant's zinc bar just to sip wine, sometimes spilling out onto the sidewalk that lies just below the eastern slope of the Sacre Coeur.

15 rue André del Sarte, 18e. © **01-42-54-88-96.** Reservations recommended. Main courses 15€–30€; fixed-price dinner 19€–24€; lunch 10€–20€. MC, V. Mon–Sat 8pm–midnight. Métro: Barbes-Rochechouart.

La Famille MODERN FRENCH This Montmartre restaurant served as the launching pad for chef Inaki Aizpitarte, who has since moved on to Le Chateaubriand. The food at La Famille remains creative but now relies more on gimmicks (dry ice, funny plating) than true gastronomic innovation. That doesn't much matter to the fashionable crowd who come for the cocktails and sparkling scene. (They don't tend to eat much, anyway.) On the bright side, the wine list is very solid and features small-scale organic producers like Foillard and Villemade.

41 rue des Trois Freres, 18e. © **01-42-52-11-12.** Reservations required. Fixed-price menus at 29€ and 35€. MC, V. Tues–Sat 8–11:30pm. Métro: Abesses.

Le Bal Café ★ ENGLISH Brunch-loving Parisians have flipped for the traditional English breakfast that's served on the weekends here. Tucked inside a cultural center and photography museum near the place de Clichy, Le Bal Café

Restaurants in Pigalle & Montmartre (18e)

Café des Deux Moulins 2
Chéri Bibi 4
La Famille 3
La Table d'Eugene 5
Le Bal Café 1

---

is more than just eggs and bacon (and scones, kippers, and pancakes). The chef, who used to work at London's renowned Saint John restaurant, prepares an impressive array of modern British cuisine, with dishes like guinea hen with endives, lamb shoulder with carrots, and head cheese with prunes. The sturdy fare is complimented by a well-chosen and affordable wine list. Kill time waiting for your reservation by browsing the adjoining bookstore or taking in some of the wonderful photography exhibits at the center.

6 impasse de la Défense, 18e. ✆ **01-44-70-75-51.** www.le-bal.fr. Reservations not required. Main courses 5.50€–21€; brunch 3.50€–12€. MC, V. Wed–Sat noon–2:30pm and 8–10:30pm; Sun brunch 11–4pm. Métro: Clichy.

La Table d'Eugene ★ 🍴 TRADITIONAL FRENCH/BISTRO   La Table d'Eugene opened in 2008 and has garnered a steady stream of critical praise, but the restaurant's location, far out in the untrendy part of northern Montmartre, ensures that it will continue to be overlooked by the tourist hordes. That's great news for anyone looking for an authentic bistro catering to a regular crowd of neighborhood locals. Expect slightly tweaked bistro fare such as crispy pig's foot with shaved daikon radish and a balsamic reduction, risotto with wild mushrooms, and venison with red wine sauce and chestnuts.

18 rue Eugène Sue, 18e. ✆ **01-42-55-61-64.** Tues–Sat noon–2:30pm and 7:30–10:30pm. Fixed-price dinner and lunch 25€. Métro: Marcadet-Poissonniers.

République, Bastille & Eastern Paris (11e & 12e)

With a mix of working-class families, hipsters, and *bobos,* the area between République and Nation is diverse, young, and fun. It's also one of the best food neighborhoods in the city, thanks to stand-out restaurants like Le Chateaubriand, Le Bistrot Paul Bert, Rino, and La Gazzetta. The atmosphere in these places is casual and buzzing, the waiters tend to be handsome and unshaved, and the wine is mostly natural. Don't let the informality trick you into believing that you don't need to book in advance.

EXPENSIVE

Au Trou Gascon BISTRO   Years ago, chef Alain Dutournier's parents mortgaged their Gascony inn to allow him to open an early 1900s-style bistro in a little-known part of the 12th arrondissement. Word spread quickly about Dutournier's authentic cuisine moderne and his exciting cave containing several little-known wines along with a fabulous collection of Armagnacs. Foie gras and Gascony-cured ham make for great starters, and delicious main dishes include a roast shoulder of milk-fed Pyrenees lamb with carrot flan, sautéed scallops with pumpkin, and cassoulet made with duck, pork, lamb, and sausage.

40 rue Taine, 12e. ✆ **01-43-44-34-26.** www.autrougascon.fr. Reservations recommended. Main courses 28€–42€; fixed-price lunch 38€; fixed-price dinner 49€. AE, DC, MC, V. Mon–Fri noon–2pm and 8–10pm. Closed Aug, and 6 days in Nov. Métro: Daumesnil.

La Gazzetta ★ MODERN FRENCH   Within one of the prettiest bistro settings in all of Paris, and just down the street from the bustling outdoor food market at Aligre, chef Petter Nilsson is serving some of the city's most avant-garde cuisine. The beautiful dining room, with its soft lighting, leafy palm trees, and dark polished wood, suggests a place serving classic bistro fare. But Nilsson's dishes are anything but traditional. A recent meal featured a soft poached egg floating in a broth of anise-scented cardoon that was spiked with briny mullet roe. That was followed by rare beef with purslane and veal knuckle with sea urchin and verbena. For fans of experimental cooking, the seven-course tasting menu at 50€ is one of the city's best values.

29 rue de Cotte, 12e. ✆ **01-43-47-47-05.** www.lagazzetta.fr. Reservations recommended. Fixed-price dinner 38€ and 50€; fixed-price lunch 16€. Tues–Sat noon–2pm and 8–11pm. Métro: Ledru-Rollin.

Le Chateaubriand ★★★ MODERN FRENCH   Chef Inaki Aizpitarte is the unofficial leader (and handsome poster boy) of France's neo-bistrot movement, and Le Chateaubriand was recently rated the 11th best restaurant in the world by *Restaurant Magazine,* the highest ranking for any French restaurant. Aizpitarte's regularly changing 45€ prix-fixe menu offers no choices, but open-minded diners are rewarded with some of the most innovative flavor pairings in Paris. You may try rare tuna slices in pink beet foam flavored with pomegranate seeds or eel flavored with orange juice and olive oil. Not every single plate is a winner, but usually at least three of four dishes tend to be brilliant. If you don't have a reservation, you can try to score a seat at the second seating, which begins around 10pm.

129 av. Parmentier, 11e. ✆ **01-43-57-45-95.** Reservations required. Fixed-price dinner 45€. AE, DC, MC, V. Tues–Sat 8–11:30pm. Métro: Goncourt.

Rino MODERN FRENCH   Chef Giovanni Passerini worked for years under Petter Nilsson at the nearby restaurant La Gazzetta (see above) and only recently ventured out on his own with Rino (pronounced like the city in Nevada, not the animal). His experience working with the avant-garde Swede has combined with his Italian heritage to produce cooking that is both inventive and delicious. A recent meal featured barley risotto with preserved lemon and fish eggs followed by a crispy-skinned chicken leg served with tapenade and turnips. The dinnertime tasting menus (at 38€ or 50€) don't offer any choice. The dining room is modern, sparse, and cool, which matches well with the surrounding hipster neighborhood.

46 rue Trousseau, 11e. **☏ 01-48-06-95-85.** www.rino-restaurant.com. Reservations recommended. Tues–Sat noon–2pm and 8–11pm. Fixed-price dinner 38€ and 50€; fixed-price lunch 20€. MC, V. Métro: Ledru-Rollin.

MODERATE

Astier TRADITIONAL FRENCH/BISTRO   Open since 1956, old-fashioned Astier has managed to avoid becoming a relic thanks to thoughtful preparations of classics like wild boar terrine, rabbit rillettes, filet of sole, duck confit, roast chicken, and tarte tatin, plus a legendary cheese tray. With red checked tablecloths, original woodwork, and café curtains, it's a picture postcard version of a Paris bistro, without the surly waiters.

44 rue Jean-Pierre Timbaud, 11e. **☏ 01-43-57-16-35.** www.restaurant-astier.com. Reservations recommended. Fixed-price dinner 30€; fixed-price lunch 26€. MC, V. Daily 12:45–2:15pm and 7:30–10:30pm. Métro: Parmentier.

L'Ebauchoir TRADITIONAL FRENCH   Tucked into a neighborhood rarely visited by foreigners, this bistro features a 1950s decor that is so out it's in; with buffed aluminum trim and plaster-and-stucco walls tinted dark orange-yellow and bordeaux, the place might remind you of a factory canteen. Specialties include a pigeon roasted in bacon fat and red wine, filet of perch in chorizo cream, lamb chops with black olive tapenade, and a grandmotherly rice pudding cake.

43 rue de Citeaux, 12e. ✆ **01-43-42-49-31.** www.lebauchoir.com. Reservations recommended for dinner. Main courses 14€–25€; fixed-price lunch 14€; fixed-price dinner 23€. AE, MC, V. Tues–Sat noon–2:30pm; Mon–Sat 8–11pm. Métro: Faidherbe-Chaligny.

Le Bistrot Paul Bert ★★ BISTRO/TRADITIONAL FRENCH   Ask any local food writer to name his or her favorite classic bistros and there's a very good chance that you'll be directed here. The chalkboard menu is long and changes with the seasons, but a typical meal might begin with a plate of sunny-side up eggs with truffle cream and shaved black truffle, followed by one of the city's best steak frites (it's crowned with a glistening morsel of marrow), and ending with a generous slice of tarte tatin (apple tart) and its accompanying pitcher of thick crème fraîche. The decor is a jumble of wooden tables, cracked tile floors, flea market finds, and a polished zinc bar—exactly how you imagine a neighborhood bistro should be. The crowd is predominantly local, although the staff is used to dealing with the occasional food-minded traveler. The wine list features many unusual and affordable bottles from small wine producers.

18 rue Paul Bert, 11e. ✆ **01-43-72-24-01.** Reservations required. Fixed-price dinner 34€; fixed-price lunch 17€. MC, V. Tues–Sat noon–2pm and 7:30–11pm. Métro: Faidherbe-Chaligny.

Le Cotte Roti BISTRO/MEDITERRANEAN   This neo-bistrot near the colorful marché Aligre has undergone a needed redecoration, though the best seat to enjoy Nicholas Michel's market cooking might be outside. There are some Mediterranean and Provençale dishes on the menu, such as an octopus salad or black risotto with clams, along with richer fare such as sweetbreads and pork belly on a bed of orzo. The name is a play on words between the address (on rue de Cotte) and the famous wine region (the Côte Rôtie), which is well represented on the list.

1 rue de Cotte, 12e. ✆ **01-43-45-06-37.** Reservations recommended. Main courses 15€–35€. MC, V. Tues–Sat noon–2:30pm and 8–11pm. Métro: Ledru-Rollin.

Le Repaire de Cartouche TRADITIONAL FRENCH   Chef Rudolph Paquin is a towering red-cheeked man whose facility with game cookery is known far and wide. A stop here during an autumn visit is almost obligatory for fans of fowl and other wild forest animals. Paquin is also known for his impressive *carte des vins* (wine list), and wine enthusiasts come regularly to eat well while making their way through the chef's treasure-studded cave. Service can at times be a little gruff, which is a shame because it detracts from the often spectacular food and wine.

8 boulevard des Filles du Calvaire, 11e. ✆ **01-47-00-25-86.** Reservations recommended. Main courses 18€–29€. MC, V. Tues–Fri noon–2pm and 7:30–11pm; Sat noon–2pm and 7:30–11:30pm. Métro: St. Sebastian Froissart.

Mansouria MOROCCAN   One of Paris's most charming Moroccan restaurants occupies a restored building midway between place de la Bastille and place de la Nation. The minimalist decor combines futuristic architecture with bare sand-colored walls, accented only with sets of antique doors and portals from the sub-Sahara. Look for eight different varieties of couscous and six different *tagines,* including versions with chicken, beef, lamb, and vegetables.

11 rue Faidherbe, 11e. ℂ **01-43-71-00-16.** www.mansouria.fr. Reservations recommended. Main courses 17€–26€; fixed-price dinner 28€–36€. AE, MC, V. Wed–Sat noon–2pm; Mon–Sat 7–11pm. Métro: Faidherbe-Chaligny.

INEXPENSIVE

Al Taglio PIZZA This Paris pizzeria does as the Romans do; the pizza here is sold by weight from rectangular pies, with a variety of fresh toppings including zucchini and ham, a straightforward margherita, and a potato and truffle cream that is not to be missed. The room is bright and minimally decorated, with communal tables and a well-sized terrace where you'll see locals, students, and families diving into the slabs, which are served on wooden boards with not enough napkins. A short Italian wine list and gelato from Pozzetto round out the offerings.

2 bis rue Neuve Popincourt, 11e. ℂ **01-43-38-12-00.** Reservations not accepted. Pizza sold by the slice 11€–30€ per kilo. MC, V. Sun–Thurs noon–11pm; Fri–Sat noon–midnight. Métro: Parmentier.

Jeanne A ★ ⌁ TRADITIONAL FRENCH/WINE BAR This new restaurant/wine bar/takeout shop represents a new trend in Paris, providing an informal place to eat and drink well for not a lot of money. Run by the renowned Astier restaurant next door (p. 207), Jeanne A turns out spit-roasted meats (Challans duck or crispy-skinned chicken) served with salad and heaping portion of *potato gratin dauphinois.* These mains are bookended by delicious charcuterie and an impressive selection of artisanal cheeses, and complemented by wines that are both easy drinking and easily priced. Order by the glass or the magnum (that's two bottles' worth), and take home what you're not able to drink.

42 rue Jean-Pierre Timbaud, 11e. ℂ **01-43-55-09-49.** Reservations recommended. Main courses 12€–17€. MC, V. Thurs–Mon 10:30am–10:30pm. Métro: Parmentier.

Mélac TRADITIONAL FRENCH/WINE BAR This cramped and cozy wine bar was founded in 1938 and not much has changed here since. You still have to walk through the kitchen to get to the main dining room, and the hearty dishes of Jacque Mélac's Aveyron region are still served the way they were decades ago. Specialties include a confit of pig's liver, veal tripe bundles, fresh and cured sausages, and a *poêlon aveyronnais* (a cast-iron casserole of chicken liver and fried eggs in a sauce made with red wine and shallots). Water consumption is discouraged in favor of the robust red wines of Aveyron.

42 rue Léon-Frot, 11e. ℂ **01-43-70-59-27.** www.melac.fr. Reservations recommended. Main courses 14€–20€; fixed-price lunch (Tues–Fri) 15€. DC, MC, V. Tues–Sat noon–4pm and 8–11pm. Closed Aug. Métro: Charonne.

Belleville & Northeast Paris (19e and 20e)

Between the two parks of Belleville and Buttes-Chaumont lie some of the city's most quirky, delightful, and wine-centered restaurants. Le Baratin and Le Chapeau Melon are both widely acknowledged as having two of the most impressive wine caves in town, with an emphasis on *vins naturels.* Relative newcomer Quedubon follows in their footsteps, serving great food and a wide selection of wine.

MODERATE

Le Baratin ★ 📱 TRADITIONAL FRENCH/BISTRO   Argentina-born Chef Raquel Carena has created a neighborhood institution with Le Baratin, serving her imaginative bistro fare to both locals and foodies. Carena cooks from the heart, changing her menu regularly to reflect the seasons and her current inspiration. The value is most compelling at lunch, when one can enjoy a leisurely two-course affair for only 16€, to be followed by a stroll in the nearby Parc de Belleville. There is an impressive wine cave here, managed by Raquel's famously grumpy husband, Philippe Pinoteau.

3 rue Jouye-Rouve, 20e. ℰ **01-43-49-39-70.** Reservations recommended. Fixed-price dinner 38€; fixed-price lunch 16€. MC, V. Tues–Fri noon–2:30pm and 8–11pm; Sat 8–11pm. Métro: Pyrénées.

Le Chapeau Melon ★ 📱 MODERN FRENCH/WINE BAR   Olivier Camus, the cofounder of Le Baratin (see above), has created one of our favorite wine bars in the city. Perched high up on the Belleville hill, not far from the beautiful Parc des Buttes-Chaumont, Le Chapeau Melon serves a no-choice four-course tasting menu for a remarkable 32€. Bright dishes such as langoustine carpaccio or vitello tonnato are often followed by slow-braised beef or lamb, signaling your move from white to red wine. The shelves that line the walls are stocked with bottles from some of the most renowned producers of natural wine, and you can buy them to go or drink them here for a modest corkage fee.

92 rue Rébeval, 19e. ℰ **01-42-02-68-60.** Reservations recommended. Prix-fixe dinner 32€. MC, V. Wed–Sun 8pm–1am. Métro: Pyrénées.

Quedubon TRADITIONAL FRENCH/BISTRO   This wine-centric bistro near the Parc des Buttes Chaumont serves classic French fare including marinated sardines, beef cheeks in red wine sauce, braised oxtail with carrots and turnips, and lentil salad with duck breast. These are complemented by a warm welcome, a killer cheese plate, and a staggering selection of wines by the bottle. The wine list is presented on a chalkboard that changes regularly, reflecting owner Gilles Bénard's preference for small-scale producers. Come on a Monday night, when many other Paris restaurants are closed, and you'll be sharing space with a room full of chefs and sommeliers who are relaxing on their night off.

22 rue du Plateau, 19e. ℰ **01-42-38-18-65.** www.quedubon-production.com. Reservations recommended. Main courses 13€–24€. MC, V. Mon–Fri noon–2:30pm and 8–11pm; Sat 8–11pm. Métro: Buttes Chaumont.

Rosa Bonheur ★ 📱 ☺ TAPAS   This restaurant inside the Parc des Buttes Chaumont boasts a sprawling terrace and one of the best panoramic views in town. A huge crowd gathers to drink and nibble tapas outside, but the menu also features main dishes such as stuffed and grilled shrimp, lamb and carrot stew, and monkfish with sage sauce. The real reason to visit is for the relaxed and friendly ambience, though—and the possibility of strolling through the city's largest and wildest park before or after your meal. That park, plus an indoor play area and kids' menu, makes Rosa Bonheur a great family option, too.

2 avenue de la Cascade, 19e. ℰ **01-42-00-00-45.** www.rosabonheur.fr. Reservations not accepted. Tapas from 5€–8€; fixed-price menus at 29€ and 35€; children's menu 14€. MC, V. Wed–Sun noon–midnight. Métro Botzaris.

THE LEFT BANK
Latin Quarter (5e)

This neighborhood, stretching south from the river near Notre Dame to the market street of Mouffetard, is one of the oldest and best preserved in the city. The chefs who have set up shop here most recently are not content to merely perpetuate tradition. Some restaurants, such as L'Agrume and Le Pré Verre, are using foreign flavors and techniques to update traditional French recipes, while others, like Dans Les Landes and Les Papilles, are trying to relax the rules and make restaurant dining a less formal experience.

VERY EXPENSIVE

La Tour d'Argent 🖐 TRADITIONAL FRENCH Although its reputation as the best in Paris has long been eclipsed, dining here remains an unsurpassed event—not because of the food, but because of its history and its view of the flying buttresses of Notre-Dame. A restaurant of some sort has stood on this site since 1582: Mme de Sévigné refers to a café here in her letters, and Dumas used it in one of his novels. The fame of La Tour d'Argent spread during its ownership by Frédéric Delair, who in the 1890s started the practice of issuing certificates to diners who ordered *caneton* (pressed duckling). The birds are numbered: The first was served to Edward VII in 1890, and now the number has surpassed 1.2 million. For decades, the restaurant was owned by Claude Terrail, but after he died in 2006, his son, André, took over. A good part of the menu is devoted to duck, but the kitchen, of course, knows how to prepare other dishes. There are plenty of other places nearby where you can order food even better than that served here—and at only half the price.

15–17 quai de la Tournelle, 5e. ☎ **01-43-54-23-31.** Fax 01-44-07-12-04. www.latourdargent.com. Reservations required far in advance. Main courses 60€–75€; fixed-price lunch 65€. AE, DC, MC, V. Tues–Sat noon–1pm; Tues–Sat 7:30–9pm. Métro: St-Michel or Pont Marie.

Restaurants in Belleville & Northeast Paris (19e & 20e)

Café de la Musique 1
Le Baratin 5
Le Chapeau Melon 4
Quedubon 3
Rosa Bonheur 2

MODERATE

Brasserie Balzar ♨ TRADITIONAL FRENCH/BRASSERIE   Opened in 1898, Brasserie Balzar is battered but cheerful, with some of Paris's most colorful waiters. The menu makes almost no concessions to modern cuisine; it includes onion soup, pepper steak, *sole meunière,* sauerkraut with ham and sausage, pigs' feet, and fried calves' liver served without garnish. Be warned that if you want just coffee or a drink, you probably won't get a table at mealtimes. But the staff, accustomed to many patrons' odd hours, will be happy to serve you dinner in the midafternoon. In the past, guests have included Sartre and Camus (who often got into arguments), and countless professors from the nearby Sorbonne. Today's clientele includes a hefty mix of tourists.

49 rue des Ecoles, 5e. ✆ **01-43-54-13-67.** www.brasseriebalzar.com. Reservations strongly recommended. Main courses 18€–35€. AE, DC, MC, V. Daily noon–11:45pm. Métro: Odéon or Cluny–La Sorbonne.

Dans Les Landes ★ 🔖 SOUTHWESTERN FRENCH   This new spot from Julien Duboué (of Afaria in the 15e, p. 223) is named after the southwestern French region that inspired the chef's long list of tapas and small plates. Go for grilled quail breasts or the unmissable fried chipirions (small squid that are crisp, golden and dusted with smoky pepper). Duboué's southwestern take on the spring roll—rice paper stuffed with foie gras, duck breast, and salad—is also compelling. Finish with an unusual dessert of warm anise-scented liquor with toasted crème anglaise.

119 bis rue Monge, 5e. ✆ **01-45-87-06-00.** Reservations recommended. Tapas 6€–15€; plat du jour 16€. MC, V. Mon–Sat noon–11pm. Métro: Censier-Daubenton.

Itinéraires TRADITIONAL FRENCH   There's always a danger when a successful restaurant moves and expands. Often its original charm and patrons are lost. Not so with acclaimed chef Sylvain Sendra and his wife, Sarah, who closed their 26-seat Le Temps au Temps in the 11th arrondissement and opened this restaurant in the Latin Quarter. Their new place is twice as large, and the cuisine is just as good as it always was. Specialties include everything from Jerusalem artichoke soup to pheasant breast accompanied by dates, pistachios, fruit compote, and the odd nugget of buckshot. One specialty is morchella mushrooms served with bacon chips and a soft-boiled egg. They have a distinctive strong taste and come in a creamy sauce. You might also order a delightful sea bass stuffed with white asparagus and served with a creamy Parmesan vanilla sauce.

5 rue de Pontoise, 5e. ✆ **01-46-33-60-11.** www.restaurantitineraires.com. Reservations required. Fixed-price lunch at 29€; fixed-price dinner at 39€ and 59€. AE, MC, V. Tues–Sat noon–2pm and 7:30–10:30pm (11:30pm Fri–Sat). Métro: Maubert-Mutualité.

L'Agrume MODERN FRENCH   Foodies began flocking to this bare-bones dining room at the southern tip of the 5th arrondissement after Franck Marchesi-Grandi took over the restaurant in late 2010. The young chef (who worked briefly at Le Bernadin in New York) serves a moderately priced menu featuring Asian-accented French dishes such as crab with green apple and lime, chicken poached in a ginger-infused kombu broth, and roasted hake with celeri rave. We're not convinced that it warrants a trip across town, but L'Agrume is certainly a welcome addition to a neighborhood that isn't flush with dining options.

15 rue des Fossés St. Marcel, 5e. ✆ **01-43-31-86-48.** Reservations required. Fixed-price dinner 37€; fixed-price lunch 16€. MC, V. Tues–Sat noon–2:30pm and 7–10:30pm. Métro: Les Gobelins.

Restaurants in the Latin Quarter & Southern Paris (5e & 13e)

Brasserie Balzar **2**
Breakfast in America **6**
Chez Gladines **11**
Dans les Landes **8**
Itinéraires **4**
L'Agrume **9**
La Tour d'Argent **5**
Le Petit Marguery **10**
Le Pré Verre **3**
Les Papilles **7**
Ribouldingue **1**

Le Pré Verre ★ 🍴 MODERN FRENCH/ASIAN FUSION   Around the corner from the Sorbonne in the heart of the Latin Quarter sits a refreshing restaurant where you can get seriously good food at an affordable price. The Delacourcelle brothers are firmly based in the French tradition but many of their chosen flavorings are inspired by Asia. In a welcoming, relaxed, and convivial atmosphere, tables are placed so close together that you're literally dining and rubbing elbows with your neighbors. For starters, dig into a well-flavored terrine—like the one made with layers of foie gras and mashed potatoes—or oysters marinated with ginger and poppy seeds or scallops with cinnamon. Main courses might include suckling pig with aromatic spices and crisp-cooked cabbage, or roasted codfish.

8 rue Thenard, 5e. ✆ **01-43-54-59-47.** www.lepreverre.com. Reservations required. Main courses 18€; fixed-price lunch 13€–29€; fixed-price dinner 29€. MC, V. Tues–Sat noon–2pm and 7:30–10:30pm. Closed Aug. Métro: Maubert-Mutualité.

Les Papilles ★ 🎁 TRADITIONAL FRENCH/BISTRO   One of the most exciting additions to Paris's culinary scene is this bustling combination bistro/wine shop run by Bertrand Bluy. The fixed price menu offers great value—four courses for 31€—but no choices. Dishes are comforting and often served family style from a cast-iron pot in the center of the table. Wine is available by the glass, but patrons are encouraged to choose a bottle from the nearby shelves and pay just a small corkage fee above retail price. This is a great place to try a good bottle because you're not paying for the usual restaurant markup on the wine.

30 rue Gay-Lussac. ✆ **01-43-25-20-79.** www.lespapillesparis.fr. Reservations not needed. Market menu 31€; fixed-price dinner 80€. AE, MC, V. Mon–Sat noon–3pm and 7–11pm. Métro: Luxembourg.

Ribouldingue TRADITIONAL FRENCH   Offal lovers flock to this bistro near St-Julien-le-Pauvre church to enjoy such old-fashioned fare as the tip of a pig's snout or thinly breaded and sautéed slices of a cow's udder. If those are unappealing, how about lamb's brain meunière, tripe cooked in white wine, or even veal kidneys in garlic sauce? For the offal timid, there are many other dishes, including veal rib with fried potatoes; pollock with eggplant caviar and crispy lardons (bacon cubes); or even a blanquette of monkfish. This Latin Quarter bistro is the creation of Nadège Varigny, who grew up without any fear of the sight of blood as the daughter of an Alpine butcher.

10 rue Saint-Julien-le-Pauvre, 5e. ✆ **01-46-33-98-80.** www.restaurant-ribouldingue.com. Reservations required. Main courses 17€–26€; fixed-price lunch 27€; fixed-price dinner 29€. MC, V. Tues–Fri noon–2:30pm and Tues–Sat 7:30–10:30pm. Closed 3 weeks in Aug. Métro: Cluny La Sorbonne or St-Michel.

INEXPENSIVE

Breakfast in America ☺ AMERICAN   Connecticut-born Hollywood screenwriter Craig Carlson opened this replica of a down-home U.S.-based diner in 2003, building it with funds from members of the California film community who donated memorabilia from their films. Its self-proclaimed mission involves dispensing proper, rib-sticking American breakfasts and diner food to Parisians. The setting replicates a 1950s-era railway car, replete with scarlet-and-black Naugahyde banquettes, faux windows with mirrored insets, and an unabashedly Americanized staff. Breakfast (heaping portions of the egg-and-waffle-and-bacon combinations, as well as omelets) is served throughout the day and evening. Also available are half a dozen variations of burgers, tacos, club sandwiches, and BLTs.

17 rue des Ecoles, 5e. ☎ **01-43-54-50-28.** Reservations not accepted. Breakfast platters 7€–11€; lunch and dinner platters and "blue-plate specials" 8€–12€; fixed-price Sun brunch 16€. MC, V. Daily 8:30am–10:30pm. Métro: Cardinal Lemoine or Jussieu.

St-Germain-des-Près & Luxembourg (6e)

Our favorite restaurants in Saint-Germain are classic bistros, serving traditional French fare with a few modern accents. Le Comptoir du Relais and Ze Kitchen Galerie are run by notable chefs and require advance reservations, but the rest of our restaurant recommendations here are more casual and accept walk-ins and same-day bookings.

EXPENSIVE

Ze Kitchen Galerie ★ INTERNATIONAL/MODERN FRENCH   Chef William Ledeuil trained in haute Parisian gastronomy under chef Guy Savoy before brazenly opening up his own place right next door to Savoy's Les Bouquinistes. The setting is a colorful loft space in an antique building with an open showcase kitchen. Most of the paintings on display are for sale (the place doubles as an art gallery). Menu items, as with the paintings, change about every 5 weeks: appetizers are subdivided into pastas, soups, and fish; and main courses are divided into meats and fish that are usually *à la plancha* (grilled). For starters, try the octopus with lemongrass and kalamenji. A pasta dish might feature homemade linguine with Bouchot mussels and dried fish eggs, and other mains of the moment include grilled mackerel with miso and Challans duck with mostarda and plums. Dessert could be the restaurant's "cappuccino of the month," a frothy dessert concoction with ingredients that change with the seasons.

4 rue des Grands-Augustins, 6e. ☎ **01-44-32-00-32.** www.zekitchengalerie.fr. Reservations recommended. Main courses 30€–35€; fixed-price lunch with wine 27€–39€; fixed-price dinner 80€. AE, DC, MC, V. Mon–Fri noon–2:30pm; Mon–Sat 7–11pm. Métro: St-Michel or Pont-Neuf.

MODERATE

Alcazar Restaurant TRADITIONAL FRENCH   This high-tech place, funded by British restaurateur Sir Terence Conran, is Paris's sleekest brasserie. It features a red-and-white futuristic decor in a street-level dining room and a busy upstairs bar (La Mezzanine de l'Alcazar). The menu includes rack of veal sautéed with wild mushrooms, roasted rack of lamb with thyme, and shellfish and oysters from the waters of Brittany. The wines are as international and diverse as you'd expect.

62 rue Mazarine, 6e. ☎ **01-53-10-19-99.** www.alcazar.fr. Reservations recommended. Main courses 17€–33€; fixed-price lunch 20€–32€; fixed-price dinner 43€; Sun brunch 32€. AE, DC, MC, V. Daily noon–2:30pm and 7pm–1am. Métro: Odéon.

Fish MODERN FRENCH/MEDITERRANEAN/SEAFOOD   This restaurant, run by Drew Harré, is the unofficial Anglo headquarters of the 6th arrondissement. Regulars fill the seats at the bar (a good spot for solo dining), where they drink wines from Juan Sanchez's La Derniere Goutte. The menu is slightly Mediterranean, offering solid if not revelatory cooking with an accent on seafood. But the service is friendly and multilingual, and the wine list is superb.

69 rue de Seine, 6e. ☎ **01-43-54-34-69.** Reservations recommended. Fixed-price dinner 31€ and 35€; fixed-price lunch 22€. M. Daily noon–3pm and 7pm–12:30am. Métro: Mabillon.

La Bastide Odéon PROVENÇAL   The sunny climes of Provence come through in the pale yellow walls, oak tables, and bouquets of wheat and dried roses. Chef Gilles Ajuelos prepares market-based cuisine for a dining room that's packed with Anglophones. His simplest first courses are the most satisfying, such as scallop risotto with Parmesan, and eggplant-stuffed roasted rabbit with olive toast and balsamic vinegar. Main courses include a warm napoleon of grilled eggplant served "in the style of the Riviera," and roasted chicken with a comfit of Provençal garlic and fried potatoes.

7 rue Corneille, 6e. ℭ **01-43-26-03-65.** www.bastide-odeon.com. Reservations recommended. Fixed-price menu 32€–45€. AE, MC, V. Tues–Sat 2:15–2pm and 7:30–10:30pm. Métro: Odéon. RER: Luxembourg.

La Ferrandaise TRADITIONAL FRENCH   This restaurant near the Luxembourg Gardens is the place for anyone in search of meat-and-potatoes cooking done right. In celebration of a certain tasty cow from the Auvergne region, La Ferrandaise is decorated with photos of the namesake breed. Beef dishes are in the spotlight here, presented in various forms from steak to *pot au feu*, but heirloom pork and seasonal game offer some variety, too. Don't leave without trying the cheese plate—it includes many raw-milk varieties from central France that you won't find anywhere else.

8 rue de Vaugirard, 6e. ℭ **01-43-26-36-36.** www.laferrandaise.com. Reservations recommended. Fixed-price dinner 32€ and 44€; fixed-price lunch 15€ and 32€. MC, V. Mon–Fri noon–3pm and 7–11:30pm; Sat 7–11:30pm. Métro: Odéon.

La Rôtisserie d'en Face TRADITIONAL FRENCH/BISTRO   This is Paris's most popular baby bistro, operated by Jacques Cagna, whose expensive namesake restaurant is across the street. The informal place features a postmodern decor with high-tech lighting, yellow walls, and red banquettes. The simply prepared food is very good and employs high-quality ingredients. Tantalizing starters include red tuna and sea bream tartare flavored with ginger and soy or rabbit pâté with pine nuts. Favorite main dishes include the signature spit-roasted free-range chicken served with buttery mashed potatoes or cold grilled salmon with coriander-marinated fresh vegetables. Few desserts top "the red berry bowl," with cassis sauce and whipped cream.

2 rue Christine, 6e. ℭ **01-43-26-40-98.** www.jacquescagna.com. Reservations recommended. Main courses 22€–27€; fixed-price lunch 23€–37€. AE, DC, MC, V. Mon–Fri noon–2:30pm; Mon–Sat 7–11pm. Métro: Odéon or St-Michel.

Le Comptoir du Relais ★★ TRADITIONAL FRENCH/BISTRO   Le Comptoir is the domain of Yves Camdeborde, the pioneering chef who kicked off the bistronomy movement, serving high-caliber food in a casual bistro setting, when he left a three-star kitchen to open his own bistro at the edge of the city. He sold La Régalade (which remains good) years ago to open this "counter," serving guests of the attached hotel and foodies who book dinner months and months in advance. Lunch is an easier table to score because reservations are not accepted—just line up before the doors open at noon and you're likely to get a table. All this fuss can be attributed to Camdeborde's well-executed bistro cuisine that reflects his southwestern roots and is made from high quality ingredients. The menu changes regularly, but dishes might include creamy slices of foie

Restaurants in St-Germain-des-Prés, Luxembourg & Montparnasse (6e & 14e)

Alcazar Restaurant 6	La Rôtisserie
Café de Flore 2	d'en Face 7
Crêperie Josselin 18	La Rotonde 16
Fish 5	L'Assiette 21
La Bastide Odéon 13	L'Avant Comptoir 11
La Cagouille 20	Le Comptoir
La Cerisaie 19	du Relais 11
La Crémerie 10	Le Cornichon 22
La Crémerie	Le Procope 9
Restaurant	Le Relais de
Polidor 12	l'Entrecôte 1
La Coupole 17	Les Deux Magots 3
La Ferrandaise 14	Le Severo 23
La Palette 4	Le Timbre 15
La Régalade 24	Ze Kitchen Galerie 8

gras with chunky prune sauce or a juicy rack of pork. It's comfort food with a touch of luxury, and it will spoil you for all subsequent bistros.

9 carrefour de l'Odéon, 6e. ✆ **01-44-27-07-97.** www.hotel-paris-relais-saint-germain.com. Reservations required for dinner weeknights; reservations not accepted for lunch and weekends. Main courses weekends 27€–35€; fixed-price dinner weeknights 50€. MC, V. Daily noon–2am. Métro: Odéon.

Le Relais de l'Entrecôte ☺ TRADITIONAL FRENCH/STEAK   For those who are tired of making decisions, Le Relais de l'Entrecôte has only one question for you: "La cuisson?" Tell them how you like your steak done (*"bien cuit"* for medium-well, *"à point"* medium rare, or *"saignant"* for rare) and then sit back and let the show begin. You'll start with a fresh green salad and then proceed to the main event: a giant silver platter of steak, doused in an addictive "secret sauce," and served with crispy golden fries. That platter is refillable, by the way—you can expect to see your server return with a second helping once you've finished. Desserts, if you can find the strength, are classic and delicious, including profiteroles and crème brûlée. The crowd that gathers inside the pretty-postcard dining room includes tourists, locals, and chefs; it also includes plenty of families with kids.

20 rue St. Benoît, 6e. ✆ **01-45-49-16-00.** www.relaisentrecote.fr. Reservations not required. Daily noon–3pm and 7–11pm. Fixed-price lunch and dinner 25€. MC, V. Métro: St. Germain des Prés.

Le Timbre TRADITIONAL FRENCH   British Chef Chris Wright opened the tiniest restaurant on the tiniest street in Paris near Montparnasse. The Manchester-born chef shops for only the finest of French regional products, including truffles and foie gras, and he gets by with no microwave or freezer. Wright prepares faultless dishes, including trout stuffed with fresh fava beans and country ham, andouillette sausages with lentils from Puy, or a filet of white fish with olives. In spite of all these *à la française* dishes, he likes to put English cheddar on his cheeseboard. If not the cheese, you might end your meal with the ruby-red strawberry soup.

3 rue Sainte Beuve, 6e. ✆ **01-45-49-10-40.** www.restaurantletimbre.com. Reservations required. Main courses 15€–21€; fixed-price lunch 24€–28€. MC, V. Tues–Sat noon–2pm and 7:30–10:30pm. Closed 3 weeks in Aug. Métro: Notre-Dame-des-Champs or Vavin.

INEXPENSIVE

La Crèmerie ★ 👜 TRADITIONAL FRENCH   New Yorker Serge Mathieu was an architect when he first entered Pierre Jancou's wine bar La Crèmerie. But after only one visit he began pleading to take over this tiny 19th century creamery. Jancou moved on to open Racines and then Vivant, but La Crèmerie, with its ceiling of hand-painted silk under glass, is still a destination for great wine and small plates. The charcuterie and cheeses are exceptional, but you can also dine on foie gras, oysters, delicately smoked tuna, and a spectacular chocolate fondant. Note that La Crèmerie doesn't serve any hot food except for grilled vegetables.

9 rue des Quatre Vents, 6e. ✆ **01-43-54-99-30.** www.lacremerie.fr. Reservations not needed. Meals from 20€. MC, V. Tues–Sat 10:30am–10pm; Sun 11am–2:30pm; Mon 2–8pm. Métro: Odéon.

La Crèmerie Restaurant Polidor ☺ TRADITIONAL FRENCH/BISTRO   Crèmerie Polidor is the most traditional (and heavily touristed) bistro in the Odéon area, serving *cuisine familiale*. Its name dates from the early 1900s, when it specialized in frosted cream desserts, but the restaurant can trace its history from 1845. The Crémerie was André Gide's favorite, and Joyce, Hemingway, Valéry, Artaud, and Kerouac also dined here. Peer beyond the lace curtains and brass hat racks to see drawers where, in olden days, regular customers used to lock up their cloth napkins. Try the day's soup followed by kidneys in Madeira sauce, *boeuf bourguignon* (beef braised in red wine), *confit de canard* (leg of duck), or *blanquette de veau* (veal ragout in cream sauce). For dessert, order a chocolate, raspberry, or lemon tart.

39 rue Monsieur-le-Prince, 6e. ℂ **01-43-26-95-34.** www.polidor.com. Main courses 11€–20€; fixed-price menu 22€–32€. No credit cards. Daily noon–2:30pm; Mon–Sat 7pm–12:30am; Sun 7–11pm. Métro: Odéon.

L'Avant Comptoir ★ WINE BAR/SOUTHWESTERN FRENCH This shoebox-size wine bar is just steps from the Odéon and run by bistro maestro Yves Camdeborde. Next door to his seminal restaurant Le Comptoir, this place sells crepes and sandwiches during the day and hors d'oeuvres to a raucous crowd at night. Basque and Béarnais-inspired nibbles include fried croquettes stuffed with from Eric Ospital's renowned Iberian ham, a filling cod brandade, oxtail canapés with horseradish cream, and chicken hearts grilled with garlic and parsley. Plates of charcuterie are meant to be eaten (and shared) with the crocks of Bordier butter and gherkins that line the counter. No more than a dozen people can crowd into this place at a time and there are no chairs.

3 Carrefour de l'Odéon, 6e. No phone and no reservations accepted. Main courses 3€–7€. MC, V. Daily 9am–1am. Métro: Odéon.

Eiffel Tower & Nearby (7e)

The chic 7th arrondissement is home to some of the city's most respected and innovative chefs, including Alain Passard (L'Arpège), Jean-François Piège, and Joël Robuchon. A table at one of their celebrated tables doesn't come cheap, but you'll never forget the experience. There are several *bistronomique* restaurants here too, including Les Cocottes and Chez l'Ami Jean, where gastronomes can go for a memorable meal at more modest prices.

VERY EXPENSIVE

Jean-François Piège ★ MODERN FRENCH This new restaurant, above the bustling brasserie Thoumieux, is the newest stage for chef Jean-François Piège. After leaving the palatial kitchens of Les Ambassadeurs, Piège partnered with Thierry Costes to open a hotel and restaurant complex near Invalides. His namesake restaurant is an intimate 20-seat showcase, which has been enthusiastically welcomed by the critics. Dishes are creative and whimsical; you might try a mussel with a heap of fried frizzled potatoes—his version of *moules frites*. For dessert, the tarte tatin (apple tart)—a puff of sweet pizza dough topped with sliced apples and cream—is excellent. Piège's cooking has been called witty and precise, and funky decor by India Mahdavi—featuring brightly colored sofas with black and white accents—has garnered almost as much attention as the food.

79 rue St. Dominique, 7e. ℂ **01-47-05-49-75.** www.jfpiege.com. Reservations recommended. Main courses 37€–69€. MC, V, Daily noon–midnight. Métro: La Tour Maubourg.

L'Arpège ★★★ MODERN FRENCH Chef Alain Passard made waves years ago when he decided to put vegetables, not meat, in the spotlight at his three-star restaurant L'Arpège. Although meat is still featured on the menu, his dedication to carrots and turnips was something previously unseen. This pristine produce, which he raises on a farm near Le Mans, is often picked in the morning and served the same day in Paris. Uneaten food from his restaurant makes the return journey to become compost. Food politics aside, the flavors that Passard coaxes from these vegetables (often with the welcome addition of butter and cream) are truly remarkable. Service is discreet, as one expects at a restaurant frequented by diplomats and executives, and the dining room, with etched glass, burnished steel, and pearwood paneling, is beautiful, if a bit dated. Don't miss the cheese course, served on a giant polished plank of wood, or the *tarte aux pommes bouquet de roses* (a tart composed of apple ribbons rolled into tiny rosettes).

84 rue de Varenne, 7e. ✆ **01-47-05-09-06.** Fax 01-44-18-98-39. www.alain-passard.com. Reservations required 2 weeks in advance. Main courses 48€–180€; fixed-price lunch 125€; fixed-price dinner 420€. AE, DC, MC, V. Mon–Fri 12:30–2:30pm and 8–10:30pm. Métro: Varenne.

EXPENSIVE

L'Atelier Saint-Germain de Joël Robuchon ★★ MODERN FRENCH
World-renowned Chef Joël Robuchon came out of a short-lived retirement in 2003 in order to open this ground-breaking culinary workshop on the left bank. He recently added the words "Saint-Germain" when he opened a second Atelier near the Arc de Triomphe (p. 104). This original location remains packed with gastronomes who want to eat well without the fuss implied by a three-star restaurant. Sitting informally upon high stools at a U-shaped bar, you can order the tasting menu or a series of sharable small plates including sea bream carpaccio, caviar with smoked eel and horseradish, grilled marrow bones, and the famous Robuchon mashed potatoes. Reservations are accepted for the extremely early and late seatings only (at 11:30am and 2pm for lunch, and 6:30pm for dinner); these spots are booked well in advance. Otherwise, it's first come, first served.

5 rue Montalembert, 7e. ✆ **01-42-22-56-56.** www.joel-rubochon.net. Reservations required. Main courses 27€–68€; dinner tasting menu 150€. AE, MC, V. Daily 11:30am–3:30pm and 6:30pm–midnight. Métro: Rue du Bac.

Les Ombres INTERNATIONAL/MODERN FRENCH
Architect Jean Nouvel named this museum rooftop restaurant for the shadows cast by the Eiffel Tower looming nearby. You dine under a canopy of "metallic lace" inspired by the tower itself. A late dinner is practically a spectacle, as the tower twinkles for the first 10 minutes of every hour. Fortunately, the chefs don't just rely on the view. The head chef, Arno Busquet, trained under the great Joël Robuchon and creates eclectic dishes like foie gras with spiced mango chutney or guinea fowl stuffed with creole sausage and served with an apple cabbage purée. Other delights include a lamb shoulder with fennel, tarragon, and coco beans and lard-roasted cod with clams and leeks.

Musée du Quai Branly, 27 quai Branly, 7e. ✆ **01-47-53-68-00.** www.lesombres-restaurant.com. Reservations required. Main courses 28€–43€; fixed-price lunch 38€; fixed-price dinner 65€. MC, V. Daily noon–2:30pm and 7–10:30pm. Métro: Pont de l'Alma.

Le Violon d'Ingres MODERN FRENCH
Christian Constant has built a sort of culinary empire in the 7th with three restaurants along the rue Saint-Dominique. Le Violon d'Ingres is his most refined restaurant, and a recent makeover has left it looking more sophisticated in tones of mushroom and red wine. Chef Stéphane Schmidt executes Constant's vision with dishes like the signature grilled wood pigeon served with a fricassee of wild mushrooms and sweet garlic;

Restaurants near the Eiffel Tower (7 & 15e)

L'Atelier Saint-Germain de Joël Robuchon 13
Le Casse-Noix 8
Les Cocottes de Christian Constant 7
Les Ombres 1
Le Violon d'Ingres 6
Lily Wang 11
Thoumieux 4

Afaria 9
Chez l'Ami Jean 2
Eric Kayser 14
Jadis 10
Jean-Francois Piège 3
La Fontaine de Mars 5
L'Arpège 12

Pedestrians only
Ⓜ Metro station
RER RER3 station
☒ Post office

0   1/4 mi
0   0.25 km

rock crab with fennel cream and herring caviar; and a spit roast turbot with baby potatoes and a mousseline sauce.

135 rue St-Dominique, 7e. ℂ **01-45-55-15-05.** Fax 01-45-55-48-42. www.leviolondingres.com. Reservations required. Main courses 27€; fixed-price menu 49€. AE, DC, MC, V. Tues–Sat noon–2:30pm and 7–10:30pm. Métro: Invalides or Ecole-Militaire.

Thoumieux MODERN FRENCH/BRASSERIE   After leaving the palatial kitchens of Les Ambassadeurs, Chef Jean-François Piège partnered with hotel scion Thierry Costes to reinvent the Paris brasserie. Critics have loved certain dishes, such as the squid carbonara and the juicy hamburger covered in Parmesan cheese, but have generally found the cooking to be uneven and unworthy of Piège. That hasn't stopped the trend-seeking set from packing the beautifully restored dining room every night. It's definitely a scene, and a very enjoyable one at that if you're more interested in gabbing than gastronomy. The chef's newer namesake restaurant (Jean-François Piège, p. 219) on the same site is even pricier, but critics have raved about the food.

79 rue St. Dominique, 7e. ℂ **01-47-05-49-75.** www.thoumieux.fr. Reservations recommended. Main courses 37€– 69€. MC, V. Daily noon–midnight. Métro: La Tour Maubourg.

MODERATE

Chez l'Ami Jean ★ BASQUE/SOUTHWESTERN FRENCH   This restaurant was originally opened by a Basque nationalist in 1931, but it was Chef Stéphane Jego who really put the bistro on the map. Jego maintained the original decor (if one can call wood panels and sports memorabilia a decor) but turned L'Ami Jean into a destination for *cuisine bistronomique*—high-caliber cooking served in a homey neighborhood setting. Reserve in advance and arrive hungry because the Basque dishes served here are anything but light—even the fish dishes here are accented by foie gras and chorizo. However much you may have already eaten, say yes to the cheese plate with Basque brebis (sheep's milk cheese) and black cherry preserves, and finish with a heaping bowl of *riz au lait* (rice pudding).

27 rue Malar, 7e. ℂ **01-47-05-86-89.** www.amijean.eu. Reservations required. Main courses 20€–40€; fixed-price dinner at 35€, 42€, and 60€. MC, V. Tues–Sat noon–2pm and 7pm–midnight. Closed Aug. Métro: Invalides.

La Fontaine de Mars BISTRO/SOUTHWESTERN FRENCH   Visiting Americans began rushing to book tables shortly after President Obama and the first lady dined at this classic French bistro. One of the old-school bistros of Paris, it's been a venerable institution since it first opened in 1908, but it's never had this kind of business before. The cooking leans toward the southwest with dishes like cassoulet, foie gras, and duck breast figuring prominently on the menu. Starters include *escargots* (snails) and *oeufs au Madiran* (eggs baked with red wine and bacon), and the dessert list is full of classics such as *île flottante*, crème brûlée, and dark chocolate mousse.

129 rue Saint Dominique, 7e. ℂ **01-47-05-46-44.** www.fontainedemars.com. Reservations required. Main courses 17€–30€. AE, MC, V. Daily noon–3pm and 7:30–11pm. Métro: Ecole Militaire.

Les Cocottes de Christian Constant ★ TRADITIONAL FRENCH   Take a seat at the long counter or a high table for Christian Constant's updated comfort food—almost all of it served in cast iron *cocottes* (casseroles). Begin with a plate of sliced Ospital ham, then move on to scallops with endive and orange butter sauce, potato-stuffed pigs' feet, or a seasonal vegetable cocotte. Desserts include an oversized waffle with Chantilly cream and Constant's signature chocolate tarte. Reservations are not accepted, which can actually be an advantage in Paris.

135 rue St. Dominique, 7e. No phone. Reservations not accepted. Main courses 20€–35€. MC, V. Mon–Sat noon–4pm and 7–11pm. Métro: École Militaire.

Lily Wang CHINESE   This audacious new Chinese restaurant is backed by the notorious Costes family and reflects the current obsession in Paris with anything Asian. The stylishly kitsch and dimly lit dining room features velvet curtains, glowing lanterns, and lacquered furniture in shades of red and black. One French critic compared Lily's looks to that of a Chinese escort working in Saint-Tropez. Dishes including fried pork ravioli, pork tenderloin marinated in fish sauce, and smoky *jian-jiao* (pork dumplings) are indisputably delicious, but the steep prices put Lily's charms out of reach for budget-minded diners.

40 avenue Duquesne, 7e. ✆ **01-53-86-09-09.** Reservations recommended. Main courses 23€–39€. MC, V. Daily noon–3pm and 7–11pm. Métro: Saint-François-Xavier.

INEXPENSIVE

Eric Kayser ★★ BAKERY/LIGHT FARE   If you're in the 7th arrondissement for breakfast or lunch, a good refueling stop is this bakery, bar, and café. Kayser's forte is bread making—he is known for the long fermentation of his dough. He's always coming up with new ideas for his breads, including one made with apricots and pistachios and another with chorizo. This Alsatian baker offers many luxe breads and pastries, and breakfast is a delight here. At lunch you have a choice of 20 different combinations of *tartines* (open-faced sandwiches), and teatime features gourmet snacks such as a sweet tartine with meringue and chestnuts.

18 rue du Bac, 7e. ✆ **01-42-61-27-63.** Sandwiches and savory tartes 4€–8€. MC, V. Tues–Sun 7am–8pm. Métro: Bac or Musée d'Orsay.

Montparnasse & Southern Paris (13e, 14e & 15e)

The largely residential 15th arrondissement has exploded with restaurants in recent years. Although this area may seem remote, those who venture here are rewarded with a large selection of fabulous and affordable bistros. Afaria and Jadis are the standouts, but newcomers Le Cornichon and Le Casse-Noix are getting rave reviews, too. The 14th has long been a bastion of bistronomy, home to the wonderfully classic bistros La Régalade, Le Cerisaie, and Le Severo.

MODERATE

Afaria ★ BASQUE/BISTRO   Many visitors skip the 15th arrondissement, but Afaria is a good reason to go there. Chef Julien Duboué lures eaters from all over town to this dull corner of the 15th with his bright Basque cooking. The bistro, which he runs with his wife, Céline, includes a bar where locals nibble tapas at a communal table, and a dining room with wooden tables decked in cheerful red and white tablecloths. Traditional recipes are revisited with an imaginative twist, including spicy pumpkin soup with scallops and artichokes; terrine of venison with fig chutney; and rosy charred duck breast on the bone served over smoking grapevines.

15 rue Desnouettes, 15e. ✆ **01-48-56-15-36.** Reservations required. Main courses 17€–19€; fixed-price lunch 22€–26€. MC, V. Tues–Sat noon–2:30pm and Mon–Sat 7–11pm. Métro: Convention.

Jadis ★ TRADITIONAL FRENCH/BISTRO   Shortly after it opened in 2009, the French daily newspaper *Le Figaro* hailed Jadis as "the best bistrot of the autumn." In the up-and-coming 15th arrondissement, Chef Guillaume Délage uses fresh seasonal ingredients to resuscitate "forgotten" bistro dishes from the past; start with an egg poached in red wine sauce and move on to beef stroganoff or stuffed breast of veal. Délage's nose-to-tail approach to cooking makes use of the whole animal, so don't be surprised to see cock's comb or kidney on the menu. Desserts, like the bittersweet chocolate soufflé and coffee-flavored *pot de crème,* are pure comfort.

208 rue de la Croix Nivert, 15e. ℭ **01-45-57-73-20.** www.bistrot-jadis.com. Reservations required. Main courses 21€; fixed-price lunch 25€; fixed-price dinner 34€. AE, MC, V. Mon–Fri 12:15–2:30pm and 7:15–10:30pm. Métro: Convention.

La Cagouille SEAFOOD   Don't expect to find meat at this temple of seafood—owner Gérard Allamandou refuses to feature it. Everything about La Cagouille is a testimonial to a modern version of the culinary arts of La Charente, the flat sandy district on the Atlantic south of Bordeaux. In a trio of oak-sheathed dining rooms, you'll sample seafood prepared as naturally as possible, with no fancy sauces or elaborate techniques. Try such dishes as fried filet of sole, grilled John Dory, or warm cockles. Red mullet might be sautéed in oil or baked in rock salt. The name derives from the regional symbol of La Charente, the sea snail, whose preparation elevates its namesake to a fine culinary art. Look for a vast list of wines and cognacs.

10-12 place Constantin-Brancusi, 14e. ℭ **01-43-22-09-01.** www.la-cagouille.fr. Reservations recommended. Main courses 16€–60€; fixed-price lunch 23€–38€; fixed-price dinner 38€. MC, V. Daily noon–2:30pm and 7:30–10:30pm. Métro: Gaité.

L'Assiette MODERN FRENCH   L'Assiette appeals to a nostalgic crowd seeking down-to-earth prices and flavorful food. The place was a *charcuterie* (pork butcher's shop) in the 1930s and still maintains some of its old accessories. The new chef and owner David Rathgeber was once a student of master chef Alain Ducasse. His twist on the bistro cooking tradition includes starters like shrimp tartare and a substantial terrine of pork and foie gras. His version of the classic steak frites dish uses beef from renowned butcher Hugo Desnoyer and features hand-cut fries. For dessert, don't miss the vanilla-flecked rice pudding with *confiture de lait* (milk jam).

181 rue du Château, 14e. ℭ **01-43-22-64-86.** www.restaurant-lassiette.com. Reservations recommended. Main courses 21€–37€; fixed-price lunch 23€. AE, MC, V. Wed–Sun noon–2:30pm and 7:30–10:30pm. Closed Aug. Métro: Gaité.

Le Casse Noix ★ 🍴 TRADITIONAL FRENCH/BISTRO   After cooking for six years at La Régalade (p. 225), Chef Pierre-Olivier Lenormand opened his own *bistronomique*—a place that serves high-caliber food in a casual setting—in 2010. The decor is nostalgic and the traditional French cooking is sincere and generous. Dishes like smoked chestnut soup, Iberian pork belly with choucroute of turnips, and the classic *petit salé aux lentilles* (lentils with smoky ham) are followed by crowd-pleasing desserts such as *île flottante* ("floating island," a meringue floating on custard). The wine list includes a good selection by the glass as well as many moderately priced bottles. This is a good option if you're looking for an affordable, traditional bistro that's not yet overrun with tourists.

56 rue de la Fédération, 15e. ✆ **01-45-66-09-01.** www.le-cassenoix.fr. Reservations recommended. Fixed-price dinner 32€; fixed-price lunch 20€. Mon–Fri noon–2:30pm and 7:30–10:30pm. Métro: Dupleix.

La Cerisaie ★ 🏠 SOUTHWESTERN FRENCH/BISTRO   This shoebox-size dining room near the Tour Montparnasse serves the soul-warming cuisine of southwestern France. Depending on the season, you might start with chestnut soup or an egg baked in porcini cream sauce, and foie gras is always on the menu. In autumn and winter, Chef Cyrill Lalanne does amazing things with wild game and his menu features every animal in the forest from hare to partridge to boar. Finish with the southwestern take on the classic *baba*, made with the region's Armagnac instead of rum. The atmosphere at La Cerisaie is informal and unpretentious, but the restaurant's popularity means that you need to reserve a few days in advance.

70 boulevard Edgar-Quinet, 14e. ✆ **01-43-20-98-98.** Reservation recommended. Main courses 15€–35€. MC, V. Mon–Fri noon–2pm and 7–9pm. Métro: Montparnasse-Bienvenüe.

La Régalade ★★ TRADITIONAL FRENCH/BISTRO   The *bistronomique* movement started here, under Chef Yves Camdeborde (who now works at Le Comptoir du Relais, p. 216), when people flocked to this sweet little bistro, with its cracked tile floors, polished wood, and burgundy banquettes, to taste excellent food in a low-key setting. Since then, the bistronomy movement has taken off, and Paris now boasts a large number of places that combine bistro ambience and prices with excellent culinary skills and ingredients. In 2006, Camdeborde sold La Régalade to Bruno Doucet, who has maintained the tradition and become a respected chef in his own right. Meals here begin with a help-yourself crock of homemade terrine, served with bread and gherkins, and continue with starters such as foie gras in asparagus bouillon or marinated sea scallops with basil and Parmesan. Mains are comforting, such as caramelized pork belly with mashed potatoes or sea bream with caramelized fennel and black olives. Dessert could be a stinky Reblochon cheese or a molten Guanaja chocolate cake.

14 av. Jean Moulin, 14e ✆ **01-45-45-68-58**. Reservations recommended. Fixed-price menu 30€–50€. MC, V. Tues–Fri noon–2:30pm; Mon–Fri 7–11:30pm. Closed Aug. Métro: Alésia

Le Cornichon TRADITIONAL FRENCH/BISTRO   Chef Matthieu Nadjar worked for years under Stéphane Jego at Chez l'Ami Jean (p. 222) before opening his own bistro in 2011. Le Cornichon (which means "The Pickle") was named by Nadjar's 6-year-old son, Elliot, and it serves southwest-inflected dishes, like monkfish with chorizo, alongside more globally inspired dishes such as skate wing with yuzu butter. Since prices are moderate and it's still relatively easy to get in, this is a great bistro option near the Montparnasse cemetery and the Fondation Cartier.

34 rue Gassendi, 14e. ✆ **01-43-20-40-19.** www.lecornichon.fr. Reservations recommended. Fixed-price dinner 30€. MC, V. Mon–Fri noon–3pm and 7:30–11pm. Métro: Denfert-Rochereau.

Le Petit Marguery TRADITIONAL FRENCH/BISTRO   This place evokes the turn of the 20th century, with antique tile floors, banquettes, vested waiters, and a dark rose color scheme. The menu is also based in old-fashioned traditions, with an emphasis on game dishes in autumn and fresh produce in summer. Excellent dishes include duck and rosemary terrine with foie gras; a *petit salé*

IN PURSUIT OF THE PERFECT Parisian pastry

Could it be true, as rumor has it, that more eggs, sugar, cream, and butter per capita are consumed in Paris than in any other city? From a modern-day Proust sampling a *madeleine* to a child munching a *pain au chocolat* (chocolate-filled croissant), everyone in Paris seems to be looking for two things: the perfect lover and the perfect pastry—and not necessarily in that order. As a Parisian food critic once said, "A day without a pastry is a day in hell!"

Who'd think of beginning a morning in Paris without a **croissant**—freshly baked, flaky, light, and made with real butter, preferably from Norman cows. The Greeks may have invented pastry making, but the French perfected it. Some French pastries have made a greater impact than others. The croissant and the **brioche,** a sweet and yeasty breakfast bread, are baked around the world today, as is the fabled **éclair au chocolat** (chocolate éclair), a pastry filled with whipped cream or pastry cream and topped with chocolate. Another pastry you should sample is the **mille-feuille** ("thousand leaves"), made by arranging thin layers of flaky pastry on top of one another, along with layers of cream or fruit purée or jam; the American version is called a napoleon.

Here are some of our favorite patisseries:

○ **Dalloyau,** 101 rue du Faubourg St-Honoré, 8e (✆ **01-42-99-90-00;** www.dalloyau.fr; Métro: St-Philippe du Roule) has been in business since Napoleon was in power, and has a name instantly recognizable throughout Paris. Dalloyau supplies pastries to the Elysée Palace (the French White House) and many Rothschild mansions nearby. Its specialties are **Le Dalloyau,** praline cake filled with almond meringue that's marvelously light-textured; the **Opéra,** composed of an almond-flavored cookie layered with butter cream, chocolate, and coffee. Unlike Stohrer, Dalloyau has a tearoom

(open daily 8:30am–7:30pm) one floor above street level, where ladies who lunch can drop in for a slice of pastry that Dalloyau warns is "too fragile to transport, or to mail, over long distances."

○ **Fauchon,** 26–30 place de la Madeleine, 8e (✆ **01-70-39-38-00;** www.fauchon.com; Métro: Madeleine). As readers of French literature know, the taste of the **madeleine** (a scalloped tea cake) triggered the memory of the narrator in Marcel Proust's *Remembrance of Things Past.* Known since the 18th century, the madeleine also inspired chef Christophe Adam at

(family-style stew) of duckling that's served with braised cabbage and garlic-flavored cream sauce; a variety of homemade terrines, including an excellent version from blood sausage; and classic dishes including roasted pigeon with red cabbage and chestnuts or *coq* (rooster), which is deboned, marinated, roasted, and served in a sauce that combines red wine, some of the animal's blood, and foie gras. Top everything off with a classic soufflé au Grand-Marnier.

9 bd. du Port-Royal, 13e. ✆ **01-43-31-58-59.** www.petitmarguery.com. Reservations recommended. 2- or 3-course lunch 23€–26€; 3-course dinner 30€–35€. AE, DC, MC, V. Daily noon–2:45pm and Mon–Sat 7:15–10:15pm. Closed Aug. Métro: Gobelins.

Fauchon to tinker with the classic cookie recipe. Today he prepares madeleines in such flavors as orange, coffee-sesame, and pistachio.

o **Ladurée Royale,** 16 rue Royale, 8e (✆ **01-42-60-21-79;** www. laduree.fr; Métro: Concorde or Madeleine), is Paris's dowager tearoom, opened in 1862, and just a few steps from La Madeleine. Its pastry chefs are known for the **macaron,** a pastry for which this place is celebrated. Karl Lagerfeld comes here and raves about them. This isn't the sticky coconut-version macaroon known to many, but two almond meringue cookies, flavored with chocolate, vanilla, pistachio, coffee, or other flavors, stuck together with butter cream. You may also want to try **Le Faubourg,** a lusciously dense chocolate cake with layers of caramel and apricots.

o **Pierre Hermé,** 72 rue Bonaparte, 6e (✆ **01-43-54-47-77;** www. pierreherme.com; Métro: St-Sulpice). While Ladurée makes our favorite classic macarons in recognizable flavors, we head to Pierre Herme for unfamiliar combinations like olive oil and vanilla, white truffle, and foie gras. Anything pastry featuring the Ispahan flavor combination (litchi, rose, and raspberry) is also delicious.

o **Sadaharu Aoki,** 56 bd. Port Royale, 13e (✆ **01-45-35-34-19;** www.sadaharu.com; Métro: Les Gobelins). Parisians started eating éclairs, that cream-filled chocolate-covered shell of choux pastry, in the 1800s. Surprisingly it is a Japanese chef who makes the best éclairs in today's Paris. He even does a mâcha green tea version.

o **Stohrer,** 51 rue Montorgueil, 2e (✆ **01-42-33-38-20;** www.stohrer.fr; Métro: Sentier or Les Halles), has been going strong ever since it was opened by Louis XV's pastry chef in 1730. A pastry always associated with this place is *puits d'amour* (well of love), which consists of caramelized puff pastry filled with vanilla ice cream. Available at any time is one of the most luscious desserts in Paris: **baba au rhum,** made with rum-soaked sponge cake, or its even richer cousin, **un Ali Baba,** which also incorporates cream-based rum-and-raisin filling. Stohrer boasts an interior decor classified as a national historic treasure, with frescoes of damsels in 18th-century costume bearing flowers and (what else?) pastries.

Le Severo TRADITIONAL FRENCH   Run by former butcher William Bernet, Le Severo is a carnivore's delight. Crispy fried pigs' feet, farmhouse *boudin noir* (blood pudding), steak tartare, and massive *cote de boeuf* (rib-eye steaks) are just some of the meaty offerings at this joint. The accompanying fries are hand-cut, and the desserts—if you still have room—are the sort that people were eating 100 years ago. One word of advice: don't ask the kitchen to cook your carefully aged steak beyond *à point* (medium rare). The majority of meat lovers here demand their meat *saingant* (rare) or even *bleu* (practically raw).

8 rue des Plantes, 14e. ✆ **01-40-44-73-09.** Reservations required. Main courses 20€–27€. MC, V. Mon–Sat noon–2pm and Tues–Fri 7:30–10pm. Closed Aug. Métro: Mouton-Duvernet or Alésia.

INEXPENSIVE

Chez Gladines ✔ BASQUE   Penny pinchers climb the cobblestone hill of the Butte aux Cailles to dine on the large portions at this dive. The setting is laid back (actually a bit grimy), but the food is hearty and authentic. This may not be the place to go to impress a date, but you can gorge on Gladines' giant "salads" (which consist of meat, cheese, garlic potatoes, and a few leaves of lettuce) and main dishes such as *pipérade* (Basque-style scrambled eggs with vegetables), cassoulet, potatoes with ham and Cantal cheese, and our favorite, ham in a creamy sauce with layers of gratin style potatoes that have been fried in duck fat. It's a bit leaden, but devotees love it.

30 rue des Cinq Diamants, 13e. ✆ **01-45-80-70-10.** Reservations not accepted. Main courses 8€–15€; fixed-price lunch 9€. No credit cards. Daily noon–3pm and 7pm–midnight; Sun noon–4pm. Closed 3 weeks in July. Métro: Corvisart or Place d'Italie.

Crêperie Josselin ★ ✔ ☺ CRÊPERIE   Josselin is just one of maybe 20 crêperies that are concentrated around the "gateway to Brittany" Montparnasse train station, but it stands above all others as the city's best. The Breton working the griddle knows exactly how to achieve the lacy, golden edges of a perfect galette, and he's not shy with the butter. Our idea of a perfect lunch (especially after too much wine the night before) is Josselin's *complete*—a buckwheat galette stuffed with egg, cheese, and ham—paired with a ceramic bowl of hard cider and followed by a salted butter caramel crepe. Priced at just 10€, that set menu is one of the best deals in town. The easy prices, continuous service and wide range of flavor combinations make this a great option for children as well.

67 rue du Montparnasse, 14e. ✆ **01-43-20-93-50.** Reservations not required. Crepes 5€–10€; fixed-price menu 10€. No credit cards. Tue–Sun noon–11pm. Métro: Montparnasse-Bienvenüe.

FAMILY-FRIENDLY RESTAURANTS

Dining with children in Paris can be tricky, especially at night. Dinner service in most restaurants begins at 8pm, which requires keeping kids awake later than they might be used to, and not many restaurants offer kids' menus. Because very few Parisians bring their children to restaurants, chefs aren't in the habit of creating special dishes that aren't on the menu. Exceptions to this rule exist, and you may find them if you're extremely charming and polite, but don't count on it. Still, you can always order a *plat du jour* or *plat garni* (a garnished main-course platter), which will be suitable for most children, particularly if a dessert is to follow.

If you'd like to introduce your children to a real French restaurant, consider bringing them for **lunch.** Prices are often half of what you might pay at dinner, and daytime dishes tend to be less intricate (and potentially off-putting for a child). **Hotel dining rooms** can also be a good choice for family dining. They usually have children's menus or at least one or two *plats du jour* cooked for children, such as spaghetti with meat sauce.

In addition to the restaurants we recommend below, **cafés** are a great option for traveling families because they're cheaper, they often serve simpler food, and they welcome children during the day and early evening. At a café, children seem to like the sandwiches (try a croque-monsieur, or toasted ham and cheese), the omelets, and the *pommes frites* (french fries). Kids will also enjoy eating crepes at a **crêperie.**

Here is our list of top restaurants that children will enjoy:

Breakfast in America (p. 214)   This American restaurant in the Latin Quarter serves breakfast all day, hamburgers and fries, milkshakes, and other familiar kid favorites.

Crémerie-Restaurant Polidor (p. 218)   This reasonably priced restaurant is so family friendly, it calls its food *cuisine familiale*. This might be a good place to introduce your child to bistro food.

Crêperie Josselin (p. 228)   This local favorite (a sit-down restaurant, not a stand on the street) is a great option for kids because they offer early dinner seating and easy prices. What kid doesn't love a crepe?

Le Relais de l'Entrecôte (p. 218)   This affordable restaurant offers unlimited servings of steak and fries, and desserts such as profiteroles never fail to make kids happy.

Rosa Bonheur (p. 210)   Located inside the city's biggest park, Parc des Buttes Chaumont, Rosa Bonheur boasts a beautiful outdoor terrace where parents can nibble on tapas while watching their kids roll down the hill. There's also an indoor play area and kids' menu.

THE TOP CAFÉS

As surely everyone knows, the café is a Parisian institution. Parisians use cafés as combination club/tavern/snack bars, almost as extensions of their living rooms. They're spots where you can sit alone and read your newspaper, do your homework or write your memoirs; meet a friend or lover; nibble on a hard-boiled egg; or drink yourself into oblivion. At cafés, you meet your dates, and then go on to a show or stay and talk. Above all, cafés are for people-watching.

Coffee (*un café*), of course, is the chief drink. It comes black, in a small cup, unless you specifically order it with milk (*un café crème*). Thé (tea, pronounced tay) is also fairly popular but generally not high quality. You can also order fruit juice, sparkling water (*un Perrier*), or soft drinks (*un Coca, un Coca Light*), but be warned that these are normally double the price of a glass of wine and may arrive without any ice. From the early afternoon onward, and especially during the *apéro* hour (the before-dinner period when friends often meet for a drink), patrons order beer (*bière*) and wine (*vin*) by the glass—either a glass of white wine (*un verre de vin blanc*) or red wine (*un verre de vin rouge*).

Now, just a few words on café etiquette: It's very likely that you won't receive a menu, because the options in most cafés are identical. The assumption, which is tricky for travelers, is that you already know what you want. Your bill will probably arrive with your order, but you're not expected to pay until you leave. *Service compris* means the tip is included in your bill, so it isn't necessary to tip extra. Still, tips are appreciated, but keep them small—a tip of small change (1€) is more than enough if you're only having a few drinks.

Café de Flore   This is perhaps the most famous café in the world, still fighting to maintain a Left Bank aura despite hordes of visitors from around the world. Jean-Paul Sartre—the granddaddy of existentialism, a key figure in the Resistance, and a renowned café-sitter—often came here during World War II. Wearing a leather jacket and beret, he sat and wrote his trilogy *Les Chemins de la Liberté* (*The Roads to Freedom*). Camus, Picasso, and Apollinaire also frequented the Flore. The café is still going strong, although the existentialists have been replaced by tourists and sometimes even fashionistas such as Karl Lagerfeld.

172 bd. St-Germain, 6e. ✆ **01-45-48-55-26.** www.cafe-de-flore.com. Café espresso 5€; glass of beer 9€; snacks from 16€; full meal 25€–45€. AE, DC, MC, V. Daily 7:30am–1:30am. Métro: St-Germain-des-Prés.

Café de la Musique   Attached to one of the grandest of Mitterrand's grands *travaux,* a concert hall within the Parc de la Villette, this café's location guarantees a crowd that's passionately devoted to music. The recorded sounds that play in the background are likely to be more diverse and more eclectic than those in any other café in Paris. The red-and-green velour setting might remind you of a modern opera house. The main attraction, however, is the sprawling outdoor terrace with thirty tables that face a bubbling lion-shaped fountain and perfectly catch the afternoon light.

In the Cité de la Musique, place Fontaine aux Lions, 213 av. Jean-Jaurès, 19e. ✆ **01-48-03-15-91.** www.cafe-de-la-musique.com. Main courses 12€–24€. AE, DC, MC, V. Daily 8am–2am. Métro: Porte de Pantin.

Café des Deux Moulins   *Amélie* was a quirky low-budget film that was nominated for five Oscars and was seen by more than 25 million people around the world following its release in 2001. The film was set in Montmartre, and the café featured in the film has developed into a mandatory stopping-off place for the constantly arriving "cult of Amélie." In the film, Amélie worked as a waitress at the Café des Deux Moulins. The musty atmosphere, with its 1950s decor, mustard-colored ceiling, and lace curtains, has been preserved—even the wall lamps and unisex toilet. The menu has retained classic, hearty dishes such as calf's liver, green frisée salad with bacon bits and warm goat cheese, and pigs' brains with lentils. They also serve hamburgers, with or without a fried egg on top.

15 rue Lepic, 18e. ✆ **01-42-54-90-50.** Main courses 11€–17€. MC, V. Daily 7am–2am. Métro: Blanche.

La Belle Hortense   This is the most literary café in a neighborhood (the Marais) that's loaded with literary antecedents and references. It contains an erudite and accessible staff; an inventory of French literary classics as well as modern tomes about art, psychoanalysis, history, and culture; and two high-ceilinged, 19th-century rooms with little changed since the days of Baudelaire and Balzac. Near the entrance is a zinc-covered bar that sells glasses of wine. If you're fluent in French, you might be interested in attending a reading, a book signing, or a lecture. Some kind of public gathering, conducted only in rapid, colloquial French, is scheduled every Tuesday, Wednesday, and Thursday, usually at 8pm.

31 rue Vieille du Temple, 4e. ✆ **01-48-04-71-60.** Glass of wine 4€–10€; coffee 1.50€; *plats du jour* 12€–24€. MC, V. Daily 5pm–2am. Métro: Hôtel-de-Ville or St-Paul.

 Did You Know?

You'll pay substantially less in a café if you stand at the counter rather than sit at a table, partly because there's no service charge, and partly because diners tend to linger at tables.

La Coupole   Born in 1927 and once a leading center of artistic life, La Coupole is now the epitome of the grand Paris brasserie in Montparnasse. Former patrons include Josephine Baker, Henry Miller, Dalí, Calder, Hemingway, Fitzgerald, and Picasso. At one of its sidewalk tables, you can sit and watch the passing scene and order a coffee or a cognac VSOP. The food is quite good, despite the fact that the dining room resembles an enormous rail-station waiting room. Try main dishes such as *sole meunière,* a very good rump steak, fresh oysters, shellfish, grilled lobster with flambéed whisky sauce, or curried lamb. The waiters are as rude and inattentive as ever, and the patrons would have it no other way.

102 bd. du Montparnasse, 14e. ✆ **01-43-20-14-20.** www.flobrasseries.com. Breakfast buffet 14€–19€; main courses 20€–40€. AE, DC, MC, V. Daily 8am–1am (breakfast buffet Mon–Fri 8:30–10:30am). Métro: Vavin.

La Palette ★ The interior of this café, inhabited by amiably crotchety waiters, consists of tiled murals installed around 1935 advertising the virtues of a brand of liqueur that's no longer manufactured. If you happen to drop in during mealtime, you'll have a limited selection of salads and croque-monsieur (toasted ham and cheese), plus one *plat du jour,* always priced at 15€, which may include roast beef, lamb stew, fish, or lamb. The real reason to come, though, is the terrace, a beautiful outdoor space not far from the river where you can get a real sense of the village life in Saint-Germain.

43 rue de Seine, 6e. ✆ **01-43-26-68-15.** Sandwiches, omelets, and *plats du jour* 6€–15€. MC, V. Café and bar daily 8am–2am. Restaurant daily noon–3pm. Métro: Mabillon or St-Germain-des-Prés.

La Rotonde Once patronized by Hemingway, the original Rotonde faded into history but is immortalized in the pages of *The Sun Also Rises,* in which Papa wrote, "No matter what café in Montparnasse you ask a taxi driver to bring you to from the right bank of the river, they always take you to the Rotonde." Having since been lavishly upgraded, its reincarnation has a paneled Art Deco elegance and shares the site with a cinema. The menu includes such hearty fare as pepper steak with french fries, shellfish in season, a superb and genuinely succulent version of *sole meunière,* and sea-bass filets with herb-flavored lemon sauce.

105 bd. du Montparnasse, 6e. ✆ **01-43-26-48-26.** www.rotondemontparnasse.com. Glass of wine 4€–11€; main courses 10€–30€; fixed-price lunch 18€–35€; fixed-price dinner 35€. AE, MC, V. Café daily 7:15am–2am; food service daily noon–1am. Métro: Vavin.

Le Procope To fans of French history, this is the holy grail of Parisian cafés. Opened in 1686, it occupies a three-story town house categorized as a historic monument. Inside, nine salons and dining rooms, each of whose 300-year-old walls have been carefully preserved and painted a deep red, are available for languorous afternoon coffee breaks or old-fashioned meals. Menu items include platters of shellfish, onion soup *au gratin, coq au vin* (chicken stewed in wine), duck breast in honey sauce, and grilled versions of various meats and fish. Every day between 3 and 6pm, the place makes itself available to sightseers who come to look but not necessarily eat and drink at the site that welcomed such movers and shakers as Diderot, Voltaire, George Sand, Victor Hugo, and Oscar Wilde. Especially charming is the ground-floor room outfitted like an antique library.

13 rue de l'Ancienne-Comédie, 6e. ✆ **01-40-46-79-00.** www.procope.com. Reservations recommended. Coffee 3€; glass of beer 5€–7€; main courses 20€–29€. AE, DC, MC, V. Daily 10:30am–1am. Métro: Odéon.

Les Deux Magots 👍 Among the two famous "philosopher cafés" of Saint-Germain, only the Café de Flore has retained any cachet among the locals. Les

Deux Magots may have once provided a haven for struggling writers, but the only tomes you'll see on the tables today are of the guidebook variety. The terrace is a good place for people-watching, but you can expect to pay outlandish prices for the privilege.

6 place St-Germain-des-Prés, 6e. ✆ **01-45-48-55-25.** www.lesdeuxmagots.fr. Café crème 6€; whisky soda 12€–16€; main courses 22€–36€. AE, DC, V. Daily 7:30am–1am. Métro: St-Germain-des-Prés.

RESTAURANTS BY CUISINE

ALGERIAN
Wally Le Saharien (**$$$,** p. 200)

ALSATIAN
Bofinger (**$$**, p. 188)

AMERICAN
Breakfast in America (**$**, p. 214)

ASIAN FUSION
Le Pré Verre ★ (**$$**, p. 214)

AUVERGNAT
L'Ambassade d'Auvergne (**$$**, p. 190)

BAKERY
Eric Kayser ★★ (**$**, p. 223)
Tartes Kluger (**$**, p. 191)

BASQUE
Afaria ★ (**$$**, p. 223)
Au Bascou (**$$**, p. 188)
Chez Gladines (**$**, p. 228)
Chez l'Ami Jean ★ (**$$**, p. 222)

BISTRO
Afaria ★ (**$$**, p. 223)
Astier (**$$**, p. 207)
Au Trou Gascon (**$$$**, p. 206)
Café des Musées (**$$**, p. 188)
Chez Janou (**$**, p. 191)
Jadis ★ (**$$**, p. 224)
Jaja (**$$**, p. 190)
La Cerisaie ★ (**$$**, p. 225)
La Crémerie Restaurant Polidor
  (**$**, p. 218)
La Fontaine de Mars (**$$**, p. 222)
La Régalade ★★ (**$$**, p. 225)

La Régalade–St. Honoré ★★
  (**$$**, p. 185)
La Rôtisserie d'en Face (**$$**, p. 216)
La Table d'Eugene ★ (**$$**, p. 205)
La Tour de Montlhéry (Chez Denise)
  ★★ (**$$**, p. 185)
Le Baratin ★ (**$$**, p. 210)
Le Bistrot Paul Bert ★★ (**$$**, p. 208)
Le Casse Noix ★ (**$$**, p. 224)
Le Comptoir du Relais ★★
  (**$$**, p. 216)
Le Cornichon (**$$**, p. 225)
Le Cotte Roti (**$$**, p. 208)
Le Pantruche ★ (**$$**, p. 202)
Le Petit Marguery (**$$**, p. 225)
Les Papilles ★ (**$$**, p. 214)
Philou ★★ (**$$**, p. 203)
Pinxo (**$$**, p. 186)
Quedubon (**$$**, p. 210)

BRASSERIE
Bofinger (**$$**, p. 188)
Brasserie Balzar (**$$**, p. 212)
Chartier (**$**, p. 203)
Garnier (**$$$**, p. 197)
Le Vaudeville (**$$**, p. 185)
Rech (**$$$**, p. 199)
Thoumieux (**$$$**, p. 222)

BRETON
Chez Michel ★★ (**$$**, p. 202)

CAFÉ
Breizh Café ★ (**$**, p. 190)

CHINESE
Lily Wang (**$$**, p. 223)
Yam'Tcha ★★★ (**$$$**, p. 183)

Key to Abbreviations:
$$$$ = Very Expensive $$$ = Expensive $$ = Moderate $ = Inexpensive

CRÊPERIE

Breizh Café ★ (**$**, p. 190)
Crêperie Josselin ★ (**$**, p. 228)

ENGLISH

Le Bal Café ★ (**$$**, p. 204)

FALAFEL

L'As du Fallafel ★ (**$**, p. 191)

FRENCH (MODERN)

Carré des Feuillants (**$$$$**, p. 182)
Cristal Room (**$$$**, p. 197)
Fish (**$$**, p. 215)
Frenchie ★★ (**$$**, p. 184)
Jaja (**$$**, p. 190)
Jean-François Piège ★ (**$$$$**, p. 219)
La Bigarrade (**$$$**, p. 197)
La Cuisine (**$$$$**, p. 194)
La Famille (**$$**, p. 204)
La Gazzetta ★ (**$$$**, p. 206)
L'Agrume (**$$**, p. 212)
L'Arpège ★★★ (**$$$$**, p. 219)
L'Assiette (**$$**, p. 224)
L'Astrance ★★★ (**$$$$**, p. 195)
L'Atelier Etoile de Joël Robuchon
   ★★ (**$$$**, p. 198)
L'Atelier Saint-Germain de Joël
   Robuchon ★★ (**$$$**, p. 220)
Le Bristol ★★ (**$$$$**, p. 195)
Le Chapeau Melon ★ (**$$**, p. 210)
Le Chateaubriand ★★★
   (**$$$**, p. 206)
Le Cinq ★★ (**$$$$**, p. 195)
Le Pré Verre ★ (**$$**, p. 214)
Les Ombres (**$$$**, p. 220)
Les Tablettes ★ (**$$$**, p. 198)
Le Verre Volé ★★ (**$$**, p. 203)
Le Violon d'Ingres (**$$$**, p. 220)
L'Hédoniste ★ (**$$**, p. 186)
Macéo (**$$**, p. 186)
Passage 53 ★★ (**$$$**, p. 182)
Pierre Gagnaire ★★★ (**$$$$**, p. 196)
Rino (**$$$**, p. 206)
Saturne ★★ (**$$$**, p. 183)
Spring ★★ (**$$$**, p. 183)
Thoumieux (**$$$**, p. 222)
Yam'Tcha ★★★ (**$$$**, p. 183)
Ze Kitchen Galerie ★ (**$$$**, p. 215)

FRENCH (TRADITIONAL)

Alcazar Restaurant (**$$**, p. 215)
Astier (**$$**, p. 207)
Au Pied de Cochon (**$$**, p. 184)
Aux Lyonnais (**$$**, p. 104)
Bar des Théâtres (**$$**, p. 199)
Benoit (**$$$**, p. 188)
Brasserie Balzar (**$$**, p. 212)
Café des Musées (**$$**, p. 188)
Caïus (**$$**, p. 199)
Chartier (**$**, p. 203)
Chéri Bibi (**$$**, p. 204)
Chez Georges (**$$**, p. 184)
Chez Grenouille (**$$**, p. 202)
Guy Savoy ★★ (**$$$$**, p. 194)
Hiramatsu (**$$$$**, p. 194)
Itinéraires (**$$**, p. 212)
Jadis ★ (**$$**, p. 224)
Jeanne A ★ (**$**, p. 209)
La Crèmerie (**$**, p. 218)
La Crèmerie Restaurant Polidor
   (**$**, p. 218)
La Ferrandaise (**$$**, p. 216)
La Grille (**$$**, p. 202)
La Maison Blanche (**$$$**, p. 198)
L'Ambassade d'Auvergne (**$$**, p. 190)
L'Ami Louis (**$$$$**, p. 187)
La Régalade ★★ (**$$**, p. 225)
La Régalade–St. Honoré ★★
   (**$$**, p. 185)
La Rôtisserie d'en Face (**$$**, p. 216)
Lasserre (**$$$$**, p. 194)
La Table d'Eugene ★ (**$$**, p. 205)
La Tour d'Argent (**$$$$**, p. 211)
La Tour de Montlhéry (Chez
   Denise) ★★ (**$$**, p. 185)
Le Baratin ★ (**$$**, p. 210)
L'Ebauchoir (**$$**, p. 208)
Le Bouchon et l'Assiette (**$$**, p. 199)
Le Bistrot Paul Bert ★★ (**$$**, p. 208)
Le Casse Noix ★ (**$$**, p. 224)
Le Comptoir du Relais ★★
   (**$$**, p. 216)
Le Cornichon (**$$**, p. 225)
Le Grand Véfour (**$$$$**, p. 182)
Le Hide ★ (**$$**, p. 200)
Le Pamphlet (**$$**, p. 190)
Le Pantruche ★ (**$$**, p. 202)
Le Petit Marguery (**$$**, p. 225)
Le Relais de l'Entrecôte (**$$**, p. 218)

Le Repaire de Cartouche (**$$**, p. 208)
Le Timbre (**$$**, p. 218)
Les Cocottes de Christian Constant ★
   (**$$**, p. 222)
Les Papilles ★ (**$$**, p. 214)
Le Severo (**$$**, p. 227)
Mélac (**$**, p. 209)
Michel Rostang (**$$$$**, p. 196)
Philou ★★ (**$$**, p. 203)
Quedubon (**$$**, p. 210)
Racines (**$$**, p. 186)
Restaurant Plaza Athénée (Alain
   Ducasse) ★★ (**$$$$**, p. 196)
Ribouldingue (**$$**, p. 214)
Tartes Kluger (**$**, p. 191)
Vivant ★ (**$$**, p. 203)

GREEK
Casa Olympe (**$$**, p. 200)

INTERNATIONAL
Juveniles (**$**, p. 187)
Les Ombres (**$$$**, p. 220)
Ze Kitchen Galerie ★ (**$$$**, p. 215)

ITALIAN
Olio Pane Vino (**$**, p. 187)
Vivant ★ (**$$**, p. 203)

LIGHT FARE
Eric Kayser ★★ (**$**, p. 223)
L'As du Fallafel ★ (**$**, p. 191)

LYONNAIS
Aux Lyonnais (**$$**, p. 184)

MEDITERRANEAN
Fish (**$$**, p. 215)
Le Cotte Roti (**$$**, p. 208)

MEXICAN
El Nopal (**$**, p. 204)

MOROCCAN
Mansouria (**$$**, p. 208)

PIZZA
Al Taglio (**$**, p. 209)

PROVENÇAL
Casa Olympe (**$$**, p. 200)
Chez Janou (**$**, p. 191)
La Bastide Odéon (**$$**, p. 216)
La Maison Blanche (**$$$**, p. 198)
Les Tablettes ★ (**$$$**, p. 198)

SCOTTISH
Juveniles (**$**, p. 187)

SEAFOOD
Fish (**$$**, p. 215)
Garnier (**$$$**, p. 197)
Goumard (**$$$**, p. 182)
La Cagouille (**$$**, p. 224)
La Grille (**$$**, p. 202)
Rech (**$$$**, p. 199)

SOUTHWESTERN FRENCH
Chez l'Ami Jean ★ (**$$**, p. 222)
Dans Les Landes ★ (**$$**, p. 212)
La Fontaine de Mars (**$$**, p. 222)
La Cerisaie ★ (**$$**, p. 225)
L'Avant Comptoir ★ (**$**, p. 219)
Le Pamphlet (**$$**, p. 190)
Pinxo (**$$**, p. 186)

STEAK
Le Relais de l'Entrecôte (**$$**, p. 218)

TAPAS
Rosa Bonheur ★ (**$$**, p. 210)

VEGETARIAN
Bob's Juice Bar (**$**, p. 190)

WINE BAR
Coinstôt Vino (**$$**, p. 184)
Jeanne A ★ (**$**, p. 209)
L'Avant Comptoir ★ (**$**, p. 219)
Le Chapeau Melon ★ (**$$**, p. 210)
Le Verre Volé ★★ (**$$**, p. 203)
Mélac (**$**, p. 209)

PRACTICAL MATTERS: THE RESTAURANT SCENE

Hours

Unless otherwise indicated (by a sign that reads *service continue*), Paris restaurants are usually open for lunch from noon to 2:30pm and dinner from 7:30 to 10:30pm. Cafés and brasseries are a good option if you need to eat a later lunch or earlier dinner.

Prices, Taxes & Tipping

Many visitors often experience sticker shock in Parisian restaurants. **Three-star dining** remains quite expensive, with appetizers sometimes priced at 60€ and dinners easily costing 185€ to 250€ per person in the top dining rooms of celebrated chefs. But, the influx of high-quality **neo-bistrots** has meant that there are many more affordable dining options in Paris today: The standard price for a very good bistro meal is 30€ to 40€ for three courses. **Cafés** offer sandwiches, soup, and salads in a relaxed setting. In a café, if you stand at the bar for a drink, coffee, or sandwich, prices are less than they would be if you were seated at a table.

However, you can get around these high price tags in many places by **dining at lunch** (when prices are always cheaper) or ordering a prix-fixe meal at lunch or dinner. In France, lunch (as well as dinner) tends to be a full-course meal with meat, vegetables, salad, bread, cheese, dessert, wine, and coffee—lunch meals can be half the price of dinner, so we strongly recommend that you splurge at lunch. The **prix-fixe (fixed price) menu** or *le menu* is a set meal that the chef prepares that day. It is most often fresh and promptly served, and represents a greater bargain than dining a la carte. Of course, it's limited, so you'll have to like the choices provided. Sometimes there are one to three menus, beginning with the least expensive and going up for a more elaborate meal. A lot depends on your pocketbook and appetite.

> Mystifying Menu?
>
> If you need help distinguishing a *coq au vin* from a *blanquette de veau*, see "Basic Menu Terms" in chapter 12.

Remember that the price you see on the menu is the full price that you'll pay at the end of the meal. Although tax and service are "hidden costs" in American restaurants (they combine to add an additional 20%–30% to the final bill), in Paris, these costs are already included in the price of your meal. Service is almost always included in your bill. (If not, look for the words *service non compris* on your bill—that means that the cost of service was not added, and you'll be expected to leave a tip.) Even when service is included, small **tips** are still appreciated, but your Parisian server earns a full salary and you don't need to leave more than 10%.

Reservations

Reservations are a necessary hurdle to overcome if you want to eat in the city's best restaurants. Travelers used to a more spontaneous approach are often surprised and disappointed when they show up without booking and are turned away. This has nothing to do with being a foreigner. It's simply that the restaurants here are relatively small, they don't offer multiple seatings throughout the night, and there's no bar where you can hang out and wait. If you haven't booked ahead, there may not be room at the table. Ask your hotel concierge to help if you're not comfortable making the call, or gather your courage and say "*Bonjour. Je voudrais faire un reservation pour diner* (dinner) *ou dejeuner* (lunch). *Vous parlez anglais?*" At this point, they may switch to English if you are polite and they are capable. If not, have the French translation for your desired date and time ready and be ready to give your name *(votre nom?)* and the number of people *(combien de personnes?)* in your party. Having a reservation is crucial, and it will open up a world of authentic and memorable dining experiences. **Paris by Mouth** (www.parisbymouth.com) offers reservation services for a small fee.

Restaurant Deals

Open Table doesn't operate in Paris, but a local version called **The Fork** (www.thefork.com) offers online booking for some restaurants, and you can select to view the site in English. Not all of the restaurants we recommend in this chapter are listed on this site, but a few very good ones are, including the Plaza Athenée, Les Ambassadeurs, Goumard, Michel Rostang, The Cristal Room, Caïus, Olio Pane Vino, Fish, and La Régalade. A few restaurants offer discounts or a free drink if you book through this site.

SHOPPING

By Kate van den Boogert

Paris is, of course, a world-famous shopping destination—and for good reason. The city marries art and commerce, elevating an afternoon of window shopping into a high-culture experience. Parisian department stores sell everything you could ever want under one elegant roof, while specialty shops hold countless small treasures, from jeweled safety pins to handcrafted candles. But true shoppers come to Paris for the fashion—Chanel, Dior, Hermès, and Louis Vuitton call Paris home. The city is also home to iconic cosmetic and perfume houses, as well as endless gourmet food shops. But you don't have to buy anything to appreciate shopping in Paris: Peer in the *vitrines* (window displays), keep an eye out for new trends, and return home with a whole new interpretation of style.

SHOPPING BY NEIGHBORHOOD
Les Halles, Louvre & Palais Royal (1er & 2e)

Subterranean shopping mall **Les Halles** is a short stroll from major shopping strip the **Rue de Rivoli.** Both these destinations are a who's-who of the major international fashion chains, including H&M, Zara, Sephora, Etam, and Gap. At another end of the 1st is the **Palais Royal,** just north of the Louvre and one of the city's best shopping secrets. The 18th-century arcade of boutiques flanks the garden of a former palace and includes some of the hottest names in fashion and accessories. It signals the beginning of the busy part of the Rue St Honoré, to the south, and to the north, behind the Palais Royal, is another sophisticated shopping destination, the **place des Victoires,** which to the east joins with the **Etienne-Marcel** shopping neighborhood, known for its jeans and street wear. In the 19th century, this area became known for its *passages*, glass-enclosed shopping streets—in fact, the world's first shopping malls. They were also the city's first buildings to be illuminated by gaslight. Many have been torn down, but a dozen or so have survived. The **Passage de Grand Cerf,** between 145 rue St-Denis and 10 rue Dussoubs (Métro: Etienne-Marcel), is filled with everything from ethnic-chic to jewelry and accessory shops. The **Place Vendome** is the city's fine jewelry quarter, set like a crown around the mythical Ritz hotel.

Annick Goutal (p. 263)
Astier de Villatte (p. 261)
Chantal Thomass (p. 254)
Christian Louboutin (p. 252)
Cadolle (p. 254)

Carrousel du Louvre (p. 242)
Cartier (p. 255)
Chanel (p. 249)
Colette (p. 256)
Dehillerin (p. 262)

PREVIOUS PAGE: **Window shopping in Paris.**

Didier Ludot (p. 253)

Dior Joaillerie (p. 255)

Francis Kurkdjian (p. 263)

Galignani (p. 247)

JC de Castelbajac (p. 251)

Jean-Paul Hévin (p. 258)

Kiliwatch (p. 253)

Lavinia (p. 259)

Le Louvre des Antiquaires (p. 245)

Les Halles (p. 242)

Maison Fabre (p. 252)

Manufacture Nationale de Sèvres (p. 261)

Morabito (p. 253)

107 Rivoli (p. 246)

Pierre Hardy (p. 253)

Salons du Palais Royal, Shiseido (p. 264)

W. H. Smith (p. 248)

Van Cleef & Arpels (p. 255)

Le Marais, Ile St Louis & Ile de la Cité (3e & 4e)

The Marais provides two dramatically different shopping experiences. The Lower Marais is concentrated around the **Rue des Francs-Bourgeois,** where you'll find a succession of charming fashion, accessories, and beauty stores. But don't be afraid to strike off into the neighborhood's medieval warren of twisting streets chockablock with up-to-the-minute fashions and trends. The Northern Marais, concentrated around the **Rue de Bretagne** is a hotbed of independent French designers. Some in-the-know shoppers are skipping St-Germain or St-Honoré and heading here instead, for guaranteed cutting-edge fashion and design.

Azzedine Alaïa (p. 248)

Bensimon (p. 249)

Bijoux Blues (p. 254)

Bonpoint (p. 252)

L'Eclaireur (p. 251)

L'Habilleur (p. 254)

Les Mots à la Bouche (p. 247)

Merci (p. 256)

Marché aux Fleurs (p. 242)

Marché des Enfants Rouge (p. 245)

Sandro Homme (p. 252)

The Different Company (p. 264)

Champs-Élysées & Western Paris (8e, 16e & 17e)

The heart of the international designer parade is here on the Right Bank. **Rue du Faubourg St-Honoré** was the traditional miracle mile until recent years, when many of the exclusive shops shunned it for the even more deluxe **avenue Montaigne** at the other end of the arrondissement. (It's a long but pleasant walk from one fashion strip to the other.) Paris's most glamorous shopping street is lined with almost unspeakably fancy shops, where you float from big name to big name and in a few hours can see Dior, Chanel, and everything in between. The neighboring **Champs-Élysées** shouts "teen scene" with hot mass-market flagships. The zone around the **Madeleine** hosts many fine specialty food shops.

Artcurial (p. 245)

Au Nain Bleu (p. 264)

Baccarat (p. 261)

Balenciaga (p. 249)

Bijoux Burma (p. 255)

Cassegrain (p. 264)

Dior (p. 249)

Fauchon (p. 258)

Givenchy (p. 250)

Hédiard (p. 259)

Hermès (p. 250)

Jadis et Gourmande (p. 258)

Lalique (p. 261)

Le 66 (p. 256)

Les Caves Taillevent (p. 260)

Jean-Paul Gaultier (p. 250)

Louis Vuitton (p. 252)

Maison de la Truffe (p. 259)

Marché Ave du Président Wilson (p. 244)

Nicolas (p. 260)

Parfums Caron (p. 263)

Réciproque (p. 254)

Sephora (p. 264)

Virgin Megastore (p. 262)

Avenue Montaigne.

Opéra & Canal St-Martin (9e & 10e)

These two neighborhoods offer wildly different shopping experiences. Opéra has at its beating heart the "other" two department stores: Le Printemps and Les Galeries Lafayette, built in a row along **Boulevard Haussmann.** Their commercial energy draws many other big names and chains. The sleepy Canal St-Martin offers boho local charm along little streets Rue de Marseille, and Beaurepaire, the Quais de Valmy, and Jemmapes.

agnès b (p. 248)

Antoine & Lili (p. 255)

Apple Store (p. 264)

Centre Commercial (p. 256)

Citadium (p. 252)

La Maison du Miel (p. 259)

Les Galeries Lafayette (p. 257)

Printemps (p. 257)

Uniqlo (p. 251)

Pigalle & Montmartre (18e)

Villagey Montmartre's charming winding streets, fanning out around Abbesses, are filled with small specialty shops, in design, fashion, jewelry, and food. Wander along the Rue des Abbesses, down the Rue Houdon, up the Rue des Martyrs for a sweet afternoon of discovery.

Chine Machine (p. 253)

Marché aux Puces St-Ouen de Clignancourt (p. 243)

Princesse Tam-Tam (p. 254)

Spree (p. 256)

République, Bastille & Eastern Paris (11e & 12e)

Shopping in Bastille is concentrated on and around the **Rue du Faubourg St-Antoine,** which heads east from the Place de la Bastille and counts big names and chains, and winding streets nearby, like the **Rue de Charonne**. The **Viaduc des Arts** running parallel to avenue Daumesnil is a collection of about 30 specialist craft stores occupying a series of narrow vaulted niches under what used to be railroad tracks.

> French Trotters (p. 250)
>
> Isabel Marant (p. 250)
>
> La Plaque Emaillées et Gravée Jacquin (p. 260)
>
> Viaduc des Arts (p. 246)

Belleville & Northeast Paris (19e & 20e)

Not a shopping zone, this is where tourists come to soak up the cosmopolitan atmosphere and explore specialty shops from the city's various immigrant communities.

Latin Quarter (5e)

More of a residential neighborhood, the Latin Quarter is better known for its major sights—the Luxembourg Gardens and the Sorbonne university—than for its shopping strips. However a host of specialist bookshops, which feed the local student population, remain a real draw.

> Diptyque (p. 263)
>
> La Quincaillerie (p. 262)
>
> La Tuile à Loup (p. 260)
>
> Librairie le Bail-Weissert (p. 247)
>
> Shakespeare & Company (p. 247)

St-Germain-des-Près & Luxembourg (6e)

This area is the soul of the Left Bank and is one of the most famous shopping districts in Paris. Traditionally a more literary neighborhood, high fashion addresses are gradually taking over the bookshops, and the Left Bank now rivals with classic Right Bank shopping zones such as St-Honoré and Avenue Montaigne. Wander the Avenue St-Germain, Rue St Sulpice, Rue du Cherche Midi, and Rue du Vieux Colombier, the Rue Bonapart and Rue Jacob down to the Seine, or gourmet paradise Rue de Buci, for some elevated shopping experiences.

> Bonpoint (p. 252)
>
> Christian Constant (p. 258)
>
> Cire Trudon (p. 260)
>
> Erès (p. 254)
>
> Fnac (p. 262)
>
> La Maison Ivre (p. 261)
>
> Marché Buci (p. 244)
>
> Pierre Hermé (p. 257)
>
> Poîlane (p. 257)

> Sabbia Rosa (p. 254)
>
> Sonia Rykiel (p. 251)
>
> Souleiado (p. 261)
>
> Taschen (p. 248)
>
> Tea & Tattered Pages (p. 248)
>
> Village Voice Bookshop (p. 248)
>
> Yves Saint Laurent (p. 251)
>
> Zadig & Voltaire (p. 251)

Eiffel Tower & Nearby (7e)

The city's most glamorous department store Le Bon Marché sets the scene for another high-voltage shopping experience. If much of this neighborhood is more dedicated to culture and architecture than fashion, along its eastern edge, some of the glamour of adjacent St-Germain rubs off, around the **Rue du Bac** and **Rue du Grenelle** for example, where you'll find all that wealth and glamour can buy.

Au Nom de la Rose (p. 260)

Barthelemy (p. 258)

Conran Shop (p. 262)

Défilé des Marques (p. 253)

Editions de Parfums Fréderic Malle (p. 263)

Le Bon Marché (p. 256)

Sennelier (p. 246)

7L (p. 247)

Montparnasse & Southern Paris (13e, 14e & 15e)

Located behind St-Germain, this neighborhood is dominated both by Paris's only skyscraper and France's tallest building, the Montparnasse tower, and a major railway station. Montparnasse might be worth a trip for the major shopping center located under the tower, and the shopping along adjacent **Rue de Rennes.**

Marché aux Puces de la Porte de Vanves (p. 243)

Montparnasse Shopping Centre (p. 242)

MALLS & MARKETS

Carrousel du Louvre ★★   If you want to combine an accessible location, a fun food court, boutiques, and plenty of museum gift shops with a touch of culture, don't miss the Carrousel. Always mobbed, this is one of the few venues allowed to open on Sunday. There's an Apple Store, Starbucks, Virgin Megastore, a branch of L'Occitane, and several other emporiums for conspicuous consumption. Check out Fragonard or Pylones for original souvenir ideas. Open daily, 10am to 8pm. 99 rue de Rivoli, 1er. (* **01-43-16-47-10.** www.carrouseldulouvre.com. Métro: Palais-Royal or Musée du Louvre.

Le Forum des Halles   This major transport and shopping hub draws suburban Parisians to its subterranean labyrinth of chain stores, including H&M, Fnac, Zara, or Muji, as well as a heated swimming pool, and the UGC cinema multiplex. Open Monday to Saturday 10am to 8pm. 101 Porte Berger, 1er. www.forumdes halles.com. Métro: Châtelet-Les Halles.

Montparnasse Shopping Centre   This shopping center is sort of a quick-fix minimall in a business center and hotel (Le Méridien) complex, with a small branch of Galeries Lafayette, a Habitat for chic homeware, and some inexpensive fashion chains. The vibe continues up neighboring commercial strip Rue de Rennes. Open Monday to Saturday 10am to 7pm. Btw. rue de l'Arrivée and 22 rue du Départ, 14e. No phone. Métro: Montparnasse-Bienvenüe.

Marché aux Fleurs ★   Artists and photographers love to capture the Flower Market on canvas and film. The stalls are ablaze with color, and each is a showcase of flowers, most of which escaped the perfume factories of Grasse on the

Food Markets

Outdoor markets are plentiful in Paris. Some of the better known are the **Marché Buci** (see below); the **rue Mouffetard market,** open Tuesday to Sunday from 9:30am to 1pm and Tuesday to Saturday from 4 to 7pm (6e; Métro: Monge or Censier-Daubenton); and the **rue Montorgueil market,** behind the St-Eustache church, open Monday to Saturday from 9am to 7pm (1er; Métro: Les Halles). The trendiest market is **Marché Biologique,** along boulevard Raspail, a tree-lined stretch lying between rue de Rennes and rue du Cherche-Midi, 6e. It's open Sunday from 8:30am to 6:30pm (Métro: Montparnasse).

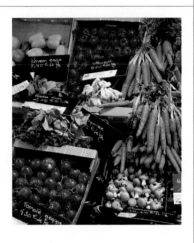

French Riviera. The Flower Market is along the Seine, behind the Tribunal de Commerce. On Sunday, it becomes the poetic **Marché aux Oiseaux (Bird Market).** Open daily 8:30am to 4pm. Place Louis-Lépine, Ile de la Cité, 4e. No phone. Metro: Cité.

Marché aux Puces de la Porte de Vanves ★★ 🎁 This weekend event sprawls along two streets and is the best flea market in Paris—dealers swear by it. There's little in terms of formal antiques and furniture. It's better for old linens, vintage Hermès scarves, toys, ephemera, costume jewelry, perfume bottles, and bad art. Asking prices tend to be high, as dealers prefer to sell to nontourists. On Sunday, there's a food market one street over. Open Tuesday to Sunday 7am to 5pm. Av. Georges-Lafenestre, 14e. No phone. Métro: Porte de Vanves.

Marché aux Puces St-Ouen de Clignancourt ★ Paris's most famous flea market is a grouping of more than a dozen flea markets—a complex of 2,500 to 3,000 open stalls and shops on the northern fringe of the city, selling everything from antiques to junk, from new to vintage clothing. The market begins with stalls of cheap clothing along avenue de la Porte de Clignancourt. As you proceed, various streets will tempt you. Hold on until you get to rue des Rosiers; then turn left. Vendors start bringing out their offerings around 9am Saturday to Monday and take them in around 6pm. Hours are a tad flexible, depending on weather and crowds. Monday is traditionally the best day for bargain seekers—attendance is smaller and merchants demonstrate a greater desire to sell.

First-timers always want to know two things: "Will I get any real bargains?" and "Will I get fleeced?" It's all relative. Obviously, dealers (who often have a pre-arrangement to have items held for them) have already skimmed the best buys. And it's true that the same merchandise displayed here will sell for less in the provinces. But for the visitor who has only a few days to spend in Paris—and only half a day for shopping—the flea market is worth the experience.

Dress casually and show your knowledge if you're a collector. Most dealers are serious and get into the spirit of things only if you speak French or make it clear you know what you're doing. The longer you stay, the more you chat and show your respect for the goods, the more room you'll have for negotiating. Most of the markets have restroom facilities; some have central offices to arrange shipping. Cafes, pizza joints, and even a few restaurants are scattered around. ***Note:*** Beware of pickpockets and teenage troublemakers while shopping the market. Open Saturday to Monday 9am to 7pm. Av. de la Porte de Clignancourt, 18e. No phone. www.marchesauxpuces.fr. Métro: Porte de Clignancourt (turn left, cross bd. Ney, and then walk north on av. de la Porte Montmartre). Métro: Porte de Clignancourt.

Wares at the Marché aux Puces St-Ouen de Clignancourt.

Marché Ave du Président Wilson

★ Even if you don't buy anything, browsing this market is a city attraction. Parisians flock to this open-air market to purchase some of the most exotic kinds of vegetables sold in the city; everything from purple cauliflower to sunflower yellow zucchini. One stallmaster even sells a type of heirloom pea, "Kelvedon Marvel," that was a particular favorite of Louis XIV, who preferred eating them to bedding one of his mistresses. A major attraction here is a vegetable stall operated by **Joel Thiebault** (✆ **01-44-24-05-77;** www.joelthiebault.fr), who supplies the city's best restaurants. Open Wednesday and Saturday from 7am to 2:30pm. On av. du Président Wilson btw. Place d'Iena and Rue Debrousse, 16e. No phone. Métro: Iena or Alma-Marceau.

Marché Buci This traditional French food market is set up at the intersection of two streets and is only a block long, but what a block it is! Seasonal fruits and vegetables cover tabletops, and chickens spin on the rotisserie. One stall is entirely devoted to big bouquets of fresh flowers. Monday mornings are light; Sunday is best. Open daily 9am to 7pm. Rue de Buci, 6e. No phone. Métro: St-Germain-des-Prés or Mabillon.

 An Open-Air Canvas Gallery

The **Paris Art Market** (✆ **01-53-57-42-60**) is "the place to go" on a Sunday. At the foot of Montparnasse Tower, this market is like an open-air gallery and has done much to restore the reputation of Montparnasse (14e) as an artistic *quartier*. Some 100 artists participate, including painters, sculptors, and photographers, even jewelers and hat makers. Head for the mall along the boulevard Edgar Quinet for the best work. Go anytime on Sunday between 9am and 7pm (Métro: Montparnasse).

A Discount Shopping Village Outside Paris

Just 35 minutes from the center of Paris, **La Vallée Village**, 3 Cours de la Garonne, 77700 Serris (𝄢 **01-60-42-35-00**; www.lavalleevillage.com), is home to some 75 outlets in a chic, purpose-built shopping village. So, it might lack some of the charm of the Avenue Montaigne, but you'll find hot French brands like agnès b, Robert Clergerie, Sandro, Maje, or Givenchy selling last season's collections at up to 70% off. From the center of Paris you can take RER to the Val d'Europe station; by car, follow the A4 motorway out of Paris to exit 12.1 (signposted from there).

Marché des Enfants Rouges ★ This charming covered fresh food market is the oldest in Paris and dates from 1777. In the heart of the rapidly gentrifying Northern Marais neighborhood, it's a lively place for stocking up on picnic supplies (organic if you like), including wine and flowers, or for sitting down for a bite at any of the food stands. We recommend traditional French dishes at L'Estaminet in the western corner, or the excellent Japanese canteen Taeko on the eastern edge. Open Monday to Saturday, 8:30am to 7:30pm, Sunday 8:30am to 2pm. 39 Rue de Bretagne, 3e. 𝄢 **01-42-72-28-12.** Métro: Filles du Calvaire.

SHOPPING A TO Z
Antiques, Collectibles & Vintage
Le Louvre des Antiquaires ★★ Across from the Louvre, this store offers three levels of fancy knickknacks and 250 vendors. It's just the place if you're looking for 30 matching Baccarat-crystal champagne flutes from the 1930s, a Sèvres tea service from 1773, or a signed Jean Fouquet gold-and-diamond pin. Too stuffy? No problem. There's always the 1940 Rolex with the eggplant crocodile strap. Prices can be high, but a few reasonable items are hidden here. What's more, the Sunday scene is fabulous, and there's a cafe with a variety of lunch menus. Pick up a free map and brochure of the premises from the information desk. Open Tuesday to Sunday 9am to 7pm. Closed Sunday. 2 place du Palais Royal, 1er. 𝄢 **01-42-97-27-27.** www.louvre-antiquaires.com. Métro: Palais-Royal.

Art & Crafts
Artcurial ★ Set within minimalist showrooms in one of the most spectacular 19th-century mansions in Paris, this is one of the best outlets in Europe for contemporary art. Since it was established in 1975, it has represented megastars such as Man Ray and the "enfant terrible" of France's postwar intelligentsia, Jean Cocteau. Today, the names of showcased artists read like a who's who of contemporary art: Arman, Sonia Delaunay, and Niki de Saint Phalle for painting and sculpture; Claude Lalanne for jewelry design; and Matta for contemporary carpets. Technically, it's an auction house, similar in some ways to Sotheby's and Christie's, albeit with a specialization in modern and contemporary art, vintage photographs by "important" photographers, antique books and posters, and sculpture. Despite an address that might be among the most expensive in the world (the intersection of av. Montaigne and Champs-Élysées), the place is more welcoming than its location implies. A great arts bookshop, and a recently

renovated daytime cafe provide respite from the shops. Open Monday to Friday 10am to 7pm; Saturday 11am to 7pm. 7 rond-point des Champs-Élysées, 8e. ☎ **01-42-99-20-20.** www.artcurial.com. Métro: Franklin-D-Roosevelt.

107 Rivoli ★★   Inside the city's Decorative Arts Museum, itself located within a wing of the Louvre, this ground floor store presents a wonderful selection of contemporary ceramic, textile, glass, and design pieces, plus a great collection of books dedicated to the arts, architecture, fashion, and design, as well as pieces inspired by the current exhibitions. Great for inspired souvenir shopping. Open Monday to Sunday 10am to 7pm. 107 rue de Rivoli, 1er. ☎ **01-42-60-64-94.** www.lesartsdecoratifs.fr. Métro: Palais-Royal.

Sennelier ★   This historic address has been keeping the city stocked in quality art supplies for over 120 years. Three generations of Senneliers have been providing students from the neighboring art school with the best pigments from this rickety shop on the quays overlooks the river. Patron Gustave developed a range of oil pastels praised by artists such as Cézanne, Degas, and Chagall and still famous in the art world today. Open Monday, 2 to 6:30pm, Tuesday to Saturday 10am to 12:45pm and 2 to 6:30pm. Closed Sunday. 3 Quai Voltaire, 7e. ☎ **01-42-60-72-15.** www.magasinsennelier.com. Métro: St Germain des Près.

Viaduc des Arts   This complex of boutiques and crafts workshops occupies the vaulted spaces beneath one of the 19th-century railway access routes into the Gare de Lyon. Around 1990, crafts artists, including furniture makers, potters, glassblowers, and weavers, began renting the niches beneath the viaduct, selling their wares to homeowners and members of Paris's decorating trades. Several trendsetting home-furnishing outfits have rented additional spaces. Stretching for more than 2 blocks between the Opéra Bastille and the Gare de Lyon, it allows one to see what Parisians consider chic in terms of home decorating. Open Monday to Saturday 11am to 7pm. 119 av. Daumesnil, 12e. ☎ **01-44-75-80-66.** www.viaduc-des-arts.com. Métro: Bastille, Ledru-Rollin, Reuilly-Diderot, or Gare-de-Lyon.

Books

If you like rare and unusual books, there's not only the choice of city's exceptional bookshops, you also have the choice to patronize one of the *bouquinistes,* the owners of those army-green stalls that line the Seine (on the Left Bank between the Quai de la Tournelle and Quai Malaquais, and on the Right Bank between Pont Marie and the Quai du Louvre). This is where tourists in the 1920s and 1930s went to buy "dirty" French postcards. You might get lucky and come across some treasured book, such as an original edition of Henry Miller's *Tropic of Cancer,* which was banned for decades in the United States.

Shops at the Viaduc des Arts.

Galignani Sprawling over a large street level and supplemented by a mezzanine, this venerable wood-paneled bookstore has thrived since 1810. Enormous numbers of books are available in French and English, with a special emphasis on French classics, modern fiction, sociology, and fine arts. Looking for English-language translations of works by Balzac, Flaubert, Zola, or Colette? Most of them are here; if not, they can be ordered. Open Monday to Saturday 10am to 7pm. 224 rue de Rivoli, 1er. ✆ **01-42-60-76-07.** www.galignani.com. Métro: Tuileries.

Les Mots à la Bouche This is Paris's largest, best-stocked gay bookstore. You can find French- and English-language books as well as gay-info magazines such as *Illico, Blue, e.m@le, Carol's Girlfriends,* and *Lesbia*. You'll also find lots of free pamphlets advertising gay/lesbian venues and events. Open Monday to Saturday 11am to 11pm; Sunday 1 to 9pm. 6 rue Ste-Croix-la-Bretonnerie, 4e. ✆ **01-42-78-88-30.** www.motsbouche.com. Métro: Hôtel-de-Ville.

Librairie le Bail-Weissert Paris is filled with rare book shops, but this one has the best collection of atlases, rare maps, and engravings from the 15th century to the 19th century. The shop sells original topographical maps of European and world cities, along with various regions of Europe. There's also a superb collection of architectural engravings. Open Monday to Friday 10am to 12:30pm and 2 to 7pm; Saturday 2 to 6pm. 13 rue Frederic Sauton, 5e. ✆ **01-43-29-72-59.** www.librairie-lebail.fr. Métro: Cluny–La Sorbonne.

7L ★ Monsieur Karl Lagerfeld is not only the creative director of Chanel, the city's emblematic fashion label, but also a prolific photographer and publisher. Here is where he sells his coffee table tomes on art, architecture, photography, and design, in an elegant space designed by Japanese architect Tadao Ando. Open Tuesday to Saturday 10:30am to 6:45pm. Closed Sunday and Monday. 7 rue de Lille, 7e. ✆ **01-42-92-03-58.** www.galignani.com. Métro: St Germain des Près.

Shakespeare and Company ★ The most famous bookstore on the Left Bank is Shakespeare and Company, on rue de l'Odéon, home to Sylvia Beach, "mother confessor to the Lost Generation." Hemingway, Fitzgerald, and Stein were frequent patrons, as was Anaïs Nin, the diarist noted for her description of struggling American artists in 1930s Paris. Nin helped her companion Henry Miller publish *Tropic of Cancer,* a book so notorious in its day that returning Americans who tried to slip copies through Customs often had them confiscated as pornography. (When times were hard, Nin herself wrote pornography for a dollar a page.) Long ago, the shop moved to rue de la Bûcherie, a musty old place where expatriates still swap books and literary gossip and foreign students work in exchange for modest lodgings. Monday nights host free readings; check the program on their site. Open daily 10am to midnight. 37 rue de la Bûcherie, 5e. 𝒞 **01-43-25-40-93.** www.shakespeareandcompany.com. Métro: St-Michel.

Taschen Taschen is a German-based publishing house known for its collection of delicious mass-market coffee-table books. Erudite, high-profile, and glossy, most of them focus on architecture, art, photography, or eroticism. Flick through their latest international releases in this sleek space designed by local design hero Philippe Starck. Open Tuesday to Saturday 11am to 7pm. 2 rue de Buci, 6e. 𝒞 **01-40-51-79-22.** www.taschen.com. Métro: Odéon.

Tea & Tattered Pages At this largely English-language paperback bookshop, you can take a break from browsing to have tea. Though it's out of the way, an extra dose of charm makes it worth the trip. Open Monday to Saturday 11am to 7pm; Sunday noon to 6pm. 24 rue Mayet, 6e. 𝒞 **01-40-65-94-35.** www.teaandtatteredpages.com. Métro: Duroc.

Village Voice Bookshop This favorite of expatriate Yankees is on a side street in the heart of the best Left Bank shopping district, near some of the gathering places described in Gertrude Stein's *The Autobiography of Alice B. Toklas.* Opened in 1981, the shop is a hangout for literati. Its name has nothing to do with the New York weekly. Regular author events are publicized on their website. Open Monday 2 to 8pm; Tuesday to Saturday 10am to 8pm; Sunday 2 to 7pm. 6 rue Princesse, 6e. 𝒞 **01-46-33-36-47.** www.villagevoicebookshop.com. Métro: Mabillon.

W. H. Smith This three-story Paris outpost of the U.K. chain store provides books, magazines, and newspapers published in English (most titles are from Britain). You can get the *Times* of London, of course, and the Sunday *New York Times* is available every Monday. There's a fine selection of maps and travel guides, plus a special children's section that includes comics. Open Monday to Saturday 9am to 7:30pm; Sunday 1 to 7:30pm. 248 rue de Rivoli, 1er. 𝒞 **01-44-77-88-99.** Métro: Concorde.

Clothing & Accessories
WOMEN'S

agnès b ★ agnès b's take on relaxed but elegant urban fashion has been winning over Parisians, and the rest of the planet, since the '70s. She produces collections for the whole family; note that you will find her menswear collections on sale around the corner at agnès b. HOMME (1 Rue Dieu, 10e). There are numerous other addresses scattered around the city. Open Monday, 1 to 7pm, Tuesday to Saturday 11am to 7pm. Closed Sunday. 13 rue de Marseille, 10e. 𝒞 **01-42-06-66-58.** www.agnesb.com. Métro: Jacques Bonsergent.

Azzedine Alaïa Alaïa, who became the darling of French fashion in the 1970s, is the man who put body consciousness back into Paris chic. If you can't afford the current collection, try the **stock shop** around the corner at 18 rue de la Verrerie, 4e (𝒞 **01-42-72-54-97;** Métro: Hôtel-de-Ville), where last season's leftovers are sold at serious discounts. Both outlets sell leather trench coats, knit dresses,

A women's clothing store.

pleated skirts, cigarette pants, belts, purses, and fashion accessories. Open Monday to Saturday 10am to 7pm. 18 rue Verrerie, 4e. ☏ **01-42-72-19-19.** Métro: Hôtel-de-Ville

Balenciaga ★ Creative director Nicolas Ghesquière took control of this floundering but mythical *maison* in 1997 and immediately brought the label bang up to date. For the last 15 years his visionary designs have been splashed across the pages of fashion magazines from Milan to Tokyo. His taste for futuristic chic is visible right down to the boutique's décor, a kind of moonscape developed in collaboration with French artist Dominique Gonzalez-Foerster. Note a dedicated menswear store is located on the Left Bank at 5 rue de Varenne, 7e. Open Monday to Saturday 10am to 7pm. 10 avenue George V 8e. ☏ **01-47-20-21-11.** www.balenciaga. com. Métro: Alma-Marceau.

Bensimon ★ This popular French label designs wearable fashion and sportswear for the whole family. They also produce an important range of accessories, including a model of canvas sneaker that has become a cult summer classic. Just down the street at no. 8 rue des Francs Bourgeois you'll find Home Autour du Monde stocking their ethnic-chic interiors range. Open Monday to Saturday 11am to 7pm, Sunday 1:30 to 7pm. 12 rue des Francs Bourgeois, 3e. ☏ **01-42-77-06-08.** www.bensimon.com. Métro: St-Paul.

Chanel ★ If you can't have the sun, the moon, and the stars, at least buy something with Coco Chanel's initials on it—either a serious fashion statement or something fun and playful. Karl Lagerfeld's designs come in all flavors and have added a subtle twist to Chanel's classicism. This mythical flagship store is located just behind the Ritz, where Mlle Chanel once lived. Check out the beautiful staircase of the *maison* before you shop the two-floor boutique—where a series of rooms display Chanel fashion, accessories, beauty, and perfumes, including store exclusives. It's well worth a peek. Open Monday to Saturday 10am to 7pm. 31 rue Cambon, 1er. ☏ **01-42-86-28-00.** www.chanel.fr. Métro: Tuileries or Madeleine.

Dior ★ This exquisite flagship on the Avenue Montaigne is set up like a small department store, selling men's, women's, and children's clothing, as well as affordable gift items, makeup, and perfume, throughout a seemingly never-ending suite of signature Dior grey rooms. Avant-garde Brit designer John Galliano built the house's reputation with a flamboyant vision of women's wear that wowed the international fashion pack. After making some inflammatory remarks, Galliano stepped down as head designer in 2011, and Riccardo Tisci from Givenchy filled the role. Unlike some of the other big-name fashion houses, Dior is very approachable. Open Monday to Saturday 10am to 7pm. 30 av. Montaigne, 8e. ☏ **01-40-73-73-73.** www.dior.fr. Métro: Franklin-D-Roosevelt.

French Trotters   A temple to urban chic, this multibrand sells hot international fashion and accessories for men and women, from brands including local talents Jerome Dreyfuss, Le Mont Saint Michel, Les Prairies de Paris, Martin Margiela, Tila March, A.P.C., Comme des Garçons, and Maison Fabre. French Trotters also develop collaborations on limited-edition pieces available exclusively in store. Note Little French Trotters selling designer children's wear is open next door at no. 28. Open Monday 2:30 to 7.30pm, Tuesday to Saturday 11:30am to 7:30pm. 30 rue Charonne, 11e. 🕐 **01-47-00-84-35.** http://frenchtrotters.fr. Métro: Bastille or Ledru-Rollin.

Givenchy ★   Hubert de Givenchy made fashion news around the world with his establishment, in 1962, of his couture company for elegant women. Today, the Italian designer Riccardo Tisci continues the Givenchy traditions, but with a distinctly contemporary take on ready-to-wear. This flagship, overseen by Tisci himself in partnership with Brit architect Jamie Fobert, presents the brand's range of women's and menswear and accessories, in an exquisite gallery-like space, where five pods display the cutting-edge collections. Open Monday to Saturday 10am to 7pm. 28 rue Fbg-St-Honoré, 8e. 🕐 **01-42-68-31-00.** www.givenchy.fr. Métro: Concorde. Other locations: 3 av. George V, 8e. 🕐 **01-44-31-50-00.** Métro: George V. Givenchy Hommes: 56 rue François Premier, 8e. 🕐 **01-40-76-07-27.** Métro: Alma-Marceau.

Hermès ★★   France's single most important status item is a scarf or tie from Hermès. Patterns on these illustrious scarves, retailing from about 220€, have recently included the galaxies, Africa, the sea, the sun, and horse racing and breeding. But the choices don't stop there—this large flagship store sells everything from beach towels and accessories, dinner plates, *prêt-à-porter* for men and women, the complete collection of Hermès fragrances (including their "24 Faubourg", named after this mythic address), to saddles; a package of postcards could be the least expensive item sold. Outside, note the horseman on the roof with his scarf-flag flying. The illustrious brand opened a magnificent new flagship on the Left Bank in late 2010, which concentrates more on homeware than on the fashion lines, and features a bookshop, florist, and pricey cafe (17 rue de Sèvres, 6e; 🕐 **01-42-22-80-83;** Mon–Sat 10:30am–7pm). Open Monday to Saturday 10:30am to 7pm. 24 rue du Faubourg St-Honoré, 8e. 🕐 **01-40-17-46-00.** www.hermes.com. Métro: Concorde.

Isabel Marant ★★   With her elegant but wearable urban fashion, Isabel Marant has defined this generation of Parisian chic, and now exports to all the fashion capitals. This is her original store, opened in 1996 when the Bastille neighborhood was where it was at. Here you'll find her signature range of trendy looks, sporting ethnic and vintage details, for women and children. Open Monday to Saturday 10.30am to 7.30pm. Closed Sunday. Also at 47 rue Saintonge, 3e, and 1 Rue Jacob, 6e. 16 rue Charonne, 11e. 🕐 **01-49 29-71-55.** www.isabelmarant.tm.fr. Métro: Bastille or Ledru-Rollin.

Jean-Paul Gaultier   Supporters of this high-camp, high-fashion mogul describe him as an avant-garde classicist without allegiance to any of the aesthetic restrictions of the bourgeoisie. Detractors call him a glorified punk rocker with a gimmicky allegiance to futurist models as interpreted by *Star Trek.* Whatever your opinion, it's always refreshing and insightful, especially for fashion buffs, to check out one of France's most emblematic designers. Open Monday and Saturday 10:30am to 7pm; Tuesday to Friday 10am to 7pm. 44 av. George V,

8e. ☎ **01-44-43-00-44.** www.jeanpaulgaultier.com. Métro: George V. Other locations: 6 rue Vivienne, 2e (☎ **01-42-86-05-05;** Métro: Bourse).

JC de Castelbajac JC/DC's vivid, multicolored world borrows from different cultural universes, like pop music and pop art. He's been working on transforming the cultural zeitgeist into fun and wearable fashion since the '70s, and he's still on the map. Open Monday to Saturday 11am to 7pm. 10 rue Vauvilliers, 1er. ☎ **01-40-41-00-30.** http://jc-de-castelbajac.com. Métro: Châtelet-Les Halles. Other locations: 61 rue des Saint Pères, 6e. ☎ **09-64-48-48-54.**

L'Eclaireur ★ You might feel as if you're stepping into an art gallery when you enter this, the latest address in this prestige string of multibrand emporiums created by the pioneering Madame and Monsieur Hadida. Their beautifully curated selection of high-end fashion is available in five exceptional stores around Paris. This Marais address was designed by Belgian artist Arne Quinze, and conceived of as a multimedia experience, or a sculpture, rather than a simple store. You'll discover women's wear from designers like Rick Owens, Maison Martin Margiela, Lanvin, Dries Van Noten and Balenciaga. Open Monday to Saturday 11am to 7pm. 40 rue Sévigné, 3e. ☎ **01-48-87-10-22.** www.leclaireur.com. Métro: St-Paul.

Sonia Rykiel ★★ The emblematic Left Bank fashion designer has been dressing the independent and audacious women of St-Germain-des-Près since 1968. Her modern wardrobe of elegant, comfortable clothes is instantly recognizable by its bestselling signature range of stripey knits. So you'll find a piece of the city's fashion history in this glamorous two-floor flagship. Open Monday to Saturday 10:30am to 7pm. 175 boulevard St Germain, 6e. ☎ **01-45-49-13-10.** www.sonia rykiel.fr. Métro: St-Germain-des-Prés.

Uniqlo All of Paris it seems worship at this temple to the low-cost basic. The cult Japanese brand sells menswear and women's wear over three floors and is particularly revered for its range of well-cut jeans, plus their winter collection of cut-price cashmere and down jackets. The colorful, upbeat designs appeal to teenagers, but the premium range designed by Jil Sander targets their mothers. Open Monday to Saturday 10am to 8pm (9pm Thurs). 17 rue Scribe, 9e. (☎ **01-58-18-30-55.** www.uniqlo.com. Métro: Havre-Caumartin or Chaussée d'Antin-La Fayette.

Yves Saint Laurent It's easy to forget the days, in the '70s and '80s, when anything the late, great Yves Saint Laurent did was touted by the international press as a sign of his genius, and the fashionable French dressed up in his luxurious versions of Cossack costumes, replete with boleros, riding boots, and copies of antique jewelry from the Russian steppes. But the master's genius continues to be conjured for today's forward-looking fashionista, and we recommend this historic place St-Sulpice boutique for getting in touch with his spirit. Monday 11am to 7pm; Tuesday to Saturday 10:30am to 7pm. 6 place St-Sulpice, 6e. ☎ **01-43-29-43-00** or 01-43-26-84-40. www.ysl.com. Métro: St-Sulpice. Other locations at 32 (men) and 38 (women) rue du Faubourg St-Honoré, 8e. ☎ **01-53-05-80-80.** Métro: Madeleine or Concorde; and 9 Rue Grenelle, 7e. ☎ **01-45-44-39-01.** Métro; St-Sulpice.

Zadig & Voltaire This trendy young French brand is doing well at capturing a contemporary European rock 'n' roll spirit. This spacious first-floor store, overlooking the Place St-Sulpice in the heart of the Left Bank, displays their popular collections of up-to-date luxury: perfectly worn jeans, comfortable cashmeres, biker boots, and more, for men, women, and children. Open Monday to Saturday 10:30am to 7:30pm. 1 rue du Vieux Colombier, 6e. ☎ **01-43-54-72-56.** www.zadig-et-voltaire.com. Métro: St-Sulpice.

MEN'S

Citadium A whole department store over four floors dedicated to streetwear and "lifestyle" for men. You'll find all the usual, international suspects like North Face, Adidas, or Diesel, but also quality local brands including Petit Bateau, Veja, or The Kooples. The Beaubourg branch is smaller, but more central. Monday to Saturday 10am to 8pm (9pm Thurs). 50/56 rue Caumartin, 9e. ℂ **01-55-31-74-00.** www.citadium.fr. Métro: Havre-Caumartin. Other location 33 rue Quincampoix, 4e. ℂ **01-70-06-99-89.** Métro: Rambuteau.

Sandro Homme If you're wanting to resemble the nonchalantly elegant gentlemen you see lounging around Parisian cafes, this newish Paris label is for you. Flannel pants in tones of charcoal or chocolate, merino turtlenecks, leather biker jackets, woolen suits, silk scarfs, and more. There's no compromising on style, but prices remain reasonable. The brand has a string of stores dedicated to its equally appealing women's wear. Open Monday to Saturday 10:30am to 7pm. 11 rue des Francs Bourgeois, 4e. ℂ **01-44-59-84-51.** www.sandro-paris.com. Métro: St-Paul.

CHILDREN'S

Bonpoint ★★ 🎁 This stylish brand helps parents transform their darlings into models of well-tailored conspicuous consumption. Though you'll find some garments for real life, the primary allure of the place lies in its tailored, fairly traditional—and expensive—garments by the "Coco Chanel of the children's garment industry," Marie-France Cohen. This breathtaking flagship is located inside a mansion set around an interior courtyard, and includes a secret cafe with chairs outside under the trees. Open Monday to Saturday 10am to 7pm. 6 rue de Tournon, 6e. ℂ **01-41-51-98-20.** www.bonpoint.com. Métro: Odéon.

Bonton ★ This fun three-floor emporium includes a candy counter, a hairdresser, a retro photo booth, toys, books, a basement knickknack and interiors department, plus the French label's signature collections of trendy clothing for boys and girls, from birth to age 16. It's hard to walk out empty-handed. Open Monday to Saturday 10am to 7pm. 5 boulevard des Filles du Calvaire, 3e. ℂ **01-42-72-34-69.** Métro: Filles du Calvaire.

SHOES & ACCESSORIES

Christian Louboutin A pair of iconic red-soled Louboutins are all any party girl needs on her pretty, pedicured feet. Sarah Jessica Parker helped launch the brand in the English-speaking market. The brand's deliciously romantic Paris flagship, inside a 19th-century covered market, is the perfect context to admire the iconic towering stilettos. Open Monday to Saturday 10:30am to 7pm. 19 rue Jean-Jacques Rousseau, 1er. ℂ **01-42-36-05-31.** www.christianlouboutin.com. Métro: Louvre-Rivoli.

Maison Fabre ★ Three generations of the Fabre family have taken this family owned glove factory in rural France to the pages of the world's finest fashion magazines. The recently revamped brand sell an exquisite range of gloves, for day and night, summer or winter, that will wow your friends back home. Open Monday to Saturday 10am to 7pm. 128-129 Galerie de Valois, 1er. ℂ **01-42-60-75-88.** www.maisonfabre.com. Métro: Palais-Royal. Other location: 60 Rue des Saints Pères, 7e. ℂ **01-42-22-44-86.**

Louis Vuitton ★★ Its luggage is among the most famous and prestigious in the world, a standard accessory aboard the first-class cabins of aircraft flying transatlantic and transpacific. Not content to cover the world's luggage with his initials, Vuitton also creates breathtaking ready-to-wear lines for men and women, as well as bags and other leather accessories, writing instruments, travel products, and publishing. The Champs-Élysées flagship rivals the Eiffel Tower as a destination for jet loads of flushed Japanese tourists, and note that the building includes a quality exhibition space (free entry) on its top floor (entry via Rue Bassano). Open Monday to Saturday 10am to 8pm, Sunday, 11am to 7pm. 101 avenue Champs-Élysées, 8e. ℂ **01-53-57-52-00.** Métro: George V. Other location 6 place St-Germain-des-Prés, 6e. ℂ **01-45-49-62-32.** Métro: St-Germain-des-Prés.

Morabito   This glamorous leather purveyor was originally established by an Italian entrepreneur on the place Vendôme in 1905. In the 1990s, it was partially acquired by an organization in Tokyo. Today, from a site on the glamorous rue François-Premier, it sells chicer-than-thou handbags. Morabito also has suitcases—some of the best in Paris—for men and women. Open Monday to Saturday 10am to 7pm. 259 rue St-Honoré, 1er. ℂ **01-53-23-90-40.** www.morabitoparis.com. Métro: George V.

Pierre Hardy ★   Another of the city's iconic cobblers. Pierre Hardy presents his cutting-edge, urban footwear collections from within sleek, black-lacquered spaces. You'll find shoes for men and women, as well as a range of leather accessories. Hardy was one of the first to propose luxury trainers. Open Monday to Saturday 11am to 7pm. 156 galerie de Valois, 1er. ℂ **01-42-60-59-75.** www.pierrehardy.com. Métro: Palais-Royal. Other location: 9 place du Palais Bourbon, 7e. ℂ 01-45-55-00-67. Métro: Assemblée Nationale.

VINTAGE CLOTHING

Chine Machine   This jumble of vintage finds in the heart of Montmartre provides an opportunity for pleasurable afternoons sifting through fashion from yesteryear in this trendy store. Open noon to 8pm daily. 100 rue des Martyrs, 18e. ℂ **08-73-75-50-50.** www.chinemachinevintage.com. Métro: Abbesses.

Didier Ludot ★   Fashion historians salivate when they're confronted with an inventory of vintage haute couture. In this frenetically stylish shop, albeit at prices that rival what you'd expect to pay for a serious antique, you'll find a selection of gowns and dresses created between 1900 and 1980 for designing women who looked *faaabulous* at Maxim's, at chic cocktail parties on the avenue Foch, in Deauville, or wherever. Open Monday to Saturday 11am to 7pm. 24 Galerie de Montpensier, in the arcades surrounding the courtyard of the Palais Royal, 1er. ℂ **01-42-96-06-56.** Métro: Palais-Royal.

Kiliwatch ★   The city's biggest central vintage emporium will not disappoint. Everything from second-hand jeans and military wear, to Hermès scarves and couture pieces. Plus there's a great arts book corner Open Tuesday to Sunday 11am to 7pm, Monday 2 to 7pm. 64 rue Tiquetonne, 1er. ℂ **01-42-21-17-37.** http://espacekiliwatch.fr. Métro: Etienne-Marcel.

DISCOUNT STORES

Défilé des Marques   French TV stars often shop here, picking up Saint Laurent, Dior, Lacroix, Prada, Chanel, Versace, Hermès, and others at a fraction of the price. Yes, it sells discounted Hermès scarves as well. Low prices here derive from the owners' skill at picking up used clothing from last year's collections in good condition and, in some cases, retro-chic clothing from collections of many years ago, sometimes from estate sales. Open Tuesday to Saturday 11am to 8pm. 171 rue de Grenelle, 7e. ☏ **01-45-55-63-47.** Métro: Latour-Maubourg.

L'Habilleur ★   This northern Marais institution discounts last season's collections of quality brands including the Italian knit brand Roberto Collina or French fashion for men and women by Paul and Joe and Antik Batik. The garments are impeccably maintained and most aesthetically organized by their color, creating a rainbow of fashion opportunities. Open Tuesday to Saturday 11am to 7pm. 44 Rue du Poitou, 3e. ☏ **01-48-87-77-12.** Métro: St-Sébastien Froissart.

Réciproque ★   Forget about serious bargains, but celebrate what could be your only opportunity to own designer clothing of this caliber. Within a series of six storefronts side by side along the same avenue, you'll find used clothing from every major name in fashion, along with shoes, accessories, menswear, and wedding gifts. Everything has been worn, but some items were worn only on fashion runways or during photo shoots. Open Tuesday to Saturday 11am to 7pm. 89–101 rue de la Pompe, 16e. ☏ **01-47-04-30-28.** www.reciproque.fr. Métro: Pompe.

LINGERIE

Cadolle   Herminie Cadolle invented the brassiere in 1889. Today, her family manages the store she founded, and they still make specialty brassieres for the Crazy Horse cabaret. This is the place to go if you want made-to-order items or are hard to fit. Open Monday to Saturday 9:30am to 1pm and 2 to 6:30pm. 4 rue Cambon, 1er. ☏ **01-42-60-94-22.** www.cadolle.com. Métro: Concorde.

Chantal Thomass ★★   This lingerie brand sells luxury French underwear for the contemporary pin-up with a penchant for suspenders and corsets. The boutique is a delicious burlesque boudoir lined in pink satin. Open Monday to Saturday 10am to 7pm. 211 rue St-Honoré, 1er. ☏ **01-42-60-40-56.** www.chantalthomass.fr. Métro: Tuileries.

Erès ★★   Minimal collections of luxury French lingerie and swimwear flaunt a subtle palette and high prices. Open Monday to Saturday 10am to 7pm. 4 bis, rue du Cherche Midi, 6e. ☏ **01-45-44-95-54.** Métro: St-Sulpice. www.eresparis.com

Princesse Tam-Tam ★   This quality lingerie chain sells quality seasonal collections of sexy French underthings, for all ages and budgets. Open Monday to Saturday 10am to 7pm. 31 rue des Abbesses, 18e. ☏ **01-42-52-34-99.** Métro: Abbesses. www.princessetamtam.com.

Sabbia Rosa   Everything here is filmy, silky, and sexy. Look for undergarments (slips, brassieres, and panties) and the kind of negligees that might have been favored by Brigitte Bardot in *And God Created Woman*. Open Monday to Saturday 10am to 7pm. 73 rue des Sts-Pères, 6e. ☏ **01-45-48-88-37.** Métro: Sèvres-Babylone or St-Germain.

JEWELRY

Bijoux Blues ★ 🎁   This Marais boutique offers unique jewelry handmade in Paris with a variety of different materials, including Austrian and bohemian crystals, natural and semiprecious stones, pearls, coral, and mother-of-pearl. Custom requests are welcomed for individually designed pieces. The store offers jewelry at what the staff calls "atelier prices." Open Tuesday to Saturday noon to 7pm, Sunday 2 to 6pm. 30 rue St-Paul, 4e. ☏ **01-48-04-00-64.** www.bijouxblues.com. Métro: St. Paul.

Bijoux Burma If you can't afford any of the spectacular and expensive bijoux at the city's world-famous jewelers, come here to console yourself with some of the best fakes anywhere. This quality costume jewelry is the secret weapon of many a Parisian woman. Open Monday to Saturday 10:30am to 6:45pm. 50 rue François-Premier, 8e. © 01-47-23-79-93. www.bijouxburma.com. Métro: Franklin D Roosevelt.

Cartier ★ One of the most famous jewelers in the world, Cartier has prohibitive prices to match its glamorous image. Go to gawk, and if your pockets are deep enough, pick up an expensive trinket. Open Monday to Saturday 10:30am to 7pm. 23 place Vendôme, 1er. © 01-44-55-32-20. www.cartier.com. Métro: Opéra or Tuileries.

Dior Joaillerie ★★ The talented Parisian aristocrat with the dreamy name Victoire de Castellane launched Dior's fine jewelry department in 1998. Colored stones, bright enamels, and flower and insect motifs are some of the signature elements. Discover her astounding, dreamy collections displayed within a jewel box of a store installed on the magnificent place Vendome. Open Monday to Saturday 11am to 7pm. 8 place Vendôme, 1er. © 01-42-96-30-84. www.diorjoaillerie.com. Métro: Tuileries.

Van Cleef & Arpels ★ Years ago, Van Cleef's designers came up with an intricate technique that remains a vital part of its allure—the invisible setting, wherein a band of sparkling gemstones, each cut to interlock with its neighbor, creates an uninterrupted flash of brilliance. Come browse with the rich and famous. Open Monday to Friday 10:30am to 7pm; Saturday 11am to 7pm. 22 place Vendôme, 1er. © 01-53-45-35-50. www.vancleef-arpels.com. Métro: Opéra or Tuileries.

Concept Stores

Antoine & Lili ★ This brightly colored string of stores sells the Paris brand's range of ethnic-inspired ready to wear for women, plus children's collections, toys, homeware, plus there's a bright canteen to refuel. The spirit of the

The Cartier store.

cosmopolitan Canal St-Martin might reside here. Open daily 11am to 7pm. 95 quai de Valmy, 10e. ✆ **01-40-37-41-55.** www.antoineetlili.com. Métro: Jacques-Bonsergent.

Colette ★★   Named after the great French writer, Colette is a swank citadel for a la mode fashion. It buzzes with excitement, displaying fashions by some of the city's most promising young talent, including Marni and Lucien Pellat-Finet. This is for the sophisticated international shopper who'd never be caught dead shopping at Galeries Lafayette and the like. Not to be overlooked are home furnishings by such designers as Tom Dixon and even zany Japanese accessories. Even if you don't plan to buy anything, check out the basement "water bar," with its fresh quiches, salads, and cakes, plus three dozen brands of bottled water. Open Monday to Saturday 11am to 7pm. 213 rue St-Honoré, 1er. ✆ **01-55-35-33-90.** www.colette.fr. Métro: Tuileries or Pyramides.

Centre Commercial ★   An innovative new collaborative, fair-trade concept store set up by the ethical French trainer brand Véja. The elegant space includes fashion for men and women, from like-minded brands including Gloverall, Grenson, Saint-James or Leaf, plus vintage furniture, secondhand bicycles, and a book and music corner. Open Monday 2 to 7:30pm. Tuesday to Saturday 11am to 7:30pm. 2 rue de Marseille, 10e. ✆ **01-42-02-26-08.** www.centrecommercial.cc. Métro: Jacques Bonsergent.

Le 66 ★★   This appealing labyrinthine space in an arcade off the Champs-Élysées provides some welcome relief from the hysteria on the Avenue. Explore the considered selection of edgy fashion and accessories for men and women at your leisure. Discover the latest pieces from an impressive list of local and international brands such as, our faves, Le Mont St Michel, Thomsen, JC de Castelbajac, and Vivienne Westwood. Plus there's a satellite Kiliwatch vintage bazaar on site. Open Monday to Saturday 11am to 8pm, Sunday 2 to 8pm. 66 ave des Champs-Élysées, 8e. ✆ **01-53-53-33-80.** www.le66.fr. Métro: George V or Franklin-D-Roosevelt.

Merci ★★   This airy, three-floor superstore brings together a carefully selected selection of furniture, home ware, fashion, and beauty. There's a delicious and healthy basement canteen overlooking a courtyard herb garden, and a literary cafe on ground level too for further refreshments. This imposing address in the Northern Marais exemplifies the neighborhood's panache and creativeness, and you don't know who you might run into. Open Monday to Saturday 10am to 7pm. 11 boulevard Beaumarchais,3e. ✆ **01-42-77-00-33.** www.merci-merci.com. Métro: Saint Sébastien-Froissart.

Spree ★ 🎁   Possibly the best store in Montmartre, Spree has been doing its bohemian thing since 2000, and slowly drawing other quality retail to the vicinity. This relaxed concept store presents an inspiring fusion of fashion and accessories, art and design, with pieces from talents including Isabel Marant, Tsumori Chisato, Vanessa Bruno, Jerome Dreyfuss, Acne, and APC. The staff is warm and helpful. Open Monday to Saturday 11am to 7:30pm, Sunday 3 to 7pm. 16 rue Vieuville, 18e. www.spree.fr ✆ **01-42-23-41-40.** Métro: Abbesses.

Department Stores

Le Bon Marché ★★   This Left Bank landmark has worked hard positioning itself as the most exclusive of the city's departments stores. Its modest size makes it manageable to wander the exclusive selection of fashion for men, women, and children; cosmetics and perfumes; furniture; upscale gifts; and housewares. It also boasts one of the largest food halls in Paris which should not be missed. The magnificent displays of the finest fresh and preserved produce from France and around the world is a feast for the senses. Open Monday to Wednesday and Saturday 10am to 8pm; Thursday and Friday 10am to 9pm. 22–24 rue de Sèvres, 7e. ℭ **01-44-39-80-00.** www.lebonmarche.fr. Métro: Sèvres-Babylone.

Les Galeries Lafayette ★ Opened in 1896, with a lobby capped by an early-1900s stained-glass cupola classified as a historic monument, the family owned Galeries Lafayette remains Paris's most popular department store. This store could provision a small city with everything from perfume to fashion: thousands of racks of clothing for men, women, and children; and a staggering array of cosmetics, and perfumes. Also in the complex is **Lafayette Gourmet,** one of the fanciest grocery stores in Paris, selling culinary exotica at prices usually lower than those at Fauchon (see "Food & Drink," later in this chapter); **Lafayette Sports; Galeries Lafayette Mariage** (for wedding accessories); and two other general-merchandise stores, both known simply as **"GL."** The floor above street level has a concentration of high-end boutiques, including Cartier, Vuitton, and Prada. The **Galerie des Galeries** is located within this luxury department and presents regular quality contemporary art exhibitions (free entry). At the street-level **Welcome Desk,** a multilingual staff will tell you where to find various items in the store, where to get a taxi back to your hotel, and so on. Across the street at 35 Boulevard Haussmann you'll find the 3-story **Lafayette Maison,** dedicated to everything you might need for the home. Open Monday to Wednesday and Friday to Saturday 9:30am to 8pm; Thursday 9:30am to 9pm. 40 bd. Haussmann, 9e. ℭ **01-42-82-34-56.** Métro: Chaussée d'Antin. RER: Auber.

Printemps ★ Take a look at the elaborate facade of this store for a reminder of the Gilded Age. Inside, the merchandise is divided into housewares (**Printemps Maison**), women's fashion (**Printemps de la Mode**), and men's clothes (**Le Printemps de l'Homme**). Since a change in ownership in 2006, the Printemps has been chasing a serious luxury market, and now displays a cavalcade of high-end brands across its selection. Turquoise light cascades through a magnificent stained-glass dome into the sixth-floor **La Brasserie Printemps,** where you can have a coffee or a full meal. Interpreters at the Welcome Service in Printemps de la Mode will help you find what you're looking for, claim your VAT refund, and so on. Printemps also has a tourist discount card, offering a flat 10% discount. Open Monday to Wednesday and Friday to Saturday 9:35am to 7pm; Thursday 9:35am to 9pm. 64 bd. Haussmann, 9e. ℭ **01-42-82-50-00.** www.printemps.com. Métro: Havre-Caumartin. RER: Auber or Haussmann–St-Lazare.

Food & Drink

BREAD & CAKES

Pierre Hermé ★★ The cult of the macaron, a delicate sweet biscuit, has swept the city over the last few years, and Monsieur Hermé is one of its pioneers. From this elegant Left Bank flagship you will find Pierre Hermé's full range, with original flavor combinations like passion fruit and chocolate, or wasabi and strawberry. There is also an incomparable selection of cakes, to eat in, take out or simply admire. Open daily 10am to 7pm. 72 rue Bonaparte, 6e. ℭ **01-43-54-47-77.** www.pierreherme.com. Métro: St-Sulpice.

Poilâne ★★ One of Paris's best-loved bakeries, Poilâne hasn't changed much since it opened in 1932. Come here to taste and admire the beautiful loaves of bread decorated with simple designs of leaves and flowers that'll make you yearn for an all-but-vanished Paris. Specialties include apple tarts, butter cookies, and a chewy sourdough loaf cooked in a wood-fired oven. Breads can be specially wrapped to stay fresh during your journey home. Cherche-Midi location open Monday to Saturday 7:15am to 8:15pm; Grenelle location Tuesday to Sunday 7:15am to 8:15pm. 8 rue du Cherche-Midi, 6e. ℂ **01-45-48-42-59.** www.poilane.fr. Métro: St-Sulpice. Also: 49 bd. de Grenelle, 15e. ℂ **01-45-79-11-49.** Métro: Dupleix.

CHOCOLATE

Christian Constant ★★ Opened in 1970, Christian Constant sells some of Paris's most delectable chocolates by the kilo. Each is a blend of ingredients from Ecuador, Colombia, or Venezuela, usually mingled with scents of spices and flowers such as orange blossoms, jasmine, the Asian blossom ylang-ylang, and vetiver and *verveine* (herbs more usually used to brew tea). Open daily 9am to 8pm. 37 rue d'Assas, 6e. ℂ **01-53-63-15-15.** Métro: St-Placide.

Jadis et Gourmande This chain of chocolatiers has a less lofty reputation than Christian Constant and more reasonable prices. Across five centrally located stores, you'll find their famous alphabetical chocolate blocks, which allow you to spell out any message (well . . . almost), in any language. *"Merci"* comes prepackaged. Specialties that are even more delectable are *pralines fondants*, a mixture of praline, nuts, and chocolate that begins to melt the moment it hits your taste buds. Open Monday 1 to 7pm; Tuesday through Saturday 10am to 7pm. 27 rue Boissy d'Anglais, 8e. ℂ **01-42-65-23-23.** www.jadisetgourmande.fr. Métro: Madeleine. An even larger premises, with greater quantities of the same inventories, is at 88 bd. du Port-Royal, 5e. ℂ **01-43-26-17-75.** Métro: Gobelins. RER: Port-Royal.

Jean-Paul Hévin ★★ One of the great chocolatiers of Paris, its owner has mastered the fusion of *chocolat* with *fromage* (cheese, of course). Sweet luscious chocolates with tart cheeses such as Camembert or Roquefort are infused to satisfy both the cheese fan and the chocolate lover's sweet tooth. Savory chocolates are also served without cheese. New offerings—unique in Paris—have caused this place to become one of the most acclaimed in Europe for chocolate devotees. Open Monday to Saturday 10am to 7:30pm. 231 rue St-Honoré, 1er. ℂ **01-55-35-35-96.** www.jphevin.com. Métro: Tuileries or Concorde.

CHEESE

Barthélémy ★ This historic cheese monger has been supplying the country's presidents since 1973 with an incredible range of specialty produce from the four corners of France. Their specialty? The Mont d'Or, a creamy cow's milk cheese from the Alps available between September and May. Open Tuesday to Saturday 7.30am to 7:30pm. 51 rue de Grenelle, 7e. ℂ **01-42-22-82-24.** Métro: Rue du Bac.

SPECIALTY

Fauchon ★★★ At place de la Madeleine stands one of the city's most popular sights—not the church, but Fauchon, a hyper-upscale mega-delicatessen that thrives within a city famous for its finicky eaters. In the original store (26 place de la Madeleine) you'll find a *pâtissier* and *boulangerie*, for breads and pastries, and a *traiteur*, for fresh produce including cheeses, terrines, pâtés, caviar, and fruits. Prices are steep, but the inventories—at least to serious foodies—are without equal. The selection of cakes is mouth-watering; try one of their famous *éclairs*, with new flavor combinations each season. Or a *Paris-Brest*, a ring in the shape of a bicycle wheel that's loaded with pastry cream, almond praline, butter cream, and hazelnut paste capped with almonds. At the second, neighboring address (30 place de la Madeleine), you'll discover an *épicerie* (for jams, crackers, pastas, and exotic canned goods), a *confiserie* selling chocolates and confectionary, a wine cellar, plus two dining areas (a casual basement lunch space, La Cantine, and upstairs more formal dining at Le Café). At some of the counters, you'll indicate to attendants what you want from behind glass display cases and get an electronic ticket, which you'll carry to a *caisse* (cash register). Surrender your tickets, pay the bill, and then return to the counter to pick up your groceries. In other cases, you simply load up a shopping basket with whatever you want and pay for your purchases at a cash register, just as you would at any grocery store. Open Monday to Saturday 9:30am to 7pm. 26 and 30 place de la Madeleine, 8e. ℂ **01-70-39-38-00.** www.fauchon.com. Métro: Madeleine.

Hédiard ★★   Another fine Parisian delicatessen, this 1850 temple of *haute gastronomie* has a more traditional style than its neighbor Fauchon. The old-fashioned decor is a series of red and black salons filled with towering displays of exotic and specialty foodstuffs, giving the store the look of an early 1900s spice emporium. Hédiard is rich in coffees, teas, jams, and spices. They have a quality wine cellar, and the fresh produce department displays exotic fruit and vegetables from the four corner of the planet, in all seasons. Open Monday to Friday 8am to 10pm, Saturday noon to 10:30pm. 21 place de la Madeleine, 8e. ℂ **01-43-12-88-99.** www.hediard.fr. Métro: Madeleine.

La Maison du Miel   Running "The House of Honey" has been a family tradition since before World War I. The entire store is devoted to products derived from honey: honey oil, honey soap, and various honeys to eat, including one made from heather. This store owes a great debt to the busy bee. Monday to Saturday 9:30am to 7pm. 24 rue Vignon, 9e. ℂ **01-47-42-26-70.** www.maisondumiel.com. Métro: Madeleine, Havre-Caumartin, or Opéra.

Maison de la Truffe ★ 🍴   Cramped and convivial, the layout of this shop was modeled after a Parisian's fantasy of an affable, cluttered, old-fashioned butcher shop in Lyon. It's *the* source for foie gras, caviar, black and white truffles, and other high-end foodstuffs. Artfully assembled gift baskets are a house specialty. One corner is devoted to a restaurant where many (but not all) of the dishes contain the costly items (especially truffles) sold in the shop. Examples include noodles or risottos with truffles and caviar with all the fixings. The restaurant is open Monday to Saturday noon to 6pm and 7 to 11pm. The store is open Monday to Saturday 10am to 9pm. 19 place de la Madeleine, 8e. ℂ **01-42-65-53-22.** www.maison-de-la-truffe.com. Métro: Madeleine or Auber.

WINES

Lavinia ★   This is the largest wine-and-spirits store in Europe, opened in 2002 to great acclaim in Paris. Spread over three floors near place de la Madeleine, it stocks more than 3,000 brands of French wine and spirits, along with more than 2,000 brands from other parts of the world. A simple lunch-only restaurant is on-site, as well as a tasting bar. Wine sales here are big business and reflective of France's marketing ideas that regard wine as a part of life. This is the only place in Paris where you can buy a good bottle of South Dakota wine. But who would want to? Open Monday to Saturday 10am to 8pm. 3–5 bd. de la Madeleine, 1er. ℂ **01-42-97-20-20.** www.lavinia.fr. Métro: Madeleine.

Les Caves Taillevent   This is a temple to the art of making fine French wine. Associated with one of Paris's grandest restaurants, Taillevent, it occupies the street level and cellar of an antique building. Stored here are more than 25,000 bottles of wine, with easy access in nearby warehouses to almost a million more. Open Monday 2 to 7:30pm; Tuesday to Saturday 9am to 7:30pm. 199 rue du Faubourg St-Honoré, 8e. ✆ **01-45-61-14-09.** www.taillevent.com. Métro: Charles-de-Gaulle–Etoile.

Nicolas 🎁   This is the flagship store of this chain of wine boutiques, and as such, its vintages are likely to be more esoteric and rare than what you'd find in any of the other 400 or so members of its chain. Scattered over three floors of a large space near La Madeleine are fairly priced bottles of mainstream wines such as Alsatian Gewürztraminers and Collioures from Languedoc-Roussillon. Nicolas also stocks some exceptionally rare vintages, such as a Romanée-Conti from Burgundy. Open Monday to Saturday 9:30am to 8pm. 31 place de la Madeleine, 8e. ✆ **01-42-68-00-16.** www.nicolas.com. Métro: Madeleine.

Gifts/Souvenirs

Au Nom de la Rose   Tasteful and frilly, this flower shop and gift boutique sells many of the floral arrangements that decorate local hotels and restaurants, as well as gift objects that are scented, emblazoned, or permeated with "the spirit or scent of the rose." Expect an overwhelming mass of flowers, many of them temporarily resting in glassed-in coolers, as well as rose-hip jams and marmalades, scented soaps and candles, rosewater-based perfumes, and decorative items for the home and kitchen. A "refinement" (their words) that you might consider either hopelessly decadent or whimsical and charming, depending on your point of view, is a perfume that's specifically designed to enhance the allure of your bedsheets. Open Monday to Saturday 9am to 9pm; Sunday 9am to 2pm. 46 rue du Bac, 7e. ✆ **01-42-22-22-12.** www.aunomdelarose.fr. Métro: Rue du Bac.

Cire Trudon ★★ 🎁   Originally the royal wax and candle makers, this historic brand dates from 1643. Still in operation, it manufactures a delicious selection of contemporary perfumed candles, and the more classic variety too, in an exquisite rainbow of colors. This charming, rickety, two-floor store is a delight. Open Monday to Saturday 10am to 7pm. 78 rue de Seine, 6e. ✆ **01-43-26-46-50.** www.ciretrudon.com. Métro: Odéon.

La Plaque Emaillées et Gravée Jacquin   Established in 1908, when the Art Nouveau craze swept Paris, the outfit has done a respectable business promoting turn-of-the-20th-century Parisian charm ever since. Its specialty is the custom manufacture of cast-iron plaques, enameled and baked, commemorating virtually any event, person (including yourself), or piece of real estate that appeals to you. Phillippe Jacquin, the owner, offers a variety of shapes, sizes, and colors for the finished product. It will take 3 to 4 weeks for your plaque to be manufactured, after which it can be shipped. Much smaller plaques, some ready-made, are also available. Open Monday to Friday 9am to 1pm and 2 to 6pm. 18 bd. des Filles-du-Calvaire, 11e. ✆ **01-47-00-50-95.** www.la-plaque-emaillee.com. Métro: St-Sébastien.

La Tuile à Loup   This emporium has been selling authentic examples of all-French handcrafts since around 1975, making a name through its concentration of hand-produced woven baskets, cutlery, and woodcarvings. Especially appealing are the hand-painted crockery and charming stoneware from such traditional manufacturers as Quimper and Malicorne and from small-scale producers in the Savoie

Alps and Alsace. Open Monday 1 to 7pm; Tuesday to Saturday 10:30am to 7pm. 35 rue Daubenton, 5e. (℃) **01-47-07-28-90.** www.latuilealoup.com. Métro: Censier-Daubenton.

Houseware

CERAMICS, CHINA & PORCELAIN

Astier de Villatte ★★   This impossibly charming two story shop sells a range of white, uncompromisingly handmade earthenware in a range of designs inspired by 18th century styles. There's regular special collections in collaboration with other Paris creatives, and a corner devoted to all sorts of other objects that appeal to the owners, from postcards to scented candles. Astier de Villatte also produces a cult range of annual diaries and notebooks. Everything they do radiates good taste. Open Monday to Saturday 11am to 7:30pm. 173 rue Saint-Honoré, 1er. (℃) **01-42-60-74-13.** www.astierdevillatte.com. Métro: Palais Royal.

La Maison Ivre   This quaint shop is perfect for country-style ceramics that add authenticity to French-country decor. It carries an excellent selection of handmade pottery from all over France, with an emphasis on Provençal and southern French ceramics, including ovenware, bowls, platters, plates, pitchers, mugs, and vases. Open Monday to Saturday 10:30am to 7pm. 38 rue Jacob, 6e. (℃) **01-42-60-01-85.** www.maison-ivre.com. Métro: St-Germain-des-Prés.

Manufacture Nationale de Sèvres ★★   Once endorsed and promoted by the mistresses of Louis XV, Sèvres today manufactures only 4,000 to 5,000 pieces of porcelain every year. Of these, many are reserved as replacements for government and historical entities. Located a short walk beyond the western edge of Paris's 16th arrondissement, in the suburb of Sèvres, it maintains a sales outlet for the porcelain manufactured inside. Open Monday to Saturday 10am to 5pm. 2 place de la Manufacture, 92310 Sèvres. (℃) **01-46-29-22-10.** Métro: Pont-de-Sèvres. More centrally located is the organization's sales outlet near the Louvre, at 4 place André Malraux, 1er ((℃) **01-47-03-40-20**). Métro: Palais-Royal.

CRYSTAL

Baccarat ★★   Opened in 1764, Baccarat is one of Europe's leading purveyors of full lead crystal. They sell luxury jewelry pieces based on colored crystal and precious gems, tableware, glassware, and contemporary chandeliers and other crystal light fittings. The most prestigious outlet is on place de la Madeleine, but the exquisite, Philippe Starck–designed **Maison Baccarat** at 11 place des Etats-Unis, 16e, is larger and includes the **Musée Baccarat** (p. 111). Branches are open Tuesday to Friday 10am to 7pm; Monday and Saturday 10am to 7:30pm. 11 place de la Madeleine, 8e. (℃) **01-42-65-36-26.** www.baccarat.fr. Métro: Madeleine. Also: 11 place des Etats-Unis, 16e. (℃) **01-40-22-11-22.** Métro: Boissière.

Lalique ★★   This historic crystal manufacturer is known for its smoky frosted-glass sculpture, Art Deco crystal, and unique perfume bottles. The shop sells a wide range of merchandise, including leather belts with Lalique buckles and silk scarves, designed to compete directly with those sold by Hermès. You'll also find a branch inside the Carrousel du Louvre. Open Monday to Saturday 10am to 7pm. 11 rue Royale, 8e. (℃) **01-53-05-12-81.** www.cristallalique.fr. Métro: Concorde.

FABRICS

Souleiado   This is the only Paris branch of one of Provence's most successful purveyors of the bright fabrics and thick pottery of France's southern tier. Fabrics are measured out by scissors-wielding saleswomen and then sold by the meter for seamstresses to whip into curtains, tablecloths, or whatever. In a separate shop just around the corner, at 78 rue de Seine (same phone), there are displays of table settings, housewares, and gift items, each reflecting the bright sunshine and colors (usually ocher, cerulean blue, and a strong medium green) of the Midi. Open Monday to Saturday 10:30am to 7pm. 3 rue Lobineau, 6e. ℂ **01-43-54-62-25.** www.souleiado.com. Métro: Odéon or Mabillon.

HOME ACCESSORIES

La Quincaillerie   This is one of those shopping oddities that seem to exist only in Paris. The owners specialize in doorknobs for front doors, windows, and cupboards. There are knobs for almost any piece of furniture, and dozens of accessories, often by top designers such as Philippe Starck. The wares in their stores at no. 3 and no. 4 are modern and designed by some of Europe's top names, including the Italian legend Gio Ponti or Portuguese architect Alvaro Siza. Open Monday to Friday 10am to 1pm and 2 to 7pm; Saturday 10am to 1pm and 2 to 6pm. 3–4 bd. St-Germain-des-Prés, 5e. ℂ **01-46-33-66-71.** www.laquincaillerie.com. Métro: St-Germain-des-Prés.

KITCHENWARE

Dehillerin ★   Established in 1820, Dehillerin is Paris's most famous cookware shop, in the "kitchen corridor" around Les Halles, where all the city's chefs once came to stock up on provisions at the central fresh food market. The shop has a professional, though dusty, feel to it, but don't be intimidated. Equipped with the right tools from Dehillerin, you too can learn to cook like a master chef. Open Monday 9am to 12:30pm and 2 to 6pm; Tuesday to Saturday 9am to 6pm. 18–20 rue Coquillière, 1er. ℂ **01-42-36-53-13.** www.e-dehillerin.fr. Métro: Les Halles.

TABLEWARE

Conran Shop   This shop might remind you of an outpost of the British Empire, valiantly imposing Brit aesthetics and standards on the French-speaking world. Inside, you'll find articles for the kitchen and dining room; glass and crystal vases; fountain pens and stationery; reading material and postcards; and even a selection of chocolates, teas, and coffees to help warm up a foggy English day. Open Monday to Friday 10am to 7pm; Saturday 10am to 7:30pm. 117 rue du Bac, 7e. ℂ **01-42-84-10-01.** www.conranshop.fr. Métro: Sèvres-Babylone.

Music

Fnac ★   This is a large chain of music, books and electronics stores known for their wide selection and discounted prices. Great for the traveler, it offers everything you need for your computer, iPod, or digital camera. Most branches include digital photo development services. Stock up on French music in the CD department, or browse the bookshelves. Seven branches are in Paris, with the largest being at 136 rue de Rennes, Montparnasse. Other locations include rue St-Lazare, avenue des Champs-Élysées, Forum des Halles, avenue des Ternes, and avenue d'Italie. All are open Monday to Saturday 10am to 7:30pm except Champs-Élysées, which is open daily noon to midnight. 136 rue de Rennes, 6e. ℂ **08-25-02-00-20.** www.fnac.com. Métro: St-Placide.

Virgin Megastore   Paris has three branches of Europe's biggest, most widely publicized CD and record store. The Champs-Élysées branch is the city's largest music store; a bookstore and cafe are downstairs. The store's opening in a landmark building helped to rejuvenate the avenue. You'll also find a Virgin Megastore at each airport. Open Monday to Saturday 10am to midnight; Sunday noon to midnight (other locations: Carrousel du Louvre, Sun–Tues 10am–8pm, Wed–Sat 10am–10pm; Gare Montparnasse, Mon–Thurs 7am–8pm, Fri 7am–9pm, Sat 7am–8pm). 52–60 av. des Champs-Élysées, 8e. ✆ **01-49-53-50-00.** Métro: Franklin-D-Roosevelt.

Perfume & Makeup

Annick Goutal ★   Although there are other branches, and you can test Goutal bathroom amenities at many upscale hotels, the sidewalk mosaic tile and the gold-accented boudoir vibe of this central flagship make it worth stopping by. Try their bestseller Eau d'Hadrien for a unisex splash of citrus and summer. Store hours are Monday to Saturday from 10am to 7pm. 14 rue Castiglione, 1er (✆ **01-42-60-52-82.** www.annickgoutal.com; Métro: Concorde.

Diptyque ★★   This contemporary Parisian perfumery and candlemaker has a truly unique range of aromatic plant based scents, including bestsellers Philosykos, a woody blend of fig tree leaves and white cedar, or Tubéreuse, an intoxicating blend based on the heady tuberose flower. Open Monday to Saturday 10am to 7pm. 34 bd St Germain, 5e. ✆ **01-43-26-77-44.** www.diptyqueparis.com. Métro: Maubert-Mutualité.

Editions de Parfums Fréderic Malle ★ 🎁   If the big brand-name perfumes that are sold at every duty-free airport in Europe bore you, consider a visit to this boutique. Founded in 2000 by master perfumer Fréderic Malle, whose nose is as sensitive as that of any wine expert, this brand edits a selection of unisex scents which come in varying intensities of floral, spice, or Oriental motifs; and carry evocative names like Iris Poudre, Noir Epices, En Passant, and one of the bestsellers, Musc Ravageur. There's a lot of elegant chichi about this place (the paneled decor was designed by superdecorators Andrée Putnam and Olivier Lempereur), and one of the things we like best about the place is the display of framed photographic portraits of each of the men and women who created the original scents sold here. Open Monday 1pm to 7pm, Tuesday to Saturday 11am to 7pm. 37 rue de Grenelle, 7e. ✆ **01-42-22-76-40.** www.editionsdeparfums.com. Métro: Rue du Bac.

Francis Kurkdjian ★★ 🎁   One of the latest arrivals on the Paris perfume scene. Francis Kurdjian has created scents for many of the most famous French perfumers, including Guerlain, Dior, or Gaultier over the past 15 years. In 2009 he set up his own *maison* and here sells an elegant range of scents for men and women, but also for the home, your laundry (!), and even perfumed bubble blowers for the kids. The store itself is a delightful homage to the city of Paris, inspired by its zinc roofs and gilded monuments. Open Monday to Saturday 11am to 7pm. 5 rue d'Alger, 1er. ✆ **01-42-60-07-07.** www.franciskurkdjian.com. Métro: Tuileries.

Parfums Caron Although you can buy scents in any duty-free or discount *parfumerie*, it's worth visiting the source of some of the world's most famous perfumes. The tiny shop boasting old-fashioned glass beakers filled with fragrances and a hint of yesteryear. Fleur de Rocaille, a Caron scent, was the featured perfume in the movie *Scent of a Woman*. Store hours are Monday to Saturday from 10am to 6:30pm. Also at 90 rue du Faubourg St Honoré, 8e. 34 av. Montaigne, 8e. ✆ **01-47-23-40-82.** www.parfumscaron.com. Métro: Franklin-D-Roosevelt.

Salons du Palais Royal, Shiseido ★★ 🎁 Shiseido, the world's fourth-largest maker of cosmetics and skincare goods, has become more prominent thanks to the efforts of its star perfumer Serge Lutens. Here in this special, secret place, it stocks more than 20 exclusive unisex fragrances created by Lutens, including one of its latest, Jeux de Peau, a nostalgic spicy scent inspired by the odor of hot bread and butter! Don't be afraid to wander in and ask for some scent strips. Open Monday to Saturday from 10am to 7pm. 142 Galerie de Valois, Palais Royal, 1er. ☏ **01-49-27-09-09.** www.salons-shiseido.com. Métro: Palais-Royal.

Sephora ★ The buzzing, late-night Champs-Élysées flagship of this international chain dedicated to cosmetics, skin care, and beauty is a great place to try many of the exclusive products you've admired in shop windows. Many of the staff speak English. Open daily 10am to midnight, and the weekend till 1am. 70 Avenue des Champs-Élysées, 8e. ☏ **01-53-93-22-50.** www.sephora.fr. Métro: Franklin-D-Roosevelt.

The Different Company ★ 🎁 Many fashionistas are deserting the fabled houses of scent and heading for this corner of counterculture chic in the Marais. The perfume shop is run by the father-daughter team of Jean-Claude and Céline Ellena. Dad is perfumer for Hermès and continues here a commitment to exceptional quality. Scents which include Osmanthus, Sel de Vétiver, and Rose Poivrée, have been called "fragrances for the 21st century." Open Tuesday to Saturday noon to 7:30 or 8pm. 10 rue Ferdinand Duval, 4e. ☏ **01-47-83-65-88.** www.thedifferent company.com. Métro: Saint-Paul.

Stationery

Cassegrain ★ Nothing says elegance more than thick French stationery and notecards. Cassegrain, originally an engraver in 1919, offers beautifully engraved stationery, most often in traditional patterns, and business cards engraved to order. Several other items for the desk, many suitable for gifts, are for sale as well; there are even affordable pencils and pens, leather wallets, and small desktop accessories. Open Monday to Saturday 10am to 7pm. 422 rue St-Honoré, 8e. ☏ **01-42-60-20-08.** www.cassegrain.fr. Métro: Concorde.

Technology

Apple Store ★ This Paris temple to the world of Apple is spread out over three stores, just steps from the Opéra Garnier and the department stores. Open Monday to Wednesday 9am to 8pm; Thursday to Saturday 9am to 9pm. Note, there's a second outlet inside the Carrousel du Louvre. 12 rue Halévy, 9e. ☏ **01-44-83-42-00.** www.apple.com. Métro: Opéra.

Toys & Games

Au Nain Bleu ★ This is the largest, oldest, and most centrally located toy store in Paris. More important, it's probably the fanciest toy store in the world. But don't panic—in addition to the expensive stuff, you'll find rows of cheaper items on the first floor. Open Monday 2 to 7pm; Tuesday to Saturday 10am to 7pm. 5 bd. Malesherbes, 8e. ☏ **01-42-65-20-00.** www.aunainbleu.com. Métro: Concorde or Madeleine.

PRACTICAL MATTERS: THE SHOPPING SCENE

Business Hours

Usual shop hours are Monday to Saturday from 10am to 7pm, but hours vary, and Monday mornings don't run at full throttle. Small shops sometimes close for a 2-hour lunch break and some do not open at all until after lunch on Monday. Thursday is the best day for late-night shopping, with stores open to 9 or 10pm.

Sunday shopping is limited to tourist areas and flea markets, though there's growing demand for full-scale Sunday hours. The department stores are now open on the five Sundays before Christmas. The **Carrousel du Louvre** (✆ 01-43-16-47-10), a mall adjacent to the Louvre, is open daily 10am to 8pm. The tourist shops lining rue de Rivoli across from the Louvre are open on Sunday, as are the antiques villages, flea markets, and specialty events. Several food markets enliven the streets on Sunday. For our favorites, see the box "Food Markets" (p. 243). Most of the shops along the Champs-Élysées stay open on Sunday.

Note: Many independent stores close for about a month at the height of summer, from late July to late August.

Getting a VAT Refund

The French **value-added tax** (**VAT**—**TVA** in French) is generally 19.6%, but you can get most of that back if you spend a minimum of 175€ on the same day, in the same, participating, store. All department and luxury stores participate in the VAT refund program. Though some people find the trouble isn't worth the refund.

When you meet your required minimum purchase amount, you qualify for a tax refund. The amount of the refund varies with the way the refund is handled and the fee some stores charge you for processing it. So the refund at a department store may be 13%, whereas at a small shop it may be 15% or 18%.

You'll receive the **Retail Export Form** in the shop; some stores, such as Hermès, have their own, while others provide a government form. Make sure you have the form stamped before leaving the store.

All refunds are processed at the point of departure from the **European Union (E.U.),** so if you're going to another E.U. country, don't apply for the refund in France. At the airport of your last stop in the E.U. look for the Detaxe counter at the airport. Then expect to stand in line for as long as half an hour. You must show your ticket, your passport, the forms you collected on the day you bought the goods, and the goods themselves, so have them on you or visit the Customs office before you check your luggage. After Customs has checked everything, keep a copy of the form for your records then drop the original in the envelope provided and in the mail. After the papers are mailed, a credit will appear, often months later, on your credit card bill.

Be sure to mark the paperwork to request that your refund be applied to your credit card so you aren't stuck with a check in euros, which may be hard to cash.

To avoid refund hassles, ask for a Global Refund form (Shopping Cheque) at a store where you make a purchase. When leaving an E.U. country, have it stamped by Customs, after which you take it to a Global Refund counter at one of more than 700 airports and border crossings in France. Your money is refunded on the spot. For information, contact **Global Blue,** 18 rue de Calais, 75009 Paris (𝄐 **01-41-61-51-51;** www.global-blue.com).

Duty-Free Boutiques

The advantage of duty-free shops is that you don't have to pay the VAT, so you avoid the red tape of getting a refund. Both Charles de Gaulle and Orly airports have shopping galore (de Gaulle has a virtual mall with crystal, cutlery, chocolates, luggage, wine, pipes and lighters, lingerie, silk scarves, perfume, knitwear, jewelry, cameras, cheeses, and even antiques). You'll also find duty-free shops on the avenues branching out from the Opéra Garnier, in the 1st and 9th arrondissements. Sometimes bargains can be found, but most often not.

Sales & Bargains

The French sales take place twice a year, over 5 weeks, beginning at the end of June for the summer collections and the beginning of January for winter. Remember, the first in are the best dressed.

Practical Matters: The Shopping Scene

SHOPPING

ENTERTAINMENT & NIGHTLIFE

By Joseph Alexiou & Meg Zimbeck

8

While the stereotype of the French may suggest a nation of hard-playing, work-adverse people, Parisians are as hardworking as the rest of us. Work ethics aside, it seems that every resident of this luminous city has a higher education in pleasure. With the workday behind them, locals head for a café or wine bar to meet with friends over a drink and perhaps a meal (see "The Top Cafés," in chapter 6). Whatever your diversional whim, Paris can answer it. Stadiums, racetracks, and city parks cater to sports enthusiasts; while theaters and concert halls captivate audiences with performances ranging from classical to postmodern. As its moniker indicates, Parisian streets and monuments remain illuminated all night. Restaurants won't expect you before 8pm, and by midnight the party is just getting started at hundreds of bars and dance clubs throughout the city.

In this chapter, we highlight the best leisure and entertainment options in Paris: the top performance spaces for live entertainment, the best bars for whistle-whetting, and the hottest clubs for dancing off all that foie gras. From a jog along the city's "green lung" to outlandish floor shows and everything in between, if it's about having fun, then you'll find it here.

THE PERFORMING ARTS

Home to a broad range of performing arts, Paris showcases everything from world-renowned opera and classical concerts to the edgy and contemporary theater. Recently, the **Opéra Garnier** and **Opéra Bastille** have been kicking out classics such as Puccini's *Madama Butterfly* and *Tosca,* as well as hosting performances from the Russian ballet powerhouse, the Bolshoi Theater. Look to companies such as the **Odéon Théâtre de L'Europe** (www.theater-odean.fr) to push the theatrical envelope by showing a trilogy of Greek tragedies by Aeschylus during the same season as punk legend Patti Smith reading passages from her autobiography, *Just Kids.* Similarly, the **Théâtre National de la Colline** (www.theater-colline.fr) is at its best when representing the theater world's virtually unrepresented, such as *Pornography* by up-and-coming English playwright Simon Stephens, or lesser-known triumphs like Eugene O'Neill's *Long Day's Journey into Night.*

LISTINGS Announcements of shows, concerts, and operas are plastered on kiosks all over town. You'll find listings in the weekly ***Pariscope,*** an entertainment guide with an English-language section, or in ***L'Officiel des Spectacles,*** available at newsstands. Also check out **en.parisinfo.com**,

PREVIOUS PAGE: **A cabaret show in Paris.**

the city's official English-language tourism website. The "What's On" section has detailed listing for every concert and show in town. *Note:* Performances tend to start later in Paris than in London or New York—from 8 to 9 pm—and Parisians tend to dine after the theater.

GETTING TICKETS Your best bet for cheap tickets is to try the theater's box office. Or head for a discount agency such as the **Kiosque-Théâtre,** 15 place de la Madeleine, 8e (© **01-42-65-35-64;** www.kiosquetheatre.com; Metro: Madeleine), offering leftover tickets for up to 50% off on the day of performance. Tickets for evening shows sell Tuesday to Saturday from 12:30 to 8pm, for matinees, Sunday 12:30 to 4pm. Other branches are in the basement of the Châtelet–Les Halles Métro station and in front of Gare Montparnasse.

Another option is **Fnac** at 136 rue de Rennes, 6e (© **08-25-02-08-02;** Métro: St. Placide); or 1–7 rue Pierre-Lescot, in the Forum des Halles, 1er (© **08-25-02-00-20;** Métro: Châtelet–Les Halles). The Virgin Megastore–type chain sells music, movies, electronics, and books, as well as tickets for festivals, concerts, and the theater. You can pick up your tickets at the *billitterie* (ticket booth) of any of these locations, or online at www. fnacspectacles.com. Another great website for reduced-price tickets is **www.ticketnet.fr**.

Tip: Students with ID can get great last-minute deals by applying for the lottery at box offices an hour before curtain time.

The easiest (and most expensive) way to get tickets is to ask your concierge to arrange for them. A service fee is added, but it's a lot easier if you don't want to waste precious hours in Paris trying to secure often hard-to-get tickets.

Theater

Comédie-Française ★★ Those with even a modest understanding of French can delight in a sparkling production of Molière at this national theater, established to keep the classics alive and to promote important contemporary authors. Nowhere else will you see the works of Molière and Racine so beautifully staged. The box office is open daily from 11am to 6pm, but the hall is dark from mid-July to early September. In 1993 a Left Bank annex was launched, the **Comédie Française-Théâtre du Vieux-Colombier,** 21 rue du Vieux-Colombier, 4e (© **01-44-39-87-00**). Though its repertoire varies, it's known for presenting serious French dramas and the occasional foreign adaptation. Discounts are available if you reserve in advance. 2 rue de Richelieu, 1er. © **08-25-10-16-80.** www. comedie-francaise.fr. Tickets range from 12€–38€. Métro: Palais-Royal or Musée du Louvre.

Opera, Dance & Classical Concerts

Cité de la Musique ★★★ This testimony to the power of music has been the most widely applauded, the least criticized, and the most innovative of the late François Mitterrand's *grands projets*. At the city's northeastern edge in what used to be a run-down neighborhood, this $120-million stone-and-glass structure incorporates a network of concert halls, a library and research center for the study of all kinds of music, and a museum (see the Musée de la Musique, p. 127, in chapter 4). The complex hosts a rich variety of concerts, ranging from Renaissance music through 19th- and 20th-century works, including jazz and traditional music from nations around the world. There's a beautiful café on site if you'd like to sip some wine on the sunny terrace before your concert. 221 av. Jean-Jaurès, 19e. © **01-44-84-45-00,** or 01-44-84-44-84 for tickets. www.cite-musique.fr. Tickets 20€–39€ for 4:30 and 8pm concerts. Métro: Porte de Pantin.

Opéra Bastille ★★   This controversial building—it has been called a "beached whale"—was designed by Canadian architect Carlos Ott, with curtains by Japanese designer Issey Miyake. Since the house's grand opening in July 1989, the Opéra National de Paris has presented works such as Mozart's *Marriage of Figaro* and Tchaikovsky's *Queen of Spades*. The main hall is the largest of any French opera house, with 2,700 seats, but the building also contains two smaller concert halls, including an intimate 250-seat room that usually hosts chamber music. Both traditional opera performances and symphony concerts are presented here, as well as classical and modern dance. 2 place de la Bastille, 4e. © **08-92-89-90-90** or 01-40-01-17-89. www.operadeparis.fr. Tickets 5€–180€ opera, 8€–89€ dance. Métro: Bastille.

Opéra Comique   This is a charming venue for light opera, on a smaller scale than Paris's major opera houses. Built in the late 1890s in an ornate style that might remind you of the Opéra Garnier, it's the site of small productions of operas such as *Carmen, Don Giovanni, Tosca,* and *Palleas and Melisande*. There are no performances from mid-July to late August. The box office, however, is open year-round Monday to Saturday 11am to 7pm; Sunday 11am to 5pm. 5 rue Favart, 2e. © **01-42-44-45-40.** www.opera-comique.com. Tickets 11€–115€. Métro: Richelieu-Drouot.

Opéra Garnier ★★★   With its grand decor, underground lake and cellars, and haunted history—a falling chandelier killed a man here in 1896—this place served as the inspiration for Gaston Leroux's 1910 novel (and later a musical hit), *The Phantom of the Opera*. Today, this is once again the premier venue for dance and opera. Charles Garnier designed this 1875 rococo wonder during the heyday of the French Empire; the facade is adorned with marble and sculpture, including *The Dance* by Carpeaux. Following a year-long renovation, during which the Chagall ceiling was cleaned and air-conditioning was added, the facade gleams as it did for Napoleon III. You can see the original gilded busts and statues, the rainbow-hued marble pillars, and the mosaics. The Opéra Garnier combines ballet and opera, and provides one of the most elegant evenings you can spend in the City of Light. Because of the competition from the Opéra Bastille, the Garnier has made great efforts to present more up-to-date dance works such as choreography by Twyla Tharp, Agnes de Mille, and George Balanchine. The box office is open Monday to Saturday from 10:30am to 6:30pm. Place de l'Opéra, 9e. © **08-92-89-90-90** or 01-40-01-18-50. www.operadeparis.fr. Tickets 5€–180€ opera, 8€–89€ dance. Métro: Opéra.

Opéra Garnier.

The Music of Angels

Some of the most moving music in Paris echoes through its churches, with sounds that can take you back to the Middle Ages. At **Eglise de St-Eustache**, 2 impasse St-Eustache, 1er ((*C*) **01-42-36 31-05**; www.saint-eustache.org; Métro: Rambuteau), High Mass with the organ playing and the choir singing is at 11am on Sunday. In summer, concerts are played on the organ, marking the church's role in holding the premiere of Berlioz's *Te Deum* and Liszt's *Messiah*. Tickets to these special concerts sell for 12€ to 40€. The church is open daily 9:30am to 7pm.

The **American Church in Paris,** 65 quai d'Orsay, 7e ((*C*) **01-40-62-05-00**; www.acparis.org; Métro: Invalides or Alma-Marceau), sponsors concerts from September to June on Sundays at 5pm. You can also attend free concerts at **Eglise St-Merry**, 76 rue Verrerie, 4e ((*C*) **01-42-71-93-93**; Métro: Hôtel-de-Ville). These performances are staged with variable musicians based on their availability, from September to July on Saturdays at 8:30pm, and again on Sundays at 4pm.

Salle Pleyel ★★★   New York has Carnegie Hall, but for years Paris lacked a permanent home for its orchestra. That is, until several years ago when the restored Salle Pleyel opened once again. Built in 1927 by the piano-making firm of the same name, Pleyel was the world's first concert hall designed exclusively for a symphony orchestra. Ravel, Debussy, and Stravinsky performed their masterpieces here, only to see the hall devastated by fire less than 9 months after its opening. The original sound quality was never recovered because of an economic downturn. In 1998, real estate developer Hubert Martigny purchased the concert hall and pumped $38 million into it, restoring the Art Deco spirit of the original and also refining the acoustics it once knew. Nearly 500 seats were removed to make those that remained more comfortable. The Orchestre Philarmonique de Radio France and the Orchestre de Paris now have a home worthy of their reputations, and the London Symphony Orchestra makes Pleyel its venue in Paris. The box office is open Monday to Friday 10am to 6pm. 252 rue du Faubourg-St-Honoré, 8e. (*C*) **01-42-56-13-13.** www.sallepleyel.fr. Tickets 10€–160€. Métro: Miromesnil.

Théâtre des Champs-Élysées   This Art Deco theater, constructed in 1913, attracts a very haute couture crowd and hosts both national and international orchestras (such as the Vienna Philharmonic) as well as opera and ballet. The box office is open Monday to Saturday from 1 to 7pm. There are no performances in August. 15 av. Montaigne, 8e. (*C*) **01-49-52-50-50** for box office. www.theatrechamps elysees.fr. Tickets 5€–140€. Métro: Alma-Marceau.

Théâtre National de Chaillot   Part of the architectural complex facing the Eiffel Tower, this is one of the city's largest concert halls. In addition to music, you might see a dance performance here or a brilliantly performed play by Marguerite Duras. The box office is open Monday to Saturday from 11am to 7pm, Sunday 1 to 5pm. 1 place du Trocadéro, 16e. (*C*) **01-53-65-30-00.** www.theatre-chaillot.fr. Tickets 8€–42€ adults, 15€–21€ seniors 60 and older, 9€–18€ 24 and younger. Métro: Trocadéro.

> White Nights *(Nuit Blanche)* in Paris

Beginning in Paris in 2002, *Nuit Blanche*, a frenetic all-night multivenue cultural bash, was launched. Since then, the concept has swept such European capitals as Madrid and Rome. Dates for this event vary from year to year. In 2011, the 10th edition of Nuit Blanche will take place on October 1. Check the website at www. nuitblanche.paris.fr, or call © **01-42-76-65-26** for programming information.

What to expect: The offerings seem endless, including everything from street entertainers to jazz jam sessions. There are modern art shows, theatrical presentations, and music of every genre, even old-fashioned French ballads.

Nuit Blanche events are free and take place, often spontaneously, throughout Paris—not just in the historic core. As many as two million people take part in the festivities, and many museums and art galleries remain open around the clock.

THE BAR & CAFÉ SCENE

Rather than go home to often-cramped apartments, Parisians socialize in the bars and cafés throughout the city. Along with coffee, wine, beer, and liquors, cafés also serve small meals and plates of meat and cheese. Besides focusing on wine, wine bars also serve small plates, but are a bit more gastronomically focused than cafés. Anglo- and Irish-style bars and pubs are also scattered throughout the city; these bars serve cocktails and beer, and are a bit more boisterous than the intimate settings of cafés.

For more information on cafés, see "The Top Cafés" in chapter 6.

Wine Bars

The wine bar, or *bar à vin,* is a welcome departure from sitting down at a typical café or restaurant. They are often calm and warmly decorated, and many have regional themes. All offer diverse and interesting selections of wines and serve simple small dishes and platters—perfect for those in the mood for a delectable snack with their drinks without the commitment to a full-blown meal.

Café de la Nouvelle Mairie   Just around the corner from the Panthéon, this tiny wine bar faces a quiet plaza with a bubbling fountain. Proprietors Benjamin Fourty and Corentin Bucillat put together an interesting selection of wines, including a delicious muscat, surrounded by equally thoughtful 1930s decor. Wine by the glass ranges from 5€ to 8€. The fresh tartines or, especially, their *charcuterie* plates are worth a try. Open Monday to Friday, from 9am to midnight Tuesdays and Thursdays, 9am to 10pm on Monday, Wednesday, and Friday. Closed in August. 19-21 rue des Fossés-Saint-Jacques, 5e. © **01-44-07-04-41**. Métro: Luxembourg or Cardinal-Lemoine.

5e Cru ★ 🍴 This shabby-chic spot, with only three pine tables as well as a few barrels converted to dining stations, is a favorite of foodies. Jean de Toalier serves more wines than just "fifth-growth" bottles as the name suggests and boasts that he's got "every *terroir* of France covered" in his kitchen, offering more than 150 different French wines. You can get a simple menu, or daily small plate special, for 14€; a glass of wine for 3€ to 8€, with bottles priced as low as 8€, rarely more than 60€. Open Tuesday to Friday 10:30am to midnight, Saturday 3pm to 1am. 7 rue du Cardinal Lemoine, 5e. ☎ **01-40-46-86-34.** www.5ecru.com. Métro: Jussieu.

Le Sancerre Enter this rustic place in the center of the chic and moneyed 7th arrondissement and—with its aging furniture and wooden bar—you'll think you've been transported somewhere in the countryside of the Loire Valley. Lovingly cared for by friendly, equally aging proprietors, this place specializes in—what else—Sancerre wine. There are other vintages as well, include chinon and saumur wine (both from the Loire Valley) among many others. The plates are as countryside as the decor: *andouillettes* (chitterling sausages), Loire cheeses, fresh oysters, and fresh quiches galore. Glasses of wine cost 4€ to 7€; simple platters of food cost 7.50€ to 16€ each. Open Monday to Friday 8 m to 4pm and 6:30 to 11pm, Saturday 8:30am to 4pm. 22 av. Rapp, 7e. ☎ **01-45-51-75-91.** Métro: Alma-Marceau.

Les Bacchantes This place prides itself on offering more wines by the glass—at least 90—than any other wine bar in Paris; prices range from 3€ to 6€. It also does a hefty restaurant trade in well-prepared *cuisine bourgeoise*, with main courses costing 14€ to 28€. Its cozy, rustic setting—with paneling, and chalkboards announcing vintages and platters—attracts theatergoers before and after performances at the Théâtre Olympia. Wines are mainly from France, but you'll also find examples from neighboring countries. Open Monday to Saturday noon to 3pm and 7pm to 2am. 21 rue Caumartin, 9e. ☎ **01-42-65-25-35.** Métro: Havre-Caumartin.

Le Tournon After a visit to the Jardin de Luxembourg, two steps up the street will find you a seat and a glass of chenin blanc at this 100-year old establishment. (Austrian writer Joseph Roth once sat at le Tournon composing his prose.) The interior is decorated with a classic zinc bar and brightly frescoed walls. With a grand selection of wines, from 6€ to 9€ a glass, and homey delicacies such as seared Landes foie gras, veal liver served in vinegar, or warmed potato tarts, there's no chance you'll leave before a second glass. Open daily 8am to 11pm (until 7pm Sun). 18 rue de Tournon, 6e. ☎ **01-43-26-16-16.** Métro: Odéon.

Mélac At his second-generation family establishment, heavily mustachioed Jacques Mélac hosts a crowd of neighborhood regulars (the area, Charonne, is off the beaten path but authentically Parisian) who are dedicated wine connoisseurs. Not only does his selection of wines include most French regional varieties, but they also serve a their own family wine, Domaine des Trois Filles, from the Boutenac terroire of Corbières. The classic French food is styled as the cooking of your *grand-mère*, that is, if she regularly prepared *oeufs cocotte* or Cantal charcuterie plates for you. Open Mondays from 9am to 2pm, and Tuesday through Sunday from 9am to 10:30pm. 42 rue Léon Frot, 11e. ☎ **01-73-70-59-27.** www.melac.fr. Métro: Charonne.

Willi's Wine Bar ★★ In an odd way, this is the granddaddy of the modern wine bar, open in 1980 and still popular among local bankers and flashy tourists. There are more than 250 varieties of wine to choose from, ranging from the reasonably priced at around 8€ per glass to outrageous, but delicious, costing upward of 20€ per glass. A fixed-price menu ranges from 22€ to 28€ at lunch, and 35€ at dinner. The restaurant is open Monday to Saturday noon to 2:30pm and 7 to 11pm; the bar, Monday to Saturday noon to midnight. 13 rue des Petits-Champs, 1er. ✆ **01-42-61-05-09.** www.willis winebar.com. Métro: Bourse, Pyramides, or Palais-Royal.

Willi's Wine Bar.

Bars & Pubs

You will find Parisians enjoying their drink at any of the ubiquitous cafés throughout town (many of which double as bars and often an extension of personal living rooms). Nonetheless, there are plenty of nooks set up in the more traditional Anglo-centric style of drinking establishment—and some cafés function more like a bar than anything else. Our selections below are among the best places to enjoy a beer or cocktail, in part because of the interesting crowds they draw. Paris is also home to quite a few grand-luxe, world-class bars: Those at the **Plaza Athénée** or **Ritz** (see p. 309 and 295 for hotel reviews), for example, are among the grandest in the world and provide a uniquely Parisian experience. Of course, you would never show up in sneakers at such an establishment—or without a titanium-level credit card. As a general rule, bars and pubs are open daily from 11am to 2am.

Andy Whaloo This bar has a Moroccan vibe, with colorful rugs and other North African collectables. The cocktails are expensive, but people-watching among the youthful and *branché* (hip) Parisians perched on the stools makes up for the prices. Open Tuesday to Saturday pm to 2am. 69 rue des Gravilliers, 3e. ✆ **01-42-71-20-38.** Métro: Arts et Métiers.

Bar Hemingway/Bar Vendôme In 1944, during the liberation of Paris, Ernest Hemingway made history by ordering a drink at the Ritz Bar while gunfire from retreating Nazi soldiers was still audible in the streets. Today the **Ritz** hotel (see p. 295 for review) commemorates the event in its Bar Hemingway with bookish memorabilia, rows of newspapers, and stiff drinks. Look for the bar's entrance, and homages to other writers such as Proust, near the hotel's rue Cambon entrance. If you develop a thirst in the daytime, when the Bar Hemingway isn't open, head for the Bar Vendôme, near the hotel's place Vendôme entrance. The setting is just as cozy and woodsy, albeit a bit more grand. Open daily 6:30pm to 2am. In the Hôtel Ritz, 15 place Vendôme, 1er. ✆ **01-43-16-30-30.** Métro: Opéra or Concorde.

Café Charbon In many ways the social center of trendy Oberkampf, this former Belle Époque dance hall has big wooden banquets, distressed mirrors, and pleasantly vaulted ceilings. Spacious but often crowded, it's a great place to start off your evening bar crawl along rue Oberkampf. Open daily 9am to 2am (until 4am Fri–Sat). 109 rue Oberkampf, 11e. ✆ **01-43-57-55-13.** Métro: Parmentier or Ménilmontant.

Experimental Cocktail Club This cosmopolitan lounge has the feel of a retro speakeasy. The cocktails here are spot-on and the crowd is fashionable—starchitect

Bar Hemingway.

Philippe Starcke and actor Adrian Grenier have been spotted sipping drinks here late into the evening. Drinks start at 12€. Open daily from 6pm to 2am, until 5am Friday and Saturday. 37 rue St-Sauveur, 2e. ℭ **01-45-08-88-09.** www.experimental cocktailclub.com. Métro: Sentier.

The Frog and the Princess It's loud, crowded, and sweaty in this English-style pub. You'll be surrounded by students and sports enthusiast, most of whom will speak English. It's so un-Parisian that it has become an especially Parisian place to go, especially if you're an "anglophile" of sorts or enjoy a good pint. A definite place to try and catch a game, match, or whatever your countrymen consider the sporting event of the day. Open from 5:30pm to 2am weekdays, noon to 2am Friday and Saturday. 9 rue Princesse, 6e. ℭ **01-40-51-77-38.** www.frogpubs.com. Métro: St Germain des Prés/Mabillon.

Hôtel du Nord Immortalized in the 1938 film of the same name by Marcel Carné, this classic charmer presides over the Canal St-Martin and is known for its creative, diverse clientele and friendly hosts. It also boasts a small library, restaurant, and quiet nooks for study. But the best time to visit is during happy hour, sipping a beer or glass of wine on the terrace while the sun sets over the Canal. It's nothing short of a Parisian dream. Open daily 9:30am to 1:30pm and 6pm to midnight. 102 quai de Jammapes, 10e. ℭ **01-40-40-78-78.** www.hoteldunord.org. Métro: République or Jacques Bonsergent.

Le Bar This classy, historic joint is all glamour and fabulousness with a shockingly 21st-century decor. It will cost you a small fortune to drink a glass of champagne, but for some it's definitely worth it. Dress to the nines if you're going—but if you're planning on making the trip, you already knew that. Drinks start at 20€. Open daily from 6 to 11pm, until 2am Thurday to Saturday. Hotel Plaza-Athénée, 25 av. Montaigne, 8e. ℭ **01-53-67-66-65.** Métro: Alma-Marceau.

Le China This site has been home to various clubs stretching back decades. In the 1930s, it was an opium den and jazz club. Today, in its latest incarnation, it is all dark colors, candles, soft lights, and intimacy. Upstairs, patrons can play backgammon. There is a fireplace and library plus a winter garden with big rattan chairs further setting a homey mood. The onsite restaurant evokes 1930s Shanghai with red-painted walls. A long zinc bar is resides on the ground floor and a bar in the basement hosts regular jazz concerts. Cocktails cost from 10€. Open daily 6pm to 2am. 50 rue de Charenton, 12e. ✆ **01-43-46-08-09.** www.lechina.eu. Metro: Ledru Rollin.

Le Forum While they cryptically claim to be twice voted the best cocktail bar in France (by whom is not entirely clear), the polished oak paneling, ornate stucco, and selection of single-malt whiskeys recalls a posh English gentleman's club. You can sample from among 180 cocktails, including many that haven't been popular since the Jazz Age. Champagne by the glass is common, as is that social lubricant, the martini. Open Monday to Thursday noon to 1am, Friday noon to 2am, Saturday 5:30pm to 2am. 4 bd. Malesherbes, 8e. ✆ **01-42-65-37-86.** www.bar-le-forum.com. Métro: Madeleine.

Le Lèche-Vin There's blasphemy and blas-for-you at this bar lit with warm red lights and decked out in kitschy religious icons—you'll know it by the glowing Virgin Mary resting in the window. Or if you're still not sure you're in the right place, look for the pornography adorning the toilets. The crowd is young and mixed, both in nationality and in orientation. Open daily from 6pm to 1:30am, closed Sunday and Monday. 13 rue Daval, 11e. ✆ **01-43-55-06-70.** Métro: Bastille.

Le Scopiton ★ Patronized by cheerful hipsters from authentic to trust fund, Le Scopiton is at the same time chic and sweaty (it's owned by another well-established night spot, Le Baron). Nightly DJs get bodies grooving in the minis-cule space. Dress up for the doormen, then head down the basement stairs dimly lit by red bordello lighting. Drinks range from 8€ to 18€, and the music is a bit rock electro. Open Tuesday to Sunday 7pm to 2am, until 6am Friday and Saturday. 5 av. de l'Opéra, 5e. ✆ **01-42-60-64-65.** Métro: Palais-Royal or Pyramides-Ligne.

Les Etages The prime spot for people-watching on a warm evening, this place also has three floors (hence the name) of art-covered walls and antique decor to appreciate while sipping cocktails. Their specialty is champagne and fruit concoctions, but if you prefer something stronger the bar staff will happily mix it for you. Watch yourself around the honey-roasted peanuts, though, because sampling more than your fair share will get you the stink-eye. Open daily from 11am to 2am. 5 rue de Buci, 6e. ✆ **01-46-34-26-26.** Métro: Odéon

The Quiet Man Named after a famous John Wayne movie set in Ireland, this is one of the best Irish pubs in Paris. Naturally, it's the watering hole for all Irish expats who gravitate to their Guinness, Irish music, and of course, darts. Open daily 5pm to 2am. 5 rue des Haudriettes, 3e. ✆ **01-48-04-02-77.** www.thequietman.eu. Métro: Rambuteau.

THE CLUB & MUSIC SCENE

The live music and club scene in Paris is legendary. The City of Light is home to everything from the swankiest of chic nightclubs—with thousand-euro bottle service and models—to the smallest and sweatiest dive bars. There is also a world-class jazz scene here, as well as a varied live music scene; clubs and concert halls host everything from cutting-edge electronica music to hip-hop to the soft glamour of indie rock, and just about everything else in between. Paris is a moveable dance floor.

Musicians.

Live Music
CABARETS

Decidedly expensive, these places give you your money's worth by providing lavishly spectacular floor shows. They generally attract an older crowd and are definitely not youth-oriented.

Chez Michou The setting is blue, the incredibly tan master of ceremonies wears blue, and the spotlights bathe performers in yet another shade of blue. Cross-dressing belles bear names such as Hortensia and DuDuche and lip-sync in costumes from haute couture to haute concierge, paying tribute to such Americans as Whitney Houston and Tina Turner and to French stars such as Mireille Mathieu, Sylvie Vartan, and Brigitte Bardot. If you don't want dinner, you'll have to stand at the bar, paying a compulsory 35€ for the first drink. Dinner is served nightly at 8:30pm (reservations required); shows begin nightly at 11pm. 80 rue des Martyrs, 18e. ✆ **01-46-06-16-04.** www.michou.com. Cover (including dinner, aperitif, wine, coffee, and show) 105€. Métro: Pigalle.

The Crazy Horse Since 1951, this sophisticated strip joint has thrived, thanks to good choreography and a sly, coquettish celebration of the female form. The Crazy Horse has been getting more attention in recent years ever since the famous burlesque performer Dita Von Teese decided to make it her home away from home in Paris. Shows last less than 2 hours. You'll find a small number of women among the audience of mainly businessmen. Shows Sunday to Friday 8:15 and 10:45pm; Saturday at 7, 9:30, and 11:45pm. 12 av. George V, 8e. ✆ **01-47-23-32-32.** www.lecrazyhorseparis.com. Reservations recommended. Entry is 100€ for the show alone, and show plus dinner packages range from 175€–209€. Métro: George V or Alma Marceau.

Folies-Bergère The Folies-Bergère has been an institution since 1869. Josephine Baker, the African-American singer who danced in a banana skirt and threw bananas into the audience, became "the toast of Paris" here. According to legend, the first GI to reach Paris at the 1944 Liberation asked for directions to the club. Don't expect the naughty and slyly permissive, skin-and-glitter revue that used to be the trademark of this place. In 1993, that all ended with a radical restoration of the theater and a reopening under new management. Today, it's a conventional 1,600-seat theater devoted to a frequently changing roster of big-stage performances in French, many of which are adaptations of Broadway blockbusters. Josephine Baker may have once performed topless here with her bananas, but those looking for nudity today should head to the Lido or the Crazy Horse. 32 rue Richer, 9e. ℭ 01-44-79-98-60 or 08-92-68-16-50. www.foliesbergere.com. Tickets 25€–84€. Métro: Grands-Boulevards or Cadet.

Le Paradis Latin Built in 1889 by Alexandre-Gustave Eiffel, with the same metallic skeleton as the famous tower, Le Paradis Latin represents the architect's only venture into theater design. The place is credited with introducing vaudeville and musical theater to Paris. In 1903 the building was a warehouse, but in the 1970s it was transformed into a successful cabaret whose singers, dancers, and special effects extol the fun, frivolity, and permissiveness of the City of Light. The show features tasteful nudity (they contrast their more dignified nudity— breasts only—with the more blatant and unabashed nudity at the Crazy Horse), and the master of ceremonies speaks in French and English. Dinner Wednesday to Monday 8pm; reviews at 9:30pm. 28 rue Cardinal-Lemoine, 5e. ℭ **01-43-25-28-28.** www.paradis-latin.com. Cover 85€ including a glass of champagne, and dinner packages range from 123€–179€. Métro: Jussieu or Cardinal Lemoine.

Lido de Paris The Lido competes with the best that Las Vegas has to offer. In explaining the concept of *Bonheur,* the Lido's current production, artistic director Pierre Rambert invites us to imagine "a bird-woman arriving on her cloud of feathers from a shore where happiness does not exist." She then discovers joy through the "four worlds of women, Paris, India, and the cinema." Don't worry if that doesn't make any sense, because you're really there just to see the topless Bluebell Girls anyway. 16 av. des Champs-Élysées, 8e. ℭ **800/227-4884** in the U.S., or 01-40-76-56-10. www.lido.fr. Tickets for the show alone are 70€ and dinner plus show packages range from 140€–280€. Price includes half-bottle of champagne per person. Métro: George V.

Moulin Rouge This place is a camp classic. The establishment that Toulouse-Lautrec immortalized is still here, but the artist would probably have a hard time recognizing it today, surrounded as it is by so many tour buses. Colette once created a scandal here by offering an on-stage kiss to Mme de Morny, but shows today have a harder time shocking audiences. Try to get a table—the view is much better on the main floor than from the bar. What's the theme? It's strip routines and the saucy sexiness of *la Belle Époque,* and of permissive Paris between the wars. Handsome men and girls, girls, girls, virtually all topless, keep the place going. Dance finales usually include two dozen of the belles doing a topless cancan. Revues begin nightly at 9 and 11pm. 82 bd. Clichy, place Blanche, 18e. ℭ **01-53-09-82-82.** www.moulinrouge.fr. Tickets for the show alone range from 80€–90€, and packages including dinner range from 150€–180€. Métro: Blanche.

CHANSONNIERS

Chansonniers (literally translated, songwriters) provide a bombastic musical satire of the day's events. This combination of parody and burlesque is a time-honored Gallic amusement and a Parisian institution. Songs are often created on the spot, inspired by the "disaster of the day."

Moulin Rouge.

Au Lapin Agile   Picasso and Utrillo patronized this little cottage near the top of Montmartre, then known as the Cabaret des Assassins, and it has been painted by many artists, including Utrillo. You'll sit at carved wooden tables in a dimly lit room with walls covered by bohemian memorabilia and listen to French folk tunes, love ballads, army songs, sea chanties, and music-hall ditties. You're encouraged to sing along, even if it's only *"oui, oui, oui—non, non, non,"* the refrain of "Les Chevaliers de la Table Ronde." Open Tuesday to Sunday 9pm to 2am. 22 rue des Saules, 18e. ✆ **01-46-06-85-87.** www.au-lapin-agile.com. Cover (includes 1 drink) 24€, 17€ students under 26 years. Métro: Lamarck Caulaincourt.

Théâtre des Deux Anes   Since 1920, this theater has staged satires of the foibles, excesses, and stupidities of French governments. Favorite targets are President Nicolas Sarkozy and other mandarins of the *hexagone française.* Cultural icons, French and foreign, receive a grilling that's very funny and sometimes caustic. The place considers itself more of a theater than a cabaret and doesn't serve drinks or refreshments. The 2½-hour show is conducted in rapid-fire French slang, so if your syntax isn't up to par, you won't appreciate its charms. Performances are given Tuesday through Saturday at 8:30pm, with matinees on Sunday at 3pm; closed July to September. 100 bd. de Clichy, 18e. ✆ **01-46-06-10-26.** www.2anes.com. Tickets 35€–42€. Métro: Place Clichy.

JAZZ CLUBS

The great jazz revival that long ago swept America is still going strong here, with Dixieland, Chicago, bop, and free-jazz rhythms being pounded out in dozens of cellars, mostly called *caveaux,* where music-lovers of all ages gather to listen to jazz.

Baiser Salé   This appealing club is housed in a cellar lined with jazz-related paintings, a large bar, and videos that show jazz greats of the past (Charlie Parker, Miles Davis). Everything is mellow and laid-back, with an emphasis on the music. Genres include Afro-Caribbean, Afro-Latino, salsa, merengue, rhythm and blues, and sometimes fusion. Open daily 5:30 pm to 6am. 58 rue des Lombards, 1er. ℂ **01-42-33-37-71.** www.lebaisersale.com. Cover Mon 7€, Tues–Sun 10€–20€ after 10pm. Free Mon. Métro: Châtelet.

Caveau de la Huchette   This celebrated jazz *caveau*, reached by a winding staircase, draws a young crowd, mostly students, who dance to the music of well-known jazz combos. In prejazz days, Robespierre and Marat frequented the place. It's open Sunday to Wednesday 9:30pm to 2:30am; Thursday to Saturday and holidays 9:30pm to 4am. 5 rue de la Huchette, 5e. ℂ **01-43-26-65-05.** www.caveau delahuchette.fr. Cover 12€ Sun–Thurs, 14€ Fri–Sat; students 24 and younger 10€. Métro/RER: St-Michel.

Caveau des Oubliettes ★   It's hard to say which is more intriguing—the entertainment and drinking or the setting. An oubliette is a dungeon with a trap door at the top as its only opening, and the name is accurate. Located in the Latin Quarter, just across the river from Notre-Dame, this night spot is housed in a genuine 12th-century prison, complete with dungeons, spine-tingling passages, and scattered skulls, where prisoners were tortured and sometimes pushed through portholes to drown in the Seine. The *caveau* is beneath the subterranean vaults that many centuries ago linked it with the fortress prison of Petit Châtelet. Today patrons laugh, drink, talk, and flirt in the narrow *caveau* or else retreat to the jazz lounge. There's a free jam session every night, perhaps Latin jazz or rock. At some point on Friday and Saturday nights concerts are staged, sometimes with a cover charge. Open daily 5pm to 4am. 52 rue Galande, 5e. ℂ **01-46-34-23-09.** www. caveaudesoubliettes.fr. Métro: St-Michel.

La Chapelle des Lombards ★ 🎁   The club's proximity to the **Opéra Bastille** seems incongruous, considering the African/Caribbean jazz and Brazilian samba that's the norm. It's a magnet for South American and African expatriates, and the rhythms and fire of the music propel everyone onto the dance floor. Open daily 11:30pm to dawn. 19 rue de Lappe, 11e ℂ **01-43-57-24-24.** www.la-chapelle-des-lombards.com. Entry is free Sun–Thurs and 20€ Fri–Sat. Women free Fri night before midnight. Métro: Bastille.

Le Duc des Lombards   Comfortable and appealing, this low-key jazz club replaced an older club 10 years ago. Performances begin nightly at 9pm and continue (with breaks) for 5 hours, touching on everything from free jazz to more traditional forms such as hard bop. Concerts begin at 9:30pm. 42 rue des Lombards, 1er. ℂ **01-42-33-22-88.** www.ducdeslombards.com. Cover 20€–30€. Métro: Châtelet.

Le Petit Journal Montparnasse ★★   This is one of the best jazz supper clubs in Paris. Music lovers come here for a dinner and show, although you can also visit just for drinks and the music (a lot cheaper). Dinner guests are given preferred seating; other patrons usually sit at the bar. Open 8pm to 2am Monday to Saturday. 13 rue du Commandant Mouchotte, 14e. ℂ **01-43-21-56-70.** www.petitjournal montparnasse.com. 3-course dinner and show 60€, cover (without dinner) 25€ including first drink. Métro: Gare Montparnasse.

Le Sunset/Le Sunside ★   This is a dual temple of jazz, one of the hottest addresses on the after-dark scene in Paris, lying between the Forum des Halles and the Centre George Pompidou. Le Sunset Jazz, created in 1983, is dedicated to electric jazz and international music, whereas le Sunside, launched in 2001, is devoted to acoustic jazz for the most part. Some of the most innovative names in European jazz appear here regularly, along with jazz legends, many from abroad.

The Club & Music Scene

ENTERTAINMENT & NIGHTLIFE

Both clubs form a single complex with two concerts every night. Open Monday to Saturday 9:30pm to 1am. 60 rue des Lombards, 1er. ☏ **01-40-26-46-60.** www.sunset-sunside.com. Tickets 20€–22€. Métro: Châtelet.

New Morning ★   Jazz maniacs come to drink, talk, and dance at this enduring club. It's sometimes a scene, attracting such guests as Spike Lee and Prince. Recent bookings have included Robin McKelle, The Klezmatics, Patricia Barber, and folk rock acts such as Steve Earle. It opens nightly at 8pm, with concerts beginning at 9pm. 7 rue des Petites-Ecuries, 10e. ☏ **01-45-23-51-41.** www.newmorning.com. Cover 18€–26€. Métro: Château d'Eau.

MODERN CONCERT HALLS

La Cigale ★   This music hall near Pigalle draws some of the biggest artists working in music today—everything from indie rock to hip-hop and jazz. Recent bookings include Band of Horses, Cee Lo Green, and the Eric Truffaz Quartet. Balcony seating is available for those who arrive early, and there's plenty of open floor space for those who want to dance. 120 boulevard de Rochechouart, 18e. ☏ **01-49-25-81-75.** www.lacigale.fr. Tickets 8€–55€. Métro: Pigalle or Anvers.

La Flèche d'Or   Set inside a converted train station and boasting beautiful windows that look out over the tracks below, this concert hall books both unknown and major label bands. Recent performances have included England's Razorlight, Yelle, the Walkmen, and a bunch of people you've never heard of. Tickets tend to be cheap here, but beers are expensive. 102 bis rue de Bagnolet, 20e. ☏ **01-44-64-01-02.** www.flechedor.fr. Tickets 8€–55€. Métro: Alexandre Dumas or Gambetta.

La Maroquinerie ★   This divey little club atop the Ménilmontant hill is the place to catch local and international music artists before they blow up big and start playing La Cigale. The roster leans heavily toward the indie rock genre but there are electro and folk acts in the mix, too. An attached restaurant and bar with a pretty outdoor courtyard are good places to hang before and after the show. 23 rue Boyer, 20e. ☏ **01-40-33-64-85.** www.lamaroquinerie.fr. Tickets 10€–18€. Métro: Ménilmontant.

Musicians at New Morning jazz club.

Olympia   Charles Aznavour and other big French names appear in this cavernous hall near the Opéra Garnier. The late Yves Montand performed once, and the show was sold out 4 months in advance. Today, you're more likely to catch the Scissor Sisters or PJ Harvey. Performances usually begin at 8:30pm Tuesday to Saturday, with Sunday matinees at 5pm. 28 bd. des Capucines, 9e. ✆ **01-55-27-10-00** or 08-92-68-33-68. www.olympiahall.com. Tickets 25€–99€. Métro: Opéra or Madeleine.

The Club Scene

From the dance halls of the cancan and raucous and energetic jazz clubs of the 1920s, Parisians have historically made it a point to get out at night and go dancing. Stepping into a Parisian club today (known as *les boîtes de nuit,* or just *une boîte*) with the locals is one of the best ways to experience a night on the town in the City of Lights. Like in any big city, Parisian clubs are divided into different scenes: some places more "see and be seen," while others tend to focus less on what you're wearing and more on the music being played—not to suggest that the glitz and glam spots don't have great music. Certain locations stay popular for years, but most will wax and wane in their level of "coolness." Also, the French love their fashion, so dressing to impress is obligatory—this includes nice shoes; sneakers rarely get you past the line outside. Check *Time Out: Paris* or *Pariscope* to get a sense of current trends. Most of these clubs don't really get going until at least 11pm, if not later.

Batofar ★   While most clubs would never last more than a few years before the crowds moved on, somehow Batofar remains fresh and consistently full. The fact that it sits on a converted barge floating on the Seine must have something to do with it. On good nights you'll see hundreds of gyrating dancers moving in rhythm to house, garage (the British one), techno, and live jazz by groups that fly in from Morocco, Senegal, and Germany. Beer costs about 8.50€ a bottle, while cover runs from free to 15€, depending on the band or DJ. Open Tuesday to Saturday from 6pm to 4am. Closed November to March. Facing 11 quai François Mauriac, 13e. ✆ **01-53-14-76-59.** www.batofar.org. Métro: Quai de la Gare.

Barrio Latino   This multilevel club-bar-restaurant in Bastille occupies a gorgeous, high-ceilinged space designed by Gustav Eiffel. Amid the margaritas, caipirinhas, and rum punches is the option of sampling Spanish tapas. Grab your drink and find a table upstairs at the restaurant that focuses on Pan-Central and South American cuisine. Be prepared to shout over the loud Latin beat since the real reason to hit Barrio Latino is for the booty shaking and hip twisting. Open Sunday through Thursday noon to 2am, Friday and Saturday noon to 4am. 46 rue du Faubourg St-Antoine, 12e. ✆ **01-55-78-84-75.** Cover 20€ for nondiners after 9pm. Métro: Bastille.

Cab ★★   Although it's not as glamorous as it once was, the former cabaret still sees crowds of rich international types, young bourgeois Parisians, and impossibly skinny fashion models. Located in an underground restaurant lounge right next to the Louvre, after 11pm the space converts into a dimly lit, classy affair. On certain nights a nook behind red velvet banquets makes a great place to cozy up, or hit the expertly lit dance floor—you'll hear the latest dance and electro-lounge hits, as well as trendy American sounds, even the occasional hip-hop. Open Wednesday to Saturday 11:30pm to 6am. 2 Place du Palais Royal, 1er. ✆ **01-58-62-56-25.** www.cabaret.fr. Cover 20€–30€, including 1 drink. Métro: Palais Royal-Musée du Louvre.

Chez Moune　This former lesbian cabaret in Pigalle was reborn in 2008 with the same name but a freshly updated and mixed crowd. Chez Moune has built a reputation as a premier spot for young *branché* (hip) Parisians and debaucherous dancing. With low ceilings and walls covered in mirrored tiles, it's all about the crowd and the music—electro, neodisco, and house—and not so much the 1930s decor. If you want to stomp around in your best dancing shoes while pumping your fist in the air, Chez Moune is the place to do it. The club generally opens at 11pm but the crowd usually swarms to the bar of Le Sans Souci across the street to start off the evening. Open Tuesday to Saturday 11pm to 5am. 54 rue Jean-Baptiste Pigalle, 9e. ✆ **01-45-26-64-64.** www.chezmoune.fr. Métro: Pigalle.

Elysée Montmartre　This expansive space near Pigalle serves the dual function of disco and major concert hall. The birthplace of the cancan, Elysée Montmartre is home to soirées that pull in more than 1,000 clubgoers. Moby, Björk, U2, and the Red Hot Chili Peppers are just some big musical acts that have headlined here. Check *Pariscope* for events and prices. This venue caught fire in March 2011, but at press time there was talk of it re-opening soon. Check on its status in advance. 72 bd. de Rochechouart, 18. ✆ **01-42-92-45-36.** www.elyseemontmartre.com. Cover 15€–35€. Métro: Anvers.

Favela Chic　The saunalike dance floor of this Brazilian *festa* is always packed with an under-40 crowd grinding to bossa jazz and samba rap. They make some of the best mojitos in town here, and if you get bored its entrance literally faces the door to le Gibus, another fine dancing destination. A *favela*, incidentally, means "slum" in Brazilian Portuguese. Open Tuesday to Thursday 8pm to 2am. 18 rue du Faubourg du Temple, 11e. ✆ **01-40-21-38-14.** www.favelachic.com. Cover 10€ Fri-Sat 8pm–4am. Métro: République.

La Balajo　Established in 1936, this dance club is where Edith Piaf won the hearts of Parisian music lovers. Today, it's easy to compare La Balajo with New York City's Roseland—an old-fashioned venue steeped in Big Band nostalgia, which sometimes manages to shake the dust out for special parties and events. Afternoon sessions focus on tangos, *pasodobles,* and waltzes, and are more staid than their late-night counterparts. Evenings attract a younger crowd (age 20–35-ish), which grooves to a mixture, depending on the DJ, of house, garage, techno, and old-fashioned disco. Open Tuesday to Thursday 7pm to 2am, Friday and Saturday 11pm to 6am, and Sunday 3 to 7pm. 9 rue de Lappe, 11e. ✆ **01-47-00-07-87.** www.balajo.fr. Cover (includes 1 drink) 8€ for afternoon sessions, 12€–20€ for night sessions. Métro: Bastille.

La Bellevilloise　This club/art space/restaurant is a little off the beaten path, but worth hunt it for its two-level dancing. If you're peckish, sample the French fusion cuisine at the attached L'Halle des Oliviers. The club regularly hosts live DJs or bands playing rock, reggae, and every indie-scene in between. Crowd-surfing has been known to occur on the basement dance floor, while the upstairs is an unpretentious lounge including a gorgeous outdoor terrace for a little fresh air. Open from Monday to Thursday 7:30 pm to 1am and until 4am Fridays and Saturdays. 19-21 rue Boyer, 20e. ✆ **01-46-36-07-07.** www.labellevilloise.com. Cover 10€–15€. Métro: Ménilmont.

Le Baron ★　Once the most expensive brothel in Paris, much of Le Baron's original decor remains, including the 1920s-era tile of frolicking nude ladies, sexy red walls, and tasseled lamps. It's long been regarded as the playground of the rich and bored, or sometimes just fabulous and occasionally androgynous. The dance floor is one of the most packed in Paris with some of the world's most beautiful people. Drinks are costly but so is being trendy. It's open daily 11pm to 6am, although hours can vary. 6 av. Marceau, 8e. ☏ **01-47-20-04-01.** www.club lebaron.com. Cover ranges from free to 15€ depending on the event and the night of the week. Métro: Champs-Élysées.

Le Bataclan   You'll never have trouble finding this place, considering its colorful exterior inspired by Chinese architecture. Inside is an equally awe-inspiring and massive space, perfect for big dance parties or concerts. Le Bataclan hosts an eclectic bevy of shows, from Swedish trip-hop star Jay Jay Johanson to indie-leaning rock groups like Morcheeba, MGMT, and Yeasayer; they also host the monthly gay-themed (but mixed) parties *Follievores* and *Crazyvores*. 50 bd. Voltaire, 11e. ☏ **01-49-23-96-33.** Cover varies depending on the show. Métro: Oberkampf.

Le Bataclan night club.

Le Gibus   One of the original venues for the French punk-rock scene (yes, apparently they had their own in the 1970s), this place pulls in the under-40s and remains one of the best-known rock clubs in Paris. It opens every night as late as a concert hall and dance club, entertaining its diverse medley of counter-culture Parisians and visitors. The themes are constantly rotating; there might be a live rock band or even a drag show presented as part of the evening's rhythms. The crowd is often mixed, and there are some gay-themed nights, but it's best to check on the website to see if there are any scheduled. Other nights of the week this place tended to be the venue for private parties or for loosely scheduled rock or pop concerts. 18 rue du Faubourg du Temple, 11e. ☏ **01-47-00-78-88.** www.gibus.fr. Cover 15€–20€. Métro: République.

Nouveau Casino   Some Paris-watchers consider this the epitome of the hyperhip countercultural scene that blossoms along the rue Oberkampf every night. In a former movie theater adjacent to the Café Charbon, it's a large, drafty space centered on a dance floor and an enormous bar crafted to resemble an iceberg. Live concerts take place nightly between 8pm and 1am; on Friday and Saturday, the party continues from 1am till dawn, with a DJ who spins some of the most avant-garde dance music in Paris. Celebrity spotters have picked out Prince Albert of Monaco and such French-language film stars as Vincent Cassel and Mathieu Kassovitz. 109 rue Oberkampf, 9e. ☏ **01-43-57-57-40.** www.nouveau casino.net. Entry ranges from free to 30€ for some concerts. Métro: St-Maur, Parmentier, or Ménilmontant.

Rex Club   With its sunken dance floors and angular nonfigurative designs gracing the walls, this space recalls the big techno-grunge clubs of London, complete

The Club & Music Scene

ENTERTAINMENT & NIGHTLIFE

with an international mood-altered crowd. The music here is usually deep and dark, bass-heavy house and other electronica. Recent luminaries to make an appearance here include rap superstar Grandmaster Flash and popular Berlin electronic band Modeselektor. Open Thursday to Saturday 11:30pm to 6am. 5 bd. Poissonnière, 2e. ✆ **01-42-36-10-96.** www.rexclub.com. Entry ranges from free to 15€.. Metro: Bonne Nouvelle.

Showcase Set almost unbelievably beneath the Pont Alexandre III, this may be the only club you'll ever enter that's literally under a bridge. Unique location aside, they have DJs and live bands, and gorgeous lighting along the endlessly long bar. The unmistakable view of the Seine doesn't hurt, either. Expect a stylish crowd with champagne bottles, Gucci blazers, and impossibly high heels. While the live bands are all over the map, the DJs play mostly electro, house, and disco beats. Open Friday and Saturday nights from 11pm until 7am. Port des Champs-Élysées under the Pont Alexandre III. ✆ **01-45-61-25-43.** www.showcase.fr. Entry ranges from free to 15€. Métro: Invalides.

GAY & LESBIAN BARS & CLUBS

Paris has a vibrant gay scene, revolving around **le Marais, les Halles,** and to some extent, **Bastille.** The area with the greatest concentration of gay and lesbian clubs, restaurants, bars, and shops is the area surrounding the Hôtel-de-Ville and Rambuteau Métro stops. Gay dance clubs come and go so fast that even the magazines devoted to them, such as *2x* and *Illico*—distributed free in the gay bars and bookstores—have a hard time keeping up. For lesbians, there is *Lesbia Magazine.* Also look *Têtu* and *PREF* (*Préférences*) magazines, sold at most newsstands—each has special nightlife inserts for gay bars and clubs.

La Bôite à Frissons Although still referred to by its former name, Tango, this old classic has music ranging from accordion (the thrill box) to disco and an emphasis on couples dancing. (No techno gets played here!) Everything is unbelievably adorable; club nights are Friday and Saturday, tea dances start late afternoon Sundays. Interested in a singles dance? Consult the website for more

The scene in le Marais.

information. Opens at 11pm and continues until 5am, except Sunday. 13 rue au Maire, 4e. ℂ **01-42-72-17-78.** www.boite-a-frissons.fr. Métro: Arts et Métiers.

La Champmeslé With dim lighting, background music, and comfortable banquettes, La Champmeslé offers a cozy meeting place for women, usually a bit older and sophisticated, and a few (about 5%) "well-behaved" men. Paris's leading women's bar is in a 300-year-old building with exposed stone, ceiling beams, and 1950s-style furnishings. Thursday night, one of the premier lesbian events in Paris, a cabaret begins at 10pm. Open daily 4pm until dawn. 4 rue Chabanais, 2e. ℂ **01-42-96-85-20.** www.lachampmesle.com. Métro: Pyramides or Bourse.

Le Central Established in 1980 in a 300-year-old town house, Le Central is a staple of gay men's life in the Marais, and the only "official" gay hotel. Outfitted with decor of battered paneling and windows that wrap around on two sides, it attracts local residents who make the place their hangout, along with good numbers of attractive male tourists and the Parisians who appreciate them. You'll meet people from all over in this place, some inevitably from your home. Open Monday to Friday from 4pm to 2am, Saturday to Sunday from 2pm to 2am. 33 rue Vieille-du-Temple, 4e. ℂ **01-48-87-99-33.** www.hotelcentralmarais.com. Métro: Hôtel-de-Ville.

Le Cox This place gets so busy early in the evening that the muscled, tank-top-wearing crowd overflows out onto the sidewalk. This is where you'll find a dependably mixed gay crowd in Paris—from hunky American tourists to sexy Parisians. 15 rue des Archives, 4e. ℂ **01-42-72-08-00.** www.cox.fr. Métro: Hôtel de Ville.

Le CUD This little lounge/basement dance club is open way late—until 7am on weekends—and has several rooms. The crowd is young and diverse. Curiously, the name stands for "Classic up and down." I think they mean what you think they mean too. 12 rue des Haudriettes, 3e. ℂ **01-42-77-44-12.** www.cud-paris.com. Métrio: Rambuteau.

Le Duplex This welcoming bar is a good choice if loud club music isn't your cup of tea. Usually piping in jazz and some hip rock, actual conversation can take place and the clientele is mostly local and quite friendly. 25 rue Michel Le Comte, 3e. ℂ **01-42-72-80-86.** www.duplex-bar.com. Métro: Rambuteau.

Le Raidd ★ The bartenders here may be hunks and so are most of the patrons. Be prepared for attitude galore. A special feature is a plexiglass shower box where nude shower boys flaunt their assets throughout the night. It's shoulder-to-shoulder action here with pickup possibilities at every turn. Only the best dressed can expect to get invited in at the door. Open daily 5pm to 5am. 23 rue du Temple, 4e. ℂ **01-92-77-09-88.** www.raiddbar.com. Métro: Hôtel-de-Ville or Rambuteau.

Le Rive Gauche This swanky joint hosts a regular lesbian party on Saturday nights for a young, stylish crowd. Men are welcome when accompanied by women. 1 rue du Sabot, 6e ℂ **01-40-20-43-23.** www.lerivegauche.com. Métro: St-Germain-des-Prés.

Le 3w Kafe The 3w means "Woman with Woman." This is the best-known lesbian bar in the Marais, where an unattached woman usually has little trouble finding a drinking buddy. On weekends there's dancing downstairs with a DJ in control of the sounds. Straight men are welcome but only if accompanied by a woman. Gay men are admitted without problem. Open Wednesday to Sunday 5pm to 2am, Friday and Saturday 5pm to 4am. 8 rue des Ecouffes, 4e. ℂ **01-48-87-39-26.** Métro: St. Paul.

Open Café   Although this bar is side-by-side with Le Cox, each is independent even if their clientele is not. Both define themselves as bars rather than dance clubs, but on particularly busy nights, someone will inevitably begin to dance. Simple café-style food is served from noon to around 5pm. Patrons include just about every type of man that roams the streets of gay Europe today. Open daily from 11am to 2 am, Friday and Saturday to 3am. 17 rue des Archives, 4e. ℭ **01-42-72-26-18.** Métro: Hôtel-de-Ville.

OUTDOOR PURSUITS

In addition to lazing about in a park or the terrace of your favorite café, there's actually quite a bit going on in outdoor Paris. Over the last decade, a somewhat more American approach to fitness has become popular, with more folks jogging and taking up gym memberships than ever before. Here are a few suggestions for getting out and exploring Paris's natural side. For information on Paris's parks, see chapter 4.

Bicycling

Bicycling through the streets and parks of Paris, perhaps with a baguette tucked under your arm, might have become your fantasy after seeing your first Maurice Chevalier film. Luckily, in the last few years the city has become even more bike-friendly than ever before.

In 2007 Mayor Bertrand Delanoë launched the **Vélib'** bicycle rental program, bringing 10,000 bikes into the city, placing them in specially built bike racks around high-pedestrian destinations. (The name Vélib' is a portmanteau of *vélo* for bicycle and *liberté* for freedom or liberty.) Today, there are more than 20,000 bicycles and more than 1,200 stations throughout Paris. The Velib' users have become ubiquitous around the city, at all hours of the day and night.

Biking in Paris.

Buy a 1-day (1€) or 7-day (5€) short-term ticket *(abonnement courte durée)* at any Vélib station or *tabac*. You will need a valid credit card (in order to charge a temporary security deposit of 150€).

The bicycle can be used for free as long as it's returned to any of the Vélib' stations within 30 minutes of its rental. Afterward, you will be charged 1€ for the next 30 minutes, then 2€ for the next 30 minutes, then afterward an additional 4€, and so on.

Bikes are one size fits all, with adjustable seats; children 13 and younger are not permitted to use the cycles. Maps showing the locations of Vélib' stations throughout Paris are available at the city hall in each of the 20 arrondissements. For more information, call ✆ **01-30-79-79-30,** or see www.velib.paris.fr.

Riding a bike around Paris is lovely, but for some well-informed commentary on what you're seeing, **Bike About Tours** (✆ **06-18-80-84-92;** www.bikeabouttours.com) has a staff of friendly and knowledgeable—and fluent-English speakers. The 3½-hour tours cost 30€ per person and includes helmet, bicycle, and insurance. All tours, which range from the big monuments to personalized "hidden Paris" adventures, leave from the statue of Charlemagne in front of Notre Dame at 10am (and 3pm during the summer). You can also organize private tours and rent bikes at a reasonable 15€ per day rate. With small groups (12 people maximum) you won't get lost in the crowd, or worse, left behind in the often-confusing maze of boulevards.

Fitness Centers

You may be shocked to see Parisians taking cigarette breaks outside gym entrances, but the fitness trend has found a foot here and is moving toward a serious approach to *le gym*. Only big corporate hotels usually offer onsite fitness centers, so hitting up the local gyms is a good way to get in your regular workout routine. **Body Gym,** 157 rue du Faubourg St-Antoine, 11e (✆ **01-43-42-42-33;** www.bodygymparis.com; Métro: Ledru Rollin), near an older building near the Gare de Lyon, looks like a corridor from a Métro station, but the machines are modern and up to date. Patronized mostly by office workers and residents of this sometimes gritty neighborhood, it offers views of Paris many visitors don't often see. A one-visit pass costs 17€, and they are open weekdays from 8am to 9:30pm, 9am to 7pm on Saturdays, and 10am to 2pm Sundays. **Club Med Gyms,** 149 rue de Rennes, 6e (✆ **01-45-44-24-35;** Métro: Montparnasse or St-Sulpice; also at 147 rue Saint-Honoré, 1er; ✆ **01-40-20-03-03;** Métro: Châtelet-Les Halles) is the largest and most popular chains of fitness centers is in France. There are 22 gyms scattered throughout Paris and its suburbs. The two noted here are the largest on the Left and Right Banks of the Seine and they offer every conceivable kind of fitness, body-building, and cardio training machine, as well as squash courts. Hours can vary, but most are open from morning to 10pm on weekdays. For additional addresses of gyms within this respected chain, check out www.clubmedgym.fr.

Ice-Skating

In the deep of winter (usually around Christmas to Feb), Paris officials set up two huge outdoor rinks, each of which is free (not counting the 4€ for skate rental). The better of the two is in front of the **Hotel de Ville** (see p. 99 for a review) in the 4th (Métro: Hôtel-de-Ville). It's open Monday to Thursday noon to 10pm, Friday noon to midnight, and Sunday 9am to 10pm. Smaller but still charming is at the **Eiffel Tower** (p. 146) in the 7th (Métro: Bir Hakeim). It's open every day from 10:30am to 10:30pm and Saturday and Sunday 9am to 8pm.

Jogging

The French say *le jogging*, and also *le footing*, although the latter is outmoded. Once pretty much ridiculed, the sport itself has gained quite a following in Paris recently. The most popular places for jogging include the **quays of the Seine** and **Jardin du Luxembourg.**

Jogging in the Promenade Plantée.

Some other lovely routes are the **Parc des Buttes Chaumont** and **Promenade Plantée ★**—the converted green rooftop of the old train trestle route. The entrance is just behind the opera house at Bastille along avenue Daumesnil, and continuing all the way to the Bois de Vincennes on the city's "green lung."

Other spots are paths around the lakes in the **Bois de Boulogne** and the **Bois de Vincennes.**

Swimming

Paris offers some three dozen public swimming pools called *piscines*. They are found throughout the city, and a complete list of them is available at **www.sport.paris.fr**. Admission to any municipal pool is 3€; you can also purchase a *carnet* granting 10 visits for 24€.

Our favorite Right Bank pool is **Suzanne Berlioux ★★**, 10 place de la Rotonde, Forum des Halles in the 1st (🕾 **01-42-36-98-44;** Métro: Les Halles). This vast pool is in the underground forum with a wall of windows streaming in natural light. On the Left Bank, **St-Germain ★** is a standout, at 12 rue Lobineau in the 6th (🕾 **01-56-81-25-40;** Métro: Mabillon or Odéon). This 25m (82-ft.) pool is in a modern underground space near Marché St-Germain.

Tennis

There are 43 public tennis courts in Paris for recreational use. The courts in the **Jardin de Luxembourg** (6e; Métro: Saint-Placide) are particularly nice. There is also in the **Marais** at 5-7 rue Neuve-Saint-Pierre (4e; Métro: Saint Paul). The fee for an hour of play is 7.50€ in an open courts, and 14€ for covered courts. *Note:* You will need to bring your own tennis equipment. More locations can be found at **www.paris.fr**.

SPECTATOR SPORTS

Aside from watching octogenarians playing *pétanques*—the lawn bowling game like Italian *bocce* that's always played in parks and always seems to draw spectators—the French love to watch quite a few sports. Paris's biggest stadium, **le Stade de France,** is in the northern suburb of St-Denis, while several smaller stadiums are within the city limits. Rugby and soccer games (known as *le football*) are the most popular to watch alongside Parisians, and the city also plays host to one of the biggest tennis events in the world, the French Open. You can also join the locals at the races, as Paris's horse tracks are a big pull with a large number of very dedicated fans. For additional spectator events and dates, see the "Calendar of Events" on p. 46.

Horse Racing

Paris boasts an army of avid horse-racing fans who get to the city's eight racetracks whenever possible. Information on current races is available in newspapers and magazines such as ***Tierce, Paris-Turf, France-Soir,*** and ***L'Equipe,*** all sold at kiosks throughout the city.

The epicenter of Paris horse racing is the **Hippodrome de Longchamp ★★★**, in the Bois de Boulogne, 16e (© **01-44-30-75-00;** RER or Métro: Porte Maillot and then a free shuttle bus on race days only). Established in 1855, during the autocratic and pleasure-loving reign of Napoleon III, it's the most prestigious track, boasts the greatest number of promising thoroughbreds, and awards the largest purse in France. The most important events at Longchamp are the **Grand Prix de Paris** in late June and the **Prix de l'Arc de Triomphe** in early October.

Another racing venue is the **Hippodrome d'Auteuil,** also in the Bois de Boulogne (© **01-40-71-47-47;** Métro: Porte Auteuil; then walk). Known for its steeplechases and obstacle courses, it sometimes attracts more than 50,000 Parisians at a time. Spectators appreciate the park's promenades as much as they do the equestrian events. Races are conducted from early March to late November.

Racing at the Hippodrome de Longchamp.

Rugby

A popular national sport is rugby, the rough-and-tumble precursor to American football. The most well known, professional level Paris-based rugby team is **Stade Français,** a team that plays matches at either the **Stade Charlety,** across the street from the **Parc des Princes,** or in the **Stade de France** (✆ 08-92-70-09-00; www.stadefrance.fr), the 81,338-person-capactiy stadium in St-Denis, Paris's northern suburb. Their seasons generally run from August to April. You can easily reserve tickets, starting at 12€ at the team's website, **www.stade. fr**. Also, if you're adventurous, check out the Dieux du Stade, a calendar and book of the French rugby stars in various states of, well, undress.

Soccer (Football)

Known throughout France as *le football,* soccer is one of France's most popular national sports. Paris is home to several football clubs—another term for a team organization—including the one professional club, the **Paris Saint-Germain Football Club,** also known as **Paris SG.** They play their home matches at the **Parc des Princes** (✆ 01-47-43-71-71; 24 rue du Commandant Guilbau, 16e; Métro: porte de Saint-Cloud), a stadium with a capacity of almost 49,000 spectators. Their season runs from January to May; match tickets start at 12€ and can easily be purchased on their website, **www.psg.fr**.

Tennis

Much like Wimbledon or the U.S. Open, France dominates the tennis world with the **French Open,** or as it's known here, **Roland Garros** (**www.fft.fr/ rolandgarros**). Matches take place over 2 weeks between late May and early June in the Roland Garros Stadium in the 16e (Métro: Porte d'Auteuil). Tickets should be purchased well in advance, as this is a world-scale tennis event.

WHERE TO STAY

by Kate van den Boogert

9

aturally, the most visited city in the world boasts an overwhelming number of hotels, which range from mythical palaces including the Ritz and the Crillon to dives so repellent that even George Orwell, author of *Down and Out in Paris and London,* wouldn't have considered checking in. (Of course, you won't find those in this guide!) We include deluxe places for those who can afford to live like the sultan of Brunei, as well as a wide range of moderate and budget choices for the rest of us.

best **PARIS HOTEL BETS**

- **Best for a Romantic Getaway:** Who doesn't take a deep sigh then murmur yes when he first pushes open this hotel's heavy wooden gate and lays his eyes on the **Pavillon de la Reine,** an enchanting ivy-covered mansion opposite the Marais' place des Vosges? See p. 301.

- **Best for Families:** You'll find all the comfort of home at the stylish **Hôtel Arvor St Georges.** Three suites include an extra single bed, and rooms can also take an extra cot. Kids will also appreciate the homemade cake in the relaxed downstairs lobby. See p. 313.

- **Best Splurge:** This new Philippe Starck–designed gem has the whole city talking. **Le Royal Monceau—Raffles Paris** offers absolute luxury for contemporary jet-setters, including a Clarins spa, an indoor pool, a state-of-the-art cinema, edgy fashion, and a mobile sound studio that can be set up in any of the soundproofed rooms. See p. 308.

- **Best Value:** The **Mama Shelter** might be off the beaten track, but this new Starck-designed hotel nonetheless attracts the in-crowd with its buzzing downstairs restaurant/bar space, high-tech setup, and low-cost rates. See p. 319.

- **Best-Kept Secret:** The **Villa Mazarin** provides elegant and spacious rooms in the thick of the lovely lower Marais, just minutes from the Pompidou Centre, the river, and Notre-Dame. See p. 302.

- **Best Service:** Of all the palace hotels in Paris, the **Hôtel Meurice** has perhaps the most warmth and contemporary style. The service here is welcoming and humorous, and not at all stuffy. See p. 294.

- **Most Rejuvenating:** The chic **Gabriel Paris Marais** is the city's first "detox" hotel, and is devoted to the well-being of its guests. After getting a good night's sleep with their revolutionary NightCove system, wake up to an organic breakfast. See p. 318.

- **Most Trendy:** The one-of-a-kind **Hôtel Amour** is run by a couple of the city's nightlife barons. Each of the 24 rooms boasts a unique, edgy, contemporary design, and you'll run into many of the city's trendsetters at the raucous downstairs bar and restaurant. See p. 312.

FACING PAGE: **A suite at the Hôtel Ritz.**

PRICE CATEGORIES

Very Expensive	400€ and up
Expensive	220€–400€
Moderate	120€–220€
Inexpensive	Under 120€

○ **Best Views:** Of the 33 rooms at the **Hôtel du Quai Voltaire,** 28 open onto views of the Seine. This 17th-century abbey was transformed into a hotel in 1856 and has been welcoming guests—including Oscar Wilde, Charles Baudelaire, and Wilhelm Richard Wagner—ever since. See p. 335.

○ **Most Charming:** In the heart of the Latin Quarter, and set within a luxuriant and peaceful little garden, the delightful **Hôtel des Grandes Ecoles** is a budget option boasting a unique, provincial charm. See p. 324.

THE RIGHT BANK
Les Halles, Louvre & Palais Royal (1er & 2e)

Located on the right bank, this area is the *très chic* center of Paris. This part of Paris—by the Seine river and clustered around the Louvre—boasts exquisite monuments, boulevards, gardens, and shopping.

Best For: Travelers who like to be in the thick of the action. The trendy area is also great for epic shopping sessions.
Drawbacks: Tourists galore!

VERY EXPENSIVE

Hôtel de Vendôme ★★　This luxury boutique hotel sits on one of Paris's most prestigious addresses, the place Vendôme, surrounded by the city's finest jewelers. The soundproof rooms are opulent and designed in classic Second Empire style, with prestige beds and well-upholstered, hand-carved furnishings. Suites have generous space and such extras as blackout draperies and quadruple-glazed windows. The security is fantastic, with TV intercoms, and the service is warm and professional. This hotel is a short walk from the Louvre and Tuileries gardens.

1 place Vendôme, 75001 Paris. www.hoteldevendome.com. ℂ **01-55-04-55-00.** Fax 01-49-27-97-89. 29 units. 535€–865€ double; 835€–1,525€ suite. AE, DC, MC, V. Parking 27€. Métro: Concorde or Opéra. **Amenities:** Restaurant; piano bar; babysitting; concierge; room service. *In room:* A/C, TV, hair dryer, minibar, MP3 docking station, Wi-Fi (free).

Hôtel Meurice ★★★　This landmark lies between the place de la Concorde and the Grand Louvre, facing the Tuileries Gardens. The hotel is more media hip, style conscious, and better located than the George V. Since the 1800s, it has welcomed the royal, the rich, and even the radical. The mad genius Salvador Dalí made the Meurice his headquarters. And in 2008 that other mad genius, Philippe Starck, overhauled the hotel's public areas, bringing an exquisite contemporary touch of the surreal to the lobby and downstairs bar and restaurant. Each room is individually decorated with period pieces, fine carpets, Italian and French fabrics, marble bathrooms, and modern features. Our favorites and the least expensive are the sixth-floor rooms. Some have painted ceilings of puffy clouds and blue skies, along with canopy beds. Suites are among the most lavish in France.

228 rue de Rivoli, 75001 Paris. www.meuricehotel.com. © **01-44-58-10-10.** Fax 01-44-58-10-15. 160 units. 665€–1,030€ double; from 1,150€ junior suite; from 1,800€ suite. AE, DC, MC, V. Parking 27€. Métro: Tuileries or Concorde. **Amenities:** 2 restaurants; bar; babysitting; concierge; health club and spa; room service. In room: A/C, TV, TV/DVD player, fax, hair dryer, minibar, Wi-Fi (20€ per day).

Hôtel Ritz ★★   The Ritz is Europe's greatest hotel, an enduring symbol of elegance on one of Paris's most beautiful and historic squares. César Ritz, the "little shepherd boy from Niederwald," converted the Hôtel de Lazun into a luxury hotel in 1898. With the help of the culinary master Escoffier, he made the Ritz a miracle of luxury. In 1979, the Ritz family sold the hotel to Mohammed al Fayed, who refurbished it and added a cooking school. The hotel annexed two town houses, joined by an arcade lined with display cases representing 125 of Paris's leading boutiques. The public salons are furnished with museum-caliber antiques. Each guest room is uniquely decorated, most with Louis XIV or XV reproductions; all have fine rugs, marble fireplaces, tapestries, brass beds, and more. Ever since Edward VII got stuck in a too-narrow bathtub with his lover, the tubs at the Ritz have been deep and big.

15 place Vendôme, 75001 Paris. www.ritzparis.com. © **800/223-6800** in the U.S. and Canada, or 01-43-16-30-30. Fax 01-43-16-31-78. 159 units. 550€–870€ double; 800€–4,370€ suite. AE, DC, MC, V. Parking 48€. Métro: Opéra, Concorde, or Madeleine. **Amenities:** Restaurant; 4 bars; babysitting; concierge; state-of-the-art health club; pool (indoor); room service. In room: A/C, TV, DVD player, hair dryer, minibar, Wi-Fi (25€ per day).

WHAT YOU'LL REALLY PAY

The prices quoted here are for hotels' rack rate, the maximum that they charge; it is, however, unlikely that you'll end up paying that rate in Paris unless you arrive during Fashion Weeks (early Mar, late Sept), or the major trade fairs (Sept, Oct). Spring is also very busy. You can typically find discounts of up to 20% for rooms when booking through the agencies listed on p. 339, or through websites such as Booking.com (see "Getting the Best Deal" on p. 339 for more tips). In March 2011, a room at the **Best Western Regent's Garden** (rack rates start at 290€) was snagged on Booking.com for 140€. During slow times (high summer and winter), it's not impossible to obtain a room at an expensive property for the same rate as a more moderate one. Rack rates at Pigalle's **Villa Royale** start at 239€, but in January 2011, just a cursory search of the usual web discount sites revealed that the going rate was actually closer to 147€.

Sometimes all you have to do is contact the hotel directly and negotiate. For example, one week in March, the **Hostellerie du Marais** was advertising a weekday rate of 190€ on its own website, but a spot check of the major discounters (Priceline, Hotels.com, Expedia, Booking. com) yielded a price of 149€. When I told the hotel what I'd been quoted online, I was offered the same rate on the spot.

Note: Quoted discount rates almost never include breakfast, hotel tax, or any applicable resort fees.

Hotels near Les Halles, Louvre, Palais Royal, Marais, Ile St-Louis, Ile de la Cité, Operá & Canal St-Martin (1-4 & 9-10e)

Park Hyatt Vendôme ★★★   American interior designer Ed Tuttle took five separate Haussmann-era buildings and wove them into a seamless entity to create this citadel of 21st-century luxury living. High ceilings, colonnades, and interior courtyards speak of the buildings' former lives, but other than the facades, all is completely modern inside—not just contemporary, but luxe modern. The third Hyatt in Paris, this palace enjoys the greatest and most prestigious location in "Ritz Hotel country." Graced with modern art, it is filled with elegant fabrics, huge mirrors, walk-in closets, mahogany doors, and Jim Thompson silk. Bedrooms and bathrooms are spacious and state-of-the-art, with elegant furnishings and glamorous bathrooms with "rain showers," plus separate tubs.

5 rue de la Paix, 75002 Paris. www.paris.vendome.hyatt.com. ✆ **800/492-8804** in the U.S. and Canada, or 01-58-71-12-34. Fax 01-58-71-12-35. 168 units. 800€–910€ double; from 1,010€ suite. AE, DC, DISC, MC, V. Métro: Tuileries or Opéra. Free parking. **Amenities:** 2 restaurants; bar; babysitting; concierge; health club and spa; room service. *In room:* A/C, TV, DVD, CD player, hair dryer, minibar, Wi-Fi (19€ per day).

EXPENSIVE

Golden Tulip Opéra de Noailles   If you're looking for a choice address in the style of Putman and Starck, this place is worth a look, in a great location. The refined Art Deco choice offers bold colors and cutting-edge style. The guest rooms come in various shapes and sizes, but all are comfortable and some have small terraces and patios. A favorite is no. 601, which has its own indoor Japanese garden.

9 rue de la Michodière, 75002 Paris. www.paris-hotel-noailles.com. ✆ **800/344-1212** in the U.S., or 01-47-42-92-90. Fax 01-49-24-92-71. 57 units. 200€–350€ double; 495€ suite. AE, DC, MC, V. Métro: 4 Septembre or Opéra. RER: Opéra. **Amenities:** Bar; babysitting; concierge; small health club; room service. *In room:* A/C, TV, hair dryer, Wi-Fi (22€ per day).

Hôtel du Louvre ★   When Napoleon III inaugurated this hotel in 1855, it was described as "a palace of the people, rising adjacent to the palace of kings." In 1897, Camille Pissarro moved into a room with a view that inspired many of his landscapes; its decor features marble, bronze, and gilt. The guest rooms are filled with souvenirs of the Belle Époque, along with elegant fabrics, carpeting, double-glazed windows, comfortable beds, and wood furniture. Suites provide greater dimensions and better exposures, as well as such upgrades as antiques, trouser presses, and robes.

Place André-Malraux, 75001 Paris. www.hoteldulouvre.com. ✆ **800/888-4747** in the U.S. and Canada, or 01-44-58-38-38. Fax 01-44-58-38-01. 177 units. 200€–700€ double; 300€–750€ junior suite. AE, DC, MC, V. Parking 20€. Métro: Palais-Royal-Louvre or Louvre-Rivoli. **Amenities:** Restaurant; bar; babysitting; concierge; exercise room. *In room:* A/C, TV, minibar, Wi-Fi (free).

Westin Paris ★ ☺   At this hotel it's location, location, location. You're 30 seconds from the Tuileries Gardens, 3 minutes from the place Vendôme, 5 minutes from the place de la Concorde, and 7 minutes from the Louvre. Renovations have breathed new life into most of the rooms, which are a bit small for the most part but comfortably furnished and well maintained. Some patrons have written in the guest book that they found the beds "heavenly." Two connecting rooms can be blocked off for families, and family rates are available. Many of the units overlook an inner courtyard.

3 rue de Castiglione, Paris 75001. www.starwoodhotels.com. ✆ **800/454-6835** in the U.S., or 01-44-77-11-11. Fax 01-44-77-14-60. 440 units. 350€–430€ double; from 600€ suite. AE, DC, MC,

V. Métro: Tuileries. **Amenities:** Restaurant; bar; babysitting; concierge; exercise room; room service. *In room:* A/C, TV, DVD player, hair dryer, minibar, Wi-Fi (25€ per day).

MODERATE

Hôtel Britannique 🎆   Conservatively modern and plush, this renovated 19th-century hotel near Les Halles and Notre-Dame is not only British in name, but it seems to cultivate English graciousness. The guest rooms are small but immaculate and soundproof, with comfortable beds. A satellite receiver gets U.S. and U.K. television shows. The reading room is a cozy retreat. Its exceptional location in the center of Paris makes this a good-value choice.

20 av. Victoria, 75001 Paris. www.hotel-britannique.com. 🕾 **01-42-33-74-59.** Fax 01-42-33-82-65. 39 units. 190€–230€ double; from 279€ suite. AE, DC, MC, V. Métro: Châtelet. **Amenities:** Bar; room service. *In room:* A/C, TV, hair dryer, minibar, Wi-Fi (free).

Hôtel du Cygne   This centrally located hotel is within walking distance of the charming gourmand–friendly rue Montorgueil, the place des Victoires, the Marais, and the Louvre. In a restored 17th-century building, the hotel combines the old with touches of the new; much of the eclectic decor has been handpicked by the hotel's friendly owner, Isabelle. The staff is helpful, but there is no elevator, so be prepared to carry your luggage up the narrow, winding stairs. Avoid the rooms overlooking the street, as they can be noisy. Room 35 is the largest.

3-5 rue du Cygne, 75001 Paris. www.cygne-hotel-paris.com. 🕾 **01-42-60-14-16.** Fax 01-42-21-37-02. 18 units. 122€ double; 167€ suite. MC, V. Métro: Etienne Marcel. **Amenities:** Breakfast room. *In room:* TV, hair dryer, Wi-Fi (free).

Hôtel Thérèse ★★   Close to the Louvre, place Vendôme, and the Tuileries Gardens, this hotel combines French charm with English classicism. For example, the library and bar evoke a London club with wood-paneled walls and plush armchairs, but the lounge is adorned with Parisian art. It's government-rated three stars but seems more like four stars in ambience, style, and comfort. Owner Sylvia de Lattre, who likes shades of pistachio and royal blue, trolled the flea markets for paintings and prints to personalize each bedroom. The rooms are unpretentious but filled with quality furnishings, from the soft, efficient lighting by Philippe Starck to the natural wool quilts.

5-7 rue Thérèse, Paris 75001. www.hoteltherese.com. 🕾 **01-42-96-10-01.** Fax 01-42-96-15-22. 43 units. 155€–320€ double. AE, MC, V. Métro: Musée du Louvre. **Amenities:** Library/bar; room service. *In room:* A/C, TV, hair dryer, Wi-Fi (free).

Le Relais du Louvre   Centrally located, Relais du Louvre overlooks the neo-classical colonnade at the eastern end of the Louvre. Between 1800 and 1941, its upper floors contained the printing presses that recorded the goings-on in Paris's House of Representatives. Its street level held the Café Momus, favored by Voltaire, Hugo, and intellectuals of the day, and where Puccini set one of the pivotal scenes of *La Bohème*. Bedrooms are outfitted in monochromatic schemes of blue, yellow, pink or soft reds, usually with copies of Directoire-style (French 1830s) furniture. Most rooms are a bit small, but some contain roomy sitting areas.

19 rue des Prêtres-St-Germain-l'Auxerrois, 75001 Paris. www.relaisdulouvre.com. 🕾 **01-40-41-96-42.** Fax 01-40-41-96-44. 21 units. 175€–260€ double; 255€–320€ suite. AE, DC, MC, V. Parking 25€. Métro: Louvre or Pont Neuf. **Amenities:** Babysitting; room service. *In room:* A/C, TV, hair dryer, minibar, Wi-Fi (free).

Timhôtel Le Louvre ☺   This hotel and its sibling in the 2nd arrondissement, the Timhôtel Palais-Royal, are part of a new breed of government-rated, two-star, family friendly hotels cropping up in France. These Timhôtels share the same manager and temperament. Though the rooms at the Palais-Royal branch are a bit larger than the ones here, this branch is so close to the Louvre that it's almost irresistible. The ambience is modern, with monochromatic rooms and wall-to-wall carpeting.

4 rue Croix des Petits-Champs, 75001 Paris. www.timhotel.fr. ☎ **01-42-60-34-86.** Fax 01-42-60-10-39. 56 units. 99€–170€ double. AE, DC, MC, V. Métro: Palais-Royal. The 46-room **Timhôtel Palais-Royal** is at 3 rue de la Banque, 75002 Paris (☎ **01-42-61-53-90;** fax 01-42-60-05-39; Métro: Bourse). **Amenities** (at both branches): Restaurant (breakfast only). *In room:* A/C, TV, Wi-Fi (free).

Le Marais, Ile St-Louis & Ile de la Cité (3e & 4e)

This busy neighborhood includes the city's gay and Jewish quarters. Most of the important contemporary galleries are here too. You'll find a concentration of great stores from independent local labels in the northern Marais, around the rue de Bretagne. But it's the architecture that really sets this area apart, as it conserves buildings dating back to the Renaissance.

Best For: Trendsetters with no time to lose.

Drawbacks: Expats from all over the world have made the lower Marais their own, so if you want to feel like you've actually left home, try a different neighborhood.

EXPENSIVE

Hôtel du Bourg Tibourg ★   Don't come here expecting large rooms with lots of elbow room: What you get is a sophisticated and supercharged color palette, a sense of high-profile design, and a deliberately cluttered venue that looks like an Edwardian town house decorated by an obsessive-compulsive individual on psychedelic drugs. It is set behind an uncomplicated, cream-colored facade in the Marais and marked only with a discreet brass plaque and a pair of carriage lamps. Its rooms have been radically overhauled by superstar decorator Jacques Garcia. Bedrooms are genuinely tiny, but rich with neo-romantic, neo-Gothic, and in some cases neo-Venetian swirls and curlicues. Each is quirky, idiosyncratic, richly upholstered, and supercharged with tassels, faux leopard skin, contrasting stripes, fringes, and lavish window treatments. Rooms facing the front get more sunlight; rooms facing the courtyard tend to be quieter.

19 rue du Bourg-Tibourg, 75004 Paris. www.hotelbourgtibourg.com. ☎ **01-42-78-47-39.** Fax 01-40-29-07-00. 30 units. 250€–270€ double; 370€ suite. AE, DC, MC, V. Métro: Hôtel-de-Ville. **Amenities:** Room service. *In room:* A/C, TV, hair dryer, minibar, Wi-Fi (free).

Hôtel du Jeu de Paume ★   This small-scale hotel encompasses a pair of 17th-century town houses accessible through a timbered passageway from the street outside. The hotel is located on the incredibly quaint and charming Ile St-Louis in the Seine, and is just a 5-minute walk from Notre-Dame. Originally, the hotel was a clubhouse used by members of the court of Louis XIII, who amused themselves with *les jeux de paume* (an early form of tennis) nearby. Public areas are outfitted in a simple version of Art Deco. Renovated in 2010, guest rooms now have a sleek contemporary style, with elegant materials such as oak floors and fine craftsmanship. Some have wooden beamed ceilings. The rooms are a bit larger than those of some nearby competitors. All bathrooms are new. The most luxurious units are the five duplexes and two junior suites, each individually decorated and opening onto an indoor courtyard.

54 rue St-Louis-en-l'Ile, 75004 Paris. www.jeudepaumehotel.com. © **01-43-26-14-18.** Fax 01-40-46-02-76. 30 units. 285€–360€ double; 360€–560€ suite. AE, DC, MC, V. Métro: Pont Marie. **Amenities:** Bar; babysitting; concierge; exercise room; room service. *In room:* A/C, TV, hair dryer, minibar, Wi-Fi (free).

Hôtel Duo ★ 💼 Fashionistas flock to this restored hotel in the Marais, which is one of the cutting-edge places to stay in Paris. The location is convenient to the Centre Pompidou, Notre-Dame, and the Louvre. The building has been in the family of Veronique Turmel since 1918. In 2002, she decided to completely convert the interior while retaining the facade. She hired Jean-Philippe Nuel, who kept many of the original architectural features, including exposed beams, old stones, and hardwood floors. He created a modern and stylish look graced with Wengé-wood furnishings, white walls, and bronzed sconces—old-world charm in a tasteful and refined setting. The midsize bedrooms are completely up-to-date, with beautiful and comfortable furnishings. The so-called breakfast "cave" is a charming room with slipcovered chairs and sea-grass matting.

11 rue du Temple, 75004 Paris. www.parishotelleduo.com. © **01-42-72-72-22.** Fax 01-42-72-03-53. 58 units. 200€–380€ double; 400€–550€ suite. AE, DC, MC, V. Métro: Hôtel-de-Ville. **Amenities:** Exercise room; room service. *In room:* A/C, TV, hair dryer, Wi-Fi (free).

Hôtel du Petit Moulin In the heart of the Northern Marais, this hotel, an enclave of bohemian chic, used to be a *boulangerie* where Victor Hugo came every morning to buy freshly baked baguettes. No more. Designer Christian Lacroix has gone behind the unpretentious facade and turned it into an idiosyncratic hotel with bold, daring designs in the bedrooms, which range in price from the Comfort Rooms to the Superior or Executive Rooms. We think room 204 is the most elegant. A well-heeled array of international guests meets in the quiet, downstairs bar or can be seen making their way through the lounge decorated with period tapestries and Flemish frescoes.

29–31 rue du Poitou, Paris 75003. www.hoteldupetitmoulin.com. © **01-42-74-10-10.** 17 units. 190€–350€ double. AE, MC, V. Métro: Bastille or Filles du Calvaire. **Amenities:** Bar. *In room:* TV, minibar, Wi-Fi (free).

Pavillon de la Reine ★★ 💼 This is the kind of hidden gem that Frommer's readers love, opening as it does onto the most romantic square in Paris. In days of yore the 1612 mansion was a gathering place for the likes of Racine, La Fontaine, Molière, and Madame de Sévigné. You enter through an arcade that opens onto a small formal garden. The Louis XIII decor evokes the heyday of the square itself, and iron-banded Spanish antiques create a rustic aura. Each guest room is individually furnished in a historic or modern style—take your pick. Some units are duplexes with sleeping lofts above cozy salons.

28 place des Vosges, 75003 Paris. www.pavillon-de-la-reine.com. © **01-40-29-19-19.** Fax 01-40-29-19-20. 56 units. 330€–450€ double; 600€–800€ suite. AE, MC, V. Métro: Bastille. **Amenities:** Bar; concierge; room service. *In room:* A/C, TV, minibar, Wi-Fi (free).

Villa Mazarin ★ 🎁   This is a special under-the-radar hotel in a great lower Marais location, across from the Hôtel de Ville. Recently refurbished, the large and bright rooms are decorated in an elegant Napoleon III style and offer a comfort that you normally only enjoy in a superior category and price range. The beds are large and comfortable with quality linens, and there are Clarins toiletries in the bathrooms. The duplex suites on the fifth floor have balconies. Open the windows and listen to the buzz of the city waft in over the rooftops; just outside is great shopping and dining.

6 rue des Archives, 75004 Paris. www.villamazarin.com. © **01-53-01-90-90**. 29 units. 220€–300€ double. AE, MC, V. Métro: Hôtel de Ville. **Amenities:** Bar; restaurant; room service. *In room:* A/C, TV, minibar, Wi-Fi (free).

MODERATE

Castex Hotel 🏷   Long known to thrifty travelers, the Castex lies on the fringe of both the Bastille sector and the Marais. Bedrooms have been restored and decorated in a 17th-century style with Louis XIII furnishings along with touches of wrought iron against Toile de Jouy wallpaper. There's a complimentary bottle of wine in every room. Several of the units open onto a courtyard patio that bursts into full bloom in the spring.

5 rue Castex, 75004 Paris. www.castexhotelparis.com. © **01-42-72-31-52.** 30 units. 155€ double; 220€ triple. AE, MC, V. Métro: Bastille. **Amenities:** Breakfast room. *In room:* A/C, TV, hair dryer, Wi-Fi (free).

Hostellerie du Marais   Half a block from the place des Vosges, this hotel occupies a corner building whose 17th-century vestiges have been preserved—this includes the remnants of a well in the cellar. Although the building façade evokes an earlier time, the hotel was recently renovated and its interior feels quite modern. Though small, the guest rooms are comfortable, with flatscreen TVs, free Wi-Fi access, and a decor of neutral gray and beige tones. Rooms on the upper floors and facing the street have great views over the gray roofs of Paris—but note that they can be noisy.

30 rue de Turenne, Paris 75003. www.hostelleriedumarais.com. © **01-42-72-73-47.** Fax 01-42-72-54-10. 24 units. 112€–230€ double. AE, MC, V. Métro: Chemin Vert or St-Paul. **Amenities:** Bar. *In room:* A/C, TV, hair dryer, minibar, Wi-Fi (free).

Hôtel Caron de Beaumarchais ★ 🏷   Built in the 18th century, this good-value choice features floors of artfully worn gray stone, antique reproductions, and elaborate fabrics based on antique patterns. Hotelier Alain Bigeard intends his primrose-colored guest rooms to evoke the taste of the French gentry in the 18th century, when the Marais was the scene of high-society dances and even duels. Most rooms retain their original ceiling beams. The smallest units overlook the courtyard, and the top-floor rooms are tiny, but have panoramic balcony views across the Right Bank.

12 rue Vieille-du-Temple, 75004 Paris. www.carondebeaumarchais.com. © **01-42-72-34-12.** Fax 01-42-72-34-63. 19 units. 145€–185€ double. AE, MC, V. Métro: St-Paul or Hôtel-de-Ville. **Amenities:** Breakfast room; babysitting. *In room:* A/C, TV, hair dryer, minibar, Wi-Fi (free).

Hôtel de la Bretonnerie   This popular and good-value hotel has plenty of character. Decorated with heavy wooden antiques and old-fashioned wallpapers and curtains, the charming 17th-century hotel also boasts exposed beams, high ceilings, and four-poster beds. Large windows look onto either the surrounding streets or a quiet inner courtyard. The hotel has an excellent location, near the atmospheric Jewish quarter and the busy Marais shopping district. It's not fancy, but it is a comfortable and clean hotel with friendly staff.

22 rue Sainte Croix de la Bretonnerie, 75004 Paris. www.hotelbretonnerie.com. ☎ **01-48-87-77-63.** Fax 01-42-77-26-78. 29 units. 135€–165€ double; 190€ suite. MC, V. Métro: Hôtel-de-Ville. **Amenities:** Breakfast room. *In room:* TV, hair dryer, minibar, Wi-Fi (free).

Hôtel de Lutèce This 19th-century hotel feels like a country house in Brittany. The lounge, with its old fireplace, is furnished with antiques and contemporary paintings. Each of the guest rooms boasts antiques, adding to a refined atmosphere that attracts celebrities such as the duke and duchess of Bedford. The suites, though larger than the doubles, are often similar to doubles with extended sitting areas. Each is tastefully furnished, with an antique or two. Located on pretty Ile St-Louis, the hotel is comparable in style and amenities to the Deux-Iles (see below), under the same ownership.

65 rue St-Louis-en-l'Ile, 75004 Paris. www.paris-hotel-lutece.com. ☎ **01-43-26-23-52.** Fax 01-43-29-60-25. 23 units. 195€ double; 230€ triple. AE, MC, V. Métro: Pont Marie or Cité. **Amenities:** Babysitting; concierge. *In room:* A/C, TV, hair dryer, Wi-Fi (free).

Hôtel des Deux-Iles ★ This is an unpretentious but charming choice in a great location. In a restored 18th-century town house, the hotel has elaborate decor, with bamboo and reed furniture and French provincial touches. The guest rooms are on the small side, but the beds are very comfortable and the bathrooms well maintained. A garden off the lobby leads to a basement breakfast room that has a fireplace.

59 rue St-Louis-en-l'Ile, 75004 Paris. www.deuxiles-paris-hotel.com. ☎ **01-43-26-13-35.** Fax 01-43-29-60-25. 17 units. 195€ double. AE, MC, V. Métro: Pont Marie. **Amenities:** Room service. *In room:* A/C, TV, hair dryer, Wi-Fi (free).

Hôtel Saint-Louis en l'Isle ★ 🖝 Proprietors Guy and Andrée Record maintain a charming family atmosphere at this antiques-filled hotel in a 17th century town house. The hotel represents an incredible value, considering its prime location on Ile St-Louis. Expect cozy, slightly cramped rooms, each with a small bathroom. With mansard roofs and old-fashioned moldings, the top-floor units sport tiny balconies that afford sweeping views. The breakfast room is in the cellar, which has 17th-century stone vaulting.

75 rue St-Louis-en-l'Ile, 75004 Paris. www.saintlouisenlisle.com. ☎ **01-46-34-04-80.** Fax 01-46-34-02-13. 19 units. 140€–220€ double. MC, V. Métro: Pont Marie or St-Michel-Notre-Dame. **Amenities:** Babysitting; concierge; smoke-free rooms. *In room:* A/C, TV, hair dryer, Wi-Fi (free).

INEXPENSIVE

Hôtel Bellevue & du Chariot d'Or Originally built in 1860 as part of the majestic redevelopment of central Paris by Baron Haussmann, this hotel has a grand facade and inexpensive, relatively comfortable and cozy, simple bedrooms. The hotel has become more desirable because of its location in the once-neglected Arts et Métiers district north of the Pompidou Center. The second part of its name—"Chariot d'Or" (Golden Carriage)—derives from the medieval custom of placing brides-to-be (along with their dowries) in a flower-draped ceremonial carriage. During the occupation of Paris during World War II, the site was commandeered as a garrison for rank-and-file Nazi troops.

39 rue de Turbigo, 75003 Paris. www.hotelbellevue75.com. ✆ **01-48-87-45-60.** Fax 01-48-87-95-04. 59 units. 72€–75€ double; 87€ triple; 98€ quad. AE, DC, MC, V. Métro: Châtelet–Les Halles or Réaumur-Sebastopol. **Amenities:** Bar; babysitting. *In room:* TV, Wi-Fi (free).

Hôtel de la Place des Vosges ★　Built about 350 years ago, during the same era as the majestic square for which it's named (a 2-min. walk away), this is a well-managed, small-scale property with reasonable prices and lots of charm. The structure was once used as a stable for the mules of Henri IV. Entirely renovated in 2010, many of the small guest rooms have beamed ceilings, flatscreen TVs, and a sense of cozy, well-ordered efficiency. The most desirable and expensive room is top-floor no. 60, overlooking the rooftops of Paris, with a luxurious bathroom. Patches of chiseled stone in various parts of the hotel add a decorative touch.

12 rue de Birague, 75004 Paris. www.hotelplacedesvosges.com. ✆ **01-42-72-60-46.** Fax 01-42-72-02-64. 16 units. 90€–160€ double. AE, DC, MC, V. Métro: Bastille. **Amenities:** Room service. *In room:* TV, hair dryer, Wi-Fi (free).

Champs-Élysées & Western Paris (8e, 16e & 17e)

This is where most of the city's money and power is concentrated. The "Golden Triangle" (Avenue Montaigne, George V, and the Champs-Élysées) is bling-bling heaven, with all the major fashion labels jostling for position. It's also a business neighborhood, so get ready to navigate the suits.

Best For: Travelers who have deep pockets, or those who want to pretend they do.

Drawbacks: Not really a residential area, this area lacks some of the authentic local charm of other neighborhoods.

VERY EXPENSIVE

Fouquet's Barrière ★★★　This deluxe boutique hotel on the corner of the Champs-Élysées may lack the historic cachet of the neighboring George V or Plaza Athénée, but it's a more contemporary brand of glitz and glamour. Standing alongside its namesake, the legendary restaurant, Fouquet's, it offers some of the most luxurious and spacious bedrooms in Paris, its decor dominated by ceiling-high padded headboards in shiny gold. The hotel contains such novel features as waterproof floating TV remotes in the bathtub, and a bedside button that, when pressed, will summon your butler. There's one butler to every eight guests, and the service is the best in Paris. That butler even arrives to unpack your luggage and serve you champagne.

46 av. George V, 75008 Paris. www.fouquets-barriere.com. ✆ **01-40-69-60-00.** Fax 01-40-69-60-05. 107 units. 750€–1300€ double; 1,100€–1,700€ junior suite; 1,700€–3,600€ suite. AE, MC, V. Métro: George V. Parking 45€. **Amenities:** 2 restaurants; 2 bars; concierge; health club and spa; pool (indoor); room service. *In room:* A/C, TV, TV/DVD, hair dryer, minibar, Wi-Fi (free).

Four Seasons Hotel George V ★★★ ☺　In its latest reincarnation, with all its glitz and glamour, this hotel is one of the best in the world. The George V opened in 1928 in honor of George V of England, grandfather of Queen Elizabeth. During the liberation of Paris, it housed Dwight D. Eisenhower. The guest rooms are about as close as you'll come to residency in a well-upholstered private home where teams of decorators have lavished vast amounts of attention and money. The beds rival those at the Ritz and Meurice in comfort. The largest units are magnificent; the smallest are, in the words of a spokesperson, *"très agréable."* Security is tight—a fact appreciated by sometimes-notorious guests. The staff pampers children with bathrobes, bedtime milk and cookies, and even special menus.

31 av. George V, 75008 Paris. www.fourseasons.com. ✆ **800/332-3442** in the U.S. and Canada, or 01-49-52-70-00. Fax 01-49-52-70-10. 245 units. 750€–1,095€ double; from 1,795€ suite. Parking 40€. AE, DC, MC, V. Métro: George V. **Amenities:** 2 restaurants; 2 bars; babysitting; concierge; health club and spa; room service. *In room:* A/C, TV, TV/DVD, CD player, hair dryer, minibar, Wi-Fi (22€).

Hôtel de Crillon ★★   The Crillon, one of Europe's grand hotels, sits across from the U.S. Embassy on the place de la Concorde. Although some international CEOs and diplomats treat it as a shrine, those seeking less pomposity might prefer the Plaza Athénée or the Meurice. The 200-plus-year-old building, once the palace of the Duc de Crillon, is owned by Jean Taittinger, of the champagne family. The salons boast 17th- and 18th-century tapestries, gilt-and-brocade furniture, chandeliers, fine sculpture, and Louis XVI chests and chairs. The guest rooms are luxurious. Think Madame Pompadour meets Louis XV. Some are spectacular, such as the Leonard Bernstein Suite, which has one of the maestro's pianos. The furniture, including the beds, offers grand comfort.

10 place de la Concorde, 75008 Paris. www.crillon.com. ✆ **01-44-71-15-00.** Fax 01-44-71-15-02. 147 units. From 950€ double; from 1,400€ junior suite; from 1,800€ suite. AE, MC, V. Free parking. **Amenities:** 2 restaurants; bar; babysitting; concierge; state-of-the-art health club; room service. *In room:* A/C, TV, TV/DVD, CD player, hair dryer, minibar, Wi-Fi (free).

Hôtel de La Trémoille ★★   In the heart of Paris and a 2-minute walk from the Champs-Élysées, this is a preferred Right Bank address for fashionistas, as it lies in the heart of the haute couture district. Built in the 19th century, the hotel preserves the building's original elegance and charm, while still incorporating modern. Originally a private residence, the hotel is outfitted in a Louis XV style, all in woodwork and tapestries. Rooms are cozy and comfortable, each decorated in harmonies of tawny, ocher, gray, and white, with much use of silks, synthetic furs, and mohair.

14 rue de la Trémoille, 75008 Paris. www.hotel-tremoille.com. ✆ **01-56-52-14-00.** Fax 01-40-70-01-08. 93 units. 545€–710€ double; 800€–1,200€ suite. AE, DC, MC, V. Métro: Alma-Marceau. **Amenities:** Restaurant; bar; concierge; exercise room; room service. *In room:* A/C, TV, hair dryer, minibar, Wi-Fi (free).

Hôtel le Bristol ★★★   This palace is near the Palais d'Élysée (home of the French president), on the shopping street parallel to the Champs-Élysées. The 18th-century Parisian facade has a glass-and-wrought-iron entryway, where uniformed English-speaking attendants greet you. Hippolyte Jammet founded the Bristol in 1924, installing many antiques and Louis XV and XVI furnishings. The guest rooms are opulent, with antiques or well-made reproductions, inlaid wood, bronze, crystal, Oriental carpets, and original oil paintings. Personalized old-world service is rigidly maintained here—some guests find it forbidding; others absolutely adore it.

112 rue du Faubourg St-Honoré, 75008 Paris. www.lebristolparis.com. ✆ **01-53-43-43-00.** Fax 01-53-43-43-01. 187 units. 670€–980€ double; 990€–1,600€ junior suite; from 1,900€ suite. AE, DC, MC, V. Free parking. Métro: Miromesnil or Champs-Élysées. **Amenities:** 2 restaurants; bar;

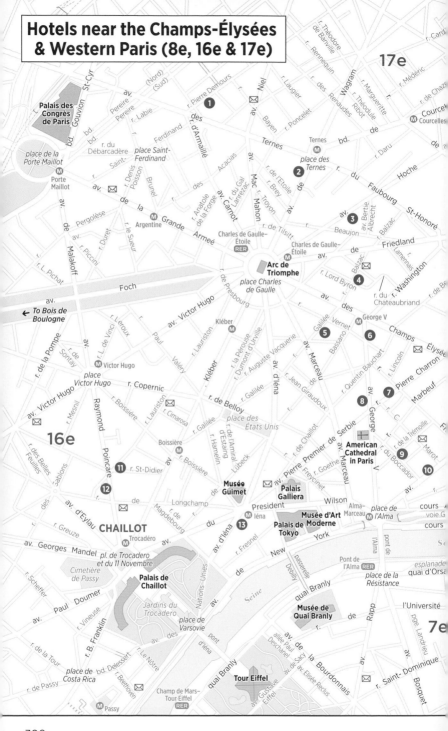

Hotels near the Champs-Élysées & Western Paris (8e, 16e & 17e)

17e

Palais des Congrès de Paris

place de la Porte Maillot

Porte Maillot

16e

CHAILLOT

Arc de Triomphe

place Charles de Gaulle

Charles de Gaulle–Étoile

place des Ternes

Ternes

Beaujon

Friedland

George V

Champs Élysées

American Cathedral in Paris

place Victor Hugo

place des États Unis

Musée Guimet

Palais Galliera

Musée d'Art Moderne

Palais de Tokyo

place de l'Alma

Pont de l'Alma

place de la Résistance

esplanade quai d'Orsay

Trocadéro

pl. de Trocadero et du 11 Novembre

Palais de Chaillot

Cimetière de Passy

Jardins du Trocadéro

place de Varsovie

Musée de Quai Branly

l'Université

7e

place de Costa Rica

Champ de Mars-Tour Eiffel

Tour Eiffel

← To Bois de Boulogne

babysitting; children's programs; concierge; health club and spa; pool (indoor); room service. *In room:* A/C, TV, TV/DVD, CD player, hair dryer, minibar, Wi-Fi (21€ per day).

Hôtel Pershing Hall ★★   Set on a hyperstylish street that parallels the avenue Montaigne, this boutique hotel was created when a late-19th-century town house was radically altered by one of France's most celebrated modern designers, Andrée Putnam. The five-story town house was built in 1890 by the Comte de Paris—who at the time was heir apparent to the French monarchy, had it been fully restored—as a home for his mistress. During World War I, it was transformed into the Paris headquarters of American Gen. John Pershing. Today, the walls of the soaring courtyard are draped in lush tropical plants from Southeast Asia, which thrive in the microclimate of the courtyard. Inside, don't expect an homage to the imperial days of the French monarchy, as all appointments have been replaced in favor of the warm, artfully minimal style favored by the woman who designed the original decor of Air France's Concorde.

49 rue Pierre Charron, 75008 Paris. www.pershing-hall.com. © **01-58-36-58-00.** Fax 01-58-36-58-01. 26 units. 470€–560€ double; 780€–1,110€ suite. AE, DC, MC, V. Métro: George V. **Amenities:** Restaurant; bar; babysitting; concierge; health club and spa; room service. *In room:* A/C, TV, CD player, hair dryer, minibar, Wi-Fi (free).

Hyatt Regency Paris-Madeleine ★★   In the heart of the financial district, this represents Hyatt's first venture into the center of the French capital. This is our top recommendation for those visiting Paris on business, as rooms are designed not only for rest, but also for work—large writing desks, three phones, modem sockets, voice mail, individual fax machines, you name it. As you enter, the hotel evokes a noble, romantic private home with a lavish use of quality materials such as sycamore wood. Some of the units boast exceptional views over the rooftops of Paris.

24 bd. Malesherbes, 75008 Paris. www.paris.madeleine.hyatt.com. © **01-55-27-12-34.** Fax 01-55-27-12-35. 86 units. 400€–600€ double; from 885€ suite. AE, DC, MC, V. Métro: Madeleine. **Amenities:** 2 restaurants; bar; babysitting; concierge; health club and spa; room service. *In room:* A/C, TV, TV/DVD, CD player, fax, hair dryer, minibar, Wi-Fi (free).

Le Royal Monceau—Raffles Paris ★★★ 🛎   This five-star Raffles hotel opened in late 2010 and immediately wowed Paris with its luxurious chic interiors designed by Philippe Starck. The decor is contemporary, but is still in tune with the Art Deco heritage of the building. The spacious rooms offer all the comfort and amenities that you would expect from a hotel of this caliber, but still have a relaxed vibe. There's even an electric guitar in each room, if you feel like expressing your inner rock star. The hotel has a unique commitment to contemporary art: it regularly hosts art exhibitions, has a fully stocked art bookstore, and it publishes a sophisticated website (www.artforbreakfast.com), which gives an insider's perspective on the Paris art scene. The hotel offers cutting-edge fashion in its satellite L'Éclaireur store. The icing on the cake? Star *pâtissier* Pierre Hermé is responsible for the desserts.

37 av. Hoche, 75008 Paris. www.leroyalmonceau.com. © **01-42-99-88-00.** Fax 01-42-99-89-00. 160 units. 780€–930€ double; from 1,200€–10,000€ suite. AE, DC, MC, V. Métro: Ternes. **Amenities:** 2 restaurants; bar; children's programs; cigar lounge; concierge; health club; movie theater; pool (indoor); room service; spa. *In room:* A/C, TV/DVD, hair dryer, iPod dock, minibar, Wi-Fi (free).

Plaza Athénée ★★★   The Plaza Athénée, an 1889 Art Nouveau marvel, is a landmark of discretion and style. About half the celebrities visiting Paris have been pampered here; in the old days, Mata Hari used to frequent the place. The **Salon Gobelins** (with tapestries against rich paneling) and the **Salon Marie Antoinette,** a richly paneled and grand room, are two public rooms that add to the ambience of this lavish hotel. There's also a calm, quiet interior courtyard draped with vines and dotted with geraniums. The quietest guest rooms overlook a courtyard with awnings and parasol-shaded tables; they have ample closet space. Some rooms overlooking avenue Montaigne have views of the Eiffel Tower. The hotel is also home to **Alain Ducasse au Plaza Athénée,** where Alain Ducasse presents a gourmet French menu. During Paris Fashion Week, the bar becomes the event's nonofficial HQ.

25 av. Montaigne, 75008 Paris. www.plaza-athenee-paris.com. © **866/732-1106** in the U.S. and Canada, or 01-53-67-66-65. Fax 01-53-67-66-66. 191 units. 830€–935€ double; 1,600€–1,700€ junior suite; 1,850€–22,000€ suite. AE, MC, V. Parking 28€. Métro: Franklin-D.-Roosevelt or Alma-Marceau. **Amenities:** 5 restaurants; bar; babysitting; concierge; state-of-the-art health club; room service. *In room:* A/C, TV, TV/DVD, CD player, hair dryer, minibar, Wi-Fi (24€ per day).

Shangri-La Hotel, Paris ★   The luxury Hong Kong hotelier opened its first Paris address at the end of 2010 inside a beautifully restored national monument, the former home of Prince Roland Bonaparte (Napoleon Bonaparte's grand-nephew), dating from 1896. This new palace hotel is located near some of the city's best museums, including the Musée d'art Moderne and the Palais de Tokyo, and has exceptional views sweeping across the Seine river to the Eiffel Tower. Grand, traditional interiors in tones of beige with gilt highlights transport you to a purely Parisian heritage setting. The rooms are exceptionally large, even for this caliber of hotel—they average 47 sq. m (506 sq. ft.). The marble bathrooms feel extra luxurious, with heated floors, rainfall shower heads and separate tubs, flatscreen TVs, and Bvlgari toiletries. The hotel is planning to open a wellness area, with spa services, in 2011.

10 avenue d'Iéna, 75016 Paris. www.shangri-la.com. © **01-53-67-19-98**. Fax 01-53-67-19-19. 81 units. From 750€ double; from 1,565€ suite. AE, DC, MC, V. Métro: Iéna. **Amenities:** 3 restaurants; bar; babysitting; concierge; exercise room; pool (indoor); room service; smoke-free rooms; Wi-Fi in public areas (free). *In room:* A/C, TV, hair dryer, high-speed Internet access (free), minibar.

EXPENSIVE

Best Western Premier Regent's Garden ★★   Near the convention center (Palais des Congrès) and the Arc de Triomphe, the Regent's Garden boasts a proud heritage: Napoleon III built this château for his physician. Renovated in 2008, the hotel prides itself on its sustainability; it was awarded a prestigious European Eco-Label for its efforts in preserving the environment by reducing the consumption of water, gas, electricity, and waste. The smart guest rooms feature tall soundproof windows, traditional French furniture, and modern textiles—the environmental approach extends to the guest rooms, as the duvets in each room are made from fair trade cotton. Even breakfast is composed of organic ingredients. Guests have access to a neighboring fitness center and spa, Eclipse & Vous. A garden with ivy-covered walls and umbrella-shaded tables makes for a perfect place to meet other guests. The hotel is smoke free throughout.

6 rue Pierre-Demours, 75017 Paris. www.hotel-regents-paris.com. ✆ **800/528-1234** in the U.S., or 01-45-74-07-30. Fax 01-40-55-01-42. 40 units. 290€–440€ double; from 490€ suite. AE, DC, MC, V. Parking 20€. Métro: Ternes or Charles-de-Gaulle–Etoile. **Amenities:** Babysitting; spa. *In room:* A/C, TV, hair dryer, minibar, Wi-Fi (free).

Hôtel Balzac ★★★   Built for the director of the Paris Opéra in 1853, and once home to Balzac himself, this is a luxurious, intimate town-house hotel overlooking the Champs-Élysées. Vibrant, warm colors such as plum and copper prevail throughout the elegant bedrooms furnished with tasteful modern pieces of varying styles. The hotel manages to recapture the romantic era but with a cutting modern edge. It underwent a multimillion-euro restoration in 2007 to attract guests who like five-star comfort but not commercial palace hotels. For atmosphere, the hotel has lithographs depicting Balzac and scenes from his works including *La Comédie Humaine*.

6 rue Balzac, 75008 Paris. www.hotelbalzac.com. ✆ **01-44-35-18-00.** Fax 01-44-35-18-05. 70 units. 350€–600€ double; 790€–870€ junior suite; from 870€ suite. AE, MC, V. Parking 23€. Métro: Champs-Élysées. **Amenities:** Restaurant; bar; health club and spa; pool (indoor); room service. *In room:* A/C, TV, TV/DVD player, hair dryer, minibar, Wi-Fi (22€ per day).

Hôtel Radisson Blu Trocadéro Dokhan's ★★   If not for the porters walking through its public areas carrying luggage, you might suspect that this well-accessorized hotel was a private home. It's in a stately 19th-century Haussmann-styled building vaguely inspired by Palladio and contains accessories such as antique paneling, Regency-era armchairs, and chandeliers. Each guest room has a different decorative style, with antiques or good reproductions, lots of personalized touches and triple-glazed windows. Beds are often antique reproductions with maximum comfort. Suites have a larger living space and spacious bathrooms with such extras as makeup mirrors and luxe toiletries.

117 rue Lauriston, 75116 Paris. www.radissonblu.com/dokhanhotel-paristrocadero. ✆ **01-53-65-66-99.** Fax 01-53-65-66-88. 45 units. 250€–350€ double; from 420€ suite. AE, DC, MC, V. Parking 30€. Métro: Trocadéro. **Amenities:** Babysitting; champagne bar; concierge; room service. *In room:* A/C, TV, fax, hair dryer, minibar, Wi-Fi (free).

Le Pavillon des Lettres ★   If you're a literature fan, this hotel—Paris's first literary-themed hotel—might just be the place for you. Located in the 8th arrondissement, this charming boutique hotel opened in 2010, and is owned by the same owners of the Pavillon de la Reine. It features 26 rooms—one for each letter of the alphabet. Each room is dedicated to the life and work of great writers, from Anderson to Proust to Zola, and you'll find excerpted texts from these writers printed on the bedroom walls. The comfortable rooms are designed to encourage relaxation and are decorated in metallic tones. Lounge in the hotel's library over a well-thumbed classic, and when you're tired of reading, just step outside to reach the many nearby shops and restaurants in the thick of Right Bank.

12 rue des Saussaies, 75008 Paris. www.pavillondeslettres.com. ✆ **01-49-24-26-26.** Fax 01-49-24-26-27. 26 units. From 300€–340€ double; 460€ suite. AE, DC, MC, V. Métro: Madeleine. **Amenities:** Restaurant; bar; library; room service. *In room:* A/C, TV, iPad, iPod docking stations, minibar, Wi-Fi (free).

Renaissance Paris Arc de Triomphe ★★   On the site of the once-famous Theatre de l'Empire, this cutting-edge hotel with its intriguing modern interiors lies only steps from the Arc de Triomphe and the Champs-Élysées. The top-floor rooms and suites open onto large terraces with the panoramic views over the heart of Paris. The upscale hotel rooms and suites are spacious, tastefully decorated, and outfitted with the latest in-room technology. Its all-glass exterior has made this a distinctive landmark, even though it opened only in 2009. This is definitely a trendy and hip hotel, so probably not the best for kids. The on-site Makassar Lounge & Restaurant blends French bistro flavors with authentic Indonesian dishes. The hotel is smoke free.

39 av. de Wagram, 75017 Paris. www.marriott.com. ✆ **01-55-37-55-37.** Fax 01-55-37-55-38. 108 units. 289€–599€ double; from 429€ suite. Parking 35€. Métro: Charles-de-Gaulle–Etoile. **Amenities:** Restaurant, bar; concierge; exercise room; room service. *In room:* A/C, TV/DVD, hair dryer, minibar, Wi-Fi (7€ per hour).

MODERATE

Hôtel Galileo ★ 🎒 This is one of the 8th's most charming hotels. Proprietors Roland and Elisabeth Buffat have won friends from all over with their Hôtel des Deux-Iles and Hôtel de Lutèce on St-Louis-en-l'Ile (see earlier in this chapter). A short walk from the Champs-Élysées, this town house is the epitome of French elegance and charm. The medium-size rooms are a study in understated taste. Within this hotel, rooms with numbers ending in 3 (specifically 103, 203, 303, 403, and 503) are more spacious than the others. Rooms 501 and 502 have private glassed-in verandas that you can use even in winter.

54 rue Galilée, 75008 Paris. www.galileo-paris-hotel.com. ✆ **01-47-20-66-06.** Fax 01-47-20-67-17. 27 units. 130€–185€ double. AE, DC, MC, V. Métro: Charles-de-Gaulle–Etoile or George V. *In room:* A/C, TV, hair dryer, minibar, Wi-Fi (free).

Relais Monceau ★ 🏷 Finding an elegant but affordable hotel in the overpriced 8th is always a challenge, but Relais Monceau is an inviting choice. A 19th-century town house with two private courtyards has been discreetly restored with a respect for the past, although all the modern amenities have been installed. A government-rated three-star hotel, it takes its name from the nearby Parc Monceau. The midsize bedrooms are furnished with elegance and taste and are spread over three floors. There are also several large public guest areas as well.

85 rue du Rocher, Paris 75008. www.relais-monceau.com. ✆ **01-45-22-75-11.** Fax: 01-45-22-30-88. 51 units. 110€–198€ double; 195€–264€ suite. AE, MC, V. Métro: Champs-Élysées. **Amenities:** Bar. *In room:* A/C, TV, hair dryer, minibar, Wi-Fi (free).

Hôtel Palais de Chaillot 🏷 Located between the Champs-Élysées and Trocadéro, the town house was restored from top to bottom in 2010, and the result is a contemporary yet informal variation on Parisian chic. The guest rooms are soundproofed, come in various shapes and sizes, and are furnished in pastel shades. Rooms 61, 62, and 63 afford partial views of the Eiffel Tower.

35 av. Raymond-Poincaré, 75016 Paris. www.hotelpalaisdechaillot.com. ✆ **01-53-70-09-09.** Fax 01-53-70-09-08. 31 units. 169€ double; 179€ junior suite; 20€ extra bed. AE, DC, MC, V. Métro: Victor Hugo or Trocadéro. **Amenities:** Room service. *In room:* A/C, TV, hair dryer, Wi-Fi (free).

INEXPENSIVE

Hôtel Eldorado 🏷 If you're looking for something to criticize, you might well find it here. But if you're an intrepid bargain hunter, and don't mind living in an offbeat neighborhood on the border of Montmartre, this is one of the best cheap hotels in an overpriced city. Of course, don't expect an elevator to take you to a room with a TV, phone, or air-conditioning. But the price is right. The manager, Anne Gratacos, continually decorates the hotel with flea market finds, including Buddha busts and Art Deco armoires. The most spacious and evocative units are in a separate pavilion separated from the main structure by a garden patio with a restaurant, Bistrot des Dames.

18 rue des Dames, 75017 Paris. www.eldoradohotel.fr. ℂ 01-45-22-35-21. Fax 01-43-87-25-97. 33 units, 23 with private bathroom. 70€–80€ double with bathroom; 80€–90€ triple with bathroom. AE, MC, V. Parking 25€. Métro: Place de Clichy. **Amenities:** Restaurant. *In room:* No phone, Wi-Fi (free).

Opéra & Canal St-Martin (9e & 10e)

Two of Paris's major department stores are located just above Opéra, and they set the tone for this dynamic shopping district which extends north via the gourmet Martyrs strip right up to the bright lights of Pigalle. The adjacent Canal St-Martin neighborhood, over to the east, has a different vibe altogether, with bohemian locals lingering over coffee by the leafy canal.

Best For: Travelers looking for proximity to monuments (Opéra) or those wanting to pretend they're Parisian in an authentic neighborhood.
Drawbacks: Can be either too busy, or too slow.

VERY EXPENSIVE

Hotel Banke ★★   In the tradition of Derby Hotels Collection, this luxurious boutique hotel is art oriented. Works of art adorn both the public rooms and the accommodations. The building dates from the Belle Epoque era and contains a majestic hall from that time, which is embellished with a great mosaic. Bedrooms are midsize to spacious and decorated with antique art and an avant-garde design. The on-site spa focuses on a self-styled "purification and regeneration of your internal ecology." Bathrooms, for the most part, are very spacious. The staff is also extremely friendly, a rarity in Paris. The terrace opens onto a panoramic view of Sacré-Coeur and the Opéra.

20 rue Lafayette, 75009 Paris. www.derbyhotels.com/Banke-Hotel-Paris. ℂ 01-55-33-22-22. Fax 01-55-33-22-28. 94 units. 630€ double; 1,265€ suite. AE, DC, MC, V. Métro: Opéra. **Amenities:** 2 restaurants; bar; exercise room; room service; smoke-free rooms; spa with steam room and sauna. *In room:* A/C, TV, hair dryer, minibar, Wi-Fi (free).

MODERATE

Hotel Amour ★★ 🎁   This hotel oozes streetwise chic and attitude. One critic claimed that thanks to the hotel bar being frequented by young European fashionistas, each flaunting his or her respective allure and neurosis, "waiting in a queue for the toilets has never been so entertaining." Each bedroom is decorated by a celebrity friend of the owner (like Sophie Calle, Marc Newson). so the trendy decor varies widely, from minimalist white-on-white with touches of faux baroque to disco balls to graffiti written directly on the walls. The relaxed downstairs bar and restaurant are a great destination at any time for seeing and being seen. And the ivy-covered courtyard is perfect for sipping champagne on warm days or nights.

8 rue Navarin, 75009 Paris. www.hotelamourparis.fr. ℂ 01-48-78-31-80. 20 units. 150€–170€ double; 280€ duplex. AE, MC, V. Métro: St-Georges. **Amenities:** Restaurant; bar; room service. *In room:* A/C, minibar, no phone, Wi-Fi (free).

Hôtel Arvor St Georges ★★ 🎁 This fresh, contemporary hotel is located in the charming "New Athens" neighborhood, off the tourist beat and nestled below Montmartre. In the 19th century, this neighborhood was frequented by Romantic artists such as Victor Hugo, George Sand, and Frédéric Chopin, but today the neighborhood is a gourmand's paradise, with the restaurant-lined rue des Martyrs nearby. The hotel is relaxed and comfortable, and you'll feel like a guest in a chic Parisian's private home as you flip through some of the art and photography titles over a cup of coffee in the airy downstairs lobby. The tasty breakfast (9€) is served here or outside in the flower-filled patio when the weather is nice. The rooms have a clean, designer style, and the six suites boast views over Paris to the Eiffel Tower. Service is friendly and professional.

8 rue Laferrière, 75009 Paris. www.arvor-hotel-paris.com. ✆ **01-48-78-60-92.** Fax 01-48-78-16-52. 30 units. 125€–190€ double. AE, DC, MC, V. Métro: St-Georges. Amenities: Bar; room service. In room: TV, hair dryer, Wi-Fi (free).

Hôtel de la Tour d'Auvergne ★ Here's a good bet for those who want to be near the Opéra or the Gare du Nord. This building was erected before Baron Haussmann reconfigured Paris's avenues around 1870. Later, Modigliani rented a room here for 6 months, and Victor Hugo and Auguste Rodin lived on this street. The interior has been recently redecorated in a chic international style. The guest rooms are meticulously coordinated, yet the small decorative canopies over the headboards can make them feel cluttered. Though the views over the back courtyard are uninspired, some guests prefer the quiet of the rear rooms.

10 rue de la Tour d'Auvergne, 75009 Paris. www.hoteltourdauvergne.com. ✆ **01-48-78-61-60.** Fax 01-49-95-99-00. 24 units. 115€–135€ double. AE, DC, MC, V. Métro: Cadet. **Amenities:** Bar; room service. In room: A/C, TV, hair dryer, minibar, Wi-Fi (2€ per day).

Hôtel Langlois ★ 🏨 This hotel used to be known as Hôtel des Croises, but when it was used as a setting for the Jonathan Demme film *The Truth About Charlie* (2002), the hotel owners changed the name to match the one used in the film. It's a well-proportioned, restored town house with a main stairwell and a spacious landing. An antique wrought-iron elevator running up the center of the building adds an old-fashioned Parisian touch. The rooms are well proportioned and spacious; those in the front get the most light. Units in the rear are darker but quieter. Rooms, with their aura of *Ecole de Nancy* (a florid Art Nouveau style), have well-chosen antiques, tasteful rugs and fabrics, even an occasional fireplace.

63 rue St-Lazare, 75009 Paris. www.hotel-langlois.com. ✆ **01-48-74-78-24.** Fax 01-49-95-04-43. 27 units. 140€–150€ double; 190€ suite. AE, DC, MC, V. Métro: Trinité. **Amenities:** Breakfast room; room service. In room: A/C, TV, hair dryer, minibar, Wi-Fi (free).

INEXPENSIVE

Hotel All Seasons Paris Gare de l'Est Magenta 🎐 Opposite the Gare de l'Est railway station, this hotel lives up to its name. It is truly a hotel for all seasons and a great convenience for passengers disembarking at Gare de l'Est, which has good taxi, bus, and Métro links to all of Paris. All Seasons is the budget chain link of the famous French hotel group, Accor, and as such, it's aimed at both vacationers and business travelers who seek affordable rates. The bedroom furnishings are fairly standard, except for the bedding, which emphasizes "anti-stress" quilts and pillows made with carbon threads said to channel the body's electricity. Breakfast is called "as much as you wish," and there is unlimited tea, coffee, and mineral water. Magazines and games for children are available. The hotel is smoke free.

87 bd. de Strasbourg, 75010 Paris. www.accorhotels.com. ☎ **01-42-09-12-28.** Fax 01-42-09-48-12. 32 units. 95€–115€ double. Rates include breakfast. MC, V. Métro: Gare de l'Est. **Amenities:** Room service. *In room:* A/C, TV, hair dryer, Wi-Fi (free).

Hôtel Chopin ✒   Enter this intimate, offbeat hotel through a passageway that includes a toy store, a bookstore, the exit from the Musée Grevin, and the architectural trappings of its original construction in 1846. Just off the Grands Boulevards, this old-fashioned hotel evokes the charm of yesteryear. In honor of its namesake, the Chopin has a piano in its reception area. The inviting lobby welcomes you behind its 1850s facade of elegant woodwork and Victorian-era glass. In the style of the Paris of long ago, the comfortably furnished bedrooms open onto a glass-topped arcade instead of the hysterically busy street, so they are rather tranquil. We prefer the bedrooms on the top floor, as they are larger and quieter, with views over the rooftops of Paris. The least expensive bedrooms lie behind the elevator bank and get less light.

10 bd. Montmartre or 46 passage Jouffroy, 75009 Paris. www.hotel-chopin.com. ☎ **01-47-70-58-10.** Fax 01-42-47-00-70. 36 units. 92€–106€ double; 125€ triple. AE, MC, V. Métro: Grands-Boulevards. **Amenities:** Wi-Fi (free). *In room:* TV, hair dryer.

Pigalle & Montmartre (18e)

The wedding cake Sacré-Coeur basilica crowns the city's highest point, on the summit of Montmartre. A neighborhood apart in Paris, with a rich artistic history and all the charm of a village, Montmartre runs into Pigalle below, a harmless red-light district with a high concentration of concert and club venues.

Best For: Dynamic travelers who want to take advantage of the nightlife.
Drawbacks: Climbing up and down the hill requires a good level of fitness.

VERY EXPENSIVE

Hôtel Particulier ★★★   No hotel in Paris seems quite as special as this one, lying between avenue Junot and rue Lepic and nestled in a "secret" passageway called le passage du Rocher de la Sorcière or the Witch's Rock Passage. Modern Paris meets Old Montmartre in this Directoire mansion from the 18th century, and the marriage is harmonious. Louis Bénech, one of the landscape architects who renovated the Tuileries, created the intimate gardens of the hotel. Each of the five suites has a different personality, the work of various artists that range in decor from an erotic window by Philippe Mayaux to poems and hats by Olivier Saillard. The most unusual is the suite "Curtain of Hair," a loft created in the attic with images of the long hair of photographer Natacha Lesueur. The downstairs bar has exceptional cocktails.

23 av. Junot, 75018 Paris. www.hotel-particulier-montmartre.com. ☎ **01-53-41-81-40.** Fax 01-42-58-00-87. 5 units. 390€–590€ suite. MC, V. Métro: Blanche. **Amenities:** Bar; breakfast room; garden. *In room:* A/C, TV, hair dryer, Wi-Fi (free).

EXPENSIVE

KUBE Hotel ★   Design-savvy clients appreciate the way the architect (Raymond Morel) made repeated use of the cube, a form that the owners refer to as "the most modern of shapes." The hotel occupies the six-story premises of what

Hotels in Pigalle & Montmartre (9e & 18e)

Hôtel des Arts **2**
Hôtel Ermitage **4**
Hôtel Particulier **1**
KUBE Hotel **5**
Timhôtel Montmartre **3**
Villa Royale **6**

was built in the late 1800s as the administrative headquarters of a now-defunct brewery (*Les bières de la Meuse*), deep inside Paris's grungy industrial heartland. There's a restaurant and a dance lounge on street level, where a DJ regularly spins tunes. Bedrooms (and everything else about the place) seem to revel in the geometry of the cube. Rectangular beds are lit from below and appear to float. Expect shag-covered sofas, fuzzy faux-fur slippers in tones of high-voltage yellow, and a sense of compact efficiency. Also on the premises is the Ice Kube Bar, a deep-cooled conversational oddity whose bar top is fashioned from—you guessed it—ice.

1–5 Passage Ruelle, 75018 Paris. www.kubehotel.com. ☎ **01-42-05-20-00.** Fax 01-42-05-21-01. 41 units. 250€–400€ double; 500€–900€ suite. Parking 15€. Métro: La Chapelle. **Amenities:** Restaurant; bar; exercise room. *In room:* A/C, TV, hair dryer, Wi-Fi (free).

Villa Royale ★ 🎁   Paris can be many things to many people, and if your vision of the city involves the scarlet-toned settings once associated with the Moulin Rouge and the paintings of Toulouse-Lautrec, this designer hotel might be for you. It does a flourishing business renting small but carefully decorated rooms, each of which evokes Paris's sometimes kitschy world of glitzy and risqué nightlife entertainment. Expect rooms outfitted Liberace-style, with rococo gew-gaws, velvet and velour upholsteries, jewel-toned walls, and TV screens that are sometimes encased in gilded frames. Each is named after someone from the world of French entertainment, including namesakes inspired by La Bardot, La Deneuve—even Claude Debussy.

2 rue Duperré, 75009 Paris. www.villa-royale.com. ✆ **01-55-31-78-78.** Fax 01-55-31-78-70. 31 units. 239€–299€ double; 289€–449€ suite. AE, DC, MC, V. Métro: Pigalle. Bus: 30 or 54. **Amenities:** Room service. *In room:* A/C, TV, hair dryer, minibar, Wi-Fi (10€).

MODERATE

Timhôtel Montmartre ★ Another address in the reliable Timhôtel chain, this two-star hotel is located in a charming square in Montmartre. The hotel is next door to the historical Bateau Lavoir building, where Picasso had a studio for many years and painted his masterpiece *Les Demoiselles d'Avignon.* The hotel rooms are decorated in a fairly basic and impersonal style, but they're clean. Rooms on the fourth and fifth floors offer excellent views over the rooftops of Paris and the Sacré-Coeur. Note that the hilltop location means that it can be a steep climb up from the closest public transport stops.

11 place Emile Goudeau, 75018 Paris. www.timhotel.com. ✆ **01-42-55-74-79.** Fax 01-42-55-71-01. 59 units. 130€–160€ double. AE, DC, MC, V. Métro: Abbesses. **Amenities:** Breakfast room; concierge. *In room:* A/C (in some rooms), TV, hair dryer, Wi-Fi (free).

INEXPENSIVE

Hôtel des Arts ★ In the center of Montmartre between place du Tertre and the Moulin Rouge, this hotel lies in a delightful quarter of Paris once made famous by poets and painters. It has a warm, welcoming atmosphere and in a former life it was a dormitory for the dancers of the Moulin Rouge. As you might expect, the rooms are small yet comfortable, with country-style curtains and bedspreads. Opt for one of the four bedrooms on the sixth floor for a panoramic view of Paris. As night falls, the area around the hotel often has its share of sex workers, although the hotel itself is a safe destination.

5 rue Tholozé, Paris 75018. www.arts-hotel-paris.com. ✆ **01-46-06-30-52.** Fax 01-46-06-10-83. 50 units. 70€–140€ double. AE, MC, V. Métro: Blanche. **Amenities:** Breakfast room. *In room:* TV, Wi-Fi (free).

Hôtel Ermitage Built in 1870 of chiseled limestone in the Napoleon III style, this hotel's facade evokes a perfectly proportioned small villa. Family run, it's set in a calm area, a brief downhill stroll from Sacré-Coeur. Views extend over Paris, and there's a garden in the back courtyard. The small guest rooms are similar to those in a countryside *auberge* (inn), with exposed ceiling beams, flowered wallpaper, and casement windows opening onto the garden or a street seemingly airlifted from the provinces.

24 rue Lamarck, 75018 Paris. www.ermitagesacrecoeur.fr. ✆ **01-42-64-79-22.** Fax 01-42-64-10-33. 12 units. 96€–100€ double; 145€ quad. Rates include breakfast. No credit cards. Métro: Lamarck-Caulaincourt. Parking 15€. **Amenities:** Babysitting; room service. *In room:* Hair dryer, Wi-Fi (free).

République, Bastille & Eastern Paris (11e & 12e)

Paris's former industrial heart has been converted into a string of cosmopolitan neighborhoods with a bohemian vibe.

Best For: Travelers wanting to look backstage, behind the glittering Paris grandeur.

Drawbacks: You might feel like you're missing out on some of the Paris mythology.

Hotels near République, Bastille, Eastern Paris, Belleville & Northeast Paris (11e, 12e, 19e & 20e)

18e

19e

10e

3e

4e

11e

12e

20e

Cosmos Hotel **5**
Gabriel Paris Marais **4**
Grand Hôtel Doré **7**
Le Général Hotel **3**
Le Pavillon Bastille **7**
Libertel Canal St-Martin **2**
Mama Shelter **8**
Résidence Alhambra **6**
St. Christopher's Inn **1**

MODERATE

Gabriel Paris Marais ★★ 🎁   This chic boutique hotel calls itself Paris's first "detox hotel." The hotel takes an active approach to purifying the bodies of its guests, with an emphasis on restful sleep and healthy food. One example of this is that some accommodations are outfitted with "NightCove," a system that uses sound and light to encourage natural sleeping patterns; the rooms are also sound-proofed to ensure a restful night. You can continue to detox with an organic breakfast and spa treatments in their Bioo Detox Room. Located close to place de la République and the Canal St-Martin, this hotel offers comfortably furnished rooms with modern amenities and stylish lighting that range from small to midsize. In the surrealist but harmoniously decorated "detox bar," guests can order a large choice of antioxidant drinks and teas.

25 rue du Grand-Prieure, 75011 Paris. www.gabrielparismarais.com. ℭ **01-47-00-13-38.** 41 units. 155€–280€ double. AE, DC, MC, V. Métro: République. **Amenities:** Cafeteria; room service; small spa. *In room:* A/C, TV/DVD, hair dryer, minibar, MP3 docking station, Wi-Fi (free).

Grand Hôtel Doré   Deep in the heart of the Daumesnil area, this venerated old hotel has been a Paris tradition since the early 20th century. Today it's been brought into the 21st century with a major restoration and vast improvements, so that once again it is a hotel of charm and character. Some of the past remains visible here, architecturally, but the hotel has been completely modernized. The bedrooms are small to midsize, but each is comfortably furnished and well maintained.

201 av. Daumesnil, 75012 Paris. www.grand-hotel-dore.com. ℭ **01-43-43-66-89.** Fax 01-43-43-65-20. 40 units. 120€–155€ double. AE, MC, V. Métro: Daumesnil. **Amenities:** Babysitting; concierge. *In room:* A/C, TV, minibar, Wi-Fi (free).

Le Général Hotel ★   As the neighborhood around place de la République, Canal St-Martin, and rue Oberkampf becomes increasingly tuned to Paris's sense of counterculture chic, this is a good example of that neighborhood's improving fortunes. Opened within the premises of a run-down hotel that was radically renovated and decorated by noted designer Jean-Philippe Nuel, the hotel's upbeat interior revolves around prominent rectilinear lines, spartan-looking decors, and an intelligent distribution of spaces. The result is a seven-story hotel with floors linked by two separate elevator banks and pale, monochromatic beige-and-off-white color schemes, and with furniture that is either dark (specifically, rosewood-toned) or pale (specifically, birch- or maple-toned).

5–7 rue Rampon, 75011 Paris. www.legeneralhotel.com. ℭ **01-47-00-41-57.** Fax 01-47-00-21-56. 46 units. 157€–252€ double. AE, MC, V. Métro: République. **Amenities:** Bar; exercise room; room service; sauna. *In room:* A/C, TV, hair dryer, Wi-Fi (free).

Le Pavillon Bastille ★   This is a modern boutique hotel in a town house across from the Opéra Bastille, a block south of place de la Bastille. It was completely renovated in 2007 when air-conditioning was installed and the rooms were made soundproof. A 17th-century fountain graces the pretty, sun-filled courtyard. The contemporary but neutral rooms have twin or double beds, partially mirrored walls, and contemporary built-in furniture. In just a few minutes' walk, you can discover the Marais district, the Faubourg Saint-Antoine, and the Opéra Bastille.

65 rue de Lyon, 75012 Paris. www.paris-hotel-pavillonbastille.com. ℭ **01-43-43-65-65.** Fax 01-43-43-96-52. 25 units. 100€–215€ double; 390€ suite. AE, DC, MC, V. Métro: Bastille. **Amenities:** Bar; babysitting; concierge; room service. *In room:* A/C, TV, hair dryer, minibar, Wi-Fi (free).

INEXPENSIVE

Cosmos Hotel 🎁 This no-frills option in the heart of the animated Oberkampf neighborhood has got to be one of the best deals in town. The simply furnished rooms are clean and have fresh towels provided on a daily basis. The staff is helpful, and the hotel is also home to a little furry feline mascot. The only downside is that the hotel can be noisy on the weekends as people spill out of the busy local bars and restaurants.

35 rue Jean-Pierre Timbaud, 75011 Paris. www.cosmos-hotel-paris.com. ✆ **01-43-57-25-88.** Fax 01-43-57-25-88. 36 units. 67€ double; 75€ triple. AE, MC, V. Métro: Parmentier. *In room:* TV, hair dryer, Wi-Fi (free).

Résidence Alhambra Named for the famous cabaret/vaudeville theater that once stood nearby, the Alhambra dates from the 1800s, and it was last renovated in 2006. In the rear garden, where breakfast is served, its two-story chalet offers eight additional guest rooms. The small accommodations are bland but comfortable, each in a dull pastel scheme with white and ocher.

13 rue de Malte, 75011 Paris. www.hotelalhambra.fr. ✆ **01-47-00-35-52.** Fax 01-43-57-98-75. 58 units. 83€–94€ double; 103€–128€ triple. AE, DC, MC, V. Métro: Oberkampf. **Amenities:** Smoke-free rooms; Wi-Fi (free) in lobby. *In room:* TV.

Belleville & Northeast Paris (19e & 20e)

Not many tourists venture to these cosmopolitan areas, located deep in the city's old industrial heartland. But up-and-coming Belleville includes one of the city's Chinatowns, a new wave of contemporary art galleries, and the must-see Buttes Chaumont Park.

Best For: Travelers looking for budget accommodations and those who want to experience a different dimension of the city.

Drawbacks: The Eiffel Tower is quite a hike!

MODERATE

Libertel Canal St-Martin ★ This hotel consists of three small typical Parisian buildings that are connected by a charming courtyard and a small garden. The largest building was entirely renovated in 2008, and the Villa Cosi was renovated in 2010. Though small, guest rooms are clean and contemporary, with flatscreen TVs and Wi-Fi access. Located in the Canal St-Martin neighborhood, the hotel is near some charming shops and restaurants, as well as the beautiful Buttes Chaumont Park; it is also very close to the Jaurès Métro stop. The hotel is entirely nonsmoking.

5 avenue Secrétan, 75019 Paris. www.hotel-canal-st-martin.com. ✆ **01-42-06-62-00**. Fax 01-42-40-64-51. 69 units. 105€–145€ double. Rates include breakfast. MC, V. Métro: Jaurès. **Amenities:** Breakfast room. *In room:* A/C (in most rooms), Wi-Fi (free).

Mama Shelter ★★ 🛎 Even though it's located off the beaten track, this recently opened Philippe Starck–designed hotel nevertheless attracts the in-crowd with its buzzing downstairs restaurant-bar space, sleek design, and high-tech features. The stylish yet simple rooms are equipped with iMac computers, offering on-demand movies, Internet access, and television programs. Plus, the low rates make the rooms a great value. This is a place for the young and hip, and the bar is a local hot spot.

109 rue de Bagnolet, 75020 Paris. www.mamashelter.com. ✆ **01-43-48-48-48**. Fax 01-43-48-48-49. 170 units. 89€–199€ double. Rates include breakfast. MC, V. Free parking. Métro: Gambetta. **Amenities:** Restaurant; bar; babysitting; bicycle rental; concierge. *In room:* A/C, iMac, microwave, minibar, Wi-Fi (free).

INEXPENSIVE

St Christopher's Inn ★ ✦   Located on the picturesque Bassin de la Villette, which connects the Canal St-Martin to the Seine, this massive hostel—opened in 2008—is close to some great bars, cinemas, restaurants, and clubs, and is particularly lovely in summer, when the banks of the canal come to life. The hostel is home to an animated bar called Belushi's.

159 rue Crimée, 75019 Paris. www.st-christophers.co.uk/paris-hostels. ✆ **01-40-34-34-40**. Fax 01-40-34-31-38. www.st-christophers.fr. 70 units. 75€–100€ double. Rates include breakfast. MC, V. Métro: Crimée or Laumière. **Amenities:** Restaurant; bar; bicycle rental. *In room:* Wi-Fi (free).

THE LEFT BANK
Latin Quarter (5e)

This is where it was all happening in May 1968. The Sorbonne University is at the heart of this Left Bank neighborhood, which gets its name from the Latin the students and professors spoke there until the end of the 18th century. To feed those minds, the area also boasts some of the city's best specialty bookshops. This neighborhood dates from the time when the Romans ruled—Paris was conquered by the Romans in 52 B.C.—and the area still conserves Roman ruins, which you can explore at the Cluny Museum.

Best For: Travelers interested in tracing the city's rich history and families grateful for some quiet close to the Luxembourg gardens.
Drawbacks: The vibe might be too bookish for some.

EXPENSIVE

Grand Hôtel Saint-Michel ★   Built in the 19th century, this hotel is larger and more businesslike than many town house–style inns nearby. It basks in the reflected glow of Brazilian dissident Georges Amado, whose memoirs recorded his 2-year sojourn in one of the rooms. The public areas are tasteful, with portraits and rich upholsteries. Improvements have enlarged some rooms, lowering their ceilings and adding amenities, but retained old-fashioned touches such as wrought-iron balconies (on the fifth floor). Triple rooms have an extra bed and are suitable for families, who share a private bathroom with tub and shower. Sixth-floor rooms have views over the rooftops.

19 rue Cujas, 75005 Paris. www.grand-hotel-st-michel.com. ✆ **01-46-33-33-02.** Fax 01-40-46-96-33. 47 units. 320€–400€ double; 450€ suite. AE, DC, MC, V. Métro: Cluny–La Sorbonne. RER: Luxembourg or St-Michel. **Amenities:** Bar; babysitting; exercise room; room service. *In room:* A/C, TV, hair dryer, minibar, Wi-Fi (free).

Hôtel Design De La Sorbonne ★★   Located near the Sorbonne University and a short walk from the Luxembourg Gardens, this boutique hotel is stylish and comfortable. Though small, guest rooms are sleek and trendy, and are decorated in bold colors and patterns; rooms feature new bathrooms and modern amenities such as Apple iMac computers. The owners, who manage several other quality hotels in Paris, demonstrate inventiveness through the hotel

Hotels in the Latin Quarter
& Southern Paris (5e & 13e)

Best Western La Tour Notre Dame 1
Familia-Hôtel 9
The Five Hotel 15
Grand Hôtel Saint-Michel 3
Hôtel Agora St-Germain 7
Hôtel des Grandes Ecoles 12
Hôtel Design De La Sorbonne 2
Hôtel des Jardins du Luxembourg 11
Hôtel du Vert Galant 16
Hôtel La Manufacture 17
Hôtel Moderne Saint-Germain 5
Hôtel Quartier Latin 10
Hôtel Résidence Saint-Christophe 13

Hotel Seven 14
Hôtel St-Jacques 4
Hôtel Sully Saint-Germain 6
Minerve Hôtel 8

design—look down at the floor to read excerpts from French literary classics woven into the hotel's carpets. The hotel is smoke-free.

6 rue Victor Cousin,75005 Paris. www.hotelsorbonne.com. ℂ **01-43-54-58-08.** Fax 01-40-51-05-18. 38 units. 250€–340€ double. AE, DC, MC, V. Métro: Cluny–La Sorbonne. RER: Luxembourg. **Amenities:** Breakfast room. *In room:* A/C, TV, Apple iMac, hair dryer, minibar, Wi-Fi (free).

Hotel Seven ★★   Run by the same team as The Five Hotel (see below), this luxury concept hotel is not for the fainthearted, taking the commitment to exceptional interiors a step beyond. Each room and suite is totally unique, with evocative names like Marie Antoinette, The Black Diamond, and On/Off; in the Levitation rooms, the bed is actually suspended off the floor. Each room is well appointed, and might include a complimentary bottle of champagne, an iPod docking base, an espresso machine, a large flatscreen TV, luxurious beds and linens, and designer bath products. Couples looking for a romantic setting will enjoy this hotel. The only downside is the slightly off-the-beaten path location.

20 rue Berthollet, 75005 Paris. www.sevenhotelparis.com. ℂ **01-43-31-47-52.** Fax 01-43-36-41-40. 37 units. 327€–397€ double; 737€–1,107€ suite. AE, DC, MC, V. Métro: Les Gobelins. **Amenities:** Bar, breakfast room, room service. *In room:* A/C, TV, iPod dock, hair dryer, minibar, Wi-Fi (free).

MODERATE

Best Western La Tour Notre-Dame ★   In the heart of the Sorbonne district, this restored Latin Quarter hotel rises seven floors over a 17th-century vaulted cellar where breakfast is served. A hotel of Rive Gauche character, it is ideally situated for Left Bank living, lying between St-Germain-des-Prés and the cathedral of Notre-Dame, opposite the Sorbonne and the Cluny Museum. Bedrooms, many with exposed beams, have been given a decorator's touch, and they are adorned with certain romantic accents. Liberty prints and Empire-era furniture decorate many of the bedrooms, which are beautifully maintained. A Vélib' bike rental station is located just outside the front door.

20 rue du Sommerard, 75005 Paris. www.la-tour-notre-dame.com. ℂ **01-43-54-47-60.** Fax 01-43-26-42-34. 48 units. 171€–245€ double. AE, DC, MC, V. Métro: Cluny–Sorbonne. RER: Saint-Michel or Notre-Dame. **Amenities:** Bar. *In room:* A/C, TV, hair dryer, minibar, Wi-Fi (free).

The Five Hotel ★ 👜   A charmer among Left Bank boutique hotels, the Five is named for the 5th arrondissement and lies in a restored 1800s town house on a U-shaped street off boulevard de Port-Royal. The funky interior design is not to everyone's taste, including a red leather paneled hall or a red-painted gas fireplace. The rooms are individually designed in various colors (blood red or Halloween orange, for example), and tiny white lights evoke a planetarium. Of course, if you want a room the color of a prune, that too is available. A Chinese lacquer artist, Isabelle Emmerique, has certainly been busy here. Some rooms are small, but all the beds are exceedingly comfortable.

3 rue Flatters, Paris 75005. www.thefivehotel.com. ℂ **01-43-31-74-21.** Fax 01-43-31-61-96. 24 units. 202€–340€ double; 392€ suite. AE, MC, V. Métro: Bastille or Gobelins. **Amenities:** Bar; room service. *In room:* A/C, TV, hair dryer, Wi-Fi (free).

Hôtel Agora St-Germain   This unpretentious hotel occupies a building constructed in the early 1600s to house a group of guardsmen protecting the brother of the king at his lodgings nearby. It's in the heart of artistic/historic Paris and offers compact, soundproof guest rooms that have been sensitively renovated. All but seven of the bedrooms have tub/shower combinations; the rest have only showers.

42 rue des Bernardins, 75005 Paris. www.agorasaintgermain.com. ☏ **01-46-34-13-00.** Fax 01-46-34-75-05. 39 units. 240€–350€ double. AE, DC, MC, V. Parking 25€. Métro: Maubert-Mutualité. **Amenities:** Room service. *In room:* A/C, TV, hair dryer, minibar, Wi-Fi (free).

Hôtel des Jardins du Luxembourg Built during Baron Haussmann's 19th-century overhaul of Paris, this hotel boasts an imposing facade of honey-colored stone accented with ornate iron balconies. Sigmund Freud stayed here in 1885. The interior is outfitted in strong, clean lines, often with groupings of Art Deco furnishings. The high-ceilinged guest rooms, some with Provençal tiles and ornate moldings, are well maintained, the sizes ranging from small to medium. Best of all, they overlook a quiet dead-end alley, ensuring relatively peaceful nights. Some have balconies overlooking the rooftops.

5 Impasse Royer-Collard, 75005 Paris. www.les-jardins-du-luxembourg.com. ☏ **01-40-46-08-88.** Fax 01-40-46-02-28. 26 units. 120€–175€ double. AE, DC, MC, V. Métro: Cluny–La Sorbonne. RER: Luxembourg. **Amenities:** Bar; babysitting; room service. *In room:* A/C, TV, hair dryer, mini-bar, Wi-Fi (10€ for 3 hr.).

Hôtel Quartier Latin Between the Sorbonne and the Musée de Cluny, this hotel captures the flavor of the Paris literati better than any other in Paris. Its original decor was conceived in 1997 by Didier Gomez, who referred to it as "contemporary with cultural references." That means walls stenciled with passages from Victor Hugo or photographs of Colette and André Gide. Even the breakfast room is stocked with bookshelves and its ceiling inscribed with quotes from Baudelaire. Bibliomania continues in the lobby, which is filled with floor-to-ceiling bookcases. Bedrooms are decorated comfortably and tastefully in blue and white, with such delicacies as linen curtains, along with fine wood furnishings, plus white-tiled bathrooms. In all, this is a "novel" hotel and ideal for bookworms.

9 rue des Ecoles, 75005 Paris. www.hotelquartierlatin.com. ☏ **01-44-27-06-45.** Fax 01-43-25-36-70. 29 units. 187€–248€ double; 242€–310€ junior suite. AE, MC, V. Métro: Cardinal Lemoine. Parking nearby: 20€. **Amenities:** Babysitting; room service. *In room:* A/C, TV, hair dryer, minibar, Wi-Fi (free).

Hôtel St-Jacques ★ 🛏 Try for a room with a balcony view of Notre-Dame and the Panthéon. The Belle Époque atmosphere of the hotel was made famous in the movie *Charade* (1963), which starred Cary Grant and Audrey Hepburn. Jean-Paul and Martine Rousseau, the owners, welcome you to this old-fashioned Latin Quarter gem, filled with Second Empire overtones, including frescoes in the breakfast room and lounge, 18th-century ceiling murals in some of the bedrooms, wedding cake plasterwork, and corridors painted with *trompe l'oeil* marble. Bedrooms are generally spacious and have been attractively and comfortably restored. Street-side rooms can be a bit noisy.

35 rue des Ecoles, 75005 Paris. www.paris-hotel-stjacques.com. ☏ **01-44-07-45-45.** Fax 01-43-25-65-50. 26 units. 142€–247€ double; 176€ triple. AE, DC, MC, V. Métro: Maubert-Mutualité. **Amenities:** Babysitting. *In room:* A/C TV, hair dryer, Wi-Fi (free).

Hôtel Sully Saint-Germain With its medieval-style decoration and its numerous antiques, this hotel is a reliable Left Bank choice with a bit of charm. At your doorstep are some of Paris's major attractions, including Notre-Dame, Cluny Abbey, the banks of the Seine, and even the Louvre and Orsay museums. The public rooms are not overly adorned but are furnished with taste and comfort in mind. The midsize bedrooms, with brass beds set against stone walls, are fairly basic but comfortable, and imbued with a touch of Parisian charisma.

31 rue des Ecoles, 75005 Paris. www.hotel-paris-sully.com. ✆ **01-43-26-56-02.** Fax 01-43-29-74-42. 61 units. 165€–200€ double; 240€ junior suite. AE, DC, MC, V. Métro: Maubert-Mutualité. Parking 26€. **Amenities:** Bar; exercise room; room service; sauna and steam bath. *In room:* A/C, TV, hair dryer, minibar, Wi-Fi (free).

Minerve Hôtel   This is a well-managed, government-rated, three-star hotel in the heart of the Latin Quarter, with good-size, comfortable rooms and a staff with a sense of humor. The comfortable bedrooms have old-fashioned mahogany furniture and walls covered in fabric. Try for one of 10 rooms with balconies where you can look out over Notre-Dame. Depending on your room assignment, bathrooms range in dimension from cramped to midsize. Street-side rooms have sweet wrought-iron decorations in front of the window, hung with geranium-filled garden boxes.

13 rue des Ecoles, 75005 Paris. www.hotel-paris-minerve.com. ✆ **01-43-26-26-04.** Fax 01-44-07-01-96. 54 units. 126€–165€ double; 165€ triple. AE, DC, MC, V. Métro: Cardinal Lemoine. Parking 20€. **Amenities:** Breakfast room, room service, Wi-Fi (in lobby). *In room:* A/C, TV, hair dryer.

INEXPENSIVE

Familia Hôtel   As the name implies, this quaint little hotel has been family run for decades. Many personal touches make the place unique. Finely executed sepia-colored frescoes of Parisian scenes grace the walls of 14 rooms. The rooms and the bathrooms are quite small; try and book one or the eight units with restored stone walls. Seven rooms boast balconies that are adorned with red geraniums and look out over the Latin Quarter and Notre-Dame. All the rooms feature flat-screen TVs and lovely custom-made carved wooden head boards or canopy beds. Eight units have restored stone walls, and seven boast balconies with delightful views over the Latin Quarter and Notre-Dame. A basic but tasty continental breakfast is included in the room rate.

11 rue des Ecoles, 75005 Paris. www.familiahotel.com. ✆ **01-43-54-55-27.** Fax 01-43-29-61-77. 30 units. 97€–117€ double; 160€ triple; 176€ quad. Rates include breakfast. Parking 20€. AE, DC, MC, V. Métro: Jussieu or Maubert-Mutualité. **Amenities:** Breakfast room. *In room:* TV, hair dryer, minibar, Wi-Fi (free).

Hôtel des Grandes Ecoles ★★ ✐   Few hotels in the neighborhood offer so much low-key charm at such reasonable prices. It's composed of a trio of high-ceilinged buildings, interconnected via a sheltered courtyard, where in warm weather, singing birds provide a worthy substitute for the TVs deliberately missing from the rooms. Accommodations, as reflected by the price, range from snug, cozy doubles to more spacious chambers. Each room is comfortable, but with a lot of luggage, the very smallest would be cramped. The decor is old-fashioned, with feminine touches such as flowered upholsteries and ruffles. Many have views of a garden where trellises and flower beds evoke the countryside.

75 rue de Cardinal-Lemoine, 75005 Paris. www.hotel-grandes-ecoles.com. ✆ **01-43-26-79-23.** Fax 01-47-47-65-48. 51 units. 115€–140€ double. Extra bed 20€. MC, V. Parking 30€. Métro: Cardinal Lemoine, Jussieu, or Place Monge. RER: Port-Royal, Luxembourg. **Amenities:** Babysitting; room service. *In room:* Hair dryer, Wi-Fi (free).

Hôtel Moderne Saint-Germain ✦ In the heart of the Latin Quarter, between the Panthéon and Saint-Michel, the Hôtel Moderne is one of the neighborhood's better three-star hotels. Its charming owner, Mr. Gibon, welcomes guests to his hotel and prides himself on its unique, futuristic decor, especially evident in the lobby and breakfast room. In the units fronting rue des Ecoles, double-glazed windows muffle the traffic noise.

33 rue des Ecoles, 75005 Paris. www.hotel-paris-stgermain.com. ✆ **01-43-54-37-78.** Fax 01-43-29-91-31. 45 units. 150€ double; 180€ triple. AE, DC, MC, V. Parking 26€. Métro: Maubert-Mutualité. **Amenities:** Exercise room; room service. *In room:* A/C, TV, hair dryer, minibar, Wi-Fi (free).

Hôtel-Résidence Saint-Christophe This hotel, in one of the Latin Quarter's undiscovered areas, offers a gracious English-speaking staff. It was created in 1987, when an older hotel was connected to a butcher shop. All the small- to medium-size rooms have Louis XV–style furniture.

17 rue Lacépède, 75005 Paris. www.charm-hotel-paris.com. ✆ **01-43-31-81-54.** Fax 01-43-31-12-54. 31 units. 130€ double. AE, DC, MC, V. Parking 24€. Métro: Place Monge. **Amenities:** Breakfast room. *In room:* TV, hair dryer, minibar, Wi-Fi (free).

St-Germain-des-Prés & Luxembourg (6e)

This glamorous neighborhood is home to great shops and cafes. Intellectuals such as Simone de Beauvoir and Jean-Paul Sartre put St-Germain on the map postwar, when they and their friends had high-minded conversations at such cafes as Les Deux Magots or the Café de Flore. The area still draws many of the city's artists and thinkers, and most of the modern art galleries are here too.

Best For: Travelers hoping to bump in to Catherine Deneuve.
Drawbacks: The lack of budget accommodations and the competition for sidewalk space between the tourists and fanatical shoppers.

VERY EXPENSIVE

Hotel Bel-Ami ★★ 🛎 This four-star hotel was designed expressly to appeal to fashion-conscious patrons in the heart of the Left Bank cafe district. Its name translates as "handsome (male) friend." You'll get the feeling that this is an arts-conscious hotel whose minimalist public areas were built only after months of careful design by a team of trend-following architects. Expect color schemes of lilac walls, acid-green sofas, copper-colored tiles, bleached ash, and industrial-style lighting fixtures. Bedrooms contain a palette of earth tones, such as pistachio ice cream or pumpkin pie, and an almost aggressively minimalist, even cubist, design. Bathrooms are artfully spartan. The suites and first-floor rooms have all been recently renovated.

7–11 rue St. Benoît, 75006 Paris. www.hotel-bel-ami.com. ✆ **01-42-61-53-53.** Fax 01-49-27-09-33. 112 units. 425€ double; 1,050€ suite. AE, DC, MC, V. Métro: St-Germain-des-Prés. **Amenities:** Bar; concierge; espresso bar; exercise room. *In room:* TV, minibar, Wi-Fi (free).

Hôtel d'Aubusson ★★ This mansion in the heart of St-Germain-des-Prés was the site of the city's first literary salon. Fully restored, it is today one of the best luxe boutique hotels in Paris. Lying 2 blocks south of Pont Neuf and the Seine, the hotel has taken over a former private residence from the 1600s, to which is attached a 1950s building. You enter a grand hall under a beamed ceiling with a baronial fireplace, original Aubusson tapestries, and furnishings in the style of Louis XV. There are also a number of smaller, more intimate lounges. The bedrooms are midsize to large, each attractively and comfortably furnished, often in a Directoire style and sometimes with exposed ceiling beams. Antiques are often placed in front of the original stone walls. For the most traditional flair, ask for one of the rooms on the top two floors. Bathrooms are stocked with Hermès toiletries.

33 rue Dauphine, Paris 75006. www.hoteldaubusson.com. ✆ **01-43-29-43-43.** Fax 01-43-29-12-62. 49 units. 305€–490€ double; 465€ suite. AE, DC, MC, V. Parking 25€. Métro: Odéon. **Amenities:** Bar; cafe; babysitting; room service. *In room:* A/C, TV, hair dryer, minibar, Wi-Fi (free).

Relais Christine ★★   This hotel welcomes you into a former 16th-century Augustinian cloister. From a cobblestone street, you enter a symmetrical courtyard and find an elegant reception area with sculpture and Renaissance antiques. Each room is uniquely decorated with wooden beams and Louis XIII–style furnishings; the rooms come in a range of styles and shapes. Some are among the Left Bank's largest, with extras such as mirrored closets, plush carpets, and some balconies facing the courtyard. The least attractive rooms are in the interior. Bed configurations vary, but all mattresses are on the soft side, offering comfort with quality linens.

3 rue Christine, 75006 Paris. www.relais-christine.com. ✆ **01-40-51-60-80.** Fax 01-40-51-60-81. 51 units. 390€–500€ double; 580€–900€ duplex or suite. AE, DC, MC, V. Free parking. Métro: Odéon or St-Michel. **Amenities:** Bar; babysitting; concierge; exercise room; room service; spa. *In room:* A/C, TV, TV/DVD, hair dryer, minibar, Wi-Fi (free).

EXPENSIVE

Hôtel de Fleurie ★ ☺   Off the boulevard St-Germain on a colorful little street, the Fleurie is one of the best of the city's updated old hotels; its statuary-studded facade recaptures 17th-century elegance, and the stone walls in the salon have been exposed. Many of the guest rooms have elaborate draperies and antique reproductions. Because some rooms are larger than others and contain an extra bed for one or two children, the hotel has long been a family favorite.

32–34 rue Grégoire-de-Tours, 75006 Paris. www.fleurie-hotel-paris.com. ✆ **01-53-73-70-00.** Fax 01-53-73-70-20. 29 units. 250€–320€ double; 465€ family room. Children 12 and under stay free in parent's room. AE, DC, MC, V. Métro: Odéon or Mabillon. **Amenities:** Bar; babysitting; room service; Wi-Fi (free). *In room:* A/C, TV, hair dryer, minibar, Wi-Fi (free).

Hôtel de l'Abbaye Saint-Germain ★   This is one of the district's most charming boutique hotels, built as a convent in the early 18th century. Its brightly colored rooms have traditional furniture, plus touches of sophisticated flair. In front is a small garden and in back is a verdant courtyard with a fountain, raised flower beds, and masses of ivy and climbing vines. If you don't mind the expense, one of the most charming rooms has a terrace overlooking the upper floors of neighboring buildings. Guest rooms are midsize to large and are continually maintained. Suites are large and full of Left Bank charm, often with antique reproductions.

10 rue Cassette, 75006 Paris. www.hotelabbayeparis.com. ✆ **01-45-44-38-11.** Fax 01-45-48-07-86. 44 units. 240€–352€ double; 442€–498€ suite. Rates include breakfast. AE, MC, V. Métro: St-Sulpice. **Amenities:** Bar; room service. *In room:* A/C, TV, hair dryer, Wi-Fi (free).

Hotels in St-Germain-des-Prés, Luxembourg & Montparnasse (6e & 14e)

Hotel La Belle Juliette ★★ 🎁 This luxury hotel, which opened in Saint-Germain-des-Prés in 2011, stands out for its chic interior design by local textile designer Anne Gelbard. The hotel is inspired by the life of Juliette Récamier, a 19th-century French socialite whose Parisian salon drew intellectuals and artists. Guest rooms feel very contemporary while still paying homage to the 19th century and Madame Récamier, with sophisticated color combinations, luxurious fabrics, original engravings, and restored antiques. Yet the rooms are also completely modern, with Apple iMac computers for entertainment.

92 rue du Cherche Midi, 75006 Paris. www.hotel-belle-juliette-paris.com. ℂ **01-42-22-97-40.** Fax 01-45-44-89-97. 34 units. 300€–450€ double; 620€–1,050€ suite. AE, DC, MC, V. Métro: St-Germain-des-Prés. **Amenities:** Bar; restaurant, room service, spa. *In room:* A/C, iMac, hair dryer, minibar, Wi-Fi (free).

Hôtel Le Sainte-Beuve ★ 🎁 Lying off the tree-lined boulevard Raspail, this quiet and charming Montparnasse choice is close to the "Lost Generation" cafés made famous in the pages of Ernest Hemingway's *The Sun Also Rises*. If you stay here, you're just 3 minutes from the Luxembourg Gardens. You enter a small reception area opening into a Georgian parlor with plush sofas, armchairs, columns, and even a marble fireplace for those nippy Paris nights. Bedrooms are often furnished in part with antiques, but have all the modern comforts. The cheaper rooms are small. If you can afford it, ask for one of the deluxe units that also has love seats and safes.

9 rue St-Beuve, 75006 Paris. www.hotel-sainte-beuve.fr. ℂ **01-45-48-20-07.** Fax 01-45-48-67-52. 22 units. 185€–315€ double; 365€ junior suite. AE, DC, MC, V. Métro: Notre-Dame-des-Champs or Vavin. **Amenities:** Bar; babysitting; room service. *In room:* A/C, TV, hair dryer, minibar, Wi-Fi (free).

Hôtel Le Six ★ 🎁 This boutique hotel is a bastion of restrained charm and low-key luxury with harmonious tones and soft lighting. Its major feature is an elegant spa offering the same products as the swank Ritz Hotel. The staff promises to leave you "gorgeous." Sturdy oak furnishings and autumnal colors fill the hotel; the best accommodations are the upper suites, opening onto views of the skyline of Paris. But all the accommodations are imbued with a high comfort level, made all the more so by the soundproofing. Guests gather in the library and lounge, sheltered under a glass roof and evoking a winter garden.

14 rue Stanislas, 75006 Paris. www.hotel-le-six.com. ℂ **01-42-22-00-75.** Fax 01-42-22-00-95. 41 units. 300€–450€ double; 402€–600€ junior suite; 700€ suite. AE, DC, MC, V. Métro: Notre-Dame-des-Champs or Vavin. **Amenities:** Room service; spa. *In room:* A/C, TV, minibar, Wi-Fi (free).

Hôtel Luxembourg Parc ★★ Near the Luxembourg Gardens for those lovely strolls, this elegant bastion of fine living has been called a small-scale version of the swank Hôtel de Crillon. In one of the Left Bank's most charming and historic districts, a 17th-century palace has been beautifully restored and decorated. The bedrooms are decorated in the styles of Louis XV, Louis XVI, and Napoleon III. The bar is an elegant rendezvous point and the library is relaxing. Bathrooms are generous in size, and units contain such thoughtful touches as bathrobes and plenty of hangers. The around-the-clock room service is actually takeout from nearby restaurants. The breakfast room on the ground floor overlooks the Luxembourg Gardens.

42 rue de Vaugirard, 75006 Paris. www.luxembourg-paris-hotel.com. ℂ **01-53-10-36-50.** Fax 01-53-10-36-59. 23 units. 290€–365€ double; 495€ suite. AE, DC, MC, V. Métro: Luxembourg. **Amenities:** Bar; exercise room; room service. *In room:* A/C, TV, hair dryer, minibar, Wi-Fi (free).

L'Apostrophe ★ 🎁 This Rive Gauche boutique hotel lies near the Café de Flore and Café des Deux-Magots, once the favorite literary haunts of some of France's most celebrated writers. This hotel pays homage to that tradition, becoming the first Parisian "poem hotel," an establishment devoted to the aesthetic, beauty, and mystery of writing. On the ground floor is painted the story of *One Thousand and One Nights*. The first floor is devoted to the markings that predate writing. On the second floor are signs indicating the alphabet, calligraphy, and music. The third floor is devoted to books and posters. A stay here is like no other in Paris. Bedrooms are beautifully decorated and comfortable, though a bit small. Be aware that the shower and water basin are actually in the room—the shower is visible through a glass door, but the toilet is in its own room.

3 rue de Chevreuse, 75006 Paris. www.apostrophe-hotel.com. (✆) **01-56-54-31-31.** 16 units. 149€–290€ standard double; 199€–350€ double with a Jacuzzi. Métro: Vavin. **Amenities:** Bar. *In room:* A/C, TV/DVD, CD player, hair dryer, Wi-Fi (free)

L'Hôtel ★ Ranking just a notch below the Relais Christine (see above), this is one of the Left Bank's most charming boutique hotels. It was once a 19th-century fleabag whose major distinction was that Oscar Wilde died in one of its bedrooms, but today's guests aren't anywhere near destitution. Guest rooms vary in size, style, and price; all have decorative fireplaces and fabric-covered walls. All the sumptuous beds have tasteful fabrics and crisp linens. About half the bathrooms are small, tubless nooks. Room themes reflect China, Russia, Japan, India, or high-camp Victorian. The Cardinal room is all scarlet, the Viollet-le-Duc room is neo-Gothic, and the room where Wilde died is Victorian.

13 rue des Beaux-Arts, 75006 Paris. www.l-hotel.com. (✆) **01-44-41-99-00.** Fax 01-43-25-64-81. 20 units. 280€–370€ double; 640€–740€ suite. AE, DC, MC, V. Métro: St-Germain-des-Prés. **Amenities:** Restaurant, bar; babysitting; room service. *In room:* A/C, TV, TV/DVD, hair dryer, mini bar, Wi-Fi (free).

Le Placide ★★ 🎁 Converted from a former family home in the 19th century, Le Placide has the aura of a private club. This small boutique hotel—there are only two rooms per floor—lies just steps from the chic Bon Marché Department Store. It was designed by a member of Philippe Starck's firm, who brought a 21st-century style of luxury and comfort to the interior, featuring white Moroccan leather, lots of glass, a bit of chrome, and a crystal pedestal table. Fresh flowers adorn each room, and rose petals are placed on your bed at night. The spacious bathrooms provide natural light.

6 rue St-Placide, 75006 Paris. www.leplacidehotel.com. (✆) **01-42-84-34-60.** 11 units. 215€–450€ double. AE, MC, V. Métro: St-Placide. **Amenities:** Bar. *In room:* A/C, TV, TV/DVD, CD player, hair dryer, minibar, MP3 docking station, Wi-Fi (free).

Relais St-Germain ★★ 🎁 It's difficult to exaggerate the charm of this deeply personalized and intimate hotel created from side-by-side 17th-century town houses. You'll navigate your way through a labyrinth of narrow and winding hallways to soundproofed bedrooms that are spacious, and artfully and individually decorated in a style that evokes late-19th-century Paris at its most sensual. Two of the rooms have terraces. Come here for a discreet escape from the anonymity of larger, less personalized hotels, and for an injection of boutique-style Parisian charm. Even *Vogue* magazine referred to this place as "an oasis of Left Bank charm." We heartily agree. The owner of the hotel is one of the city's best chefs;

hotel guests have priority booking at the attached restaurant, Le Comptoir, where Parisians often wait 6 months for a reservation.

9 Carrefour de l'Odéon, 75006 Paris. www.hotelrsg.com. ✆ **01-43-29-12-05.** Fax 01-46-33-45-30. 22 units. 285€–370€ double; 395€ suite. Rates include breakfast. AE, DC, MC, V. **Amenities:** Restaurant. *In room:* A/C, TV, TV/DVD, hair dryer, minibar, Wi-Fi (free).

Villa Madame ★   In the heart of St-Germain-des-Prés, this hotel is a smart Left Bank address in a neighborhood of tiny boutiques and fashionable hair salons, just a short walk from Jardin du Luxembourg. The bedrooms are sleek and modern with the latest gadgets. We prefer the accommodations on the top floor, with their balconies overlooking the rooftops of Paris. There is an inside courtyard, where you can order breakfast or else drinks in the evening. The Big Salon is actually a tearoom with a fireplace.

44 rue Madame, 75006 Paris. www.hotelvillamadameparis.com. ✆ **01-45-48-02-81.** Fax 01-45-44-85-73. 28 units. 225€–325€ double; 505€ suite. AE, DC, MC. Métro: Rennes or St-Sulpice. RER: Luxembourg. *In room:* A/C, TV, minibar, Wi-Fi (free).

MODERATE

Grand Hôtel des Balcons   The Corroyer-André family welcome you to this restored 19th-century building, once patronized by Baudelaire and the poets Henri Michaux and Endré Ady. You enter an Art Nouveau setting with stained-glass windows and tulip-shaped molten glass lamps and chandeliers. The hotel lies behind a restored facade studded with small balconies—hence, its name. Bedrooms are not only affordable, but also harmonious in decor and comfort. Close to the gardens of Luxembourg, the rooms are not large but ample enough for big closets and full-length dressing mirrors.

3 Casimir Delavigne, 75006 Paris. www.balcons.com. ✆ **01-46-34-78-50.** Fax 01-46-34-06-27. 50 units. 125€ double; 220€ triple or quad. AE, MC, V. Métro: Odéon. RER: Luxembourg. *In room:* TV, hair dryer, Wi-Fi (5€ per day).

Hôtel Delavigne   Despite modernization, you still get a sense of the 18th-century origins of the building, which is next to the Luxembourg Gardens. The public areas reveal a rustic use of chiseled stone, some of it original. The high-ceilinged guest rooms are tasteful, sometimes with wooden furniture, Spanish-style wrought iron, and upholstered headboards.

1 rue Casimir Delavigne, 75006 Paris. www.hoteldelavigne.com. ✆ **01-43-29-31-50.** Fax 01-43-29-78-56. 34 units. 160€–230€ double; 230€ triple. AE (accepted for Internet reservations only), MC, V. Métro: Odéon. **Amenities:** Babysitting; concierge; room service. *In room:* TV, hair dryer, Wi-Fi (free).

Hôtel des Deux Continents   Built from three interconnected historic buildings, each between three and six stories high, this hotel is a reliable choice with a sense of Latin Quarter style. The carefully coordinated guest rooms range from small to medium size and include reproductions of antique furnishings and soundproof, upholstered walls.

25 rue Jacob, 75006 Paris. www.2continents-hotel.com. ✆ **01-43-26-72-46.** Fax 01-43-25-67-80. 41 units. 185€ double; 230€ triple. MC, V. Métro: St-Germain-des-Prés. *In room:* A/C, TV, hair dryer, Wi-Fi (8€).

Hôtel des Marronniers   In the heart of St-Germain-des-Prés, this is one of those hidden gems that is nestled in the back of a courtyard on a street lined with antiques stores. At the rear of this "secret" address is a small garden with a veranda, where you can linger over afternoon tea. Some of the rooms open onto views of the steeple of the church of St-Germain-des-Prés. The midsize bedrooms are furnished with period pieces placed under exposed beams and enveloped by fabric-covered walls in rich tones.

21 rue Jacob, 75006 Paris. www.paris-hotel-marroniers.com ✆ **01-43-25-30-60.** Fax 01-40-46-83-56. 37 units. 180€–195€ double. MC, V. Métro: St-Germain-des-Prés. *In room:* A/C, TV, hair dryer, Wi-Fi (free).

Hôtel Le Clément ★   This charming two-star hotel sits on a narrow street within sight of the towers of St-Sulpice church. The building dates from the 1700s, but was renovated several years ago. Rooms are comfortably furnished, with elegant upholstered walls, but many are small.

6 rue Clément, 75006 Paris. www.hotelclementparis.com. ✆ **01-43-26-53-60.** Fax 01-44-07-06-83. 28 units. 126€–148€ double; 165€ suite. AF, DC, MC, V. Métro: Mabillon. **Amenities:** Bar; room service. *In room:* A/C, TV, fax, hair dryer, Wi-Fi (12€ for 2 hr.).

Hôtel Louis II ★   In an 18th-century building on the rue St-Sulpice, this elegant boutique hotel offers guest rooms decorated in modern French tones. Afternoon drinks and morning coffee are served in the reception salon, where gilt-framed mirrors, fresh flowers, and antiques radiate a provincial aura, as though something out of Proust. The generally small, soundproof rooms with exposed beams and lace bedding complete the impression. Many visitors ask for the romantic attic rooms.

2 rue St-Sulpice, 75006 Paris. www.hotel-louis2.com. ✆ **01-46-33-13-80.** Fax 01-46-33-17-29. 22 units. 195€–220€ double; 310€ junior suite. AE, DC, MC, V. Métro: Odéon. **Amenities:** Bar; room service. *In room:* A/C, TV, hair dryer, minibar, Wi-Fi (free).

Hôtel Pas-de-Calais   The Pas-de-Calais dates from the 17th century. It retains its elegant facade, with wooden doors. Novelist Chateaubriand lived here from 1811 to 1814, but its most famous guest was Jean-Paul Sartre, who struggled with the play *Les Mains Sales (Dirty Hands)* in room no. 41. The hotel is a bit weak on style, but as one longtime guest confided, "We still stay here for the memories." Rooms are small; inner units surround a courtyard with two garden tables and several trellises. From January until the end of March, the hotel often grants substantial discounts.

59 rue des Sts-Pères, 75006 Paris. www.hotelpasdecalais.com. ✆ **01-45-48-78-74.** Fax 01-45-44-94-57. 38 units. 180€–255€ double; 315€ suite. AE, DC, MC, V. Parking 25€. Métro: St-Germain-des-Prés or Sèvres-Babylone. **Amenities:** Bar; babysitting; room service. *In room:* A/C, TV, hair dryer, Wi-Fi (free).

La Villa St Germain ★   This hotel's facade resembles those of many of the other buildings in the neighborhood. Inside, however, the decor is a minimalist ultramodern creation rejecting traditional French aesthetics. The public areas and guest rooms contain Bauhaus-like furniture; the lobby's angular lines are softened with bouquets of leaves and flowers. Most unusual are the tubs, with decidedly postmodern stainless steel and pink, black, or beige marble.

29 rue Jacob, 75006 Paris. www.villa-saintgermain.com. ✆ **01-43-26-60-00.** Fax 01-46-34-63-63. 31 units. 160€–370€ double; from 470€ suite. AE, DC, MC, V. Métro: St-Germain-des-Prés. **Amenities:** Bar; babysitting; room service. *In room:* A/C, TV, hair dryer, minibar, Wi-Fi (5€ per day).

Prince de Condé   In the heart of St-Germain-des-Prés, with all its art galleries, this 18th-century building has been restored and turned into the epitome of Left Bank charm. Guests gather in the elegant lounge with its cozy ambience, carved stone walls, and arches. The wallpapered bedrooms, small to midsize, are comfortably furnished and intimate, each tidily maintained with double-glazed windows.

39 rue de Seine, 75006 Paris. www.prince-de-conde.com. ✆ **01-43-26-71-56.** Fax 01-46-34-27-95. 11 units. 146€–234€ double; 280€ suite. AE, MC, V. Métro: St-Germain-des-Prés. *In room:* A/C, TV, hair dryer, minibar, Wi-Fi (free).

INEXPENSIVE

Hotel Mayet ★ 🏨   This budget hotel has a great location close to shopping heaven Le Bon Marché and St-Germain. The compact rooms are clean, comfortable, and contemporary, designed in a bordeaux and gray color scheme. The low-key lobby sets the scene: deep, comfortable sofas are set against a brightly painted wall with some original graffiti by Parisian artist André. There's an iMac computer in the lobby with Internet access. Service goes the extra mile.

3 rue Mayet, 75006 Paris. www.mayet.com. ✆ **01-47-83-21-35**. Fax 01-40-65-95-78. 23 units. 130€–150€ double. Rates include breakfast. AE, DC, MC, V. Métro: Duroc. **Amenities:** Bar, breakfast room. *In room:* A/C, minibar, TV, Wi-Fi (free).

Eiffel Tower & Nearby (7e)

Running along the Seine on the Left Bank, from the Musée d'Orsay to the Eiffel Tower and opposite the Louvre, this elegant residential neighborhood counts Monsieur Karl Lagerfeld as one of its well-heeled inhabitants.

Best For: Its proximity to major monuments and museums.
Drawbacks: Can be a touch bourgeois for some.

VERY EXPENSIVE

Hôtel Montalembert ★★   The elegant Montalembert dates from 1926, when it was built in the Beaux Arts style. Its beige, cream, and gold decor borrows elements of Bauhaus and postmodern design. The guest rooms are spacious except for some standard doubles that are small unless you're a very thin model. Frette linens decorate roomy beds topped with cabana-stripe duvets that crown deluxe French mattresses, and bathrooms boast L'Occitane products.

3 rue de Montalembert, 75007 Paris. www.montalembert.com. ✆ **800/786-6397** in the U.S. and Canada, or 01-45-49-68-68. Fax 01-45-49-69-49. 56 units. 300€–520€ double; 650€–900€ suite. AE, DC, MC, V. Parking 33€. Métro: rue du Bac. **Amenities:** Restaurant; bar; concierge; access to nearby health club; room service. *In room:* A/C, TV, hair dryer, minibar, Wi-Fi (29€).

EXPENSIVE

Bourgogne & Montana ★   Across from the Palais Bourbon and just 2 blocks from the Seine, this boutique hotel dates from 1791. A 1924 cage elevator takes visitors to the accommodations, which are midsize for the most part, although some are small and have no view whatsoever. Two of the bedrooms open onto the Grand Palais or the Assemblée Nationale. Each room is individually decorated, often in Empire style or with Empire reproductions. The fifth and sixth floors were recently renovated.

Hotels near the Eiffel Tower (7 & 15e)

Bourgogne & Montana **1**
Derby Eiffel **10**
Eiffel Seine **12**
Hôtel de l'Académie **7**

Hôtel de l'Université **5**
Hôtel de Londres Eiffel **11**
Hôtel du Palais Bourbon **8**
Hôtel du Quai Voltaire **3**

Hôtel Le Bellechasse **2**
Hôtel Le Tourville **9**
Hôtel Montalembert **6**
Hôtel Verneuil **4**

Pedestrians only
M Metro station
RER RER station
⊠ Post office

1/4 mi
0.25 km

3 rue de Bourgogne, 75007 Paris. www.bourgogne-montana.com. ☏ **01-45-51-20-22.** Fax 01-45-56-11-98. 32 units. 230€–305€ double; 410€ junior suite. Rates include breakfast. AE, DC, MC, V. Métro: Invalides. **Amenities:** Bar; babysitting; room service. *In room:* A/C, TV, hair dryer, minibar, Wi-Fi (free).

Hôtel Le Tourville ★★   This is a well-managed, personalized town house between the Eiffel Tower and Les Invalides. It originated in the 1930s as a hotel and was revitalized much later into the charmer of today. Bedrooms offer original art, antique furnishings or reproductions, and wooden furniture covered in modern, sometimes bold, upholsteries. Four of the rooms, including the suite, have private terraces. Beds are queens or twins, each of which was recently replaced. The staff is well trained, with the kinds of personalities that make you want to linger at the reception desk. Breakfast is the only meal served, but you can get a drink in the lobby.

16 av. de Tourville, 75007 Paris. www.hoteltourville.com. ☏ **01-47-05-62-62.** Fax 01-47-05-43-90. 30 units. 210€–300€ double; 380€–470€ suite. AE, MC, V. Métro: Ecole Militaire. **Amenities:** Bar; concierge; room service. *In room:* A/C, TV, hair dryer, Wi-Fi (free).

MODERATE

Derby Eiffel   This hotel faces the Ecole Militaire and contains airy public areas. Our favorite is a glass-roofed conservatory in back, filled with plants and used as a breakfast area. The soundproof and modern guest rooms are fairly basic, but employ thick fabrics and soothing neutral colors. Most front-facing rooms have balconies with views of the Eiffel Tower.

5 av. Duquesne, 75007 Paris. www.hotelsderby.com. ☏ **01-47-05-12-05.** Fax 01-47-05-43-43. 43 units. 135€–155€ double; from 165€ triple. AE, DC, MC, V. Métro: Ecole Militaire. **Amenities:** Bar; babysitting; concierge; room service. *In room:* A/C, TV, hair dryer, minibar, Wi-Fi (5€ per day).

Hôtel de l'Académie ★   The exterior walls and old ceiling beams are all that remain of this 18th-century residence of the Duc de Rohan's private guards. Other than its associations with the Duc de Rohan, this place is locally famous for having housed poet and novelist Antonio Marchado, "the Victor Hugo of Spain," between 1909 and 1914. Guest rooms have a lush Ile-de-France decor and views over the neighborhood's 18th- and 19th-century buildings. Rooms are smallish.

32 rue des Sts-Pères, 75007 Paris. www.academiehotel.com. ☏ **800/246-0041** in the U.S. and Canada, or 01-45-49-80-00. Fax 01-45-44-75-24. 34 units. 199€–229€ double; from 299€ junior suite. AE, DC, MC, V. Parking 23€. Métro: St-Germain-des-Prés. **Amenities:** Babysitting; room service. *In room:* A/C, TV, hair dryer, minibar, Wi-Fi (free).

Hôtel de l'Université   This 300-year-old, antiques-filled town house enjoys a location in a discreetly upscale neighborhood. Room no. 54 is a favorite, containing a rattan bed, period pieces, and a terrace. Another charmer is room no. 35, which has a nonworking fireplace and opens onto a courtyard with a fountain. Beds have plush comfort and discreet French styling. You'll sleep well here. A complete renovation in 2011 has increased the comfort of rooms and public areas, and the prices are sure to follow.

22 rue de l'Université, 75007 Paris. www.hoteluniversite.com. ☏ **01-42-61-09-39.** Fax 01-42-60-40-84. 27 units. 185€ double. AE, DC, MC, V. Métro: St-Germain-des-Prés. **Amenities:** Room service. *In room:* A/C, TV, hair dryer, minibar, Wi-Fi (5€ per hour).

Hôtel de Londres Eiffel ★★   Small and charming, this independently run hotel is just a 2-minute walk from the Eiffel Tower. Completely renovated, it is "dressed" in colors of yellow and raspberry, which is far more harmonious and elegant than the combination sounds. In a residential district (one of the best in Paris), the bedrooms are midsize and tastefully decorated, each with an individual decor. The top floors open onto views of the illuminated Eiffel Tower at night.

1 rue Augereau, 75007 Paris. www.londres-eiffel.com. **℃ 01-45-51-63-02.** Fax 01-47-05-28-96. 30 units. 185€–220€ double; 380€ suite. AE, DC, MC. Parking 34€. Métro: Ecole Militaire. **Amenities:** Concierge. *In room:* A/C. TV. hair dryer, minibar, Wi-Fi (free).

Hôtel du Palais Bourbon ★   The solid stone walls of this 18th-century building aren't as grand as those of the embassies and stately homes nearby. But don't be put off by the tight entranceway and rather dark halls: Though the guest rooms on the upper floors are larger, all the rooms are comfortable and pleasantly decorated, with carefully crafted built-in furniture.

49 rue de Bourgogne, 75007 Paris. www.hotel-palais-bourbon.com. **℃ 01-44-11-30-70.** Fax 01-45-55-20-21. 29 units. 195€–220€ double. Rates include breakfast. MC, V. Métro: Varenne. **Amenities:** Room service. *In room:* A/C, TV, hair dryer, minibar, Wi-Fi (free).

Hôtel du Quai Voltaire   Built in the 1600s as an abbey and transformed into a hotel in 1856, the Quai Voltaire is best known for such illustrious guests as Wilde, Richard Wagner, and Baudelaire, who occupied room nos. 47, 55, and 56, respectively. Camille Pissarro painted *Le Pont Royal* from the window of his fourth-floor room. Most rooms have exceptional views overlooking the bookstalls and boats of the Seine and the Louvre on the other side, though these can be noisy.

19 quai Voltaire, 75007 Paris. www.quaivoltaire.fr. **℃ 01-42-61-50-91.** Fax 01-42-61-62-26. 33 units. 150€–160€ double; 180€ triple. AE, DC, MC, V. Parking 14€. Métro: Musée d'Orsay or rue du Bac. **Amenities:** Bar; room service. *In room:* Hair dryer, Wi-Fi (free).

Hôtel Le Bellechasse ★★ 🏠   This gem of a hotel, seconds on foot from the Musée d'Orsay, is still one of the city's most fanciful designer hotels. It's the creation of couturier Christian Lacroix, who let his imagination go wild. A stay here is like wandering into a psychedelic garden. Each guest room is different in a pastiche of colors with baroque overtones. One French critic called Lacroix's designs "magpie sensibility," perhaps a reference to one room where top-hatted, frock-coated Paris dandies with butterfly wings wrap around both walls and ceilings. The helpful staff is part of the fun—that and taking a bath in a fiberglass tub.

8 rue de Bellechasse, 75007 Paris. www.lebellechasse.com. **℃ 01-45-50-22-31.** Fax 01-45-51-52-36. 34 units. 160€–245€ double. MC, V. Métro: Solferino. RER: Musée d'Orsay. **Amenities:** Dining room (breakfast). *In room:* A/C, TV, TV/DVD, CD player, hair dryer, minibar, MP3 docking station, Wi-Fi (free).

Hôtel Verneuil ★★ 🏠   Small scale and personal, this hotel feels modern, while still evoking nostalgia for *la vieille France* (old-fashioned France). Built in the 1600s as a town house, it is a creative and intimate jumble of charm and coziness inside. Expect a mixture of antique and contemporary furniture; lots of books; and, in the bedrooms, *trompe l'oeil* ceilings, antique beams, quilts, and walls covered in fabric that comes in a rainbow of colors.

8 rue de Verneuil, 75007 Paris. www.hotelverneuil.com. ☎ **01-42-60-82-14.** Fax 01-42-61-40-38. 26 units. 178€–240€ double. AE, DC, MC, V. Métro: St-Germain-des-Prés. **Amenities:** Bar; babysitting; room service. *In room:* A/C (in some), TV, hair dryer, minibar, Wi-Fi (free).

Montparnasse & Southern Paris (13e, 14e & 15e)

Back in the early days of the 20th century, Montparnasse was a hotbed of creativity. Between the two World Wars, artists, expats, and extravagant figures such as Kiki de Montparnasse and Gertrude Stein reinvented the world in the bars and cafes of the area.

Best For: Travelers looking for a quiet residential zone with a rich history.
Drawbacks: Much of the area shuts down early in the evening.

MODERATE

Apollon Montparnasse   This privately owned hotel lies in Montparnasse, former home of such famous Left Bank residents as Gertrude Stein and Alice B. Toklas. Since opening in 1990, the hotel has established a reputation for its good rates and very comfortable bedrooms, which are midsize and furnished with flower spreads and draperies. The building was originally constructed in the 1930s as private apartments, and was completely renovated in 2009. The clean and simple rooms are decorated with pale wood and gray-and-white-striped wall paper.

91 rue de l'Ouest, 75014 Paris. www.apollon-montparnasse.com. ☎ **01-43-95-62-00.** Fax 01-43-95-62-10. 33 units. 120€–142€ double. AE, DC, MC, V. Métro: Pernety. Parking 18€. **Amenities:** Room service. *In room:* A/C, TV, hair dryer, minibar, Wi-Fi (free).

Eiffel Seine ★   Rising on the banks of the Seine, this Art Nouveau–style hotel lies only 5 minutes by foot from the Eiffel Tower. That style pervades the hotel from the reception lounge to the personalized doubles and family rooms. Two ground floor rooms, opening onto an interior garden, are suited for persons with disabilities. Each room has its own special decoration, and the decor is harmonious from the tiles to the wallpaper to the mirrors and wall lamps. The quiet rooms are filled with modern technology as well as comfy beds.

3 bd. De Grenelle, 75015 Paris. www.paris-hotel-eiffelseine.com. ☎ **01-45-78-14-81.** Fax 01-45-79-46-95. 45 units. 180€–250€ double. MC, V. Métro: Bir Hakeim. **Amenities:** Exercise room. *In room:* A/C, TV, TV/DVD, room service, Wi-Fi (free).

Hôtel La Manufacture ★ 🎁   With good rooms and decent prices, this place is a real find. Lying on a small street near place d'Italie in the 13th arrondissement, it is only 10 minutes by Métro from the stations at Montparnasse and Gare de Lyon. Small to midsize bedrooms are decorated in printed fabrics and soothing pastels. The most desirable room is no. 74 because of its distant views of the Eiffel Tower. This restored 19th-century building has a wrought-iron door and is graced with iron lamps, wicker chairs, oak floors, and bright paintings. It contains a number of old-fashioned armoires called *chapeau de gendarme* (police hat).

8 rue Philippe de Champagne (av. des Gobelins), 75013 Paris. www.hotel-la-manufacture.com. ☎ **01-45-35-45-25.** Fax 01-45-35-45-40. 56 units. 145€–195€ double; 310€ triple. AE, DC, MC, V. Métro: Place d'Italie. **Amenities:** Bar; room service. *In room:* A/C, TV, hair dryer, Wi-Fi (10€ per 3 hr.).

INEXPENSIVE

Hôtel du Vert Galant   Verdant climbing plants and shrubs make this family run hotel feel like an *auberge* (inn) deep in the French countryside. The smallish guest rooms have tiled or carpeted floors, unfussy furniture, and (in most cases) views of the private garden or the public park across the street. One of the hotel's best aspects is the Basque restaurant next door, the Auberge Etchegorry, sharing the same management; hotel guests receive a discount

41 rue Croulebarbe, 75013 Paris. www.vertgalant.com. ✆ **01-44-08-83-50.** Fax 01-44-08-83-69. 15 units. 90€–130€ double. AE, MC, V. Parking 15€. Métro: Corvisart or Gobelins. RER: Gare d'Austerlitz. **Amenities:** Restaurant; room service. *In room:* TV, hair dryer, minibar, Wi-Fi (free).

NEAR THE AIRPORTS
Orly
MODERATE

Hilton Paris Orly Airport ★   Boxy and bland, the Hilton at Orly is a well-maintained and convenient business hotel. Noise from incoming planes can't penetrate the guest rooms' sound barriers, giving you a decent shot at a night's sleep. (Unlike the 24-hr. Charles de Gaulle Airport, Orly is closed to arriving flights from midnight–6am.) The midsize rooms are standard for a chain hotel; each has been renovated.

Aéroport Orly, 267 Orly Sud, 94544 Orly Aérogare Cedex. www.hilton.com. ✆ **800/445-8667** in the U.S. and Canada, or 01-45-12-45-12. Fax 01-45-12-45-00. 351 units. 90€–250€ double; 300€ suite. AE, DC, MC, V. Parking 14€. Transit to and from airport by complimentary shuttle bus. **Amenities:** Restaurant; bar; babysitting; concierge; exercise room; room service. *In room:* A/C, TV, TV/DVD player, hair dryer, Wi-Fi (17€ per 12 hr.).

INEXPENSIVE

Air Plus   This 1990s hotel offers standard rooms that are comfortable, insulated against airport noise, and a bit larger than you might expect. The location is in an out-of-the-way, leafy residential zone. It is connected with Orly by 10-minute complimentary shuttle-bus rides, which can be irregular, so it's worth checking the timetable with the hotel directly.

58 voie Nouvelle (near the Parc Georges Méliès), 94310 Orly. www.hotelairplus.com. ✆ **01-41-80-75-75.** Fax 01-41-80-12-12. 72 units. 70€–110€ double. AE, DC, MC, V. Free parking. Transit to and from airport by complimentary shuttle bus. **Amenities:** Restaurant; room service. *In room:* A/C, TV, hair dryer, Wi-Fi (free).

Charles De Gaulle
MODERATE

Hyatt Regency Paris–Charles de Gaulle ★   This property is adjacent to the Charles de Gaulle Airport. Lying only a 25-minute drive from Disneyland Paris and a half-hour from the attractions of central Paris, the Roissy property was designed by the renowned architect Helmut Jahn. He created a stunning five-story structure of sleek design and tech-smart features. Jet-lagged passengers find comfort in the elegantly furnished and soundproof guest rooms, which meld modern convenience with European style.

351 av. du Bois de la Pie, 95912 Roissy. www.paris.charlesdegaulle.hyatt.fr. ✆ **01-48-17-12-34.** Fax 01-48-17-17-17. 388 units. 155€–255€ double; 265€–400€ suite. AE, DC, MC, V. RER-B train to its final destination (Aéroport Charles de Gaulle-Terminal Two). From there, take the hotel's shuttle bus (departures every 20 min.) directly to the hotel. Parking 29€. Free shuttle to and from airport. **Amenities:** Restaurant; bar; babysitting; concierge; exercise room; pool (indoor); room service; 2 tennis courts. *In room:* A/C, TV, TV/DVD, hair dryer, minibar, Wi-Fi (12€ per day).

Novotel Convention & Wellness Roissy CDG ★★ ☺   This comfortable four-star hotel located on the airport grounds is ideal for business travelers, families, or for people who need to be near the airport to make a flight. The hotel offers a Wellness Club, with a heated pool, hammam, sauna, gym, and beauty treatments to help exhausted travelers unwind. There are regular free shuttles that go between the hotel and the airport.

Allée des Vergers, 95700 Roissy. www.novotel.com. ✆ **01-30-18-20-00.** Fax 01-34-29-95-60. 289 units. 129€–295€ double. AE, DC, MC, V. Free shuttles 5:15am–12:30am btw. the RER/TGV train stations at Paris CDG airport and the hotel. Transit to and from airport terminals by free shuttle. Parking 21€ per day. **Amenities:** Restaurant; bar; babysitting; concierge; exercise room; pool (indoor); room service. *In room:* A/C, TV, hair dryer, minibar, Wi-Fi (free).

Pullman Paris Aéroport CDG ★   Many travelers pass through this bustling, somewhat anonymous member of the French chain. It employs a multilingual staff accustomed to accommodating international business travelers. The conservatively furnished guest rooms are soundproof havens against the all-night roar of jets. Suites are larger and more comfortable, although they are not especially elegant.

Aéroport Charles de Gaulle, Zone Central, 20248, 95713 Roissy. www.pullmanhotels.com. ✆ **800/221-4542** in the U.S. and Canada, or 01-49-19-29-29. Fax 01-49-19-29-00. 350 units. 140€–370€ double; 450€–1,100€ suite. AE, DC, MC, V. Parking 12€. Free shuttle to and from airport. **Amenities:** Restaurant; bar; concierge; exercise room; room service. *In room:* A/C, TV, hair dryer, minibar, Wi-Fi (free).

INEXPENSIVE

ibis Paris CDG Terminal Roissy   Conveniently located near CDG's Terminal 3, this two-star hotel is the cheapest option near the airport. Freshly renovated, the hotel rooms are clean and comfortable, though they are decorated in that bland aesthetic common to airports.

Roissy Aéroport, 95701 Roissy en France. www.ibishotel.com. ✆ **01-49-19-19-19.** Fax 01-49-19-19-21. 556 units. 79€–139€ double. AE, DC, MC, V. Parking 16€ per day. Transit to and from airport by complimentary shuttle bus. **Amenities:** 2 restaurants; bar; room service. *In room:* A/C, TV, hair dryer, minibar, Wi-Fi (free).

PRACTICAL MATTERS: THE HOTEL SCENE

As in most large cities, accommodation choices in Paris vary widely. France rates its hotels by an official government star system, which is based on a complex formula of room sizes, facilities, plumbing, elevators, dining options, renovations, and so on. In the past, hotels ranged from one star (for a simple inn) to four stars (for a luxury hotel), but in July 2012, this star-rating system will change to a five-star classification, putting it more in line with international standards. In one-star hotels, the bathrooms can be shared, the facilities are extremely limited (such as no elevator), the rooms may not have phones or TVs, and breakfast is often the only meal served. Despite limited amenities, they may be perfectly clean and decent places. Two- or three-star hotels usually have elevators, and rooms will likely have bathrooms, phones, and TVs. In four- and five-star establishments, you'll get all the amenities plus facilities and services such as room service, concierges, elevators, and perhaps even health clubs. Do remember that the system can be deceptive, and a charming two-star hotel in a historic building can be more appealing than a brand-new three-star hotel with all the amenities.

Because hot weather rarely lasts long in Paris, air-conditioning is not a standard feature in the city's hotels. If you're trapped in a garret on a hot summer night, you'll have to sweat it out. Noise can be an issue too, particularly in those rooms facing the street. Check if a room has double-glazed windows or ask for a room off the street. Expect rooms to be small unless you pay for a suite. Some hotel websites explain the differences between different room categories by including average room surface. Beds are usually standard doubles, or queen size for superior rooms and the pricier hotels; it's rare to find a king-size bed. Be warned that you'll have to carry your bags to and from your room in most hotels—don't expect to find bellboys unless you're staying at a luxury hotel. Free Wi-Fi in rooms has become a standard offer for most hotels.

Getting the Best Deal

If you're looking for budget options, Paris has some good-value places in the lower price ranges, and we've included reviews for the best of these properties in this chapter.

Prices dip during Paris's low season over winter from November to February. The height of summer, during July and August, can be quiet too. Most visitors, at least those from North America, come to Paris at this time, but many French people are on vacation, and trade fairs and conventions come to a halt, so there are usually plenty of rooms available. Peak periods are from March to July and September to November; the major trade show season in September and October; and seasonal events like Fashion Week in early March and late September. Book ahead if you come during these times. If you arrive without a reservation, you may have to take what you can get, often at a much higher price than you'd like. It's true that you can almost always get a room at a deluxe hotel if you're willing to pay the price.

Online travel booking sites offer considerable discounts off of room rates. Check sites like **Expedia, Priceline, ebookers.com, Hotels.com, venere. com, france-hotel-guide.com,** or **Booking.com** to find discount rates on hotel rooms.

Reservation Services

Most hotels require a credit card number to confirm a reservation. You can usually cancel a room reservation one week ahead of time without paying a deposit. A few hotel keepers will return your money up to 3 days before the reservation date, but some will keep a deposit, even if you cancel far in advance. To secure special Internet deals, you often must pay up-front. If you'd prefer someone to take care of the details for you, check out **Mondiale Tourisme** (© **01-42-46-83-29;** www.mondialfrance.com), a Paris-based travel agency with an international team and 15 years of experience booking vacations both in Paris and throughout France.

Alternative Accommodations

More intimate than a hotel, a bed-and-breakfast within a private home can be an affordable and interesting option. The **Hôtes Qualité Paris** (www.hotesqualite paris.fr) is the city's official agency for professional B&Bs in selected private homes; it offers rooms for about 50€ to 140€ per person per night, based on double occupancy. **Alcôve & Agapes** (🕿 **01-44-85-06-05;** www.bed-and-breakfast-in-paris.com) is a reliable private agency that promotes upmarket B&B accommodations in Paris. These services provide a bridge between travelers who seek rooms in private homes and Parisians who wish to welcome visitors. Most hosts speak at least some English, range in age from 30 to 75, and have at least some points of view about entertainment and dining options within the neighborhood. Available options include individual bedrooms, usually within large, old-fashioned private apartments, as well as "unhosted" accommodations where the apartment is otherwise empty and without the benefit (or restrictions) of a live-in host.

If you'd prefer to live like an expat, it is also possible to rent an apartment in Paris. A number of agencies lease apartments that are centrally located, furnished, and well-equipped; short- or long-term rentals are available. To rent an apartment in Paris, contact one of the following agencies: **Paris Attitude** (🕿 **01-42-96-31-46;** www.parisattitude.com); **Parisian Home** (🕿 **01-45-08-0337;** www.parisianhome.com); **France Lodge** (🕿 **01-56-33-85-85;** www.france lodge.fr); **Paris Appartements Services** (🕿 **01-56-33-85-85;** www.paris-appartements-services.com); **Appartement de Ville** (🕿 **01-40-28-01-28;** www.appartementdeville.com); or **Flip Key** (www.flipkey.com). Through these organizations, you will likely deal with the agency (not the owners), and the minimum stay is usually 1 week.

It is possible to get a good deal at an *aparthotel,* a cross between a hotel and an apartment. Short on charm, these rentals are good on convenience, each with a kitchenette. Although rates are more than short-term studios, you get more of the services of a hotel, including fresh towels and a reception desk. The best known agency renting *aparthotels* is **Citadines** (🕿 **08-25-33-33-32;** www. citadines.com). The cheapest rentals are the studios with pull-out beds; a studio for two might range from 140€ to 250€ a night—or even more in such highly priced locations as the Louvre area or St-Germain-des-Prés.

Finally, it's a bit riskier than the previously inspected and approved recommendations, but it is possible to rent cheap apartments independently. To do so, checking out the classified ads in **FUSAC** (France-USA Contacts; www.fusac. com), a free biweekly magazine that is widely distributed in bookstores, cafes, and restaurants catering to English-speaking visitors.

SIDE TRIPS FROM PARIS

By Lily Heise

10

P arisians generally feel that their capital is the center of the universe. They may be correct, if only geographically speaking. Paris is at the heart of the region of *Ile-de-France* (the Island of France), and is encircled by seven suburban *départements* (administrative divisions) commonly and regally referred to as the *petite* and *grande couronne*s. These "crowns" are dotted with cultural and historic treasures, from majestic palaces to picturesque artistic villages, and are only a short journey from the city center.

Opulent **Versailles** is usually at the top of visitors' list, but the magnificent châteaux of **Fontainebleau** and **Vaux-le-Vicomte** shouldn't be overlooked. The towns of **Giverny** and **Auvers-sur-Oise** are ideal destinations for art fans. Medieval church aficionados should make the pilgrimage south to the world-renowned **Chartres Cathedral** with its spectacular stained-glass windows, while those looking for some animated adventure or family fun can head east to **Disneyland Paris.** In this chapter, we offer only a handful of the possibilities for day jaunts. For a more extensive list, see *Frommer's France 2012.*

For pretrip planning, abundant visitor information can be found on the various websites listed in the details of our side trip destinations or on the office website for **Ile-de-France tourism** (www.new-paris-ile-de-france.co.uk). Once in Paris, you can also obtain more information at the main **Tourist Information Office** (25 Rue des Pyramides, 75001 Paris; ✆ **01-49-52-42-63**). Train tickets for all of these destinations do not require reservations and can be bought the day of an excursion at the departing train or subway station. You can find more information about the train schedule of suburban trains at **www.transilien.com;** for national trains (only required for Chartres and Vernon/Giverny), check **www.voyages-sncf.com**. You can also enquire directly at any Paris train station (most have an information desk with staff who speak English).

VERSAILLES ★

21km (13 miles) SW of Paris, 71km (44 miles) NE of Chartres

Just 45 minutes southwest of Paris, Le Château de Versailles is the most sumptuous castle in Europe and forever associated with the Sun King, Louis XIV, and the doomed Queen Marie Antoinette. The palace's regal gardens were designed by the famous landscape architect, Le Nôtre, to create a French Eden and give the grounds a bucolic feel. But the town of Versailles—practically synonymous with its decadent royal palace—has its pleasures too, with stately streets ringing the Cathédrale St-Louis, colorful markets, and antiques shops.

PREVIOUS PAGE: **A statue at Versailles.**

Île-de-France

Gisors
Méru
A16
Senlis
Crépy-en-Valois
Chambly
Chantilly
Forêt d'Halatte
Le Plessis-Belleville
Magny-en-Vexin
non
Giverny
Bonnières-sur-Seine
A13
Auvers-sur-Oise
Pontoise
Charles de Gaulle (Roissy)
Meaux
Mantes-la-Jolie
Seine
Le Bourget
St-Denis
A1
N2
Poissy
Nanterre
Bobigny
Marne
A4
St-Germain-en-Laye
PARIS
Disneyland Paris
Boulogne-Billancourt
Houdan
N12
Château de Versailles
Versailles
Champigny-sur-Marne
Créteil
Coulommiers
Châteaufort
Massy
Orly
Cernay-la-Ville
Saint-Rémy-lès-Chevreuse
N4
Rambouillet
Limours
Évry
A5
Eure
Forêt de Rambouillet
A10
Arpajon
Vaux-le-Vicomte
Melun
Nangis
N20
Dourdan
A6
A11
Ablis
Chartres Cathedral
Étampes
Barbizon
Chartres
A10
Forêt de Fontainebleau
Montereau-Fault-Yonne
Fontainebleau

Things to Do   Get gold fever inside the palace's extravagantly gilded **Petits & Grands Appartements,** where royals and their sycophants lived under constant scrutiny. Few superlatives aptly describe the beauty of the chandeliered **Hall of Mirrors** where the treaty ending WWI was signed in 1919. The gardens contain a line-up of noble statuary, hidden *bosquets* (groves) and fountains adorned with frolicking Greek gods. Just outside the gates, wander the Sun King's vegetable garden, before exploring boutiques around the quartier St. Louis.

Where to Eat   The Trianon Palace Hotel is home to Gordon Ramsey's wonderfully decadent restaurant, **Gordon Ramsay au Trianon,** which offers a Michelin-starred English take on French classics. Sample royal veggies at **Le Potager du Roy** or head to affordable **rue de Satory**, where crêperies, Thai, and Lebanese restaurants line the street.

Nightlife & Entertainment   Try to catch the famous *Grands Eaux Musicales,* when the fountains dance majestically to the rhythm of classical music. During the summer, the gardens are also the setting for nighttime spectacles of opera, theater, fireworks and music, which capture the pomp of the celebrations the Sun King once hosted. If you're lucky, you can also catch "Les Fêtes de Nuit de Versailles," an impressive fireworks display around late August.

Essentials

GETTING THERE   To get to Versailles, catch the **RER** line C1 to Versailles–Rive Gauche at the Gare d'Austerlitz, St-Michel, Musée d'Orsay, Invalides, Ponte de l'Alma, Champ de Mars, or Javel stop, and take it to the Versailles–Rive Gauche station. The trip takes 35 to 40 minutes. Do not get off at Versailles Chantier, which will leave you on the other end of town, a long walk from the château. The round-trip fare is 6€; Eurailpass holders travel free on the RER but need to show the pass at the ticket kiosk to receive an RER ticket. **SNCF trains** (Société Nationale des Chemins de Fer) make frequent runs from Gare St-Lazare and Gare Montparnasse in Paris to Versailles: Trains departing from Gare St-Lazare arrive at the Versailles Rive Droite railway station; trains departing from Gare Montparnasse arrive at Versailles Chantiers station, a long walk as mentioned.

The Versailles–Rive Gauche station is within a 10-minute walk of the château, and we recommend the walk as a means of orienting yourself to the town, its geography, its scale, and its architecture. If you can't or don't want to walk, you can take bus B, or (in midsummer) a shuttle bus marked CHATEAU from either station to the château for either a cash payment of around 2€ (drop the coins directly into the coin box near the driver) or the insertion of a valid ticket for the Paris Métro. Because of the vagaries of the bus schedules, we highly recommend the walk. Directions to the château are clearly signposted from each railway station.

If you're **driving,** exit the *périphérique* (the ring road around Paris) on N10 (av. du Général-Leclerc), which will take you to Versailles; park on place d'Armes in front of the château.

You can purchase individual entrance tickets to the various sights, but the easiest option is an all inclusive **Château Passeport,** which grants you access to the main chateau, the gardens (on special entrance days), the Trianon Palaces, and the Marie Antoinette Hamlet. From April to October the passport costs 18€ Monday to Friday, rising to 25€ on Saturday and Sunday. From November to March it costs 18€ per day. You can avoid the long lines at the château by purchasing the pass online at www.chateauversailles.fr or at the tourist office in Versailles. If you hold the **Paris Museum Pass,** on the weekend or the evening spectacles). You can also avoid the long ticket lines with the Paris Museum Pass.

VISITOR INFORMATION   The **Office de Tourisme** is at 2 bis av. de Paris (© **01-39-24-88-88;** fax 01-39-24-88-89; www.versailles-tourisme.com). Open April to October Tuesday to Sunday 9am to 7pm, Monday 10am to 6pm; November to March Tuesday to Saturday 9 to 6pm, Sunday and Monday 11am to 5pm.

EVENING SPECTACLES   Recognizing the value of the palace as a national symbol, the French government offers a program of fireworks and illuminated fountains, "Les Fêtes de Nuit de Versailles," on about 7 to 10 widely publicized dates between late August and early September, usually beginning at 9:30pm. Observers, who sit in bleachers near the palace's boulevard de la Reine entrance, close to the Fountain *(Bassin)* of Neptune, are treated to a display of fireworks, prerecorded classical music, and up to 200 players

Versailles

(none of whom utter a line) in period costume, portraying the glories of France as symbolized by Louis XIV and the courtiers of the *ancien régime*. Shows are big on pomp and visuals, and last about 90 minutes. Tickets range from 15€ to 85€. Gates open around 90 minutes prior to showtime. For information, see www.chateauversailles-spectacles.fr or call ✆ **01-30-83-78-89.**

DAYTIME SPECTACLES   *Les Grandes Eaux Musicales* are held Saturdays and Sundays from April to early October, between 11:30am and noon and 3:30 and 5pm,. The spectacles showcase the landscaping vision of the palace's designers and encourage participants to walk, promenade, or meander the vast park, enjoying the juxtaposition of supremely grand architecture with lavish waterworks. On Tuesdays music is also broadcast in the gardens, however, the fountains are not running. Admission to any part of the park during these spectacles can vary from 6€ to 10€. For information, see www.chateauversailles-spectacles.fr or call ✆ **01-30-83-78-89.**

You can purchase tickets to all spectacles at Versailles up until about a half-hour prior to the day or night of any performance from the ticket office in the *Accueil-Billeterie* on Place d'Armes, immediately across from the main facade of the palace, online at www.chateauversailles-spectacles.fr or from any French branch of the Fnac department store (Fnac's central phone number is ✆ **01-55-21-57-93**).

Touring Versailles

In 1661, Louis XIV set out to build a palace that would be the envy of Europe and created a symbol of opulence copied, yet never duplicated, the world over. Less than 40 years and more than 40,000 workmen later, the Château de Versailles was transformed from Louis XIII's humble hunting lodge into an extravagant palace.

Wishing (with good reason) to keep an eye on the nobles of France, Louis XIV summoned them to live at his court. Here he amused them with constant

Le Château de Versailles.

Grands Appartements.

Hall of Mirrors.

entertainment and lavish banquets. To some he awarded such tasks as holding the hem of his robe. While the aristocrats played at often-silly intrigues and games, the peasants on the estates sowed the seeds of the revolution.

When Louis XIV died in 1715, his great-grandson Louis XV succeeded him and continued the outrageous pomp, though he is said to have predicted the outcome: *"Après moi, le déluge"* ("After me, the deluge"). His Polish wife, Marie Leszczynska, was shocked by the blatant immorality at Versailles.

The next monarch, Louis XVI, found his grandfather's behavior scandalous—in fact, on gaining the throne, he ordered that the "stairway of indiscretion" (secret stairs leading to the king's bedchamber) be removed. The well-intentioned but weak king and his queen, Marie Antoinette, were well liked at first, but the queen's frivolity and spending led to her downfall. Louis and Marie Antoinette were at Versailles on October 6, 1789, when they were notified that mobs were marching on the palace. As predicted, *le déluge* had arrived.

Château de Versailles ★★★ ROYAL BUILDING/MUSEUM/GARDEN
The château gets increasingly crowded as the day goes on, so aim to visit the inside first and pick up one of their free audioguides to help you navigate the vast interior. Before going up to the second floor where the main highlights of the castle are, have a quick glance at the **Chapel.** Designed by Hardouin-Mansart, it was the fifth chapel to be built at Versailles. This was where the Sun King attended Mass every morning and where Louis XVI married Marie Antoinette in 1770, while he was the Dauphin.

Upstairs, step into the magnificent **Grands Appartements** ★★★. In the Louis XIV style, each bears the name of the allegorical painting on the ceiling. The best-known and largest is the **Hercules Salon** ★★, with a ceiling painted by François Lemoine depicting the Apotheosis of

Contemporary Versailles

Despite being one of France's most visited sights, Versailles has been trying to enter the 21st century through a program of controversial exhibits by contemporary artists such as Jeff Koons and Takashi Murakami. The Sun King might be rolling in his grave, but the shows have drawn in huge crowds of new admirers to the Château.

Palace Opéra.

Hercules. In the **Mercury Salon** (with a ceiling by Jean-Baptiste Champaigne), the body of Louis XIV was put on display in 1715; his 72-year reign was one of the longest in history.

The most famous room at Versailles is the 71m-long (233-ft.) **Hall of Mirrors ★★★**. Begun by Mansart in 1678 in the Louis XIV style, it was decorated by Le Brun with 17 arched windows faced by beveled mirrors in simulated arcades. Several important events took place here, including the proclamation of the German Empire in 1871 and the Treaty of Versailles was signed here on June 28, 1919, officially ending World War I.

The royal apartments were for the public life of the kings, but Louis XV and Louis XVI retired to the **Petits Appartements ★★** to escape the demands of court etiquette. Louis XV died in his bedchamber in 1774, a victim of smallpox. In a second-floor apartment, which you can visit only with a guide, he stashed away his mistresses, first Mme de Pompadour and then Mme du Barry. Despite being pillaged in the revolution, the Queen's Apartments have been restored to their appearance in the days of Marie Antoinette, when she played her harpsichord in front of special guests.

Louis XVI had a sumptuous **Library,** designed by Jacques-Ange Gabriel. Its panels are delicately carved, and the room has been restored and refurnished. The **Clock Room** contains Passement's astronomical clock, encased in gilded bronze. Twenty years in the making, it was completed in 1753. The clock is supposed to keep time until the year 9999. At age 7, Mozart played for the court in this room. Gabriel also designed the **Opéra ★★** for Louis XV in 1748, though it wasn't completed until 1770. In its heyday, it took 3,000 candles to light the place. Recently restored, it now has a regular program of opera performances.

Spread across 100 hectares (247 acres), the **Gardens of Versailles ★★★** were laid out by landscape artist André Le Nôtre. He created a Garden of Eden using ornamental lakes and canals, geometrically designed flower beds, and

---

Versailles's *Jardin's Secrets*

Tucked away in the wooded areas of the gardens on each side of the Grand Canal are various *bosquets* (groves). These hidden gardens each have a specific theme, and several have significant links to certain royals. The **Apollo Baths,** surrounded by a mix of English and Chinese gardens, were constructed on the request of Louis XIV's mistress Mme de Montespan. The **Queen's Grove** was the setting of the infamous 1785 Affair of the Diamond Necklace (when Marie Antoinette was wrongly accused of arranging the purchase of an exorbitantly priced diamond necklace), which forever tarnished Marie Antoinette's image—despite her innocence. Today they offer visitors a quiet escape from the masses marching along the Grand Canal.

avenues bordered with statuary. In the days of Louis XIV, 1,400 fountains spewed forth. *The Buffet* is an exceptional fountain, designed by Mansart. One fountain depicts Apollo in his chariot pulled by four horses, surrounded by Tritons rising from the water. Louis XV used to take gondola rides with his favorite mistress of the moment.

Developments within the sprawling estate include *Les Grandes Ecuries* (the Stables) and avenue Rockefeller, immediately opposite the château's main front façade, where the horses and carriages of the kings were housed. Visitors can watch a team of up to a dozen riding school students, with their mounts, strut their stuff during hour-long riding demonstrations within the covered, 17th-century amphitheater of the historic stables. Horse lovers will appreciate the equestrian maneuvers that this riding school shows off during these presentations, but they shouldn't go with any expectations that the horsemanship will re-create exclusively 17th- and 18th-century styles. Demonstrations are conducted Tuesday to Thursday, and Saturday and Sunday, at 11:15am. There's an additional presentation every Saturday and Sunday at 2pm. The price of tickets can vary, perhaps 12€ to 25€. It is possible to tour the stables without attending a show, however, usually only in the mornings and on certain days. For additional information, contact the château directly at © **01-30-83-78-00** or check on the Versailles website.

Gardens of Versailles.

Grand Trianon.

Place d'Armes. ℭ **01-30-83-78-00.** www.chateauversailles.fr. Palace 15€ adults; free for 18 and under. Both Trianons and Le Hameau (see listing below) 10€ adults; everything free for children 17 and younger. Palace Apr–Oct Tues–Sun 9am–6:30pm; Nov–Mar Tues–Sun 9am–5:30pm. Trianons and Le Hameau Tues–Sun noon–6pm. Grounds daily dawn–dusk.

The Trianons & The Hamlet ROYAL BUILDING/GARDEN   A long walk across the garden (or reachable by the little train), will take you to the **Grand Trianon (Grand Pavilion)** ★★, in pink-and-white marble. Le Vau built a Porcelain Trianon here in 1670, covered with blue-and-white china tiles, but it was fragile and soon fell into ruin. So, in 1687, Louis XIV commissioned Hardouin-Mansart to build the Grand Trianon. Traditionally, it has been a place where France has lodged important guests, though de Gaulle wanted to turn it into a weekend retreat. Nixon once slept here in the room where Mme de Pompadour died. Mme de Maintenon also slept here, as did Napoleon. The original furnishings are gone, of course, with mostly Empire pieces there today.

Le Hameau (Hamlet).

Gabriel, the designer of place de la Concorde in Paris, built the **Petit Trianon ★★** in 1768 for Louis XV. Louis used it for his trysts with Mme du Barry. When he died, Louis XVI presented it to his wife, and Marie Antoinette adopted it as her favorite residence, a place to escape the rigid life and oppressive scrutiny at the main palace. Many of the current furnishings, including a few in her rather modest bedchamber, belonged to the ill-fated queen.

Rousseau's theories about recapturing the natural beauty and noble simplicity of life were much in favor in the late 18th century, and they prompted Marie Antoinette to have Mique build her the 12-house **Le Hameau (Hamlet)** on the banks of the Grand Trianon Lake in 1783. She wanted a chance to experience the simplicity of peasant life—or at least peasant life as seen through the eyes of a frivolous queen. Dressed as a shepherdess, she would come here to watch sheep being tended and cows being milked, men fishing, washerwomen beating their laundry in the lake, and donkey carts bringing corn to be ground at the mill. The interiors of the hamlet buildings cannot be visited, but the surrounding informal landscaping—in obvious contrast to the formality of the other gardens at Versailles—and bizarre origins make views of their exteriors one of the most popular attractions here.

Follow the signs from the place d'Armes (to the immediate right after entering the Palace of Versailles). See previous entries for admission times and hours to visit.

Exploring the Town

If you have some extra time, or want to escape the hoards of tourists at the château, take a stroll through center of Versailles, and you'll see the real life of this elegant Parisian suburb. The heart of the town is the **Saint-Louis Cathedral.** To make room for the burgeoning palace, the village church of Saint-Julien of Brioude was demolished in 1679. With Versailles' rising importance, Louis XIV commissioned a new church, not surprisingly in honor of his namesake; St-Louis. Finished almost a century later in the rococo style, it was converted into a "temple of Abundance" during the revolution and, with the revival of religion, consecrated a cathedral in 1843.

A short distance from the cathedral is the vibrant **Notre Dame market,** a gastronomic paradise held in the 1841 covered market building Tuesday to Sunday mornings and overflowing into the neighboring streets on Tuesdays, Fridays and Sundays. Antiques fans will be in heaven exploring the dozens of shops in the **Passage de la Geôle,** occupying the former royal jail. More shops can be found continue in the picturesque **Les Carrés Saint-Louis.** Built by Louis XV in 1755, these square blocks of low slate-roofed houses make up one of the first ever shopping malls. Even if you're not looking to buy, it's fun to imagine what could fill the gorgeous 18th-century mansions scattered around Versailles, constructed by aristocrats during the city's heyday as seat of the French government.

Where to Eat

Gordon Ramsay au Trianon ★★★ FRENCH/INTERNATIONAL   One of the kings of cuisine reigns over this Art Deco restaurant in the swanky **Trianon Palace Hotel**—and he's not French. Scottish-born and Michelin laureate Gordon Ramsay, the *enfant terrible* of chefs, offers up a seasonal traditional French menu with modern flair. Treat yourself to the exceptional tasting menu or choose from ravioli with langoustines, roasted Périgord foie gras with gingerbread and carrot purée, royal Bresse pigeon served with potato and artichoke mille-feuille, quince and cinnamon purée. The service, the setting—everything here is a delight. The food is of the highest order—and so are the prices. For more relaxed dining, opt for its little sister **Le Veranda** in the terrace of the hotel, perfect in summer.

In the Hotel Trianon Palace, 1 bd. de la Reine. ☎ **01-30-84-55-55.** www.gordonramsay.com. Reservations required. Main courses 55€–72€; fixed-price menu 160€. AE, DC, MC, V. Fri–Sat 12:30–2:30pm and Tues–Sat 7–10:30pm. Closed Jan and 1 week in Mar.

L'Angélique MODERN FRENCH   Chef Régis Douysset's creative menu has earned him one Michelin star. In a renovated 17th-century *hôtel particulier* a few minutes' walk from the château, you will find *bistronomie* at its best, and without breaking the bank. Tantalize your taste buds with the zucchini and tomato confit with hermit crab and bouillabaisse broth, before moving on to the braised *ris de veau* (veal sweetbreads) paired with black chanterelles and shallot preserve or venison accompanied by grilled turnip. If the fermier cheese plate doesn't tempt you, try the delicious layered praline meringue and Ecuadorian Guayaquil chocolate cake with rosemary ice cream.

27 Avenue de Saint-Cloud ☎ **01-30-84-98-85.** www.langelique.fr. Fixed-price menu 41€–60€. MC, V. Tues–Sat noon–2:30pm and 7:30–10:00pm.

Le Potager du Roy ★ MODERN FRENCH   It's not often you can eat as the kings did—or at least from their vegetable garden. Philippe Letourneur spent years perfecting a distinctive cuisine—his skillfully prepared menu highlights seasonal vegetables grown in the château's garden. Examples include foie gras with glazed celery, *pot-au-feu* of vegetables with foie gras, cream of asparagus soup with smoked bacon, roasted duck with *navarin* of vegetables, and roasted codfish with roasted peppers in the style of Provence. The wine list might not date back as far as the château, but it's equally impressive.

1 rue du Maréchal-Joffre. ☎ **01-39-50-35-34.** www.potager-du-roi.fr. Reservations required. Main courses 28€; fixed-price menu 34€–42€. AE, MC, V. Tues–Sat 12:30–2pm and 7:30–9:30pm.

Le Resto du Roy FRENCH   This informal bistro lies in an 18th-century building overlooking the western facade of the palace at Versailles. The chef prepares an appetizing array of dishes, including specialties such as duck foie gras with fresh fig compote or salmon smoked with birch branches. For a main course, we recommend such dishes as poached tuna steak with coconut milk and lime sauce or supreme of chicken stuffed with wild mushrooms. There are also large *salades* including the vegetarian Estivale with hot goat cheese on toast and melon. For dessert, try the divine profiterole *royale* with grilled almonds.

1 av. de St-Cloud. ☎ **01-39-50-42-26.** www.restaurant-versailles.com. Reservations recommended. Main courses 15€–16€; fixed-price menu 16€–38€ lunch menu 13€. AE, MC, V. Daily 11:45am–2:30pm and 7–10:30pm.

THE CATHEDRAL OF CHARTRES ★★★

97km (60 miles) SW of Paris, 76km (47 miles) NW of Orléans

An hour south of Paris, amid a sea of wheat fields, rises the city of Chartres. Crowned with one of the world's most breathtaking cathedrals and quaint historic center, it gives visitors the perfect glimpse of a quintessential French town.

In a half-day excursion you'll be captivated by the splendid Notre-Dame spend a full day to explore the local farmers market, enjoy a lunch of *pâté de Chartres* before wandering along its medieval laneways, or visiting its lovely Fine Arts Museum.

Essentials

GETTING THERE From Paris's Gare Montparnasse, **trains** run directly to Chartres, taking about an hour. Tickets cost 28€ round-trip. Call *℄* **08-92-35-35-35.** If **driving,** take A10/A11 southwest from the *périphérique* and follow signs to Le Mans and Chartres. (The Chartres exit is clearly marked.)

VISITOR INFORMATION The **Office de Tourisme** is on place de la Cathédrale (*℄* **02-37-18-26-26;** fax 02-37-21-51-91; www.chartres-tourisme.com).

Notre-Dame de Chartres

- Chapelle St-Piat
- Chapelle St-Sacrement
- Notre-Dame du Pilier
- Sacristy
- Ambulatory
- Choir Screen
- Choir
- Choir Screen
- Crypt Entrance
- Notre Dame de la Belle Verrière
- North Portal
- North Rose Window
- North Transept
- Crossing
- South Transept
- South Rose Window
- South Portal
- Nave
- North Aisle
- South Aisle
- Chapelle Vendôme
- Labyrinth
- New Bell Tower
- West Rose Window
- Old Bell Tower
- Royal Portal

Seeing the Cathedral

Cathédrale Notre-Dame de Chartres ★★★ CHURCH It's not hard to understand why visitors flock to see the awe-inspiring Cathédrale de Chartres, a UNESCO World Heritage Site since 1979. With its mixed-and-matched bell towers, its weather-worn, revolution-damaged exterior, and above all, its shimmering stained-glass windows, the phenomenal church seduces the eyes and the spirit. Reportedly, Rodin once sat for hours on the sidewalk, admiring the sculptures on the facade. His opinion: Chartres is the French Acropolis. If you take the time to absorb the cathedral's intricacies, you will most certainly come to the same conclusion.

The cathedral's origins are uncertain; some have suggested it grew up over an ancient Druid site that later became a Roman temple. As early as the 4th century, there was a Christian basilica here. An 1194 fire destroyed most of what had by then become a Romanesque cathedral but spared the western facade and crypt. The cathedral you see today dates principally from the 13th century, when it was rebuilt with the efforts and contributions of kings, princes, churchmen, and pilgrims from all over Europe. One of the world's greatest high Gothic cathedrals, it was one of the first to use flying buttresses to support the soaring dimensions within.

As you approach the building, stop to admire the beautiful 12th-century sculptures on the **Royal Portal ★★★**. A landmark in Romanesque art, the

Chartres Cathedral.

sculptured bodies are elongated, often stylized, in their long, flowing robes. But the faces are amazingly (for the time) lifelike, occasionally winking or smiling. In the central tympanum, Christ is shown at the Second Coming, with his descent depicted on the right and his ascent on the left. Before entering, walk around to both the **North Portal** and the **South Portal,** each from the 13th century. Look carefully and you can read some of the biblical scenes depicted such as the expulsion of Adam and Eve from the Garden of Eden.

Upon entering the cathedral visitors are immediately overcome by the amazing light from the **stained glass ★★★**. Covering an expanse of more than 2,500 sq. m. (26,910 sq. ft.), the glass is unlike anything else in the world. The stained glass, most of which dates from the 12th and 13th centuries, was spared in both world wars by being painstakingly removed, piece by piece, and stored away. See the windows in the morning, at noon, in the afternoon, at sunset—as often as you can. Like the petals of a kaleidoscope, they constantly change. It's difficult to single out one panel or window above the others, but an exceptional one is the 12th-century *Vierge de la Belle Verrière* (**Our Lady of the Beautiful Window**) on the south side. Of course, there are three fiery rose windows, but you couldn't miss those if you tried.

Though you might be too transfixed by the heavenly light, don't neglect to take in the

Stained-glass windows at the Chartres Cathedral.

celebrated **choir screen;** work on it began in the 16th century and lasted until 1714. The niches, 40 in all, contain statues illustrating scenes from the life of the Madonna and Christ—everything from the *Massacre of the Innocents* to the *Coronation of the Virgin.*

Before exiting, have a look at the floor of the **nave,** which still contains its ancient floor labyrinth, a 262m-long (858 ft.) pilgrimage path that used to be walked by pilgrims in prayer or often traveled on one's knees as an act of repentance. The wooden *Notre-Dame du Piller* **(Virgin of the Pillar),** to the left of the choir, dates from the 14th century. The crypt was built over 2 centuries, beginning in the 9th century. Enshrined within is *Our Lady of the Crypt,* a 1976 Madonna that replaced one destroyed during the revolution.

Try to take a tour conducted by Malcolm Miller (✆ **02-37-28-15-58;** fax 02-37-28-33-03; millerchartres@aol.com), an Englishman who has spent 3 decades studying the cathedral and giving tours in English. His rare blend of scholarship, enthusiasm, and humor will help you understand and appreciate the cathedral. He usually conducts 75-minute tours at noon and 2:45pm Monday to Saturday for 10€ for adults or 5€ students. Tours are canceled during pilgrimages, religious celebrations, and large funerals.

If you're fit enough, don't miss the opportunity, especially in summer, to climb to the top of the tower.

After your visit, stroll through the **Episcopal Gardens** and enjoy yet another view of this remarkable cathedral.

16 Cloître Notre-Dame. ✆ **02-37-21-22-07.** http://cathedrale-chartres.monuments-nationaux. fr. General admission to the cathedral is free. Admission to the treasury and towers 7€ adults; 4.50€ adults 18–25; free for children 17 and under. Daily 8:30am–7:30pm.

Exploring the Old Town

If time remains, you may want to explore the medieval cobbled streets of the **Vieux Quartier (Old Town)** ★. Wandering around the narrow lanes near the cathedral, you will find many gabled houses, including the colorful facades of **Rue Chantault,** one of which is 8 centuries old. Seek out rue du Bourg, where you'll find the famous Salmon House, and some lovely medieval sculptures (including a certain fish). In the lower town, you can stroll along the picturesque Eure River with its stone bridges and ancient wash-houses. From the Pont de Bouju, you can see the lofty spires in the background. If you go on a Saturday morning you can enjoy the atmosphere of a local farmers market held in Place Billard (until 1 pm), the perfect place to grab picnic supplies for a casual lunch in the park behind the wcathedral or along the river.

Musée des Beaux-Arts de Chartres ★ Located next to the cathedral, a stop here will be a highlight of your visit. A former Episcopal palace, the building at times competes with its exhibitions—one part dates from the 15th century and encompasses a courtyard. This museum of fine arts boasts a collection covering the 16th to the 20th centuries, including the work of masters such as Zurbarán, Watteau, and Brósamer. Of particular interest is David Ténier's painting *Le Concert.* Allot about 1 hour for your visit.

10

SIDE TRIPS FROM PARIS

The Cathedral of Chartres

Vieux Quartier (Old Town), Chartres.

29 Cloître Notre-Dame. 📞 **02-37-90-45-80.** May 3–Oct 30 Mon, Wed–Sun 10am–noon and 2–6pm (closed Sun mornings); the rest of the year, until 5pm. Admission 3.20€ adults, 1.60€ 18 and under, extra fee for temporary exhibits.

Where to Eat

La Vieille Maison ★★ MODERN FRENCH   Even if the food here wasn't superb, the 14th-century building would still be visited for its historic value. The dining room, outfitted in the Louis XIII style, is centered on a narrow ceiling vault, less than 2m (6½ ft.) across, crafted of chiseled white stone blocks during the 9th century. Bruno Letartre, the only *maître cuisinier de France* (master French chef) in Chartres, supervises the cuisine. The menu changes four or five times a year, reflecting the seasonality of the region and its produce. Some good examples include steamed scallops with roasted lobster salad, foie gras with fig chutney and Indian spices, brochettes of lobster and scallops with spaghetti and smoked bacon, *blanquette* of turbot with mushroom and oat pilaf, and noisettes of venison fried with juniper berries and heirloom vegetables. Dessert fans should go with the caramel and chocolate ganache lava cake on a delicate pear coulis.

5 rue au Lait. 📞 **02-37-34-10-67.** www.lavieillemaison.fr. Reservations recommended. Main courses 28€–32€; fixed-price menu 30€–58€. MC, V. Tues–Sun noon–2:15pm; Tues–Sat 7–10pm. Closed 1 week in Aug.

Le Georges ★★ FRENCH   The best food and the most upscale dining ambience in Chartres is not surprisingly found at the town's best hotel. The friendly staff makes you feel comfortable in its elegant dining room, which expands in summer to the courtyard terrace. Its excellent gastronomic menu changes with the seasons, but usually includes savory portions of *pâté de Chartres*, made with a combination of minced meats that includes wild duck baked in a giant puff pastry; a steamed combination of crayfish with scallops in wine sauce; and a superb version of roasted veal "Grand Monarque," served with a casserole of mushrooms and cheese. Local products are also highlighted in the beauceron rabbit *à la Royale* or the Eure and Loire raised saddle of lamb with mint pistou.

Desserts are sumptuous, especially the *Grand Marnier Soufflé,* and the cheese cart will warm the heart of any Francophile.

In the Grand Monarque Best Western, 22 place des Epars. ℂ **02-37-18-15-15.** www.bw-grand-monarque.com. Reservations recommended. Main courses 18€–36€; fixed-price menu 48€–85€. AE, DC, MC, V. Tues–Sun noon–2:45pm; Tues–Sat 7–10pm.

Where to Stay

Grand Monarque Best Western   Located in the town center, this is certainly the most appealing and desirable hotel in Chartres. Functioning as an inn since its original construction in the 15th century and expanded and improved many times since then, it's a grand hotel that remains under the direction of the hard-working members of the Jallerat family. It attracts guests who enjoy its old-world charm—such as Art Nouveau stained glass and Louis XV chairs in the dining room. The 55 guest rooms are decorated with reproductions of antiques; many have sitting areas in addition to the five more spacious suites. Request a room facing the courtyard for a peaceful night's sleep or one facing the main square for a nice view of the city. The hotel provides solid and reliable comfort but not great style. Its new spa complex provides a relaxing break after a day's touring.

22 place des Epars, 28005 Chartres. www.bw-grand-monarque.com. ℂ **800/528-1234** in the U.S., or 02-37-18-15-15. Fax 02-37-36-34-18. 55 units. 130€–180€ double; 250€ suite. AE, DC, MC, V. Parking 8€. **Amenities:** 2 restaurants; bar; room service; spa. *In room:* A/C (in some), TV, hair dryer, minibar, Wi-Fi (free).

GIVERNY ★

80km (50 miles) NW of Paris

When artist Claude Monet moved to Giverny in 1883, looking for some peace and quiet, little did he know he would forever change the fate of this sleepy Norman village. Soon after his arrival, the town was invaded by eager young artists who'd come from all over the world in search of the Impressionist master. Today, artists and art lovers alike still trek out to Giverny to tour his restored home and gardens, and to be inspired themselves. If you fall in love with the amazing Monet paintings at the Orsay, Orangerie, or Marmottan museums in Paris, Giverny should be next on your list.

Essentials

GETTING THERE   It takes a half day to get to Giverny and see its sights or a full day to take your time, have a nice lunch and perhaps visit the picturesque old town of nearby Vernon. It's best to visit in the morning on a weekday to avoid the crowds. Take the Paris-Rouen train from Paris's Gare St-Lazare to the Vernon station, where you can either take a taxi (around 15€) or local bus (4€, located just outside the station) the 5km (3 miles) to Giverny. Vernon itself lies 40km (25 miles) southeast of Rouen. Another option is to take a 5-hour bus tour from Paris, for 72€ per person, that focuses on Monet's house and garden. For ages 3 to 11, the fare is 36€. Tours depart at 1:45pm Monday to Saturday and 8:15am on Sunday between April and October. These tours can be booked through **Cityrama,** 149 rue St-Honoré, 1er (ℂ **01-44-55-61-00;** www.pariscityrama.com; Métro: Palais-Royal–Musée du Louvre) in summer, or year-round through **American Express,**

11 rue Scribe, 9e (© **01-47-14-50-00;** Métro: Opéra), **Context Travel** runs small group excursions with art historians regularly from April to October from 85€ per person. See www.contexttravel.com.

If you're **driving,** take the Autoroute de l'Ouest (Port de St-Cloud) toward Rouen. Leave the highway at Bonnières, and then cross the Seine on the Bonnières Bridge. From here, a direct road with signs leads to Giverny. Expect it to take about an hour; try to avoid weekends. Another approach is to leave the highway at the Bonnières exit and go toward Vernon. Once there, cross the bridge over the Seine and follow signs to Giverny or Gasny (Giverny is before Gasny). This is easier than going through Bonnières, where there aren't many signs.

VISITOR INFORMATION The **Office de Tourisme des Portes de l'Eure** is shared by Giverny and the nearby hamlet of Vernon (36 rue Carnot 27200 Vernon; © **02-32-51-39-60;** www.cape-tourisme.fr). Open October to April Tuesday to Saturday 9am to 12:30pm and 2 to 5:30pm, May to September 9am to 6pm.

Exploring Giverny

Claude Monet Foundation ★★★ MUSEUM/GARDEN   Monet is certainly one of France's most renowned artists. One of the founders of Impressionism, it was his painting titled *Impression, Sunrise* (at the **Musée Marmottan,** p. 113) that gave the movement its name. A brilliant innovator, he excelled at presenting the effects of light at different times of the day. His paintings of the Rouen cathedral and of water lilies are just a few of his masterpieces.

Monet was born in Le Havre in 1840. His career flowed along the path of the Seine River—as a young man, he lived in Paris before leaving the bustling city for the suburbs, then the town of Vernon before finally settling in Giverny. Once here, Monet barely left, preferring to stay in his peaceful gardens. However, many of his friends came to visit him here at *Le Pressoir,* including Clemenceau, Cézanne, Rodin, Renoir, Degas, and Sisley. When Monet died in 1926, his son,

Claude Monet Foundation.

The gardens and lily pond at Giverny.

Michel, inherited the house, but left it abandoned until it decayed. The gardens became almost a jungle, inhabited by river rats. In 1966, Michel died and left the property to the Académie des Beaux Arts. It wasn't until 1977 that Gerald van der Kemp, who restored Versailles, decided to work on Giverny.

Unfortunately, you won't find any original Monet paintings at the foundation; however, you can stroll the garden and view the thousands of flowers, including the *nymphéas*. The Japanese bridge, hung with wisteria, leads to a setting of weeping willows and rhododendrons. Monet's studio barge was installed on the pond.

84 rue Claude-Monet Parc Gasny. (C) **02-32-51-28-21.** www.fondation-monet.com. Admission 8€ adults, 5€ students, 3.50€ children 7–12, free for children 6 and under. Apr–Oct daily 9:30am–6pm. Closed Nov–Mar.

Where to Eat

Baudy FRENCH   While the hotel Baudy might be overrun with tourists, it's still well worth dining at this legendary *auberge* (inn), especially for true art fans. In Monet's time, it was an *epicerie-buvette* (casual hangout) run by the painter's friends Angelina and Gaston Baudy. During the town's 19th-century heyday, the American painters used the pink villa as their lodging. The place no longer has its "legendary two tables," at which Mme Baudy fed the artists, but the fare hasn't changed much since then. Classic French standards are offered, such as chicken liver terrine with Armagnac liquor, the Baudy omelet with *confit de canard* and sautéed potatoes, or deluxe "wine merchant" *faux filet*. Grab a table on the terrace to escape the crowds and be sure to pop your head into the back gardens before leaving to experience a second Giverny garden wonder.

81 rue Claude-Monet. (C) **02-32-21-10-03.** Reservations recommended. Main courses 14€–21€; fixed-price menu 24€. MC, V. daily 10am–9:30pm; Sun 10am–3pm. Closed Nov–Mar.

 Giverny's Other Sites

After you've explored the Claude Monet Foundation, take a stroll along the main street up the cemetery to visit the Monet family tomb. The **Musée des Impressionismes** (99 rue Claude Monet; (C) **02-32-51-94-65;** www.museedesimpressionnismes giverny.com), the former American museum, also has notable temporary exhibits that occasionally feature some Monet works.

L'Esquisse Gourmande FRENCH   Located at the far end of town near the church, this is a refreshing alternative to the tourist traps near le Fondation Monet. This combined tea salon and restaurant is perfect for a relaxing summer lunch. Service is friendly, yet tends to be a little slow on busy days—while you wait you can admire the works of the new generation of Giverny artists adorning the walls. The seasonal menu is inspired by regional specialties and the apple reigns. Start with a *kir-normand,* local cider with crème de cassis, followed by the Camembert crumble, one of their creative salads or daily specials such as lamb brochettes or supreme of quail with caramelized baby vegetables and apples. Save room for their tasty desserts, which include *crème brûlée normand* with cooked apples or apple cheesecake.

73 bis rue Claude-Monet. ✆ **02-32-51-86-95.** www.lesquissegourmande.fr. Main courses 8€–20€. AE, MC, V. Wed–Sun noon–2pm; Tues–Sat 7:30–10pm.

AUVERS-SUR-OISE

30km (18 miles) N of Paris

"Here we are far from Paris, far enough for it to be the real country . . . Auvers is truly beautiful," was how post-Impressionist master Vincent van Gogh described scenic Auvers-sur-Oise. While the town itself has not changed much since the artist's brief stay in 1890, his 70-day sojourn here and his tragic death immortalized this country nook both on canvas and in history. Terribly poor his whole adult life, financially supported by his brother Theo, van Gogh has since become an artistic icon. Ironically, a century after his death, **van Gogh's *Portrait of Dr. Gachet***—the reason he came to Auvers—fetched a record sale price of $82.5 million. Come pay homage to van Gogh in his last resting place and tour the town that so inspired him.

Essentials

GETTING THERE   The easiest way is by taking the direct train to Auvers-sur-Oise that runs every Saturday, Sunday, and public holidays April to October departing from Gare du Nord at 9:56am and a direct return train to Paris at 6:15pm (approx. 35 min. either way). Alternatively, take a suburban train at Saint-Lazare or Gare du Nord toward Pontoise. Change at St-Ouen L'Aumone. Be careful, it's the second St-Ouen stop, not the first (approx. 1 hr.). Switch to the Persan Beaumont Creil line (walk downstairs and change to opposite platform; consult screens for departures) and get off at Gare d'Auvers-sur-Oise (approx. 15 min.) 11€ round-trip.

BY CAR: From Porte Maillot or la Porte de Clignancourt take the A15

Van Gogh's *Portrait of Dr. Gachet.*

Auvers-sur-Oise

ATTRACTIONS

Absinthe Museum **3**
Auberge Ravoux **8**
Auvers Cemetery **7**
Château d'Auvers **2**
L'Atelier de Daubigny **4**
Maison du Docteur
  Gachet (Doctor
  Gachet's Home) **1**
Manoir des
  Colombières **5**
Notre Dame church **6**

RESTAURANTS

Auberge Ravoux **8**
Chemin des Peintres **9**

highway direction Cergy-Pontoise. After 5km (3 miles) take the A115, in the direction of Amiens-Beauvais. Exit at Méry-Auvers-sur-Oise, follow signs to "Maison de Van Gogh" (30 min.). If you are driving you may want to combine Auvers with Giverny to make a full day trip.

There are also full day **bus tours** from Paris visiting both Auvers and Giverny, for 166€ per person, 84€ for children aged 3 to 11. Tours depart at 8:30am Wednesday and Saturday April to October. You can arrange these through **Cityrama,** 149 rue St-Honoré, 1er (✆ **01-44-55-61-00;** www.pariscityrama.com; Métro: Palais-Royal–Musée du Louvre). Private or group tours of Auvers are also available through the Office du Tourisme.

VISITOR INFORMATION   The **Office du Tourisme** is located in the Manoir des Colombières, rue de la Sansonne, across from the entrance to the Maison de Van Gogh (✆ **01-30-36-10-06;** www.lavalleedeloise.com). Open April to October Tuesday to Sunday 9:30am to 12:30pm and 2 to 6pm and November to March Tuesday to Sunday 2 to 5pm (5:30pm on weekends).

EVENTS   Auvers is far from a sleepy town in summers, with an annual international music festival, frequent jazz concerts, a contemporary artist open house during the Fête des Peintres, and minicruises along the Oise River on Sundays (see "Events'" at www.lavalleedeloise.com).

Exploring Auvers

Like Monet, in the mid–19th century many artists started to break out of their Parisian studio and traveled to towns in and around Ile de France to paint *en plein air*. One day, **Charles Daubigny,** an early open-air painter, docked his floating studio on the banks of the Oise and instantly fell in love with Auvers. He was soon followed by future Impressionist **Camille Pissarro,** who convinced his friend **Dr. Gachet** to come up to Auvers. Gachet, a painter himself and friend to many artists, also fell under the town's spell, and in no time his Auvers house became a central meeting point for visiting artists, including **Paul Cézanne,** who stayed for nearly 2 years. Cézanne encouraged his disturbed friend **Vincent van Gogh** to leave the asylum he was at in the south of France and come to Auvers where he could relax in the tranquil atmosphere of the country while being treated by Dr. Gachet. From the moment he arrived at the end of May 1890, Dr. Gachet pushed van Gogh to paint to help overcome his psychological problems. And paint he did, with frenetic energy, creating virtually a painting a day.

At first the country proved beneficial to Vincent; however, as the weeks went on his mood, along with his palette, darkened. He remained forever tormented and overwhelmed by the feeling he was a burden to his art-dealer brother, Theo. The ultimate reasons for his suicide will never really be known; nonetheless, this guilt surely played a role in his act.

There are several interesting sights to see in Auvers, all reachable on foot. Van Gogh fans will definitely want to visit the **Auberge Ravoux** (see below). Afterward, amble along the *Chemin des Peintres* to visit the various intriguing sights around Auvers (all well indicated with signposts). Hike up the gentle hill to visit the **Notre-Dame church,** which features one of van Gogh's tableaux (now at the Musée d'Orsay). Follow the signs a further 7 minutes up the hill by foot to visit the **Auvers Cemetery,** the final resting place of both Vincent and Theo, who died 6 months after Vincent. You'll find their ivy-covered graves side-by-side against the far left cemetery wall.

Near the Auberge Ravoux (also called the Maison de Van Gogh), you'll find two sites linked to the first known artist of Auvers, Charles Daubigny. You can visit a museum in his honor, the **Manoir des Colombières,** Rue de la Sansonne (© **01-30-36-80-20;** www.musee-daubigny.com), and just down the road you can also visit his **L'Atelier de Daubigny,** his home and studio, 61 rue Daubigny (© **01-30-36-60-60;** www.atelier-daubigny.com). If you have enough energy, keep walking along the rue Flery and you'll reach the 17th-century **Château d'Auvers,** rue de Léry (© **01-34-48-48-48;** www.chateau-auvers.fr), which has a multimedia display on Impressionist artists. Another 10 minutes along the road, which turns into rue Dr Gachet, you'll come to **Maison du Docteur Gachet** (Dr. Gachet's home), 78 rue du Docteur Gachet (© **01-30-36-81-27**), which also has thematic exhibits. However, his wonderful art collection was donated to the Louvre by his son in the 1950s.

To end your visit with a little fun, head to the **Absinthe Museum,** 44 Rue Alphonse Callé (© **01-30-36-83-26;** www.musee-absinthe.com), where you'll learn about the strong liquor—also known as "the green fairy"—which was much enjoyed by the Impressionist artists. The museums of Auvers are only open from spring to late autumn.

Auberge Ravoux (Maison de Van Gogh).

Auberge Ravoux MUSEUM/HISTORIC BUILDING   An inn and restaurant since 1876, l'Auberge Ravoux is often referred to as the Maison de Van Gogh, as the artist lodged here during his time in Auvers. He rented the tiny 7 sq. m (75 sq. ft.) room for 3.5 francs a day. The room also acted as van Gogh's studio, and after a day of painting in the village he would stack his works in his room or outside on the landing. On July 27, 1890, the artist headed out to the fields armed with his brushes, easel, and apparently a pistol. At the end of the day, he came crawling back to the Auberge with a fatal gunshot wound to the chest. As he lay dying for almost 2 days in his bed, with Theo by his side, it is hoped they reconciled any disputes. "Sadness goes on forever," are his supposed last words. You can't stay at the Auberge today, and there's really not much to see here besides Vincent's room (no. 5), but it remains exactly as it was in 1890. Visiting it can be a deeply moving experience.

52 Rue du Général de Gaulle. ☎ **01-30-36-60-63.** www.maisondevangogh.fr. Admission 6€ adults, 4€ ages 12–17 and under, free for children 11 and under. Mar to mid-Nov Wed–Sun 10am–6pm. Closed mid-Nov to Feb.

Where to Eat

Auberge Ravoux FRENCH   We can wholeheartedly recommend the Auberge Ravoux, which distinguishes itself with its unique, historically accurate approach to cuisine. The restaurant aims, with great success, to re-create the ambience of the van Gogh era, right down to the use of historic recipes and 19th-century furniture and tableware. Chef Laurent Gattuso's menus feature seasonal Ile-de-France produce to prepare both traditional working-class and bourgeois dishes. Start off with the homemade Ravoux pâté or rabbit loaf with lentil salad and onions marmalade, before savoring the veal blanquette or perhaps in honor of van Gogh, the *waterzooï du pêcheur* (a type of fish stew). Tempt yourself with the rich mousse au chocolat, or, if you're coming from the Absinthe Museum, you may want to try the Muse Ravoux—anise ice cream.

52 Rue du Général de Gaulle ✆ **01-30-36-60-63.** www.maisondevangogh.fr. Reservations recommended. Main courses 18€–32€; fixed-price menu 29€–38€. MC, V. Restaurant open early Mar to end of Nov. Wed–Fri lunch 12–2:30pm, tea and coffee from 3pm Sat, Sun and public holidays: 1st sitting at noon, 2nd sitting at 2:15pm, tea and coffee from 4pm. Fri-Sat: dinner 7:30pm–9:30pm.

Chemin des Peintres FRENCH   As the Auberge Ravoux, various other restaurants in Auvers are returning to authentic gastronomic philosophies and recipes, and the Chemin des Peintres is among the best. Set in a restored 19th-century barn, it serves tasty traditional dishes with a dash of creativity using local organic and farm products. The atmosphere is friendly and relaxed, fitting its country locale. Some mouthwatering dishes include warm Chauvy goat-cheese salads, local Commency rabbit seasoned with cumin and ginger, and free-range chicken with a red wine reduction. It's also a teahouse, so you can stop in after trekking up to the cemetery for a coffee and pear tart draped with chocolate and almond slivers.

3 bis, rue de Paris. ✆ **01-30-36-14-15.** Main courses 12€–24€; fixed-price menu 18€–24€. MC, V. Mon–Fri 11am–4pm; Sat 11am–11pm; Sun 11am–7pm.

DISNEYLAND PARIS

32km (20 miles) E of Paris

It might be an ocean away from the other Disney parks, but Disneyland Paris looks, tastes, and feels like the ones in California and Florida—except this fairytale château belongs to *Belle au Bois Dormant* instead of Cinderella, and Mickey might greet you with a friendly *bonjour*! The controversy over the opening of Disneyland Paris in 1992 has long been forgotten, and the resort has surpassed the Eiffel Tower and the Louvre to become France's number-one tourist attraction—drawing a whopping 50 million visitors annually. Take a day to get your fill of thrills at the main park or two to enjoy the full Disney atmosphere and movie action at the Walt Disney Studios.

Essentials

GETTING THERE   The RER commuter express **rail** network (Line A) stops within walking distance of the park. Board the RER in Paris at Charles-de-Gaulle–Etoile, Châtelet–Les Halles, or Nation. Get off at Line A's last stop, Marne-la-Vallée/Chessy, 45 minutes from central Paris. The round-trip fare is 14€ or

 Fast Pass Those Long Lines

Disneyland Paris has instituted a program that's done well at the other parks. With the **Fast Pass** system, visitors reserve a 1-hour time block at various rides, by printing a fast pass from the machine at the entrance to the attraction. Within that block, the wait is usually no more than 8 minutes.

6.70€ one-way. Trains run daily, every 10 to 20 minutes from 5:30am to midnight.

Shuttle buses connect Orly and Charles de Gaulle airports with each hotel in the resort. Buses depart the airports every 30 to 45 minutes. One-way transport to the park from either airport is 14€ for adults, 12€ for children 3 to 11.

If you're **driving,** take A4 east from Paris and get off at exit 14, DISNEY-LAND PARIS. Parking begins at 8€ per day, but is free if you stay at one of the park hotels. A series of moving sidewalks speeds up pedestrian transit from parking areas to the park entrance.

VISITOR INFORMATION   All the hotels we recommend offer general information on the theme park. For details and reservations at any of its hotels, contact the **Disneyland Paris Guest Relations Office,** located in City Hall on Main Street, U.S.A. (© **01-60-30-60-53** in English, or 08 25 30-60-30 in French; www.disneylandparis.com). For information on Disneyland Paris and specific details on the many other attractions and monuments in the Ile de France and the rest of the country, contact the **Maison du Tourisme,** Disney Village (B.P. 77705), Marne-la-Vallée (© **01-60-43-33-33**).

ADMISSION   Admission varies depending on the season. In peak season, a 1-day park ticket (for either the main park or Walt Disney Studios) costs 54€ for adults, 49€ for children 3 to 12, and is free for children 2 and younger; a 2-day park-hopper ticket is 113€ for adults, 102€ for kids; and a 3-day park-hopper ticket is 140€ for adults, 126€ for kids. See the official Disneyland website (www.disneylandparis.com) for ticket specials, especially in low season. Peak season is from mid-June to mid-September as well as Halloween, Christmas and Easter weeks. Entrance to Disney Village is free, though there's usually a cover charge at the dance clubs.

HOURS   Hours vary throughout the year, but most frequently they are 10am to 7pm. Be warned that autumn and winter hours vary the most; it depends on the weather and national holidays. It's a good idea to phone ahead if you're contemplating a visit at this time.

Spending the Day at Disney

Disneyland Paris ★★★ AMUSEMENT PARK   Situated on a 2,000-hectare (4,942-acre) site (about one-fifth the size of Paris) in the suburb of Marne-la-Vallée, the resort was designed as a total vacation destination: In one enormous unit, the park includes five "lands" of entertainment, a dozen hotels, a campground, an entertainment center, a 27-hole golf course, and dozens of restaurants, shows, and shops. **Disney Village** contains dance clubs, shops, restaurants (one of which offers a dinner spectacle based on the original *Buffalo Bill's Wild West Show*), bars for adults trying to escape their children, a French Government Tourist Office, a post office, and a marina.

Visitors stroll among flower beds, trees, reflecting ponds, fountains, and a large artificial lake flanked with hotels. An army of smiling employees and Disney characters—many of whom are multilingual, including Buffalo Bill, Mickey and Minnie Mouse, and of course, the French-born Caribbean pirate Jean Laffite—are on hand to greet the thousands of *enfants.*

Disneyland Paris's Sleeping Beauty Castle.

Main Street, U.S.A., abounds with horse-drawn carriages and barbershop quartets. Steam-powered railway cars embark from the Main Street Station for a trip through a Grand Canyon diorama to **Frontierland,** with its paddlewheel steamers reminiscent of Mark Twain's Mississippi River. Kids will love the Critter Corral petting zoo and parents can take a break in the Lucky Nugget Saloon, its cancan show inspired from the cabarets of turn-of-the-20th-century Paris.

The park's steam trains chug past **Adventureland**—with its swashbuckling pirates, Swiss Family Robinson treehouse, and re-enacted Arabian Nights legends—to **Fantasyland.** Here you'll find the **Sleeping Beauty Castle (*Le Château de la Belle au Bois Dormant*),** whose pinnacles and turrets are an idealized (and spectacular) interpretation of French châteaux. In its shadow are Europeanized versions of Blanche Neige et Les Sept Nains (Snow White and the Seven Dwarfs), Peter Pan, Dumbo, Alice (from Wonderland), the Mad Hatter's Teacups, and Sir Lancelot's Magic Carousel.

Visions of the future can be found in **Discoveryland,** where tributes to invention and imagination draw from the works of Leonardo da Vinci, Jules

A pirate ship in Adventureland.

Walt Disney Studios

You don't need to go all the way to Hollywood to experience movie magic—**Walt Disney Studios** takes guests on a behind-the-scenes interactive discovery of film, animation, and television through four thematic Studio Lots.

The main entrance to the studios, called the **Front Lot,** consists of "Sunset Boulevard," an elaborate sound stage complete with hundreds of film props. The **Toon Studio** allows visitors to learn the trade secrets of Disney animators,

here families can have gigantic fun in the oversized **Toy Story Playland,** speed around on the **RC Racer,** get dizzy on the **Slinky Dog Zigzag Spin,** or soar through the skies on the **Toy Soldiers Parachute Drop.** The **Production Courtyard** lets guests take a look behind the scenes of film and TV production; bigger and braver kids enter the spooky Hollywood Tower Hotel at their own risk. The abandoned hotel's rickety elevator sends you flying 13 floors to the depths of the **Twilight Zone Tower of Terror.** Finally, the **Back Lot** is home to special-effects and stunt workshops. A live stunt show features cars, motorbikes, and jet skis.

Big thrill seekers turn up the volume on the **Rock 'n' Roller Coaster,** a roller-coaster featuring the music of Aerosmith that combines a state-of-the-art rock video with high-speed scary twists and turns.

Admission is 54€ for adults, 49€ for children. Hours are daily from 10am to 7pm.

Verne, H. G. Wells, the modern masters of science fiction, and the *Star Wars* series, before sending visitors on their own intergalactic adventure on Space Mountain: Mission 2.

Throughout the park or during the daily parades you'll see characters from *Aladdin; The Lion King; Pocahontas; Toy Story;* and *Monsters, Inc.* As Disney continues to churn out animated blockbusters, look for the newest stars to appear in the theme park.

Where to Eat

Disneyland Paris offers a gamut of cuisine in more than 45 restaurants and snack bars. You can live on burgers and fries, or you can experiment at the following upscale restaurants.

California Grill ★★ ☺ CALIFORNIAN/FRENCH   The resort's showcase restaurant serves cuisine that's equal to the fare at a one-Michelin-star restaurant. Focusing on the lighter specialties for which the Golden State is famous, with various French inspirations the elegant restaurant accommodates both adults and children gracefully. East meets West in their wonderful range of appetizers such as the crispy rock shrimp salad with Asian pears, red onions, and wasabi cream. For excellent fusion try the pan-seared Florida snapper with roasted fig risotto, forest mushrooms, and pinot noir reduction. Another winning selection is the oak-fired filet of beef, served with *dauphinoise* potatoes with smoked bacon, ginger-scented carrots, and teriyaki barbecue. If you want a quiet, mostly adult venue, go here as late as your hunger pangs will allow.

In the Disneyland Hotel. ℰ **01-60-45-65-76.** Reservations required. Fixed-price menu 57€–71€; children's menu 17€–20€. AE, DC, MC, V. Daily 6:30–10:30pm.

Inventions ℰ INTERNATIONAL   This may be the only buffet restaurant in Europe where animated characters from the Disney films (including Mickey and Minnie) go table-hopping. With views over a park, Sleeping Beauty's Castle, and Space Mountain, the restaurant contains four enormous buffet tables devoted to starters, shellfish, main courses, and desserts. Selections are wide, portions can be copious, and no one leaves hungry. Don't expect *grande cuisine*—however, the quality is much better than your average buffet, topped with a mix of French and international delicacies such as chilled asparagus, Italian prosciutto, or even escargot and bouillabaisse, plus lots of kid-friendly dishes from spaghetti with meatballs to Buzz Lightyear éclairs.

In the Disneyland Hotel. ℰ **01-60-45-65-83.** Buffet 49€ adults, 25€ children 7–11, 19€ children 3–6. AE, DC, MC, V. Daily 12:30–3pm and 6–10:30pm.

Disneyland After Dark

The fun doesn't stop at the park gates; head to the Disney Village to continue your magical day. Experience the world in 3-D at the **Gaumont Disney Village IMAX cinema,** grab a drink at the sophisticated **New York City Bar** (located in the Hotel New York) or dance the night away to the hottest international hits at the **Hurricanes nightclub.** The whole family will enjoy **Le Legende de Buffalo Bill** in Disney Village (ℰ **01-60-45-71-00**). The twice-per-night stampede of entertainment recalls the show that once traveled the West with Buffalo Bill and Annie Oakley. You'll dine at tables arranged amphitheater-style around a rink where sharpshooters, runaway stagecoaches, and dozens of horses and Indians ride fast and perform alarmingly realistic acrobatics. Don't be surprised if you see a few special cowboys, or rather cow-mice. A Texas-style barbecue adds to the lively far West atmosphere served in an assembly line by waiters in 10-gallon hats. Shows start at 6:30 and 9:30pm; the cost (dinner included) is 59€ for adults, 45€ for children 3 to 11.

Where to Stay

You can easily make Disneyland a day trip from Paris—the transportation links are excellent—or spend the night. The resort's seven theme hotels share a reservation service. In North America, call ℰ **011-33-1-60-30-60-53.** In France, contact the **Central Reservations Office,** Euro Disney Resort, S.C.A., B.P. 105, F-77777 Marne-la-Vallée Cedex 4 (ℰ **08-25-30-60-30;** for more information and specials and packages see www.disneylandparis.com).

Disneyland Hotel ★★   Mouseketeers who have rich daddies and mommies frequent Disney's poshest resort. Located right at the park entrance, this flagship four-story hotel is Victorian, with red-tile turrets and jutting balconies. The spacious guest rooms are plushly furnished but evoke the image of Disney, with cartoon depictions and candy-stripe decor. The beds are king-size, double, or twin; in some rooms armchairs convert to beds. Accommodations in the rear overlook Sleeping Beauty Castle and Big Thunder Mountain; however, some less desirable units open onto a parking lot. The luxurious bathrooms have marble vanities, showers and tubs, and twin basins. The exclusive Castle Club on the third floor pampers guests with a separate elevator, reception desk and addition perks as free newspapers, all-day beverages, and access to a well-equipped private lounge.

Disneyland Paris, B.P. 111, F-77777 Marne-la-Vallée Cedex 4. ℂ **01-60-45-65-89.** Fax 01-60-45-65-33. www.disneylandparis.com. 495 units. 564€–897€ double; from 770€ suite. Rates include breakfast. AE, DC, MC, V. **Amenities:** 2 restaurants; bar; babysitting; health club and spa; pool (indoor); room service. *In room:* A/C, TV, TV/DVD player, hair dryer, minibar, Wi-Fi (10€ for 3 hr.).

Newport Bay Club ★★   The Disney lake might not be the Atlantic, but with its central cupola, balconies, awnings, and pergolas, The Newport Bay mirrors a harborfront New England hotel (ca. 1900). The yacht club atmosphere carries over to the nautically decorated blue and cream rooms, arranged in various shapes and sizes. Try to book a corner unit, which is the most spacious; in one of these you'll hardly realize you are staying in the biggest hotel in France. The hotel is a good balance for everyone with such distractions as the **Sea Horse Club Game Arcade** for the little ones and the **Fisherman's Wharf bar** for tired parents.

Disneyland Paris, B.P. 105, F-77777 Marne-la-Vallée Cedex 4. ℂ **01-60-45-55-00.** Fax 01-60-45-55-33. www.disneylandparis.com. 1,093 units. 310€–454€ double; 572€–840€ suite. Rates include breakfast. AE, DC, MC, V. **Amenities:** 2 restaurants; 2 bars; state-of-the-art health club; 2 pools (indoor and outdoor); room service. *In room:* A/C, TV/DVD player, minibar, Wi-Fi (15€ per day).

Hotel Cheyenne/Hotel Santa Fe ☺   Head to the far West for the best hotel bargains at the resort. These two Old West–style lodgings stand side-by-side near a re-creation of Texas's Rio Grande. The Cheyenne consists of 14 two-story buildings along Desperado Street; the desert-themed Santa Fe encompasses four "nature trails" winding among 42 adobe-style pueblos. The Cheyenne is a favorite among families, offering a double bed and bunk beds. Children have an array of activities, including a play area in a log cabin with a lookout tower and a section where you can explore the "ruins" of an ancient Anasazi village. The only disadvantage is the absence of a pool.

More recently constructed, the nearby **Kyriad Hotel,** a government-rated two-star hotel designed for families that evokes the aesthetics and layout of a French country inn. Whenever the Cheyenne and the Santa Fe are full, Disney usually directs the overflow to the Kyriad.

Disneyland Paris, B.P. 115, F-77777 Marne-la-Vallée Cedex 4. ℂ **01-60-45-63-12** (Cheyenne), or 01-60-45-79-22 (Santa Fe). Fax 01-60-45-62-33 (Cheyenne), or 01-60-45-78-33 (Santa Fe). www.disneylandparis.com. 2,000 units. Hotel Cheyenne 140€–310€ double; Hotel Santa Fe 120€–274€ double. Rates include breakfast. AE, DC, MC, V. **Amenities:** Restaurant; bar; babysitting. *In room:* A/C, TV, Wi-Fi (15€ per 100 min.).

FONTAINEBLEAU ★

60km (37 miles) S of Paris, 74km (46 miles) NE of Orléans

From the elegant Renaissance castle of François I to 19th century Napoleonic stronghold, the hallways and vast forest of Fontainebleau have played host to some of the most important figures and events in French history. Far from the overwhelming glitz and pomp of Versailles, Fontainebleau, which Napoleon referred to as "the house of the centuries," offers visitors a more intimate look at the real lives of French monarchs and its immense forest provides a great getaway from hectic Paris for lovers of the great outdoors.

GETTING THERE   Allow for a half day with lunch or a full day with a visit to the gardens and forest. **Trains** to Fontainebleau depart from the Gare de Lyon in Paris. The trip takes 45 minutes each way and costs 7.50€ one-way. Fontainebleau's railway station lies 3km (1¾ miles) north of the château, in the suburb of Avon. A local bus (marked simply CHATEAU and part of line A) makes the trip to the château at 15-minute intervals Monday through Saturday and at 30-minute intervals on Sunday; the fare is 1.40€ each way. If you're **driving,** take A6 south from Paris, exit onto N191, and follow the signs.

VISITOR INFORMATION   The **Office de Tourisme** is at 4 rue Royale, Fontaine-bleau (𝄐 **01-60-74-99-99;** www.fontainebleau-tourisme.com), opposite the main entrance to the château.

Exploring Fontainebleau

Musée National du Château de Fontainebleau ★★★ HISTORIC BUILDING/MUSEUM/GARDEN   Napoleon's affection for this palace is understandable. He followed the pattern of a succession of French kings who used

Château de Fontainebleau.

Fontainebleau as a resort and hunted in its forests. François I converted the hunting lodge into a royal palace in the Italian Renaissance style, bringing artists, including Benvenuto Cellini, there to work for him. Under this patronage, the School of Fontainebleau gained prestige, led by painters Rosso Fiorentino and Primaticcio. The artists adorned the 63m-long (207-ft.) **Gallery of François I ★★★**, where stucco-framed panels depict such scenes as *The Rape of Europa* and the monarch holding a pomegranate, a symbol of unity. The salamander, the symbol of the Chevalier king, is everywhere.

Sometimes called the Gallery of Henri II, the **Ballroom ★★★** displays the interlaced initials "H&D," referring to Henri and his mistress, Diane de Poitiers. Competing with this illicit tandem are the initials "H&C," symbolizing Henri and his dowdy wife, Catherine de Medici. At one end of the room is a monumental fireplace supported by two bronze satyrs, made in 1966 (the originals were melted down during the Revolution). At the other side is the **Balcony of the Musicians**, with sculptured garlands. Looking up, you can see a wonderful example of a Renaissance ceiling displaying octagonal coffering adorned with rosettes. Above the wainscoting is a series of frescoes, painted between 1550 and 1558, that depict subjects such as *The Feast of Bacchus*. An architectural curiosity is the richly adorned **Louis XV Staircase ★★**. To make room for th

Gallery of François I.

The Ballroom at the Château de Fontainebleau.

monumental stairway, the floor was removed from the upper level bedroom of the duchesse d'Etampes, but luckily the beautiful sculpture and paintings by artist Primaticcio, which decorated the duchess's suite, were incorporated into the final staircase design. Of the Italian frescoes that were preserved, one depicts the queen of the Amazons climbing into Alexander the Great's bed.

When Louis XIV ascended to the throne, Fontainebleau was all but forgotten due to the Sun King's preoccupation with Versailles. However, he wasn't opposed to using the palace for houseguests, specifically such unwanted ones as Queen Christina, who had abdicated the throne of Sweden in 1657 in a fit of religious fervor. Fontainebleau was conveniently on her way to Naples, which she was plotting to seize. Though Louis XV and Marie Antoinette took an interest in Fontainebleau, the château found its renewed glory under Napoleon, who used it as one of his bases. Imperial influences include the **throne room** where he abdicated rule of France, his **offices,** his monumental **bedroom,** and his **bathroom.** Some of the smaller Napoleonic rooms contain his personal mementos and artifacts. You will leave the chateau via the very horseshoe-shaped stairway where Napoleon stood to bid farewell to his shattered army before departing for Elba.

After your trek through the palace, visit the **gardens** and especially the **carp pond;** the gardens, however, are only a prelude to the Forest of Fontainebleau.

Place du Général-de-Gaulle. (✆ **01-60-71-50-70.** www.musee-chateau-fontainebleau.fr. *Grands appartements* 10€ adults, 8€ students 18–25 (includes audioguide); ticket to *petits appartements* and Napoleonic rooms 6.50€ adults, 5€ students 18–25, Combination ticket including the *Grands Appartements* plus another section 15 adults, free 17 and under. Apr–Sept Wed–Mon 30am–6pm; Oct–Mar Wed–Mon 9:30am–5pm.

The gardens at the Château de Fontainebleau.

Where to Eat

Le François-1er—Chez Bernard ★ TRADITIONAL FRENCH   The premier dining choice in Fontainebleau has Louis XIII decor, winemaking memorabilia, and walls that the owners think are about 200 years old. If weather permits, sit on the terrace overlooking the château and the cour des Adieux. Chef Bernard Crogiez's cuisine is meticulous, with an undeniable flair. Game from the royal hunting grounds is featured on the menu, seasonally ranging from hare, duck, and partridge. Modern variations of traditional dishes include a cassoulet of snails with flap mushrooms and garlic-flavored cream sauce, magret of duckling with cassis sauce, *rognon de veau* (veal kidneys) with mustard sauce, and a salad of baby scallops with crayfish. Cheese lovers should save room for some regional Brie de Meaux.

3 rue Royale. ✆ **01-64-22-24-68.** Reservations required. Main courses 23€–45€; fixed-price lunch Mon–Fri only 15€; fixed-price dinner daily 25€. AE, MC, V. Tues–Sun noon–2pm; Mon–Sat 7:30–10pm. Closed 2 weeks in Aug and 1 week in Dec.

Hiking Along Trails Left by French Kings

The Forest of Fontainebleau is riddled with *sentiers* (hiking trails) made by French kings and their entourages who went hunting in the forest. A *Guide des Sentiers* is available at the tourist information center (see above). Bike paths also cut through the forest. You can rent bikes at the Fontainebleau-Avon rail depot. At the station, go to the kiosk, **A La Petite Reine** (✆ **01-60-74-57-57**). The cost of a bike is 5€ per hour, 15€ for a half or full day. The kiosk is open Tuesday to Saturday from 9:30am to 7:30pm, and Sunday from 9am to 6pm.

La Table des Marechaux FRENCH   Located close to the château in the Hotel Napoleon, this is a great value gastronomic restaurant, especially lunch. Its modern sophisticated decor mirrors its traditional beautifully presented dishes. Start with the light vegetable mousse with scallop petals or splurge on the rich sautéed foie gras with apple jelly. Main courses include crispy cod with tapenade and filet of beef Rossini, a nod to of the château's main artists. Service is friendly and professional. In the summer, try to get a table on the terrace in the private garden.

9, rue Grande. ☎ **01-60-39-50-50.** www.naposite.com. Reservations recommended. Main courses 20€–32€; fixed-price menu 28€–40€. AE, MC, V. Daily noon–2pm and 7–10:30pm.

Where to Stay

Grand Hôtel de l'Aigle-Noir (The Black Eagle) ★   This 17th-century mansion, once the home of Cardinal de Retz, has been a hotel since 1764 and is certainly the finest lodging in Fontainebleau. Conveniently situated opposite the château, it fits into this regal setting with its formal courtyard entrance surrounded by a high iron grill-gate and pillars crowned by black eagles. The rooms are decorated with Louis XVI, Empire, or Regency-era antiques or reproductions, with plush beds and elegant bathroom amenities. Enjoy a drink in the Napoleon III–style piano bar before dinner.

27 place Napoleon-Bonaparte, 77300 Fontainebleau. www.hotelaiglenoir.fr. ☎ **01-60-74-60-00.** Fax 01-60-74-60-01. 51 units. 170€–240€ double; 380€ suite. AE, DC, MC, V. Parking 10€. Closed 2 last weeks of Dec. **Amenities:** Restaurant; bar; exercise room; pool (indoor); room service. *In room:* A/C, hair dryer, minibar, Wi-Fi (free).

VAUX LE VICOMTE

55km (34 miles) SE of Paris

Ambition, jealousy and treachery underlie the troubled history of the château de Vaux-le-Vicomte, the most influential baroque castle in all of Europe. For the first time, a château's architectural plan, its interior, and grounds were designed in unison by the era's top artistic minds, creating a perfectly harmonious effect. However, the lavish château would become the theater of the tragic downfall of its owner, Nicolas Fouquet, and the birth of an even more extravagant palace: the Château de Versailles.

Essentials

GETTING THERE   Vaux might not be the easiest place to get to, but it's well worth the effort. Take the RER line D to Melun at Châtelet-Les Halles, Gare de Lyon, or Gare du Nord (30 min.–1hr.; round-trip 16€). In Melun take the shuttle bus to the château (6€–8€ round-trip, weekends and public holidays only) or take a taxi (around 15€). If you don't take the shuttle back to the station, the château staff can call you a taxi, or call ☎ **01-64-52-51-50.** You can arrange bus tours through **ParisVision** (☎ **01-42-60-30-01;** www.parisvision.com; 25€–154€); also contact them for dinner and a visit to candlelight shows Saturdays at 6pm May to October (154€). If you're driving, take Autoroute A4 or A6 at Porte de Charenton or Ivry and follow the direction of Troyes-Nancy via the A5. Take the first exit at Saint-Germain-Laxis and follow the signs 1km (½ mile) to the château.

VISITOR INFORMATION Tourist help can be obtained at the **Service Jeunesse et Citoyenneté,** 2 av. Gallieni (✆ **01-60-56-55-10;** www.ville-melun.fr), located next to the train station in Melun. Open Tuesday to Saturday 10am to noon and 2 to 6pm.

EVENING SPECTACLES Candlelight evenings in the Vaux gardens take place on Saturdays from May through October. On the first and third Saturday of the month you can enjoy an extraspecial show including a fireworks display around 10:30pm. More information about tickets is on Vaux-le-Vicomte website listed above; excursions on these special evenings are also available through **Cityrama,** 149 rue St-Honoré, 1er (✆ **01-44-55-61-00;** www.pariscityrama.com)

Exploring Vaux le Vicomte

Le Château de Vaux le Vicomte HISTORIC BUILDING/MUSEUM/GARDEN Nicolas Fouquet, an aristocrat from an important noble family, acquired the estate of Vaux, well located between the royal castles Vincennes and Fontainebleau, in 1641 at the age of 26. Ambitious and clever, he quickly rose in the political ranks, soon reaching the prestigious position of superintendent of finance. In 1757, to create a stunning dwelling worthy of his status, Fouquet assembled an artistic dream team comprised of the architect Louis Le Vau, the landscape architect André le Nôtre, and the painter-decorator Charles Le Brun.

To inaugurate his spectacular residence, Fouquet organized a celebration on August 17, 1661, which would outshine any previously held at the court of Louis

Le Château de Vaux le Vicomte.

XIV. The king and several hundred courtiers were treated to a sumptuous banquet served on solid silver and gold tableware, followed by an original ballet-comedy written by Molière, during which guests were also presented with diamonds and other gifts. To top everything off, a phenomenal fireworks display showered the night sky. However, Fouquet had gone too far with his opulent fete, enraging the jealousy of the young king, which was further fueled by the malicious advice of the equally ambitious Jean-Baptiste Colbert, Fouquet's archrival, who lead the king to believe that Vaux had been built using misappropriated state funds. Within 2 weeks of his party, poor Fouquet was arrested, charged with embezzlement, and spent the rest of his days, not in the beautiful château he had just created, but in a decrepit prison cell. The king proceeded to "acquire" most of Vaux's tapestries, garden statues, and orange trees.

After the destitute Mrs. Fouquet sold Vaux in 1705, the château had various subsequent owners. Members of the Sommier family, which has owned it since the end of the 19th century, have done a lovely job restoring it to its original splendor.

The symmetrical château is flanked on either side by service buildings and is surrounded by a three-quarter rectangular moat. The front facade is rather simple; however, the south facade facing the gardens is where the grandeur is displayed, with an Italian-inspired central oval salon that soars up two stories and is crowned with an oval dome. Look carefully at the rear walls and you will also find "F" motifs and squirrels (Fouquet means squirrel), as well as images of the sun, a symbol that would be adopted by Louis XIV. The interior is beautifully decorated and has a much more intimate feel than Versailles. Many rooms feature allegorical Le Brun wall and ceiling paintings; some of the finest are in **King's Apartments** and **Fouquet's bedroom,** known as the Chambre des Muses. The kitchens add insight into the life of the era and it's also interesting to have a look at the vast cellars where there is usually a temporary exhibit. If you have enough energy, climb up to the top of the dome for the best views of the impressive gardens.

The true highlight of Vaux is the famed **Le Nôtre gardens.** Here, Le Nôtre fused various new landscaping principles developed in the first half of the 17th century, creating what would become the model *jardin à la française.*

Le Nôtre gardens at le Château de Vaux le Vicomte.

Grandes Fêtes in the Glowing Gardens

Experience a classic 17th-century *grande fête* (lavish party) during one of its *Chandelle* evenings, when the gardens and the castle are illuminated with 2,000 candles and costumed actors help re-create the ambience of the extravagant feasts in honor of the Sun King. For more information, see "Evening Spectacles," above

Walking through the garden, you will be surprised to find the distance between the different sections much farther away than it appears from the château's terrace. Le Nôtre designed the perspective so that the composition is balanced from every point of view, creating an optical illusion with widening canals, water basins, and patterned parterres (mirror motifs that Le Brun also used indoors), which extend nearly 3km (1½ miles) along the central axis. If you can make it all the way to the end to where the Farnese Hercules statue is perched, you will be rewarded with the vista of the whole grounds and the château.

Vaux Le Vicomte 77950 Maincy. ℭ **01-64-14-41-90.** www.vauxlevicomte.com. Admission day pass 16€ adults, 13€ students. Candlelight visit pass 19€ adults, 17€ students. Gardens only ticket 8€ adults and students. Mid-Mar to Oct and some public holidays such as Christmas Thurs–Tues 10am–6pm (daily in July–Aug). Candlelight evenings until midnight. Closed Nov to mid-Mar.

Where to Eat

Le Pouilly FRENCH   A 15-minute drive from Vaux is one of the region's best restaurants. Set in an old farmhouse, the dining room's stone walls covered with antique tapestries, the high ceiling with wooden beams, and the large fireplace add to its ageless charm. Michelin-starred Chef Anthony Vallette prepares traditional French cuisine with a dash of innovation. Taste the freshness of his daily "from the market" specials or try the "from the past to today" gastronomic menu, which could include mignon of deer with lime served with lobster and hazelnut cream, or braised pork with scallops a l'orange accompanied by turnips sprinkled with olive juice. For dessert, sample the American-inspired pumpkin flan.

1 rue de la fontaine, Pouilly le For, 77240 Vert Saint Denis. ℭ **01-64-09-56-64.** www.restaurant-lepouilly.com. Main courses 25€–45€; fixed-price menu 45€ and 78€. MC, V. Tue–Sun 12:15–1:30pm and 7:30–9:30pm. Closed Sun for dinner.

 Vaux on the Silver Screen

You may recognize Vaux-le-Vicomte even if you haven't been there yet. The château is a popular location for French and Hollywood movie shoots, most recently featured in *The Man in the Iron Mask* with Leonardo DiCaprio and Sophia Coppola's *Marie Antoinette*.

Les Charmilles MODERN FRENCH Located on the Diane parterre, facing the south facade of the château and the gardens, Les Charmilles' menu includes a variety of dishes from light salads to more elaborate plats du jour. Take a break from the summer heat with their chilled white asparagus soup or savor the succulent *magret de canard* with foie gras and finish off with roasted seasonal fruit draped in a spicy chocolate sauce. It is also open on the candlelight evenings, making it ideal for a romantic *dîner-à-deux* or glass of champagne under the stars before the fireworks begin.

Located in the Vaux Gardens ✆ **01-60-66-95-66.** Reservations recommended for candlelight evenings; ask about their special packages for these evenings. Main courses 10€–18€; fixed-price menu 35€. MC, V. Daily 11:30am–6pm and 11pm on candlelight evenings. Closed Nov–Mar.

PLANNING YOUR TRIP TO PARIS

by Sophie Nellis

GETTING THERE
By Plane

Paris has two international airports: **Aéroport d'Orly,** 18km (11 miles) south of the city, and **Aéroport Roissy-Charles-de-Gaulle,** 30km (19 miles) northeast. An Air France bus (Line 3; 19€ for a single journey) makes the 50- to 75-minute journey between the two airports every 30 to 45 minutes. A budget airport, **Beauvais,** is located about 70km (40m) from Paris.

ROISSY-CHARLES-DE-GAULLE AIRPORT There are two terminals at Roissy-Charles-De-Gaulle Airport (✆ 00-33-1-70-36-39-50 from abroad, or **39-50** from France only; www.aeroportsdeparis.fr), which are linked by a free train called the CDGVAL.

The quickest way into central Paris is the fast **RER B** (Réseau Express Régional; www.ratp.fr), local trains that leave every 10 to 15 minutes between 5am and midnight. It takes about 40 minutes to get to Paris, and RER B stops at several Métro stations including Gare du Nord (sometimes referred to as Paris Nord), Châtelet-Les-Halles, Saint-Michel-Notre-Dame, Luxembourg, Port-Royal, and Denfert-Rochereau. A single ticket costs 8.70€ and you can buy it from the machines located in the stations at both terminals.

You can also take an **Air France bus** (Line 2; ✆ 08-92-35-08-20; www.cars-airfrance.com) to central Paris for 15€ one-way; children 2 to 11 pay 7.50€. It stops at the Palais des Congrès (Porte Maillot) and continues to place Charles de Gaulle–Etoile, where you can take the Métro to anywhere in Paris. The journey, depending on the traffic, takes 45 to 55 minutes. The bus leaves every 20 minutes between 6am and 10pm and there are two additional buses that leave the airport at 10.30pm and 11pm.

The **Roissybus** (✆ 08-92-69-32-46; www.ratp.fr) departs from the airport daily from 6am to 11pm and costs 9.40€ for the 40- to 50-minute ride. Departures are every 15 to 20 minutes, and the bus leaves you in the center of Paris, at the corner of rue Scribe and rue Auber, near the Opera House.

A **taxi** from Roissy into the city will cost at least 50€, and the fare is 15% higher from 5pm to 10am, as well as on Sundays and Bank Holidays. Long, orderly lines for taxis form outside each of the airport's terminals.

ORLY AIRPORT Orly (✆ 00-33-1-70-36-39-50 from abroad, or **39-50** from France) has two terminals—Orly Sud (south) for international flights and Orly Ouest (west) for both domestic and international flights.

There are no direct trains from Orly to the center of Paris; however, you can take the 8-minute monorail **OrlyVal** to the RER station "Anthony" to get **RER B** into the center. Combined travel time is about 45 to 55 minutes, and it stops at several Métro stations including Denfert-Rochereau, Port-Royal, Luxembourg, Saint-Michel-Notre-Dame, Châtelet-Les-Halles, and Gare du Nord (sometimes referred to as Paris Nord). Trains run between 6am and 11pm and the one-way fare for the OrlyVal plus the RER B is 10€.

PREVIOUS PAGE: **A taxi on the Champs-Élysées.**

Air France buses (Line 1; ✆ **08-92-35-08-20;** www.cars-airfrance. com) leave from Exit L of Orly Sud and from Exit B-C of Orly Ouest every 20 minutes between 6am and 11:30pm, stopping at Gare Montparnasse, Invalides, and Charles de Gaulle-Etoile. The fare is 12€ one-way, 19€ round-trip, and 5.50€ for children ages 2 to 11. Depending on the traffic, the journey takes between 30 and 50 minutes.

A **taxi** from Orly to central Paris will cost at least 50€, and the fare is 15% higher from 5pm to 10am, as well as on Sundays and Bank Holidays. Lines for taxis form outside Exit L of Orly Sud and Gate B on the arrivals level of Orly Ouest.

BEAUVAIS AIRPORT   Beauvais airport (✆ **08-92-68-20-66;** www.aeroport beauvais.com) is located 70km (40 miles) from Paris and is served by budget airlines such as Ryanair, Wizzair, and Blueair. Buses leave 15 to 20 minutes after each flight has landed, and, depending on the traffic, take about an hour to get to Paris. The bus drops you at Porte Maillot (Métro: Porte Maillot). To return to Beauvais, you need to be at the bus station 3 hours and 15 minutes before the departure of your flight. A one-way ticket costs 15€.

By Train

Paris has six major stations: **Gare d'Austerlitz** (55 quai d'Austerlitz, 13e), serving the center of France, with trains to and from the Loire Valley and Limousin, as well as night trains to Nice and Spain; **Gare de Lyon** (Place Louis-Armand, 12e), serving the center and southeast, with trains to and from Burgundy, the Alpes, Provence, the Côte d'Azur (Nice, Cannes, St-Tropez), and beyond, to Geneva and Italy; **Gare Montparnasse** (17 bd. Vaugirard, 15e), serving the west, and southwest with trains to and from Brittany, Normandy, Bordeaux, as well as trains to the northwest of Spain; **Gare St-Lazare** (13 rue d'Amsterdam, 8e), serving the northwest, with trains to and from Normandy. **Gare de l'Est** (Place du 11-Novembre-1918, 10e), serving the east, with trains to and from Strasbourg, Reims, and beyond, to Germany, Switzerland and Austria; and **Gare du Nord** (18 rue de Dunkerque, 10e), serving the north, with trains to and from Picardy, and beyond, to the U.K., Holland, Denmark, and Germany. Each station can be reached by bus or Métro; further information on each station can be obtained from **SNCF** (La Société Nationale des Chemins de Fer Français; ✆ **36-35;** www.gares-connexions.com/en).

Eurostar services from Paris to London and Brussels arrive at and depart from the Gare du Nord (www.eurostar.com). Thanks to the new high-speed track, the journey between Paris and London St. Pancras now only takes 2hrs15 (it's a little longer if the train goes via Ashford or Lille). Cheap return tickets to London are available for 88€ if you are flexible about the times and dates of your trip.

For information about train travel from Paris to other parts of France or other destinations in Europe, and to make reservations, use SNCF (www. voyages-sncf.com). Prices depend on the distance of the journey, when you make the reservation, and the type of train you book (the **TGV,** France's high-speed train service, for example, is usually more expensive than regional trains). For further information about international train travel try **Rail Europe** (www.raileurope.com). **Warning:** As in most major cities, the stations and surrounding areas are rather seedy and frequented by pickpockets. Be alert, especially at night.

By Bus

Most coaches arrive at the **Eurolines France** station, 28 av. du Général-de-Gaulle, Bagnolet (✆ **08-92-89-90-91;** www.eurolines.fr; Métro: Gallieni).

By Car

Driving in Paris is *not* recommended. Parking is difficult and the traffic dense. If you drive, remember that Paris is encircled by a ring road, the *périphérique.* Always obtain detailed directions to your destination, including the name of the exit (called *portes*) on the *périphérique* (exits aren't numbered). Avoid rush hours.

The major highways into Paris are A1 from the north; A13 from Rouen, Normandy, and other points northwest; A10 from Spain and the southwest; A6 and A7 from the French Alps, the Riviera, and Italy; and A4 from eastern France.

The Channel Tunnel—the undersea rail tunnel that connects France and the U.K.—accommodates not only trains but cars, buses, taxis, and motorcycles. The Chunnel, as it is informally known, carries the Eurostar and the **Eurotunnel,** a train that carries vehicles under the English Channel (✆ **08-10-63-03-04** in France, or 08444 63 00 00 in the U.K.; www.eurotunnel.com), connecting Calais, France, with Folkestone, England; the journey takes a mere 35 minutes. It operates up to four shuttles an hour and prices start at 30€ per car.

Rental cars are available at all the major airports and train stations in Paris. You must be over 25 and have held a driving license for at least a year. The major car rental companies are **Hertz** (✆ **01-55-31-93-21;** www.hertz.fr), **Europcar** (✆ **01-53-64-16-24;** www.europcar.fr), **Avis** (✆ **08-21-23-07-60;** www.avis.fr), and **Ada** (✆ **01-48-06-58-13;** www.ada.fr).

By Ferry from England or Ireland

Ferry travel to France appears to be in its waning days, since more and more travelers are opting for low-cost flights or a much speedier passage through the Channel Tunnel. In England the two leading operators of ferries are **P&O Ferries** (✆ **08716 64 21 21** in the U.K.; www.poferries.com), which runs ferries from Dover to Calais, and **Britanny Ferries** (✆ **08712 44 07 44** in the U.K.; www.britanny-ferries.com), which runs ferries from Portsmouth to Le Havre. **Irish Ferries** (✆ **0818 300 400** in Ireland; www.irishferries.com) operates an overnight ferry from Cherbourg to Rosslare. Call or check websites for specific times, prices, and points of departure/arrival.

GETTING AROUND

Finding an Address

The river Seine divides Paris into the **Rive Droite (Right Bank)** to the north and the **Rive Gauche (Left Bank)** to the south. Paris is divided into 20 municipal districts called arrondissements. Arrondissements spiral out clockwise from the 1st, which is the geographical center of the city. The 2nd through the 8th form a ring around the 1st, and the 9th through the 17th form an outer ring around the inner ring. The 18th, 19th, and 20th are at the far northern and eastern reaches of the Right Bank. Arrondissements 5, 6, 7, 13, 14, and 15 are on the Left Bank.

Most city maps are divided by arrondissement, and addresses include the arrondissement number (in Roman or Arabic numerals and followed by "éme" or "e," for example, 10éme). Paris also has its own version of a zip code. The mailing address for a hotel is written as, for example, "Paris 75014." The last two digits, 14, indicate that the address is in the 14th arrondissement—in this case, Montparnasse.

Numbers on buildings running parallel to the Seine usually follow the course of the river—east to west. On perpendicular streets, the lowest building numbers are closest to the river.

MAPS

If you're staying more than 2 or 3 days, purchase an inexpensive pocket-size book called *Paris Pratique par arrondissement*, available at newsstands and bookshops for around 7€. This guide provides you with a Métro map and maps of each arrondissement, with all streets listed and keyed. Free maps of the Paris Métro and bus and RER networks are available at all Métro stations.

By Public Transport

The majority of Paris's public transport is run by **RATP** (Régie Autonome des Transports Parisiens; *C* **08-92-69-32-46,** or 32-46 in France; www.ratp.fr). Paris and its suburbs are divided into six travel zones, and the city itself is covered by zones 1 and 2.

RATP tickets are valid on the Métro, bus, and RER. You can buy tickets over the counter or from machines at most Métro entrances. A **single ticket** costs 1.70€ and a *carnet* of 10 tickets costs 12€. Tourists can benefit from a **Paris Visite** pass, which offers unlimited travel in zones on bus, Métro, and RER, and discounts on some attractions. A 1-day pass for zones 1 to 3 costs 9.30€, 2-day pass 15€, a 3-day pass 21€ and a 5-day pass 30€. Slightly cheaper is the 1-day **Mobilis** ticket, which offers unlimited travel in zones 1 and 2 and costs 6.10€. For travelers under 26, look out for the **Ticket Jeune,** which can be used on a Saturday, Sunday, or bank holiday, and which provides unlimited travel in zones 1 to 3 for 3.40€.

If you're staying for a while, it's worth getting the **Navigo Découverte,** a swipe card that you can buy at most stations for 5€. You must provide a passport photo, but once you have the card it offers unlimited travel in the relevant zones. The weekly tariff (which runs Mon–Sat) for zones 1 and 2 is 18€, and the monthly tariff (which runs from the first to the last day of the month) is 60€.

BY MÉTRO (SUBWAY)

The Métro is the fastest and most efficient way to get around Paris. All lines have a different number and color, and the final destination of each line, which will tell you which direction the train is going in, is clearly marked on subway maps, and in the system's underground passageways. The Métro runs daily from 5:30am to 12:40am (last departure at 1:30am Fri–Sat). It's reasonably safe at any hour but beware of pickpockets.

To familiarize yourself with the Métro, check out the color map on the inside back cover of this book. Most stations display a map of the Métro at the entrance. To locate your train on a map, find your destination, follow the line to the end of its route, and note the name of the final stop, which is that line's direction. In the station, follow the signs for your direction in the passageways until you come to the right platform.

To change lines follow the signs saying *Correspondances*, which usually indicate the numbers of the other Métro lines. Some stations such as Châtelet-Les-Halles, République, and Montparnasse-Bienvenüe require long walks. Don't follow a *Sortie* (exit) sign, or you'll have to pay again to get back on the train.

At the turnstile entrances to the Métro, insert your ticket and pass through. Hold onto your ticket as you occasionally need it to change trains or exit a station. There are also occasional ticket checks on trains in Métro stations.

BY RER

A suburban train system, **RER** (Réseau Express Regional), passes through the heart of Paris, traveling faster than the Métro and running daily from 5:30am to 1am. This system works like the Métro and requires the same tickets (if you stay within zones 1 and 2). The major stops on Paris's Right Bank, linking the RER to the Métro, are Nation, Gare de Lyon, St-Lazare, Charles-de-Gaulle–Etoile, Gare de l'Est, Gare du Nord, as well as Châtelet-Les-Halles. On the Left Bank, RER stops include Denfert-Rochereau, St-Michel, Invalides, and Champ de Mars Tour Eiffel. The five RER lines are marked A through E, and each line corresponds to a different color. Different branches are labeled by a number, for example the C5 Line serving Versailles-Rive Gauche. Electric signboards next to each track outline all the possible stops along the way. Make sure that the little square next to your intended stop is lit.

BY BUS

Buses are obviously slower than the Métro. The majority run from 6:30am to 9:30pm (a few operate until 12:30am) and service is limited on Sundays and holidays. You can use Métro tickets on the buses or you can buy tickets directly from the driver (1.80€). Tickets need to be validated in the machine next to the driver's cabin.

There is usually a map of the bus route at the bus stop, which lists all of the stops, highlights which stop you are currently at, and indicates the direction of travel. Each bus route has a different number and a corresponding color. Inside the bus, the next stop is usually written on an electronic panel on the ceiling of the bus. Press the red button when you want to get off.

At night, after the bus and Métro services stop running, there are a number of night bus lines called **Noctilien** (www.noctilien.fr). Most of the lines leave from Place du Châtelet and pass by the main train stations, crossing the city's major streets before leaving Paris for the suburbs (Mon–Thurs every hour 12:30am–5:30am; Fri–Sat every 30 min.). Although often a little rowdy, the night buses are usually quite safe. Tickets cost 1.80€ if bought from the driver but travel passes are valid.

BY TRAM

Paris has three tramway lines, but these lines are currently being extended and four new lines are being added. The projects are due to be completed by the end of 2012. Line 1 runs from Saint-Denis RER station to Noiry-le-Sec; Line 2 runs from La Défense to Porte de Versailles–Parc des expositions; and Line 3 from Pont du Garigliano to Porte d'Ivry. All three lines connect to bus stops and both Métro and RER stations, and tickets are the same price as the Métro. However, because they run along the outskirts of Paris, most visitors are not likely to take them.

By Bicycle

Cycling in Paris has been revolutionized by the hugely successful **Vélib'** scheme (the name comes from *vélo* meaning bicycle and *liberté* meaning freedom) launched in 2007 (www.velib.paris.fr). There are now more than 20,000 bicycles available at 1,500 stations—that's one every 300m (186 ft.)—around Paris. The service can be accessed at any time of day and to get a bike you need to have an account. Creating one is reasonably easy to do on the machines located at every Vélib' stand, but make sure you select the English-language option before you read the instructions. You can choose either a 1-day (1€) or 7-day (5€) account (which you have to pay for using a credit card) and you will be asked to choose a PIN code. This will give you unlimited access to the Vélib' service. You then use the PIN to select a bike from the bikes available at your stand. Journeys under 30 minutes are free, and after that the price goes up by 1€ every half an hour. If you arrive at a Vélib' station to return a bike and discover it is full, you can enter your code in the machine and have 15 minutes to find another terminal. To use the services you will be asked to pay a 150€ *caution* (deposit), which freezes the money in your account until the bike is returned. With foreign credit cards this can sometimes take a couple of days. **Note:** It is preferable to cycle in cycle lanes—there are 400km (250 miles) of green cycle paths in Paris—and it's illegal to cycle on footpaths or down one-way streets. Remember to cycle on the right-hand side of the street and to give way to your right. Remember that the bikes do not come with helmets.

Alternatively, you can rent a bike from **Paris à vélo, c'est sympa!** (22 rue Alphonse Baudin; ✆ 01-48-87-60-01; www.parisvelosympa.com; Métro: St-Sébastien-Froissart or Richard Lenoir). Rentals cost 12€ for half a day and 15€ for a full day, but they do require 250€ or a passport as a deposit. Open Monday to Friday from 9:30am to 1pm and 2 to 6pm, Saturday and Sunday 9am to 7pm. Closed Tuesday.

Vintage Vespas are available for rent from **Left Bank Scooters** (✆ 06-78-12-04-24; www.leftbankscooters.com) for 90€ per day, and the company will deliver the scooters to your hotel or apartment. A credit card deposit of 1,200€ is required, but this can be reduced to 500€ for an additional fee. This amount is held rather than charged on a credit card.

Note that bicycles are not allowed on buses or the Métro, except on Line 1 on Sundays and public holidays, until 4:30pm. Bikes can be taken aboard all RER trains except during rush hours (Mon–Fri 6:30–9am and 4:30–7pm).

By Boat

The **Batobus** (✆ 08-25-05-01-01; www.batobus.com) is a 150-passenger boat that operates along the Seine, stopping at such points of interest as the **Eiffel Tower, Musée d'Orsay,** the **Louvre, Notre-Dame,** and the **Hôtel de Ville.** Unlike the Bateaux-Mouches (p. 52), the Batobus does not provide recorded commentary. The only fare option available is a day pass valid for either 1, 2, or 5 days, each allowing as many entrances and exits as you want. A 1-day pass costs 13€ for adults, and 7€ for children 16 and under. Boats operate daily (closed most of Jan) every 15 to 30 minutes, starting between 10 and 10:30am and ending at 4:30pm from November to March, 7pm in April and May and September and October, and 9:30pm from June to August. The timetable changes slightly every year so it's always worth double-checking on the website.

By Taxi

Taxi drivers are organized into a union that limits their number to around 15,000, which can make it difficult to find a taxi in Paris. It's virtually impossible to get a taxi at rush hour, and your best option for finding a taxi is often to wait at a *station de taxis*. Located across the city, you'll find a *station de taxi* by looking for a blue sign saying TAXI above a turquoise column.

You can hail regular cabs on the street when their signs are lit with a white light. An orange light means a taxi is occupied. Taxis are easier to find at the many stands near Métro stations. The flag drops at 2.20€ and the rates are then based on time and zone. From 10am to 5pm you pay .89€ per kilometer, from 5pm to 10am you pay 1.14€ to 1.38 € per kilometer. Journeys within Paris usually cost between 6€ and 20€, and there is a minimum fee of 6€.

You're allowed several pieces of luggage free if they're transported inside and are less than 5 kilograms (11 lb.). Heavier suitcases carried in the trunk cost 1€ to 2€ apiece. For radio cabs, call or reserve on the internet: **Les Taxis Bleus** (✆ 01-49-36-29-48; www.taxis-bleus.com), **Taxi G7** (✆ 01-47-39-47-39; www.taxisg7.fr). Avoid minicabs or unlicensed taxis and make sure the meter is at 2.20€ when you first get in.

On Foot

Paris is made for walking; this is the only real way to explore the city in any depth. Stroll the streets and absorb the sights and smells. On almost every block you will find something of interest—a Belle Epoque shopping arcade, a Renaissance square, a medieval rampart. After walking through an arrondissement, stop in a cafe for coffee and a spot of people-watching. If you'd like more guidance instead of an aimless stroll, you can always refer to chapter 5, "Strolling Around Paris."

[FastFACTS]

Area Codes The country code for France is 33 and the area code for Paris is 01. See "Telephones," later in this section, for further information.

Business Hours Opening hours in Paris are erratic. Most museums close on 1 day a week (usually Mon or Tues) and some national holidays. Museum hours tend to be from 9:30am to 6pm. Some museums, particularly the smaller ones, close for lunch from noon to 2pm. Generally, **offices** are open Monday to Friday from 9am to 6pm, but don't count on it—always call first. **Banks** tend to be open from 9am to 5pm Monday to Friday but some branches are also open on Saturday. **Large stores** are open from around 10am to 6 or 7pm without a break for lunch. Some **small stores** have a lunch break that can last for up to 2 hours, from noon onward, but this is becoming increasingly rare. Most shops, except those in the Marais or on the Champs-Élysées, are closed on Sunday. Restaurants are typically closed on Mondays and many businesses across the city are closed in August.

Car Rental See "Getting There by Car," earlier in this chapter.

Cellphones See "Mobile Phones," later in this section.

Crime See "Safety," later in this section.

Customs What you can bring into France: Citizens of E.U. countries can bring in any amount of goods as long as the goods are intended for their personal use and not for resale. Non-E.U. citizens are entitled to 200 cigarettes, 100 small cigars, 50 cigars, or 250g of tobacco duty-free. You can also bring in 2 liters of wine or beer and 1 liter of spirits (more than 22% alcohol). In addition, you can bring in 50g (1.76oz) of perfume.

What you can take out of France:

Australian Citizens: A helpful brochure is available from the Australian Customs and Border Protection Service *Know Before You Go,* online under "Information for travelers." For more information, call the **Australian Customs Service** (✆ **1300/363-263** in Australia, or 612/6275-6666 if you're abroad; www.customs.gov.au). The duty-free allowance in Australia is A$900 or, for those 17 or younger, A$450. If you're returning with valuables you already own, you should file the "Goods Imported in Passenger Baggage" form.

Canadian Citizens: For a clear summary of Canadian rules, ask for the booklet *I Declare* issued by the **Canada Border Services Agency** (✆ **800/461-9999** in Canada, or 204/983-3500 from abroad; www.cbsa-asfc.gc.ca, under "Going on Vacation?"). Canada allows its citizens a C$750 exemption and you're allowed to mail gifts to Canada from abroad valued at less than C$60 a day, provided they're unsolicited and don't contain alcohol or tobacco (write on the package "Unsolicited gift, under C$60 value"). All valuables, including serial numbers of valuables you already own, should be declared on the Y-38 form before departure from Canada.

New Zealand Citizens: The answers to most questions regarding customs can be found on the website of the **New Zealand Customs Service** (✆ **0800/4-CUSTOMS,** 0800/428-786, or 649/300-5399 from outside New Zealand; www.customs.govt.nz). The duty-free allowance for New Zealand is NZ$700. Fill out a certificate of export, listing the valuables you are taking out of the country so that you can bring them back without paying duty.

U.K. Citizens: When returning to the U.K. from an E.U. country such as France, you can bring in an unlimited amount of most goods. There is no limit on what you can bring back from an E.U. country, as long as the items are for personal use (this includes gifts) and you have already paid the duty and tax. However, if you bring in more than these levels, you may be asked to prove that the goods are for your own use. For information, contact **HM Revenue Customs** (✆ **0845 010 9000;** www.hmrc. gov.uk).

U.S. Citizens: For specifics on what you can bring back and the corresponding fees, download the invaluable free pamphlet *Know Before You Go* online at **www.cbp.gov**. Or, contact the **U.S. Customs & Border Protection (CBP)** (✆ **877/CBP-5511** [877/227-5511] in the U.S. or 703/526-4200 from outside the U.S.) Returning U.S. citizens who have been away for 48 hours or more are allowed to bring back, once every 30 days, $800 worth of merchandise duty-free. You're charged a flat rate of duty on the next

$1,000 worth of purchases, and any dollar amount beyond that is subject to duty at whatever rates apply. On mailed gifts, the duty-free limit is $200. To avoid having to pay duty on foreign-made personal items you owned before your trip, bring along a bill of sale, insurance policy, jeweler's appraisal, or receipt of purchase or register items before you leave. You cannot bring fresh foodstuffs into the U.S.

Disabled Travelers Paris is an old city and therefore not particularly well equipped to welcome disabled travelers. However, this is changing, and if you visit the tourist office's website (www.parisinfo.com) and click on "Paris Pratique," you'll find links to a number of guides and websites dedicated to travelers with disabilities. This includes a link to *Access Paris,* a guidebook that can also be downloaded in PDF format. With the exception of Line 14 and several other stations, most Métro lines do not have disabled access, and are not always equipped with either escalators or elevators. Buses are a much better option for disabled visitors, as many lines are now equipped with lowering floors and space for wheelchairs. RER lines and some SNCF services are wheelchair-accessible (call 📞 **08-10-64-64-64,** or see www.infomobi.com for a useful disabled-access version of the Paris Métro map). Paris taxis are legally obliged to take passengers in wheelchairs.

Doctors Doctors are listed in the Pages Jaunes (French equivalent of the Yellow Pages, www. pagesjaunes.fr) under *Médecins: Médecine générale.* If you're using the website, you can search for a doctor in your neighborhood by typing your post code (for example 75006 if you're staying in the 6th arrondissement) in the "Où" box. The minimum fee for a consultation is about 23€—for this rate look for a doctor who is described as "conventionée secteur 1." The higher the "secteur," the higher the fee. **SOS Médecins** (📞 **36-24** or 01-47-07-77-77) makes house calls that cost 70€ before 7pm and from 110€ after 7pm or on holidays (prices quoted are for people without French social security). The **Urgences Médicales de Paris** (📞 **01-53-94-94-94**) also makes house calls and some doctors speak English. During the day it costs 60€, until midnight 80€, and after midnight 90€ (if you don't have French social security). See also "Emergencies" and "Health," later in this section.

Drinking Laws Supermarkets, grocery stores, and cafes sell alcoholic beverages. The legal drinking age is 18, but persons under that age can be served alcohol in a bar or restaurant if accompanied by a parent or legal guardian. Wine and liquor are sold every day of the week, year-round. Hours of cafes vary. Some open at 6am, serving drinks to 3am; others are open 24 hours. Bars and nightclubs may stay open as late as they wish.

The law regarding drunk driving is tough. A motorist is considered "legally intoxicated" if his or her blood-alcohol limit exceeds .05%. If it is under .08% (the limit in the U.K., Ireland, and some U.S. states) the driver faces a fine of 135€. Over .08% and it could cost 4,500€ or up to 2 years in jail. If you cause an accident while drunk driving the fine could be increased to 30,000€, and if you cause serious injury or death, you face 10 years in jail and a fine of up to 150,000€.

Driving Rules The French drive on the right. At junctions where there are no signposts indicating the right of way, cars coming from the right have priority. Many roundabouts now give priority to those on the roundabout. If this is not indicated, priority is for those coming from the right.

Drugstores You'll spot French *pharmacies* by looking for the green neon cross above the door. If your local pharmacy is closed, there should be a sign on the door indicating the nearest one open. *Parapharmacies* sell medical products and toiletries, but they don't dispense prescriptions. Both the **Pharmacie des Champs-Élysées** (84 av. des Champs-Élysées; Métro: George V; ☎ **01-45-62-02-41**) and the **Pharmacie Européene de la Place de Clichy** (6 Place de Clichy; Métro: Place de Clichy; ☎ **01-48-74-65-18**) are open 24 hours daily. See also "Emergencies" and "Health," later in this section.

Electricity Electricity in France runs on 220 volts AC (60 cycles). Adapters or transformers are needed to fit sockets, which you can buy in branches of Darty, FNAC, or BHV. Many hotels have two-pin (in some cases, three-pin) sockets for electric razors.

Embassies & Consulates If you have a passport, immigration, legal, or other problem, contact your consulate. Call before you go—they often keep odd hours and observe both French and home-country holidays.

The Embassy of **Australia** is at 4 rue Jean-Rey, 15e (☎ **01-40-59-33-00;** www. france.embassy.gov.au; Métro: Bir Hakeim), open Monday to Friday 9am to noon and 2 to 4pm.

The Embassy of **Canada** is at 35 av. Montaigne, 8e (☎ **01-44-43-29-00;** www. amb-canada.fr; Métro: Franklin-D-Roosevelt or Alma-Marceau), open Monday to Friday 9am to noon and 2 to 5pm.

The Embassy of **Ireland** is at 4 rue Rude, 16e (☎ **01-44-17-67-00;** www.embassy ofireland.fr; Métro: Etoile), open Monday to Friday 9:30am to noon.

The embassy of **New Zealand** is at 7ter rue Léonard-de-Vinci, 16e (☎ **01-45-01-43-43;** www.nzembassy.com; Métro: Victor Hugo), open Monday to Thursday 9am to 1pm and 2 to 5.30pm, Friday 9am to 1pm and 2 to 4pm.

The Embassy of the **United Kingdom** is at 35 Rue du Faubourg St-Honoré, 8e (☎ **01-44-51-31-00;** http://ukinfrance.fco.gov.uk; Métro: Concorde or Madeleine), open Monday to Friday 9:30am to 1pm and 2:30 to 6pm.

The Embassy of the **United States,** 2 av. Gabriel, 8e (☎ **01-43-12-22-22;** http:// france.usembassy.gov; Métro: Concorde), is open Monday to Friday 9am to 6pm.

Emergencies In an emergency, call ☎ **112** from a mobile phone, or the fire brigade (*Sapeurs-Pompiers*) (☎ **18**), who are trained to deal with all kinds of medical emergencies, not just fires. For an ambulance, call ☎ **15**. For the police, call ☎ **17.**

Etiquette & Customs Parisians like pleasantries and take manners seriously: Say *bonjour, madame/monsieur,* when entering an establishment and *au revoir* when you depart. Always say *pardon* when you accidentally bump into someone. With strangers, people who are older than you, and professional contacts, use *vous* rather than *tu* (*vous* is the polite form of the pronoun you).

Family Travel To locate accommodations, restaurants, and attractions that are particularly kid-friendly, look for the "Kids" icon throughout this guide.

Health For travel abroad, non-E.U. nationals should consider buying medical travel insurance. For U.S. citizens, Medicare and Medicaid do not provide coverage for medical costs incurred abroad, so check what medical services your health insurance covers before leaving home. U.K. nationals will need a **European Health Insurance Card (EHIC)** to receive free or reduced-cost medical care during a visit to a European Economic Area (EEA) country or Switzerland (go to www.ehic.org.uk for further information).

If you suffer from a chronic illness, consult your doctor before your departure. Pack prescription medications in your carry-on luggage and carry them in their original containers, with pharmacy labels—otherwise they won't make it through airport security. Carry the generic name of prescription medicines, in case a local pharmacist is unfamiliar with the brand name.

For further tips on travel and health concerns, and a list of local English-speaking doctors contact the **International Association for Medical Assistance to Travelers** (**IAMAT;** ✆ **716/754-4883** in the U.S., or 416/652-0137 in Canada; www.iamat.org). You can also find listings of reliable medical clinics overseas at the **International Society of Travel Medicine** (www.istm.org). See also "Doctors," "Drugstores," "Emergencies," and "Hospitals."

Holidays Major holidays are New Year's Day (January 1), Easter Sunday and Monday (Late Mar/Apr), May Day (May 1), VE Day (May 8), Ascension Thursday (40 days after Easter), Pentecost/Whitsunday and Whitmonday (seventh Sun and Mon after Easter), Bastille Day (July 14), Assumption Day (Aug 15), All Saints Day (Nov 1), Armistice Day (Nov 11), and Christmas Day (Dec 25). For more information on holidays, see "Paris Calendar of Events," p. 46.

Hospitals Open Monday to Saturday from 8am to 6/7pm, **Central Médical Europe,** 44 rue d'Amsterdam, 9e (✆ **01-42-81-93-33;** www.center-medical-europe.com; Métro: Liège or St-Lazare), maintains contacts with medical and dental practitioners in all fields.

The following hospitals have 24 hour accident and emergency services: **Hôpital Hôtel Dieu** (1 Place du Parvis Notre-Dame, 4e; ✆ **01-42-34-82-34**), **Hôpital St-Louis** (1 av. Claude-Vellefaux, 10e; ✆ **01-42-49-49-49**), **Hôpital St-Antoine** (184 Rue du Faubourg-St-Antoine, 12e; ✆ **01-49-28-00-00**), **Hôpital de la Pitié-Salpêtrière** (47-83 Bld de l'Hôpital, 13e; ✆ **01-42-16-00-00**), **Hôpital Cochin** (27 Rue du Faubourg St-Jacques, 14e; ✆ **01-58-41-41-41**), **Hôpital Européen Georges Pompidou** (20 Rue Leblanc, 15e; ✆ **01-56-09-20-00**), **Hôpital Bichat-Claude Bernard** (46 Rue Henri-Huchard, 18e; ✆ **01-40-25-80-80**), and **Hôpital Tenon** (4 Rue de la Chine, 20e; ✆ **01-56-01-70-00**).

There are two private hospitals with English-speaking staff that operate 24 hours daily: the **American Hospital of Paris** (63 bd. Victor-Hugo, Neuilly, 17e; ✆ **01-46-41-25-25;** www.american-hospital.org; Métro: Pont de Levallois or Pont de Neuilly; bus: 82) and **Hertford British Hospital, Hôpital Franco-Britannique** (3 Rue Barbès, 92300 Levallois-Perret; ✆ **01-46-39-22-22;** www.british-hospital.org; Métro: Anatole-France).

Hot Lines S.O.S. Help is a hot line for English-speaking callers in crisis at ✆ **01-46-21-46-46;** www.soshelpline.org. Open 3 to 11pm daily.

Internet & Wi-Fi Many Parisian hotels and cafes have internet access, and Wi-Fi (pronounced *wee-fee*) is becoming increasingly common in cafes and public spaces. To find cybercafes in Paris, check **www.cybercaptive.com** and **www.cybercafe.com**. The latter lists 20 such cafes scattered throughout central Paris. Cybercafes tend to be pretty pricey, but a reasonably priced option is **Luxembourg Micro,** 81 bd. Saint-Michel, 5e (✆ **01-46-33-27-98;** Métro: Luxembourg; www.luxembourg-micro.com). For 15 minutes, you pay .90€, for 30 minutes 1.80€, and for an hour 2.50€. It's open daily from 9am to 10pm.

Language English is widely understood in Paris, and is common in all the tourist areas—museums, hotels, restaurants, cafes, and nightclubs. For handy French words and phrases, as well as food and menu terms, refer to chapter 12, "Useful Terms & Phrases." A good phrasebook is *Frommer's French PhraseFinder & Dictionary.*

Legal Aid In an emergency, especially if you get into trouble with the law, your country's embassy or consulate will provide legal advice. See "Embassies & Consulates," above.

LGBT Travelers France is one of the world's most tolerant countries toward gays and lesbians. "Gay Paree" boasts a large gay population, and an openly gay mayor, Bertrand Delanoë. The center of gay and lesbian life is Le Marais, particularly on Rues St-Croix-de-la-Bretonnerie, des Archives, and Vieille-du-Temple. The annual Gay Pride March takes place on the last Sunday in June. Information and resources can be found in Paris's largest, best-stocked gay bookstore, **Les Mots à la Bouche,** 6 rue Ste-Croix-de-la-Bretonnerie, 4e (ℂ **01-42-78-88-30;** www.motsbouche.com; Métro: Hôtel-de-Ville), which carries publications in both French and English. *Têtu* (www.tetu.com) and *Préf* (www.prefmag.com) are two magazines dedicated to gay life that have texts in English. *La Dixième Muse* (www.ladixiememuse.com) is the lesbian equivalent. In addition, both www.paris-gay.com and www.gayvox.com have updated listings about the gay and lesbian scene and events.

Lost & Found All lost objects—except those found in train stations or on trains—are taken to the **Bureau des Objets Trouvés** (36 Rue des Morillons, 15e; ℂ **08-21-00-25-25;** www.prefecture-police-paris.interieur.gouv.fr). It's better to visit in person than to call, but be warned that there are huge delays in processing claims. It's open from Monday to Thursday 8:30am to 5pm and Friday 8:30am to 4:30pm. Objects lost on the Métro are held by the station agents before being sent onto the Bureau des Objets Trouvés. If you lose something on a train or in a train station, go to the Lost Property office of the SNCF station in question.

Mail Most post offices in Paris are open Monday to Friday from 8am to 5pm and every Saturday from 8am to noon. The main post office (52 rue du Louvre Métro: Louvre-Rivoli) is open 24 hours daily. Stamps are also sold in *tabacs* (tobacconists). Tariffs depend on the weight and size of the letter or package but more information can be found on www.laposte.fr.

Medical Requirements Unless you are arriving from an area of the world known to be suffering from an epidemic, especially cholera or yellow fever, inoculations or vaccinations are not required for entry in France.

Mobile Phones The three letters that define much of the world's wireless capabilities are **GSM** (Global System for Mobile Communications), a big, seamless network that makes for easy cross-border mobile phone use throughout Europe and dozens of other countries worldwide. You can use your mobile phone in France provided it is GSM and tri-band or quad-band, just confirm this with your operator before you leave.

Using your phone abroad can be expensive, and you usually have to pay to receive calls, so it's a good idea to get it "unlocked" before you leave. This means you can buy a SIM card from one of the three French providers: **Bouygues Télécom** (www.bouygues telecom.fr), **Orange** (www.orange.fr), or **SFR** (www.sfr.fr). A SIM card with 5€ call credit costs about 10€. Alternatively, if you're phone isn't unlocked, you could buy a cheap mobile phone. To top-up your phone credit, buy a Mobicarte from *tabacs,* supermarkets, and mobile phone outlets. Prices range from 5€ to 100€.

Money & Costs

THE VALUE OF THE EURO VS. OTHER POPULAR CURRENCIES

Euro (€)	US$	C$	UK£	A$	NZ$
1	1.37	1.36	0.86	1.38	1.77

Frommer's lists exact prices in the local currency. The currency conversions quoted above were correct at press time. However, rates fluctuate, so before departing consult a currency exchange website such as www.oanda.com/convert/classic to check up-to-the-minute rates.

For decades Paris was known as one of the most expensive cities on earth. It still is a pricey destination, but London has not only caught up with Paris, it has surpassed it. Paris is not as expensive as Tokyo or Oslo, but it's increasingly difficult to find even an average hotel for less than 150€.

ATMs are widely available in Paris, but if you're venturing into rural France, it's always good to have cash in your pocket. Be sure you know your personal identification number (PIN) and daily withdrawal limit before you depart. Many banks impose a fee when you withdraw money abroad, and that fee can be higher for international transactions than for domestic ones. In addition, the bank from which you withdraw cash may charge its own fee. Currency exchange is available at Paris airports, train stations, and along most of the major boulevards—just look out for a sign saying *Bureau de Change*. They charge a small commission.

Visa (known as Carte Bleue in French) is the most common credit card in France, but most international credit cards are widely used. In an attempt to reduce credit card fraud, French credit cards are issued with an embedded chip and a PIN to authorize transactions. Non-French cards (which don't have a chip) do work but they print a slip that requires a signature. This does mean, however, that they cannot be used in automated machines, such as those in Métro stations. Check for hidden fees when using your card abroad—some bank charges can be up to 3% of the purchase price. Use the following numbers in France to report your lost or stolen credit card: **American Express** (*✆* **01-47-77-72-00;** www212.americanexpress.com); **MasterCard** (*✆* **08-00-90-13-87;** www.mastercard.com); **Visa** *✆* **08-00-90-11-79;** www.visa europe.com). It may be difficult to get a new card until you get home, so carrying two cards is better than one. There are still shops, restaurants and bars, often family-run, that don't accept credit or debit cards so it's always good to both check in advance and have cash on you. The minimum amount you have to spend to use a credit or debit card is slowly decreasing, but in some shops and bars, again often smaller businesses, it can be as high as 15€.

You can buy traveler's checks at most banks, and they are widely accepted in France, although frankly, merchants prefer cash. Because of difficulties with credit cards (see above) or ATMs that can reject your card for no apparent reason, travelers are once again buying traveler's checks for security in case something goes wrong with their plastic. They are offered in denominations of $20, $50, $100, $500, and sometimes $1,000. Generally, you'll pay a service charge ranging from 1% to 4%. The most popular traveler's checks are offered by **American Express, Visa,** and **MasterCard.** You can

WHAT THINGS COST IN PARIS	EURO
Taxi from the airport to downtown Paris	70.00
Métro ticket	1.70
Double room, expensive	220.00–400.00
Double room, moderate	120.00–220.00
Double room, inexpensive	90.00–120.00
Three-course dinner for one without wine, moderate	25.00 30.00
Bottle of beer	3.00–5.00
Espresso	1.00–2.50
1 gallon/1 liter of premium gas	1.30–1.50
Admission to most museums	7.00–10.00

change traveler's checks at most post offices. If you carry traveler's checks, keep a record of their serial numbers separate from your checks in the event that they are stolen or lost—you'll get your refund faster.

For help with currency conversions, tip calculations, and more, download Frommer's convenient Travel Tools app for your mobile device. Go to www.frommers.com/go/mobile/ and click on the "Travel Tools" icon.

Multicultural Travelers See "Safety," below.

Newspapers & Magazines Only 20% of French people read a national paper. The most famous is the serious, center-left **Le Monde,** which is strong on both politics and economic issues. **Le Figaro** is more conservative, and tends to favor lifestyle features over controversial issues. **Libération,** founded in the late 1960s by Jean-Paul Sartre and Simone de Beauvoir, has good news and arts coverage and is considered more left-wing. For more local news, try **Le Parisien.**

English-language newspapers are available at kiosks across the city. Published Monday to Saturday, the Paris-based *International Herald-Tribune* is the most widely available English-language newspaper. The most popular British and American papers and magazines can be found at kiosks. **WH Smiths** (248 Rue de Rivoli; ✆ **01-44-77-88-99**) has a good selection of English-language press.

Passports Citizens of the U.K., New Zealand, Australia, Canada, and the United States need a valid passport to enter France. The passport is valid for a stay of 90 days. To prevent international child abduction, E.U. governments have initiated procedures at entry and exit points. These often (but not always) include requiring documentary evidence of relationship and permission for the child's travel from the parent or legal guardian not present. Having such documentation on hand, even if not required, facilitates entries and exits. All children must have their own passports.

Allow plenty of time before your trip to apply for a passport; processing normally takes 3 weeks but can take longer during busy periods (especially spring). Keep in mind that if you need a passport in a hurry, you'll pay a higher processing fee.

For Residents of Australia: You can pick up an application from your local post office or any branch of Passports Australia. Visit the government website at www.passports.gov.au for more details.

For Residents of Canada: Passport applications are available at Passport Canada agencies throughout Canada. Forms and further information can be found at www.ppt.gc.ca.

For Residents of Ireland: You can apply for a passport using the Passport Express service at most post offices. Further information can be found at www.foreignaffairs.gov.ie.

For Residents of New Zealand: You can pick up a passport application at any New Zealand Passports Office or download it from their website www.passports.govt.nz.

For Residents of the United Kingdom: To pick up an application for a passport visit your nearest passport office, major post office, or download the forms from the website www.ips.gov.uk.

For Residents of the United States: Whether you're applying in person or by mail, you can download passport applications from the U.S. State Department website at http://travel.state.gov.

Police In an emergency, call ✆ **17** or **112** from a mobile. The Préfecture de Police has 94 stations in Paris. To find the nearest police station call ✆ **08-91-01-22-22** or go to www.prefecture-police-paris.interieur.gouv.fr. See also "Emergencies," earlier in this section.

Safety In general, Paris is a safe city and it is safe to use the Métro late at night. However, certain Métro stations (and the areas around them) are best avoided at night: Châtelet-Les Halles, Gare du Nord, Barbès Rochechouart, and Strasbourg St-Denis. Violent incidents and robberies have been known on the RER, particularly RER B, so it is best find alternative transport to and from the airport (such as buses or taxis) late at night or early in the morning.

The most common crime in Paris is the plague of pickpockets. They prey on tourists around popular attractions such as the Louvre, the Eiffel Tower, Notre-Dame, St-Michel, Center Pompidou, and Sacré-Coeur, in the major department stores, and on the Métro. Take precautions and be vigilant at all times: don't take more money with you than necessary, keep your passport in a concealed pouch or leave it at your hotel, and ensure that your bag is firmly closed at all times. Also, around the major sites it is quite common to be approached by a young Roma girl and asked if you speak English. It's best to avoid these situations, and any incident that might occur, by shaking your head and walking away.

In cafes, bars, and restaurants, it's best not to leave your bag under the table or on the back of your chair. Keep it between your legs or on your lap to avoid it being stolen. Never leave valuables in a car, and never travel with your car unlocked.

The government of France maintains a national antiterrorism plan; in times of heightened security concerns, the government mobilizes police and armed forces, and installs them at airports; train and Métro stations; and high-profile locations such as schools, embassies, and government installations.

Paris is a cosmopolitan city and most nonwhite travelers won't experience any problems. Although there is a significant level of discrimination against West and

North African immigrants, there has been almost no harassment of African-American tourists to Paris or France itself. In fact, many expatriate Americans, including such cultural figures as Josephine Baker and author James Baldwin, fled to Paris in decades past to escape the racism of America. **S.O.S. Racisme** (51 av. de Flandre, 19e; ✆ **01-40-35-36-55;** www.sos-racisme.org) offers legal advice to victims of prejudice and will even intervene to help with the police.

Female travelers should not expect any more hassle than in other major cities and the same precautions apply. Avoid walking around the less safe neighborhoods (Barbès Rochechouart, Strasbourg St-Denis, Châtelet-Les-Halles) alone at night and never get into an unmarked taxi. If you are approached in the street or on the Métro, it's best to avoid entering into conversation and walk away.

Senior Travel Many discounts are available to seniors—men and women over 60. Although they often seem to apply to residents of E.U. countries, it pays to announce at the ticket window of a museum or monument that you are 60 years old or more. You may not receive a discount, but it doesn't hurt to ask. "Senior," incidentally, is pronounced *seenyore* in France. Senior citizens do not get a discount for traveling on public transport in Paris, but there are senior discounts on national trains. Check out www.voyages-sncf.com for further information. Frommers.com offers more information and resources on travel for seniors.

Smoking Smoking is now banned in all public places, including cafes, restaurants, bars, and nightclubs.

Student Travel Student discounts are less common in France than other countries, but simply because young people under 26 are usually offered reduced rates. Some discounts only apply to residents of E.U. countries, but it's worth carrying ID to prove your age and announcing it when buying tickets. Look out for the **Ticket Jeune** when using the Métro. It can be used on a Saturday, Sunday, or bank holiday, and provides unlimited travel in zones 1 to 3 for 3.40€ (see "Public Transport," above). SNCF also offer discounts for under-26-year-olds traveling on national trains (www.voyages-sncf.com).

Taxes As a member of the European Union, France routinely imposes a value-added tax (VAT in English; *TVA* in French) on most goods. The standard VAT is 19.6% and prices that include it are often marked TTC (*toutes taxes comprises,* "all taxes included"). If you're not an E.U. resident, you can get a VAT refund if you're spending less than 6 months in France; you purchase goods worth at least 175€ at a single shop on the same day; the goods fit into your luggage; and the shop offers *vente en détaxe* (duty-free sales or tax-free shopping). Give them your passport and ask for a *bordereau de vente à l'exportation* (export sales invoice). This is then signed by the retailer and yourself. When you leave the country, you need to get all three pages of this invoice validated by France's customs officials. They'll keep one sheet and you must post the pink one back to the shop. Once the shop receives its stamped copy, it will send you a *virement* (fund transfer) using the payment method you requested. It may take several months.

Telephones Public phones can still be found in France. They all require a phone card (known as a télécarte), which can be purchased at post offices, tabacs, supermarkets, SNCF ticket windows, Métro stations, and anywhere you see a blue sticker reading *télécarte en vente ici* ("phone card for sale here"). They cost 7.50€ for 50 calling units and 15€ for 120 units.

The country code for France is 33. To make a local or long distance call within France, dial the 10-digit number of the person or place you're calling. Mobile numbers begin with 06. Numbers beginning with 0 800, 0 804, 0 805, and 0 809 are free in France, other numbers beginning with 8 are not. Most four-digit numbers starting with 10, 30, or 31 are free of charge.

To make international calls from Paris, first dial 00 and then the country code (U.S. and Canada 1, U.K. 44, Ireland 353, Australia 61, New Zealand 64). Next you dial the area code and number. For example, if you want to call the British Embassy in Washington, D.C., you would dial ✆ **001 202/588-7800**.

For operator assistance and French directory enquiries dial ✆ **12.**

Time France is on Central European Time, which is 1 hour ahead of Greenwich Mean Time. French daylight saving time lasts from the last Sunday in March to the last Sunday in October, when clocks are set 1 hour ahead of the standard time. France uses the 24 hour clock. So 13h is 1pm, 14h15 is 2:15pm, etc. For help with time translations, and more, download our convenient Travel Tools app for your mobile device. Go to www.frommers.com/go/mobile and click on the "Travel Tools" icon.

Tipping By law, all bills in **cafes, bars, and restaurants** say *service compris,* which means the service charge is included. However, it is customary to leave 1€ or 2€ depending on the quality of the service. **Taxi drivers** usually expect a 5% to 10% tip, or for the fare to be rounded up to the next euro. The French give their **hairdressers** a tip of about 15%, and if you go to the theater, you're expected to tip the **usher** 2€ or 3€. For help with tip calculations, currency conversions, and more, download our convenient Travel Tools app for your mobile device. Go to www.frommers.com/go/mobile and click on the "Travel Tools" icon.

Toilets Paris is full of gray-colored, automatic street toilets, which are free to use and are washed and disinfected after each use. If you're in dire need, duck into a cafe or brasserie to use the toilet but expect to make a small purchase if you do so. In older establishments, you can still find Turkish toilets, otherwise known as squat toilets.

VAT See "Taxes," above.

Visas E.U. nationals don't need a visa to enter France. Nor do U.S., Canadian, Australian, New Zealand, or South African citizens for trips of up to 3 months. Nationals of other countries should make inquiries at the nearest French embassy or consulate before they travel to France. If non-E.U. citizens wish to stay for longer than 3 months, they must apply to French embassy or consulate for a long-term visa.

Visitor Information The **Office du Tourisme et des Congrès** (25 Rue des Pyramides, 1er; ✆ **08-92-68-30-00;** www.parisinfo.com) has information on hotels, restaurants, monuments, shopping, excursions, events, and transport. Open Monday to Saturday 10am to 7pm and Sunday 11am to 7pm. There are several other offices around Paris: **Montmartre** (21 Place du Tertre, 18e; daily 10am–7pm); **Anvers** (72 Bld Rochechouart, 9e; daily 10am–6pm); **Gare du Nord** (18 Rue de Dunkerque, 10e; daily 8am–6pm); **Gare de l'Est** (Place du 11-novembre-1918, 10e; Mon–Sat 8am–7pm); **Gare de Lyon** (20 Bld Diderot, 12e; Mon–Sat 8am–6pm); and **Porte de Versailles** (1 Place de la Porte de Versailles, 15e; daily 11am–7pm during trade fairs).

There are lots of interesting blogs written in English about Paris, but some of the best are **GoGo Paris** (www.gogoparis.com), an insider guide to Paris's fashion, food, art and gigs; **Paris by Mouth** (www.parisbymouth.com), a collaborative website edited by established food writers where you can find all the latest food gossip and a guide to Paris restaurants; and **Chocolate & Zucchini** (http://chocolateandzucchini.com), the hugely successful food blog written by a 30-something Parisian called Clotilde.

Water Drinking water is generally safe. To order tap water in a restaurant ask for *une carafe d'eau*.

Wi-Fi See "Internet & Wi-Fi," earlier in this section.

Women Travelers See "Safety," above.

USEFUL TERMS & PHRASES

FRENCH-LANGUAGE TERMS

Although Parisians can seem aloof and uninterested in foreigners and tourists, it's amazing how a word or two of uncertain French can change their dispositions. At the very least, try to learn the basic greetings, a few numbers, and—above all—the life raft, *"Parlez-vous anglais?"* You'll discover that many Parisians speak passable English and will use it liberally if you initiate the courtesy by greeting them in their language. Go out, try a few phrases from this chapter, and don't be bashful. *Bonne chance!*

BASICS

English	French	Pronunciation
Yes/No	Oui/Non	**Wee/Nohn**
Okay	D'accord	**Dah-*core***
Please	S'il vous plaît	**seel voo *play***
Thank you	Merci	**Malr-*see***
You're welcome	De rien	**duh ree-*ehn***
Hello (during daylight)	Bonjour	**Bohn-*jhoor***
Good evening	Bonsoir	**bohn-*swahr***
Good-bye	Au revoir	**O ruh-*vwahr***
What's your name?	Comment vous appellez-vous?	**Ko-*mahn* voo za-pell-ay-*voo*?**
My name is . . .	Je m'appelle . . .	**Jhuh ma-*pell* . . .**
Happy to meet you	Enchanté(e)	**Ohn-shahn-tay**
Miss	Mademoiselle	**Mad-mwa-*zel***
Mr.	Monsieur	**muh-*syuh***
Mrs.	Madame	**Ma-*dam***
How are you?	Comment allez-vous?	**Kuh-*mahn* tahl-ay-*voo*?**
Fine, thank you, and you?	Très bien, merci, et vous?	**Tray bee-*ehn,* mair-*see,* ay *voo*?**
Very well, thank you	Très bien, merci	**tray bee-ehn, mair-*see***
So-so	Comme ci, comme ça	**Kum-*see*, kum-*sah***
I'm sorry/excuse me	Pardon	**pahr-*dohn***
I'm so very sorry	Désolé(e)	**Day-zoh-*lay***
That's all right	Il n'y a pas de quoi	**Eel nee ah pah duh kwah**

GETTING AROUND/STREET SMARTS

English	French	Pronunciation
Do you speak English?	Parlez-vous Anglais?	**Par-lay-*voo* ahn-*glay*?**
I don't speak French.	Je ne parle pas Français	**Jhuh ne parl pah frahn-*say***
I don't understand.	Je ne comprends pas	**Jhuh ne kohm-*prahn* pas**
Could you speak . . .	Pouvez-vous parler un peu . . .	**Poo-vay-*voo* par-*lay* un puh**
. . . more loudly?	. . . plus fort?	**. . . ploo for?**
. . . more slowly?	. . . plus lentement?	**. . . ploo lan-te-*ment*?**
Could you repeat that?	Répetez, s'il vous plaît?	**Ray-pay-*tay,* seel voo *play***

English	French	Pronunciation
What is it?	Qu'est-ce que c'est?	**Kess kuh *say*?**
What time is it?	Quelle heure est-il?	**Kel uhr eh-*teel*?**
What?	Quoi?	**Kwah?**
How?/What did you say?	Comment?	**Ko-*mahn*?**
When?	Quand?	**Kahn?**
Where is . . . ?	Où est . . . ?	**Ooh eh . . . ?**
Who?	Qui?	**Kee?**
Why?	Pourquoi?	**Poor-*kwah*?**
I'm American.	Je suis Américain(e).	**Jhuh sweez a-may-ree-*kehn***
. . . British.	. . . Anglais(e).	**ahn-glay (*glaise*)**
. . . Canadian.	. . . Canadien(e).	**can-ah-dee-*en***
I'm sick.	Je suis malade	**Jhuh swee mal-*ahd***
Fill the (gas) tank, please.	Le plein, s'il vous plaît	**Luh plan, seel voo play**
I'm going to . . .	Je vais à . . .	**Jhe vay ah . . .**
I want to get off at . . .	Je voudrais descendre à . . .	**Jhe voo-*dray* day-*son*-drah ah**
. . . the airport	. . . l'aéroport	**lair-o-*por***
. . . the bank	. . .la banque	**lah bahnk**
. . . the bridge	. . . le pont	**luh pohn**
. . . the bus station	. . . la gare routière	**lah gar roo-tee-*air***
. . . the bus stop	. . . l'arrèt de bus	**lah-*ray* duh boohss**
by bicycle	en vélo/par bicyclette	**ahn *vay*-low/par bee-see-*clet***
by car	en voiture	**ahn vwa-*toor***
cashier	la caisse	**lah *kess***
castle/palace	un château	**uh sha-*tow***
cathedral	la cathédrale	**lah ka-tay-*dral***
church	l'église	**lay-*gleez***
dead end	une impasse	**ewn am-*pass***
driver's license	un permis de conduire	**uh per-*mee* duh con-*dweer***
elevator	l'ascenseur	**lah-sahn-*seuhr***
entrance (to building/city)	une porte	**ewn port**

English	French	Pronunciation
exit (from building/ freeway)	une sortie	**ewn sor-*tee***
garden	un jardin	**uh jhar-*dehn***
gasoline	du pétrol/de l'essence	**doo pet-*role*/de lay-*sahns***
ground floor	rez-de-chaussée	**ray-de-show-*say***
here/there	ici/là	**ee-*see*/lah**
highway to . . .	la route pour . . .	**la root por**
hospital	l'hôpital	**low-pee-*tahl***
insurance	les assurances	**lez ah-sur-*ahns***
left/right	à gauche/à droite	**a goash/a drwaht**
luggage storage	la consigne	**lah kohn-*seen*-yuh**
museum	le musée	**luh mew-*zay***
no entry	sens interdit	**sehns ahn-ter-*dee***
no smoking	défense de fumer	**day-*fahns* de fu-may**
on foot	à pied	**ah pee-*ay***
one-day pass	ticket journalier	**tee-kay jhoor-nall-ee-*ay***
one-way ticket	aller simple	**ah-*lay* sam-pluh**
police	la police	**lah po-*lees***
rental car	une voiture de location	**ewn vwa-*toor* de low-ka-see-*on***
round-trip ticket	aller-retour	**ah-*lay*-re-*toor***
second floor	premier étage	**prem-ee-*ehr* ay-*taj***
slow down	ralentir	**rah-lahn-*teer***
store	un magasin	**uh luh ma-ga-*zehn***
straight ahead	tout droit	**too drwah**
street	la rue	**lah roo**
suburb	banlieu/environs	**bahn-*liew*/en-veer-*ohns***
subway	le Métro	**luh *May*-tro**
telephone	le téléphone	**luh tay-lay-*phone* port-arb-*le***
ticket	un billet	**uh *bee*-yay**
ticket office	vente de billets	**vahnt duh bee-*yay***
toilets	les toilettes/les WC	**lay twa-*lets*/les Vay-Say**

NECESSITIES

English	French	Pronunciation
How much does it cost?	C'est combien?/Ça coûte combien?	**Say comb-bee-*ehn*?/Sah coot comb-bee-*ehn*?**
That's expensive.	C'est cher/chère	**Say share**
That's inexpensive.	C'est raisonnable/C'est bon marché	**Say ray-son-*ahb*-bluh/Say bohn mar-*shay***
Do you take credit cards?	Est-ce que vous acceptez les cartes de credit?	**Es-*kuh* voo zak-sep-*tay* lay kart duh creh-*dee*?**
I'd like . . .	Je voudrais . . .	**Jhe voo-*dray***
I'd like to buy . . .	Je voudrais acheter . . .	**Jhe voo-dray ahsh-*tay***
. . . an aspirin	. . . des aspirines/des aspros	**dayz ahs-peer-*eens*/ deyz ahs-*prohs***
. . . cigarettes	. . . des cigarettes	**day see-ga-*ret***
. . . condoms	. . . des préservatifs	**day pray-ser-va-*teefs***
. . . a dictionary	. . . un dictionnaire	**uh deek-see-oh-*nare***
. . . a dress	. . . une robe	**ewn robe**
. . . envelopes	. . . des envelopes	**days ahn-veh-*lope***
. . . a gift (for someone)	. . . un cadeau	**uh kah-*doe***
. . . a handbag	. . . un sac	**uh sahk**
. . . a hat	. . . un chapeau	**uh shah-*poh***
. . . a magazine	. . . une revue	**ewn reh-*vu***
. . . a map of the city	. . . un plan de ville	**unh plahn de *veel***
. . . a computer	. . . un ordinateur	**unh ord-ee-nat-*uhr***
. . . a laptop	. . . un laptop	**unh lap-top**
. . . a charger (telephone/computer)	. . . un chargeur	**unh charg-uhr**
. . . a cell phone	. . . un téléphone portable	**uh tay-lay-*phone* port-ahb-*le***
. . . matches	. . . des allumettes	**dayz a-loo-*met***
. . . a necktie	. . . une cravate	**uh cra-*vaht***
. . . a newspaper	. . . un journal	**uh zhoor-*nahl***
. . . a phone card	. . . une carte téléphonique	**uh cart tay-lay-fone-*eek***
. . . a postcard	. . . une carte postale	**ewn carte pos-*tahl***
. . . a road map	. . . une carte routière	**ewn cart roo-tee-*air***
. . . a shirt	. . . une chemise	**ewn che-*meez***

12

French-Language Terms

USEFUL TERMS & PHRASES

English	French	Pronunciation
. . . shoes	. . . des chaussures	**day show-*suhr***
. . . a skirt	. . . une jupe	**ewn jhoop**
. . . soap	. . . du savon	**dew sah-*vohn***
. . . socks	. . . des chaussettes	**day show-*set***
. . . a stamp	. . . un timbre	**uh *tam*-bruh**
. . . trousers	. . . un pantalon	**uh pan-tah-*lohn***

IN YOUR HOTEL

English	French	Pronunciation
Are taxes included?	Est-ce que les taxes sont comprises?	***Ess*-keh lay taks son com-*preez*?**
Is breakfast included?	Petit dé jeuner inclus?	**Peh-*tee* day-jheun-*ay* ehn-*klu*?**
We're staying for . . . days.	On reste pour . . . jours.	**Ohn rest poor . . . jhoor.**
balcony	un balcon	**uh bahl-*cohn***
bathtub	une baignoire	**ewn bayn-*nwar***
Internet	l'Internet	**luhn-tair-*net***
key	la clé (la clef)	**lah *clay***
room	une chambre	**ewn *shahm*-bruh**
shower	une douche	**ewn dooch**
sink	un lavabo	**uh la-va-*bow***
suite	une suite	**ewn sweet**
two occupants	pour deux personnes	**poor duh pair-*sunn***
water (cold)	l'eau froide	**low fwad**
water (hot)	l'eau chaude	**low showed**
Wi-Fi	avec une connexion Wi-Fi	**ah-*vek* ewn con-neks-*iohn* wee-*fee***
with air-conditioning	avec climatisation	**ah-*vek* clee-mah-tee-zah-see-*on***
without	sans	**sahn**
youth hostel	une auberge de jeunesse	**oon oh-*bayrhj* duh jhe-*ness***

IN THE RESTAURANT

English	French	Pronunciation
Is the tip/service included?	Est-ce que le service est compris?	**Ess**-ke luh ser-**vees** eh com-**pree?**
I would like . . .	Je voudrais	**Jhe voo-*dray***
. . . to eat	manger	**mahn-*jhay***
. . . to order	commander	**ko-mahn-*day***
Please give me . . .	Donnez-moi, s'il vous plaît . . .	**Doe-nay-*mwah,* seel voo play . . .**
. . . a bottle of . . .	. . . une bouteille de . . .	**ewn boo-*tay* duh . . .**
. . . an ashtray	. . . un cendrier	**uh sahn-dree-*ay***
. . . a cup of . . .	. . . une tasse de . . .	**ewn tass duh . . .**
. . . a glass of . . .	. . . un verre de . . .	**uh vair duh . . .**
. . . a plate of . . .	. . . une assiette de . . .	**ewn ass-ee-*et* duh . . .**
Can I buy you . . .	Puis-je vous offrir . . .	***Pwee*-jhe vooz-off-*reer***
. . . a drink?	. . . un verre?	**uh *vahr*?**
. . . a cocktail?	. . . un aperitif?	**uh ah-pay-ree-*teef*?**
appetizer	une entrée	**ewn en-*tray***
breakfast	le petit déjeuner	**luh puh-*tee* day-zhuh-*nay***
check/bill	l'addition/la note	**la-dee-see-*ohn*/la noat**
Cheers!	à votre santé	***ah* vo-truh sahn-*tay***
cheese tray	le plâteau de fromage	**luh plah-*tow* duh fro-*mahj***
course	un plat principal	**uh plah pran-see-*pahl***
for dinner	pour dîner	**poor dee-*nay***
dish of the day	le plat du jour	**luh plah dew jhoor**
drinks not included	boissons non comprises	**bwa-*sons* no com-*preez***
fixed-price menu	un menu	**uh may-new**
fork	une fourchette	**ewn four-*shet***
knife	un couteau	**uh koo-*toe***
napkin	une serviette	**ewn sair-vee-*et***
salt	du sel	**dew sell**
soup	une soupe/un potage	**ewn soop/uh poh-*tahj***
spoon	une cuillère	**ewn kwee-*air***
sugar	du sucre	**dew *sook*-ruh**

English	French	Pronunciation
tasting menu	menu dégustation	**may-new day-gus-ta-see-*on***
tip included	service compris	**sehr-*vees* cohm-*preez***
Waiter!/Waitress!	Monsieur!/Mademoiselle!	**Mun-*syuh*/Mad-mwa-*zel***
wine list	la carte des vins	**lah cart day *van***

SHOPPING

English	French	Pronunciation
antiques store	un magasin d'antiquités	**uh maga-*zan* don-tee-kee-*tay***
bakery	une boulangerie	**ewn boo-lon-zhur-*ree***
bank	une banque	**ewn bonk**
bookstore	une librairie	**ewn lee-brehr-*ree***
butcher	une boucherie	**ewn boo-shehr-*ree***
cheese shop	une fromagerie	**ewn fro-mazh-*ree***
dairy shop	une crémerie	**ewn krem-*ree***
delicatessen	une charcuterie	**ewn shar-koot-*ree***
department store	un grand magasin	**uh grah maga-*zan***
drugstore	une pharmacie	**ewn far-mah-*see***
fishmonger	une poissonerie	**ewn pwas-son-*ree***
gift shop	un magasin de cadeaux	**uh maga-*zan* duh ka-*doh***
greengrocer	un marchand de légumes	**uh mar-*shon* duh lay-*goom***
hairdresser	un coiffeur	**uh kwa-*fuhr***
market	un marché	**uh mar-*shay***
pastry shop	une pâtisserie	**ewn pa-tee-*sree***
supermarket	un supermarché	**uh soo-pehr-mar-*shay***
tobacconist	un tabac	**uh ta-*bah***
travel agency	une agence de voyages	**ewn azh-*ahns* duh vwa-*yazh***

COLORS, SHAPES, SIZES & ATTRIBUTES

English	French	Pronunciation
black	noir	**nwahr**
blue	bleu	**bleuh**
brown	marron/brun	**mar-*rohn*/bruhn**
green	vert	**vaihr**
orange	orange	**o-*rahnj***
pink	rose	**rose**
purple	violet	**vee-o-*lay***
red	rouge	**rooj**
white	blanc	**blahnk**
yellow	jaune	**jhone**
bad	mauvais(e)	**moh-*veh***
big	grand(e)	**gron/gronde**
closed	fermé(e)	**fer-*meh***
down/below	en bas	**on *bah***
early	de bonne heure	**duh bon *urr***
enough	assez	**as-*say***
far	loin	**lwan**
free, unoccupied	libre	***lee*-bruh**
free, without charge	gratuit(e)	**grah-*twee*/grah-*tweet***
good	bon/bonne	**bon/bun**
hot	chaud(e)	**show/shoad**
near	près	**preh**
open (as in "museum")	ouvert(e)	**oo-*ver*/oo-*vert***
small	petit(e)	**puh-*tee*/puh-*teet***
up	en haut	**on *oh***
well	bien	**byehn**

NUMBERS & ORDINALS

English	French	Pronunciation
zero	zéro	**zare-*oh***
one	un	**uh**
two	deux	**duh**
three	trois	**twah**

English	French	Pronunciation
four	quatre	*kaht*-ruh
five	cinq	sank
six	six	seess
seven	sept	set
eight	huit	wheat
nine	neuf	nuf
ten	dix	deess
eleven	onze	ohnz
twelve	douze	dooz
thirteen	treize	trehz
fourteen	quatorze	kah-*torz*
fifteen	quinze	kanz
sixteen	seize	sez
seventeen	dix-sept	deez-*set*
eighteen	dix-huit	deez-*wheat*
nineteen	dix-neuf	deez-*nuf*
twenty	vingt	vehn
twenty-one	vingt-et-un	vehnt-ay-*uh*
twenty-two	vingt-deux	vehnt-*duh*
thirty	trente	trahnt
forty	quarante	ka-*rahnt*
fifty	cinquante	sang-*kahnt*
sixty	soixante	swa-*sahnt*
sixty-one	soixante-et-un	swa-sahnt-et-*uh*
seventy	soixante-dix	swa-sahnt-*deess*
seventy-one	soixante-et-onze	swa-sahnt-et-*ohnze*
eighty	quatre-vingts	kaht-ruh-*vehn*
eighty-one	quatre-vingt-un	kaht-ruh-vehn-*uh*
ninety	quatre-vingt-dix	kaht-ruh-venh-*deess*
ninety-one	quatre-vingt-onze	kaht-ruh-venh-*ohnze*
one hundred	cent	sahn
one thousand	mille	meel
one hundred thousand	cent mille	sahn meel
first	premier	*preh*-mee-ay

English	French	Pronunciation
second	deuxième	***duhz*-zee-em**
third	troisième	***twa*-zee-em**
fourth	quatrième	**kaht-ree-em**
fifth	cinquième	***sank*-ee-em**
sixth	sixième	***sees*-ee-em**
seventh	septième	***set*-ee-em**
eighth	huitième	***wheat*-ee-em**
ninth	neuvième	***neuv*-ee-em**
tenth	dixième	***dees*-ee-em**

THE CALENDAR

English	French	Pronunciation
January	Janvier	***jhan*-vee-ay**
February	Février	***feh*-vree-ay**
March	Mars	**marce**
April	Avril	**a-*vreel***
May	Mai	**meh**
June	Juin	**jhwehn**
July	Juillet	***jhwee*-ay**
August	Août	**oot**
September	Septembre	**sep-*tahm*-bruh**
October	Octobre	**ok-*toh*-bruh**
November	Novembre	**no-*vahm*-bruh**
December	Decembre	**day-*sahm*-bruh**
Sunday	Dimanche	**dee-*mahnsh***
Monday	Lundi	***luhn*-dee**
Tuesday	Mardi	***mahr*-dee**
Wednesday	Mercredi	***mair*-kruh-dee**
Thursday	Jeudi	***jheu*-dee**
Friday	Vendredi	***vawn*-druh-dee**
Saturday	Samedi	***sahm*-dee**
yesterday	hier	**ee-*air***
today	aujourd'hui	**o-jhord-*dwee***

English	French	Pronunciation
this morning/this afternoon	ce matin/cet après-midi	**suh ma-*tan*/set ah-preh-mee-*dee***
tonight	ce soir	**suh *swahr***
tomorrow	demain	**de-*man***

BASIC MENU TERMS

Note: No need to get intimidated when ordering in French. Simply preface the French-language menu item with the phrase *"Je voudrais"* (jhe voo-*dray*), which means, "I would like . . ." *Bon appétit!*

MEATS

English	French	Pronunciation
beef stew	du pot au feu	**dew poht o *fhe***
brains	de la cervelle	**duh lah ser-*vel***
chicken	du poulet	**dew poo-lay**
warm dumplings of creamed chicken, veal, or fish (often pike)	des quenelles	**day ke-*nelle***
chicken with mushrooms and wine	du coq au vin	**dew cock o vhin**
gooseliver	du foie gras	**dew fwah grah**
ham	du jambon	**dew jham-bohn**
haunch or leg of an animal, especially that of a lamb or sheep	du gigot	**dew *jhi*-goh**
kidneys	des rognons	**day *row*-nyon**
lamb	de l'agneau	**duh lahn-*nyo***
lamb chop	une cotelette de l'agneau	**ewn koh-te-*let* duh lahn-*nyo***
liver	du foie	**dew fwah**
pork	du porc	**dew poor**
potted and shredded pork	des rillettes	**day ree-*yet***
rabbit	du lapin	**dew lah-*pan***
sirloin	de l'aloyau	**duh lahl-why-*yo***
steak	du bifteck	**dew beef-*tek***
filet steak, served with a pepper sauce	un steak au poivre	**uh stake o *pwah*-vruh**

English	French	Pronunciation
thick filet steak from the tenderloin, usually serves two	du chateaubriand	**dew *sha*-tow-bree-ahn**
snails	des escargots	**dayz ess-car-*goh***
stewed meat with white sauce	de la blanquette	**duh lah blon-*ket***
sweetbreads	des ris de veau	**day *ree* duh voh**
veal	du veau	**dew *voh***

FISH

English	French	Pronunciation
fish	du poisson	**dew pwoiss-*ohn***
herring	du hareng	**dew ahr-*rahn***
lobster	du homard	**dew oh-*mahr***
mussels	des moules	**day *moohl***
mussels in white wine and shallots	des moules marinières	**day moohl mar-ee-nee-*air***
oysters	des huîtres	**dayz hoo-*ee*-truhs**
pike	du brochet	**dew broh-*chay***
shrimp	des crevettes	**day kreh-*vette***
smoked salmon	du saumon fumé	**dew sow-*mohn* fu-*may***
trout	de la truite	**duh lah tru-eet**
tuna	du thon	**dew tohn**
wolffish (Mediterranean sea bass)	du loup de mer	**dew loo duh *mehr***

SIDES/APPETIZERS

English	French	Pronunciation
bread	du pain	**dew pan**
butter	du beurre	**dew bhuhr**
fries	des frites	**day freet**
rice	du riz	**dew ree**
salad	de la salade	**duh lah sa-*lard***
vegetables	des légumes	**day lay-*goom***

BEVERAGES

English	French	Pronunciation
beer	de la bière	**duh lah bee-*aire***
coffee	un café	**uh ka-*fay***
coffee (black)	un café allongé	**uh ka-*fay* all-on-*jay***
coffee (decaf)	un café décaféiné (slang: un déca)	**uh ka-*fay* day-kah-fay-*nay***
coffee (espresso)	un café express	**uh ka-fay ek-*sprehss***
coffee (with cream)	un café crème	**uh ka-*fay* krem**
coffee (with milk)	un café au lait	**uh ka-*fay* o *lay***
milk	du lait	**dew *lay***
orange juice	du jus d'orange	**dew joo d'or-*ahn*-jhe**
tea	un thé	**uh *tay***
tea (herbal)	une tisane	**ewn tee-*zahn***
tea (w/lemon)	du thé au citron	**uh tay o see-*tran***
water	de l'eau	**duh lo**
wine (red)	du vin rouge	**dew vhin *rooj***
wine (white)	du vin blanc	**dew vhin *blahn***

SPICES/CONDIMENTS

English	French	Pronunciation
mayonnaise	de la mayonnaise	**duh lah may-o-nayse**
mustard	de la moutarde	**duh lah moo-*tard*-uh**
ketchup	du ketchup	**dew ketch-up**
pepper	du poivre	**dew *pwah*-vruh**
salt	du sel	**dew *sel***
sour heavy cream	de la crème fraîche	**duh lah krem *fresh***
sugar	du sucre	**dew *sooh*-kruh**

Index

Accommodations

Restaurants and Cafes

Photo Credits